SOCIAL PROBLEMS

in a diverse society

SOCIAL PROBLEMS
in a diverse society

Diana Kendall
Baylor University

Vicki L. Nygaard
University of Victoria

Edward G. Thompson
McMaster University

PEARSON
and
Toronto

Library and Archives Canada Cataloguing in Publication

Kendall, Diana Elizabeth
    Social problems in a diverse society / Diana Kendall, Vicki L.
Nygaard, Edward G. Thompson. — 2nd Canadian ed.

Includes bibliographical references and indexes.
ISBN-13: 978-0-205-48260-3
ISBN-10: 0-205-48260-0

    1. Social problems—Textbooks. I. Thompson, Edward G., 1945-
II. Nygaard, Vicki Leanne, 1964- III. Title.

HN17.5.K45 2008   361.1   C2006-905485-1

ISBN-13: 978-0-205-48260-3
ISBN-10: 0-205-48260-0

Editor-in-Chief, Vice-President of Sales: Kelly Shaw
Senior Acquisitions Editor: Laura Paterson Forbes
Executive Marketing Manager: Judith Allen
Associate Editor: Emily Jardeleza
Production Editor: Amanda Wesson
Copy Editor: Lisa Berland
Proofreader: Nancy Mucklow
Production Coordinator: Avinash Chandra
Composition: Laserwords
Photo Research: Lisa Brant
Art Director: Julia Hall
Cover Design: Geoff Agnew
Interior Design: Julia Hall
Cover Image: Corbis Canada

 3 4 5   12 11 10 09 08

Printed and bound in the United States of America.

DEDICATION

This book is dedicated to my parents, Marilyn and Peter Hardy, and my brother Adrian Nygaard, who have always been there for me and to my two wonderful daughters, Freja Nygaard and Phoenix Nygaard, who are my life, now and always.

Vicki L. Nygaard

This book is dedicated to my dear partner, Helen.

Edward G. Thompson

CONTENTS

Preface   xv

CHAPTER ONE
TAKING A NEW LOOK AT SOCIAL PROBLEMS   1

What Is a Social Problem?   2

BOX 1.1   Social Problems in Global Perspective: Violence around the World   3

Why Study Social Problems?   4

The Sociological Imagination and Social Problems   5

Sociological Perspectives on Social Problems   5

The Functionalist Perspective   6

The Conflict Perspective   8

BOX 1.2   Social Problems in the Media: The New Canadian *Youth Criminal Justice Act:* Selling Canadians a "Sheep in Wolf's Clothing"?   10

The Interactionist Perspective   11

Feminist Perspectives   13

Social Change and Reducing Social Problems   15

Microlevel Attempts to Solve Social Problems   15

Mid-Range Attempts to Solve Social Problems   16

Macrolevel Attempts to Solve Social Problems   19

BOX 1.3   Social Problems in Global Perspective: The Lysistrata Project   19

In Sum   24

Summary   25

Key Terms   27

Questions for Critical Thinking   28

CHAPTER TWO
WEALTH AND POVERTY   29

Wealth and Poverty in Global Perspective   31

Analyzing Canadian Class Inequality   32

Wealth and Income Inequality   33

Divisions in the Canadian Class Structure   36

Poverty in Canada   38

Poverty Lines: LICOs and LIMs   39

Who Are the Poor?   40

BOX 2.1   Social Problems in the Media: How You Can Tell When the Media Poor-Bash   41

Consequences of Poverty   43

How Canada Deals with Poverty   46

Social Welfare in Canada   47

BOX 2.2   Social Problems and Social Policy: Workfare in Canada: Betraying a National Trust   47

Perspectives on Poverty and Class Inequality   50

The Symbolic Interactionist Perspective   50

The Structural Functionalist Perspective   52

The Conflict Perspective   53

Feminist Perspectives   53

Can Class-Based Inequality Be Reduced?   54

What Can You Do?   54

Summary   55

Key Terms   56

Questions for Critical Thinking   57

Weblinks   57

CHAPTER THREE
RACISM AND ETHNIC INEQUALITY   59

Racism and Ethnic Inequality as a Social Problem   61

What Are Ethnicity, "Race," and Racialization?   61

Historical and Political Roots of "Race"   63

The Meaning of Majority and Minority Groups   63

White Privilege and Internalized Dominance   63

Racism, Prejudice, and Discrimination   64

Historical Roots of Racism   67

The Many Forms of Racism in Canadian Society   68

BOX 3.1   Social Problems in Global Perspective: Organized Racism—Canada's Links to a World of Hatred   **68**

BOX 3.2   Social Problems and Social Policy: Undermining Democratic Racism in Canada   **72**

Perspectives on Racialized and Ethnic Inequality   75

The Symbolic Interactionist Perspective   75

The Structural Functionalist Perspective   76

The Conflict Perspective   76

Feminist and Anti-Racist Perspectives   78

Can Racialized and Ethnic Inequalities Be Reduced?   79

What Can You Do?   79

Summary   81

Key Terms   82

Questions for Critical Thinking   82

Weblinks   83

CHAPTER FOUR
GENDER INEQUALITY   84

Gender Inequality as a Social Problem   86

Defining Sex and Gender   87

Biological and Social Bases for Gender Roles   88

BOX 4.1   Social Problems and Social Policy: *Transgressing Gender Norms*   **88**

Gender Inequality and Socialization   93

BOX 4.2   Social Problems in Global Perspective: Female Genital Surgery or Female Genital Mutilation?   **93**

Gender Socialization by Parents   95

Peers and Gender Socialization   96

Education and Gender Socialization   97

The Media and Gender Socialization   100

Contemporary Gender Inequality   101

The Gendered Division of Paid Work   102

The Wage Gap   104

Sexual Harassment   105

The Glass Ceiling and the Glass Escalator   108

The Double Shift   109

Perspectives on Gender Inequality   111

The Interactionist Perspective   111

The Functionalist Perspective   113

Conflict Perspectives   113

Feminist Perspectives   114

Can Gender Inequality Be
  Reduced?   115

What Can You Do?   116

Summary   117

Key Terms   118

Questions for Critical Thinking   119

Weblinks   119

CHAPTER FIVE
INEQUALITY BASED
ON AGE   121

Ageism as a Social Problem   122

  Age-Based Stereotypes   123

  Social Inequality and the Life
  Course   123

  BOX 5.1 Social Problems in the Media:
            Media Ageism: Reporting on and Preferring
            Age Groups   125

  Suicide and the Life Course   129

  Death and Dying   130

Problems Thought to Be Associated
  with Aging   131

  BOX 5.2 Social Problems and Social Policy:
            Euthanasia   132

  Workplace Discrimination   132

  Retirement and Changing Roles   133

  Health, Illness, and Health Care   133

  Victimization   134

  Family Problems and Social
  Isolation   134

  Housing Patterns and
  Long-Term-Care Facilities   135

Perspectives on Aging and Social
  Inequality   136

  The Functionalist Perspective   136

  The Interactionist Perspective   136

  The Conflict Perspective   137

  The Feminist Perspective   137

Can Age-Based Inequality Be
  Reduced?   137

What Can You Do?   139

Summary   139

Key Terms   140

Questions for Critical Thinking   141

Weblinks   141

CHAPTER SIX
INEQUALITY BASED ON
SEXUAL ORIENTATION   142

Nature and Extent of Inequality Based
  on Sexual Orientation   144

Ideological Bases of Inequality Based
  on Sexual Orientation   145

  Religion and Sexual Orientation   146

  Law and Sexual Orientation   147

Discrimination Based on Sexual
  Orientation   153

  Housing Discrimination   153

  BOX 6.1 Social Problems and Social Policy: Coming Out:
            Risky Business in a Homophobic Culture   153

  Discrimination in Medical Care   154

  Occupational Discrimination   155

  Victimization and Hate Crimes   156

Perspectives on Sexual Orientation
  and Social Inequality   157

  BOX 6.2 Social Problems and Social Policy:
            School's Out: Closing the Books on
            Homophobia   158

  Interactionist Perspectives   159

  Functionalist and Conflict Perspectives   159

  Feminist and Queer Perspectives   161

Can Inequalities Based on Sexual
  Orientation Be Reduced?   163

What Can You Do?   165

Summary   166

Key Terms   168

Questions for Critical Thinking   168

Weblinks   168

CHAPTER SEVEN
THE SEX INDUSTRY IN CANADA AND BEYOND 170

Prostitution in Historical and Global Perspective 171

The World's Oldest Profession? 172

The Global Sex Industry 172

BOX 7.1 Social Problems in Global Perspective: The Global Sex Trade—A Canadian Case 173

Prostitution in Canada 176

Some Characteristics of Prostitution in Canada 181

The Extent of Prostitution in Canada 185

Prostitution and Age, Class, Racialization, and Ethnicity 185

A Closer Look at "Johns" 186

Perspectives on Prostitution 188

The Functionalist Perspective 188

The Interactionist Perspective 189

Conflict and Feminist Perspectives 189

Pornography 191

The Social Construction of Pornography as a Social Problem 192

The Nature and Extent of Pornography 193

BOX 7.2 Social Problems and Information Technology: Canada's Role in Cracking Down on Internet Child Pornography 194

Research on Pornography 196

Pornography and Age, Gender, Class, Racialization, and Ethnicity 197

The Future of Pornography and the Sex Industry 198

What Can You Do? 200

Summary 200

Key Terms 202

Questions for Critical Thinking 202

Weblinks 202

CHAPTER EIGHT
ALCOHOL AND OTHER DRUGS 204

Drug Use and Abuse 205

Defining Drug Abuse 205

Drug Addiction 205

Alcohol Use and Abuse 206

Heavy Alcohol Consumption and Gender, Age, Marital Status, and Class 207

Alcohol-Related Social Problems 207

BOX 8.1 Social Problems in the Media: Maintaining a Drumbeat against Drunken Driving 210

Tobacco (Nicotine) Use as a Social Problem 211

Prescription Drugs, Over the Counter Drugs, and Caffeine 212

Prescription Drugs 212

Over-the-Counter Drugs 212

Caffeine 213

Illegal Drug Use and Abuse 213

Marijuana 214

BOX 8.2 Social Problems and Social Policy: The Battle over Marijuana: Medicalization, Availability, Decriminalization, Legalization? 216

Stimulants 217

Depressants 218

Narcotics 219

Hallucinogens 219

Inhalants 220

Overall Harm from Drug Use 221

Explanations of Drug Abuse 221

Biological Explanations 221

Psychological Explanations 221

The Interactionist Perspective 222

The Functionalist Perspective 222

The Conflict Perspective   223

The Feminist Perspective   223

The Future of Alcohol and Drug Abuse   224

Prevention Programs   224

Treatment Programs   225

What Can You Do?   227

Summary   228

Key Terms   229

Questions for Critical Thinking   230

Weblinks   230

CHAPTER NINE
CRIME AND CRIMINAL JUSTICE   231

Crime as a Social Problem   232

Problems with Official Statistics   232

Defining Crime and Delinquency   233

Types of Crimes   234

Violent Crime   234

Gang Violence   237

Property Crime   239

Crime Comparisons between Canada and the United States   240

Occupational (White-Collar) Crime   241

Corporate Crime   241

Organized Crime   242

Youth Crime   242

BOX 9.1   Social Problems in Global Perspective: Organized Crime: The Global Empire   243

Biological and Psychological Explanations of Crime   244

Biological Explanations   244

Psychological Explanations   245

Sociological Explanations of Crime   245

The Functionalist Perspective   245

The Conflict Perspective   248

The Interactionist Perspective   248

Feminist Perspectives   249

The Criminal Justice System   250

The Police   250

The Courts   251

BOX 9.2   Social Problems and Social Policy: Plea Bargains and Later Restrictions: The Case of Karla Homolka   252

Punishment and the Prisons   252

Restorative Justice   253

BOX 9.3   Social Problems and Social Policy: To Collect or Not Collect Racialization and Ethnicity Statistics   254

The Death Penalty   255

What Can You Do?   255

Summary   255

Key Terms   257

Questions for Critical Thinking   257

Weblinks   258

CHAPTER TEN
HEALTH, ILLNESS, AND HEALTH CARE AS SOCIAL PROBLEMS   259

Health and Illness as Social Problems   260

Acute and Chronic Diseases and Disability   261

BOX 10.1   Social Problems in Global Perspective: HIV/AIDS Worldwide   262

Sex and Gender, Class, and Indigenous Status   264

Obesity   265

Mental Illness as a Social Problem   266

Treatment of Mental Illness   268

The "Crisis" in Canadian Health Care   269

Development of the National Health Care System   270

Current Issues in the Health Care System   270

BOX 10.2   Social Problems and Social Policy: Health Care: The American Model   **272**

Perspectives on Illness and Health Care Problems   276

The Functionalist Perspective   276

The Conflict Perspective   277

The Interactionist Perspective   278

The Feminist Perspective   279

What Can You Do?   280

Summary   280

Key Terms   282

Questions for Critical Thinking   282

Weblinks   282

CHAPTER ELEVEN
THE CHANGING FAMILY   284

The Nature of Families   285

Changing Family Structure and Patterns   285

Are Canadian Families in Decline?   286

BOX 11.1   Social Problems in Global Perspective: The Changing Family around the World   **287**

Changing Views on Marriage and Families   288

Perspectives on Family-Related Problems   289

The Functionalist Perspective   289

The Conflict Perspective   290

The Feminist Perspective   290

The Interactionist Perspective   290

Diversity in Intimate Relationships and Families   291

Singlehood   291

Postponing Marriage   292

Common-Law, Cohabitation, and Domestic Partnerships   292

Dual-Earner Marriages   293

Comparing Two-Parent and One-Parent Households   294

Child-Related Family Issues   295

Reproductive Freedom, Contraception, and Abortion   295

Infertility and New Reproductive Technologies   296

Adoption   297

Parenting Style   298

Teen Pregnancies and Unmarried Motherhood   299

Same-Sex Parenting   300

Divorce and Remarriage   300
Domestic Violence   302

Child Abuse   302

BOX 11.2   Social Problems in the Media: Speaking Out on Incest   **304**

BOX 11.3   Social Problems and Social Policy: Should Spanking Be Permitted?   **305**

Spouse Abuse   306

Social Responses to Domestic Violence   306

Family-Related Problems in the 21st Century   306

What Can You Do?   307

Summary   307

Key Terms   309

Questions for Critical Thinking   309

Weblinks   309

CHAPTER TWELVE
PROBLEMS IN EDUCATION   311

Perspectives on Education   312

Functionalist Perspectives   313

BOX 12.1   Social Problems in Global Perspective: Change in Education in Japan: Becoming More Like Us?   **314**

Conflict Perspectives   315

Interactionist Perspectives   316

BOX 12.2 Social Problems in the Media: Students Challenge the Ghetto Image 317

Feminist Perspectives 318

Problems in Canadian Education 318

What Can Be Done about Illiteracy? 319

Educational Problems of Immigrants 320

Educational Opportunities and Ascribed Statuses 320

Bullying and School Violence 323

Residential Schools 324

Problems in Financing Education 325

Elementary and Secondary Education 325

Post-secondary Education 325

Commercialization of Post-secondary Education 327

Educational Problems in the 21st Century 327

What Can You Do? 330

Summary 331

Key Terms 333

Questions for Critical Thinking 333

Weblinks 334

CHAPTER THIRTEEN
POPULATION, URBANIZATION, AND THE ENVIRONMENTAL CRISIS 335

Global Population Problems 336

Population Growth 337

BOX 13.1 Social Problems in Global Perspective: Challenges and Opportunities Presented by Worldwide Migration 339

The Impact of Population Growth 340

World Hunger 341

Controlling Fertility 343

Family Planning 344

Zero Population Growth 344

Immigration and Its Consequences 344

Changes in Canadian Cities 346

Early Urban Growth and Social Problems 346

Contemporary Urban Growth 346

Urban Problems in Canada 348

Fiscal Crisis in Cities 348

BOX 13.2 Social Problems and Social Policy: Saving Our Cities 348

The Crisis in Urban Health Care 349

Housing Problems 350

Spatial Separation of the Poor and Visible Minorities 353

Problems in Global Cities 354

Perspectives on Urban Problems 356

The Functionalist Perspective 357

The Conflict Perspective 357

The Interactionist Perspective 358

BOX 13.3 Social Problems in the Media: Different Perceptions about Regent Park 359

The Feminist Perspective 360

Urban Problems in the Future 360

Environmental Problems 360

Economic Growth and Environmental Degradation 361

Air Pollution and Smog 362

BOX 13.4 Social Problems and Social Policy: The Ratification of the Kyoto Protocol 365

Problems with Water, Soil, and Forests 367

Solid, Toxic, and Nuclear Wastes 368

Perspectives on Population and the Environment 370

The Functionalist Perspective 370

The Conflict Perspective 372

The Interactionist Perspective 372

Feminist Perspectives 373

Population and the Environment in the Future 374

What Can You Do?   374

Summary   375

Key Terms   379

Questions for Critical Thinking   379ˆ

Weblinks   380

Epilogue   381

Glossary   387

References   393

Name Index   422

Subject Index   429

Photo Credits   443

PREFACE

[A social problems course] can provide a mind-opening . . . overview of a field of study, providing a method of perceiving and understanding the social realities we construct, playing a central role in leading students through the cognitive developmental processes that turn unchallenged dualism and other oversimplifications about everyday life into the complex formulations that better represent the social world in which we live.

Sociologists Michael Brooks and Kendal Broad describe the social problems course in the Instructor's Resource Manual on Social Problems (Brooks and Broad 1997:1)

This statement sums up the main reasons why we wrote *Social Problems in a Diverse Society*. Learning about social problems can be a highly rewarding experience. Although we live in difficult and challenging times, the social problems course provides an excellent avenue for developing patterns of critical thinking and for learning how to use sociological concepts and perspectives to analyze specific social concerns ranging from drug addiction, violence, and crime to inequalities of racialization and ethnicity, class, age, sexual orientation, and gender.

Our first and foremost goal in writing this book is to make the study of social problems interesting and relevant for students. To stimulate interest in reading the chapters and participation in class discussions, we have used lived experiences (personal narratives of real people) and statements from a wide variety of analysts to show how social problems impinge on people at the individual, group, and societal levels. Moreover, we have applied sociological imagination and relevant sociological concepts and perspectives to all the topics in a systematic manner.

The second Canadian edition of *Social Problems in a Diverse Society* focuses on the significance of racialization and ethnicity, age, sexual orientation, class, and gender in understanding social problems in Canada and around the globe. Throughout the text, people—especially those from marginalized groups—are shown not merely as "victims" of social problems, but also as individuals who resist discrimination and inequality and seek to bring about change in families, schools, workplaces, and the larger society. To facilitate the inclusion of previously excluded perspectives, Chapters 2 through 6 examine wealth and poverty, racialized/ethnic inequality, gender inequality, and inequalities based on age and sexual orientation. Thereafter, concepts and perspectives related to racialization and ethnicity, class, sexual orientation, age, and gender are intertwined in the discussion of specific social problems, such as education, health care, and the environment.

This second Canadian edition is balanced in its approach to examining social problems. However, it includes a more comprehensive view of feminist and postmodern perspectives on a vast array of subjects—such as the effect of new technologies and how the media depict social issues—than other social problems textbooks. As sociologists who integrate social theory into our lectures, we were disheartened by the minimal use of sociological theory in most social problems texts. Those that discuss theory typically do so in early chapters but then fail to use these theories as a systematic framework for examining specific social issues in subsequent chapters. Similarly, many texts give the impression that social problems can be solved if people reach a consensus on what should be done. But *Social Problems in a Diverse Society*, Second Canadian Edition, emphasizes that how people view a social problem is related to how they believe the problem should be reduced or solved. Consider poverty, for example: People who focus on individual causes of poverty typically believe that individual solutions (such as teaching people the work ethic and reforming welfare) are necessary to reduce the problem, whereas those who focus on structural causes of poverty (such as chronic unemployment and inadequate educational opportunities) typically believe that solutions must come from the larger society. Moreover, what some people see as a problem, others see as a solution for a problem (e.g., the sex industry as a source of income, or abortion to terminate a problematic pregnancy). The Epilogue allows students to fully explore the question, "Can social problems be solved?"

Finally, we wrote *Social Problems in a Diverse Society*, Second Canadian Edition, in hopes of providing students and instructors with a text that covers all the major social concerns of our day but does not leave students believing that the text—and perhaps the course—was a "depressing litany of social problems that nobody can do anything about anyway," as many students have stated about different texts. We have written this book in hopes of resolving those students' concerns, because we believe the sociological perspective has much to add to our national and global dialogues on a host of issues, such as environmental degradation; international terrorism; discrimination based on racialization and ethnicity, class, gender, age, sexual orientation, or other attributes; and problems in education. Welcome to an innovative examination of social problems—one of the most stimulating and engrossing fields of study in sociology!

ORGANIZATION OF THIS TEXT

Social Problems in a Diverse Society, Second Canadian Edition, has been organized with the specific plan of introducing disparities in wealth and poverty, racialization and ethnicity, gender, age, and sexual orientation early on so that the concepts and perspectives developed in these chapters may be applied throughout the text. All chapters offer theoretical analyses from structural functionalism, conflict or Marxist perspectives, symbolic interactionism, and feminist theories. In addition, other theories are introduced where relevant. Following several reviewers' suggestions, the total number of chapters has been reduced to better fit the number of classes in a term.

- Chapter 1 explains the sociological perspective and provides an analysis of attempts at problem solving at the microlevel, mid-range, and macrolevel of society and highlights the issue of worldwide violence and the new Canadian *Youth Criminal Justice Act*.

- Chapter 2 looks at wealth and poverty in Canada and around the world. Students will gain new insights into disparities between the wealthy and the poor and into problems such as workfare, homelessness, food insecurity, and poverty. The chapter concludes with a thematic question, "Can class-based inequality be reduced?" This question will be asked throughout the text as new topics are discussed.

- Chapter 3 integrates the previous discussion of class-based inequalities with an examination of racialized and ethnic inequality. The chapter looks at issues of democratic racism and White privilege in Canada, and at the ways that racism manifests itself throughout Canadian institutions and practices.

- Chapter 4 highlights factors such as mainstream gender socialization and social barriers that contribute to the unequal treatment of women in the workplace, in the family, at school, and at other social institutions. Transgender issues and global gender issues are also introduced for discussion.

- Ageism and inequality based on age are discussed in Chapter 5, and inequality based on sexual orientation is examined in Chapter 6, placing these important topics in a context similar to the studies of prejudice and discrimination rooted in racism and sexism in contemporary societies. In addition, Queer theory is highlighted as a way of analyzing sexual orientation issues.

- Chapter 7 links previous discussions of racialization and ethnicity, class, and gender to an analysis of prostitution, pornography, and the sex trade. The chapter provides up-to-date information on the globalization of prostitution and gives students insight into "johns" and how sex workers view themselves, why they engage in this line of work, and why some people view sex workers as a social problem.

- In Chapter 8, social problems caused by the use of alcohol and other drugs are discussed in depth, and students are provided with information about the drug commonly called the "date rape" drug and the abuse of prescription drugs, over-the-counter drugs, and caffeine.

- Chapter 9 discusses crime and criminal justice and takes an incisive look at sociological explanations of crime.

- Beginning with Chapter 10, a look at health care and its problems, we examine some of the major social institutions in our society and note aspects of each that constitute a social problem for large numbers of people.

- Chapter 11 explores the changing family, emphasizing diversity in intimate relationships and families, and child-related family issues. It also explores the dark side of family life.

- Chapter 12 presents contemporary problems in education, tracing the problems to such issues as what schools are supposed to accomplish, how they are financed, and why higher education may become less widely accessible with increasing tuition fees.

- Chapter 13 provides a survey of problems associated with population and the environmental crisis, focusing particularly on the causes and consequences of high rates of global migration and particular types of pollution. It also includes a look at urban problems, detailing the powerful impact of urbanization on both high-income and low-income nations of the world.

- The Epilogue asks, "(How) Can social problems be solved?" and includes a review of the four main sociological theories used to explain social problems, plus a set of perceived problems and possible solutions.

DISTINCTIVE FEATURES

A number of special features have been designed to incorporate racialization and ethnicity, class, sexual orientation, and gender into our analysis of social problems and to provide students with new insights on the social problems that they hear about on the evening news. The following sections discuss the text's distinctive features.

Lived Experiences throughout Each Chapter

These authentic, first-person accounts are used as vignettes—"real words from real people"—to create interest and show how the problems being discussed affect people as they go about their daily lives. Lived experiences provide opportunities for students to examine social life beyond their own experiences ("to live vicariously," as one student noted) and for instructors to systematically incorporate into lectures and class discussions examples of relevant, contemporary issues that have recently been on the evening news and in newspaper headlines.

- Fyre Jean Graveline, a college professor, describes her experience teaching in a "Native-controlled" college in Canada where nevertheless dominant White values are implicit and must be adhered to (Chapter 3, Racism and Ethnic Inequality).

- Gordon Brent Ingram discusses how his views of public spaces are informed by his sexual orientation (Chapter 6, Inequality Based on Sexual Orientation).

- Anonymous Canadian youth from across the country speak about how they became involved in the sex trade (Chapter 7, The Sex Industry in Canada and Beyond).

- Helen Stauffer, former Vice President of PRIDE (People to Reduce Impaired Driving Everywhere), and mother of a son who was killed by an impaired driver describes how that driver "took the sunshine from [her] life" (Chapter 8, Alcohol and Other Drugs).

- Plea bargains and restrictions after release, as shown in the case of Karla Homolka, are discussed, following a reviewer's suggestion (Chapter 9, Crime and Criminal Justice).

- Jeannie Hilton relates her experience of incest from her father, a former world-champion boxer in a new book (Chapter 11, The Changing Family).
- Ainsworth Morgan, an inner-city teacher and former Toronto Argonauts football player, outlines his ideas and projects to help his students succeed and help others (Chapter 12, Problems in Education).

Interesting and Highly Relevant Boxed Features

Four different boxes—Social Problems and Information Technology, Social Problems in the Media, Social Problems and Social Policy, and Social Problems in Global Perspective—highlight current hot topics involving various long-term social problems. Examples of each type of box are

- *Social Problems and Information Technology:* "Canada's Role in Cracking Down on Internet Child Pornography" (Chapter 7, The Sex Industry in Canada and Beyond);
- *Social Problems in the Media:* "Media Ageism: Reporting on and Preferring Age Groups" (Chapter 5, Inequality Based on Age);
- *Social Problems and Social Policy:* "The Battle over Marijuana: Medicalization, Availability, Decriminalization, Legalization?" (Chapter 8, Alcohol and Other Drugs); and
- *Social Problems in Global Perspective:* "Female Genital Surgery or Female Genital Mutilation?" (Chapter 4, Gender Inequality).

Built-in Study Features

These pedagogical aids promote students' mastery of sociological concepts and perspectives:

- Chapter Outlines: A concise outline at the beginning of each chapter gives students an overview of major topics.
- What Can You Do? Section: This section gives students suggestions about how they can tackle social problems on their own, as individuals, or collectively in a group.

- Key Terms: Major concepts and key terms are defined and highlighted in bold print within the text. Definitions are also available in the glossary at the back of the text.
- Summary in question-and-answer format: Each chapter concludes with a concise summary in a convenient question-and-answer format, to help students master the key concepts and main ideas in each chapter.
- Questions for Critical Thinking: End-of-chapter questions provide opportunities for students to develop important critical-thinking skills about the issues raised in each chapter.
- Weblinks: Several websites are listed to encourage students to pursue their interests, from a variety of perspectives, and gain more up-to-date material on social issues they are interested in following up.

Supplements

- For the Instructor: The Instructor's Resource CD-ROM that accompanies this text contains a variety of supplements, including an Instructor's Manual, Test Item File, TestGen, and PowerPoint Presentation. Please contact your local sales representative for more information about these supplements.
- For the Student: A wealth of online resources can be found on the Companion Website for this text at **www.pearsoned.ca/kendall**.

ACKNOWLEDGMENTS

We wish to personally thank the many people who have made this new edition a reality. First, we offer our profound thanks to the following reviewers who provided valuable comments and suggestions on how to make this text outstanding. Whenever possible, we have incorporated their suggestions into the text. The reviewers are Winston Barnwell, Dalhousie University; Andrew Hathaway, McMaster University; Uldis Kundrats, Nipissing University; Thomas Groulx, St. Clair College; Dana Lennox, Algonquin College; Cecelia Reilly, Loyalist College; G. Frank Trovato, Humber Institute of Technology & Advanced Learning; and Deirdre Way, Loyalist College.

The second Canadian edition of *Social Problems in a Diverse Society* has also involved the co-operative efforts of many people who have made this book possible. We wish to thank Ky Pruesse, Executive Acquisitions Editor; Jon Maxfield, Associate Editor and Emily Jardeleza, Associate Editor; Amanda Wesson, Production Editor; and Lisa Berland, Copy Editor.

I could not have written this book without the assistance of my husband, Terrence Kendall, who has done so much outstanding advising, editing—and sometimes consoling—on this and other texts I have written that I have declared him to be not only a lawyer but also an "Honorary Sociologist."

—Diana Kendall

My heartfelt thanks go to my beautiful daughters, Freja Aramaia Nygaard and Phoenix Taran Nygaard and to my dearest friend, Maya K Gislason, who kept me grounded and focused on what's really important in life and who continually offered me the gifts of their time and support throughout the research and writing of this book.

—Vicki L. Nygaard

I could not have written this book without the assistance of my partner, Helen Barron, who has not only provided continuing support, but also edited each of my chapters.

—Edward G. Thompson

To each of you reading this preface, we wish you the best in teaching or studying social problems and hope that you will share with us any comments or suggestions you have about *Social Problems in a Diverse Society*, Second Canadian Edition. The text was written with you in mind, and your suggestions (with appropriate attribution) will be included whenever possible in future editions. Let's hope that our enthusiasm for "taking a new look at social problems" will spread to others so that together we may seek to reduce or solve some of the pressing social problems we encounter during our lifetime.

Diana Kendall
Vicki L. Nygaard
Edward G. Thompson

1

TAKING A NEW LOOK AT SOCIAL PROBLEMS

WHAT IS A SOCIAL PROBLEM?

    Box 1.1 Social Problems in Global Perspective:
    Violence around the World

WHY STUDY SOCIAL PROBLEMS?

THE SOCIOLOGICAL IMAGINATION AND
SOCIAL PROBLEMS

SOCIOLOGICAL PERSPECTIVES ON
SOCIAL PROBLEMS

    The Functionalist Perspective

    The Conflict Perspective

    Box 1.2 Social Problems in the Media: The New
    Canadian *Youth Criminal Justice Act:* Selling
    Canadians a "Sheep in Wolf's Clothing"?

    The Interactionist Perspective

    Feminist Perspectives

SOCIAL CHANGE AND REDUCING SOCIAL
PROBLEMS

    Microlevel Attempts to Solve Social
    Problems

    Mid-Range Attempts to Solve Social
    Problems

    Macrolevel Attempts to Solve Social
    Problems

    Box 1.3 Social Problems in Global Perspective:
    The Lysistrata Project

    In Sum

Gosset did something wrong, we all knew that. Gosset murdered my son. He used the law. He hid behind it. There's no way we could have gotten justice.... I'm not a racist person but I believe that both juries did not give us justice and I'm going to say freely that I do not think white people can give justice to black people... I think in their hearts they just can't.

Orberth Griffin, speaking out after the acquittal of the police officer who fatally shot Griffin's son (Pedicelli 1998:94)

In no way am I racist. Where I used to live in Lasalle, there were many black people and I often vacation in countries that are predominantly black.

Constable Allan Gosset in response to accusations of racism in the shooting death of Anthony Griffin (Pedicelli, 1998:78)

To steal that [the touch of her son] away from you, it's like death to you.

Julia Farquharson speaks of her son's shooting to people trying to deal with the killing of over 100 Black youths by other Black youths in Toronto since 1996 (CBC 2003)

Whether it takes place in an inner-city schoolyard or on a city street or in Iraq, Afghanistan, or Kosovo, violence leaves shock and anguish behind. **Violence is the use of physical force to cause pain, injury, or death or damage to property.** Around the world, violence is a major social problem. On an almost daily basis, the Internet and television news channels quickly spread word of the latest bombing, the latest massacre, the latest sexual assault, the latest murder. In Canada, a place not known for the violence reported daily in the United States, murders of youth by other youth have made sensational headlines. Along with several recent murders of youth in Toronto, a young South Asian woman, Reena Virk, was beaten and later killed by a group of mainly female peers in Victoria, B.C. The other youth were white, adding a racialized dimension to the tragedy. In Vancouver in 2003, 17-year-old Jomar Lanot was beaten to death on his way home from playing basketball at a nearby school by a group of teens led by 16-year-old Muzil Abdullah. Additionally, following the Columbine High School murders in Littleton, Colorado, on April 20, 1999, a 14-year-old boy in Taber, Alberta, brought a gun to school and shot 17-year-old Jason Lang to death and injured another boy.

In the wake of each new episode of violence, a renewed call for gun control goes out from advocates of restricted access to guns and other weaponry. Advocates of gun control point to Department of Justice information showing that the province with the highest percentage of homes with guns is Alberta, followed by New Brunswick and Saskatchewan; the provinces with the highest rate of youth, aged 15 to 25, killed by firearms are, in order, New Brunswick, Saskatchewan, and Alberta (CBC 1999). A corresponding cry arises from gun enthusiasts across the country and such organizations as the National Firearms Association, who oppose further tightening of gun laws. In fact, in a 2002 news release, the National Firearms Association called the federal government's gun control program, which required Canadian citizens to register their firearms with a government gun registry, "a dog and pony show." Seemingly, in accordance with this viewpoint and after millions of dollars in overspending, in June of 2006, the Harper government introduced legislation to abolish the long-gun registry. The handgun registry and bans on automatic weapons will remain in place, however.

Many of us are ambivalent about violence. We condemn drive-by shootings and cold-blooded murders, yet enjoy watching action movies with lots of "blood and guts" or contact sports such as wrestling, hockey, football, and boxing. However we explain this contradictory behaviour, violence is seen by many as a major social problem, in this country and around the world.

WHAT IS A SOCIAL PROBLEM?

Although not all sociologists agree about what constitutes a social problem, most would agree with this general definition: A *social problem* **is a social condition (such as poverty) or a pattern of behaviour (such as violence against women) that people believe warrants public concern and collective action to bring about change.** Social conditions or certain patterns of behaviour are defined as social problems when they systematically disadvantage or harm a significant number of people (or number of "significant" people?) or when they are seen as harmful by many of the people who wield power, wealth, and influence in a group or society. To put it another way, social problems are social in their causes, consequences, and possible sources of resolution.

The study of social problems is one area of inquiry within *sociology*—**the academic and scholarly discipline that engages in systematic study of human society and social interactions.** A sociological examination of social problems focuses primarily on issues that affect an entire *society*—**a large number of individuals who share the same geographical territory and are subject to the same political authority and dominant cultural expectations**—and the groups and organizations that make up that society. Because social problems are social in their causes, public perception of what constitutes a social problem can change. Consider, for example, how public perception of what constitutes a social problem has changed over the last 50 years. In the 1950s, people worried about the problem of nuclear war. More recently, people have been worried about unemployment (early 1980s and early 1990s), government debt (mid-1990s), and, in the last few years, cutbacks to health care, education, and social services (*Maclean's* 1999, 2002).

SOCIAL PROBLEMS IN GLOBAL PERSPECTIVE

BOX 1.1   Violence around the World

In its first *World Report on Violence and Health,* released in October 2002, the World Health Organization (WHO) stated that violence kills 1.6 million people annually. About one-half of these deaths are due to suicide; one-third are due to homicide; and 20 percent are due to armed conflict. One person commits suicide every 40 or so seconds; one person is the victim of a homicide every minute; and one person is killed in armed conflict every two minutes. During the 20th century, about 191 million people were killed in armed conflict. Many more people are injured, physically and psychologically. Young people aged 15 to 44 are especially affected. Violence is a major cause of death for this group: 14 percent of young males and 7 percent of young females die violently.

Some patterns of victimization are experienced worldwide. For example, in Canada, nearly half of murdered women are killed by an intimate or former intimate partner (see Chapter 9); about 20 percent of women and 5 to 10 percent of men experience sexual abuse (see Chapter 11); and about 4 percent of the elderly experience abuse (see Chapter 5). Other patterns show wide differences in rates of victimization. For example, the rate of violent death is twice as high in low- and middle-income countries than in high-income countries; in some countries, up to 70 percent of women are killed by intimate or former intimate partners, and one-third of adolescent girls report forced sexual initiation. Patterns also vary by region. In Europe and Asia, suicides exceed homicides; in Latin America, homicides exceed suicides.

Following its mandate, the WHO promotes a public health approach to understanding the problem of violence. Thus, its *World Report on Violence and Health* could be considered part of the process of the medicalization of crime and deviance (see Chapter 9). To solve the problem of violence, the report recommends dealing with the social, cultural, economic, and psychological root causes of violence and taking advantage of opportunities to prevent violence. Developing community projects such as parent training and gun-safety training, strengthening responses of victims to violence, collecting better data on violence, and seeking practical international agreements to combat the drug and arms trades are among the recommendations put forward.

In November 2005, the World Health Organization released findings from another major study about violence called the *WHO Multi-Country Study on Women's Health and Domestic Violence Against Women.* This study reported data from 10 countries, including Ethiopia, Bangladesh, Peru, and the United Republic of Tanzania, where few data were available, and one high-income country, Japan. A sample size of 24 000 women was obtained from cities and rural parts of these countries, and topics of physical and sexual violence were studied. The percentage of women who had experienced physical and sexual violence by an intimate partner in their lifetime ranged from 15 percent in Japan to 71 percent in Ethiopia. In Ethiopia, Bangladesh, Peru, and the United Republic of Tanzania, more than 50 percent of married women experience both physical and sexual violence. Other topics studied were abuse outside marriage, abuse before age 15, forced sex in marriage (a major problem because of the inability of women to protect themselves from HIV infection), and abuse during pregnancy. The report included several recommendations to create programs to help women, to enlist local leadership, and to make physical environments safer for women.

Sources: World Health Organization (WHO), 2002, *World Report on Violence and Health.* Retrieved July 23, 2006 (http://www.who.int/violence_injury_prevention/violence/world_report/en/); WHO, 2005, *WHO Multi-Country Study on Women's Health and Domestic Violence Against Women.* Retrieved July 23, 2006 (http://www.who.int/gender/en/).

Sociologists apply theoretical perspectives and use a variety of research methods to examine social problems. Some social problems—such as violence and crime—are commonly viewed as conditions that affect all members of a population (see Box 1.1). Other social problems—such as racialized discrimination and sexual harassment—may be viewed (correctly or incorrectly) as conditions that affect some members of a population more than others. However, all social problems may be harmful to all members in a society whether they realize it or not. Sociological research, for example, has documented the extent to which white racism wastes the energies and resources of people who engage in racist actions as well as those of the targets of the actions (see Feagin and Sikes 1994; Feagin and Vera 1995).

Social problems often involve significant discrepancies between the ideals of a society and their actual achievement. For example, in Canada, the rights of individuals are guaranteed by the *Charter of Rights and Freedoms*, which also provides the legal basis for remedying injustices. Significant discrepancies exist, however, between the democratic ideal and its achievement. One such discrepancy is *discrimination*—**actions or practices of dominant group members (or their representatives) that have a harmful impact on members of subordinate groups.** Sociologists define the *dominant group* as **the group whose members are disproportionately at the top of the hierarchy, "with maximal access to the society's power resources, particularly political authority and control of the means of economic production"** (Marger 1999:273). *Subordinate groups* are all **those whose members, in relation to the dominant group (or groups), do not occupy such positions of power.** The term usually used for a subordinate group is *minority group* (see Chapter 3).

Discrimination may be directed along a number of lines—class, racialization, gender, and age. It also may be directed against subordinate group members whose sexual orientation, religion, nationality, disability, or other attributes or characteristics are devalued by those who discriminate against them. Sometimes, discrimination is acted out in the form of violence. This type of violent act is referred to as a *hate crime*—**an act of violence motivated by prejudice against people on the basis of racialized identity, ethnicity, religion, gender, or sexual orientation. This can include the dissemination of materials intended to incite hatred.** Although hate crimes have been added to the *Criminal*

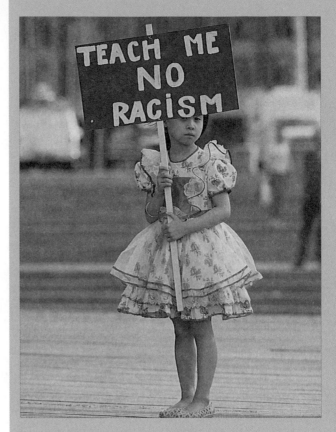

What does this photo show us about the discrepancies that exist between the democratic ideals and the social realities of our society? Does discrimination against subordinate group members take place in other societies as well?

Code only quite recently, the crimes themselves date back hundreds of years (see Chapters 3, 6, and 9 for further discussion of hate crimes).

WHY STUDY SOCIAL PROBLEMS?

Studying social problems helps us understand the social forces that shape our lives on both personal and societal levels. In our daily lives, we rely on common sense—"what everybody knows"—to guide our conduct and make sense of human behaviour. But many common-sense notions about why people behave the way they do, who makes the rules, and why some people break rules and others follow them are *myths*—beliefs that persist even when the actual truth is different. Myths about social problems frequently garner widespread acceptance and sometimes extensive media coverage.

A sociological examination of social problems enables us to move beyond common-sense notions, to gain new insights into ourselves, and to develop an awareness of the connection between our own world and the worlds of other people. According to sociologist Peter Berger (1963:23), a sociological examination allows us to realize that "things are not what they seem." Indeed, most social problems are multifaceted. When we recognize this, we can approach pressing local, national, and global concerns in new ways and make more effective decisions about those concerns. In taking a global perspective on social problems, we soon realize that the lives of all people are closely intertwined, and that any one nation's problems are part of a larger global problem.

THE SOCIOLOGICAL IMAGINATION AND SOCIAL PROBLEMS

Just like other people, sociologists usually have strong opinions about what is "good" and "bad" in society and what might be done to improve conditions. However, sociologists know their opinions are subjective. Thus, they use systematic research techniques and report their findings to other social scientists for consideration. In other words, sociologists strive to view social problems *objectively.* Of course, complete objectivity may not be an attainable—or desirable—goal in studying human behaviour. Max Weber (1864–1920), an early German sociologist, acknowledged that complete objectivity might be impossible and pointed out that *verstehen* ("understanding," or "insight") was critical to any analysis of social problems. According to Weber, *verstehen* enables individuals to see the world as others see it and to empathize with them. *Verstehen,* in turn, enables us to develop what is called the sociological imagination.

According to sociologist C. Wright Mills (1959b), the *sociological imagination* **is the ability to see the relationship between an individual's experiences and the larger society in which they are contextualized.** The sociological imagination enables us to connect the private troubles of individuals to the public issues of a society. Public issues (or social problems) are matters beyond a person's control that originate at the regional or national level and can be resolved only by collective action. In *The Sociological Imagination*, Mills used

unemployment as an example of how people may erroneously separate personal troubles from public issues in their thinking. The unemployed individual may view his or her unemployment as a personal trouble concerning only the individual, other family members, and friends. However, widespread unemployment resulting from economic changes, corporate decisions (downsizing or relocating a plant abroad), or technological innovations (computers and advanced telecommunications systems displacing workers) is a public issue. The sociological imagination helps us to shift our focus to the larger social context and see how personal troubles may be related to public issues.

Sociologists make connections between personal and public issues in society through microlevel and macrolevel analysis. *Microlevel analysis* **focuses on small-group relations and social interaction among individuals.** Using microlevel analysis, a sociologist might investigate how fear of unemployment affects workers and their immediate families. In contrast, *macrolevel analysis* **focuses on social processes occurring at the societal level, especially in large-scale organizations and major social institutions such as politics, government, and the economy.** Using macrolevel analysis, a sociologist might examine how globalization and the attendant labour market restructuring has impacted Canadian workers and their families.

As Mills suggested, a systematic study of a social problem such as unemployment gives us a clearer picture of the relationship between macrolevel structures such as the Canadian economy and microlevel social interactions among people in their homes, workplaces, and communities. It does not get the individual his or her job back, but it provides a better understanding of how the situation happened. With a clearer understanding of how we find ourselves in the situations we do, we may be able to develop more effective levels of prevention and intervention.

SOCIOLOGICAL PERSPECTIVES ON SOCIAL PROBLEMS

To determine how social life is organized, sociologists develop theories and conduct research. A *theory* **is a set of logically related statements that attempt to describe, explain, or predict social events.** Theories are useful for explaining relationships between social concepts or phenomena, such as "ethnicity and unemployment" or "gender and poverty." They also help us interpret social reality in a distinct way by giving us a framework for organizing our observations. Sociologists refer to this theoretical framework as a ***perspective***—**an overall approach or viewpoint toward some subject.** Four major theoretical perspectives have emerged in sociology: the functionalist perspective, which views society as a basically stable and orderly entity; the conflict perspective, which views society as an arena of competition and conflict; the interactionist perspective, which focuses on the everyday, routine interactions among individuals; and, the feminist perspective, which focuses on the gendered (and racialized and classed) inequalities between groups and on strategies for positive social change. The functionalist and conflict perspectives are based on macrolevel analysis because they focus on social processes occurring at the societal level. The interactionist perspective is based on microlevel analysis because it focuses on small-group relations and social interaction. The feminist perspective involves both macro- and microlevel analysis by looking at the ways, for example, that the dominant gender ideology (macro) impacts the specific interactions (micro) between woman X and man Y within a capitalist and patriarchal, white-dominant culture.

The Functionalist Perspective

The functionalist perspective grew out of the works of early social thinkers such as Auguste Comte (1798–1857), the founder of sociology. Comte compared society to a living organism. Just as muscles, tissues, and organs of the human body perform specific functions that maintain the body as a whole, the various parts of society contribute to its maintenance and preservation. According to the ***functionalist perspective***, **society is a stable, orderly system composed of several interrelated parts, each of which performs a function that contributes to the overall stability of society** (Parsons 1951). These interrelated parts are social institutions (such as families, the economy, education, and the government) that a society develops to organize its main concerns and activities so that it meets social needs. Each institution performs a unique function, contributing to the overall stability of society and the well-being of individuals (Merton 1968). For example,

the functions of the economy are producing and distributing goods (such as food, clothing, and shelter) and services (such as tourism services and dry-cleaning), whereas the government is responsible for coordinating activities of other institutions directed to such ends as health care, education, maintaining law and order, dealing with unmet social needs, and handling international relations and peace.

Manifest and Latent Functions

Though the functions of the economy and the government seem fairly clear-cut, functionalists suggest that not all the functions of social institutions are intended and overtly recognized. In fact, according to the functionalist perspective, social institutions perform two different types of societal functions: manifest and latent. *Manifest functions* are intended and recognized consequences of an activity or social process. A manifest function of education, for example, is to provide students with knowledge, skills, and cultural values. In contrast, *latent functions* are the unintended consequences of an activity or social process that are hidden and remain unacknowledged by participants (Merton 1968). The latent functions of education include the babysitter function of keeping young people off the street while their parents work and out of the full-time job market, and the matchmaking function whereby schools provide opportunities for students to meet and socialize with potential marriage partners. These functions are latent because schools were not created for babysitting or matchmaking, and most organizational participants do not acknowledge that these activities take place.

Dysfunctions and Social Disorganization

From the functionalist perspective, social problems arise when social institutions do not fulfill their functions or when dysfunctions occur. *Dysfunctions* are the undesirable consequences of an activity or social process that inhibit a society's ability to adapt or adjust (Merton, 1968). For example, a function of education is to prepare students for jobs; but if schools fail to do so, then students have problems finding jobs, employers or governments have to spend millions of dollars on employee training programs, and consumers have to pay higher prices for goods and services to offset worker training costs. In other words, dysfunctions in education threaten other social institutions, especially families and the economy.

Dysfunctions can occur in society as a whole or in a part of society (a social institution). According to functionalists, dysfunctions in social institutions create social disorganization in the entire society. ***Social disorganization* refers to the conditions in society that undermine the ability of traditional social institutions to govern human behaviour.** Early in the 20th century, sociologists Robert E. Park (1864–1944) and Ernest W. Burgess (1886–1966) developed a social disorganization theory to explain why some urban areas had higher rates of *social deviance,* which they defined as a pattern of rule violation, than other areas had. Social disorganization causes a breakdown in the traditional values and norms that serve as social control mechanisms, which, under normal circumstances, keep people from engaging in nonconforming behaviour. ***Values* are collective ideas about what is right or wrong, good or bad, and desirable or undesirable in a specific society** (Williams 1970). Although values provide ideas about behaviour, they do not state explicitly how we should behave. Norms, on the other hand, have specific behavioural expectations. ***Norms* are established rules of behaviour or standards of conduct.** French sociologist Emile Durkheim (1858–1917) suggested that social problems arise when people no longer agree on societal values and norms. According to Durkheim, periods of rapid social change produce *anomie*—a loss of shared values and sense of purpose in society. During these periods, social bonds grow weaker, social control is diminished, and people are more likely to engage in nonconforming patterns of behaviour, such as crime.

Early sociologists, examining the relationship between social problems and rapid industrialization and urbanization in Britain, Western Europe, and the United States in the late 19th and early 20th centuries, noted that rapid social change intensifies social disorganization. ***Industrialization* is the process by which societies are transformed from a dependence on agriculture and handmade products to an emphasis on manufacturing and related industries.** At the beginning of the Industrial Revolution, thousands of people migrated from rural communities to large urban centres to find employment in factories and offices. New social problems emerged as a result of industrialization and ***urbanization*, the process by which an increasing proportion of a population lives in cities rather than in rural areas.** During this period of rapid technological and social change, urban social problems such as poverty, crime, child labour, inadequate housing, unsanitary conditions, overcrowding, and environmental pollution increased sharply.

Applying the Functionalist Perspective to Problems of Violence

Some functionalists believe that violence arises from a condition of anomie, in which many individuals have a feeling of helplessness, normlessness, or alienation. Others believe that violence increases when social institutions such as the family, schools, and religious organizations weaken, and the main mechanisms of social control in people's everyday lives are external (i.e., law enforcement agencies and the criminal justice system).

Other functionalist explanations of violence focus on how changes in social institutions put some people at greater risk of being victims of violent crime than others. According to the ***lifestyle–routine activity approach*, the patterns and timing of people's daily movements and activities as they go about obtaining such necessities of life as food, shelter, companionship, and entertainment are the keys to understanding violent personal crimes and other types of crime in our society** (Cohen and Felson 1979). Several changes over the past 50 years that may have put people at increased risk for violent crime victimization in Canada, such as more people living by themselves, shopping hours extended into the night, and more people eating outside the home (Parker 1995). Social structure may also put constraints on behaviour, thus making certain people more vulnerable to violent attack (e.g., people who are required to work at night). The lifestyle–routine activity approach suggests that people who willingly put themselves in situations that expose them to the potential for violent crime should modify their behaviour, or that society should provide greater protection for people whose lifestyle routine leaves them vulnerable to attackers. The lifestyle–routine activity approach offers some insight, but it does not address the issue of violence in the home and other supposedly safe havens. Further, it does not explain the violence itself; it simply points out that people are at risk, which tells us nothing that would assist in eliminating violence.

How would a functionalist approach the problem of violence? Most functionalists emphasize shared moral values and social bonds. They believe that when rapid social change or other "disruptions" occur, moral values may erode, and problems such as school violence or hate crimes are likely to occur more frequently. Functionalists believe that to reduce violence, families, schools, religious organizations, and other social institutions should be strengthened so that they can regenerate shared values and morality. Most functionalists also believe that those who engage in violent criminal behaviour should be prosecuted to the full extent of the law.

The Conflict Perspective

The *conflict perspective* **is based on the assumption that groups in society are engaged in a continuous power struggle for control of scarce resources.** Unlike functionalist theorists, who emphasize the degree to which society is held together by a consensus on values, conflict theorists emphasize the degree to which society is characterized by conflict and discrimination. According to some conflict theorists, certain groups of people are privileged while others are disadvantaged through the inequitable use of political, economic, or social power. Not all conflict theorists hold the same views about what constitutes the most important form of conflict. We will examine two principal perspectives: the value conflict perspective and the critical-conflict perspective.

The Value Conflict Perspective

According to value conflict theorists, social problems are conditions that are incompatible with group values. From this perspective, value clashes are ordinary occurrences in families, communities, and the larger society, in which individuals commonly hold many divergent values. Although individuals may share certain core values, they do not share all values or a common culture. *Culture* refers to the knowledge, language, values, customs, and material objects that are passed from person to person and from one generation to the next in a human group or society.

Discrepancies between ideal and real culture are a source of social problems in all societies. *Ideal culture* refers to the values and beliefs that people claim they hold; *real culture* refers to the values and beliefs that they actually follow. In Canada, members of such diverse groups as B'nai Brith, the Heritage Front, the Aryan Nations, and the Urban Alliance on Race Relations all claim to adhere to ideal cultural values of equality, freedom, and liberty; however, these ideal cultural values come into direct conflict with real cultural values when issues of racialized/ethnic relations arise.

The brutal murder of 14-year-old Reena Virk, a high-school student of South Asian descent, in Victoria, B.C., in 1997 by eight other youths produced an outcry in her community. Some people were concerned that hate crimes against individuals because of ethnic origin, class, or gender might go unpunished. However, two young people, Warren Glowatski and Kelly Ellard, were eventually convicted of second-degree murder.

The value conflict perspective has been criticized by critical-conflict theorists, who argue that it overlooks the deeper social problems of inequality and oppression based on class, "race," and gender.

Critical-Conflict Perspective

Unlike the value conflict approach, critical-conflict theorists suggest that social problems arise out of the major contradictions inherent in the way societies are organized. Some critical-conflict perspectives focus on class inequalities in the capitalist economic system; others focus on inequalities based on "race"/ethnicity or gender.

Most class perspectives on inequality have been strongly influenced by Karl Marx (1818–1883), a

German economist and activist, who recognized that the emergence of capitalism had produced dramatic and irreversible changes in social life. ***Capitalism* is an economic system characterized by private ownership of the means of production, from which personal profits can be derived through market competition and without government intervention.** According to Marx, members of the *capitalist class* (the *bourgeoisie*), who own and control the means of production (e.g., the land, tools, factories, and money for investment), are at the top of a system of social stratification that affords them different lifestyles and life chances from those of the members of the *working class* (the *proletariat*), who must sell their labour power (their potential ability to work) to capitalists. In selling their labour power, members of the working class forfeit control over their work, and the capitalists derive profits from the workers' labour.

Marx believed that capitalism leads workers to experience increased levels of impoverishment and *alienation*—a feeling of powerlessness and estrangement from other people and from oneself (Marx and Engels 1847/1971:96). He predicted that the working class would eventually overthrow the capitalist economic system. Although Marx's prediction has not come about, Erik Olin Wright (1997) and other social scientists have modified and adapted his perspective to apply to contemporary capitalist nations. In today's capitalist nations, according to Wright (1997), ownership of the means of production is only one way in which people gain the ability to exploit others. Two other ways in which individuals gain control are through *control* of property and *control* over other people's labour. In this view, upper-level managers and others in positions of authority gain control over societal resources and other individuals' time, knowledge, and skills in such a manner that members of the upper classes are able to maintain their dominance.

Some critical-conflict perspectives focus on racialized and gender subordination instead of class-based inequalities. Critical-conflict theorists who emphasize discrimination and inequality based on "race" or ethnicity note that many social problems are rooted in the continuing exploitation and subordination of people of colour and Indigenous people by white people, or more accurately, by institutions and systems set up by and for white people. For example, Frideres (1999:142–44) has shown how Indigenous people in Canada are greatly disadvantaged relative to any other ethnic groups: they have considerably lower family incomes and substantially higher rates of unemployment than non-Indigenous people.

Throughout this text, where we discuss conflict theory, we will use critical-conflict theory (rather than the value conflict approach) to highlight the power relations that result in social problems.

Applying the Conflict Perspective to Problems of Violence

Conflict theorists who focus on class-based inequalities believe that the potential for violence is inherent in capitalist societies. In fact, say these theorists, the wealthy engage in one form of violence, and the poor engage in another. They note that the wealthy often use third parties to protect themselves and their families from bodily harm as well as to secure their property and investments in this country and elsewhere in the world. For example, the wealthy who live in Canada or other high-income nations and who own factories (or own stock in factories) in middle- and low-income nations use the governments and police of those nations—third parties—to control workers who threaten to strike. The wealthy also influence Canadian government policy, by supporting or not supporting peacekeeping or military intervention in nations where they may have investments or desire to have investments.

In contrast, these theorists say, when the poor engage in violence, the violence is typically committed by the individual and may be a reaction to the unjust social and economic conditions he or she experiences daily on the bottom rung of a capitalist society. The economic exploitation of the poor, these theorists note, dramatically affects all aspects of the individual's life, including how the person reacts to daily injustices, stress, and other threatening situations. In violent street crimes, the vast majority of offenders—as well as victims—are poor, unemployed, or working in low-level, low-paying jobs. In fact, most violent street crime is an intra-class phenomenon. Arrest and conviction data suggest that poor and working-class people typically victimize others who are like themselves. In part, this is due to the fact that violence committed by middle-and upper-class individuals is not investigated and/or prosecuted to the same degree. Moreover, middle- and upper-class individuals are likely to enlist the services of people from lower classes when they wish to commit violence. For example, in a televised interview, Brett Hayes, a past member of a neo-Nazi skinhead organization in Canada, stated that certain individuals are targeted for violence by the organization's elite (many allegedly in prominent positions in society), but the actual violence is commissioned and carried out by the "foot soldiers," or "dogs," of the movement, the mainly working-class and youthful "skins" (CTV 1995).

The conflict perspective argues that the criminal justice system is biased in favour of the middle and upper classes. Because it is, its definition of violence depends on where a person's ethnicity, class, and gender locate him or her in the system of stratification. In this way, violent crimes are but one part of a larger system of inequality and oppression. Sexism and racism are reinforced by the overarching class structure that benefits the powerful at the expense of the powerless. The conflict perspective that focuses on racialized/ethnic inequalities points out that racism is an important factor in explaining such violent acts as hate crimes. Recently, a number of white supremacists spouting racist and anti-Semitic dogma have been convicted of violent crimes. This kind of brutality, for example the 1998 murder of a Sikh man in Surrey, British Columbia, by a group of white supremacists, is fuelled by racist ideologies that suggest that problems with the economy and growing unemployment for young people are due to increased immigration. Leaders of white supremacist groups foster these discourses as a way of fuelling hate and inciting violence (see Chapter 3).

No matter what approach conflict theorists take, they all agree on one thing: Violence is unlikely to diminish significantly unless inequalities based on class and ethnicity are reduced at the macrolevel in society.

SOCIAL PROBLEMS IN THE MEDIA

BOX 1.2   The New Canadian *Youth Criminal Justice Act:* Selling Canadians a "Sheep in Wolf's Clothing"?

On February 4, 2002, the Canadian House of Commons passed Bill C-7, bringing into effect on April 1, 2003, Canada's *Youth Criminal Justice Act* (YCJA). The new act replaced the 1984 Canadian *Young Offenders Act* (YOA). There are several differences between the two acts, but most notable are the changes that allowed children to be tried as adults and penalized as adults, particularly for violent crimes such as murder and sexual assault. Under the old act, children aged 12–17 were viewed as having not reached full maturity and as such should be shown leniency. However, even under the old act, a youth aged 14 or over who was charged with murder, attempted murder, manslaughter, or aggravated sexual assault could be transferred to adult court and receive an adult sentence. Adult sentences were imposed if the court felt that a youth sentence would be insufficient in making the youth accountable for the crime (Department of Justice 2006b).

The repeal of the 1984 YOA and subsequent creation of the 2002 YCJA were accomplished after much heated debate in Canada; the result, some say, of a multi-pronged public relations campaign begun in 1998 by the Government of Canada. On the one side were the advocates of the "law and order" agenda, who painted youth as "out of control," "super-predators" who were "getting away with murder" (Martin 2002: 96; Young and Gainsborough 2000: 2). As Hartnagel states,

> The YOA was under frequent criticism almost from its inception in 1984. Many argued that the act was too soft on young offenders and that the available sentences were too light, particularly for repeat or more serious offences. The minimum age of legal culpability (12) was claimed to be too high; and the age of adulthood (18) was seen as 'mollycoddling' young adult criminals (2004: 361).

On the other side of the debate were those who followed a "children's rights" discourse, believing the new YCJA would be too harsh, "too & offence oriented' and/or too & tough' on young people" (Doob and Sprott 2006: 229).

The "law and order" approach to youth violence was aided by a concept Stanley Cohen and Jock Young have advanced, called a "moral panic" (1971/1980), where "the youth of today" are presented as "a threat to the established way of life" (Thompson 1998: 1). A moral panic is defined as a campaign sustained over a period of time that appeals to people worried about the risks of a disintegrating social order, that lacks clear moral guidelines, that politicians and media are eager to act on in order to be seen as suppressing the threat, and that leaves the real causes of social breakdown (if a breakdown exists) unaddressed (Thompson 1998: 3). Moral panics, as described by Kenneth Thompson, have five key stages or elements:

1. Something or someone is defined as a threat to values or interests.
2. This threat is depicted in an easily recognizable form by the media.
3. There is a rapid buildup of public concern.
4. There is a response from authorities and opinion makers.
5. The panic recedes or results in social changes (1998:8).

For at least 100 years, society has endured moral panics of one sort or another, disproportionately with youth as the perceived threat. That media and politicians created a moral panic in the 1980s and 1990s about the so-called rising tide of youth violence cannot be in doubt.

Several Canadian criminologists argue that public opinion in Canada about youth crime and youth justice has been carefully socially constructed through savvy government public relations strategies (including well-timed "leaks" to the media) and relentless media sensationalism that implies that statistically rare serious and violent crimes committed by youth have, in fact, become commonplace. The perceived goal of this PR was the political ejection of a party that was viewed as being too soft on youth crime (Doob and Gainsborough 2006; Hartnagel 2004; Martin 2002; Pedicelli 1998). Various Canadian public opinion polls over these years indicated that Canadians believed violent youth crime was on the rise, and as a result, they became increasingly fearful of youth (Hartnagel 2004). Hartnagel, citing the work of Schissel (1997), states:

> [T]he Canadian media constructed folk devils of youth, symbolically targeting them as scapegoats for various ills of society. [Schissel] illustrated his argument with newspaper articles claiming that youth crime had become endemic, characteristic of a certain kind of youth, and required stern intervention [and he] concluded that the media present an ideological

portrait of youth crime and criminals by using selected extraordinary crimes as evidence of a general crime wave (2004:366).

We can see clear evidence of Hartnagel's (and Schissel's) argument in the sensationalized media accounts of the trials of Kelly Ellard and Warren Glowatski, convicted April 2005 (Ellard) and June 1999 (Glowatski), of killing Reena Virk in Victoria, B.C.; of Muzil Abdullah, convicted July 2006 of killing Jomar Lanot in Vancouver, B.C.; and of Sonny Head, convicted June 2002 of killing Barbara Danelesko in Edmonton, Alberta.

What is significant about these well-publicized trials and Canadians' newfound comfort with the YCJA is that there are actually no demonstrable changes in our responses to youth who commit violent crimes. In fact, the level of punitiveness, demonstrated for example by increased rates of imprisonment, increased transfers to adult court, and harsher penalties, toward serious and violent youth offenders has not increased since the YCJA came into effect. Certainly the sensationalized cases mentioned earlier bear this out. Ellard and Glowatski were sentenced to life imprisonment and are eligible for parole after seven years. Head was sentenced to seven years in prison. Abdullah was sentenced to seven years in prison, with Judge Bernard stating that he would have sentenced Abdullah to ten years in an adult jail *but for his age*, the fact that he pleaded guilty, and that he had expressed remorse for the crime.

It remains the case that Canadian youth are still incarcerated at a high rate, higher than any other Western country, and that most Canadian youth, even violent offenders, are sentenced to alternatives to incarceration. Whether or not you view this as positive or negative, the evidence stemming from research on Canadian youth justice over the past 15 years appears to demonstrate that the new YCJA was a political tool used by politicians, via the media, to ensure political victory. In no appreciable way has it impacted either the rate or type of violent crimes committed by Canadian youth, nor the penalties for committing such crimes. Those who worried the YCJA would be too harsh should feel more at ease now, despite the media sensationalism.

The Interactionist Perspective

Unlike the conflict perspective, which focuses on macrolevel inequalities in society, the interactionist perspective focuses on microlevel analyses of how people act toward one another and how they make sense of their daily lives. The *interactionist perspective* views **society as the sum of the interactions of individuals and groups.** Most interactionists study social problems by analyzing how certain behaviour comes to be defined as a social problem and how individuals and groups come to engage in activities that a significant number of people and/or a number of significant people view as a major social concern.

German sociologist Georg Simmel (1858–1918), a founder of the interactionist approach, investigated the impact of industrialization and urbanization on people's values and behaviour within small social units. Simmel (1902/1950) noted that rapid changes in technology and dramatic urban growth produced new social problems by breaking up the "geometry of social life," which he described as the web of patterned social interactions among the people who constitute a society. According to Simmel, alienation is brought about by a decline in personal and emotional contacts. How people *interpret* the subjective messages that they receive from others and the situations that they encounter in their daily life greatly influences their behaviour and perceptions of what constitutes a social problem.

Labelling Theory and the Social Construction of Reality

While Simmel focused on how people interpret their own situations, other interactionists have examined how people impose their shared meanings on others. According to sociologist Howard Becker (1963), *moral entrepreneurs* are people who use their own views of right and wrong to establish rules and *label* others as deviant (nonconforming). *Labelling theory,* as this perspective is called, suggests that behaviour that deviates from established norms is deviant *because* it has been labelled as such by others. According to this theory, deviants (nonconformists) are people who have been successfully labelled as such by others. Labelling theory raises questions about why certain individuals and certain types of behaviour are labelled as deviant but others are not. The answer is suggestive of an analysis of power, which this theory has no real view of.

According to some interaction theorists, many social problems can be linked to the *social construction of reality*—the process by which people's perception of reality is shaped largely by the subjective meaning that they give to an experience (Berger and Luckmann 1967). From this perspective, little shared reality exists beyond that which people socially create. It is, however, this social construction of reality that influences people's beliefs and actions. Other interactionists suggest that how we define a situation affects our reactions to it. According to sociologist W. I. Thomas (1863–1947), when people define situations as real, the situations become real in their consequences.

Elaborating on the Thomas Theorem, as it has come to be called, sociologist Robert Merton (1968) has suggested that when people perceive a situation in a certain way and act according to their perceptions, the end result may be a *self-fulfilling prophecy*—**a false definition of a situation that evokes a new behaviour that makes the original false conception become true.** For example, a teenager who is labelled a "juvenile delinquent" may accept the label and adopt the full-blown image of a juvenile delinquent as portrayed in television programs and films: wearing "gang" colours, dropping out of school, and participating in violence or other behaviour that is labelled as deviant. If the teenager is subsequently arrested, the initial label becomes a self-fulfilling prophecy.

Applying Interactionist Perspectives to Problems of Violence

Interactionist explanations of violence begin by noting that human behaviour is learned through social interaction. Violence, interactionists state, is a learned response, not an inherent characteristic, in the individual. Some of the most interesting support for this point of view comes from studies done by social psychologist Albert Bandura (1973), who studied aggression in children. Showing children a film of a person beating, kicking, and hacking an inflatable doll produced a violent response in the children, who, when they were placed in a room with a similar doll, duplicated the behaviour shown in the film and engaged in additional aggressive behaviour. Others have noted that people tend to repeat their behaviour if they feel rewarded for it. Thus, when people learn that they can get their way by inflicting violence or the threat of violence on others, their aggressive behaviour is reinforced. It is important to point out that the "reward" may only be perceived as a reward in the eyes of that person.

Interactionists also look at the types of social interactions that commonly lead to violence. According to the ***situational approach***, **violence results from a specific interaction process, termed a "situational transaction."** Criminologist David Luckenbill (1977) has identified six stages in the situational transaction between victim and offender. In the first stage, the future victim does something behavioural or verbal that is considered an affront by the other (e.g., a glare or an insult). In the second, the offended individual verifies that the action was directed at him or her personally. In the third, the offended individual decides how to respond to the affront and may issue a verbal or behavioural challenge (e.g., a verbal threat or a raised fist). If the problem escalates at this point, injury or death may occur in this stage; if not, the participants enter into the fourth stage. In this stage, the future victim further escalates the transaction, often prodded on by onlookers siding with one party or the other. In the fifth stage, actual violence occurs when neither party is able to back down without losing face. At this point, one or both parties produce weapons (if these have not already appeared), which may range from guns and knives to bottles, pool cues, or other bludgeoning devices, and the offender kills the victim. The sixth and final stage involves the offender's actions after the crime; some flee the scene, others are detained by onlookers, and still others call the police themselves.

The situational approach is based, first, on the assumption that many victims are active participants in the violence perpetrated against them and, second, on the idea that confrontation does not inevitably lead to violence or death. As Robert Nash Parker (1995) has noted, in the first four stages of the transaction, either the victim or the offender can decide to pursue another course of action and most often does.

According to interactionists, reducing violence requires changing those societal values that encourage excessive competition and violence. These changes must occur at the microlevel, which means agents of socialization must transmit different attitudes and values toward violence. The next generation must learn that it is an individual's right—regardless of gender, racialized status, class, religion, or other attributes or characteristics—to live free from violence and the devastating impact it has on individuals, groups, and the social fabric of society.

Feminist Perspectives

Feminist theorists begin their analysis by pointing out that mainstream sociological thought and theory is both *androcentric* and *Eurocentric* (Alvi, DeKeseredy, and Ellis 2000:19). This means most sociological theory is based on the experiences, ideas, and issues of concern for males of European and Western extraction. European and male perspectives are valid, of course, *and* they are partial. All perspectives are partial, but in the past, these perspectives were treated as though they were representative of the experiences, ideas, and issues of all people. Today, we know this is impossible; hence, feminist theories, anti-racist theories, post-colonial theories, Indigenous theories, and so on have been created and employed to account for more of social life, in addition to maintaining the mainstream theories previously discussed.

There are no "feminist issues" per se. Every issue is a feminist issue. Basically, when feminist theorists engage in analysis, they "gender" the issues under study. This means that theorists look at the differential impacts of social phenomena for men and women, and more recently for transgendered or non-gendered people as well. This does not mean that feminists study only gender, although, in the past, that may have been more true than today. Feminist theories typically examine dynamics of power in relationships between individuals, roles, structures, and so on. This focus on power differentials is shared with conflict and Marxist theories, but feminist theories add a focus on gendered power and patriarchy. A final defining feature of feminist theories is the idea of beginning one's analysis from a particular "standpoint." This is to say that social life is examined from the situated vantage points of the individuals and/or groups involved.

Since there is no one feminist perspective, there is no one feminist perspective on social problems. Many authors put forth summaries of numerous variations of feminist theory (liberal, Marxist, radical, socialist, anti-racist, lesbian, cultural, and so on); however, it may be more useful to distinguish between the types of theories instead of the specific variants. Lengermann and Niebrugge-Brantley (1992:319) provide a classification system that categorizes various feminist theories either as (a) theories of difference, (b) theories of inequality, or (c) theories of oppression. Theories are distinguished from one another by the approach taken to answering the question: Why are women's situations as they are? Theories of difference are premised on the idea that men and women experience different realities, based on their differential locations within most situations. Theories of inequality assert that women's situations are not only different from men's but are also less privileged or are disadvantaged relative to men's. Theories of oppression suggest that not only are women's situations different from and unequal to men's but that women are actively subordinated and kept disadvantaged, both by patriarchal structures and individuals reinforcing sexist socialization and ideologies.

Feminist theories and the people who advance them have been appropriately criticized for perpetuating the same kinds of injustice based on "difference" that mainstream sociological theories perpetuated because of their androcentrism and Eurocentricity. Most feminist theory in the past (and today) comes from a white, middle-class, heterosexual, educated women's bias. The issues assumed to be central by these theories, then, are the issues of interest and concern to these groups of people. Criticism arose, for example, because where White and educated feminists saw men and patriarchy denying them reproductive freedom (e.g., access to birth control and abortion), Indigenous women and women of colour saw racism and acts of discrimination (e.g., in employment or housing) affecting both the men and the women of racialized groups as *the* issue of importance. Poor feminists saw academic elitism and poverty as *the* issue of importance for men and women. Lesbians and women with disabilities saw their perspectives silenced or marginalized. So, the locations or situations of the particular theorists determine what issues are defined as the quintessential feminist issues to be taken up.

Modern-day feminist theories, if they are reflexive, turn the lenses back upon themselves. If one is supporting a particular theory, is it sexist? Is it racist? Is it homophobic? Is it classist? Is it ableist? Many contemporary feminists spend a good deal of time deconstructing the theories they favour; the underlying assumptions, the exclusions, the inclusiveness, the impacts of the analysis, and the dissemination of the analysis. While this exercise may seem academic—and it is, in some senses—it is also important to know where the theory is weak, where it cannot be used to see an issue clearly, what the bias is, whose voice is missing, and so on. Several feminist theorists today call for simultaneous analyses of interlocking oppressions (see Chapter 3). These feminist theorists view the social world as a matrix of domination, where sexism, racism, heterosexism, classism, and other marginalized statuses meet in myriad ways over issues. Theoretical analysis focuses on the ways that these interlocking oppressions play out in different contexts. Other concepts important to contemporary feminist theorists are "public and private spheres, ideology [and] relations of ruling" (Swingewood 2000:240). Focusing on these concepts allows us to analyze macro and micro issues and the interplay between the two, an important feature if we are to have the ability to understand social life from a broader perspective. This leads to a final defining feature of feminist theory—a propensity to propel its adherents toward engaged social action.

Applying Feminist Perspectives to Problems of Violence

Feminist perspectives of violence highlight issues of dominance and power. Inequalities between groups result in violence. People who enjoy power and privilege likely commit as many acts of violence as those who are disenfranchised. The main difference between groups is that those without power are disproportionately targeted as the perpetrators or viewed as bringing it on themselves. So, for example, in an analysis of Reena Virk's murder in Victoria, B.C., the media chose to focus on personal characteristics of the murdered young woman—her apparent "flaws"—while ignoring structures of domination and sexist and racist ideologies that create the context for this type of violence and that support and perpetuate gendered and racialized violence. In an incisive anti-racist feminist analysis, Yasmin Jiwani (1997:2–3) concludes that

> [the murderers'] power and dominance, legitimized by and rooted in the sexism and racism of the dominant white culture and its attendant sense of superiority, was used to force [Virk] into submission—a submission that amounted to her death and erasure from society.... The implicit message [in the media] was that had she been white and had she been thin, she would have fit in, and there would have been no reason for her to be killed.... What happened to Reena could have happened to any number of us who are visibly different and doubly or triply marked in this society by virtue of race (sic), gender, sexual orientation and disability.

Feminists also add social class oppression as a location of domination. For example, in Chapter 4, the fact that the 1989 Montreal Massacre at École Polytechnique gained such notoriety is contrasted with the relatively little stir created by the murders of many poor women from the downtown East Side of Vancouver.

Finally, one feminist perspective suggests that violence against women is a means of reinforcing patriarchy. According to this feminist analysis, in a patriarchal system, the sexual marketplace is characterized by unequal bargaining power, making transactions between men and women potentially coercive in nature. Gender stratification is reinforced by powerful physical, psychological, and social mechanisms of control, including force or the threat of force. Fear of violence forces women to adapt their ways of being in the world—living, acting, and dressing—to ensure they are not in a position to be victimized by men, and thus, they are deprived of many basic freedoms (see Gardner 1995).

SOCIAL CHANGE AND REDUCING SOCIAL PROBLEMS

The concept of social change is important to any discussion of reducing social problems. *Social change* **is the alteration, modification, or transformation of public policy, culture, or social institutions over time** (Kendall 2000). Notice that this definition states that social change occurs "over time." Thus social change has a temporal dimension. Some efforts to deal with social problems are *short-term* strategies, whereas others are *middle-term* remedies, and still others constitute *long-term* efforts to alleviate the root causes of a social problem. In other words, efforts to alleviate individual unemployment or reduce unemployment rates in a community have a different temporal dimension than efforts to change the political economy in such a manner that high levels of employment and greater wage equity are brought about throughout a nation or nations. Clearly, efforts to alleviate individual unemployment are a short-term solution to the problem of unemployment, while efforts to reduce unemployment in a community or to change the entire political economy are middle-term and long-term solutions, respectively. Sometimes discussions of social change sound idealistic or utopian because they are middle-term or long-term strategies that attempt to target the root causes of a social problem. For most social problems, however, a combination of strategies is required to eliminate, or even reduce, social problems.

Microlevel Attempts to Solve Social Problems

Earlier in this chapter, we described sociologist C. Wright Mills's (1959b) belief that we should apply the sociological imagination to gain a better understanding of social problems. According to Mills, the sociological imagination is the ability to see the relationship between individual experiences and the larger society. For Mills, social problems cannot be *solved* at the individual level because they are more than personal troubles or private problems. However, sometimes social institutions cannot deal with a problem effectively, and political and business leaders are unwilling, or unable, to allocate the resources necessary to reduce a problem. In these situations, we typically begin to deal with the problem in an individualized way.

Seeking Individual Solutions to Personal Problems

Microlevel solutions to social problems focus on how individuals operate within small groups to try to remedy a problem that affects them, their family, or their friends. Usually, when individuals have personal problems, they turn to their *primary groups*—**small, less specialized groups in which members engage in face-to-face, emotion-based interactions over an extended period of time** (Kendall 2000). Primary groups include one's family, close friends, and other peers with whom one routinely shares the more personal experiences in life.

How can participation in primary groups help us reduce personal problems? According to sociologists, members of our primary groups usually support us even when others do not. For example, some analysts believe that there are many more people without a domicile (technically homeless) than current statistics suggest, but whenever possible, these people live with relatives or friends, many of whom already live in overcrowded and sometimes substandard housing. Many people who seek individualized solutions to personal troubles believe the situation will be temporary. However, if the problem is widespread or embedded in the larger society, it may stretch out for months or years without resolution. At best, individualized efforts to reduce a problem are short-term measures that some refer to as a "band-aid approach" to a problem because they do not eliminate the causes of the problem: they merely ameliorate the effects of it for a few, for a while.

Microlevel attempts to solve social problems often focus on how individuals operating within small groups can try to remedy a problem that affects them. An example is people using their extended families as a source of economic, social, and spiritual support in "tough times." Here, several generations of one family live under the same roof in an effort to minimize housing expenses.

Some microlevel approaches to reducing social problems focus on how individuals can do something about the problems they face. For example, a person who is unemployed or among the "working poor" because of low wages, seasonal employment, or other factors may be urged to get more education or training and work experience in order to find a "better" job and have the opportunity for upward mobility. Individuals who appear to have eliminated problems in their own lives through such efforts are applauded for their "determination," and they are often held up (sometimes unwillingly or unknowingly) as examples that others are supposed to follow.

Mid-Range Attempts to Solve Social Problems

Mid-range solutions to social problems focus on how secondary groups and formal organizations can assist individuals in overcoming problems such as drug addiction or domestic violence. Some groups help people cope with their own problems, and some groups attempt to bring about community change.

Groups That Help People Cope with Their Problems

Most mid-range solutions to social problems are based on two assumptions: (1) some social problems can best be reduced by reaching one person at a time; and, (2) prevention and intervention are most effective at the personal and community levels. Groups that attempt to reduce a social problem by helping individuals cope with it, or eliminate it from their own lives, are common in our society. Among the best known are Alcoholics Anonymous (AA) and Narcotics Anonymous (NA); however, a broad range of "self-help" organizations exists in most Canadian communities. Typically, self-help groups bring together individuals who have experienced the same problem and have the same goals. For example, a shared goal may be quitting a particular behaviour that has caused the problem, which can be anything from abuse of alcohol, tobacco, and other drugs to overeating, gambling, and chronic worrying. Volunteers who have had similar problems (and believe they are on the road to overcoming them) often act as role models for newer members. For example, AA and NA are operated by recovered alcoholics and/or other recovered substance abusers who try to provide new members with the support they need to overcome alcohol addiction or drug dependency. According to some analysts, AA is a subculture with distinct rules and values that alcoholics learn through their face-to-face encounters with other AA members (Maxwell 1981). Social interaction is viewed as central for individual success in the programs. Confessing one's behavioural problems to others in an organizational setting is believed to have therapeutic value to those who are seeking help.

Like other mid-range approaches, organizations such as AA and NA may bring changes in the individual's life; however, they usually do not systematically address the structural factors (such as unemployment, work-related stress, and aggressive advertising campaigns) that may contribute to the problems. For example, AA typically does not lobby for more stringent laws pertaining to drunk driving or the ready sale and consumption of alcoholic beverages. In British Columbia, for example, recent legal changes have made the purchase of alcohol easier by expanding the hours it can be made available to consumers and expanding the kinds of outlets where it can be sold. As a result, larger societal intervention is necessary to reduce the problems that contribute to individual behaviours.

Grassroots Groups That Work for Community-Based Change

Some grassroots organizations focus on bringing about a change that may reduce or eliminate a social problem in a specific community or region. ***Grassroots groups are organizations started by ordinary people who work in concert to deal with a perceived problem in their neighbourhood, city, province or territory, or nation.*** Using this approach, people learn how to empower themselves against local, provincial, territorial, and national government officials, as well as corporate executives; and media figures who determine what constitutes the news in their area:

> By their nature, grassroots groups emerge to challenge individuals, corporations, government agencies, academia, or a combination of these when people discover they share a grievance. In their search for redress, they have encountered unresponsive, negative public agencies, self-serving private businesses, or recalcitrant individuals and groups. The answer for them is to select specific issues and find like-minded others. (Adams 1991:9)

A central concern of those who attempt to reduce a social problem through grassroots groups is the extent to which other people are apathetic about the problem. Some analysts suggest that even when people are aware of problems, they do not think that they can do anything to change them or they do not know how to work with other people to alleviate them:

> The biggest problem . . . is not those issues that bombard us daily, from homelessness and failing schools to environmental devastation and the federal deficit. Underlying each is a deeper crisis. Some see that deeper problem in the form of obstacles that block problem solving: the tightening concentration of wealth, the influence of money in politics, discrimination, and bureaucratic rigidity, to name a few. These are powerful barriers. But for us the crisis is deeper still. The crisis is that *we as a people don't know how to come together to solve these problems*. We lack the capacities to address the issues or remove the obstacles

that stand in the way of public deliberation. Too many [people] feel powerless. (Lappé and Du Bois 1994:9)

According to social analysts, more community dialogue is needed on social issues, and more people need to become involved in grassroots social movements. A ***social movement*** **is an organized group that acts collectively to promote or resist change through collective action** (Goldberg 1991). Because social movements are not institutionalized and are outside the political mainstream when they begin, they empower outsiders by offering them an opportunity to have their voices heard (Kendall 2000).

An example of a mid-range group is Pollution Probe, a Canadian environmental organization, whose purposes, according to its website (**www.pollutionprobe.org**), are

- to define environmental problems through research;
- to promote understanding through education; and
- to press for practical solutions through advocacy.

The organization has four major programs:

1. An air program to promote tougher controls on urban smog;
2. A water program to ensure safe, clean drinking water and to help develop a global water ethic;
3. An energy conservation program; and
4. An indoor air quality program.

Pollution Probe started in 1969, when a few University of Toronto students began working with faculty members, such as Donald Chant, then chair of the Department of Zoology. Early concerns were dangers of pesticides for birds, high levels of phosphates in detergents for freshwater lakes, and smog in cities. To help deal with these concerns, Pollution Probe undertook a variety of programs. For example, in 1970, a community development project was devised to send people to different parts of southern Ontario's cottage country to encourage summer camp participants, cottage association members, and townspeople to look into problems of water pollution and waste management in their area. Over its 30-year history, Pollution Probe has had a wide variety of accomplishments, including limiting the phosphate content of detergents, encouraging household recycling, helping to launch the Coalition on Acid Rain, contributing to an Ontario act that guarantees the right of residents to participate in environmental decisions, and being instrumental in the passage of an act for mandatory emissions testing of vehicles in Ontario. Although the Ontario government has not always agreed with the ideas and methods of Pollution Probe, on the occasion of Pollution Probe's 30th anniversary celebration, in 1999, then Minister of the Environment Tony Clement said,

> But trust is exactly what Pollution Probe has earned. It's trust that has enabled you to be at the centre of the environmental debate all these years. And it's trust that will ensure your continued role in protecting and improving our air, water and land.

Pollution Probe has an enviable combination of accomplishments and trust that should ensure its continued effectiveness.

Many social movements, such as Mothers Against Drunk Driving (MADD), begin as community-based grassroots efforts (see Box 8.1 on page 210). Over time, many mid-range organizations evolve into national organizations; however, their organization and focus often change in the process (Adams 1991). Table 1.1 provides examples of activist organizations that seek to reduce specific social problems in communities.

Grassroots organizations and other local structures are crucial to national social movements because national social movements must recruit members and gain the economic resources that are necessary for nationwide or global social activism. Numerous sociological studies have shown that the local level constitutes a necessary microfoundation for larger-scale social movement activism. In fact, Bob Ratner (1997:275), a UBC sociologist, notes that the politics of new social movements have prompted a shift from national politics to local grassroots action and the formation of a vast and profound solidarity grounded in the validity of communal experience. Such movements, as they multiply and spread, represent a different sort of globalization, one tantamount to a "globalization from below."

To understand how grassroots organizations aid national social movements, consider the problem of environmental degradation. Leaders of national environmental organizations often participate in local or

TABLE 1.1 Selected Organizations That Seek to Reduce a Social Problem

Category	Organization	Website Address
Environment:	Earth First	www.earthfirst.org
	Greenpeace	www.greenpeace.ca
	Sierra Club	www.sierraclub.org
	Student Environmental Action Coalition	www.seac.org
	Western Canada Wilderness Committee	www.wildernesscommittee.org
Driving while drinking:	Mothers Against Drunk Driving	www.madd.ca
Wages and working conditions:	Canadian Labour Congress	http://clc-ctc.ca
	Industrial Workers of the World	http://iww.org
Poverty, hunger, and homelessness:	Canadian Association of Food Banks	www.cafb-acba.ca
	National Anti-Poverty Organization	www.napo-onap.ca
	Poverty Net	www.povnet.org
	Raising the Roof (Homelessness)	www.raisingtheroof.org
Violence and war:	Food Not Bombs	www.foodnotbombs.net
	Peace and anti-war	www.wagepeace.org
	Canadian Peace Alliance	www.acp-cpa.ca/en/index.html
	The Nonviolence Web	www.nonviolence.org

Note: Web addresses often change. Those given here were accurate at the time of publication.

regional rallies, protests, and letter-writing or e-mail campaigns, particularly when politicians are making decisions that environmentalists believe will have a negative effect on the environment. By working with local and regional activists and seeking to influence local and regional power structures—city councils, provincial and territorial planning commissions, and legislatures—national organizations assert the need for their existence and attempt to garner additional supporters and revenue for their efforts nationwide or around the globe. By intertwining local, regional, and national organizational structures, these groups create a powerful voice for social change. In this sense, then, many social movement groups participate in what the well-known Canadian sociologist William Carroll (1997:29) has defined as counter-hegemonic practice—"a coherent practical and ethical alternative" to prevailing hegemony. The danger of creating counter-hegemonies is one that social movement groups need to be aware of: by defining a group's issues as "the" issues of the day, thereby relegating other group's issues to the back burner, a group risks the possibility of creating new injustices (Carroll 1997). However, a paradigm shift that moves people away from notions and practices of competition is one way of ensuring this does not happen. If social movements are truly counter-hegemonic, then they leave us with a "hopeful prognosis for social and political transformation" (Carroll 1997:25).

Macrolevel Attempts to Solve Social Problems

Macrolevel solutions to social problems focus on how large-scale social institutions such as the government and the media may be persuaded to become involved in remedying social problems. Sometimes individuals who view themselves as individually powerless bind together in organizations to make demands on those who make decisions at the national or global level. As two social analysts explain,

> Most individuals are largely powerless in the face of economic forces beyond their control. But because millions of other people are affected in the same way, they have a chance to influence their conditions through collective action. To do so, people must grasp that the common interest is also their own personal interest. This happens whenever individuals join a movement, a union, a party, or any organization pursuing a common goal. It happens when people push for a social objective—say universal health care or human rights—which benefits them by benefiting all those similarly situated. It underlies the development of an environmental movement which seeks to preserve the environment on which all depend (Brecher and Costello 1998:107).

SOCIAL PROBLEMS IN GLOBAL PERSPECTIVE

BOX 1.3   The Lysistrata Project

I am positive. If we douse ourselves in perfume but ignore them when they pine—if we cook there'll be no resisting us. If we truly shut them out, it will drive them mad. They will miss us! Not just our husbands and boyfriends, but all of our fathers, brothers, sons and male friends! Our men will do whatever it takes to get back with us. The longer we neglect them on account of the war, the more desperate they'll be to end it.

Lysistrata, planning a sex strike to end the Peloponnesian War (Aristophanes)

Approximately 2400 years ago, Aristophanes wrote a play, *Lysistrata*, about a group of women, led by Lysistrata, who, in

protest against the 28-year-old Peloponnesian War, withheld sex from their husbands until the men laid down their swords. In early 2003, the Lysistrata Project—to have coordinated readings of the play—was conceived by Sharron Bower and Kathy Blume, who were frustrated that "We could do nothing but sit and watch in horror as the Bush Administration drove us toward a unilateral attack on Iraq" (Greene 2003). So they decided to e-mail "all [their] friends and put up a website. The response has been enormous." Blume added, "Many people have e-mailed us to say they now feel empowered to do something, and foster dialogue in their own communities about the dangers of this war."

The Lysistrata Project took off via the internet. Over 900 play readings in over 50 countries were planned for

March 3, 2003. Countries participating included Russia, China, Thailand, Greece, and Iceland. Many famous actors volunteered to participate, including F. Murray Abraham, Kevin Bacon, and Julie Christie in New York and Los Angeles, and David Hare and Vanessa Redgrave in London. In Canada, at least 37 readings took place, with some in almost every province. Any money raised was to be donated to humanitarian charities in the Middle East. In some cases, the readings were accompanied by presentations by various peace groups. For example, in one location in Toronto, besides having a reading of the play, the organizers of the production planned to have presentations from the Council of Canadians, Ploughshares, Artists Who Oppose War, the Humanist Delegation from the United Nations, and the Voice of Women for Peace.

The web has frequently been harnessed for peace demonstrations, but this was the first worldwide theatre event for peace. The website (**www.lysistrataproject.com**) is still active. One of its latest concerns is the effects of Uranium 238 ("depleted" uranium), which is being experienced by U.S. troops and Iraqis.

Source: The Lysistrata Project. 2006. Retrieved July 28, 2006, from www.lysistrataproject.com

---

For example, when Canadian workers organize to support the rights of workers in low-income nations and are able to bring about changes that keep them from competing with these workers, they not only help workers abroad, but they also help themselves (Brecher and Costello 1998).

Working through Special-Interest Groups for Political Change

At the national level, people seeking macrolevel solutions to social problems may become members of a *special-interest group*—a political coalition composed of individuals or groups sharing a specific interest they wish to protect or advance with the help of the political system (Greenberg and Page 1993; see Box 1.3). Examples of special-interest groups include the Canadian Labour Congress, the Reform Party, and REAL Women. In the United States, special-interest groups that fund campaigns to help elect (or defeat) candidates based on their positions on specific issues are known as *political action committees* (PACs).

Through special-interest groups, which are sometimes called *pressure groups* or *lobbies,* people seek to change social situations by exerting pressure on political leaders. These groups may be categorized on the basis of four factors:

1. *Issue focus:* Some groups focus on *single issues*, such as abortion, gun control, or teaching acceptance for family diversity in Canadian schools; others focus on *multiple issues,* such as equal access to education, employment, and health care (Ash 1972; Gamson 1990).

2. *View of the present system of wealth and power:* Some groups make *radical demands* that would involve the end of patriarchy, capitalism, governmental bureaucracy, or other existing power structures; others do not attack the legitimacy of the present system of wealth and power but insist on specific social reforms (Ash 1972; Gamson 1990).

3. *Beliefs about elites:* Some groups want to *influence* elites or incorporate movement leaders into the elite; others want to replace existing elites with persons whom they believe share their own interests and concerns (Ash 1972; Gamson 1990).

4. *Type of political action:* In recent decades, many special-interest groups have been single-issue groups that focus on electing and supporting politicians who support their views. There may be more than one single-issue group working to reduce or eliminate a specific social problem. Usually, however, these groups do not agree on the nature and extent of the problem or on proposed solutions for the problem. For this reason, competing single-interest groups may aggressively place their demands in front of elected officials and bureaucratic policy-makers.

Working through National Social Movements to Reduce Problems

Collective behaviour and national social movements are significant ways in which people seek to resolve social problems. ***Collective behaviour* is voluntary, often spontaneous activity of a large number of people that typically violates dominant group norms and values** (Kendall 2000). Public demonstrations and riots are examples of collective behaviour. Since the civil rights movement in the United States in the 1960s, one popular form of public demonstration has been *civil disobedience*—**non-violent action that seeks to change a policy or law by refusing to comply with it** (Kendall 2000). People often use civil disobedience in the form of sit-ins, marches, boycotts, and strikes to bring about change. When people refuse to abide by a policy or law and challenge authorities to do something about it, they are demanding social change with some sense of urgency. Protestors at the 1999 WTO meeting in Seattle used civil disobedience strategies by sitting on the street, linking arms together, and chanting over and over the words "non-violent protest" in response to the advancing lines of the National Guard in full riot gear.

Groups that engage in activities that they hope will achieve specific political goals are sometimes referred to as *protest crowds*. For example, on February 23, 2002, in Victoria, B.C., thousands of demonstrators blocked traffic in the downtown core for an entire afternoon as they marched to the parliament buildings in an extensively organized and festive "Provincial Day of Action" against the budget-cutting measures of the newly elected government of Gordon Campbell and the B.C. Liberals. The protest included members of a huge range of groups: seniors, union activists, students, firefighters, hospital employees, teachers, children, Indigenous groups, environmentalists, religious leaders, peace activists, and others joined together in one of the largest and most multi-stakeholdered demonstrations ever to take place in the province. It was reminiscent of the scope of the WTO protest that had preceded it.

Other protests have been organized, for example, in resistance to the recent B.C. government referendum on treaty issues. Organizations that help plan such protests are usually said to be engaged in emancipatory politics rather than in life politics. *Emancipatory politics* involve "liberating people from adverse constraints on their life chances through the reduction or elimination of exploitation, inequality, and oppression, and through the promotion of justice, equality, and participation" (Buechler 2000:150).

Collective behaviour is a powerful form of social protest against perceived injustices. Numerous protests have been staged in Canada against environmental degradation caused by logging, pollution, hunting, and other activities. Why do sociologists refer to this form of protest as emancipatory politics rather than as life politics?

Unlike emancipatory politics, *life politics* involves lifestyles, particularly those issues and social problems pertaining to the self, sexuality, reproduction, and the human body. The women's movement is an example of the life politics approach, which is often expressed as "the personal is political" (Buechler 2000:150). However, life politics also reaches outward to look at global concerns, such as ecological survival and nuclear devastation (Buechler 2000).

What types of national and international social movements may be used to reduce social problems? National social movements may be divided into five major categories: reform, revolutionary, religious, alternative, and resistance movements. *Reform movements* seek to improve society by changing some specific aspect of the social structure. Environmental groups and disability rights groups are examples of groups that seek to change (reform) some specific aspect of the social structure. Reform movements typically seek to bring about change by working within the existing organizational structures of society, whereas *revolutionary movements* seek to bring about a total change in society. Examples of revolutionary movements include utopian groups and radical terrorist groups that use fear tactics to intimidate and gain—at least briefly—concessions from those with whom they disagree ideologically. Some radical

Religious movements are one kind of national social movement. Religious movements, such as the Promise Keepers (shown here), seek to renovate or renew people through "inner change." What are the strengths of this approach in bringing about personal change and reducing social problems? What are the limitations?

terrorists may kill people in their pursuit of a society that more closely conforms to their worldview.

Religious movements (also referred to as *expressive movements*) seek to rejuvenate people through inner change. Because they emphasize inner change, religious movements are often linked to local and regional organizations that seek to bring about changes in the individual's life. National religious movements often attempt to persuade political officials to enact laws that will reduce or eliminate what they perceive to be a social problem. For example, some national religious movements view abortion as a social problem and thus lobby for a ban on abortions. In contrast, *alternative movements* seek limited change in some aspects of people's behaviour. Currently, alternative movements include a variety of so-called New Age movements that emphasize such things as the development of a collective spiritual consciousness.

Finally, *resistance movements* seek to prevent change or to undo change that has already occurred. In public debates over social policies, most social movements advocating change face resistance from reactive movements, which hold opposing viewpoints and want social policy to reflect their own beliefs and values. Examples of resistance movements include groups opposing same-sex marriage initiatives for gay or lesbian couples;

anti-abortion groups, such as "Operation Rescue," which seek to close abortion clinics and make abortion illegal; and anti-immigrant groups seeking to close Canadian borders to outsiders or place harsher demands on immigrant workers.

Can national activism and social movements bring about the changes that are necessary to reduce social problems? Some analysts believe that certain social problems can be reduced through sustained efforts by organizations committed to change. An example of national social movements is the Council of Canadians. The not-for-profit council was formed in 1985 by Maude Barlow and associates and has become Canada's pre-eminent citizen watchdog organization. According to its website (**www.canadians.org**),

> Strictly non-partisan, the Council lobbies Members of Parliament, conducts research, and runs national campaigns aimed at putting some of the country's most important issues into the spotlight: safeguarding our social programs, promoting economic justice, renewing our democracy, asserting Canadian sovereignty, advancing alternatives to corporate-style free trade, and preserving our environment.

The Council of Canadians is sustained by volunteers and wholly financed by its members, who now number over 100 000 in over 70 chapters across the country. As a public interest organization, it does not take money from corporations or governments. Past campaigns include combatting bank mergers, control of newspapers by conglomerates, and changes in public pensions. Current issues include energy deregulation, sustainable development, media concentration, health care, and water. In June 2006, for example, the newly formed Whistler, B.C., chapter successfully lobbied against the privatization of their wastewater management.

A major successful campaign was the fight against the Multilateral Agreement on Investments (MAI) in 1998. The Council of Canadians called it a charter of rights and freedoms for global corporations. As part of the campaign to free up the movement of capital and protect investors, the MAI was criticized for wanting standardized national policies that could potentially erode environmental legislation, culture, and sovereignty and bring in a two-tiered health system. The council sent a letter to Prime Minister Chrétien, supported by prominent Canadians such as Carol Shields, David Suzuki, Judy Rebick, and Buzz Hargrove, emphasizing five principles that should govern all international trade and investment agreements. The principles were

1. Upholding the rights of citizens;

2. Protecting the common good;

3. Promoting the development of sustainable communities;

4. Guaranteeing the sovereignty of democratically elected governments over corporations; and

5. Ensuring effective citizen participation in the development of trade and investment policies. (Council of Canadians 1999)

The Council of Canadians called on Canada to pull out of MAI negotiations. The MAI was defeated because, in 1998, France, and later Australia, also concerned about the MAI's encroachment on their national sovereignty, pulled out of the negotiations.

What about global activism? Once again, we turn to the environmental movement for an example. According to Jared Diamond (2000), a physiology professor and director of the World Wildlife Fund, some transnational corporations are becoming aware that they have a responsibility for the environment. Diamond believes that a new attitude has taken hold of corporations such as Chevron and Home Depot, both of which now claim to realize that it is better to have a clean operation than to have costly industrial disasters. Of course, consumers have also demanded that corporations become more accountable for their actions: "Behind this trend lies consumers' growing awareness of the risks that environmental problems pose for the health, economies, and political stability of their own world and their children's world" (Diamond 2000: A31). For example, growing consumer awareness has led some companies that buy and retail forest products to no longer sell wood products from environmentally sensitive areas of the world and instead give preference to certified wood—that is, lumber that has been derived from forests where guidelines for environmentally sound logging practices have been met (Diamond 2000). Consumer power should not be underestimated when it comes to impacting corporations' profits.

According to some analysts, what is needed is the "globalization from below" mentioned above (Brecher and Costello 1998). In other words, people cannot rely on corporations to solve environmental problems. Indeed, it is necessary to develop a human agenda that will offset the corporate agenda that has produced many of the problems in the first place. Social activists Jeremy Brecher and Tim Costello (1998) suggest these criteria for any proposed human agenda:

- It should improve the lives of the great majority of the world's people over the long run.

- It should correspond to widely held common interests and should integrate the interests of people around the world.

- It should provide handles for action at a variety of levels.

- It should include elements that can be at least partially implemented independently but that are compatible or mutually reinforcing.

- It should make it easier, not harder, to solve social problems such as environmental degradation and war.

- It should grow organically out of social movements and coalitions that have developed in response to the needs of diverse peoples.

Based on these guidelines, the only way that a major global social problem, such as environmental degradation or world poverty, can be reduced is through a drastic redirection of our energies, as Brecher and Costello (1998:184) explain:

> The energies now directed to the race to the bottom need to be redirected to the rebuilding of the global economy on a humanly and environmentally sound basis. Such an approach requires limits to growth—in some spheres, sharp reductions—in the material demands that human society places on the environment. It requires reduced energy and resource use; less toxic production and products; shorter individual worktime; and less production for war. But it requires vast growth in education, health care, human caring, recycling, rebuilding an ecologically sound production and consumption system, and time available for self-development, community life, and democratic participation.

Do you believe such human co-operation is possible? Will it be possible for a new generation of political leaders to separate *politics* from *policy* and focus on discovering the best courses of action for Canada and the world? Where do ideas regarding possible social policies come from? Some of the ideas and policies of tomorrow are being developed today in public policy organizations and think tanks like the right-wing Fraser Institute or the left-leaning Canadian Centre for Policy Alternatives. If, as some analysts believe, these think tanks are increasingly setting the Canadian government's agenda, how much do we know about these groups, their spokespersons, and the causes they advocate?

Perhaps gaining more information about the current state of Canadian and global affairs is the first step toward individual efforts to be part of the solution rather than part of the problem in the future.

In Sum

Sociologists view social problems from a variety of perspectives. Each perspective involves different assumptions. Functionalists, who emphasize social cohesion and order in society, commonly view social problems as the result of institutional and societal dysfunctions, social disorganization, or cultural lag, among other things. Conflict theorists, who focus on value conflict or on structural inequalities based on class, ethnicity, or other socially constructed attributes, suggest that social problems arise either from disputes over divergent values or from exploitative relations in society, such as those between capitalists and workers or between different ethnic groups. In contrast, interactionists focus on individuals' interactions and on the social construction of reality. For interactionists, social problems occur when social interaction is disrupted and people are dehumanized, when people are labelled deviant, or when the individual's definition of a situation causes him or her to act in a way that produces a detrimental outcome. Feminist theorists focus on gendering their analyses of inequalities that are maintained and perpetuated by structures and ideologies of domination. The ways that individuals play out oppressive relationships together can be traced to the unequal ways that structures and relations are organized in a capitalist, patriarchal society. This is the root of social problems, according to feminist theorists. We will use these theoretical perspectives, along with selected others, throughout the book.

It is important not only to have an analysis of social problems but also to see a means for solving them. The concept of social change is important to any discussion of reducing social problems. Strategies people use to deal with social problems are either *short-term, middle-term,* or *long-term.* An example of a short-term strategy is an attempt to help individuals find jobs, through a "back-to-work" program or a resumé writing service. An example of a middle-term strategy may be to reduce unemployment in a community by developing a new resort and golf course. An example of a long-term strategy could be to shift the whole political economy of a nation to a system that endorses 100 percent employment. For most social problems, a combination of strategies is required to eliminate or reduce them.

The remedies that people seek to social problems are microlevel, mid-range, or macrolevel remedies. Microlevel solutions to social problems focus on that ways that individuals work within small groups to try to solve a problem that affects them, their family, or their friends. Mid-range solutions focus on how secondary groups and formal organizations can deal with problems or assist individuals or groups in overcoming problems. Macrolevel solutions focus on getting large-scale social institutions such as the government or media to become involved in remedying social problems.

This chapter has examined violence from four sociological perspectives. As with many other social problems, people do not always agree on the causes of violence. They also do not always agree on what should be done about violence. However, this does not mean that we should simply give up and do nothing. The perspective taken by the authors of this text is that Canadians do have a number of pressing social problems to address and that it is our responsibility to work toward a better world, however we conceive that world and however we decide to do that work. This book explores a range of social issues—and ways by which we may eliminate or reduce the harmful effects of those issues we collectively define as "problems." If an issue sparks something in you and you want to get involved, you will find some ideas for social action in the "What Can You Do?" section of each chapter. Of course, there are many more ideas and ways of being involved in the issue(s) of your choice than those we have indicated. Feel free to explore and do your part to make the world a better place. We would love to hear about it! As summarized by UNICEF in 1995 in *The Progress of Nations* (Ecumenical Coalition for Economic Justice 1996),

The day will come when the progress of nations will not be judged by their military or economic strength, nor by the splendour of their capital cities and public buildings, but by the well-being of their peoples: by their levels of health and education; by their opportunities to earn a fair reward for their labours; by their ability to participate in the decisions that affect their lives; by the respect that is shown for their political and civil liberties; by the provision that is made for those who are vulnerable and disadvantaged; and by the protection that is afforded to the growing minds and bodies of their children.

Please join us now in exploring many of the crucial issues of the 21st century.

SUMMARY

HOW DO SOCIOLOGISTS DEFINE A SOCIAL PROBLEM?

According to sociologists, a social problem is a social condition (such as poverty) or a pattern of behaviour (such as substance abuse) that people believe warrants public concern and collective action to bring about change.

HOW DO SOCIOLOGISTS VIEW VIOLENCE?

Sociologists view violence as a social problem that involves both a subjective awareness and objective reality. We have a subjective awareness that violence can occur in such public settings as schools, daycare centres, businesses, and churches. Our subjective awareness becomes an objective reality when we can measure and experience the effects of violent criminal behaviour.

HOW DO SOCIOLOGISTS EXAMINE SOCIAL LIFE?

Sociologists use both microlevel and macrolevel analyses to examine social life. Microlevel analysis focuses on small-group relations and social interaction among individuals; macrolevel analysis focuses on social processes occurring at the societal level, especially in large-scale organizations and major social institutions.

HOW DOES THE FUNCTIONALIST PERSPECTIVE VIEW SOCIETY AND SOCIAL PROBLEMS?

In the functionalist perspective, society is a stable, orderly system composed of interrelated parts, each of which performs a function that contributes to the overall stability of society. According to functionalists, social problems such as violence arise when social institutions do not fulfill the functions that they are supposed to perform or when dysfunctions occur.

HOW DOES THE CONFLICT PERSPECTIVE VIEW SOCIETY AND SOCIAL PROBLEMS?

The conflict perspective asserts that groups in society are engaged in a continuous power struggle for control of scarce resources. This perspective views violence as a response to inequalities based on "race," class, gender, and other power differentials in society.

HOW DOES THE VALUE CONFLICT PERSPECTIVE DIFFER FROM THE CRITICAL-CONFLICT PERSPECTIVE?

According to value conflict theorists, social problems are conditions that are incompatible with group values. From this perspective, value clashes are ordinary occurrences in families, communities, and the larger society, where people commonly hold many divergent values. In contrast, critical-conflict theorists suggest that social problems arise out of major contradictions inherent in the way societies are organized.

WHY ARE THERE SO MANY DIFFERENT APPROACHES IN THE CONFLICT PERSPECTIVE?

Different conflict theorists focus on different aspects of power relations and inequality in society. Perspectives based on the works of Karl Marx emphasize class-based inequalities arising from the capitalist economic system.

HOW DOES THE INTERACTIONIST PERSPECTIVE VIEW SOCIETY AND SOCIAL PROBLEMS?

Unlike the functionalist and conflict perspectives, which focus on society at the macrolevel, the interactionist perspective views society as the sum of the interactions of individuals and groups. For interactionists, social problems occur when social interaction is disrupted and people are dehumanized, when people are labelled deviant, or when the individual's definition of a situation causes him or her to act in a way that produces a detrimental outcome.

WHAT IS THE FEMINIST PERSPECTIVE?

Feminist perspectives focus on patriarchy—a system of male dominance in which males are privileged and women are oppressed. Other perspectives emphasize that "race," class, and gender are interlocking systems of privilege and oppression that result in social problems. However, these perspectives are based on the assumption that inequality and exploitation, rather than social harmony and stability, characterize contemporary societies.

WHAT IS SOCIAL CHANGE? WHY IS IT IMPORTANT IN REDUCING SOCIAL PROBLEMS?

Social change refers to the alteration, modification, or transformation of public policy, culture, or social institutions over time. Social change is important in reducing social problems because a combination of strategies, some previously untried, are usually required to reduce major social problems.

WHAT ARE MICROLEVEL SOLUTIONS TO SOCIAL PROBLEMS? WHAT ARE THE LIMITATIONS OF THIS APPROACH?

Microlevel solutions to social problems focus on how individuals operate within small groups to try to remedy a problem that affects them, their family, or their friends. Most people turn to their primary groups for help in dealing with a problem. However, solving social problems one person at a time does not take into account the fact that secondary groups and societal institutions play a significant part in creating, maintaining, and exacerbating many social problems.

WHAT ARE MID-RANGE ATTEMPTS TO DEAL WITH SOCIAL PROBLEMS? WHAT ARE THE LIMITATIONS OF THIS APPROACH?

Mid-range attempts to deal with social problems focus on how secondary groups and formal organizations deal with problems or seek to assist individuals in overcoming problems, such as addiction to drugs or alcohol. Grassroots groups often work to change a perceived wrong in their neighbourhood, city, province or territory, or nation. Although local efforts to reduce problems affecting individuals and collectivities in a specific city or region have brought about many improvements in the social life of individuals and small groups, they usually lack the sustained capacity to produce the larger systemic changes needed at the national or international levels to reduce or eliminate the problems.

WHAT ARE MACROLEVEL ATTEMPTS TO DEAL WITH SOCIAL PROBLEMS? WHAT ARE THE LIMITATIONS OF THIS APPROACH?

Macrolevel solutions to social problems focus on how large-scale social institutions such as the government and the media may become involved in remedying social problems. Some people work through social movements, others through special-interest groups, and still others through various forms of collective behaviour. While macrolevel approaches are necessary for reducing or eliminating many social problems, some analysts believe that these approaches overemphasize structural barriers in society and give people the impression that these barriers constitute insurmountable walls that preclude social change. Macrolevel approaches may also de-emphasize the importance of individual responsibility.

WHAT ARE FOUR KEY FACTORS THAT DIFFERENTIATE SPECIAL-INTEREST GROUPS?

The four factors by which special-interest groups may be categorized are (1) issue focus (single-issue vs. multiple demands); (2) view of the present system of wealth and power (positive vs. negative); (3) beliefs about elites (whether to try to influence elites or seek to replace them); and (4) type of political action.

WHAT IS COLLECTIVE BEHAVIOUR? HOW DOES CIVIL DISOBEDIENCE OCCUR?

Collective behaviour is voluntary, often spontaneous activity of a large number of people that may violate dominant-group norms and values. As a form of collective behaviour, civil disobedience refers to non-violent action that seeks to change a policy or law by refusing to comply with it. In 1999, in Seattle, many WTO protestors engaged in this form of direct action by linking arms, sitting in the streets, and chanting "non-violent protest" over and over again in the face of advancing lines of the armed National Guard.

HOW DOES EMANCIPATORY POLITICS DIFFER FROM LIFE POLITICS?

Emancipatory politics involves the liberation of people from adverse conditions by reducing or eliminating exploitation, inequality, and oppression, or through the promotion of justice, equality, and participation. In contrast, life politics focuses on lifestyles, particularly those issues and social problems pertaining to the self, sexuality, reproduction, and the human body. Life politics also reaches outward to look at global concerns, such as ecological survival and nuclear devastation.

WHAT ARE THE KEY CHARACTERISTICS OF THE FIVE MAJOR CATEGORIES OF NATIONAL SOCIAL MOVEMENTS?

National social movements are divided into five major categories: reform, revolutionary, religious, alternative, and resistance movements. Reform movements seek to improve society by changing some specific aspect of the social structure. Revolutionary movements seek to bring about a total change in society. Religious movements seek to renovate or renew people through "inner change." Alternative movements seek limited change in some aspects of people's behaviour and currently include a variety of so-called New Age movements. Resistance movements seek to prevent change or undo change that has already occurred.

KEY TERMS

capitalism,   p. 9
civil disobedience,   p. 21
collective behaviour,   p. 21
conflict perspective,   p. 8
discrimination,   p. 4
dominant group,   p. 4
functionalist perspective,   p. 6

grassroots groups,   p. 17
hate crime,   p. 4
industrialization,   p. 7
interactionist perspective,   p. 11
lifestyle–routine activity approach,   p. 7
macrolevel analysis,   p. 5
microlevel analysis,   p. 5

norms, p. 7
perspective, p. 6
primary groups, p. 15
self-fulfilling prophecy, p. 12
situational approach, p. 12
social change, p. 15
social disorganization, p. 7
social movement, p. 17
social problem, p. 2

society, p. 3
sociological imagination, p. 5
sociology, p. 3
subordinate group, p. 4
theory, p. 5
urbanization, p. 7
values, p. 7
violence, p. 2

QUESTIONS FOR CRITICAL THINKING

1.   What are some of the impacts on a nation when high levels of violence exist within its borders?

2.   Value conflict theorists suggest that social problems are conditions that are incompatible with group values. How would value conflict theorists view debates over gun control laws?

3.   Some critical-conflict theorists believe that social problems arise from the major contradictions inherent in capitalist economies. What role does violence play in a capitalist economy?

4.   Using feminist and interactionist perspectives, what kind of arguments can you make to explain why males are more frequently involved in acts of physical violence than females? What do your own observations tell you about the relationship between social norms and violent behaviour?

5.   Do you believe that corporations can be trusted to "do the right thing" when it comes to reducing or eliminating existing social problems? Is good corporate citizenship a possibility in the global economy today? Why or why not?

6.   Suppose you were given the economic resources and political clout to reduce a major social problem. Which problem would you choose? What steps would you take to alleviate this problem? How would you measure your success or failure in reducing or eliminating the problem?

2

WEALTH AND POVERTY:

CANADIAN AND GLOBAL ECONOMIC INEQUALITIES

WEALTH AND POVERTY IN GLOBAL PERSPECTIVE

ANALYZING CANADIAN CLASS INEQUALITY

Wealth and Income Inequality

Divisions in the Canadian Class Structure

POVERTY IN CANADA

Poverty Lines: LICOs and LIMs

Who Are the Poor?

Box 2.1 Social Problems in the Media: How You Can Tell When the Media Poor-Bash

Consequences of Poverty

How Canada Deals with Poverty

SOCIAL WELFARE IN CANADA

Box 2.2 Social Problems and Social Policy: Workfare in Canada: Betraying a National Trust

PERSPECTIVES ON POVERTY AND CLASS INEQUALITY

The Symbolic Interactionist Perspective

The Structural Functionalist Perspective

The Conflict Perspective

Feminist Perspectives

CAN CLASS-BASED INEQUALITY BE REDUCED?

WHAT CAN YOU DO?

Poverty is not just the outstretched hand or the figure slumped in a doorway. It's not just the single mother down on her luck in line at the food bank, or the street kid looking for a safe place to spend the night. It isn't always genteel or hopeful, the person who might turn his life around with a little well-timed, benevolent help. It's a face that, no matter how charitable we might feel, we would probably rather not see.

Pat Capponi (1999:xi)

We can't depend on charity to do the work of inadequate social services.

Loren Freid, Executive Director, North York Harvest Food Bank, Ontario (HungerCount 2005)

We keep hearing threats of more things being taken away, like "snow suit allowance" or we'll have to pay $2 prescription fees. That $2 buys two cans of juice, or two loaves of bread, or bus fare.

A participant in the YWCA of Metropolitan Toronto's Teen Mother Program (Ricciutelli et al. 1998:57)

The Child Tax Benefit is supposed to go to the child—for clothing etc.—but it has to go for food. That's not fair.

A participant in the YWCA of Metropolitan Toronto's Teen Mother Program (Ricciutelli et al. 1998:57)

Hunger is related to economic security. . . . A comprehensive set of policy measures—including living wages, adequate employment insurance and social assistance programs and more affordable housing and childcare—along with concrete measurable objectives, are essential to improving the income security of low-income Canadians and consequently in helping to reduce the need for food banks. . . . [Y]ear after year members of the Canadian Association of Food Banks state that what is needed is not more food or more food banks but effective public policies to end poverty.

Dr. Mustafa Koc, Ryerson University Sociologist and Director of the Centre for Studies in Food Security (Canadian Association of Food Banks 2005:4–5).

Last week I went two days without food (I had some for the kids) until I got my cheque. They want me to get a job but I can't afford to send out resumes or take the bus to deliver them, as well as there is the cost of photocopying.

A participant in the YWCA of Metropolitan Toronto's Teen Mother Program (Ricciutelli et al. 1998:57)

The cuts have augmented my struggles against the constant pressure of economic survival, part-time attendance at the University of Toronto, a part-time job, and full-time work as a single parent. I really can see no sense in cutting funding for subsidized childcare, funding for the Ontario Student Assistance Program, and funding for the Family Benefits Act. For women like myself, such increased economic and emotional stress makes it more difficult, if not near impossible, to imagine a successful future for myself and my child.

Diane Aiken (Flynn 1998:147)

Canadians expect people who work to be able to live decently. Citizens articulated a vision of a "working society" where everyone who can work gets a chance to earn a living wage. Yet we have people working full-time who are poor.

Ron Saunders, on the findings from Canadian Policy Research Networks' 2003 study "Citizen's Dialogue on Canada's Future: A 21st Century Social Contract" (Saunders 2005: executive summary).

Out of a Women of Action Day meeting, held in Ontario in the late 1990s, a resource book was put together to document some of the impacts of the social services cuts on the daily lives of women and children in that province. Several groups and organizations participated in researching and writing the pieces, from which several of the above quotations were taken. The cuts in federal funding and provincial funding in several provinces today make the realities described in the Ontario resource book a reality for people right across Canada. Decreases in real wages, as well as unemployment and underemployment, mean that cuts to services not only impact those people who are on income assistance but also mean increased poverty for those who work full- and part-time. This chapter examines these issues as well as the ways that poverty is measured, the types of people who live in poverty in Canada, the differences in wealth and income among Canadians, and the ways we deal with poverty and income inequalities as a nation.

For decades, Canada has been described as the "land of opportunity"—or a place where the "American Dream" can be realized. Simply stated, the American Dream is the belief that the members of each generation can have a higher standard of living than that of their parents

(Danziger and Gottschalk 1995). Implicit in the American Dream is the belief that all people—regardless of ethnicity, colour, national origin, gender, ability, age, sexual orientation, or religion—should have an equal opportunity for success. This is the same as saying that Canadians view themselves as living in a *meritocracy*, **a nation where the best person can rise to the top in any situation, despite his or her antecedents.** Sociologists John Macionis and Linda Gerber (2002:257) define a meritocracy as a "system of social stratification based on personal merit." But do all the people in this nation and other parts of the world really have an equal opportunity for success? How equally divided are national and global resources? What kinds of inequalities exist in the Canadian and worldwide class system today?

A *class system* **is a system of social inequality based on the ownership and control of resources and on the type of work people do** (Rothman 1993). A primary characteristic of any class system is social mobility. *Social mobility* refers to the upward or downward movement in the class structure that occurs during a person's lifetime and from one generation to another.

WEALTH AND POVERTY IN GLOBAL PERSPECTIVE

On a global basis, there is a vast disparity in economic resources, both across nations and within nations. In any one nation, there are both very wealthy and very poor individuals and families. When sociologists conduct research on these disparities, they frequently analyze secondary data that originally were collected by the World Bank and the United Nations. These data focus on quality-of-life indicators, such as wealth, income, life expectancy, health, sanitation, the treatment of women, and education, for high-income, middle-income, and low-income nations. *High-income nations* **are countries with highly industrialized economies; technologically advanced industrial, administrative, and service occupations; and relatively high levels of national and per capita (per person) income.** Examples include Australia, New Zealand, Japan, the European nations, Canada, and the United States. *Middle-income nations* **are countries undergoing transformation from agrarian to industrial economies.** Columbia, Guatemala, Panama, Poland, and Romania are examples of middle-income nations. These

nations still have many people who work the land, and national and per capita incomes remain relatively low. *Low-income nations* **are primarily countries with agrarian economies, little industrialization, and low levels of national and personal income.** For example, the countries in sub-Saharan Africa have experienced little or no benefit from recent changes in global economic markets (United Nations Development Programme 1999). Examples of low-income nations include Rwanda, Mozambique, Ethiopia, Nigeria, Cambodia, Vietnam, Afghanistan, Bangladesh, and Nicaragua.

Comparisons of high-income and low-income nations reveal a growing gap between the rich and the poor, both within and among nations. Indeed, throughout the world today, the wealthiest and poorest people are living in increasingly separate worlds (Crossette 1996b). By the late 1990s, the fifth of the world's population living in the highest-income countries had 86 percent of the world's gross domestic product. The gross domestic product (GDP) is a measure of all of the goods and services produced *within* a country's economy during a given year (revenue from sources outside the country is not included in the GDP). The world's GDP, then, is the total of the GDP for each nation. By contrast, the bottom fifth of the world's population had only 1 percent of the world's GDP. Similarly, the highest-income countries contained 82 percent of world export markets, whereas the lowest-income countries had only 1 percent of those markets (United Nations Development Programme 1999). Perhaps the easiest way to bring these statistics to life is to think in terms of the common telephone line: 74 percent of all the telephone lines in the world are in the highest-income countries; the bottom one-fifth of the world's nations have only 1.5 percent of all the telephone lines.

Disparity in the GDPs of high-income and low-income nations reflects disparity in the life chances of the populations of these nations. *Life chances* **are the extent to which individuals have access to important societal resources such as food, clothing, shelter, education, and health care.** Poverty, food shortages, hunger, and rapidly growing populations are pressing problems in many middle- and low-income nations. Today, more than 1.3 billion people live in *absolute poverty*, **a condition that exists when people do not have the means to secure the most basic necessities of life (food, clothing, and shelter).** Absolute poverty is life threatening. People living in absolute poverty may suffer from chronic malnutrition or die from hunger-related diseases. Current estimates suggest that more than 600 million people suffer from chronic malnutrition and more than 40 million people die each year from hunger-related diseases. To put this figure in perspective, the number of people worldwide dying from hunger-related diseases each year is the equivalent of more than 300 jumbo jet crashes *per day* with no survivors and half the passengers being children (Kidron and Segal 1995). In recent years, the numbers of people living in absolute poverty in high-income nations like Canada has also been increasing, drawing the criticism of many worldwide, including the United Nations.

In addition, experts project that the populations of middle- and low-income nations will increase by almost 60 percent by the year 2025, while the populations of high-income nations increase by about 11 percent, all of which will magnify the problems of the disparity in life chances and the prevalence of absolute poverty. Because half the world's population of about 6 billion people already lives in low-income nations, this rapid increase in population can only compound existing problems and increase inequality on a global basis.

How do social scientists explain the disparity between wealth and poverty in high-income and low-income nations? According to the "new international division of labour" perspective, the answer lies in the global organization of manufacturing production (Bluestone and Harrison 1982). Today, workers in several low-income nations primarily produce goods such as clothing, electrical machinery, and consumer electronics for export to Canada and other developed nations. Using this global assembly line, transnational corporations find they have an abundant supply of low-cost (primarily female) labour, no corporate taxes, few or no environmental regulations, and no labour unions or strikes to interfere with their profits (Petras 1983). Thus, owners and shareholders of transnational corporations benefit, along with subcontractors and managers in middle- and low-income nations, while workers remain in poverty despite working long hours in sweatshop conditions.

ANALYZING CANADIAN CLASS INEQUALITY

Despite the notion that anyone can get ahead if only she or he tries hard enough, one of this country's most persistent social problems is that Canada is a highly stratified society. *Social stratification* **is the hierarchical arrangement of large social groups on the basis of their control over basic resources** (Feagin and Feagin 1997). Today, the gap between the rich and the poor in this nation is wider than it has been for decades.

This widening gap, which is linked with global systems of stratification, has a dramatic impact on everyone's life chances and opportunities. Affluent people typically have better life chances than the less affluent because the affluent have greater access to quality education, safe neighborhoods, high-quality nutrition and health care, police and private security protection, and an extensive array of other goods and services. In contrast, people who have low and poverty level incomes tend to have limited access to these resources.

How are social classes determined in Canada? Most contemporary research on class has been influenced by either Karl Marx's means of production model or Max Weber's multidimensional model. In Marx's model, class position is determined by people's relationship to the means of production. Chapter 1 described Marx's division of capitalist societies into two classes: the bourgeoisie, or capitalist class, which owns the means of production; and the proletariat, or working class, which sells its labour power to the capitalists to survive. According to Marx, inequality and poverty are inevitable by-products of the exploitation of workers by capitalists (Vanneman and Cannon 1987:39).

Like Karl Marx, the German sociologist Max Weber (1864–1920) believed that economic factors were important in determining class location and studying social inequality, but he also believed that other factors were important. Weber developed a multidimensional class model that focused on the interplay of wealth, power, and prestige as determinants of people's class position. *Wealth* **is the value of all economic assets, including income and savings, personal property, and income-producing property, minus one's liabilities or debts.** While some people have great wealth and are able to live off their investments, others must work for wages. *Power* **is the ability of people to achieve their goals despite opposition from others.** People who hold positions of power can achieve their goals because they can control other people; on the other hand, people who hold positions that lack power must carry out the wishes of others. *Prestige* **is the respect, esteem, or regard accorded to an individual or group by others.**

Individuals who have high levels of prestige tend to receive deferential and respectful treatment from those with lower levels of prestige.

Recent theorists have modified Marx's and Weber's theories of economic inequality. According to the sociologist Erik O. Wright (1997), neither Weber's multidimensional model of wealth, power, and prestige nor Marx's two-class system fully define classes in modern capitalist societies or explain economic inequality. Wright sets forth four criteria for placement in the class structure: (1) ownership of the means of production; (2) purchase of the labour of others (employing others); (3) control of the labour of others (supervising others on the job); and (4) sale of one's own labour (being employed by someone else). Based on these criteria, Wright (1979, 1985) has identified four classes: the capitalist class, the managerial class, the small-business class, and the working class.

Although most people are aware of the wide disparity in lifestyles and life chances between the rich and the poor, far fewer of us stop to analyze the differences between middle-class and poverty-level living arrangements in Canada. Should social policies be implemented to equalize opportunities for the young people shown in these photos? Why or why not?

Wealth and Income Inequality

According to Forbes.com, a U.S. business e-publication, Bill Gates is the richest person in the world today. At age 49, he was worth US$46.5 billion. Down 9 ranks from Gates was the richest Canadian, Kenneth J. Thomson whose total net worth before his death in 2006 was US$19.6 billion, or approximately CN$23 billion. No other Canadian comes close to owning that kind of wealth, although Canada has a respectable number of billionaires (see Table 2.1), like the Westons, the Bronfmans, and the Irvings, and even British Columbia's own "rags to riches" story maker, Jimmy Pattison. The vast majority of Canadians will never amass even a fraction of the wealth these people possess. In fact, although wealth for Canadian families increased by 10 percent overall between 1984 and 1999, it did not increase for all family types (Statistics Canada 2002r). For example, wealth, or "net worth," for young families (aged 25 to 34) with children dropped a dramatic 30 percent in this 15-year period (from a net worth of $44 000 in 1984 to

$30 800 in 1999). Additionally, the proportion of families with a zero net worth rose from 10 percent in 1984 to 16 percent in 1999. Conversely, families where the main income earner had a university degree rose 18 percent in this time period, for a net worth in 1999 of $118 000. Families in which the main income earner was 65 or older had an increase of 56 percent to a net worth of $126 000. Among immigrants to Canada, those who have been in Canada fewer than 10 years saw wealth fall 25 percent, while those who have been in Canada for 20 years or more saw wealth rise (Statistics Canada 2002r). The face of poverty is increasingly diverse with regard to family type, as more Canadians experience layoffs, lack of real wage gains, and reduced work hours. We will look at this in more depth later in the chapter.

How is the unequal distribution of wealth associated with social problems? According to sociologists Melvin L. Oliver and Thomas M. Shapiro (1995:2), wealth is a particularly important indicator of individual and family access to life chances:

> Wealth signifies the command over financial resources that a family has accumulated over its lifetime along with those resources that have been inherited across generations. Such resources, when

TABLE 2.1   Canada's Billionaires, 2006[1]

Rank	Name	Worth (US$ bil)
9	Thomson, Kenneth, and family	19.6
59	Weston, Galen, and family	8.4
106	Irving, James, Arthur, and John	5.5
114	Skoll, Jeffery	5.0
174	Desmarais, Paul	3.8
181	Sherman, Bernard (Barry)	3.7
194	Pattison, Jim	3.5
224	Miller, Robert	3.0
224	Rogers, Edward	3.0
258	Bronfman, Charles	2.7
335	McCain, Wallace	2.3
365	Lee-Chin, Michael	2.1
382	Riddell, Clayton	2.0
486	Katz, Daryl	1.6

[1]Rank = rank in world

Source: Forbes.com (January 2006). Reprinted by permission of Forbes Magazine © 2006 Forbes Inc.

Housing is one reflection of larger economic inequalities that exist in Canada. What economic realities are shown by this multi-storey house in a wealthy suburban neighbourhood as compared with these apartment units in a low-income urban area?

combined with income, can create the opportunity to secure the "good life" in whatever form is needed—education, business, training, justice, health, comfort, and so on. Wealth is a special form of money not used to purchase milk and shoes and other life necessities. More often it is used to create opportunities, secure a desired stature and standard of living, or pass class status along to one's children.

Like wealth, income is extremely unevenly divided in Canada (see Table 2.2). ***Income* is the economic gain derived from wages, salaries, and income transfers (governmental aid such as income assistance [welfare], or ownership of property)** (Beeghley 1989). According to a recent international study on income conducted by Statistics Canada, Canada has higher income inequality than Europe and lower inequality than the United States (Statistics Canada 2005i). In 2003, in Canada, the median income, adjusted for inflation, for all families was $56 000, one-half a percent less than the year previous (Statistics Canada 2005e). Median income means exactly one-half of families make below $56 000 and one-half make above $56 000. Lone-parent families in 2003, in contrast, earned a median income of $28 600, down 1 percent from 2002. Economic gains associated with economic expansion in Canada through the 1990s, as one might predict, mainly went to higher income families, and the result was an increase in family income inequality. Overall, the incomes of the richest 20 percent of families rose by approximately 10 percent, while family income stagnated among Canada's poorest families. Additionally, the low income rate unexpectedly continued to rise. Statistics Canada attributes this "to earning difficulties among poorer families and declining social transfers in the mid to late 1990s." (Statistics Canada 2005j).

When we look at market wages in comparison, average market wages, again adjusted for inflation, were $61 634 in 2000, the equivalent of an annual increase of 2.5 percent per year since 1993. This average market wage is, however, exactly that—an average. When we examine which families are benefiting most from market increases, a clearer picture emerges. The distribution of market income for each quintile of the Canadian population has remained amazingly stable since 1951. The share of income in the highest quintile rose from 42.8 percent in 1951 to 44.5 percent in 1996. The share for the lowest quintile went from 4.4 percent in 1951 to 4.6 percent in 1996. It is noteworthy that in 1998, the share for the highest quintile was up to 45.2 and down to 3.1 for the lowest (Statistics Canada 2000; see Figure 2.1). The gap between the richest and the poorest in the nation continues to widen.

The increase in after-tax income was not shared by all family types, however. Among senior or "elderly" families (those in which the main income earner was aged 65 and over), median after-tax income remained virtually unchanged at $38 500. However, it was up 12 percent in real terms compared with 1996.

According to Statistics Canada (2006c), an estimated 684 000 families had low income in 2004, which

TABLE 2.2   Median Total Income for Families (not adjusted for tax—i.e., before tax), 2003

	All families		Couple families		Lone-parent families	
	Amount $	% Change 2002/03	Amount $	% Change 2002/03	Amount $	% Change 2002/03
Canada	$ 56 000	–0.9%	$ 62 600	–0.5%	$ 28 600	–1.0%
St. John's	$ 55 800	0.9%	$ 64 300	0.4%	$ 25 000	–1.5%
Halifax	$ 59 200	–0.7%	$ 66 800	–0.3%	$ 26 800	–0.1%
Saint John	$ 52 900	0.5%	$ 60 800	0.8%	$ 24 500	–0.7%
Montreal	$ 54 400	–1.1%	$ 61 000	–0.9%	$ 29 800	–0.4%
Quebec	$ 59 600	–0.4%	$ 64 800	–0.5%	$ 33 800	–0.3%
Saguenay	$ 54 300	–1.1%	$ 59 100	–1.4%	$ 28 100	–1.6%
Sherbrooke	$ 52 100	–0.2%	$ 57 600	–1.0%	$ 29 200	0.4%
Trois-Rivières	$ 50 500	–0.5%	$ 56 700	–0.6%	$ 26 800	2.7%
Ottawa-Gatineau	$ 71 100	–1.5%	$ 79 600	–1.2%	$ 34 700	–1.6%
Hamilton	$ 65 200	–0.6%	$ 72 400	–0.1%	$ 31 500	–0.5%
Kingston	$ 61 900	0.6%	$ 69 100	1.1%	$ 30 100	1.3%
Kitchener	$ 67 000	–1.1%	$ 73 400	–0.7%	$ 32 900	–1.2%
London	$ 61 200	–0.4%	$ 68 500	–0.1%	$ 29 800	0.3%
Oshawa	$ 72 400	0.2%	$ 80 300	0.3%	$ 34 600	3.3%
St. Catharines-Niagara	$ 57 300	–1.5%	$ 63 800	–1.0%	$ 29 100	–0.3%
Greater Sudbury	$ 59 200	–1.2%	$ 67 600	–0.2%	$ 26 100	–1.2%
Thunder Bay	$ 63 400	–0.2%	$ 71 000	0.2%	$ 28 500	2.7%
Toronto	$ 58 500	–2.2%	$ 65 700	–1.3%	$ 32 300	–3.6%
Windsor	$ 67 800	–1.7%	$ 76 600	–1.0%	$ 30 600	–0.8%
Winnipeg	$ 57 300	–0.8%	$ 64 300	–0.4%	$ 28 800	–1.3%
Regina	$ 63 300	0.1%	$ 72 700	–0.1%	$ 28 800	–0.6%
Saskatoon	$ 57 500	–0.3%	$ 65 300	–0.1%	$ 24 900	–1.5%
Calgary	$ 67 800	–1.1%	$ 74 500	–0.7%	$ 34 500	–1.6%
Edmonton	$ 64 800	–0.5%	$ 72 200	–0.4%	$ 31 300	–1.8%
Abbotsford	$ 51 000	–1.5%	$ 56 300	–1.3%	$ 25 100	–1.5%
Vancouver	$ 54 100	–1.6%	$ 59 700	–1.0%	$ 29 400	–3.7%
Victoria	$ 61 700	–0.6%	$ 68 100	–0.5%	$ 32 100	1.2%

Source: Statistics Canada, 2005, "Family Income, 2003," The Daily, May 20, Catalogue no. 11-001.

FIGURE 2.1   Share of Total Income by Quintiles, 2003

Source: National Council of Welfare Reports, Poverty Profile, 2002 and 2003. Summer 2006, Volume 124. Reproduced with the permission of the Minister of Public Works and Government Services Canada, 2006.

represents 7.8 percent of all families. Some 865 000 children under 18 were living in low-income families, 12.8 percent of the total number of children in families.

Divisions in the Canadian Class Structure

Canada has several class divisions characterized by widely diverse lifestyles and life chances. The upper, or capitalist, class, the wealthiest and most powerful class, is made up primarily of those whose wealth is inherited. In Canada, this accounts for fewer than 1 percent of Canadians. The children of these elite Canadians attend private schools and exclusive universities, studying liberal arts, not vocations (Macionis and Gerber 2002:77). Elite women often involve themselves in charity work, which, as Macionis and Gerber point out, "also builds networks that put these families at the center of the nation's power elite." The "lower upper" class, the remaining 2 to 4 percent of the capitalist class, derive their income from investments in income-producing property, such as media conglomerates, high-rise hotels, apartment buildings, and office parks; others earn their wealth as entrepreneurs, presidents of major corporations, sports or entertainment celebrities, or top-level professionals.

The middle class in Canada, approximately 40 to 50 percent of the population, is more ethnically diverse than the WASPish upper class. The upper-middle class is composed typically of university-educated professionals (for example, physicians and attorneys), business analysts, owners of small businesses, stockbrokers, and corporate managers. These individuals generally do not own the means of production but have substantial control over production and other workers and can amass considerable wealth (Wright 1979, 1985). The "middle-middle" class includes white-collar office workers, middle-management personnel, and people in support positions (for example, medical technologists, nurses, and legal and medical secretaries), semiprofessionals, and non-retail salesworkers. Typically people in this class are high-school graduates and homeowners who are able to accumulate a small amount of wealth.

The working class, approximately one-third of the Canadian population, is composed of people who work as semiskilled machine operators in industrial settings and in non-manual, semiskilled positions (for example, daycare workers, checkout clerks, cashiers, and counter help in fast-food restaurants). People in this class have little or no accumulated wealth and, if they are homeowners, typically own homes in low-cost neighbourhoods. They are unlikely to go to university or have incomes above the national average (unless unionized), and their jobs are often highly supervised and give little personal satisfaction (Macionis and Gerber 2002).

The lower class in Canada, approximately 20 percent of the population, comprises the working poor and the chronically poor. The working poor are those who work full-time in unskilled positions, such as seasonal or migrant agricultural workers or the lowest-paid service sector workers, but still remain at the edge of poverty. When the minimum wage was introduced in Canada in 1974, an individual with full-time, full-year employment earning minimum wage could expect to live 10 percent above the poverty line. Today, an individual needs to earn more than $10 per hour, full-time, full-year to even reach the poverty line. It is easy, therefore, to see why so many Canadians fall into this class, despite the overall wealth of the nation. No minimum wages in any part of Canada reach anywhere near the poverty line (see Table 2.3).

In an interview with sociologist Mark Robert Rank (1994:43), Jack Collins, a married father with six children, described the transitory nature of work for the working poor:

> You name it, I've done it. I started out cooking. I've been a janitor. I've been an auto mechanic. I drove a school bus for five years. I drove a semi [truck] coast to coast. I've worked in a foundry. I've worked in a shoe factory. I've worked in other factories, warehouses. I'll do just about anything. . . . The main problem was findin' [a job] with starting pay that's enough to really get by on.

Jack Collins and his family may be only one paycheque away from the chronically poor, the very bottom of the Canadian class system.

The National Council of Welfare (2001b) demonstrated, by way of examples, how working people can remain poor in Canada. The poverty line for a two-person family in a large city in 1998 was $22 452. Working 40 hours per week at minimum wage in Ontario ($6.85/hour), a person could earn $14 248. These wages can keep people just above the poverty line if there are two adults working 52 weeks per year. However, if the other person in the two-person family is a child, even with the federal child tax benefit of

TABLE 2.3   Minimum Hourly Wages for Experienced Adult Workers in Canada, 2000–2007

Jurisdiction	2000	2001	2002	2003	2004	2005	2006	2007
Alberta						1-Sep $7.00		
British Columbia	1-Nov $7.60	1-Nov $8.00						
Manitoba		1-Apr $6.25	1-Apr $6.50	1-Apr $6.75	1-Apr $7.00	1-Apr $7.25	1-Apr $7.60	1-Apr $8.00
New Brunswick	1-Jan $5.75	1-Jul $5.90	1-Aug $6.00		1-Jan $6.20	1-Jan $6.30	1-Jan $6.50 1-Jul $6.70	
Newfoundland and Labrador			1-May $5.75 1-Nov $6.00			1-Jun $6.25	1-Jan $6.50 1-Jun $6.75	1-Jan $7.00
Northwest Territories				28-Dec $8.25				
Nova Scotia	1-Oct $5.70	1-Oct $5.80	1-Oct $6.00	1-Oct $6.25	1-Apr $6.50	1-Oct $6.80	1-Apr $7.15	
Nunavut				3-Mar $8.50				
Ontario					1-Feb $7.15	1-Feb $7.45	1-Feb $7.75	1-Feb $8.00
Prince Edward Island	1-Jan $5.60	1-Jan $5.80	1-Jan $6.00	1-Jan $6.25	1-Jan $6.50	1-Jan $6.80	1-Apr $7.15	1-Apr $7.50
Quebec		1-Feb $7.00	1-Oct $7.20	1-Feb $7.30	1-May $7.45	1-May $7.60	1-May $7.75	
Saskatchewan			1-May $6.35 1-Nov $6.65			1-Sep $7.05	1-Sep $7.55	1-Mar $7.95
Yukon							1-May $8.25	

Source: Adapted from Human Resources and Skills Development Canada, 2006, Minimum Wages for Canadian Adult Workers since 1965. *Reproduced with the permission of Her Majesty the Queen in Right of Canada 2006.*

$1625 for one child, plus a GST refund of $503, the family receives only $16 376 per year to live on—a figure not even close to the poverty line. In 1999 in Winnipeg, a single parent would have to work 80 hours per week to get to the poverty line, while a two-parent family with two children would have to work 118 hours per week to reach the poverty line. There are only 168 hours in a week, so this scenario assumes each parent could get the equivalent of a 59-hour-per-week job (not easy in the current economy) and also assumes that daycare or after-school care is not needed. Vancouver had the highest minimum wage, and still a single parent had to work 61 hours per week while a couple with two children had to work 89 hours per week to get to the poverty line. Minimum wages in this country no longer keep people out of poverty, despite the fact that that was what they were designed to do.

Although the poor constitute approximately 15 percent of the Canadian population, they receive only about 5 percent of the overall Canadian income. Individuals who are chronically poor include people of working age who are unemployed or outside the labour force and children who live in poor families caught in long-term deprivation. Overrepresented among low-income and poverty-level individuals are those who are unable to work because of age or disability and lone-parent mothers who are heads of households, along with their children. The term *underclass* is sometimes used to refer to people who are chronically poor, but this term not only negatively labels poor people, it also puts them outside the mainstream of society.

POVERTY IN CANADA

The fact that Canada is such a wealthy nation, but one in which such a high proportion of the population lives in low income and poverty situations, has made Canada the target of international criticism, particularly by the United Nations. In Canada, the picture of poverty is multifaceted. Estimates of the homeless population range in the hundreds of thousands (Duffy and Mandell 2001), while people trying to survive on social assistance number in the hundreds of thousands as well. Along with affordable housing, one of the most critical issues facing people on a limited or poverty-level income is food security. As a woman interviewed by the Peterborough Social Planning Council (1998:126) reported, "I've been visiting my doctor regularly. He feels I'm not eating properly. My kids are fed three times per day, whereas I eat three times per week. I've lost 60 lbs. in the last year."

In *Hunger Count 2002—Eating Their Words: Government Failure on Food Security*, the Canadian Association of Food Banks (2002:4) outlined some of the impacts of poverty and deprivation:

> Food insecurity . . . elicits feelings of alienation, impoverishment and social exclusion. While parents deprive themselves in order to protect their children from the impacts of poverty and food insecurity, some simply do not have the resources to ensure an adequate diet for their children. Inadequately nourished children are more likely to experience compromised health, iron deficiency, frequent stomach aches and head aches, colds, ear infections, anemia, and asthma. Children with poor diets also have slower recovery periods from illness and reduced immune systems. Food insecurity is associated with major depression in adults, hyperactivity in children, and dysthymia, suicidal ideation and attempted suicide in adolescents.

Recently, in many provinces, governments have been introducing severe cuts, disqualifying many previous recipients of income assistance, and changing criteria so fewer people qualify for benefits. The result has been, in some provinces, a reduction in the numbers of people receiving income assistance benefits but not a reduction in need. What happens to people who no longer qualify for social assistance? Evidence suggests that more people are joining the ranks of the homeless, erecting cardboard huts, sleeping in cars, or staying in urban shelters. In fact, one-third of all homeless people are entire families. Children are the fastest growing group of homeless people in Canada (Macionis and Gerber 2002:289), and recent studies of shelter use indicate that one-fifth of shelter users are children under the age of 18 (Duffy and Mandell 2001:95).

In Toronto, the issue of inclusion has surfaced in a challenging way: There are approximately 100 homeless transgendered people (see Chapter 4) who have trouble finding even temporary shelter. In February 2001, the Salvation Army banned "trans" people from its facility because it was contracted "to provide space for only 100 percent females' and couples" (Appelbe 2001). Everyone should feel safe, but "trans" males (F to M), for example, may not feel safe in shelters for men. An equally valid point is that women in women's shelters may not feel safe in close quarters with females who they perceive are men (M to F). Advocates for "trans" people say that "the only acceptable solution is education and legal action that results in full acceptance of all transgender people in any situation" (Appelbe 2001:2).

Sociologists make a distinction between absolute poverty and relative poverty. ***Relative poverty* exists when people may be able to afford basic necessities, such as food, clothing, and shelter, but cannot maintain an average standard of living in comparison to that of other members of their society or group** (Ropers 1991). Many Canadians do not suffer from absolute poverty, but do experience relative poverty on the basis of what is available to other people in Canada.

Canada has a very high rate of poverty compared with other advanced industrial nations, although the United States has the highest (Rothchild 1995). The ***poverty rate* is the proportion of the population whose income falls below the government's official poverty line—the level of income below which a family of a given size is considered to be poor.** In Canada, the government has never actually established a formal "poverty line" as such, but rather has created a low income cut-off (LICO) line, which allows us to see how many people in Canada spend significantly more than the average on the necessities of life. LICOs also allow us to see how far below the cut-off some people live. As stated in a recent report by the National Council of Welfare (2001b), "All measures of poverty are relative. The issue is not so much about measurement as it is about values. How poor and excluded are we willing to allow some people to be in our wealthy society?"

The number of families who live below the unofficial poverty (LICO) line in Canada increased throughout most of the 1980s and 1990s, although since 1996, the numbers have dropped marginally each year, signifying better overall economic conditions in more recent years (Statistics Canada, 2002f). The National Council of Welfare (2001b) cautions, though, that the drop in numbers living in poverty is not equivalent to the economic increases experienced by the nation overall, suggesting, for poor people, stagnation at best.

Poverty Lines: LICOs and LIMs

The Canadian government, through Statistics Canada, has established two measures that are commonly used to measure poverty in Canada, although neither measure is

an actual measure of poverty per se. The first is the low income cut-off (LICO) line, discussed earlier. It uses information on family spending patterns and family and community size from a specified base year. The base year is updated periodically. Currently, Statistics Canada is using 1992 data for its base-spending year. Every year, the LICO is updated to reflect changes in inflation, as per the Consumer Price Index (CPI). When the LICO was first established in 1959, the average Canadian family spent 50 percent of its pre-tax income on food, shelter and clothing, according to the Family Expenditures Survey (FAMEX). Twenty points were added to this number with the rationale that a family spending 70 percent of its pre-tax income on these necessities would be "in strained circumstances" (Statistics Canada 2002i:11). Using the 70 percent, the government then calculates LICOs for five community sizes and seven family sizes (see Table 2.4).

Another measure often used to calculate the well-being of the population is the low income measure (LIM). The LIM takes a fixed percentage of per capita family income and adjusts it for family size *and* the age of family members. The rationale is that a family of two adults and one child is cheaper to feed than a family of three adults. LIMs are calculated on a before-tax and an after-tax basis. Neither LICOs nor LIMs are measures of poverty, although they are typically used

TABLE 2.4   Low Income Cut-Off Lines (LICOs), Canada, 2005

	Population of Community of Residence				
Family Size	500 000 +	100 000–499 999	30 000–99 999	Less than 30 000*	Rural
1	$20 778	$17 895	$17 784	$16 273	$14 303
2	$25 867	$22 276	$22 139	$20 257	$17 807
3	$31 801	$27 386	$27 217	$24 904	$21 891
4	$38 610	$33 251	$33 046	$30 238	$26 579
5	$43 791	$37 711	$37 480	$34 295	$30 145
6	$49 389	$42 533	$42 271	$38 679	$33 999
7+	$54 987	$47 354	$47 063	$43 063	$37 863

Note: This table uses the 1992 base. Income refers to total pre-tax household income.

*Includes cities with a population between 15 000 and 30 000 and small urban areas (under 15 000).

Example: A family of four living in a very large Canadian city with a before-tax income of less than $38 610 in 2005 would have been living below the poverty line.

Source: Prepared by the Canadian Council on Social Development using Statistics Canada's Low Income Cut-Offs, from Low Income Cut-offs for 2005 and Low Income Measures for 2004, Catalogue # 75F0002MIE, www.ccsd.ca.

as such, since they do indicate relative circumstances for citizens. Furthermore, Canada lacks other measures of poverty, a curious fact given that such a high proportion of Canadians live below the LICOs set by the federal government.

Who Are the Poor?

If poverty were equally distributed among all social groups in Canada, all people regardless of their age, ethnicity, gender, household composition, ability, or other attributes would have an equal chance of being among the poor in any given year. However, poverty is not distributed equally: People in some categories are at greater risk for poverty than are people in other categories.

Age, Gender, Household Composition, and Poverty

The vast majority of poor people in Canada are women and children, particularly lone parent women and their children. Sociologist Diana Pearce (1978) refers to the association between gender and poverty as the *feminization of poverty*—**the trend whereby women are disproportionately represented among individuals living in poverty.** On the basis of research on the feminization of poverty, some sociologists suggest that high rates of female poverty are related to women's unique vulnerability to event-driven poverty—poverty resulting from the loss of a job, disability, desertion by a spouse, separation, divorce, or widowhood (Bane 1986; Kurz 1995; Weitzman 1985; see Chapter 4 for a full discussion of the feminization of poverty). In 2001, 15.7 percent of all families in Canada were headed by a lone parent (1 311 190 lone-parent families). Of those, more than 80 percent were headed by females. Four out of five of these women had earnings in 2000, and over 40 percent of those employed lived in low-income situations. Of the lone-parent women who had no earnings in 2003, 94.6 percent lived in poverty (National Council of Welfare 2006; Statistics Canada 2002f). Statistics Canada estimates that families below the low-income line would have needed, on average, an additional $6707 per year, after tax, to rise above that line, and the total amount of money required to bring all poor people in Canada up to the poverty line in 2003 was $21.6 billion (National Council of Welfare 2006). As a comparison, Canada's gross domestic product (GDP) in 2003 was $1.2 trillion. In 2003, the poverty

FIGURE 2.2 Poor Children by Family Type, 2001

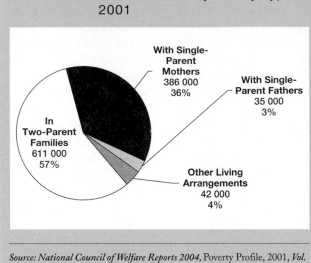

Source: National Council of Welfare Reports 2004, Poverty Profile, 2001, *Vol. 122, Autumn. Reproduced with the permission of the Minister of Public Works and Government Services Canada, 2006.*

rate for lone-parent women was 48.9 percent, compared with the rate of 20.0 percent for lone-parent men.

Because so many of Canada's lone-parent women live in poverty, so too do their children, although the biggest proportion of impoverished children live in two-parent families (National Council of Welfare 2004; see Figure 2.2).

In 2003, 17.6 percent of children lived in poverty in Canada, an appalling number given the federal government's commitment to the United Nations during the mid-1990s to eradicate "child poverty" by the year 2000. The term *child poverty* is an Orwellian exercise in language use—clearly, children are poor *because* their parents are poor. By having governments speak of "child poverty," we are able to simultaneously hold children blameless (appropriately) for their situations while targeting their parents as "shiftless," "lazy," "welfare cheats" (see Box 2.1). As Freiler and Cerny (1998:17) point out, "child and family poverty is being redefined as a personal problem arising out of immoral or irresponsible behaviour, rather than out of external social and economic factors." Similarly, by speaking of "lone-parent" women, we do not focus on the behaviours of the men they may have been involved with and their potential contributions to the rise in the lone-parent female population or the relative poverty of lone-parent females in comparison with lone-parent male.

SOCIAL PROBLEMS IN THE MEDIA

BOX 2.1   How You Can Tell When the Media Poor-Bash

Sometimes poor-bashing is obvious. Calling people on welfare names like "cheats" or "criminally inclined opportunists" is blatant poor-bashing. But subtle poor-bashing can be just as devastating. You must read or listen critically to make sure you're not being taken in by it.

When Newfoundland anti-poverty activist Bev Brown gives workshops on poverty and the media, she asks these questions about media coverage of poverty issues:

What's left out of the story?
Issues usually left out of articles about welfare and EI are the high unemployment rate, the poor quality of jobs that are available (when they are), an explanation of who benefits from poverty, information about the laws that cause poverty (like low welfare rates and minimum wages), and information about who has the funds or could create the jobs or pay the wages to reduce poverty.

Who is speaking?
Do poor people or groups that represent poor people have any voice in the story? Do we hear directly from people in poverty or only from people who work for agencies or charities or from researchers who theorize about them?

Is the story based on false assumptions?
Is it assumed that jobs are available when they aren't? That welfare is generous? That people on welfare are lazy? That welfare is easily available? That people on welfare and EI don't have to look for work? That single moms aren't productive? That people have to be forced to look for work? That training programs will create enough jobs for all who need them?

What are the subtle messages of the story?
Does it suggest—without clearly stating it—that people who have paid work are better than people who have unpaid work (child care, for example)? Does it imply that people on welfare prefer this to a range of other options?

Does the story use facts, or gossip and insinuation?
Are the sources named? Are the sources right-wing think tanks that have a vested interest in policies that cut the taxes and

reduce the wages that their member corporations pay? Are the sources "authorities" that promote the typical stereotypes about people on welfare or EI? Would a similar standard of accuracy apply when reporting about a person or a group with a lot of power?

Does the story use the social policy newspeak words?
Does it use words or phrases like "dependent," "incentive," "disincentive," and others... that blame the poor and take the pressure off the rich?

Brown recommends these supplementary questions:

1. Does the story ask how to end poverty, or does it merely expose the suffering of poor individuals?
2. Does it ask who benefits from poverty?
3. Does it investigate what laws cause poverty instead of focusing on individual characteristics of poor people?
4. Does it deal with the morality of poverty in the midst of great wealth?
5. If a publication includes stories advising upper-income people how to use RRSPs, does it also print stories advising poor people how to use welfare and EI? If there are stories about welfare fraud, are there any about tax fraud, or corporate fraud?
6. Does the story assume charity is the only way to deal with poverty?

A final test: How would it sound if the statements about poor people were made about women or people of colour? Would it be okay to say that women are "criminally inclined opportunists"? That would be sexist. Would it be okay to say that people of colour are "criminally inclined opportunists"? No, that would be racist. Then it's poor-bashing to say that people on welfare are "criminally inclined opportunists."

Source: Jean Swanson, 2001, Poor-Bashing: The Politics of Exclusion, *Toronto: Between the Lines, 191–92. Reprinted by permission of Between the Lines Publishing.*

Ethnicity, Racialization, and Poverty

As of the May 15, 2001 census, Canada experienced its greatest number of foreign-born citizens (18.4 percent of the total population) since 1931 (22.2 percent). Along with people reporting "aboriginal identity" (approximately 3.3 percent of the population) and those reporting "visible minority" status (13.4 percent of the population), foreign-born people have a heightened risk of poverty over Canadian-born individuals. With regard to what Statistics Canada called "unattached individuals," the poverty rate in 2003 for immigrants was 40.1 percent compared to 36.4 percent for those Canadian-born. The picture intensifies for those who are in families where the major income earner is an immigrant. In 2003, the poverty rate for immigrants was 18.6 percent, versus 9.8 percent for Canadian-born people (National Council of Welfare 2006) Further, one-quarter of recent immigrant workers made less than $10 per hour in 2000, compared with one-sixth of those Canadian-born (Saunders 2005:23). There are many confounding reasons for the overrepresentation of people from marginalized groups at or below the low income cut-off line: discrimination due to racism, education level, age, unemployment, labour market attachment, language, and culture, to name a few (see Chapter 3). Consistently, Indigenous people in Canada have the highest unemployment rates of all Canadians and the lowest employment incomes. For example, average full-time, full-year earnings for Indigenous people were 23 percent lower than the national average. Further, average earnings for Indigenous people are considerably lower at every education level (Saunders 2005:22). A Centre for Social Justice study, using Statistics Canada income data from 1996 and 1998, showed that white Canadians had a poverty rate of 17.6 percent, compared to 35.6 for racialized minorities (Fleras and Elliott 2003:120). The dramatic differences in poverty rates between white Canadians and members of racialized minorities have been referred to as "economic apartheid" (Galabuzi, in Fleras and Elliott 2003:120).

The contrast in poverty rates within racialized categories becomes especially evident if household composition is considered. According to sociologist Demie Kurz (1995), the feminization of poverty is intensified by the racialization of poverty—the process by which the effects of low income are made even worse by racialized discrimination, which is experienced by all people of colour and Indigenous people but is particularly acute for women who are single heads of household.

This phenomenon (discussed in Chapter 3) is known as *intersectionality*: **when people experience oppression in more than one aspect of their lives (e.g., sexism plus racism plus homophobia), the resulting oppression is greater than the sum of these oppressions.**

Education Level, Ability, and Poverty

Statistics from 1998 show that even higher education does not protect Canadians from poverty. One-third of high school graduates and more than one-fifth of people with baccalaureate degrees lived in poverty in 2003 (see Figure 2.3), and families with female major income earners had higher rates of poverty at every level of education (National Council of Welfare 2006:48).

In fact, an emergent problem seems to be the difficulty many students today experience in paying back enormous student loans. As a 2006 report created by Human Resources and Skills Development Canada (HRSDC) states,

> Findings revealed a picture of heavier student debt burden. While the proportion of graduates who borrowed money did not change between 1990 and 2000, the average student debt size increased. As a result, the median-debt-to-earnings ratio increased significantly for both college and bachelor graduates (from 0.21 to 0.33 and from 0.28 to 0.44) over the ten-year period. The proportion of students reporting problems in repaying loans also increased over the period, reaching 41% for college graduates and 31% for bachelor graduates in 2000. . . . Borrowing and more particularly heavy debt burden can have an adverse impact on future personal decisions such as the timing for buying a home, starting a family, saving for retirement, participation in adult education, etc. (Dubois 2006: "Abstract")

One Canadian website, in fact, is dedicated to recording people's student loan experiences and supporting them through them (see CanadaStudentDebt.ca in Weblinks at the end of this chapter). Structural shifts in the labour market are responsible for many people's inability to get a job that pays more than minimum wage, even when they hold a baccalaureate degree. People with a master's degree do fare better, but the question is, for how long? Many, particularly those who have amassed a small fortune in student loan debt, wonder if they would have been better off financially without the post-secondary education.

FIGURE 2.3   Poverty Rates by Highest Level of Education Completed, 2003

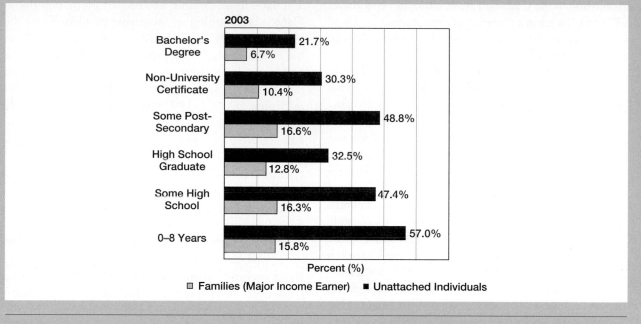

Source: *National Council of Welfare Reports, 2006* Poverty Profile, 2002 and 2003, *Vol. 124. Reproduced with the permission of the Minister of Public Works and Government Services Canada, 2006.*

The impact of intersectionality on the population's risk of poverty is substantial. According to the 2001 Participation and Activity Limitation Survey (PALS), in addition to risks of poverty associated with education, 12.4 percent of the Canadian population lives with a disability. Indigenous people have significantly higher rates of disability than the population generally (as reported in the 2000–01 Canadian Community Health Survey). The most common disabilities experienced by Canadians are mobility, agility, and pain conditions (HRDC 2002). For people with disabilities in Canada, many lack the education to participate fully in the workforce. In 2001, just over one-half had completed high school (46 percent for Indigenous) and only 7 percent (2 percent for Indigenous) had a university degree. This contrasts with the population at large, in which over 70 percent graduate from high school and 17 percent hold university degrees. As noted by Human Resources Development Canada, stable employment is a critical factor in financial security. The employment rate in 1996 for men with a disability was 41 percent and for women was 32 percent. Again, compared to the Canadian population as a whole, this rate is abysmal: In 1996, 83 percent of men without disabilities and 70 percent of women without disabilities were employed. In the Indigenous population, 56 percent of the general population was employed, while only 28 percent of Indigenous people with a disability were employed. Lastly, according to 1998 income statistics, working-age people with a disability earned 76 percent of what non-disabled Canadians earned, after taxes, while Indigenous people with disabilities earned only half. People with a disability are doubly disadvantaged here as well, since extra expenses often accompany the disability itself, besides dramatically lower after-tax incomes.

Consequences of Poverty

Poverty statistics are more than just a snapshot of who is poor and how the poor live: these statistics are also predictors. As such, they tend to predict a grim future for individuals who live below the poverty line and for the entire nation (Gleick 1996). As one social analyst (Ropers 1991:25) has noted, "Poverty narrows and closes life chances. . . . Being poor not only means economic insecurity, it also wreaks havoc on one's mental and physical health."

Health and Nutrition

According to the Canadian Association of Food Banks (2002:5), "[w]ithin a domestic context, hunger and food insecurity are best understood as consequences of extreme poverty."

Good nutrition, which is essential to good health, depends on the food purchased; and when people are poor, they are more likely to go without food or to purchase cheap but filling foods such as beans, rice, and potatoes that may not meet all daily nutritional requirements. Poor children particularly are at risk for inadequate nutrition and hunger (Community Childhood Hunger Identification Project 1995). Emergency food assistance is especially pronounced in urban areas, but recently, there has been greater need in rural communities as well. Since 2000, 51 food banks have opened in rural areas. In a recent study of food insecurity in the Canadian North, 51 percent of children in 2000–2001 went hungry at some points during the year (Canadian Association of Food Banks [CAFB] 2005:24).

Increasing numbers of people annually are relying on food banks to meet their needs, consistently more than 40 percent of whom are children. The majority of food banks allow only one food bank visit per month and provide on average five days' worth of food (CAFB 2005). Evaluating the contents of food bank hampers, nutritionists found that the donated groceries did not allow a person to meet basic daily nutritional requirements (CAFB 2002:15). When these hampers are used in emergency situations, as they were originally intended, that does not present many problems. However, when people are reliant on food bank hampers over the long term, the consequences are detrimental and severe. Prolonged malnutrition can contribute to or result in such medical problems as rickets, scurvy, parasitic worms, and developmental disabilities. Between one-third and one-half of all children living in poverty consume significantly less than the federally recommended guidelines for caloric and nutritional intake (Children's Defense Fund 1999).

Problems associated with food and shelter are intricately linked. When parents have to decide between paying the rent and putting food on the table, many choose to pay the rent in hopes of keeping a roof over their children's head. Sometimes, however, they cannot afford to do either.

Housing

The lack of affordable housing in many regions in Canada is becoming an increasing problem. Over the last two decades, low-cost housing units in many areas have been replaced by expensive condominiums or single-family residences for affluent residents in a process known as "gentrification." This shift to condominiums and single-family residences has made finding housing even more difficult for individuals and families living in poverty. When low-income housing is available, it may be located in high-density, often overcrowded areas. The housing often has inadequate heating and plumbing facilities, infestations of insects or rodents, and dangerous structural problems due to faulty construction or lack of adequate maintenance. Studies conducted by food banks in Canada show that most food-bank users spend more than 30 percent of their income on housing (CAFB 2002:14). The Canadian Mortgage and Housing Corporation (CMHC) describes people in this situation as "in core housing need and at risk of becoming homeless" (CAFB 2002:14).

Recently, the federal government signed agreements with seven provincial and territorial governments to match $680 million over five years for social housing. The 2005 federal budget promised to continue existing programs. This is a welcome shift away from funding cuts but unfortunately still does not meet need. The Federation of Canadian Municipalities and the National Housing and Homelessness Network have estimated that an annual budget of $2 billion over 10 years is closer to what is needed (CAFB 2002:15). As of 2005, approximately $800 million is sitting, untouched, in the Affordable Housing initiative due to "intergovernmental wrangling" (CAFB 2005: 30). Another issue is the redirection of housing funds to other budgets, after political promises were made. For example, British Columbia has approximately 10 000 people on waiting lists for social housing and had federal funding of $89 million dollars for social housing between 2002 and 2007. That money, which could have provided up to 2500 new affordable family housing units, is now being redirected into the health care system (CAFB 2005: 16). With the provision of additional social housing in Canada, a

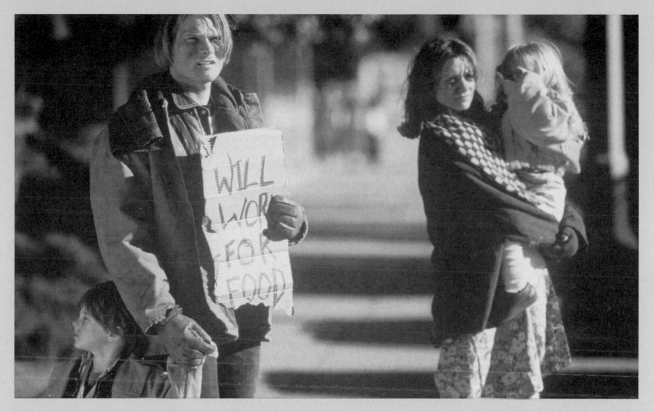

The sight of homeless individuals and families has become all too familiar in Canada, primarily in larger cities but also in rural areas. What social factors do you think have caused an increase in homeless families in recent years

central question remains regarding affordability. As the Canadian Association of Food Banks points out in *HungerCount 2002*, "There is no suggestion that federal government will intervene to ensure affordability of this new housing" (CAFB 2002:15).

In recent years, increasing rates of homelessness reflect one of the most devastating effects of poverty. As described earlier, the composition of the homeless population has shifted to include many more families, young children, youth, and elderly (see studies by Liebow 1993; Lundy 1995; Rossi 1989). Regardless of age or marital status, homeless people are among the poorest of the poor.

Education

A crucial relationship exists between educational opportunities and life chances. Children from low-income families tend to have inadequate educational opportunities; this keeps them at the bottom of the class system (Bowles and Gintis 1976). They get fewer years of schooling and are less likely to graduate from high school or a post-secondary institution than are children from more affluent families. The schools that poor children attend are more likely to be in areas with lower property values and more limited funding bases for education than are the schools attended by more affluent students, who often live in property-rich suburbs. Schools located in high-poverty rural areas or central cities often are dilapidated, have underpaid and overworked teachers, and must rely on outdated equipment and teaching materials.

Lack of educational opportunity can result in lower levels of educational attainment among people from lower-income and poverty-level families and tends to perpetuate poverty by making it significantly more difficult for these individuals to acquire well-paying jobs or a more secure economic future.

How Canada Deals with Poverty

In Canada, as part of an overall retrenchment of government programs and services, structural poverty is dealt with as though it is an individual problem. Rather than examine ways of eliminating poverty or dealing with poverty at a societal level, we offer temporary assistance, not through our governments, but through charity—both individual charity, such as serving a meal at a soup kitchen on Christmas Day and making a donation of money or goods, or through the existence of charitable organizations, such as soup kitchens like the Open Door and food banks like The Mustard Seed in Victoria, B.C., which typically rely on volunteer labour and community donations and, sometimes, some base year-to-year funding from government. In 1980 there were no food banks in Canada. In 2005, 650 food banks, along with 2864 affiliated agencies, provided "emergency" food rations and meals to Canadian citizens. Food bank use in Canada to 2002 had increased an incredible 97.8 percent since 1989, although Canada made a commitment in 1996, as a signatory to the Rome Declaration on World Food Security, to attain food security and end hunger (CAFB 2002). Forty-one percent of food bank users are children, despite the federal government's 1989 pledge to end "child poverty." The number of shelters has grown in recent years as well and still there are not enough available beds for all who need them. Sociologists Ann Duffy and Nancy Mandell (2001: 95) state that Toronto frontline workers estimate that two to four homeless people die each week in the city and, as mentioned earlier, that the number of homeless in Canada in the late 1990s was approximately 200 000, one-third of whom are whole families (Macionis and Gerber 2002:289).

We temporarily fund shelters and food banks in Canada, as though the problems associated with poverty in our nation are fleeting aberrations. Yet poverty is not significantly decreasing, despite good overall economic growth. State welfare programs, such as Employment Insurance (EI) and Social Assistance, continue to be retrenched, resulting in heightened risks of poverty for income-insecure individuals. As Macionis and Gerber (2002:289) state,

> Structural changes in the Canadian economy coupled with declining government support for lower-income people have all contributed to homelessness.

By way of example, revisions to the employee- and employer-funded Employment Insurance program have resulted in drastically narrowed eligibility criteria and shorter benefit periods, even though the program has always run at a surplus. Most recent data demonstrate that a mere 37 percent of the applicants meet new criteria, compared to more than 74 percent one decade ago (Canadian Labour Congress 2005). Additionally, waiting periods for benefit receipt have been lengthened, and individuals who need social assistance while waiting for a decision about their EI claim must agree to pay that money back when they receive EI benefits. In the past, unemployed workers were able to achieve EI benefits of up to 75 percent of their previous earnings, so this wait would not be as problematic in the short term. Today, however, workers typically are only able to receive *up to* 55 percent of their previous earnings.

Since its inception, the Employment Insurance Program has run at a surplus—perhaps the only government-handled program that has. Employers and employees both continue to pay into the EI fund, so why have there been so many cuts? Where has the EI money gone? As of 2005, the federal government had siphoned more than $45 billion to pay off the deficit, pay for tax cuts, and pay down government debt (CAFB 2005:32). Currently there is an additional $45 billion dollars in EI surplus (CAFB 2005:29). If you are laid off tomorrow, your chances of accessing any of the surplus you and your employer helped create are very low. Think about what you would do to survive for a month or more while your eligibility was being determined. *If you were successful in getting EI, how well could you make ends meet on half of your current monthly income? What about your parents, if they are still in the labour market?*

SOCIAL WELFARE IN CANADA

Canada, like many other advanced capitalist nations, is a *welfare state*—**a nation in which the government intervenes in the welfare of its citizens through various social policies, programs, standards, and regulations** (see Olsen 2002 and Teeple 2000 for a thorough discussion). Most Canadians are so accustomed to the benefits of the Canadian welfare state that we take them for granted. All of our social programs, such as universal health care, education, pension plans, worker's compensation, minimum wage, employment standards, environmental regulations, health and safety standards, social or income assistance, child tax benefits, and so on, are subsumed under the mantle of the welfare state. From their inception, government programs have been viewed as "good" if recipients are thought to be deserving of assistance and "bad" if recipients are considered undeserving (see Box 2.2).

The modern welfare state, or Keynesian welfare state, came into existence in Canada following World War II. The economist John Maynard Keynes proposed that nation states intervene between their citizens and capitalism in order to create

> a political compromise with the working classes. This compromise included the goals of moderating the business cycle (to prevent a repeat of the unrest of the 1930s), helping rebuild the war-destroyed economies of Europe (to ensure the re-establishment of capitalism), and containing or diminishing the growing interest in socialism stemming from the experience of the 1930s and the devastation of war. (quoted in Teeple 2000:440)

SOCIAL PROBLEMS AND SOCIAL POLICY

BOX 2.2   Workfare in Canada: Betraying a National Trust

In 1966, the federal government brought into effect the Canada Assistance Plan (CAP). The purpose of the plan was to outline the ways the federal government would cost-share income assistance with the provinces and to establish national social assistance standards. The criterion upon which people could access CAP was need, based on the idea that all Canadian citizens had certain basic human rights. These rights, enshrined in CAP, were (a) the right to income assistance when in need; (b) the right to an amount of income assistance that meets basic requirements; (c) the right to appeal decisions if the person disagrees; (d) the right not to have to work or train in order to collect income assistance; and (e) the right to collect income assistance, regardless of the province of origin (Swanson 2001:108). Historically derived from a charity model, income assistance based upon need became a right for all citizens in Canada.

Following a Keynesian economic model, the government had great incentive to stabilize the domestic market. Unemployment had to be kept low. Business cycles needed to be stabilized. All of this protected corporations and citizens from the worst of the cyclical nature of capitalism (Shragge 1997). CAP was just one of many social programs that were part of the welfare state, along with universal health care and education, pension plans, and unemployment insurance.

In July 1995, the Liberal government passed Bill C-76, which signalled the end of the Canada Assistance Plan, and on April 1, 1996, they replaced it with the *Canada Health and Social Transfer Act* (CHST). Replacing CAP with CHST was part of a broader strategy of retrenchment by the government, decreasing its responsibilities in general for the welfare of citizens through the reduction of various social services (Morel 2002). Sociologist Gregg M. Olsen (2002), in a comparative analysis between Canada, the United States, and Sweden, states that while all three are advanced capitalist nations, Canada has always existed somewhere between the other two with regard to policies and programs and their effects. With globalization stepping up, Canada has been becoming increasingly similar to the United States in terms of social policies, cost-cutting measures, and cutbacks in social services and programs (Olsen 2002:3). Welfare state retrenchment in Canada has had farther reaching and more "acute, punitive, and brutal" changes, because we are becoming more like the United States than like Sweden (Olsen 2002:3). Political scientist Sylvie Morel (2002:19) has noted that one of the distinctive features of Canadian welfare policy reform is the classification of social assistance recipients according to a criterion of fitness for work. One of the major effects of replacing CAP with the CHST was that it ended our participation in the United Nations Covenant of Social, Economic, and Cultural Rights, which we signed in 1976. Among other things, the covenant declared that all citizens have the right to "freely chosen" employment and to "an adequate standard of living . . . including adequate food, clothing and housing and . . . the continuous improvement of living conditions" (UN 1992, in Swanson 1997:158). Every five years, each nation that has signed the covenant must report to the UN how it is complying. In the past, Canada used the CAP to demonstrate its commitment to the covenant.

Another and related effect of the CHST was to make workfare legal in Canada. The term *workfare* is generally used to describe a particular direction taken by governments as they reform social assistance, with a particular focus on the shift from income assistance based on need to some type of mandatory employment activity in exchange for benefits (Morel 2002; Shragge 1997). Workfare programs are based on the assumption that there are two groups of poor: the deserving and the undeserving. The deserving poor are those who, for reasons completely beyond their control (for example, extreme old age or extreme disability) are unable to work. The undeserving poor, rated as the vast majority of people on income assistance, are those who suffer from the "damaging consequences of dependence on the welfare system" (Shragge 1997:17). According to proponents of workfare schemes, the undeserving poor need the "tough love of workfare" to give them a hand up and not merely a hand out (Shragge 1997:19). Ideally, this tough love would improve the moral conduct of the undeserving poor, who, it is supposed, must be taught "appropriate sexual conduct" and a "life of thrift and humility," rather than squandering their meagre incomes on alcohol, tobacco, bingo, and other luxuries (Hardina 1997; Shragge 1997; Swanson 2001).

The official rationale for retrenchment and for workfare is to save money and reduce welfare dependency. It is believed by many that "the poor" are unmotivated, or do not value work, or have no work ethic, or have, through a "culture of poverty," "cultural values and attitudes which preclude a commitment to work" (Hardina 1997:132). In fact, social scientist Donna Hardina, following a comprehensive analysis of U.S. workfare programs, noted that conservatives throughout the 1990s have blamed "single mothers [on income assistance] for both the federal deficit and moral decay." Swanson (1997) calls this "Newspeak," based on the language made up by government officials in George Orwell's famous novel *1984*. In Orwell's novel, new terms are created in order to shape and direct citizen's understandings of social life in particular ways. Activist Jean Swanson (1997:151) argues that "social policy experts," corporate lobby groups, and right-wing politicians" have devised a new language of blame that serves to obscure the truth about welfare and workfare programs and to create a climate where cuts can be justified. Newspeak about workfare is based on two myths: (1) that people on welfare need to be forced to take employment because they are lazy, and (2) that enough employment, paying living wages, exists. A coalition of social justice groups concerned with poverty, End Legislated Poverty, catalogued at least 15

Newspeak terms currently in use and their meanings (Swanson 1997). The following reflects a small sampling of some of these terms. Have you heard these expressions before?

Breaking the Cycle of Poverty: This phrase implies that children are taught to be poor by poor adults who pass their preference for poverty onto their children. ELP notes that "no one is exhorted to 'break the cycle of wealth' where rich people pass their wealth on to children who pass it on to their children, perpetuating inequality of income distribution" (Swanson 1997:152–153).

Bring Social Programs into the 21st Century: This phrase typically means to "cut and slash social programs so that people will have to work at low-wage jobs [if they can find them] so they can compete with people in Mexico making $5 a day" (Swanson 1997:153).

Self-Esteem: This phrase is most often used in conjunction with the idea that people need employment to build and maintain their self-esteem. "It implies that a single parent must build her self-esteem at a low-wage, exploitative paid job, rather than by staying home to raise her children to be good citizens" (Swanson 1997:154).

Training for the Jobs of the Future: Swanson (1997) states this one best, saying that this "phrase is used to imply that if only we got ourselves trained in computer programming or air traffic controlling, we could get off welfare or UI and be set for the future. In fact, we don't need 1.5 million (the number of unemployed in Canada) people in new high-tech jobs. Training does not create jobs. Available jobs are mostly low wage. Tens of thousands of people get trained and then can't find work. They are pushed out into the labour force to compete with those who do have jobs and pull wages down . . ." (Swanson 1997:154–155).

Newspeak therefore attempts to suggest that workfare programs are good for people on welfare, as a way of curbing their dependence on the system, on "taxpayers." Nowhere does Newspeak suggest that people's, usually short-term and temporary, sojourns on income assistance are caused by the lack of decent-paying jobs, by downsizing and restructuring and other structural shifts in the paid labour market.

This reflects an individualizing of poverty, where the cause of poverty is viewed as resting with the individual instead of being found in social and structural factors. Critics of workfare point to these structural factors as the reason workfare schemes and the retrenchment of other social programs and services will not work to eradicate poverty.

In fact, long-term research in the U.S. and in Canada has shown that workfare programs are not successful in moving people off of income assistance in the long term (Hardina 1997; Shragge 1997; Swanson 1997). As Hardina (1997:131) states,

There is no sound empirical research that confirms that mandatory work and job training programs are effective in helping people leave the welfare system. On the contrary, most evaluations of welfare state reform projects have not produced statistically significant differences in job acquisition, earnings or decreases in welfare benefits.

Swanson (1997:150), citing 40 years of research in British Columbia, makes the further point that "welfare benefits are so low, the welfare system so controlling and demeaning, that the vast majority of people engineer their own escapes from it as soon as they can." Her comments are based on research showing that only 10 percent of assistance recipients stay on it for more than two years. Hardina (1997:137) further points out that conservative politicians assert that income assistance is the "cause" of deficits, but in Canada, *all* social program spending (including health and education spending) accounts for a mere 2 percent of the budget, and in the United States, AFDC (Aid to Families with Dependent Children) spending accounts for less than 1 percent. Income assistance programs in Canada cost taxpayers as much money as tax breaks to RRSP holders do, and yet the latter class of citizens is not held to blame for Canadian deficit problems (Swanson 1997, 2001). If it is true that most people only use income assistance as a safety net in times of real need, as was intended, and if forced work programs have not been shown to be effective for their stated purpose (to save money and reduce welfare rolls), and if these social programs do not cost us much money, why do governments persist in moving ahead with workfare programs and the like?

Several writers have developed incisive critiques of workfare, putting forth alternative reasons for governmental promotion of workfare programs while cutting benefits and eligibility for income assistance and EI. Tying people's income assistance benefits to training and/or to low-waged, temporary employment threatens existing jobs and wages and depresses labour standards throughout society (A Commitment for Training and Employment for Women [ACTEW] 1998; Hardina 1997; Morel, 2002; Shragge, 1997; Swanson, 1997, 2001). Basically, these programs create a pool of cheap, subsidized, and "flexible" (disposable) labour that governments, the private sector, and community organizations can access. In effect, workfare creates the perfect reserve army of labour, a pool of workers who can be moved into and out of the labour market as needed, without regard to the creation of permanent jobs, living wages, or benefits. This pool of labour is not only flexible (available to serve the cyclical expansion and contraction of a capitalist market), but is also used to undermine so-called good jobs (those with decent wages, labour practices, stability, and benefits) and help bust unions. Social scientist Eric Shragge (1997:30–31) summarizes, "Workfare becomes a means of mobilizing a surplus population to undermine the conditions of public sector and community employment."

What are the social policy implications following from these analyses? Long-term forecasts for employment predict that, with globalization, generally, unemployment in Canada will get worse. Shragge (1997) suggests that in shaping future social policy we need to look at the polarizations that are taking place in the labour market and in society in general between those with wealth and employment and those without. Many people find themselves forced to work longer hours and take more jobs while others are being "downsized" right out of the labour market. In order to create a more equitable distribution of income and employment, then, some policies may need to address restrictions on overtime and shorter average work weeks (Shragge, 1997). Further, the National Council of Welfare recently conducted a study that found that if minimum wage was raised to $10 or $11 dollars per hour, people would have no disincentive to work, as they could live on that wage (Swanson 1997).

Canadian social welfare policy has been based, in the past, on two distinct traditions. The first of these is the British Poor Laws of the 1600s, which established notions of deserving and undeserving poor (Graham et al. 2000:64). Social scientist Francis J. Turner (1995:6), in an overview of social welfare in this country, described the nature of this historical dichotomy:

> The *deserving* were those persons and groups who, through no fault of their own, but by birth, accident, or disaster, were not able to care for themselves, either temporarily or permanently. Since they were deemed not to be responsible for their state of need, it was considered fitting that society, through one of its subsystems, provide assistance to them. What has never been clear in this matter is who decided, and on what grounds, what criteria could be applied in determining who was deserving or undeserving.

> The *undeserving* were those people who, in the opinion of persons of influence, were in need through their own fault or failings. Such persons were considered to be lazy, irresponsible, improvident—and indeed, evil—members of society and thus were not considered to have a claim on assistance. To help such persons was considered as an unfair drain on the resources of society and as a way of contributing to further indolence. Any help that was made available was provided only grudgingly, was made as unattractive as possible, and was kept to an absolute minimum.

The second tradition informing Canadian social welfare policies has been the racist Social Darwinism of the 19th century, which helped to establish ideas about hierarchies and majority–minority relations (Graham et al. 2000:64). Poverty in Canada kills more people than cancer, despite the fact that we have a cure for poverty, through changes to social policies (see Table 2.5), should we choose to exercise it (Swanson 2001:185). So far, however, we have chosen not to. What do you think will happen in the future if we refuse to intervene in the problem of poverty in Canada?

One of the unintended, but useful, consequences of the welfare state has been to ameliorate the worst contradictions created by capitalism's normal "ebb and flow" cycle; therefore, as Teeple (2000:442) points out, the welfare state soothes "the worst effects of economic inequality and . . . placate[s] resistance to all political and social implications of such inequality." A harsher view of this is proposed by sociologists Shahid Alvi, Walter DeKeseredy, and Desmond Ellis (2000:60), who observe that capitalists and conservatives view the poor as

> "social junk" because they are not formally attached to the capitalist economy, . . . [and] are seen by the ruling class as requiring discipline. Thus, the "invisible hand" of the capitalist market is replaced by the "visible fist" of the government. For example, the government intervenes to ensure that the process of capital accumulation is not hindered by these potential troublemakers.

In the early 1970s, capitalism shifted from a national to an international economic system—in short, capitalism became global. Capitalist enterprises were no longer reliant on the purchasing power of any particular nation-state when a whole world was now the market. Additionally, workers in any particular nation no longer had to be placated when capitalist enterprises could easily move production from nation to nation. Under various trade agreements, capitalists sought to level ("harmonize") social and economic policies between nations so as to facilitate easier and more profitable trade (see Chapter 13). A newly internationalized capitalism put increased pressure on governments to enact new neo-liberal policies that would have the effect of reducing government interventions, sometimes called "barriers to trade" by neo-liberals. These "interventions," in the form of social programs and public protections, are being retrenched or cut back more each year, using a variety of justifications, from "deficit-mania" hysteria to superficially convincing arguments that Canadian health care is "just too expensive," when the facts underlying these sophisticated advertising campaigns demonstrate much different realities. Can a welfare state provide a solution to poverty? The answer to this question may depend on how poverty itself is explained.

PERSPECTIVES ON POVERTY AND CLASS INEQUALITY

Social class inequality and poverty can be understood from various perspectives and can be explained in individualistic, cultural, or structural terms. The framework that is applied influences people's beliefs about how poverty might be reduced. We will look at each perspective separately.

The Symbolic Interactionist Perspective

Symbolic interactionists examine poverty from the perspective of meanings, definitions, and labels. How is poverty defined? How are people who are poor viewed by non-poor society members? How do people who are poor define themselves and their situations? What stigma is attached to poverty, and how do people live with, or manage, that stigma? What are the consequences of being labelled as "poor" or "low income"?

Canada is a meritocracy, and much of contemporary rhetoric suggests, then, that if people wish to succeed, they can. Definitions of *success* are rarely explicitly discussed; instead, a common understanding of the term is assumed and taken for granted. If someone fails to succeed, the fault lies with the individual, who is "irresponsible," "lazy," "immoral," "lacking in motivation," and so on. This is the "land of opportunity," and people who do not succeed have none but themselves to blame for their lacks and flaws (Feagin 1975). Workfare programs for social assistance recipients are based on individualistic explanations for poverty. To many sociologists, however, individual explanations of poverty amount to *blaming the victim*—**a practice used by people who view a social problem as emanating from within the individual who exhibits the problem** (Ryan 1976). Conversely, symbolic interactionists also examine what it means to be wealthy. How are those with wealth viewed by others? While impoverished people tend to be negatively stigmatized, wealthy individuals tend to be seen as hard working and deserving of their wealth. Where do we get information about the relative merits of whole groups of people? As author and journalist Jeremy Seabrook (2002:129) points out, "while it

TABLE 2.5   Differences in Canadian and Western European Family Policies

	Canada	Western Europe
Value assigned to children and the role of parents	• children considered "life style choices" or "private commodities" to be pursued with private means • family presumed to be essentially private and self-sufficient • government role/community support only when children are "at risk" or families "in need" • parenting role is undervalued because children are undervalued	• children considered collective responsibility or "public goods" who contribute to the well-being of the whole society • important contribution parents make to the larger society is recognized • state commitment to contribute to the cost of raising children
Ideas about who should benefit from social programs	• "public charity" model results in growing unwillingness to contribute to "undeserving" welfare poor • pits modest-income families against poor families; threatens social cohesion • privatization of child rearing and targeting basic benefits primarily to the poor • median-income families excluded from significant benefits	• willingness of people to contribute public revenues for the common good of *all* families • not only those with the lowest incomes benefit from social programs • policies provide significant benefits to all or most families, reflecting sense of collective responsibility • universality and higher family allowances
Ways of supporting families/women	• reducing/preventing poverty are explicit goals of public policy, yet unsuccessful at preventing poverty • women not supported adequately as mothers or workers • mothers of young children expected to be in the labour market yet very little support is provided (income support, child care, parental leave programs) • gender-neutral individual responsibility model	• reduction/prevention of poverty among families with children are by-products of family support policies and programs • two different approaches: family-oriented or employment-oriented • both approaches extremely successful at preventing poverty, even among lone parents • social responsibility model to support family ethic and/or care ethic for women
Different outcomes	• social assistance primary form of income support for many families with children • high poverty rates for children, particularly in female lone-parent families • large income gaps and inequalities	• social assistance truly residual • low poverty rates even for female lone-parent families • smaller income disparities generally

Source: Christa Freiler and Judy Cerny, 1998, Benefiting Canada's Children: Perspectives on Gender and Social Responsibility, *Ottawa, ON: Research Directorate, Status of Women Canada. March. Reproduced with the permission of the Minister of Public Works and Government Services Canada, 2003.*

is easy to find a table of the 20 richest people in the world, it would be impossible to do the same with the 20 poorest."

Symbolic interactionists are also interested in what it means to people to be poor and what impact stigma has on people's self-concepts. Some researchers have focused on how cultural background affects people's values and behaviour (see Table 2.5). Among the earliest of these explanations is the "culture of poverty" thesis by anthropologist Oscar Lewis (1966). According to Lewis, poor people have different values and beliefs than people from the middle and upper classes and so develop a separate and self-perpetuating system of attitudes and behaviours that keeps them trapped in poverty. Among these attitudes and behaviours are the inability to defer gratification or plan for the future; feelings of apathy, hostility, and suspicion toward others; deficient speech and communication patterns; female-headed households; and a decided lack of participation in major societal institutions. People trapped in the "culture of poverty" socialize their children into this cycle of poverty, and hence the culture perpetuates. The "culture of poverty" thesis has provided political leaders, social analysts, and many ordinary Canadian citizens with a reasonable-sounding rationale for blaming the situations endured by poor people on the poor themselves. The "culture of poverty" thesis, while popular, is not without criticism. Critics point out that people who are poor, just like people who are not poor, develop attitudes and behaviours as responses and ways of coping with stigma and other limitations and barriers placed on their participation. The "culture of poverty" thesis has also been critiqued for suggesting that poor people both enjoy their impoverished situations and do not know any better. Both notions are paternalistic and erroneous.

More recent cultural explanations of poverty have focused on the lack of *cultural capital* — **social assets, such as the values, beliefs, attitudes, and competencies in language and culture, that are learned at home and required for success and social advancement** (Bourdieu and Passeron 1990). From this perspective, low-income people do not have adequate cultural capital to function in a competitive global economy. According to some sociologists, cultural explanations

again deflect attention from the true sources of poverty (unemployment, racism, sexism, and so on) and shift blame from the affluent and powerful to the poor and powerless (Sidel 1996:xvii–xviii).

The Structural Functionalist Perspective

Unlike individual and cultural explanations of poverty, which operate at the microlevel, structural explanations of poverty focus on the macrolevel, the level of social organization that is beyond an individual's ability to change. One structural explanation of poverty (Wilson 1996) points to changes in the economy that have dramatically altered employment opportunities for people, particularly those who have the least wealth, power, and prestige. According to the functionalists who espouse this explanation, social inequality serves an important function in society because it motivates people to work hard to acquire scarce resources. In 1945, Kingsley Davis and Wilbert Moore published a paper explaining that social stratification exists in every society in some form and must, therefore, be functional. Davis and Moore asserted that some occupations require more training and investment than others, or are difficult or unpleasant to do, so should be compensated more, through prestige and pay. This explains, they felt, why doctors and judges have high prestige and pay, while restaurant servers and truck drivers do not. This thesis has been criticized for several reasons, among them the idea that inequities in pay and prestige are functional for society. Why are women paid less than men? Who is this functional for? Is the work of a child-care provider really worth millions of dollars less, per year, than the "work" of an NHL star? Why are occupations that are dirty or dangerous not rewarded with high salaries? Functionalists also assert that it is functional to maintain a pool of more desperate workers in order to fill the occupations that no one wants to do. This is deemed "functional" but is likely problematic for those who are forced to work in unfavourable conditions for low wages. This is a main criticism of functionalist perspectives generally—we must always ask the question, functional for whom? Lastly, sociologists Linda Mooney, David Knox, Caroline Schacht, and Adie Nelson (2001:312) point out that functionalists may see poverty as functional for those who work in the "poverty industry" (for example, financial assistance workers) and for those who need a market for second-rate or "inferior goods such as older dilapidated homes and automobiles."

The Conflict Perspective

Another structural explanation for poverty is based on a conflict perspective that suggests poverty is a side effect of the capitalist system. Using this explanation, analysts note that workers are increasingly impoverished by the wage squeeze and high rates of unemployment and underemployment. The *wage squeeze* is the steady downward pressure on the real take-home pay of workers that has occurred over the past two decades. During these same decades, shareholders in major corporations have had substantial increases in dividends, and chief executive officers have received extremely lucrative salaries and compensation packages (Gordon 1996). In a February 2006 interview with Vancouver's local publication *The Georgia Straight,* Barry Cook, an executive-compensation expert at Western Management Consultants, stated that executive pay has risen at a faster rate than pay for other occupations every year since the early 1990s (Smith 2006). As an example, the average increase in CEO pay at "Standard and Poor 500" firms from 1993 to 2003 was 146 percent! In contrast, average workers wages increased very little and in some cases declined. (CLC 2005:2). Corporate downsizing and new technologies that replace workers have further enhanced capitalists' profits and contributed to the impoverishment of middle- and low-income workers by creating a reserve army of unemployed people whom the capitalists use for casual labour and as a means to keep other workers' wages low. Corporations' intense quest for profit results in low wages for workers, a wide disparity in the life chances of affluent people and poor people, and the unemployment and impoverishment of many people. Sociologist Harley D. Dickinson (2000) notes that unemployment is a normal consequence of capitalism and, in fact, is necessary for capitalism. Conflict between the capitalists (Marx's bourgeoisie) and the workers (Marx's proletariat) has, in part, been ameliorated in past decades by welfare state programs like EI or social assistance (Dickinson 2000). What effect will continued retrenchment have on class conflict in Canada? Although some analysts suggest that high rates of poverty will always exist in advanced capitalist societies, others believe that inequality and poverty could be reduced, if not eliminated, if the political will existed.

Feminist Perspectives

Many feminist perspectives on poverty or class inequality focus in on the gendered character of stratification and poverty. Most of the people living in poverty are women and their children. As discussed earlier in the chapter, this has been called the "feminization of poverty." Feminist theorists look at the differential valuing of occupations and roles within Canadian society, noting who has power and prestige, which occupations are deemed more or less valuable, and so on. In work that later became the foundation of a socialist–feminist analysis of the intersection of gender and class, or patriarchy and capitalism, Engels theorized that the fact of private property was at the heart of patriarchy. With capitalism came private property. With private property came the desire to pass it on along with the wealth it generated to the children of the bourgeoisie. This then made knowing one's genetic offspring very important to the bourgeoisie, which then made the establishment of a system for ensuring paternity very important. In order to ensure a man's children were indeed his own, monogamy and the subjugation of women became necessary. Engels (1884/1972:120) referred to this, in a famous phrase, as "the world-historical defeat of women." One of the criticisms of a socialist–feminist perspective is that it is deterministic; it lacks an explanation of why capitalism must unfold this way (Muszynski 2000). More recently, instead of seeing women and men as oppositional classes, scholars have analyzed the variety of ways that gender, racialization, and class intersect within a capitalist economic system, recognizing the complexities in an analysis of who is poor and who is wealthy, who is an oppressor and who is oppressed. In addition to the fact that poverty is gendered, Kazemipur and Halli (2000:112) point out in their book on poverty in Canada that

> poverty is too diverse and complicated a phenomenon to be adequately explained by a uni-dimensional theory. It varies, for example, from one city to another; from one ethnic group to another; from one segment of population

(e.g., immigrants) to another; and even within each segment, it varies from one generation to another.

If we are going to understand poverty, if indeed this is a necessary precursor to ending it, our explanations will need to become more comprehensive. Is it possible to reduce or eliminate class inequality and poverty without a theoretical understanding?

CAN CLASS-BASED INEQUALITY BE REDUCED?

Chapter 1 made the point that how people view a social problem is related to how they believe the problem should be reduced or solved. Poverty and social inequality are no exceptions. Analysts who focus on individualistic explanations of poverty typically suggest individual solutions: "Low-income and poverty-level people should change their attitudes, beliefs, and work habits." For example, economist George Gilder (1981) has stated that "the only dependable route from poverty is always work. . . . The poor must not only work, they must work harder than the classes above them."

Similarly, people who use cultural explanations seek cultural solutions; they suggest that poverty can be reduced by the enhancement of people's cultural capital. They urge the development of more job training and school enrichment programs to enhance people's cultural capital and counteract negative familial and neighbourhood influences. Seeking cultural solutions, the federal government developed job training and young entrepreneur programs to provide children and adolescents from low-income families with the cultural capital (white middle-class values, for example) that they need to succeed in the (white, middle-class) world (see Quadagno and Fobes 1995).

Although some analysts seeking structural solutions suggest that poverty can be eliminated only if capitalism is abolished and a new means of distributing valued goods and services is established, others state that poverty can be reduced by the creation of "a truly open society—a society where the life chances of those at the bottom are not radically different from those at the top and where wealth is distributed more equitably" (MacLeod 1995:260). These analysts feel that federal, territorial, and provincial governments should play a

vital role in reducing poverty and lessening people's need for social assistance. Recent proposals based on this structural solution include the following strategies:

- establishing a coordinated employment policy that emphasizes the creation of jobs with livable wages and benefits;
- building individual assets through government policies that provide incentives and resources for low-income families to acquire and build economic assets;
- providing tax benefits to assist low-income workers;
- giving economic assistance to help families deal with divorce, unwanted pregnancies, and child care; and
- investing in lower-income areas of communities and empowering residents to organize and address problems such as affordable housing and better schools (Rank 1994).

Although these proposals, if enacted, would not "solve" the problem of poverty, they might temper and reduce the price poor people pay for living in the "land of opportunity" (Rank 1994).

WHAT CAN YOU DO?

- Lobby politicians to support real job-creation strategies, higher minimum wages, universal child care, and affordable housing.
- Volunteer at a local food bank or shelter or soup kitchen.
- Donate money, food, or time to an organization such as a food bank or an anti-poverty organization.
- Write a letter to the local newspaper or your university or college paper, outlining some little known facts about poverty or welfare or "wealthfare" or workfare or hunger in your region. Send a copy of your letter to the Canadian Association of Food Banks at **info@cafb-acba.ca**.
- Participate in alternate economies such as food-share programs and car-share programs.
- Bookmark on a computer you use some of the websites for organizations that keep up-to-date statistics on hunger and homelessness in Canada (see pages 57 and 58).
- Engage a homeless person in conversation and find out about his or her life.

- Make a phone call to your local city hall and ask what programs the municipality has in place for homeless people. Use your voice!

- Become a member of the Canadian Association of Food Banks or a local anti-poverty organization.

- Attend demonstrations and protests on poverty issues in order to gain information about what the issues are locally. For example, recently in Victoria, B.C., a group of temporary shelters made of cardboard, erected in an out-of-the-way place, was torn down by police at the directive of the municipality. Taking away people's belongings and a semi-dry place to sleep did not stop the problem of homelessness in that city. Use your privilege, as a literate person with more media access than most homeless people, to get these issues heard.

- Organize a food drive for a local food bank. For example, at Christmastime in some urban centres, municipal garbage collection workers, organized through the Canadian Union of Public Employees (CUPE), ask citizens to leave wrapped, non-perishable food donations outside on garbage collection days and they will ensure they get to the local food bank.

- Visit a local grocery store, deli, or bakery and ask if they donate leftover food to the local food banks or soup kitchens. Call places that do and thank the managers of those stores. This encourages people to continue to operate with their civic responsibilities in mind.

- Send a donation to the Canadian Association of Food Banks (an organization whose member food banks and agencies feed over 90 percent of Canada's hungry). For every dollar you donate, the CAFB can move $75 worth of food.

- Intervene when you hear someone poor-bashing or negatively stereotyping poor people. Educate friends, family members, and classmates or professors who are not as knowledgeable about the issues. Keep up to date about the facts so you are comfortable educating others.

SUMMARY

WHY IS SOCIAL STRATIFICATION A SOCIAL PROBLEM?

Social stratification refers to the hierarchical arrangement of large social groups based on their control over basic resources. In highly stratified societies, low-income and poor people have limited access to food, clothing, shelter, education, health care, and other necessities of life.

WHAT ARE THE MAJOR PROBLEMS OF THE LOW-INCOME NATIONS?

Studies of global inequality distinguish between high-income nations—countries with highly industrialized economies and relatively high levels of national and per capita (per person) income, middle-income nations—countries that are undergoing transformation from agrarian to industrial economies, and low-income nations—countries that are primarily agrarian with little industrialization and low levels of national and personal income. Poverty, food shortages, hunger, and rapidly growing populations are pressing problems in many low-income nations.

HOW DOES THE "NEW INTERNATIONAL DIVISION OF LABOUR" PERSPECTIVE EXPLAIN GLOBAL INEQUALITY?

According to this perspective, transnational corporations have established global assembly lines of production in which workers in middle- and low-income nations, earning extremely low wages, produce goods for export to high-income nations such as Canada, the United States, and Japan.

HOW IS THE CANADIAN CLASS STRUCTURE DIVIDED?

The Canadian population is divided into several classes. The upper, or capitalist, class, the wealthiest and most powerful class, is made up of investors, heirs, and executives. The upper-middle class is composed of professionals, business analysts, owners of small businesses, stockbrokers, and business analysts. The middle class includes white-collar office workers, middle-management personnel, people in technical support positions, semiprofessionals, and non-retail sales workers. Members of the working class hold occupations such as semiskilled machine operator or counter help in a fast-food restaurant. The poor include the working poor and the chronically poor. The working poor are those who are attached to the labour market but whose wages are not sufficient to provide them with the necessities. The chronically poor include individuals of working age who are outside the labour force and children who live in poor families.

WHO ARE THE POOR IN CANADA?

While poverty cuts across every gender, age, sexual orientation, ethnicity, and ability, the major categories of poor people in Canada are women, children under age 18, people with disabilities, and visible minorities, especially Indigenous people.

WHAT ARE INDIVIDUAL AND CULTURAL EXPLANATIONS OF POVERTY?

Individual explanations of poverty focus on the attitudinal and motivational problems of individuals or the amount of human capital a person possesses. Cultural explanations of poverty focus on how cultural background affects people's values and behaviour. These explanations focus on the microlevel, and many sociologists view them as attempts to blame the victim for the problem.

WHAT ARE STRUCTURAL EXPLANATIONS OF POVERTY?

Structural explanations of poverty focus on the macrolevel, the level of social organization that is beyond an individual's ability to change. These explanations consider how changes in the economy have altered employment opportunities or how inequality and exploitation are inherent in the structure of class relations in a capitalist economy.

WHAT SOLUTIONS HAVE BEEN SUGGESTED FOR POVERTY?

Most individual and cultural solutions focus on the importance of work. Individual perspectives suggest that people should work harder. Cultural perspectives suggest enhancing people's cultural capital to make them better prepared for employment. Structural perspectives are based on the assumption that society can reduce poverty by creating real jobs and training programs and investing in people through provision of child care, health care, and affordable housing. Intersectionality approaches highlight the need for multipronged strategies.

KEY TERMS

absolute poverty,   p. 31
blaming the victim,   p. 50
class system,   p. 31
cultural capital,   p. 52
feminization of poverty,   p. 40
high-income nations,   p. 31
income,   p. 34
intersectionality,   p. 42
life chances,   p. 31
low-income nations,   p. 31

meritocracy,   p. 31
middle-income nations,   p. 31
poverty rate,   p. 38
power,   p. 32
prestige,   p. 32
relative poverty,   p. 38
social stratification,   p. 32
wealth,   p. 32
welfare state,   p. 47

QUESTIONS FOR CRITICAL THINKING

1.   What would happen if all the wealth in Canada were redistributed so that all adults had the same amount? Some analysts suggest that within five years most of the wealth would be back in the possession of the people who hold it today. What arguments can you give to support this idea? What arguments can you give to refute this idea?

2.   Forcese (1997:215) stated that "Employers can, if obliged, produce jobs as well as products. Educational institutions, if obliged, can generate mobility. Political parties, if obliged, can legislate benefits." Assess the implications of "obliging" employers, educational institutions, and political parties to do these things.

WEBLINKS

Caledon Institute for Social Policy

www.caledonist.org

The Caledon Institute for Social Policy is a think tank that produces research, analysis, and practical proposals and seeks to inform public opinion on social policy and reform social programs. It contributes articles, some of which are available on the site in PDF format, to major newspapers and media institutions.

Canadian Association of Food Banks (CAFB)

www.cafb.ca

The CAFB represents member food banks in every province in Canada. It coordinates the distribution of goods to food banks throughout the country and works to find solutions to Canada's growing hunger problem. The site enables you to get involved in its activities.

Canadian Centre for Policy Alternatives (CCPA)

www.policyalternatives.org

The Canadian Centre for Policy Alternatives is a national organization that undertakes and promotes research on issues of social and economic justice. The centre produces publications that offer accurate facts and ideas on how to best understand and choose the policies that affect our lives.

Canadian Council on Social Development (CCSD)

www.ccsd.ca

The Canadian Council on Social Development is a non-profit social policy and research unit whose work focuses on issues such as poverty, disability, cultural diversity, housing, and employment and seeks to improve social and economic security. The site offers links to many other social organizations.

Centre for Social Justice

www.socialjustice.org

The Centre for Social Justice is an advocacy organization that seeks to make policy changes that promote economic and social justice. The site offers information, lists of publications and articles, and opportunities to join and make donations.

CanadaStudentDebt.ca

www.canadastudentdebt.ca

This site is a moderated Canadian Student Loans discussion site that provides support for student loan problems.

National Anti-Poverty Organization (NAPO)

www.napo-onap.ca

NAPO works to foster awareness of and respect for low-income people across Canada. Its aim is to eradicate poverty by researching, mobilizing, and lobbying.

National Council of Welfare

www.ncwcnbes.net

The National Council of Welfare is a citizens' advisory body that advises the Minister of Human Resources Development on the needs and problems of low-income Canadians. The site offers welfare incomes reports, publications, and public statements in HTML and PDF formats.

Poverty Network

www.povnet.org

The PovNet site provides general, up-to-date information about welfare and housing laws in Canada.

It is designed for advocates and people on welfare or involved in anti-poverty work. It also offers numerous links to other anti-poverty organizations and resources in Canada and worldwide.

Statistics Canada

www.statcan.ca

Statcan.ca is the official source for Canadian social and economic statistics and products. It provides detailed information on nearly every aspect of Canada's products and services. Some of the content is also available in PDF format.

3

RACISM AND ETHNIC INEQUALITY

RACISM AND ETHNIC INEQUALITY AS A SOCIAL PROBLEM

What Are Ethnicity, "Race," and Racialization?

Historical and Political Roots of "Race"

The Meaning of Majority and Minority Groups

White Privilege and Internalized Dominance

RACISM, PREJUDICE, AND DISCRIMINATION

Historical Roots of Racism

The Many Forms of Racism in Canadian Society

Box 3.1 Social Problems in Global Perspective: Organized Racism—Canada's Links to a World of Hatred

Box 3.2 Social Problems and Social Policy: Undermining Democratic Racism in Canada

PERSPECTIVES ON RACIALIZED AND ETHNIC INEQUALITY

The Symbolic Interactionist Perspective

The Structural Functionalist Perspective

The Conflict Perspective

Feminist and Anti-Racist Perspectives

CAN RACIALIZED AND ETHNIC INEQUALITIES BE REDUCED?

WHAT CAN YOU DO?

We looked around at the other women at the table. Nobody said hello. They looked and I looked back. . . . We sat and we waited. The other women talked amongst themselves in what resembled a huddle. They glanced furtively in our direction. We sat and waited—I watched. Whispers. Whispers coming from the huddle. Whispers that called out, too loud, clanging around in my ears, "Smells like Indians!" Instinctively I breathed in deeply. Did they mean us? I could see them staring at us. My mother's head was down. Tears? I looked back at them. I knew it was us. We moved to another table. We do not speak about what was said about us. We do not recognize them. We cannot give them more power. My anger grows. My mother's spirit staggers. . . . How can they make a judgment about Native people without knowing or caring to know about us?—judgments made in ignorance. I decided that someday I would tell them about things they did not want to hear, about things they were afraid to ask. I decided to talk back. There was nothing to lose. People hated us anyway.

Valerie Bedassigae Pheasant recollecting "growing up different" in Canada (2001:39–40)

I grew a second head—an English one. Depending on the time or issue, I would inhabit one or the other of my two heads. But for many of my interlocutors, this meant at times exhibiting behaviours that appeared to be, or were effectively, "out of place"—that of a Quebecoise in Toronto, and a somewhat Torontonian in Quebec. . . . Since moving to Hull-Ottawa, where living a bilingual existence has meant spending about 70 percent of my time speaking English, I have found myself (still), and not without paradox, a Quebecoise francophone. This situation makes me wonder if I can escape Papineau's fate, and at this point in history the question remains pertinent not only for me as an individual but also on the collective and political levels.

Angele Denis, speaking of her experience coming to English Canada from Quebec. She theorizes about the potential similarities between her experience, Canada's experience, and Papineau's experience. In a novel by Jacques Godbout, the character Papineau is a person with two heads, one French and one English. When deciding to merge, as half-French and half-English, the English persona takes over the French, resulting in an Anglo personality (2001:135, 137).

"We're all the same. Just because you're Black doesn't matter." I realized there was a lot more work to do than just explaining my feelings. I was shocked to realize that many of my classmates—professional people living in Canada, one of the most multicultural countries in the world—simply didn't get it. For them, the Canadian Mosaic was not much of a reality. . . . I asked my classmates, "How can I, an African, be the same as you, an Irish immigrant?" . . . "Our experiences are not the same, our lives are not the same, and by God I am thankful that we are not the same." My reaction surprised them.

Gifty Serbeh-Dunn speaking about when she realized that many Canadians had no desire to discuss culture and "race" (Dunn and Dunn 2001:270)

I expect that being an interracial couple in Toronto would be a very different experience. Our smaller community seems at times to exoticize my Indianness and at other times to ostracize us as a couple. I remember when we decided to tell my parents about our relationship and felt as though the burden of the world had been lifted from our shoulders. Walking down the street for the first time, hand-in-hand, without fear that we would be seen was like walking on cloud nine. Do you remember? What popped my balloon was that guy on the park bench who yelled out to us, "You fucking White bastard, what are you doing with that Paki woman?" It jarred me into a reality that our differences were not just cultural but also racial, and that we would not only have to deal with the problem of my family's acceptance of you as my husband, but also that of society's acceptance of us. This is the difference that has been the most difficult with which to cope. The cultural stuff like food, language and clothing can be negotiated. But racism is something not so easily negotiated.

Bina Mehta in a dialogue with her husband, Kevin Spooner (2000:155)

I am always unprepared for the backlash of White authority. How the words and actions of myself and my students were twisted and used against me. Twisted and used against the students. Twisted and used against our traditions. . . . "You are to teach in the expected mode, exactly what the calendar says." Why is White monocultural reality now the expected norm on our ancestral lands, I want to know.

Fyre Jean Graveline, describing an experience teaching in a "Native-controlled college [that] was not" (2000:284)

It is not enough to imagine a better and more just future; without a commitment to action, we will continue to suffer. . . . We cannot expect a better future in the absence of a commitment to take action, to attack and destroy the heart of colonialism. There is no hope—or sense—in attacking the state with physical force, or in seeking peace by unpeaceful means. The goals that flow from our traditions demand an approach based on undermining the intellectual and moral foundations of colonialism and exposing internal contradictions of states and societies that promise justice and practice oppression. Non-Indigenous people need to be brought to the realization that their notion of power and its extension over Indigenous peoples is wrong by any moral standard. This approach holds the greatest promise for the freedom of Indigenous people.

Taiaiake Alfred, Director of the Indigenous Governance Program at the University of Victoria (1999:144)

As the preceding quotations illustrate, racism in Canada continues unabated in both subtle and overt forms. While many in Canada know that racism is unacceptable, their privileged positions blind them to ways they participate in and perpetuate it. Non-White Canadians, regardless of class position, gender, sexual orientation, ability, age, size, educational level, or occupation, all experience prejudice and discrimination every day in what many people claim is a multicultural society. We know from experience that right now several people reading this are wondering if we are non-White people writing this, because our socialization in Canada teaches us that issues of racialized prejudice and discrimination are not White issues; that they are issues for Indigenous people or visible minorities only. We are White people, and therefore are every bit as implicated in the racism we speak about, as are most of the readers. This chapter will not only discuss the many manifestations of racist discrimination in Canada but also raise issues of privilege and dominance and examine possibilities for change.

As described in Chapter 1, *discrimination* is the actions or practices of dominant group members that have a harmful impact on members of subordinate groups (Feagin and Feagin 1999). Like many other social problems, racialized and ethnic discrimination signals a discrepancy between the ideals and realities of Canadian society today. While equality and freedom for all—regardless of country of origin, skin colour, creed, or language—are stated ideals of this country, many subordinate group members experience oppression based on racializing factors, regardless of their other statuses.

RACISM AND ETHNIC INEQUALITY AS A SOCIAL PROBLEM

As we enter the 21st century, racism is among the most divisive social problems facing Canada. At the same time, sociologists such as William J. Wilson (1996) suggest that we all—regardless of racialized or ethnic background—share certain common interests and concerns that cross "race" and class boundaries. Some of the problems are unemployment and job insecurity, declining real wages, escalating medical and housing costs, a scarcity of good-quality child-care programs, worries about the quality of public education, and violence in many neighbourhoods. From this perspective, racialized and ethnic inequality is a problem for everyone, not only for people of colour. Additionally, all people can be allies in working toward the elimination of racism. While the anti-racism torch has been lit and carried by non-White people for many years in Canada, it is time for White people to exercise some of their considerable privilege to join this campaign. Who better to speak out against racism than those who benefit most from it? Who better than those who are viewed as credible sources (as opposed to those viewed as "whining special interest groups") to take up this discussion publicly and to press for the necessary changes? Changes for the better have already been made and there is no doubt, despite backlash, that they will continue. The process of change could, however, move more quickly when alliances are formed.

What Are Ethnicity, "Race," and Racialization?

In Canada, the terms *ethnicity* and *"race"* are often used interchangeably, while *racialization* is a term many people have never heard of. It is useful, therefore, to define these concepts at the outset. In Canada, we talk mainly of "ethnicity," and Statistics Canada censuses have, historically, collected data based primarily on ethnic group.

An *ethnic group* **is a category of people who are distinguished, by others or by themselves, on the basis of cultural or nationality characteristics (Feagin and Feagin 1999). These can include language, country of origin, and adherence to a culture.** Briefly stated, members of an ethnic group share five main characteristics: (1) unique cultural traits; (2) a sense of community; (3) a feeling that one's own group is distinct; (4) membership from birth; and, (5) a tendency, at least initially, to occupy a distinct geographic area (such as a Chinatown, Little Italy, or Greektown). "White ethnics," such as Norwegian Canadians, Ukrainian Canadians, and Jewish Canadians, are also examples of ethnic groups. Ethnicity can be, and often is, used as a basis to judge an individual or group as inferior or superior. Ethnicity is a contested issue. Some, like sociologist J. Milton Yinger (1994), support a more narrow definition of ethnicity based on three criteria: members of a group must view themselves as distinct; others must view the group as distinct; and group members must participate in collective "activities that have the intent or the effect of affirming their distinctiveness" (Fleras and Elliott 1999:104). Sociologists Augie Fleras and Jean Leonard Elliott (1999) point out that these criteria would leave out the most dominant group—White Canadians—a conclusion they find problematic. It is problematic to assert that most members of the dominant group have no ethnicity. It presents White existence as a neutral standard and masks the ethnicized nature of our institutions, practices, and beliefs (see Box 3.2 on page 72). Moreover, it suggests that ethnicity is really a euphemism for "minority group," which again puts White experience at the centre, a standard against which "others" (non-White ethnics) are measured. Fleras and Elliott (1999:104) caution, "To ignore white ethnicity is to redouble its hegemony by naturalizing whiteness."

Where ethnic groups are defined on the basis of cultural or nationality characteristics, sociologists note that racialized groups are usually defined on the basis of real or alleged physical characteristics. Many sociologists view "race" as a *social construct*—**a classification of people based on social and political values—rather than a biological given** (see Omi and Winant 1994). How does a sociological definition of "race" differ from a biological one? A *biological definition of a "race"* is "a population that differs from other populations in the incidence of some genes." In the past, some anthropologists classified diverse categories of peoples into "races" on the basis of skin colour (pigmentation) and features and build (morphology). Contemporary anthropologists classify "races" in terms of genetically determined immunological and biochemical differences. There exist clusters of phenotypes (observable characteristics) and genotypes (more internal attributes that are not as easily discernable) that can occur more frequently if a subpopulation has been isolated for quite a long time. However, humans have not existed long enough in isolated groups for speciation to occur. Anthropologists and other scientists have therefore concluded that because of multiple generations of interbreeding, no "pure races" exist. In humans, genetic differences by population do not exist—we share a generalized gene pool. The only "race" that exists with regard to humans is the "human race," or human species. Socio-culturally, however, the concept of "race" has been salient. European, Chinese, and Arab people were active in attempting to classify humans into racialized groups as early as the 15th century, although Europeans became the first to use "science" to legitimate and popularize "race" as a classification system (Fleras and Elliott 1999).

In contrast to an attempted biological definition of "race," sociologists define a *racialized group* **as a category of people who have been singled out, by others or themselves, as inferior or superior, on the basis of subjectively selected physical characteristics such as skin colour, hair texture, and eye shape.** Blacks, Whites, Asians, and "Aboriginals" are all examples of categories of people that have been racialized. Racialization is therefore a process that occurs to or with a group in that it becomes "racialized," or comes to be seen as having certain distinct traits that are supposed to mean something. In addition to persistent efforts to classify people along "racial" lines despite the continued lack of biological substantiation, it is in the definition and ranking of traits where racism can be seen, because definitions applied to certain features or characteristics are completely arbitrary: They vary across cultures and change over time. This is not the same as saying "race" doesn't matter. "Race" does matter, not because of innate differences between people, but because racialized individuals and groups have been treated as though certain characteristics matter in certain ways (discussed later in Box 3.2).

Historical and Political Roots of "Race"

Fleras and Elliott (1999:47) define "race" as the classification of people into categories on the basis of preconceived attributes . . . each group is defined as different by virtue of predetermined properties that are seen as fixed and permanent because of real or alleged characteristics.

Several classification schemes were developed from the 1700s onward, beginning with Swedish naturalist Carl von Linne's (Linnaeus') four-category scheme from 1735. Others since have come up with anywhere from 30 to 150 categories (Fleras and Elliott 1999). The best known of these typologies is the one still employed today: Mongoloid (for Yellow people), Caucasoid (for White people), and Negroid (for Black people). It is curious that this three-category typology has remained so stubbornly in our lexicon when there are such serious flaws with its use, not the least of which is, under which category do we classify the Red people and the Brown people? Several other arguments against the use of "racial" typologies deserve mention. Discrete boundaries between "races" are indefinable and, hence, arbitrary. "Racial" purity is a myth. The selection of traits defined as meaningful in some way is arbitrary. Why skin colour, for example, and not eye colour (Fleras and Elliott 1999:48)? It is important to understand that there is more variation on any criterion within a supposed "race" than between "races"; for example, there are more variations in skin tone within any racialized grouping than between two racialized groupings.

The politics of "race" are hotly debated and highly divisive because people who are attached to "racial" classifications often attempt to "rank diversity along an ascending/descending order," with implicit and explicit messages about concomitant superiority or inferiority (Fleras and Elliott 1999:49). Others acknowledge that racialization is what is significant and not the socially constructed notion of "race." In any case, no one disputes the significance of the concept in justifying or legitimating ways of treating people. The concept of "race" has historically been used to justify inequitable treatment—sometimes economic and social disadvantage, sometimes death—in all cases, not contributing anything satisfactory to our understanding of human behaviour. As summarized by Fleras and Elliott (1999:36), "Race matters because people perceive others to be different and rely on these perceptions to justify unequal treatment and condone indifference."

The Meaning of Majority and Minority Groups

When sociologists use the terms *majority group* and *minority group*, they are referring to power differentials among groups, not to the numerical sense in which the words *majority* and *minority* are generally used. A **majority (or dominant) group is one that is advantaged and has superior resources and rights in a society** (Feagin and Feagin 1999). Majority groups often are determined on the basis of racialized factors or ethnicity, but they can also be determined on the basis of gender, sexual orientation (homosexuality, heterosexuality, or bisexuality), age, or physical ability. A **minority (or subordinate) group is one whose members, because of physical or cultural characteristics, are disadvantaged and subjected to negative discriminatory treatment by the majority group and regard themselves as objects of collective discrimination** (Wirth 1945). In Canada, people of colour, all women, people with disabilities, and gay men, lesbians, and trans people tend to be considered minority group members, regardless of their proportion in the overall Canadian population.

White Privilege and Internalized Dominance

In Canada, the racialized and ethnic majority group is associated with *White privilege,* privilege that accrues to the people who have "white" skin, trace their ancestry to Northern and Western Europe, and think of themselves as European Canadians or WASPs (White Anglo-Saxon Protestants). Women's studies scholar Peggy McIntosh describes White privilege as "an invisible package of unearned assets that I can count on cashing in each day, but about which I was 'meant' to remain oblivious. White privilege is like an invisible weightless knapsack of special provisions, assurances, maps, guides, codebooks, passports, visas, clothes, compass, emergency gear, and blank cheques" (McIntosh 1995:76–77).

In a paper called "Deconstructing Whiteness," Gabriel Bedard (2000:45) makes the point that "In

Canada, Whiteness holds political, economic and moral power." In addition, Whiteness is a condition that White people every day can count on to ease their lives *because* they are White. In general, having "white" skin in Canada confers two overarching benefits: the normalization of privilege and the choice of whether or not to struggle against racialized oppression (Wildman and Davis 2002). The normalization of privilege means that characteristics and attributes associated with Whiteness or White people's cultures are viewed as the standard, as the "normal" way of doing things. Normalization of privilege is manifested when all members of a society are judged against the characteristics or attributes of those who are privileged, and typically this is seen as a neutral process—the standard is typically invisible to those who do the judging. Objectivity is the dominant group's subjectivity. In this system, when people—usually those who are most like the privileged norm—succeed, it is seen as the result of individual effort or merit, not due to privilege (Wildman and Davis 2002:93). Janet Sawyer (1989) called this " ***internalized dominance***"—**all the ways that White people learn they are normal, feel included, and do not think of themselves as "other" or "different."** White people carry this privilege around with them at all times, everywhere they go, and they are generally unaware of it. Sawyer (1989:23) concludes a discussion of internalized dominance by saying,

> In any way we are in a dominant group, we have been taught to internalize our own dominance. That is not our fault. It does not mean we are bad people. It does mean that our learned values, assumptions and behaviours are actively hurting other people. It does mean that it is our responsibility to change.

The second benefit conferred on people with "white" skin is having the choice about whether to work against oppression. If White people choose, they do not have to engage in working against racist oppression. This privilege is commonly exercised as silence when witnessing racist behaviour or hearing racist comments. As legal scholars Stephanie Wildman and Adrienne D. Davis (2002:94) conclude, "Privilege is not visible to its holder; it is merely there, a part of the world, a way of life, simply the way things are. Others have a *lack,* an absence, a deficiency." Most White Canadians are unaware of the benefits that they derive

from White privilege (see Frankenberg 1993; Hacker 1995; McIntosh 1995; Wellman 1993). What is also true is that many White people in Canada suffer from a clear lack of privilege, associated with class, gender, ability, age and/or sexual orientation or preference. What White privilege does for people who experience oppression on other measures is that it reflects one place where they are not discriminated against. Non-White people may experience gendered oppression or be impoverished and *also* have to contend with racialized oppression, the kind of multiple jeopardy, or intersectionality, discussed elsewhere in this chapter and text. Nevertheless, the advantage/disadvantage and power/exploitation relationships of majority and minority groups in this country are deeply rooted in patterns of prejudice and discrimination.

RACISM, PREJUDICE, AND DISCRIMINATION

Racism **is a set of attitudes, beliefs, and practices used to justify the superior treatment of one racialized or ethnic group and the inferior treatment of another racialized or ethnic group.** In sociology, racism is sometimes referred to as White racism. *White racism* refers to socially organized attitudes, ideas, and practices that deny visible minorities the dignity, opportunities, freedoms, and rewards that are typically available to White Canadians (Feagin and Vera 1995:7). From this perspective, people of colour pay a direct, heavy, and immediately painful price for racism, while White discriminators pay an indirect and seldom-recognized price.

Prejudice **is a negative attitude about people based on such characteristics as racialization, gender, age, religion, or sexual orientation** (Allport 1958). If we think of prejudice as a set of negative attitudes toward members of another group simply because they belong to that group, we quickly realize that all people have prejudices, whether or not they acknowledge them. Prejudice is rooted in *ethnocentrism*—**the assumption that one's own group and way of life are superior to all others.** For example, most school children are taught that their own school and country are the best. Singing the national anthem is a form of *positive ethnocentrism.* However, *negative ethnocentrism* can result if individuals come to believe, because of constant emphasis on the superiority or "normalcy" of their own group or nation, that other groups or nations are inferior and should be treated accordingly (Feagin and Feagin 1999). Negative ethnocentrism is manifested in stereotypes that adversely affect many people.

Stereotypes **are overgeneralizations about the appearance, behaviour, or other characteristics of all members of a group.** For example, non-White-looking Canadians, regardless of how many generations their families have been in Canada and who may even be of mixed ethnic origins, are assumed to be from somewhere other than Canada, in ways White-looking Canadians are not. Greg Taylor (2000:61), a man with a White mother and Black father, recollects a fairly typical experience he had growing up in eastern Ontario:

> I was playing at a soccer game at a local high school in Grade 10 or 11 and developed what I thought was a friendly competitive rivalry between myself and the guy on their team I was always paired up against. This happens a lot and generally isn't much of a big deal. Anyway, this other guy decides to increase the competition by elbowing me. I (because I hate conflict) started walking away. To my back he says to me: "Why don't you go back to your own fucking country, you fucking nigger?" . . . I always thought it was interesting that he told me to go back to my own country. Where would that be exactly, if not Canada? This is my country and I belong here as much as he does.

Discrimination may be carried out by individuals acting on their own or by individuals operating within the context of large-scale organizations or institutions, such as schools, corporations, and government agencies. *Individual discrimination* **consists of one-on-one acts by members of the dominant group that harm members of the subordinate group or their property** (Carmichael and Hamilton 1967). Individual discrimination results from the prejudices and discriminatory actions of bigoted people who target one or more subordinate group members. The taxi driver who refuses to pick up passengers who are members of Indigenous groups in Canada is practising individual discrimination. The neo-Nazi member of an organized racist group who paints a swastika on a synagogue is practising individual discrimination.

In contrast, *institutional discrimination* **consists of the day-to-day practices of organizations and institutions that have a harmful impact on members of**

subordinate groups. For example, many mortgage companies are more likely to make loans to White people than to people of colour or to members of Indigenous groups (see Squires 1994). Institutional discrimination is carried out by the individuals who implement policies and procedures that result in negative and differential treatment of subordinate group members. Jewish immigrants in the late 1800s experienced institutional discrimination in accommodations and employment. Signs in hotel windows often read "No Jews Allowed," and many "help wanted" advertisements stated "Christians Only" (Levine 1992:55). Such practices are referred to as *anti-Semitism*—**prejudice and discriminatory behaviour directed at Jews.** Anti-Semitism is not the same as racism, although both have to do with prejudice and discrimination against a group of people presumed to have certain characteristics.

Anti-Semitism is one of the longest standing forms of discrimination recorded in history (Fleras and Elliott 1999). A little-known fact about Canada is that in 1939, authorities refused to admit to Canada, as refugees, 900 German Jews who were fleeing the Holocaust. They were forced to return to Nazi Germany where many were imprisoned in concentration camps. In Toronto, Jews (and dogs) were disallowed public beach access at Lake Ontario. Public signage warning Jews (and Catholics) not to apply for police work was posted by the Metropolitan Toronto Police Force, and many other types of employment and education in Canada were closed to Jews (see Abella 1989; Abella and Troper 1991). Today, discrimination against Jews is often carried out through the destruction and defacing of property and the distribution of hate propaganda, increasingly over the internet. Based on the pernicious history of intolerance and overt discrimination against Jews in Canada, there is a longstanding debate about whether or not anti-Semitism should be taken up under the anti-racism banner. In defence of keeping the issues separate, but co-operating as allies with common interests, activist Joshua Goldberg (1998), a White Jew, wrote in correspondence to a friend, "Solidarity is not built on pretending we all experience the same struggles. As a white Jew, I get all the race-based privileges afforded Gentile white people." While this is no doubt true, Jewish people today still experience being on the receiving end of negative stereotyping, prejudice, and discrimination. In fact, with the upsurge of organized racist activity around the world, Jews are active targets of virulent hatred. In addition to this, they are often disbelieved when they try to raise issues of anti-Semitism. Short (1991:37), for example, states that even "anti-racists appear to have eschewed any interest in anti-Semitism." Reasons for the neglect of anti-Semitism in anti-racist work may be remnants of anti-Semitism among those who are active anti-racists or a belief in the stereotype of Jews as powerful people in society who are therefore not subject to economic and educational disadvantage in the same ways that people of colour (Jewish or not) or Indigenous people are. Racism and anti-Semitism come from different histories of oppression: colonization and slavery on the one hand and expulsion and persecution on the other.

In all anti-oppression work, it is important to acknowledge people's distinct histories and distinct struggles and not become complicit in furthering people's

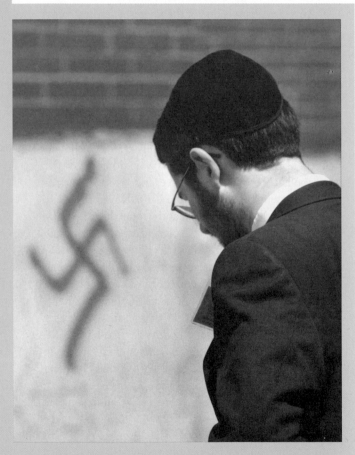

Anti-Semitism is one of the longest-standing recorded forms of discrimination in history. Today, in Canada and throughout the world, discrimination against Jews is often carried out in the destruction and defacing of property, as this photo illustrates, and in the distribution of hate propaganda.

oppression through competition. Isobel Yrigoyei, a student of professor bell hooks, wrote,

> We are not equally oppressed. There is no joy in this. We must speak from within us, our own experiences, our own oppressions—taking someone else's oppression is nothing to feel proud of. We should never speak for that which we have not felt. (in hooks 1984:57)

This last point speaks also to the issue of analogizing, as a way of unintentionally furthering the oppression of people as we try to understand their situations. Legal scholars Tina Grillo and Stephanie Wildman (1996:86) talk about the contradictory use of analogies as both "the key to greater comprehension and the danger of false understanding." Trying to understand another's experience by comparing it with an experience one has had is common. This can ease the process of comprehension and pave the way for greater understanding. It can, however, perpetuate existing relations of domination and, thus, cause more pain by centring on and shifting the focus back to the analogizer's issues or by taking over or denying the existence of pain through the analogizer's belief that she or he understands the pain the other is experiencing. As Grillo and Wildman (1996:98) conclude,

> The use of analogy exacerbates this natural desire to have our own struggles receive recognition. For if we can convince ourselves that another's experience is "just like" ours, we are then exempt from having fully to comprehend that experience.

A final type of institutional discrimination that deserves mention occurs in what American anti-racism trainer and diversity consultant Byron Kunisawa (1996) refers to as an "institutional design of omission." Kunisawa points out that the design of the whole range of systems, from education through health care through not-for-profit organizations through government through judicial systems, reflects the needs, values, practices, and priorities of those who created them. Members of every group in society were not consulted. Their needs and priorities were not considered. It may have nothing to do with intentional exclusion but rather may reflect the (racist) protocols and values consistent with the era in which the systems were developed. Kunisawa's contribution to understanding and overcoming racism is that he points out that we have never actually dealt with the exclusionary nature of the system design. Rather, we attempt to remedy situations by "adding on" another piece. For example, in his model, Institutional Designs of Omission (see Figure 3.1), Kunisawa shows, in phase one, how a system or an organization gets designed by people who represent 70 percent of the population but who *think* they represent 100 percent. In phase two, those left out of the original design want inclusion. The way of balancing people's demands for inclusion is to create separate systems, add-ons, with the belief that these add-ons will sufficiently meet the needs of those previously excluded. The add-ons do not, however,

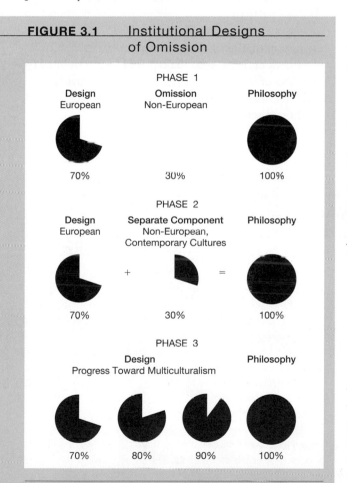

FIGURE 3.1   Institutional Designs of Omission

Source: Byron Kunisawa, www.byronkunisawa.com. Reproduced by permission of the author.

Historically, Canada and the United States have maintained a philosophy of equality and opportunity. However, our systems and institutions have never had the design to match this philosophy. The three phases illustrated here reflect the past and present system designs and future design for systemic change. If we are going to become truly, multicultural nations in the 21st century, we will need to work toward the model reflected in phase three.

because people are still not included in systems. People are still set apart and, given how pervasive racism is, not treated equally. What we need to do, according to Kunisawa, is work toward changing the fundamental design criteria of the organizations and systems we take part in by including historically marginalized people in their redesign. This process will take time but will yield an inclusive and truly multicultural society; however, we still have a long way to go when one considers how little progress we have made historically.

Historical Roots of Racism

As Europeans participated in campaigns to expand their empires, they increasingly came into contact with "exotic others." Their responses to these others ranged from benign curiosity to outright hostility. As a way of making sense of the diversity they encountered, they employed the pseudoscientific "race" theories that were gaining a foothold in society. It was the time known as the Enlightenment, and people searched for rational and scientific ways to classify and explain their worlds. Using the legitimacy of the scientific enterprise (but arbitrary criteria), these theories explained that some people were superior to others. That these systems of classification also aided Europeans in colonization, by justifying the exploitation and domination of people all over the world, is not accidental:

> Europeans not only racialized the "other" as unassimilable or as a threat; they also racialized themselves by defining Europeans as a group held together by the inevitable superiority of white to non-white. (Fleras and Elliott 1999:53)

The most common doctrine of "racial" supremacy, widely accepted in the first part of the 19th century, was what became later known as social Darwinism, (Fleras and Elliott 1999). Notions of "survival of the fittest" and the "struggle for survival" and the notion of unilinear evolution legitimized colonial expansion with the rationale that those who were better adapted would thrive; those less adapted would become extinct. As with all who have the power to define, the Europeans defined themselves at the top of the evolutionary hierarchy, with all others ranked according to how closely they emulated European civilization and Christianity. Therefore, colonialism was viewed as a "natural" and inevitable process, just like capitalism and imperialism. Colonialists saw themselves as assisting those whom they were exploiting in their evolutionary progression from savagery through barbarism to civilization. Civilization meant European and Christian civilization, of course. This doctrine added legitimacy to many practices, such as slavery and forced labour, the appropriation of land and resources, and the destruction of whole cultures and ways of life.

The Many Forms of Racism in Canadian Society

Racism is not a uniform process. It has many permutations and varieties, demonstrating its complexity and multidimensionality. Several authors have created a typology of the diversity of forms of racism in Canada as a way of pointing to the necessity for a range of diverse solutions to the problem (Fleras 2001; Fleras and Elliott 1999; Henry et al. 2000). Fleras and Elliott (1999) outline three broad categories of racism, each with specific subcategories: interpersonal, which includes redneck racism and polite racism; institutional, which includes systematic racism and systemic racism; and societal, which includes everyday racism and cultural racism.

Interpersonal Racism

Interpersonal racism occurs between individuals and gets directed at an individual because of who or what that individual stands for. The typical depiction of a racist is the redneck racist whose racism is explicit and who generally is not intimidated by the label "racist." This is the "Bubba" stereotype of our collective view. "Bubba" participates in highly personalized attacks on others, such as name calling or "racial" slurs, based on the notion that his or her culture is superior. Examples of redneck racism can be the type of racism exhibited by members of White supremacist groups in Canada, such as the Heritage Front or the Aryan Nations (see Box 3.1 for more discussion).

SOCIAL PROBLEMS IN GLOBAL PERSPECTIVE

BOX 3.1   Organized Racism—Canada's Links to a World of Hatred

Organized racist groups have been increasing in membership around the world since the fall of apartheid in South Africa and the fall of communism in Europe and the former U.S.S.R. Racist groups worldwide have fairly easily traceable links to a number of racists networks and groups in Canada. While it may be surprising to many Canadians, the history of organized hate groups in Canada is, unfortunately, a long one. The Ku Klux Klan (KKK), which began as a U.S. group, became a thriving organization in Canada in the 1920s and 1930s and has recently resurfaced here. Along with the KKK, however, we have seen the growth and proliferation of more of these groups, both in Canada and abroad. British Columbia and Ontario see the highest rates of organized racist activity, hardly surprising as these two provinces have, along with Quebec, the highest rates of immigration into Canada.

Organized racism is often referred to as neo-fascism, neo-Nazism, White supremacism, or organized hate. It differs from other forms of Canadian racism in both its virulence and its intent. Organized racists differ from regular racists in that their hatred of non-White people, and of Jews in particular, coupled with their active membership in a hate group gives them a predisposition to *act* on their racism, by committing violence, by publishing messages of hate, by recruiting others to their cause, and by participating in a host of other activities.

The intent of the many hate groups ranges; however, they do have one basic activity in common—to rid the province/state/nation/world of *undesirables*; to fight against what they view as the "racial takeover" of "their" geographic space. As anthropologists Frances Henry and Carol Tator, lawyer Winston Mattis, and race relations and diversity specialist Tim Rees (2000:99) state, "All these groups share an ideology that supports the view that the Aryan, or White, 'race' is superior to all others, morally, intellectually, and culturally, and that it is Whites' manifest destiny to dominate society." Also, as the term implies, organized racism is an organized activity. Typically, the group has a designated leadership and a well-established hierarchy of followers. Most Canadians are completely unaware of this kind of organized activity. Those who are aware of the existence of such groups tend to dismiss their adherents as "nutters" or people on the fringe. Contrary to what many people believe or want to believe about these groups, they do exist, they have resources, and they are dangerous. While many of us do not wish to believe it, when a 65-year-old Sikh janitor is beaten to death at a Surrey, B.C., temple, or an elderly Calgary journalist is beaten savagely in a surprise attack at his home, or Jewish synagogues are defaced across Canada, or burning crosses are placed on the lawns of people believed to be non-White or Jewish, it is difficult to discount these White supremacists as harmless.

Fleras and J. L. Elliott reported in 1999 that in Canada there may only be "1500 hard-core supremacists" who are members of a proliferation of groups including known racist groups such as the KKK, the Western Guard, the Aryan Nations, White Aryan Resistance, the Heritage Front, the Nationalist Party, Posse Comitatus, and the Church of the Creator, and alleged groups such as the Canadian Free Speech League, the Council on Public Affairs, and the Coalition for Humanistic British Canada. Information about organized hate groups in Canada is now easy to access through the internet and telephone call-in lines, such as Canadian Liberty Net, although organized hate groups still carry out physical recruitment drives as well.

The question is, What do these people want? Different groups have different aims. Some of the more radical right-wing groups desire the downfall of the Canadian state (viewed as traitorous because it has allowed non-White and Jewish immigration) and political control over a bounded territory (a sovereign "Aryan Nation") completely free of non-White and Jewish people and of "race traitors" (those who associate with non-Whites or Jews). For many, violence is an acceptable means for achieving these ends, and in preparation for the coming "race war," paramilitary training is carried out in several areas of Canada (for example, northern British Columbia, Alberta, and Ontario) and at some "Whites only" compounds in the United States (Hayden Lake, Idaho, and other areas in the southern United States, for example).

Organized hate groups adhere to an extreme right-wing and very often Christian ideology. Sociologist Stanley Barrott (1991:90–91) reports that the main tenets of the White supremacist's ideology are "anticommunism, antiliberalism, racism and anti-Semitism" and a belief that the "survival of the whites is precarious." Barrett (1991:90) also points out that, in contrast to their views of Jewish people, who are supposedly responsible for all of society's ills, "White supremacists see themselves as the saviours of the white race (sic) and Western Christian civilization." In this way, many right-wing racists interpret their racism as a positive force rather than a negative one, "a natural preference of people for their own race and repugnance for other races" (Barrett, 1991:95). Many believe that it will take an extreme incident, like the near-extinction of Whites, before White people will wake up and realize they need to join supremacist groups and "take back" their nation. While some are content to wait for the majority of Whites to "wake up," many others take matters into their own hands by actively recruiting members.

Recruitment into hate groups takes many forms. It may be a simple pamphlet left in a mall washroom or on a city bus seat. It may be a racist comic book given out to elementary school children. It can be a book table at a public lecture. It can be a personal visit to a person's home. It can be through political platforms in legitimate democratic elections. (Wolfgang Droege, now deceased Heritage Front leader, ran in a municipal election in Scarborough, Ontario, in 1993 and won an alarming 14 percent of the vote. It is worth noting that Droege, a very public racist figure, was murdered outside of his Ontario apartment in April 2005.) Recruitment can be through music. For example, the alternative hate rock band RaHoWa (which stands for Racial Holy War), was managed by George Burdi, who was also the band's lyricist and vocalist. Burdi was also a self-proclaimed leader of the violent Church of the Creator and a Heritage Front member. Bands like RaHoWa and others, such as Odin's Law from Surrey, B.C., market and distribute their hate-filled lyrics worldwide. George Burdi, whose real name is George Eric Hawthorne, recently left the White Power movement after a stint in prison for assault. He is now married to a non-White woman, lives mainly Buddhist spiritual practice, and is involved in a multi-ethnic music group called Novacosm. Late in April 2004, Burdi was interviewed by Vanguard News Network about his departure from the White Power movement and his new life. Vanguard News Network asserts itself as,

a group of disgusted and disaffected writers driven out of academia and journalism by the Semitical Correctness that has denatured our culture. We have come together on the Internet to reclaim the American mind from the Jews. In short, we are the Antibodies, and our advent heralds the day a White political force rises and reasserts civilization (VNN Homepage, http://www.vanguardnewsnetwork.com/whoweare.htm, retrieved June 1, 2006).

Interviewers for VNN asked Burdi, now Hawthorne, if he had listened "to any White Power music today? Which bands? Do you have any opinions you want to share on Resistance, Panzerfaust, or any other WN music-related companies or people? How would you sum up the evolution of WP music since your departure? Do you have any advice for today's WP musicians?" (Vanguard News Network 2004).

Burdi's response to VNN is indicative of his shift. He says,

I have not heard any current WP music, nor of Panzerfaust (which I assume is a label).

My advice for today's WP musicians is to remember that every lyric you ever write will be read by your children someday, that once it's out there you can't take it back, and that you have to speak out to the kids who listen to your records, keep them out of jail, and make the concerts more family oriented and culturally uplifting. Focus more on what you love, not what you hate. Also

George Burdi

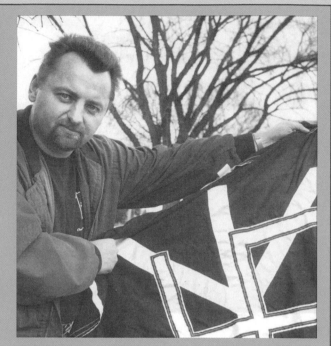

Wolfgang Droege, 1992

do not concentrate only on your racial identity, for can "what is impermanent, changeable, and non-substantial be considered thus: this is mine, this am I, this is my self?" (http://www.vanguardnewsnetwork.com/2004b/42704burdiinterview.htm, retrieved June 1, 2006)

While membership in organized hate groups tends to increase during economic recessions, membership is by no means restricted to the working class. On the contrary, although much of the membership may be from economically disenfranchised classes, the leadership and financial support are often from middle- and upper-middle classes (CTV 1995).

Dhiru Patel (1980, cited in Barrett 1991:85–86) distinguishes three explanations for racism. The first views racism from the perspective of the deviant individual. Acts such as racist graffiti or the beating of a member of a minority group are seen as being caused by poorly socialized individuals. The second perspective, a social forces perspective, sees a rise in racism as accompanying aberrant social factors, such as an increase in immigration, unemployment, or inflation. From this view, racism is, again, not integral to society but atypical, and will abate when the event abates. The third view, the institutional racism perspective, suggests that acts of racism can occur because there is widespread institutional and social structural support for racism. Based on this view, Barrett (1991:87) concludes that "it is improbable that such organizations could exist unless there was some degree of compatibility with the institutional fabric of the larger society." This last view may best explain how it is that organized hate groups are able to access tolerance from many liberal thinkers who otherwise claim to be non-racist. The racists play on people's deep emotions about personal freedoms and democracy. Making a heartfelt case for an issue such as freedom of speech, organized racists say that even if most Canadians do not like exactly what they are saying, as Canadians they should have the right not to be censored. Fleras and Elliott (1999:80) point out that because of a deeply rooted history of racism and the ability of organized racists to hide behind this liberal façade, "these extremists have the potential to destabilize a society where prejudice is pervasive."

Apparently the federal government of Canada agreed with Fleras and Elliott, since in July 2006, Justice von Finckenstein sentenced Tomasz Winnicki of London, Ontario, to nine months in jail for ignoring a court order to stop spreading hate messages on the internet against Jews, people of colour, and immigrants. While approximately two dozen people in Canada have been jailed for internet hate crimes, Winnicki, an immigrant himself to Canada, was the first to be jailed without being criminally convicted and the first to be sentenced for contempt of court for defying an order to stop posting hate messages on the internet. Leo Adler, the Director of National Affairs for a Toronto Jewish human rights organization, was quoted as saying, "Hopefully, it will send a message to people that, firstly, they should not be practicing hate in Canada, and secondly, if you are going to do it, and the courts tell you to stop, they mean it" (Tibbetts 2006). Adler noted that there are approximately 6000 internet sites operating today that promote hatred. What do you think? Do you think people in Canada should have the freedom to publicly express views and messages of hatred against groups?

The use of the "Bubba" stereotype in our cultural view can be dangerous for two reasons. First, it is a stereotype and, as such, can be misleading and inaccurate and can be applied to people erroneously. Second, and more subtle, is the fact that if we define racism as only the type of behaviour exhibited by "Bubba," we miss the majority of racism that goes on in Canada; the stereotype provides a cover for other harmful attitudes and practices. Human rights legislation and the *Charter of Rights and Freedoms* have done a great deal to erode redneck racism in public discourse. In its place, due to increasing risks of legal and social consequences, polite racism has evolved. *Polite racism* refers to the ways that people may couch criticisms of racialized others in bland tones or use language that appears non-prejudicial on the surface. Polite racists are often good at phrasing a sentence so as to deliver the racist message to anyone looking for it but make it obscure enough to enable him or her to deny that there was any racist intent. Unsurprisingly perhaps, polite racists tend to be those with higher education. Polite racism can be difficult to prove and therefore difficult to combat. An example is when a member of a dominant group makes a comment to another member of a dominant group about a subordinate group that he or she would not make, knowingly, to a member of the subordinate group in question. The comment is often carefully benign on the surface, to allow room for the denial of racism, but the receptor of the comment *knows* what the thrust of the comment is.

Institutional Racism

Institutional racism refers to various organizational practices, policies, and procedures that discriminate, either purposely or inadvertently. If there is the intent to deny privilege or to exclude, it is referred to as systematic. If not, it is referred to as systemic. *Systemic racism* is embedded in the design of the organization, is formalized, and is legally sanctioned by the state. Discriminatory practices reflect the values of the dominant culture and act to deliberately prevent certain groups from participating in the culture. Examples are the exclusion of Black Canadians from movie theatres and restaurants until the 1950s, the restricting of the enrolment of Jewish Canadians in Canadian universities in the 1940s, and the disallowing of Japanese Canadians from voting in British Columbia until 1949 (Fleras and Elliott 1999). Indigenous people were only allowed the vote provincially starting between 1949 and 1969 and were disenfranchised federally until 1960.

Systemic racism is also embedded in the organization, procedures, and norms of an organization. It tends to be impersonal and unconscious in that discrimination is unintended but has the effect of discriminating anyway. It occurs because seemingly neutral rules get applied evenly to all, even when this may be inappropriate. The impact is the favouring of certain groups whose members most closely resemble the rule makers while disadvantaging those who are different. An example is the height and weight requirements for police recruits in Canada, which inadvertently disallowed most Asians, Indigenous people, and women from participation. A well-publicized example was the headgear policy for the RCMP that stated that members had to wear RCMP-issue headgear. This policy, which was fought and defeated, effectively disenfranchised Sikhs who, for religious reasons, must wear a turban.

Societal Racism

Societal racism refers to the generalized, and typically unconscious, patterns of interaction between people that perpetuate a racialized social order. It is part of the general functioning of the society and is said to precede other forms of racism (Henry et al. 2000). *Everyday racism* refers to general, and seemingly benign, ideas of the relative superiority and inferiority of certain groups. These ideas are widely accepted as normal by dominant group members. The main way that ideas are perpetuated is through language that is held to be neutral. Language, of course, is far from neutral, as through it we socially construct our reality. Words convey images and associations, both positive and negative, that we draw upon to order our worlds. As Fleras and Elliott (1999:84) point out, "[Language] provides a cultural frame of reference for defining what is desirable and important."

Some examples of everyday racism are found in the use of colour symbolism (e.g., associating white with good, black with evil) or the use of emotionally loaded terms like "Indian massacres" (Fleras and Elliott 1999:85). Everyday racism can be further distinguished into active and passive racism (Henry et al. 2000:55). *Active racism,* according to social psychologist Philomena Essed (1990), includes any act (including the use of language) that is motivated by the intention of excluding or making a person or group feel inferior *because* of his/her/their minority group status. *Passive racism*

What does the act of employing ethnic "seasonal" labourers for extremely low wages by Canadian businesses, especially in the agricultural sector, suggest about the existence of racist beliefs among Canadians?

includes being complicit in another's racism, for example laughing at a racist joke or "not hearing" racist comments (Essed 1990). *Cultural racism* refers to cultural values that reinforce the interest of the dominant group while undermining the interests of subordinate groups. Cultural racism is manifested in the notion that minority groups are acceptable in Canada, as long as they know and understand their place in society and act in ways the dominant majority wants them to. Cultural values support equality, but measures toward ensuring that it happens are resisted. An example can be cultural support for the notion of equal opportunity in employment in all sectors but hostility toward employment equity programs or the *Canadian Employment Equity Act.* This type of racism is discussed in depth in Box 3.2, below.

Racism manifests in a diversity of ways. This being so, it is imperative that strategies and measures to combat it be equally diverse and multidimensional.

SOCIAL PROBLEMS AND SOCIAL POLICY

BOX 3.2   Undermining Democratic Racism in Canada

Most non-White Canadians know that prejudice and discrimination based upon racializing factors is still very much alive and well in Canada. While there are many White Canadians who are aware of this as well, there are more who are perplexed when they hear allegations of racism in Canada. Pointing to our official multiculturalism policies, our recent hate crimes legislation, our Federal Employment Equity policy, and our *Charter of Rights and Freedoms,* people question how racism can coexist with policies and laws that enshrine people's rights to be culturally and linguistically different from the mainstream. The fact of these liberal democratic policies and laws may be precisely what makes racism in Canada so elusive. Frances Henry and Carol Tator (1999:107) have published a number of articles and books addressing this paradox. In fact, they assert "social inequality continues to operate and is reproduced and legitimated through the state." Racism in Canada, although often cloaked, is thus made possible by way of a process called "democratic racism."

Democratic racism refers to the tension between two contradictory sets of values, and the process enabling them to simultaneously exist (Henry and Tator 1999, 2000; Henry et al. 2000). This gets played out in Canada through, on the one hand, ideologies consistent with liberal democracies, with ideals like "justice," "fairness," "equality," "tolerance," "acceptance," and "individual rights," and, on the other hand, pervasive and widespread racist practices, beliefs, and attitudes. This racism is inherent in, and promoted by not only individuals but also institutions and the Canadian state itself through its policies and practices. As Henry and Tator (1999:89–90) state:

> State responses have largely failed to achieve the goal of eliminating or even controlling racial bias and discrimination because racism and notions of racial superiority are deeply embedded in the collective belief system and in the norms and practices of Canadian society.

We typically think of racism as the attitudes and actions of individuals. More dangerous, perhaps, because it is more easily hidden, is the racism, rooted in our collective belief system, that holds up one culture's beliefs, values, norms, and practices as superior and others as inferior. Individuals' attitudes and practices are connected, however, to institutions and the whole system: "Racist attitudes are derivative in nature and grow out of and are sustained by the structures of social relations of which they are a mere reflection" (Henry and Tator 2000:286).

We have developed a set of arguments in Canada that justify and rationalize racism. Philosopher Michel Foucault used the term *discourse* to describe these sets of arguments as a form of communication that is used as a "vehicle for social processes" (1980, quoted in Henry and Tator 2000:291). In deconstructing an overall discourse of domination, Henry and Tator (2000:292–298) outline 12 myths or discourses that support and perpetuate democratic racism. Each one is briefly featured below.

The Discourse of Denial: The main assumption underpinning this discourse is that racism simply does not exist here. The systemic nature and embeddedness of racism is ignored. Examples of this discourse include, "Canada is not a racist nation"; "I am not a racist"; "The justice system is not racist."

The Discourse of Political Correctness: The main feature of this neo-conservative discourse is that it discredits any moves toward social justice—for example, the inclusion of marginalized people or groups, or critiques of exclusionary practices—as "overzealous" and "illegitimate" or "whining." The term *political correctness* (as in, "I don't even know what the 'politically correct' term for Indians is these days") is used derisively to "stifle dissent."

The Discourse of Colour Blindness: The overriding feature of this discourse is a lack of acknowledgment of the privileges that accompany skin colour in Canada. For example, many White people will insist they "don't even notice skin colour." Minimizing or ignoring the impact of skin colour allows people to ignore the very real power differences and the fact that "race matters" in terms of the experiences that people have had.

The Discourse of Equal Opportunity: The point of this discourse is to convey the message that if we treat everyone equally, fairness will follow. The unexplored, ahistorical, and incorrect assumption is that everyone is coming from an equivalent place and has an equal opportunity to succeed or fail. This discourse ignores the power and privilege assigned to people based on gender, language, skin colour, sexual orientation, and so on.

The Discourse of "Blame the Victim": This discourse builds upon the assumption of equal opportunity. Any person or group who is not successful must therefore, clearly, be flawed in some way, due either to genetic inferiority or upbringing (for example, as promoted by the culture of poverty thesis discussed in Chapter 2).

The Discourse of White Victimization: The main tenet of this discourse is that White immigrants also have experienced prejudice and discrimination and that all immigrants should expect to start at the bottom and work their way up. One problematic piece of this argument is that it confounds "race," ethnicity, and immigrant experiences, lumping them all together, as though they are the same. Another problematic piece is the refusal to acknowledge that, for non-White immigrants, prejudice and discrimination do not go away in the second or third generation but are still in effect in ongoing oppressive practices.

The Discourse of Reverse Racism: The main point of this discourse is the assertion that White people are now on the receiving end of oppression and exclusion. Policies and programs that are designed to redress inequities in Canadian society are viewed as anti-democratic and symptomatic of a "creeping totalitarianism" that discriminates against Whites.

The Discourse of Binary Polarization: This discourse rests on the fragmenting of Canadian society into "us" and "them." An example of an implicit message is, "We are 'Canadian Canadians'—law-abiding, hard-working members of society. They are the "others" who, it must be assumed, have opposite characteristics" (Henry et al. 2000:384).

The Discourse of "Moral Panic": The major point underlying this discourse is that the dominant group, in the wake of economic and political uncertainty, is no longer in control. Instead of targeting processes that accompany the globalization of capital, for example, the threat to "the Canadian way of life" is seen to come from immigrants and other, usually racialized, "others." Henry and Tator (2000) refer to this sort of propaganda as a "moral panic."

The Discourse of Multiculturalism—Tolerance, Accommodation, Harmony, and Diversity: The main point of this discourse is that while the ways of "others" must be tolerated (but not necessarily accepted or enjoyed) in a multicultural society, the dominant ways are superior and people *should* adapt. Cultural practices that are viewed as too distant from those of the mainstream are viewed as disruptive to overall Canadian harmony. "Tolerance has its limits."

The Discourse of Liberal Values—Individualism, Truth, Tradition, Universalism, and Freedom of Expression: The main feature of this discourse is the notion that there is "a" truth, one overarching, authentic view. An example of this discourse is, "There is a universal form of expression that includes and transcends all cultural and racial boundaries." (Henry et al. 2000:385).

The Discourse on National Identity: The major feature of this discourse is the exclusion of all but English Canadians and French Canadians from the national identity. Despite the fact that groups other than the British or French settled in the region long before Confederation, the national identity is based on the two Charter groups. Everyone else is treated as "other." As Henry and Tator (2000:297) point out, "erasures, omissions and silences mark the discourse of Canada's national identity."

After identifying these 12 discourses that underlie democratic racism in Canada, Henry and Tator (2000:298) conclude:

> Many Canadians see themselves as egalitarian and have little difficulty in rejecting the more overt expressions of racism. They may make symbolic gestures of inclusivity. However, beyond these tokenistic efforts, the struggles of people of colour [and Indigenous people] are met with arbitrary use of political, economic, and cultural institutional power in the interest of "maintaining democracy."

Democratic racism plays out at all levels in Canadian society and carries with it many consequences for all citizens. One consequence of democratic racism is a general lack of support for anti-racist or equity initiatives. As an example, employment equity strategies, or affirmative action strategies by employers, get painted in mainstream society as "unfair" and "undemocratic." The argument is based on the idea that these hires are not based on "merit" but rather are based on some ascribed characteristic such as skin colour, ancestry, or gender. What is conveniently overlooked in this argument is that we have always had precisely this kind of affirmative action— *for members of dominant groups*. When people from the dominant groups are no longer automatically preferred or privileged, they cry "unfair," " *reverse* racism," "discrimination," and so on. While, strictly speaking, affirmative action is discriminating and selectively preferring, as an interim strategy, it is necessary if we are to build a truly fair and just society, based on something other than ascription. This is not to suggest that people hired through employment equity strategies are in any way unqualified. Unfortunately, often a member of a minority group must be many times more qualified than a member of the dominant group in order to be hired. A message of "lack of qualifications" is often the implicit message in these complaints, however, and it needs to be exposed for its underlying racism. We must make an effort, even if temporarily, to redress past exclusion and discrimination. When we have true equity, we will no longer need specific policies and legislation.

Many Canadians seem to resist equity and anti-racist initiatives because it is easier to believe the rhetoric of democratic racism. It is easier to believe that things are running smoothly for us all and to blame the victim when we hear stories that contradict our beliefs. It is easier to do this than critically question our own deeply held beliefs and value systems because, ultimately, upon examination, if our real practices do not support our stated values, we are placed in an untenable position. If we know about this contradiction and we choose to do nothing, it makes us hypocrites; and if we choose to do something, where and how do we begin? Additionally, we may be in the uncomfortable predicament of having to give up some of our invisible and often uncontested privilege. As philosopher Elizabeth Kamarck Minnich (1995:424) noted more than a decade ago, "Most seem to want to give up the harm without giving up the privilege."

Given the pervasive and sometimes subtle nature of democratic racism, it is difficult to know how to approach meaningful change. Henry and colleagues (2000) offer five strategies as starting points that offer hope that we can work toward the elimination of racism in Canada. Each strategy will be reviewed briefly.

The Development of Reflective Skills and Practices

Most White people do not experience the marginalization, exclusion, and discrimination that non-White people in Canada do, and hence, it is very difficult for many White people to see or understand the kind of impact these everyday experiences have on a person. Much of the privilege that Whites in Canada have is invisible to them. As an example, Grillo and Wildman (1996) have pointed out that part of the privilege of Whiteness is the ability not to think about "race." One of the necessary skills that is absent from professional socialization and curricula is reflective practice. Incorporating critical thinking and reflection into university training for professionals (social workers, judges, lawyers, teachers, and so on) could have a widespread and beneficial effect of giving people the tools to deconstruct privilege, critically examine racism and its impacts, and allow people with privilege to gain a more complete understanding of what others in Canadian society face (Henry et al. 2000:390–392).

Responses to Allegations of Racism

Responses to allegations of racism are usually emotional for all parties concerned. First, the individuals involved (the person saying the complaint and the person hearing the complaint) both need to acknowledge that the issue is emotional, without getting defensive or distraught. Second, White people need to recognize that their realities, as dominant group members, can be quite different from those of non-White Canadians. Third, both parties need to make a "commitment to negotiate, implement, and institutionalize change." This process can also take place at the community and/or institutional levels (Henry et al. 2000:392–393).

The Empowerment of Communities

Communities should be empowered to push for peaceful social change, based on different groups' differing needs and interests. This may bring racialized communities into conflict with dominant structures and institutions, which should be regarded as a positive sign (within reason) as it may be indicative of more efforts to reduce inequality underway. Community pressure has always been a major impetus for change. Direct and sustained community actions should include "organizational resources (financial and human); legitimacy (support from media and other communities); expertise (legal, media, and organizational); and leadership (training and development) (Henry et al. 2000:393–395).

The Monitoring of Anti-Racism Initiatives

In Canada, a number of policies and acts of legislation have been put into place to address disadvantage occurring due to prejudice and discrimination. However, the main activities that have taken place have been around determining if racism is happening, how much is occurring, how it occurs, and how it may be prevented.

While these considerations are very important, it is equally important to emphasize the analysis of outcomes. "In other words, initiatives must show definable results that reduce racial injustices in a measurable way" (Henry et al. 2000:396). Anti-racist initiatives too often are based on vague (and immeasurable) concepts like "encouraging," "improving," and "promoting." Instead of attempting to measure the process of "promoting diversity," what is needed are ways to measure the *impact* of a particular program or policy in reducing disadvantage. Moreover, information about initiatives, processes, and impacts needs to be shared across the nation much more broadly than is currently occurring. If people have information about the problem and the impact of anti-racist measures, more can be achieved (Henry et al. 2000:395–397).

The Emphasis on the Role of Major Institutions

Institutions need to articulate specific statements regarding racism, coming from upper management first. Currently, they operate as though racism does not exist and is in no way connected with them, if it does exist. Coherent statements and measures need to be implemented in institutions so that people understand the ways in which racism negatively impacts all citizens (not just people "of colour" or "visible" minorities). Monitoring systems need to be set up in institutions so that people can assess the progress toward a racism-free institution. The development of a coherent anti-racism strategy in an institution requires "a total system effort that must be comprehensive, systematic, and long term with clearly enunciated goals, not so much concerned with maintaining order and harmony as with responding to grievances and correcting inequities." At a very basic level, ensuring that people from all groups are represented at the decision-making level of any organization is an important first step (Henry et al. 2000:399–400).

Despite measures that have been taken in Canada to reduce inequalities based on ethnicity and racialization, they persist at alarming levels. The concept of democratic racism, with its confounding discourses, allows us to understand how it is possible to hold two sets of conflicting values simultaneously. The impact of these values contradictions is not merely intellectual but, rather, has serious and derogatory impacts on the real material conditions of people's lives—their abilities to participate equally and be treated equally as citizens in a rich and prosperous land. We must all take action to eliminate racism. Besides being morally and ethically wrong, it is a shocking waste of human potential.

PERSPECTIVES ON RACIALIZED AND ETHNIC INEQUALITY

Over the course of the past 100 years, sociologists have developed different perspectives to explain why racialized and ethnic inequality occurs and why it persists. Some perspectives focus on sociological factors such as migration, assimilation, conflict, and exploitation.

The Symbolic Interactionist Perspective

Somewhat related to social-psychological explanations of prejudice and discrimination are theories based on the interactionist perspective. One interactionist approach emphasizes how racialized socialization contributes to feelings of solidarity with one's own racialized or ethnic group and hostility toward all others. *Racialized socialization* is a process of social interaction that contains specific messages and practices concerning the nature of one's racialized or ethnic status as it relates to (1) personal and group identity; (2) inter-group and inter-individual relationships; and (3) one's position in the social stratification system. Although racialized socialization may occur through direct statements about "race" made by parents, peers, teachers, and others, it may also include indirect modelling behaviours, which occur when children imitate the words and actions of parents and other caregivers (Thornton et al. 1990). Racialized socialization affects how people view themselves, other people, and the world. Here, for example, racialization and ethnic relations scholar and historian Manning Marable (1995:1) describes how racialized socialization makes "race" a prism through which Canadians who are Black or members of other visible minorities view their daily lives:

> Black and white. As long as I can remember, the fundamentally defining feature of my life, and the lives of my family, was the stark reality of race. . . . It was the social gravity which set into motion our expectations and emotions, our language and dreams. . . . Race seemed granite-like, fixed and permanent, as the centre of the social universe. The reality of racial discrimination constantly fed the pessimism and doubts that we as Black people felt about the apparent natural order of the world, the inherent unfairness of it all, as well as limiting our hopes for a better life somewhere in the distant future.

Though all groups practise racialized socialization, White racialized socialization emphasizes White "racial" bonding. According to multicultural education scholar Christine E. Sleeter (1996), White "racial" bonding occurs when White people act in ways that reaffirm the common stance on ethnic or cultural issues and draw "us–them" boundaries, thus perpetuating racism and discrimination. Such people choose to live near other Whites, to socialize with other Whites, and to vote for other Whites, thus maintaining racialized solidarity. Although many Whites do not support racist beliefs, actions, or policies, they fear breaking bonds with other Whites and may simply remain silent in the face of prejudice and discrimination (Sleeter 1996).

The Structural Functionalist Perspective

To functionalists, social order and stability are extremely important for the smooth functioning of society. Consequently, "racial" and ethnic discord, urban unrest, and riots are dysfunctional and must be eliminated or contained. One functionalist perspective focuses on *assimilation*—**the process by which members of subordinate racialized and ethnic groups become absorbed into the dominant culture.** Functionalists view assimilation as a stabilizing force that minimizes differences that otherwise might result in hostility and violence (Gordon 1964). In its most complete form,

assimilation becomes *amalgamation* **, a process in which the cultural attributes of diverse racialized or ethnic groups are blended together to form a new society incorporating the unique contributions of each group.** Amalgamation occurs when members of dominant and subordinate racialized or ethnic groups intermarry and procreate to produce "mixed-ethnicity" children.

Early assimilation in Canada focused primarily on the Anglo-conformity model, rather than amalgamation. The *Anglo-conformity model* **refers to a pattern of assimilation in which members of subordinate racialized/ethnic groups are expected to conform to the culture of the dominant (White) Anglo-Saxon population.** Assimilation does not always lead to full social acceptance. For example, many successful members of minority groups have been excluded from membership in elite private clubs and parties in the homes of co-workers.

Another functionalist perspective emphasizes *ethnic pluralism*—**the coexistence of diverse racialized/ethnic groups with separate identities and cultures within a society.** In a pluralistic society, political and economic systems link diverse groups, but members of some racialized/ethnic groups maintain enough separation from the dominant group to guarantee that their group and ethnic cultural traditions continue (Gordon 1964). Ethnic pluralism is the formal model of ethnic relations in Canadian society; however, Anglo-conformity is such a strong force that pluralism may be more of a myth than a reality for ethnic groups. In Canada, pluralism can take the form of *segregation* because subordinate racialized/ethnic groups have less power and privilege than do members of the dominant group (Marger 1994). *Segregation* **is the spatial and social separation of categories of people by racialization, ethnicity, class, gender, religion, or other social characteristics.** Recent sociological studies have found that when high levels of segregation based on racialization are followed by inter-ethnic contact, competition may ensue, tending to increase ethnic unrest and the potential for intense conflict between groups (Olzak et al. 1996).

The Conflict Perspective

Conflict theorists explain racialized and ethnic inequality in terms of economic stratification and access to power. As discussed in Chapter 1, there are a number of conflict perspectives. However, this chapter focuses on the critical-conflict approach, which explains racialized and ethnic inequality in terms of economic stratification and unequal access to power. We will briefly examine class perspectives, split-labour market theory, internal colonialism, and the theory of "racial" formation.

Class perspectives on racialized and ethnic inequality highlight the role of the capitalist class in racialized exploitation. For example, according to sociologist Oliver C. Cox (1948), the primary cause of slavery was the capitalist desire for profit, not racialized prejudice. People were enslaved because, through force, they could be made to do heavy labour and other duties for basically the costs of feeding and housing them. A contemporary class perspective suggests that members of the capitalist class benefit from a split-labour market that promotes racialized divisions among workers and suppresses wages. According to the *split-labour market theory*, the economy is divided into two employment sectors: a primary sector composed of higher-paid workers in more secure jobs and a secondary sector composed of lower-paid workers in jobs that often involve hazardous working conditions and little job security (Bonacich 1972, 1976). Dominant group members are usually employed in primary sector positions; subordinate group members are concentrated in the secondary sector. Workers in the two job sectors tend to have divergent interests and goals because of their different relations to the labour market; therefore worker solidarity is difficult (Bonacich 1972, 1976). Members of the capitalist class benefit from these divisions because workers are less likely to band together and demand pay increases or other beneficial changes in the workplace. White workers in the primary sector who accept racist arguments attempt to exclude subordinate group members from higher-paying jobs by barring them from labour unions, lobbying against employment equity, and opposing immigration.

A second critical-conflict perspective examines *internal colonialism*—**a process that occurs when members of a racialized/ethnic group are conquered or colonized and forcibly placed under the economic and political control of the dominant group.** According to sociologist Robert Blauner (1972), people in groups that have been subjected to internal colonialism remain in subordinate positions in society

much longer than do people in groups that voluntarily migrated to this country. For example, Indigenous peoples were forced into subordination when they were colonized by Europeans. Hundreds of culturally and linguistically diverse Indigenous groups lost property, political rights, components of their culture, and often their lives; some Indigenous groups were virtually extinguished, victims of *genocide*—**the deliberate, systematic killing of an entire people or nation.** Meanwhile, the capitalist class acquired cheap labour and land, frequently through government-sanctioned racialized exploitation (Blauner 1972). The legacy of internal colonialism remains visible today in the number of Indigenous people who live in poverty, particularly those who live on federal reserves, often lacking essential services such as water, electricity, and sewage disposal.

The last critical-conflict perspective we will look at is the ***theory of racial formation,* which states that the government substantially defines racialized and ethnic relations.** From this perspective, racialized bias and discrimination tend to be rooted in government actions, ranging from passage of "race"-related legislation to imprisonment of members of groups that are believed to be a threat to society. According to sociologists Michael Omi and Howard Winant (1994), governments are responsible for shaping the politics of racialized inequality through actions and policies that have resulted in the unequal treatment of Indigenous people and visible minorities. Immigration legislation, for example, reveals specific racialized biases. Fleras and Elliott (1992:39–40), for example, note that "initial policies could be described as essentially racist in orientation, assimilationist in content, and segregationist in intent." As examples, until the 1960s, Western Europeans were the preferred immigrants; and when this was extended to Eastern Europeans, Jewish and Mediterranean people required special permits. Further, Asians of Chinese and Indian origin were only reluctantly admitted during times of capitalist expansion, when the state required large pools of cheap labour, and then, only males were permitted to immigrate. Family members were not allowed. Overtly racially selective immigration policies, closely following Canada's nation-building requirements, were in force until the first major revision in 1962. As sociologist Victor Satzewich (1989) has pointed out,

Racism is an ideology imposed from above by those who own the means of production on those who do not: racism acts to mystify social reality, justifies the exploitation of certain groups of people's labour power, and contributes to the maintenance of the status quo.

Feminist and Anti-Racist Perspectives

One feminist perspective is based on a critical-conflict perspective and links racialized inequality and gender oppression. *Gendered racism* **may be defined as the interactive effect of racism and sexism in exploiting Indigenous and visible minority women.** According to Essed (1991), not all workers are exploited equally by capitalists. For many years, the majority of jobs in the primary sector of the labour market were held by White men, while most people of colour and many White women were employed in secondary sector jobs. Below the secondary sector, in the underground sector of the economy, many Indigenous women and women of colour worked as domestic servants and nannies, in sweat shops, or the sex trade, just to survive. Work in this underground sector is unregulated, and people who earn their income in it are vulnerable to exploitation by many people, including unscrupulous employers, greedy pimps, and corrupt police officers (Amott and Matthaei 1991).

In Canada, anti-racist feminist theorizing—deconstructing the interconnectedness of racism and sexism, colonialism and imperialism—has been engaged in since the 19th century (Dua 1999). Anti-racist feminist theorizing differs from mainstream feminist theorizing: it challenges the notion of a common experience that all women share under capitalism; it focuses on the specific ways that class, gender, *and* ethnicity play out as interconnections. Anti-racist feminist scholar and critical theorist Hamani Bannerji (1995:77) points out that "the erasure of the factors 'race,' racism, and continual immigration prevents an adequate understanding of the Canadian economy." Building on this, women's studies scholar Enakshi Dua (1999:21) concludes that "the discourse of race is as 'foundational' to the creation and maintenance of the Canadian political economy as are capitalist relations and patriarchy." Dua (1999:16) outlines three priorities within much

of Canadian anti-racist feminist thought: (1) to interrogate feminist theory and practice to assess its complicity in perpetuating racism; (2) to raise questions about ways of theorizing about the connections between gender and racialization; and (3) to continue to document the ways that racialized differences are created and maintained among women.

Many proponents of anti-racist feminism also investigate the impacts of racism on women of colour, examining the ways that gender, racialization, and class intersect, for example, when well-to-do White women employ racialized and poor women from non-industrialized nations to do domestic labour for them on temporary work visas. Other impacts that have been examined are the wages of women of colour and Indigenous women compared to White women's wages and the ways that equity measures for women disproportionately privilege White women relative to non-White women. Some anti-racist feminist theorists have suggested a *standpoint analysis,* that is, beginning theorizing and analysis from the situated standpoint of the person and her experiences—employing a kind of "outsider-within" perspective (Dua 1999:19). However, women's experiences with racialization vary along class lines, according to sexual orientation and personal history. Therefore, it is important to account for the whole of a person's identity or locations.

Taking anti-racist feminism a step further, sociologist and editor Daiva Stasiulis (1999) makes a convincing case for feminist intersectional theorizing. Feminist intersectional theorizing is a trend away from what Stasiulis (1999:350–351) calls the "race-gender-class trinity" or the "iron triangle of race-gender-class" and a move toward an understanding of the myriad ways that oppressions are linked and the impacts on individuals and groups of those intersections. In addition to a focus on the triad of issues mentioned, nationality, language, religion, sexuality, citizenship, ability, and so on are interrogated, with the emphasis on seeing the ways these social divisions play out. With the increase in economic globalization, interest in this mode of analysis was heightened and developed. However, in developing an analysis of intersectionality, the challenge is to steer clear of the trap of essentializing all women this way and all people of colour that way and so on, as well as to avoid using terms euphemistically, such that "gender" means "women" and "racialized" means "brown," and so on.

CAN RACIALIZED AND ETHNIC INEQUALITIES BE REDUCED?

According to symbolic interactionists, prejudice and discrimination are learned, and what is learned can be unlearned. As sociologist Gale E. Thomas (1995:339) notes, "In the areas of race, ethnic, and human relations, we must learn compassion and also to accept and truly embrace, rather than merely tolerate, differences . . . through honest and open dialogue and through the formation of genuine friendships and personal experiential . . . exchanges and interactions with different individuals and groups across cultures." In other words, only individuals and groups at the grassroots level, not government and political leaders or academic elites, can bring about greater "racial" equality. Many authors point to anti-racist education as an important means of promoting change and building alliances (Bishop 2002; Fleras 2001; Fleras and Elliott 1999; Henry et al. 2000; Kivel 2002/1996; Robertson 1999).

How do functionalists suggest reducing racialized/ ethnic inequality? Because they believe a stable society requires smoothly functioning social institutions and people who have common cultural values and attitudes, functionalists suggest restructuring social institutions to reduce discrimination and diffuse racialized/ethnic conflict. According to sociologist Arnold Rose (1951), discrimination robs society of the talents and leadership abilities of many individuals, especially people of colour. Rose suggests that societies invest time and money fostering racialized/ethnic inclusion and eliminating institutionalized discrimination in education, housing, employment, and the criminal justice system. Employing a global perspective, functionalists argue that Canadian racialized discrimination should be reduced because it negatively affects diplomatic and economic relations with other nations made up of diverse racialized/ethnic groups (Feagin and Vera 1995).

From a conflict perspective, racialized and ethnic inequality can be reduced only through struggle and political action. Conflict theorists believe that inequality is based on the exploitation of subordinate groups by the dominant group, and that political intervention is necessary to bring about economic and social change. They agree that people should mobilize to put pressure on public officials. According to social activist Paul Kivel (2002/1996), racialized inequality will not be reduced until this country has significant national public support and leadership for addressing social problems directly and forcefully.

Feminists and anti-racist feminists advocate critical analysis that begins from the myriad standpoints and situated experiences of people. In addition to building on insights developed from various standpoints, they advocate rendering the connections between locations or standpoints visible so that silences can be heard, hypocrisies can be exposed, and myths can be evaporated. When White people become more clearly aware of their complicity in perpetuating racism and systems of domination, the foundation for solid alliances can be built. We must work toward those ends tirelessly if we intend to create a better place for all.

Whether or not the people of Canada will work for greater equality for all racialized/ethnic groups, one thing is certain: The Canadian population is rapidly becoming increasingly diverse. Statistics Canada released its latest analysis of 2001 census data on ethnic diversity in January, 2003, and stated that 18.4 percent of the population in Canada today is foreign-born. This is the highest rate of foreign-born Canadians since 1931, when 22.2 percent of the population was foreign-born. Foreign-born citizens are increasingly diverse, both culturally and linguistically, adding credence to the notion of a "Canadian mosaic," a concept that in recent decades has been little more than a catchphrase. For example, in 2001, four million people, or 13.4 percent of the population, claimed "visible minority" status. The population of Indigenous people in Canada has also been increasing, accounting for a total of 4.4 percent of the population (1.3 million people). In addition to responding to the challenges and richness accompanying increased diversity, we also need to deal with longstanding tensions between Indigenous peoples and White people based on a legacy of colonization. A vision of the future in Canada must be inclusive and be based on a collective endeavour to bring about the thorough eradication of racism at all levels of society—the individual, the institutional, and the societal. The time to begin is immediately.

WHAT CAN YOU DO?

■ Join (or start) a local anti-racism group and develop or take part in a "social action" mandate.

■ Learn how to address racist comments and jokes when you hear them. This can sometimes be accomplished by asking people for clarification about their comments and providing information counter to their stereotypes. This can also sometimes meaning just clearly telling the perpetrator that you find these remarks upsetting or unsettling and do not wish to hear them.

■ Join and/or monitor anti-racist discussion groups online such as **http://icare.to**.

■ Make an effort to get to know people from cultural groups different from your own. Take stock of your friendship circle right now. Do you regularly hang out with people who are different from you? If not, why do you think that is?

■ Attend cultural activities that are open to the public in order to get to know people different from you and find out about cultures different from your own. What things do you have in common? What things are different? What differences can you celebrate?

■ Do not assume that eating sushi or falafel or listening to "world music" gives you broad enough cross-cultural experience! It's often a beginning. Challenge yourself and others to broaden that knowledge.

■ To begin to learn how to unlearn racism, enroll in an anti-racism or diversity course or workshop.

■ Get educated about contemporary Indigenous issues such as sovereignty, land claims, treaty rights, and self-determination. Recognize that what you may read or hear in the media is usually only one perspective and that careful attention to information from legitimate sources on both (or more) sides of an issue may be something you need to research to find out.

■ Attend public forums on issues concerning immigration, refugees, and Indigenous people. Check into Canada's immigration and refugee policies and investigate recent immigration and refugee statistics to get a better understanding of what is fact and what is fiction.

■ Look at the cultural makeup of the boards and staff and volunteers at organizations you belong to or at places you frequent. Where there is diversity, what positions do people fill in your organization? Are there any non-White people in positions of authority or working on the front lines (e.g., visible to the public as soon as they walk in?).

■ Carefully read the policies of organizations you are part of. Are they inclusive? Are they welcoming of diversity? If you are unsure, contact a local anti-racism organization and have them come in to do a policy workshop, or consult with them, using your policies as examples.

■ Address stereotypical comments that may be made by your family and friends. Do not let any such remarks go by. Ask them for more information about a stereotype they hold, or why they believe the stereotype to be true; or, if they really believe the stereotype to be true, ask them what evidence they have that it is. Ask yourself what investment they may have, if any, in continuing to hold a certain view.

■ March in solidarity with people of all backgrounds when the opportunity to publicly declare your stance against racism arises. If you are a White person, demonstrate your position as an ally.

■ Write letters or editorials for your local or post-secondary newspaper, debunking stereotypes. Interview people of diverse groups.

■ If you are White, do not make your unlearning of racism the work of people of colour or Indigenous people. Make this your own project. Read. Talk to other White people who are grappling with these issues. Be reflective about the biases and stereotypes you hold and analyze them critically. Do not wallow in guilt. This serves no one. Become a force for positive change. "No one is free, until all are free."

■ Think about your social locations and determine which of your statuses confer privilege on you and which ones confer disadvantage. Think carefully about what you are willing to give up or to do to ensure equality for all people in Canada. This is a hard one!

SUMMARY

HOW DO RACIALIZED AND ETHNIC GROUPS DIFFER?

According to sociologists, racialized groups are defined on the basis of arbitrarily selected characteristics, and ethnic groups are defined on the basis of cultural or nationality characteristics. "Race" does not exist biologically but does exist as a socio-cultural phenomenon.

WHAT ARE MAJORITY AND MINORITY GROUPS?

When sociologists use the terms *majority group* and *minority group,* they are referring to power differentials. A majority (or dominant) group is one that is advantaged and has superior resources and rights in a society. A minority (or subordinate) group is one whose members, because of physical or cultural characteristics, are disadvantaged and subjected to unequal treatment by the dominant group and regard themselves as objects of collective discrimination.

HOW ARE PREJUDICE AND DISCRIMINATION RELATED?

Prejudice is a negative attitude that may or may not lead to discrimination, which is an action or practice of dominant group members that has a harmful impact on subordinate group members.

HOW DO INDIVIDUAL DISCRIMINATION AND INSTITUTIONAL DISCRIMINATION DIFFER?

Although individual discrimination and institutional discrimination are carried out by individuals, individual discrimination consists of one-on-one acts by members of the dominant group; institutional discrimination refers to actions and practices that are built into the day-to-day operations of large-scale organizations and social institutions.

HOW DO THE INTERACTIONIST AND FUNCTIONALIST PERSPECTIVES VIEW RACIALIZED AND ETHNIC RELATIONS?

Interactionists focus on microlevel issues, such as how people develop a racialized/ethnic identity and how individuals from diverse racialized/ethnic groups interact with each other. Functionalists focus on macrolevel issues, such as how entire groups of people assimilate or do not assimilate into the mainstream of the society.

WHAT ARE THE MAJOR CONFLICT EXPLANATIONS FOR RACIALIZED/ETHNIC INEQUALITY?

Conflict perspectives include class perspectives, split-labour market theory, internal colonialism, and racial formation theory.

HOW DO FEMINIST AND ANTI-RACIST FEMINIST THEORIES EXPLAIN RACIALIZED/ETHNIC INEQUALITY?

Feminists and anti-racist feminists advocate using critical analysis, beginning from the lived experiences of people. Additionally, they advocate an analysis that examines the intersections of locations, such as gender and ethnicity.

WHAT TYPES OF DISCRIMINATION HAVE BEEN EXPERIENCED BY MINORITY GROUP MEMBERS IN CANADA?

Minority group members have experienced every type of discrimination in Canada, from exclusion and expulsion to cultural genocide, slavery, and internment; from discrimination in hiring and retention and in housing to physical violence on a personal level. The legacy of racism for Indigenous people is particularly acute.

WHAT COMMONALITIES CAN BE SEEN IN THE EXPERIENCES OF ALL SUBORDINATE RACIALIZED/ETHNIC GROUPS?

Members of most subordinate racialized/ethnic groups have these commonalities in their experiences in Canada: (1) each has been the object of negative stereotypes and discrimination; (2) each has resisted oppression and continued to strive for a better life for their members and their children; and, (3) each has been the object of some government policy that has shaped its place (or lack thereof) in Canadian ethnic relations over the past four centuries.

KEY TERMS

amalgamation, p. 76
Anglo-conformity model, p. 76
anti-Semitism, p. 65
assimilation, p. 76
ethnic group, p. 62
ethnic pluralism, p. 76
ethnocentrism, p. 64
gendered racism, p. 78
genocide, p. 77
individual discrimination, p. 65
institutional discrimination, p. 65

internal colonialism, p. 77
internalized dominance, p. 64
majority (dominant) group, p. 63
minority (subordinate) group, p. 63
prejudice, p. 64
racialized group, p. 62
racism, p. 64
segregation, p. 76
social construct, p. 62
stereotypes, p. 65
theory of racial formation, p. 77

QUESTIONS FOR CRITICAL THINKING

1. Do you consider yourself part of the majority or dominant racialized/ethnic group or part of a minority or subordinate racialized/ethnic group in Canada? Consider what specific ways your life might be different if you were in another group.

2. Sociologists suggest that we acquire beliefs about our self and others through socialization. What specific messages have you received about your racialized/ethnic identity? What specific messages have you received about dealing with people from other racialized/ethnic groups? What hidden messages have you received about your cultural group and others?

3. Have all White Canadians, regardless of class, gender, or other characteristics, benefited from racialized prejudice and discrimination in Canada? Why or why not? In what ways have White people benefited from racism against non-Whites? In what ways have they been harmed by racism against non-Whites?

4. Compare recent depictions of Indigenous people, Black Canadians, Asian Canadians, and other racialized/ethnic groups in Canada in films, television shows, and advertisements. To what extent have we moved beyond the traditional stereotypes of those groups? To what extent have the stereotypes remained strong?

WEBLINKS

Assembly of First Nations (AFN)

www.afn.ca
The AFN represents over 630 First Nations communities in Canada. The national lobby organization is designed to present the views of the various First Nations through their leaders in areas such as Aboriginal and treaty rights, economic development, education, and health and housing, among others.

Canadian Ethnic Studies Journal

www.ss.ucalgary.ca/ces
A tri-annual interactive journal dedicated to the study of ethnicity, immigration, inter-group relations, and the history and cultural life of ethnic groups in Canada. It also offers book and film reviews, opinions, immigrants' memoirs, and other resources.

Canadian Race Relations Foundation

www.crr.ca
The CRRF seeks to strengthen the struggle for racial harmony, for the eradication of racism. The site presents the foundation's activities, research projects, and other publications.

Canadian Research Centres in the Field of Ethnic Relations

www.ceetum.umontreal.ca/english/links.htm
The Centre for Research and Interdisciplinary Training in the Ethnic Studies Field's links page leads to other Canadian and international research centres.

Crosspoint Antiracism

www.magenta.nl/crosspoint/cnd.html
Magenta is a foundation that combats racism and discrimination. Its Crosspoint is the internet's largest directory of links in the field of human rights and anti-racism.

Internet Centre Anti Racism Europe

http://icare.to
ICARE is the information disseminator for the European non-governmental organization community working in the field of anti-discrimination

National Antiracism Council of Canada

www.narc.freeservers.com
The National Antiracism Council of Canada brings together community-based organizations and individuals to ensure that the country actively contributes to the United Nations World Conference Against Racism and that work to fight racism is implemented locally.

The Nizkor Project

www.nizkor.org
The Nizkor project is devoted to shedding light on the phenomenon and history of hate (especially the Nazi Holocaust) and seeks to offer non-violent methods for combatting such hate.

UN World Conference Against Racism: NGO Virtual Forum

www.unwcar.freeservers.com
This site offers a discussion forum and an online community fighting to eliminate racism. Also available are a search engine and a variety of links.

4

GENDER
INEQUALITY

GENDER INEQUALITY AS A SOCIAL PROBLEM

    Defining Sex and Gender

    Biological and Social Bases for Gender Roles

    Box 4.1 Social Problems and Social Policy: *Trans*-gressing Gender Norms

GENDER INEQUALITY AND SOCIALIZATION

    Box 4.2 Social Problems in Global Perspective: Female Genital Surgery or Female Genital Mutilation?

    Gender Socialization by Parents

    Peers and Gender Socialization

    Education and Gender Socialization

    The Media and Gender Socialization

CONTEMPORARY GENDER INEQUALITY

    The Gendered Division of Paid Work

    The Wage Gap

    Sexual Harassment

    The Glass Ceiling and the Glass Escalator

    The Double Shift

PERSPECTIVES ON GENDER INEQUALITY

    The Interactionist Perspective

    The Functionalist Perspective

    Conflict Perspectives

    Feminist Perspectives

CAN GENDER INEQUALITY BE REDUCED?
WHAT CAN YOU DO?

Would you note that if I commit suicide today 89-12-06 it is not for economic reasons (for I have waited until I have exhausted all my financial means, even refusing jobs) but for political reasons. Because I have decided to send the feminists, who have always ruined my life, to their Maker. For seven years life has brought me no joy and being totally blasé, I have decided to put an end to those viragos . . . Even if the Mad Killer epithet will be attributed to me by the media, I consider myself a rational erudite that only the arrival of the Grim Reaper has forced to take extreme acts. . . . The feminists have always enraged me. They want to keep the advantages of women . . . while seizing for themselves those of men . . . .

Partial text of the suicide letter left by the shooter who killed 14 women on December 6th, 1989, at Montreal's École Polytechnique. The letter was followed by a list of names of 19 women and the following appended note . . . "The lack of time (because I started too late) has allowed these radical feminists to survive." (Quoted in Malette and Chalouh 1991:180–181)

The killing of 14 women in Montreal, Quebec, on December 6, 1989, shocked the nation. Most news reports in the days and weeks following cited the act as that of a madman—an isolated, bizarre event carried out by a deranged individual. While there can be no doubt that the act was extreme, feminists and other analysts continue to question this individualistic analysis, pointing instead to the pervasiveness of sexism in a patriarchal society, a pervasiveness they say creates a climate for actions such as this, and other forms of violence against women, to play out. **Sexism is the subordination of one sex, female, based on the assumed superiority of the other sex, male**, while **patriarchy refers to a hierarchical system of social organization in which cultural, political, and economic structures are controlled by men.** According to some social analysts, problems of sexism have been overblown: Sexism was a problem in the past when women were under-represented in organizations and the paid labour force generally; now, however, women have made significant inroads in education and employment. In 2003, for example, 62 percent of women aged 15 and over were employed for pay, up from 30 percent in 1961 (Nelson 2006:215). Many more women today have gained post-secondary degrees and are employed in an increasing variety of professional fields; women are also increasingly represented among the self-employed. With increases such as these, some people believe that women should just be happy and stop complaining

about the "past." Many feel that, while the events of December 6, 1989, were tragic, conditions that may (assuming a social versus an individualized analysis) have caused such an event to occur are over now—they are historical conditions that we have overcome in recent years. These people believe that today women and men in Canada are equal.

However, despite women's advances in the labour market and education and so on, gender inequality persists. Nowhere is this more clearly illustrated than in the persistence of violence against women. As Charlotte Bunch, past president of MATCH, a Canadian NGO, stated in a public speech in the early 1990s, "Violence against women is the most pervasive human rights abuse in the world today. If any other group in society were as systematically battered and killed in order to be controlled, it would be a civil emergency . . . the war on women must end."

The B.C. Ministry of Community Services reports that every minute of every day, a woman or girl is sexually assaulted somewhere in Canada—as of 1999, 60 percent of those assaulted are under the age of 18 (B.C. Ministry of Community Services 2006). The 1993 National Violence Against Women Survey conducted by Statistics Canada represents (still) the only comprehensive report on women's experience of violence. The survey, which asked a sample of 12,300 women to report their lifetime experiences of assault, sexual assault, and sexual harassment, found that most assaults go unreported to police. Only 14 percent of all assaults had been reported; wife assaults were reported at a rate of 26 percent. Fifty-one percent of Canadian women had experienced at least one incidence of physical or sexual assault since the age of 16. Forty-five percent of these women were assaulted by men known to them, and an additional 23 percent were assaulted by a stranger. Thirty-nine percent of women experienced sexual assault; 34 percent of women experienced non-sexual assault. Some of the sexual assaults and most of the non-sexual assaults were perpetrated by the women's spouses (Johnson 1996:49).

Every week in Canada, a woman is murdered by her boyfriend or spouse (B.C. Ministry of Community Services 2006). In a study of 448 women's shelters and transition houses in Canada, in a one-year period ending March 31, 2000, 57,182 women and 39,177 of their children were admitted (Dauvergne and Johnson 2001). Forty-one percent of the children were under age 5, and 32 percent were between the ages of 5 and 9. A previous study of 413 shelters, conducted in 1997–98, found that 47 962 women and 42 830 children had been admitted (Trainor 1999). A further study of women who experience violence found that one million Canadian children have witnessed violence by their fathers against their mothers (Fitzgerald 1999).

In 2000, a national study of 166 police departments was conducted. Researchers found that of all *crimes against the person,* females represented the vast majority of victims in cases of sexual assault (86 percent), criminal harassment (e.g. "stalking"; 78 percent), and kidnapping/hostage taking or abduction (67 percent; Status of Women Canada 2005). Seventy-seven percent of female victims were victimized by someone they knew. Clearly, violence against women by men is a tremendous social problem linked to sexism.

Just as women are not viewed as equal to men, not all women are viewed as equal to one another. For example, the murders of the 14 women in Montreal sparked annual December 6th memorials to raise awareness of the violence against women that continues today. The White Ribbon campaign, begun and carried out by men to raise awareness of violence against women, continues to gain support each year. A national monument in Vancouver's Thornton Park commemorates women's deaths at the hands of male violence. Women's groups from Vancouver's downtown East Side question why the disappearances of at least 68 Vancouver women since 1983 have not created the same kind of public concern. No one criticizes the increased attention to issues of violence against women, but many point out the difference in public interest and attention the two groups of women have received. Analysts highlight the class, ethnic, and lifestyle differences between the groups; for instance, the Montreal Massacre, as it quickly came to be called, involved 14 young, White, middle-class women, most of whom were enrolled as students in engineering at the "Poly." The disappearances in Vancouver have mainly involved women believed to be drug users and/or sex-trade workers, many of whom are also Indigenous. These women are commonly viewed as "disposable" people, societal "throwaways." In a critique of the way the 68 disappearances have been handled by the RCMP to date, John Lowman of Simon Fraser University's Department of Criminology stated in a February 2002 newspaper interview, "If [68] women in any other category, whether housewives or women of a certain age or anyone else, went missing, believe me, the police reaction would have been entirely different" (Matas 2002).

Violence against women in its many forms is one result of sexism and gender inequality. Other manifestations of sexism that are discussed on the following pages include inequalities in the paid labour force and in domestic labour. The ways that gender socialization perpetuates these inequalities is highlighted, as are various theories for analyzing gender inequality.

GENDER INEQUALITY AS A SOCIAL PROBLEM

Similar to the ways that racialized ethnic group members experience discrimination based on supposed innate characteristics, women experience discrimination based on their sex. Since 51 percent of the people in Canada are female, women constitute a numerical majority. However, they are sometimes referred to as the country's largest minority group, because as a group, they do not possess as much wealth, power, or prestige as men. As a telling example involving income alone, for all full-time workers in Canada in 1967, the first year the data were gathered on male to female earnings, women earned 58.4 percent of what men earned. In 1991, women earned 69.4 percent, and in 1995, this increased to 73.0 percent. But by 2000, the earnings differential had decreased again, to 72.0 percent; and by 2003, it was 71.0 percent (Nelson 2006:227; Statistics Canada 2002a; Statistics Canada 2006e). The differences between women's and men's earnings are more striking when we examine all earners' wages, since women are more often only employed part-time. Sometimes this is by choice, though often it is not by choice but is the result of persistent gender stereotypes that women's incomes are "pin money" or otherwise merely "supplemental" to men's. In 1991, for all Canadian earners, full- and part-time, women earned 61.3 percent of men's earnings. In 1995, a banner year, they earned 64.8 percent, and in 2000, women earned 64.0 percent of what men earned (Statistics Canada 2002a). More recent data state that women today earn approximately 61 percent of what men earn (Fleras 2005:115). If the pattern from past decades continues to hold, we cannot expect much change.

Defining Sex and Gender

What is the difference between sex and gender? Although many people use these terms interchangeably, sociologists believe that there are significant differences in their meanings. *Sex* **refers to the biological differences between females and males.** Our sex is the first label we receive in life and is an ascribed status. Before birth or at the time of birth, we are identified as either male or female on the basis of our sex organs and genes. Despite the fact that many children do not exhibit the genitalia or chromosomes consistent with either a male or female designation, most people act as though there are only two dichotomous and "opposite" sexes. For example, when a child is born *intersexed*, that is **with either unrecognizably male or female genitalia or with both male and female genitalia**, we surgically alter the child to fit the two-sex model of reality that is currently in vogue. Within the two-sex model, males are seen as the central or standard sex, against which females, the "opposite" sex, are measured. This practice of **putting males at the centre** is known as *androcentricity*. As an illustration of the fluidity of our notions, even in biology, in the past, Westerners had a one-sex model of humanity, the one sex being male. Females and their bodies were viewed as imperfect or flawed versions of the male. Historian Thomas Laqueur (1992:4), in a book called *Making Sex*, states that several early "scientists," such as Galen and Herophilus,

> demonstrated at length that women were essentially men in whom a lack of vital heat—of perfection—had resulted in the retention, inside, of structures that in the male are visible without ... In this world the vagina is imagined as an interior penis, the labia as foreskin, the uterus as scrotum, and the ovaries as testicles ... for two centuries, the ovary ... had not even a name of its own.

Scholars and lay people alike were "caught up in the female-as-male model" (see Figure 4.1) until approximately 1800, when many began to insist that there "were fundamental differences between the male and female sexes" (Laqueur 1992:5).

Following, then, from a two-sex model, *gender* **refers to the culturally and socially constructed differences between females and males based on meanings, beliefs, and practices that a group or society associates with**

FIGURE 4.1   The One-Sex Model

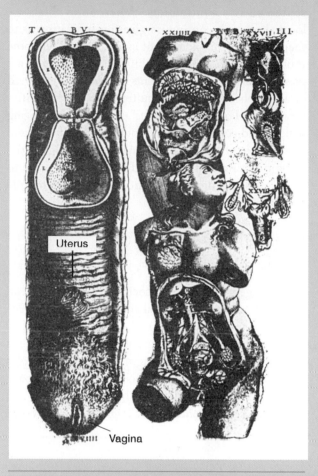

Source: From Making Sex: Body and Gender from the Greeks to Freud, *by Thomas Laqueur, 1992, Cambridge: Harvard University Press. Originally published in Andreas Vesalius,* De Humani Corporis Fabrica *(Basel, 1543).*

femininity or masculinity. For many people, being *masculine* means being aggressive, independent, and not showing emotions, and being *feminine* means the opposite—being passive, dependent, and emotional. Understanding the difference between sex and gender is important, according to sociologists, because what many people think of as *sex differences*—for example, being aggressive or independent—are actually socially constructed *gender differences* based on widely held assumptions about men's and women's attributes (Gailey 1987). In other words, males are supposed to be aggressive and independent not because they have male sex organs but because that is how people in this society think males should act. Psychologist S. L. Bem (1974) talked about masculinity and femininity being represented on two continuums. Where individuals are located on each continuum gives an indication as to their personal combination of masculine and feminine traits. Again, though, masculinity and femininity are presented as the central elements in a dichotomy instead of as simply two out of a multiplicity of possibilities for genders. For example, "trans" people are challenging widely held conceptions of gender (see Box 4.1), and queer theorists (see Chapter 6) are challenging the appropriateness of long-held binary categories to encompass and describe the fluidity of gender many people experience.

Biological and Social Bases for Gender Roles

To study gender inequality, sociologists begin with an examination of the biological and social bases for *gender roles*, which are the rights, responsibilities, expectations, and relationships of women and men in a society (Benokraitis and Feagin 1995). Gender roles have both a biological and a social basis and, as a concept, need to be problematized in terms of power and inequality. The biological basis for gender roles is rooted in the chromosomal and hormonal differences between men and women. When a child is conceived, the mother contributes an X chromosome, and the father contributes either an X chromosome (which produces a female embryo) or a Y chromosome (which produces a male embryo). As the embryo's male or female sex glands develop, they secrete the appropriate hormones (more androgens for males, more estrogens for females), which circulate through the bloodstream, producing sexual differentiation in the external genitalia, the internal reproductive tract, and possibly some areas of the brain. At birth, medical personnel and family members distinguish male from female infants by their *primary sex characteristics,* the genitalia used in the reproductive process. At puberty, hormonal differences in females and males produce *secondary sex characteristics,* the physical traits that, along with the reproductive organs, identify a person's sex. Females develop secondary sex characteristics such as menstruation, more prominent breasts, wider hips and narrower shoulders, and a layer of fatty tissue throughout the body. Male secondary sex characteristics include the development of larger genitals, a more muscular build, a deeper voice, more body and facial hair, and greater height. Although both males and females have androgens and estrogens, it is the relative proportion of each hormone that triggers masculine or feminine physical traits.

SOCIAL PROBLEMS AND SOCIAL POLICY

BOX 4.1 *Trans*-gressing Gender Norms

On October 15, 2002, directors and chairs at the University of Victoria received a memo from the Office of the President. The University of Victoria president, along with the vice-president, academic, and the new dean of graduate studies, were advising the university community that the dean of graduate studies, also a tenured professor in the Department of Sociology, wished henceforth to be known as a man. The memo communicated the upper administration's "unequivocal personal support for this decision and . . . a great appreciation for his valued contributions to the university" and called for people's understanding and consideration of the wishes of the Dean to now "live as a man." Aaron (formerly Holly) Devor is the well-known Canadian author of many publications on gender and transgender issues, including the books *Gender Blending: Confronting the Limits of Duality* (1989) and *FTM: Female to Male Transsexuals in Society* (1997).

Aaron Devor's experience of "unequivocal" institutional support, economic well-being, and a high-status, high-profile position is precisely what we wish to see achieved for all "trans" people. The unfortunate reality, however, is that this experience is not at all typical among transgendered people. A recent study by "trans" activist Emilia L. Lombardi and her colleagues (2001) documents that violence and economic discrimination are more common responses to gender nonconformity. Several other studies confirm that "trans" people experience high rates of prejudice, marginalization, discrimination, harassment, stalking, and other violence (Appelbe 2001; Donavon 2001; MacDonald 1998/2000; Nangeroni 2001; Towle and Morgan 2002). In addition to the

Dr. Aaron Devor, 2003

external threats, pervasive victimization has been shown to lead to a higher incidence of depression, substance abuse, and suicide by "trans" people (Donavon 2001; Lombardi et al. 2001; Nangeroni 2001). As with homophobia and biphobia (see Chapter 6), it is important to remember that it is not the fact of being a transsexual or transgendered person that causes ill health and heightened risks, but rather, it is transphobia, or the hatred and fear of "trans" people, that does. Sadly, transphobia may come as much from gays and lesbians as it does from heterosexuals.

"Trans" people have begun to speak out about their experiences and the issues that they face living in a transphobic culture. As Nick Matte, a graduate student studying the history of gender and sexuality, points out,

> When we're thinking about the barriers faced by "trans" people, what's really sad is that people often have to spend so much time educating themselves and breaking down the barriers they help to create, that it's easy to forget to make time to celebrate the fact that "trans" people have already been breaking those barriers down for them/ourselves. (2003, author's files)

Recently, Tina Donavon (2001:20), a member of Senior Action in a Gay Environment (SAGE)/Queens, described a little of her experience coming out as a transgendered woman in the mid-1970s:

> I am a woman, 61 years old and transgender. I have lived the last 27 years as a woman, much to the chagrin of my parents and some friends. They did not understand the nature of my struggles since early childhood. I knew all along that I was female, not a male. When I revealed this information to my parents, my father said I was "nuts" and my mother cried. They both thought that my gender identification was a result of their failing to raise me in the correct way.

"Trans" issues have increasingly come into public focus over the last decade. Ethnographic research, largely by anthropologists, has been used to provide supposed cross-cultural "proofs" that the "Western binary gender system is neither universal nor innate" (Towle and Morgan 2002:469). In many publications, examples of people who belong to a "third gender" are presented: the Hijras in India, the so-called Berdache[1] of North America, the female husbands of West Africa, the Xanith of the Arabian Peninsula, and the Sambia of Papua New Guinea. While these people around the world provide interesting examples of a variety of socially constructed roles and statuses, they cannot just be slotted unproblematically into the North American context; one must carefully examine the cultural and historical contexts from which these groups spring. As anthropologists Evan B. Towle and Lynn M. Morgan (2002:490) point out,

> Invoking "third gender" examples in an oversimplified way or citing them out of context to underwrite Western social agendas is an unwitting kind of neocolonial (or at least ethnocentric) appropriation that distorts the complexity and reality of other people's lives.

The term *transgender* was originally coined by Virginia Prince in a 1970s conference presentation titled "The Transsexual and His Wife" (MacDonald 1998/2000). We use and have used in the past a great many terms to refer to "trans" people: transgendered, transsexual, transvestite, butch, femme, drag king, drag queen, female to male (F to M), male to female (M to F), intersex, third gender, non-op, pre-op, post-op, androgyne, epicene, and two-spirited—to name only a few. Providing definitions of a range of "trans" experiences is beyond the scope of this feature. Moreover, it is not necessarily appropriate, given that an often common thread of "trans" experiences is precisely the challenge to identity-based categories and to the way we think about identity. Political scientist Eleanor MacDonald (1998/2000:284), for example, provides this provocative notion:

> What transgender identity specifically problematizes is identity itself. Transgender identity is about identity experienced as problematic; the experience of being transgender problematizes the relationship of the self to the body, and the self to others. In doing so, it also

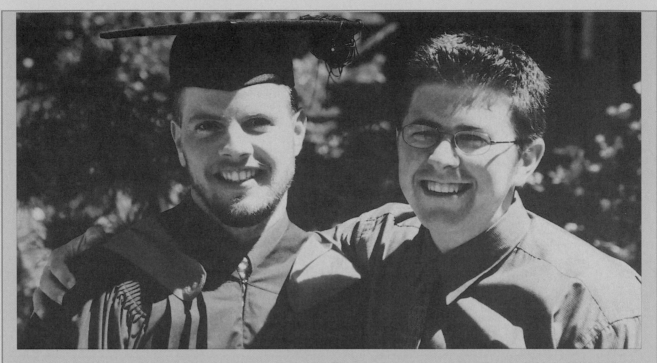

This young F to M couple are celebrating graduation from university. They have to contend not only with transphobia in their daily lives, but also with homophobia.

problematizes issues of identity boundaries, stability and coherence . . . . What is radical, then, to the definition of "transgender" is its origin in problem, a disjunction between one's feelings of who one is or is not, and how one is (or has once been) perceived, recognized, and understood by others.

The existence of "trans" people, "trans" bodies, and "trans" identities may be useful in understanding all gender relations, the normative and the transgressive. Towle and Morgan (2002) suggest that through an interrogation of "trans" we may be able to get at what the differences between men and women really are: Through what acts is gender identity communicated? What consequences are there for social interactions if one fails to communicate a gender identity? and, What is the meaning of inhabiting a gendered body? David Valentine and Riki Anne Wilchins subvert the typical lines of questioning with their point that "[bodies that] are suspect . . . are not what have to be explained. Rather, the requirement that they explain themselves should itself be investigated" (in Towle and Morgan 2002:491–492). Konnor Brett, a recent sociology and women's studies graduate, adds, "I'm not sure that my transitioning broke down many aspects of the binary gender system in our society as a whole. I do know that I see my future with happiness" (2003, author's files).

The Canadian general public has responded to "trans" issues in a range of ways, from support, to confusion, to intolerance or hostility. Recent movies such as *Transamerica* and *Kinky Boots* have given the mainstream more balanced insights in some of the issues faced by "trans" people. While many people are supportive and may even constitute a "silent majority" in some sectors of the population, MacDonald (1998/2000) outlines three general responses to "trans" people that she has observed and that can present problems. One response has been hostility and/or exclusion in the form of denouncing "trans" people as dangerous to progressive enterprises, such as women's centres, for example. "Trans" people, particularly F to M, have been viewed by some as traitors or turncoats, while M to F have been treated as deceptive, as "Trojan horses," and as violators of women-only spaces. It is interesting to note both the essentialism and the sexism inherent in this response: Essentialist because "trans" people are stereotyped a certain way, using the sex they were born into; and sexist because women are often portrayed, through sexist stereotypes, as "sneaky deceivers." Further, females who transition may be seen as "switching sides," suddenly developing all the characteristics supposedly attributed to males, including a complete inability to understand women's concerns, issues, or experiences.

A second response has been to medicalize "trans" people's experiences, seemingly rendering them "apolitical." Finally, a third response has been to "celebrate trans identity as emblematic of the subversiveness of post modern theory"—where

```
        8th Annual GROOVEFEST 2003—Saturday,
February 15—Vertigo Nightclub
Tickets: $9 advance/$11 at the door/
Doors open at 9 pm.
        Groovefest is an annual event promot-
ing and facilitating the self-expression and
empowerment of individuals and communities
who do not fit dominant, imposed, standards
of beauty. An evening of high energy, fun-
filled and politically charged performances,
Groovefest sets out to challenge mainstream
beauty standards, the fashion industry, con-
sumerism, white supremacy, ableism, sexism,
homophobia, racism, transphobia, ageism,
classism, fatphobia and all other forms of
inequality.
        This year's Groovefest will feature a
wide variety of performances, including drag
acts, non-traditional fashion features (the
infamous "anti-fashion" show), poetry,
dance, spoken word, skits and surely a few
surprises. The evening will end with a fine
round of booty shakin' tunes provided by DJs
Mama Miche and Marlee. All proceeds go to
local groups working for social change, and
this year's beneficiaries are P.E.E.R.S and
the S.E.X.Y. Queer Youth Group. This is a
licensed event.
```

of them. We need to contest, rather than support ideologies that assert that queer, gay, lesbian, bisexual, questioning, and transgender kids are pathological.

In the study about the extent to which "trans" people are at risk for violence and discrimination, Lombardi and colleagues (2001:99) report that "trans" youth are exposed to heightened risks of "attempted suicide, substance abuse, unsafe sexual practices, of being exposed to STDs (including HIV), of being homeless, dropping out of school, and of experiencing high levels of distress, as well as experiencing many forms of discrimination, harassment and violence." Widespread transphobia and its devastating consequences indicate that a series of policies is required to create ways to protect "trans" Canadians' fundamental human rights, such as,

- Tracking all incidences of violence against members of "trans" communities in order to better understand the nature of these hate crimes.
- Designing and implementing education for law enforcement personnel, social service workers, and other professionals who come into contact with members of "trans" communities, so that they can recognize issues and lend assistance.
- As with other "hate crimes" in Canada, ensuring that penalties for hate-motivated crimes against members of "trans" communities are enhanced (e.g., made more severe). This will require the addition of gender identity and/or presentation to be added to hate crimes legislation.
- Ensuring that unless it is absolutely necessary to know, "sex" should not have to be reported to bureaucracies, employers, and other officials. As with other personal information, such as age, sexual orientation, or ability, knowing someone's sex is usually unnecessary, and requiring this information could violate human rights. To require this information complicates the lives of "trans" people unnecessarily and may even set them up for negative or harmful experiences.
- Where possible, providing gender-neutral washroom spaces, either in addition to male and female washrooms or place of them. We often provide gender-neutral washroom space in public places already, so there is no logical reason why "trans" people should not also be afforded this measure of privacy. As the public becomes more relaxed about co-ed worlds, many public spaces, such as restaurants, are already doing away with gendered designations. (Appelbe 2001; Devor 2003; Lombardi et al. 2001).

In addition to legislated change, measures may be taken by communities wishing to celebrate the diversity and richness of a society that is working to transcend gender norms. In Victoria, B.C., for example, several community groups, along

"gender doesn't [or shouldn't] matter" (MacDonald 1998/2000:282, 285). This can create a lot of inappropriate pressure for "trans" people to think and feel and act in certain ways.

While this third response is more supportive, it does not adequately capture the complexity of lived experiences of "trans" identities. "Trans" people may "playfully or seriously" choose identities that are grounded firmly in gender-stereotypical notions of masculinity or femininity. What is sometimes overlooked is that a sense of relief and pleasure can accompany the ability to identify with a recognizable and easily understood gender, especially for those for whom a gender identity has been denied or has felt uncertain. Additionally, becoming firmly situated within a recognizable gender may be necessary from a strategic perspective, as many physicians and psychiatrists view this as the "proof" necessary to endorse a sex change or to dispense hormones.

Political scientist and activist Paisley Currah (2001:192) takes a different stance, stating that it is imperative that "trans" (and non-"trans") people push beyond the gender stereotypes that "reinforce heteronormative notions":

[rather] we need to give sustenance to gender-variant traditions, to preserve them, to make sure they get reproduced, not play into the larger ideological erasure

with some university campus groups, organize an annual "Groovefest" in February, the proceeds of which go to selected not-for-profit, anti-oppression groups (see advertisement on previous page).

While "trans" issues are often misunderstood and marginalized (even writing this feature as a "boxed item" instead of as part of the "regular" text may illustrate this fact), "trans" issues are finally coming into the mainstream in positive and empowering ways. As you read at the beginning of this box, some "trans" people are experiencing support in their workplaces. Many "trans" people experience support for their transitions through their relationships with family, friends, and peers. One "trans" person, in a relationship with another "trans" person, related that "the most common question we get asked is about family support and I have to say that both our families love and support us in all aspects" (2003, author's files). Many "trans" people also report feelings of joy in having the ability to finally feel as though they are living authentically, in ways they have chosen. As one undergraduate student recently stated:

> Before I knew about transitioning, I basically had accepted my life would be lived in a depressed state.

Since my transition, I have been constantly amazed about what I was missing. I feel truly happy and balanced for the first time in my life. (2003, author's files)

These positive reports do not in any way diminish the ongoing need to be vigilant about ridding Canadian society of prejudice and discrimination against "trans" people, but they do help us to see that life as a "trans" person is not all negative and, in fact, can be cause for celebration. As one "trans" person concluded, "What you see in the media is only going to give you the miserable story" (2003, author's files). Clearly, there is much more to "trans" life than that.

Note: [1]Use of the term "Berdache" reflects the mistaken assumptions about same-sex relations among Indigenous peoples made by Europeans at contact. The word "Berdache" originated as a Persian term meaning "slave youth." It later came to mean a "kept boy" in a gay relationship. Neither meaning depicts any North American Indigenous traditions or practices, nor was either term accepted as appropriate by Indigenous people. The continued widespread use of the term demonstrates, if nothing else, the pervasiveness of colonialism (Roscoe 1995, in Goldie 2001:10).

Is there something in the biological and genetic makeup of boys or girls that makes them physically aggressive or passive? As sociologist Judith Lorber (1994:39) notes, "When little boys run around noisily, we say 'Boys will be boys,' meaning that physical assertiveness has to be in the Y chromosome because it is manifest so early and so commonly in boys." Similarly, when we say "She throws like a girl" we mean, according to Lorber, that "she throws like a female child, a carrier of XX chromosomes." However, Lorber questions these widely held assumptions: "But are boys universally, the world over, in every social group, a vociferous, active presence? Or just where they are encouraged to use their bodies freely, to cover space, take risks, and play outdoors at all kinds of games and sports?"

According to Lorber, boys and girls who are given tennis racquets at the age of three and encouraged to become champions tend to use their bodies similarly. Even though boys gradually gain more shoulder and arm strength and are able to sustain more concentrated bursts of energy, after puberty girls acquire more stamina, flexibility, and lower-body strength. Coupled with training and physical exercise, these traits enhance, compensate for or override different physical capabilities (Lorber 1994). Thus, the girl who throws "like a girl" is probably a product of her culture and time: She has had more limited experience than many boys at throwing the ball and engaging in competitive games at an early age. Still, the implication that social roles "are an unproblematic reflection of biology (sex)" is analytically flawed (Marshall 2000:24).

The social basis for gender roles is known as the gender belief system or *gender ideology*—**ideas of masculinity and femininity that are held to be valid in a given society at a specific historical time** (Lorber 1994). Gender ideology is reflected in what sociologists refer to as the *gendered division of labour*—**the process whereby productive tasks are separated on the basis of gender.** How do people determine what constitutes "women's work" or "men's work"? Evidence from cross-cultural studies shows that social factors, more than biological factors, influence the gendered division of labour in societies. In poor agricultural societies, for example, women work in the fields and tend to their families' daily needs; men typically produce and market cash crops but spend no time on household work. In industrialized nations, an increasing proportion of women are in paid employment but still have heavy household and family responsibilities. For example, in Canada in 2005, men spent 2.4 hours per day on housework and other unpaid work while women spent 4.3 hours per day (Statistics Canada 2006b). Across cultures, women's domain is viewed as the private and domestic, and men's domain is viewed as the public, economic, and political. This difference in how labour is divided, how workers are rewarded, and what cultural value is accorded to paid versus unpaid labour affects access to scarce resources such as wealth, power, and prestige. Given their domain, men have greater access to wealth, power, and prestige, a situation that leads to gender inequality in other areas.

To explain gender inequality, some sociologists use a *gender role approach,* focusing on how the socialization process contributes to male domination and female subordination. Other sociologists use a *structural approach,* focusing on how large-scale, interacting, and enduring social structures determine the boundaries of individual behaviour. Let's look first at how socialization can perpetuate gender stereotyping and inequality.

GENDER INEQUALITY AND SOCIALIZATION

Numerous sociological studies have found that gender-role stereotyping is one of the enduring consequences of childhood gender socialization. Socialization into appropriate "feminine" behaviour makes women less likely than men to pursue male-dominated activities, and socialization into appropriate "masculine" behaviour makes men more likely than women to pursue leadership roles in education, religion, business, politics, and other spheres of public life (Peterson and Runyan 1993). We learn our earliest and often most long-lasting beliefs about gender roles from a variety of *agents of socialization*—people, groups, or institutions that teach us what we need to know to participate in society. Among the most significant agents of socialization are parents, peers, the education system, and the media.

SOCIAL PROBLEMS IN GLOBAL PERSPECTIVE

BOX 4.2   Female Genital Surgery or Female Genital Mutilation?

It is estimated that up to 140 million women have undergone the practice of genital cutting, with each year 2 million more women (6000 per day) joining their ranks (F.L. Gordon 2000; Seager 1997; World Health Organization (WHO) 2000). The practice, variously known as female genital surgery, female genital mutilation, or female circumcision, depending in part on the feelings of the person describing the practice, has been performed in at least 30 countries worldwide, including Canada, Europe, Australia, and the United States, for as long as 6000 years (Ward 1999). Surgeries are typically performed on girls aged from 5 to 13 but have been performed on days-old infants and adult women as well (WHO 2000).

There are at last three distinct types of surgery performed, all often confusingly referred to as "circumcision." Circumcision, the least severe and least practised, refers to the removal of the prepuce, or hood, of the clitoris. A similar practice, called

sunna, meaning "religious duty" in Arabic, refers to the removal of the sheath, or tip, of the clitoris. Excision, or clitoridectomy, practised in approximately 80 percent of surgeries, refers to the removal of all or some of the clitoris and all or part of the inner genitals (*labia minora*). The most severe form of surgery is infibulation, which refers to the removal of the clitoris, the labia minora, and most or all of the outer genitals (*labia majora*). The vulva is then fastened together through stitching or with thorns, and a reed or other small object is inserted in order to allow for urination and menstruation as the surgery heals. The girl's legs may then be bound from hip to ankle for up to 40 days to allow scar tissue to form (F.L. Gordon 2000:270; WHO 2000; Wood 2001:322–323).

Surgeries are nearly always carried out by older women, in less-than-sterile surroundings, using special knives, scissors, pieces of glass, or tin or razor blades (F.L. Gordon 2000; Wood

2001). Further, the people performing the surgeries rarely have medical training, and no anesthesia is used (Ward 1999; WHO 2000; Wood 2001).

Westerners decry the custom of female genital cutting as "barbaric" and call for its immediate end. Many people within cultures who practise it criticize Westerners' approaches to the issue as "colonialism in disguise" (El Saadawi 1980, cited in Ward 1999:252). Those who support it say that it is a time-honoured cultural tradition that Westerners have no business involving themselves in: "Stop groping about in our panties" was a comment heard from many African women at the 1985 United Nations Decade for Women Conference in Kenya when the issue was debated (quoted in Ward 1999:252). In contrast, many women who do not support the practice retort that "Torture is not culture" (Walker 1993, quoted in Ward 1999:252).

There are many reasons given for the continuation of support for female genital surgery, reasons that are viewed by some as merely a means to mask and/or justify patriarchal practices. Here, Frances L. Gordon, a travel writer specializing in Africa, (2000:271); Julia Wood, a communications scholar (2001:325); and the World Health Organization (2000) bring several such reasons to light:

- *Hygiene*: Removal of the genitals is thought to foster cleanliness.
- *Aesthetics:* Women's genitals are considered unclean and unattractive.
- *Myth*: Some believe that a woman's genitals will continue to grow if not removed, while some believe that a woman will be unable to conceive, or if she does conceive, some believe that the resulting child will be murdered by coming into contact with the clitoris.
- *Social solidarity*: Engaging in the operation means a woman will be accepted as a fully participating member of her culture and will be able to reap the rewards of womanhood in that culture (namely marriage and children and a sense of belonging).
- *Social control of sexuality*: Operations such as this are said to lessen or completely extinguish women's ability to experience sexual pleasure or to experience orgasm; therefore, it may be less likely for her to practise infidelity. Additionally, in some countries where polygamy is practised, it is said to result in many wives making fewer sexual demands on only one husband. Where infibulation is practised, it is clear if the woman has been sexually active previous to her marriage; thus, men can be assured of marrying virgins. This is important because virginity "reflects the moral prestige of the girl's family, ensures a good market value for the bride and establishes the paternity of future children." Lastly, infibulation, in particular, may also heighten men's sexual pleasure.

These operations often result in a variety of possible physical complications, such as hemorrhaging; scarring; painful urination, menstruation, intercourse, and childbirth; and infections and death (estimated to occur as much as 15 percent of the time); there are psychological costs reported as well: for example, depression, anxiety, and low self-esteem (F. L. Gordon 2000:271; WHO 2000).

It may seem clear that female genital surgery is a barbaric practice that should be halted. However, some critics of this view suggest that rather than deflecting our attention elsewhere, we need to consider our own cultural practices that result in body modification, pain, and death. Male circumcision, while similar to female circumcision, is rarely viewed as barbaric. This practice, the removal of the sheath, or prepuce, of the penis, demonstrates no clear health or cleanliness advantages yet is often performed routinely at birth in Canada. The age at which this typically happens is what sets it apart, say some. Additionally, male circumcision does not adversely impact on men's sexual pleasure (Wood 2001).

Increasingly, younger and younger women (mainly) are availing themselves of dieting pills, rigid exercise regimes, cosmetic surgeries, tummy tucks, breast implants, and the like, all in search of the perfect body (Abu-Laban et al. 2001; Boddy 1991, in Ward, 1999; Nelson 2006). Girls in elementary school, as young as age 7, report being "too fat," and rates of anorexia and bulimia, disproportionately affecting females (85 to 97 percent) are on the rise (Nelson 2006; Nelson and Robinson 2002). The typical anorexic or bulimic is White, middle-class, and under the age of 25 (Nelson and Robinson 2002:146). A recent study of 2279 Ontario girls, aged 10–14, found that nearly one-third (31 percent) of healthy weight girls described themselves as "too fat," and 29 percent were currently dieting. 10.5 percent had disturbed eating patterns, with 4 percent binge-eating regularly and 1.5 self-inducing vomiting (Nelson 2006; Picard 2004). A 1990 Saskatoon study of high school girls found that 76 percent diet, 17 percent vomit, and 12 percent use diet aids (Abu-Laban et al. 2001). With the profusion of extremely thin media icons today, as compared even with 1990, it is certain these numbers would be higher today. As sociologists Adie Nelson and Barry W. Robinson (2002:146) state, "The vast majority of North American women engage, to some degree, in a regimen of self-restraint and dieting . . . . Women's concern with dieting within North America has become a 'normative obsession' and a 'cultural obsession'." There are a number of websites aimed at teens that teach girls how to achieve the ultra thin "look" that is in fashion today, websites that are increasingly being blocked by parents and school districts (author's files). Moreover, we teach girls to "put on their faces" using make-up and to wear precariously high heels and impractical, tight clothing that restricts their freedom of movement (Abu-Laban et al. 2001).

If beauty standards in Canada are narrow, they are also racialized, with Whiteness being the beauty norm (healthily tanned Whiteness, that is). We find non-White women using products that will straighten hair or lighten skin and undergoing surgery to "Westernize" their eye shape, nose shape and size, lips, body size, and so on (Abu-Laban et al., 2001:123; Nelson and Robinson, 2002:145).

Given Canadian culture's preoccupation with thinness, youthfulness, restrictive fashions, and strict standards of facial beauty, can we truly say that we do not engage in harmful practices, practices that even result in death (e.g., diet pills, poisoning from breast implants, and so on)? In addition, female genital surgery was practised in North America and Europe as well. Clitoridectomies were seen by many physicians as appropriate cures for masturbation, "nymphomania," and orgasm in women, even as late as the 20th

century; and "until the mid-1940s, clitoridectomies were routine for female patients in many mental hospitals" (Wood 2001:323).

People contrasting these practices with those in countries practising genital surgery today point out that unlike girls in those countries, Canadian girls and women have choices about which practices they will engage in or take seriously. Given the increasingly rigid beauty standards Westerners "must" conform to and given most people's desperate desires to "fit in" and "be accepted," is it really true that we have more freedom of choice? Really? Perhaps, as some suggest, we should be turning our lens on ourselves more critically and allow female genital surgery to be dealt with by women's movements and other grassroots groups in nations that practise it. What do you think?

Gender Socialization by Parents

From birth, parents maintain gender distinctions and hierarchies between girls and boys through differential treatment. Because boys are believed to be tougher than girls, parents offer them more autonomy and are more likely to bounce an infant son, to hold him up in the air, and to play with him more vigorously than they are an infant daughter (Lindsay 2005; MacDonald and Parke 1986). Parents believe that girls require most help and tend to cuddle infant girls, treat them gently, and provide them with verbal stimulation through cooing, talking, and singing to them (Basow 1992; Lindsay 2005). Further, parents are more prone to reward assertiveness and accomplishments by their sons, while reacting positively to their daughters' skills in interpersonal and social situations (Leaper et al. 1998; National Public Radio 1992). Studies over several decades continue to support that within 24 hours of birth, parents react to the label of their child as male or female by describing their sons as being *strong, active, hardy, alert,* and *big* and describing their daughters as being *gentle, dainty, quiet, delicate, awkward, and small* (Beitel and Park 1998; Delk et al. 1986; Lindsay 2005; Rubin et al. 1974; Stern and Karracker 1989).

Parents reinforce these gender distinctions through their selection of infants' and children's clothing. Most parents dress boys in boldly coloured "rough and tough" clothing and dress girls in softly coloured clothing encumbered with easily dirtied and torn bows, frills, and lace. Parents further reinforce gender stereotyping and gender distinctions through the toys they buy. For example, parents buy blocks and building sets, vehicles, sporting equipment, and action toys such as guns, tanks, and soldiers for boys, and they buy dolls, doll clothing, dollhouses, play cosmetics, and homemaking items such as dishes, ovens, irons, brooms, and mops for girls (Leaper 1994; Lindsay 2005). These toys and games develop different types of skills and clearly demonstrate for children what type of activities they should expect to be proficient at in the future. Moreover, "masculine" toys require little verbal interaction and promote competition and independence, while "feminine" toys promote verbal communication, interaction, and nurturance (Wood 2001). Interestingly, children themselves show few differences in toy preference until about age two or three, but their parents often actively discourage interest in toys and games deemed to be appropriate for the "opposite" sex (Lytton and Romney 1991; Wood 2001). As Lindsay (2005: 63) notes,

By preschool, children have a firm commitment to own-gender toys and tend to reject children playing with other-gender toys, especially if a boy is seen playing with a girl's toy.

Chores also reinforce gender distinctions. Most research confirms that parents use toys and chores to encourage their sons more than their daughters toward greater independence (Basow 1992; Lindsay 2005). Thus, boys frequently are assigned such maintenance chores as carrying out the garbage, cleaning up the yard, or helping dad or an older brother (a "taking care of things" orientation). Girls, on the other hand, are given domestic chores such as shopping, cooking, clearing the table, and doing laundry (a "taking care of others" orientation) (Lindsay 2005; Weisner et al. 1994; Wood 2001). Mothers are more likely than fathers, however, to encourage both genders to take on chores that would normally be assigned to the other gender (Lindsay 2005). When parents and others purchase gender-specific toys and give children gender-stereotypical household assignments, they send a powerful message about the gendered division of labour. In addition, in terms of preparing children for their futures, which will likely include performing *all* activities equally dexterously, gender-typed socialization does not do children any favours. Interestingly, many parents today support gender equity but continue to fall back on age-old socialization patterns. Linda Lindsay, a sociologist, notes however that "[a]s beliefs about gender equity become more widespread, the next generation of parents should socialize their children in less traditional ways than they were socialized" (2005:66). In any case, gender socialization varies widely, and peer group involvement is an important factor.

Peers and Gender Socialization

Peer groups are powerful socializing agents that can reinforce existing gender stereotypes and pressure individuals to engage in gender-appropriate behaviour. *Peer groups* are social groups whose members are linked by common interests and, usually, by similar age. Children are more widely accepted by their peer group when they conform to the group's notion of gender-appropriate behaviour (Lindsay 2005; Maccoby and Jacklin 1987; Martin 1989). Male peer groups place more pressure

on boys to do "masculine" things than female peer groups place on girls to do "feminine" things (Fagot 1984; Lindsay 2005). For example, most girls today wear jeans and many play soccer and softball, but boys who wear dresses or play hopscotch with girls would be banished from most male peer groups. In a study of gendered activity with elementary school children, Thorne (1998) found three salient themes related to male–female playground interactions:

- Girls play closer to buildings than boys, where they are more closely supervised by adults, and boys control approximately 10 times more playground space than girls.

- Boys invade and interrupt girl's space and girl's games much more than the reverse.

- Girls are more often defined as contaminating than boys, as in "girl germs" or "cooties."

These themes reinforce that "the worlds of boys and girls may be separate but they are not parallel, nor are they equal" (Thorne 1998:94).

During pre-adolescence, male peer groups also reinforce gender-appropriate emotions in boys. Kyratzis, in a recent study of same-sex preschool friendship groups, found that if boys exhibit feelings of being

Take a close look at this picture. What do you notice about the two lines? Social scientists have pointed out that gender socialization occurs in many ways, including how teachers organize school activities by sex.

frightened, for example, they are mocked by other boys who associate the emotion with girl's characteristics, which they do not value (2001). In an earlier study of a Little League baseball team, for example, sociologist Gary A. Fine (1987) found that the boys were encouraged by their peers to engage in proper "masculine" behaviour—acting tough even when they were hurt or intimidated, controlling their emotions, being competitive and wanting to win, and showing group unity and loyalty. Boys who failed to display these characteristics received instantaneous negative feedback from their teammates. Boys learn the contours of masculine behaviour through sports and through membership in boys clubs and organizations. For example, a study of the inception of the Boy Scouts in the United States points out that Scout programs began in order to specifically indoctrinate young boys into stereotypical ideals of masculinity, based on the "manliness" learned through a pioneering life in the wilderness: "The hardships and privations of pioneer life which did so much to develop sterling manhood are now but a legend in history, and we must depend on the Boy Scout Movement to produce the MEN of the future" (Beard 1914, in Hantover 1998:104).

Peers are important in both female's and male's development of gender identity and their aspirations for the future (Maccoby and Jacklin 1987). Nelson and Robinson (2002:133) report that the influence of peers on children begins around age 7 or 8 and peaks between ages 14 to 16. A study of Canadian teens showed that 91 percent reported that friendship was "very important" while only 65 percent rated family life equally important (Bibby and Posterski 1985). Peer friendship was seen as outweighing sports, sexuality, music, partying, and family activities (Bibby and Posterski 1992). In adolescence, peer friends assist the individual in developing his or her self-identity. Boys' culture comes to be characterized by "coolness," "autonomy," and "physicality," while girls' culture comes to be characterized by "compliance and conformity," "romance," and "domesticity" (Adler et al. 1992/1995:136). Boys tend to have more extensive peer groups but interact in a less communal style, whereas girls tend to have smaller peer groups that exhibit higher levels of intimacy and self-disclosure, which leads to higher levels of trust, particularly between best friend pairs (Lindsay 2005). As sociologist Linda Lindsay concludes, "when boys and girls meet as teenagers they may do so as strangers"

(2005:67). Among post-secondary students, peers play an important part in career choices and the establishment of long-term, intimate relationships (Huston 1985; Martin 1989). Even in kindergarten and the early grades, peers influence how and what we do in school and our perceptions of self and other.

Education and Gender Socialization

The education system is charged with the responsibility of transmitting cultural values. These values are far from gender-neutral. Like parents and peers, and despite being unaware of it, teachers reinforce gender distinctions by communicating to students that males and male-dominated activities are more important than females and female-dominated activities. Research on education continues to show the existence in schools of *gender bias—a situation in which favouritism is shown toward one gender.* For example, education scholars Myra Sadker and David Sadker (2002/1994) found that teachers subtly convey the message to their students that boys (White boys, in particular) are more important than girls by devoting more time, effort, and attention to boys than to girls. In day-to-day interactions, teachers are more likely to allow boys to interrupt them and give boys more praise, criticism, and suggestions for remediation than girls. Boys are more likely to be called on in class, whether they volunteer or not. When boys make comments, teachers often follow up with additional questions or suggestions; but when girls make comments, teachers often respond with a superficial "okay" and move on to the next student. Teachers praise girls for their appearance or for having a neat paper, but boys are praised for their accomplishments. Most teachers believe they do not treat boys and girls differently in the classroom, yet research consistently demonstrates that it is "aggressive boys and dependent girls who gain their attention" (Lindsay 2005: 298). This is not to suggest that Canadian boys experience no problems in the school system. Recent research suggests that boys' experiences in the education system are becoming increasingly negative, an issue that will be taken up more extensively in Chapter 12.

The pervasive gender bias in the Canadian education system was recognized by the 1970 Royal Commission on the Status of Women. The main thrusts of the recommendations were the elimination of gender stereotypes in textbooks and in curricula, changing teachers' gender-stereotypical treatment of students, changing girl's feelings about mathematics, and broadening career information for females (Mackie 1991). Textbooks today have changed somewhat to depict boys in a few non-traditional roles such as babysitters; however, the roles of fathers and husbands, which most boys will take on in their lives, are still downplayed in ways that the roles of mothers and wives are not. Despite decades of awareness and reform, studies conducted at the Ontario Institute for Studies in Education demonstrated that the self-esteem of girls aged 12 to 16 dropped significantly. It was postulated that the decrease in self-esteem was, in large part, the result of marginalization and silencing of females in co-ed classrooms (cited in Nelson and Robinson 2002:152). One way of countering this problem has been the introduction of all-female schools. While all-female schools, like the Linden School in Toronto, Emily Murphy Junior High School in Edmonton, and Queen Margaret's School for Girls in Duncan, B.C., provide girls with the opportunity to learn more about women's contributions to social, political, and economic life, typically they are set up as independent or private schools with hefty tuitions attached to gender-balanced curricula (for example, $650 to $1000 or more per girl, per month). Therefore, whatever advantages these schools may mete out to girls in terms of maintaining high self-esteem and high academic standards are likely to be realized only by girls from wealthier families. In addition, graduates of these all-female schools will still face sexism and gender bias in their post-secondary education and in the paid labour force.

The effects of gender bias become evident when teachers take a "boys will be boys" attitude about derogatory remarks and aggressive behaviour against girls. *Sexual harassment*—**unwanted sexual advances, requests for sexual favours, or other verbal or physical conduct of a sexual nature**—is frequently overlooked by teachers and school administrators. Larkin (1994:53), an education researcher, reports that "male students are by far the most frequent harassers of girls in schools . . . [but] according to the results of a recent survey of 4200 girls . . . three percent were harassed by their teachers. In all but one incident the teacher harasser was male." Unfortunately, media stories like the one about the grade 1 boy who was suspended from school for kissing a female classmate on

the cheek trivialize gender bias and sexual harassment, both of which create a hostile environment that makes it more difficult for many girls and young women to learn and accomplish as much as their male counterparts (see Orenstein 1996; Sadker and Sadker 1994). These outcomes should not be surprising to us if we consider research on elementary school children. Myra and David Sadker (1994) asked children what they thought it would be like to be suddenly turned into a member of the "opposite" gender. While both genders preferred their own, unsurprisingly, girls found the idea "intriguing and interesting," stating things like "I will be able to be almost anything I want" and "I will make more money now that I am a boy" (Lindsay 2005: 68). Boys found the idea to be "appalling, disgusting and humiliating," saying things like "my teachers would treat me like a little hairy pig-headed girl" and "if I were turned into a girl today I would kill myself" (Lindsay 2005: 68). Even in elementary school, boys and girls are very clear about the relative societal worth of each gender.

Researchers have found that in some schools, male students regularly refer to females as "sluts," "bitches," and "hos" without fear of reprimand from teachers, and the females' fear of reprisal keeps them from speaking out against their harassers (Orenstein 1996). One high-school student described her experience in a shop class in this way: "The boys literally pushed me around, right into tables and chairs. They pulled my hair, made sexual comments, touched me, told sexist jokes. And the thing was that I was better in the shop class than almost any guy. This only caused the boys to get more aggressive and troublesome" (Sadker and Sadker 1994:127). Teachers who fail to challenge or stop harassing behaviour in their classrooms are perceived by students as being unconcerned (Larkin 1994). A survey of 4200 North American females found that 4 in 10 experienced sexual harassment daily at school (Mann 1993). Moreover, the Ontario Secondary School Teacher's Federation 1994 study of sexual harassment at Ontario schools found that a disturbing 83 percent of female students had been sexually harassed in the school setting (Larkin and Staton 1998). Harassment has the result of making girls feel ill at ease, lose confidence, exhibit reluctance to attend school or to draw attention to themselves in classrooms, and/or drop out of classes or school altogether (Larkin and Staton 1998; Nelson and Robinson 2002). Larkin (1994:33), citing Jacqui Halson, states that "schools help to reproduce the existing power imbalance between men and women by failing to recognize the significant impact of sexual harassment on the lives of female students and by failing to intervene." Although it may seem that boys benefit from sexual harassment and teachers' gender bias (or at least are not harmed by it), that is not the case.

Boys, too, are limited by stereotypical notions of masculinity and gender-appropriate behaviour. According to Sadker and Sadker (2002/1994), boys confront the "frozen boundaries" of the male role at every turn in their school life. They are taught to "Be cool, don't show emotion, repress feelings, be aggressive, compete, and win"—the same messages that sociologist Gary Fine (1987) found Little Leaguers use to reinforce each other. Such teachings not only limit the range of emotions boys are allowed to feel but also encourage boys to see themselves—and other males—as better than girls and to distance themselves from any activity that is considered "feminine," even though it may be an activity they enjoy.

Male gender norms, which require boys to be active, aggressive, and independent, often conflict with school norms, which require students to be quiet, passive, and conforming. Many boys walk a tightrope between compliance and rebellion. They tend to receive lower grades than girls do and are more likely to drop out of school (Sadker and Sadker 2002/1994). Although female gender norms conflict less with school norms than male gender norms, sociologist Michelle Fine (1991) found in one study that for many girls, the price of academic success is being compliant and muting their own voices.

Gender bias also occurs at the post-secondary level. Lindsay reports that "academic life exemplifies a male mode of performance . . . the values of competition, individualism and aggressive classroom debates are stronger than in high school" (2005:306). Research consistently shows that more educational resources, ranging from athletic programs and dormitories to course offerings and career advising, are targeted primarily at men, even though women constitute more than half of all Canadian college and university students today. In the classroom, many professors give more attention to men than to women (Hall 1984; Hall and Sandler 1982; Lindsay 2005). Women tend to be called on less frequently and to receive less encouragement. When they speak out in class, women are more likely to be interrupted, ignored, or devalued than men are (Fox 1995). In graduate school, women are less often mentored and taken on as "protegés," a key to academic success. While men's self-esteem tends to increase in the post-secondary milieu, women typically experience a drop in self-esteem, being negatively affected by gender bias "in terms of their self-image, aspirations, concerns and expectations" (Reynolds 2001:247; Sandler 2004). More than one-third of women post-secondary students report that they have experienced gender discrimination on the part of instructors, administrators, and classmates (Lindsay 2005: 306). Despite their negative experiences in academic settings, women tend to have higher grade-point averages and earn a higher percentage of baccalaureate and master's degrees than Canadian men do. Even so, women are under-represented in fields such as economics, engineering, computer and information sciences, and physical sciences, and overrepresented in the number of degrees awarded in education, psychology, and nursing and allied health fields (McAdie 1998; Reynolds 2001; Women's Research and Educational Institute 1996). Recent research demonstrates that nearly one-half of women who enter post-secondary studies with science-related interests switch to other non-science majors (Lindsay 2005). Some analysts attribute the under-representation of women in math, science, and engineering to the way these courses are taught: "The traditions are based on military applications. The programs started out in military schools and colleges" (Jane Daniels, Women in Engineering, Purdue University, quoted in Urschel 1996:2D; Nelson 2006). Additionally, many young women lack the high school math and science backgrounds necessary to enter these courses at the post-secondary level. They also lack female role models and female peers in many post-secondary concentrations. Even though more women than men achieve college diplomas and undergraduate and graduate university degrees, the trend does not continue when looking at doctoral (Ph.D.) degrees: Men still outnumber women as recipients of degrees: 41 percent of doctoral degrees granted in 2001 were awarded to women. As expected, the only discipline where women outnumber men is education, while men outnumber women in all the so-called "hard" sciences (see Table 4.1 on page 103). In part, fewer numbers of women at the Ph.D. level can be seen as resulting from the difficulties experienced disproportionately by women as they attempt to reconcile employment and a disproportionate share of domestic responsibilities with the rigorous demands of typically full-time doctoral programs (Benoit 2000; Husk 1998; Nelson 2006). In part, it may also be the result of the culmination of women's low wages relative to men's and chronic underfunding of post-secondary education. Additionally, persistent cultural values and norms that suggest that education is "wasted" on women and that women's rightful sphere is the household, not higher education or the professional labour force, are to blame (Dagg and Thompson 1988; Nelson and Robinson 2001).

The Media and Gender Socialization

From television and radio to the internet, from magazines and newspapers to billboards, we are relentlessly bombarded by media on a daily basis. Because media are socially constructed, they reflect the realities and/or fantasies of their creators. Wood (2001) identifies three themes in contemporary media that represent gender. The first theme is the under-representation of women and other minority groups. The overrepresentation of able-bodied, youngish, White men in media conveys the message that they make up the majority of the population (and in Canada they do not) and, as such, that they are the cultural standard. When women and other minority groups are depicted in media, they are typically shown in ways that reinforce and perpetuate negative stereotypes about the group. The second theme is the stereotypical fashion in which males and females are presented. Males continue to be presented as competent, powerful, serious, confident, and independent, while females continue to be presented as incompetent, unintelligent, young, thin, beautiful, dependent, and passive sex objects (Wood 2001:283–284). To redress past voids, some media have made a limited attempt to show women involved in activities outside the domestic sphere (not that these same media portray these women necessarily in a positive light); however, they have not made a corresponding attempt to show men involved in the domestic sphere. Where men are shown involved in domestic labour or child care at all, they are typically portrayed as helpless ("hopeless"?) buffoons (Wood 2001:284), reinforcing men's lack of "suitability" to domestic activities. The third theme is the portrayal of

male–female relations along traditional lines and in ways that perpetuate and normalize violence against women (Wood 2001:281). Communications scholar Julia T. Wood (2001:287–294) suggests there are four themes that reflect and promote gender-stereotypical, and perhaps even dangerous, relations between the sexes: (1) women's dependence and men's independence; (2) women's incompetence and men's authority; (3) women as primary caregivers and men as primary breadwinners; and (4) women as victims and sex objects and men as aggressors.

While some critics argue that the media simply reflect existing gender roles in society, others point out that the media have a unique ability to shape ideas. Lindsey (2005:69) notes that "[h]eavy television viewing is strongly associated with traditional and stereotyped gender views, a pattern that is demonstrated for all [ethnic groups] and age groups." From children's cartoons to adult shows, television programs offer more male than female characters. Furthermore, the male characters act in a strikingly different manner than female ones. Male characters in both children's programs and adult programs are typically aggressive, constructive, and direct, while female characters defer to others or manipulate them by acting helpless, seductive, or deceitful (Basow 1992). Some have argued that even educational programs, such as *Sesame Street,* perpetuate gender stereotypes because most of the characters have male names and masculine voices and participate in "boys' activities." Wood (2001:287) reports that this is no accident: "Beginning in 1991, television executives deliberately and consciously adopted a policy of having dominant male characters in all Saturday morning children's programming."

Recent studies of televised music videos have found that these videos often show stereotyped gender roles and condone harassment of and discrimination against women. In the words of sociologist Linda Lindsey, "[t]he misogyny in most rock videos is blatant" (2005:358). A 1992 study found most female characters were dressed in revealing clothing, made sexual advances toward men, and usually were presented as sex objects. Further studies from 1999 and 2002 demonstrate that women do not appear at all or appear only in the background in over half of music videos, but where they do appear, sexual images are increasingly combined with violence. Male characters routinely pursued fantasy adventures or engaged in aggression and violence

(Seidman 1992). Further, music-video women are shown either satisfying male sexual fantasies or being ostracized or punished for not engaging in this way. Sociologist Sut Jhally, in the documentary *Dreamworlds II* (1991), describes the fantasy world of music videos as the male videomaker's and consumer's dreamworld. This "dreamworld" objectifies and dehumanizes women and denies them subjectivity, all of which puts women at risk for violence by reinforcing a *rape culture*—**the pervasive system of cultural values, attitudes, and practices that support and perpetuate sexualized violence against women.** It includes rigid gender scripts for males and females and equally rigid notions of gender-appropriate behaviours. Many music videos overtly depict male violence against women, and increasingly, over the years, rape scenes are enacted in music videos (Lindsey 2005). Research by Dieter (1989) demonstrated that women who watched sexualized violence on MTV were more accepting of violence in their own intimate relationships with men than women who did not view the images (cited in Wood 2001).

While changes have occurred in the roles men and women play in movies, most roles still embrace stereotypes. Even though there are many movie stars who are female, few notable roles exist for women, and even fewer films examine women's lives and issues from their own perspectives. (Exceptions include *The Divine Secrets of the Ya-Ya Sisterhood, Shirley Valentine, Fried Green Tomatoes, A League of Their Own,* and *Thelma and Louise.*) Recently, boys have saved the world from an evil wizard (*Harry Potter*), saved the universe from destruction (*Star Wars*), and saved a parent from evil government agents (*Clockstoppers*). Meanwhile, girls and young women, in films such as *Clueless,* are depicted as "bimbos," shopaholics, and uninterested in school. Things may be changing somewhat: In *Scooby Doo,* the ditzy character, Daphne, is an accomplished martial artist and wins a fight with a burly wrestler, and Velma, the token "smart female," is portrayed as attractive and, in fact, even manages to hook up with a man. However, like characters in *Harry Potter* and *The Phantom Menace,* even when females are portrayed positively as smart *and* attractive, they are still only supporting characters to the males who save the day. Recently, there has been a spate of movies featuring "kick-ass" females (*Aeon Flux, Underworld, The Matrix*); however, these women are depicted as cold-blooded killers, very masculine in their approach to the world, and dressed in highly sexualized attire. According to social psychologist Hilary Lips (1993:19), "We are surrounded with the message that masculine males can be powerful, but feminine females cannot, or that women's only effective source of feminine influence is beauty and sex appeal." Moreover, the dominant message conveyed remains that females must use their influence, however paltry, in an attempt to garner the pinnacle of feminine achievement and self-definition—an intimate relationship with a man (Nelson and Robinson 2002).

Why is awareness of gender socialization important for understanding gender discrimination and gender inequality? Social analysts who use a gender-role approach say that because parents, peers, teachers, and the media influence our perceptions of who we are and what our aspirations should be, gender-role socialization contributes to a gendered division of labour, creates a *wage gap* between women and men workers, limits occupational and other choices for women and men, and perpetuates gendered violence and shapes our (lack of) responses to it. It is important, therefore, to keep in mind that gender is a social construction and, as such, can be deconstructed and reconstructed. In this way, social change is possible. In the words of sociologist Judith Lorber (1986:576), "what is socially constructed can be reconstructed, and social relations can be rearranged."

However, some social analysts say that no direct evidence links gender role socialization to social inequality and that it is therefore important to use social structural analysis to examine gender inequality (see Reskin and Hartmann 1986). In other words, these analysts believe that the decisions that people make (such as the schools they choose to attend and the occupations they choose to pursue) are linked not only to how they were socialized but also to how society is structured. We now examine structural features that contribute to gender inequality.

CONTEMPORARY GENDER INEQUALITY

How do tasks in a society get defined as either "men's work" or "women's work," and why are they differentially rewarded? Many sociologists believe that through various social institutions and structures, people assign different roles and responsibilities to women and men based on notions of gender appropriateness and, in the process, restrict women's opportunities. According to feminist scholars, gender inequality is maintained and reinforced through individual and institutionalized sexism. The term *individual sexism* refers to individuals' beliefs and actions that are rooted in anti-female prejudice and stereotypical beliefs. The term *institutionalized sexism* refers to the power that men have to engage in sex discrimination at the organizational and institutional levels of society. This pattern of male domination and female subordination is known as *patriarchy*—**a hierarchical system of social organization in which cultural, political, and economic structures are controlled by men.** According to some analysts, the location of women in the work force and on the economic pyramid is evidence of patriarchy (Epstein 1988). In this section, we focus on five structural forms that contribute to contemporary gender inequality: the gendered division of labour, the wage gap, sexual harassment, the glass ceiling and the glass escalator, and the double shift.

The Gendered Division of Paid Work

Whether by choice or economic necessity, women have entered the paid labour force in unprecedented numbers in recent years. Today, Canadian women have among the highest labour force participation rates in the world (Wilson 2001). In 1946, fewer than 20 percent of women over the age of 25 were employed in the Canadian paid labour force. This number had risen to 30 percent as of 1961. Today, women represent nearly 50 percent of the total Canadian work force (46.4 percent in 2003), and nearly 60 percent of all Canadian women 25 years or older are in the paid labour force (Nelson 2006; Nelson and Robinson 2002). Until the 1950s, employed women were typically single, young, and childless. Today, however, many women with preschool children are in the paid labour force. In fact, between 1981 and 1991, women with preschool children accounted for 60 percent of the increase in employed women; and in 2003, 66 percent of women with children under age 6 were in the labour force (Nelson 2006; Nelson and Robinson 2002; Wilson 2001).

There are several reasons for these dramatic increases in women's labour force participation. First, structural pressures such as inflation necessitated higher incomes generally, and the shift from a goods-producing or manufacturing economy to a service economy, with the attendant lower wages, drove the increase in dual-earner families. As well, service jobs are ones in which we disproportionately find women. Along with this, cultural values about gender, paid employment, marriage, and parenting shifted to the point where today, women working for pay, regardless of their marital or parental status, are no longer so negatively stigmatized as they once were (Nelson, 2006; Nelson and Robinson, 2002; Wilson, 2001). Even as women's labour force participation has been increasing, male participation has been gradually declining due to layoffs in the industrial sector, downsizing of business and government, and the long-term trend toward early retirement, either voluntary or involuntary (i.e., "buyouts"; Nelson 2006; Nelson and Robinson 2002).

While many people who know these statistics are optimistic about the gains Canadian women have made in paid employment, it should be noted that women's position in the labour force is lower than men's in terms of status, opportunities, and salaries. Today, most women and men remain concentrated in occupations that are segregated by gender (see Table 4.1). The term *gender-segregated work* refers to the extent to which men and women are concentrated in different occupations and places of work (Reskin and Padavic 1994). For example, women are predominant in word-processing pools and child-care centres, whereas men are predominant in the construction trades. In some settings, both men and women are employed. In these settings, however, women are employed predominantly in clerical or other support positions, while men hold supervisory, managerial, or other professional positions. For example, despite the increasing number of women entering the legal profession, most attorneys are men, and most support-staff workers, such as legal secretaries and paralegals, are women (see Epstein 1993; Pierce 1995). In medicine, female doctors tend to become general practitioners or to have "family practices," whereas more male doctors tend to specialize and/or become surgeons, with the attendant higher pay and status than are allocated to general practitioners or those in family medicine (Nelson 2006).

Despite the fact that females and males are still segregated into highly gendered types of occupations, there may be some room for optimism. Occupational

TABLE 4.1   Women as a Percentage of Total Employed in Occupation, 1987, 1994, 1999, 2003

	1987	1994	1999	2003
Managerial				
Senior management	16.9	19.8	26.8	24.2
Other management	30.6	36.9	35.7	36.1
Total management	28.9	35.1	35.1	35.4
Professional				
Business and finance	40.7	44.6	49.4	48.4
Natural sciences/engineering/mathematics	16.7	17.0	19.6	22.0
Social sciences/religion	47.8	56.5	58.2	63.8
Teaching	57.3	59.4	62.1	62.9
Doctors/dentists/other health	44.1	48.7	47.1	52.1
Nursing/therapy/other health-related	87.3	87.1	86.5	87.7
Artistic/literary/recreational	50.4	53.6	54.6	53.4
Total professional	49.8	52.2	51.8	53.4
Clerical and administrative	74.4	74.9	75.3	75.1
Sales and service	55.7	56.4	58.7	58.7
Primary	20.0	21.3	21.6	19.7
Trades, transport, and construction	5.3	5.4	6.2	6.6
Processing, manufacturing, and utilities	30.2	29.2	29.8	28.9
Total*	43.0	45.3	45.9	46.6

*Includes occupations that are not classified.

Source: *Adapted from Statistics Canada*, Women in Canada: Work Chapter Updates, 2003, *Cat. No. 89F0133X (March, 25, 2004). Adapted in* Gender in Canada, Third Edition *by Adie Nelson, 2006, p.219, Pearson Canada. Reprinted with permission of Pearson Canada Inc.*

segregation by gender has decreased in some categories. For example, in the publication *Canadian Social Trends*, Best (1995:33) reports that the proportion of female doctors and dentists rose to 26 percent in 1993, up from 18 percent in 1982. The latest Statistics Canada data (2001g:8) suggest that figure has risen to 53 percent today (see Chapter 10). Of new law graduates, 53 percent of new lawyers called to the bar are women, accounting for approximately a third of the practising law profession today (Tyler 2002:A18). On the not-so-optimistic side, in 1987, 74 percent of the women employed in the paid labour force could be found in just a handful of occupations: teaching, nursing and health-related, clerical and other administration, and sales or service occupations. By 2003, the percentage had declined only 4 percentage points to 70 percent, largely because of a modest decrease of women working in clerical and

related administrative positions (Statistics Canada, 2004a). As sociologist Susannah Wilson (2001:225) reports, "the concentration of women in service and sales jobs has been a persistent aspect of the labour force since these figures were first calculated in the 1891 census."

The persisting concentration of a high proportion of employed Canadian women in only three occupational areas has been described as a ***pink-collar ghetto***—**where the jobs primarily held by women are relatively low-paying, non-manual, and semiskilled**—such as clerical work, counter help in fast-food restaurants, medical assistance, and child-care work.

Women are overrepresented in the contingent work force as well. ***Contingent work* is part-time work, temporary work, and subcontracted work that offers advantages to employers but can be detrimental to workers' welfare.** Many employers stress that having more contingent workers and fewer permanent, full-time employees keeps corporations competitive in the global marketplace. One of the reasons contingent work is so attractive to employers is that, in addition to its "flexible" nature, it allows employers to avoid providing benefits and contributing to health care premiums and pension plans. While many women are found in contingent work because it often provides them greater flexibility to work around family responsibilities, in 2003, consistent with earlier surveys, close to 30 percent of women who were employed part-time reported that they would prefer to be employed full-time (Nelson 2006; Statistics Canada 1999a). Although all contingent workers experience problems related to this type of work, women especially are affected by the fact that many contingent workers receive little monetary remuneration, are unlikely to qualify for any or adequate un/employment insurance when they lose their jobs, do not qualify for pension coverage or other job-related benefits enjoyed by many full-time workers, and have difficulty finding suitable child-care arrangements (Nelson 2006; Nelson and Robinson 2002).

Women continue to be concentrated in jobs where they receive lower wages, less prestige, and fewer benefits, on average, than men. However, this inequity is even more compounded by racialization and (dis)ability, a situation known as *multiple jeopardy*. Multiple jeopardy is often manifested as an inability to get hired or to maintain employment, to gain a promotion, and/or to obtain adequate compensation and benefits. For example, as pointed out by Nelson and Robinson (2002:228–229), the unemployment rate for Indigenous people is more than double that for all Canadians; visible minority women are more likely than other Canadian women to be found in manual labour; and women with disabilities are more likely than men with disabilities to be unemployed. Following the pattern of gender disparities in income, Indigenous people earn less than non–Indigenous people, visible minority people earn less than non–visible minorities, and people with a disability earn less than people without disabilities. Across all categories, women earn less than men. People with disabilities, visible minority people, and Indigenous people all earn average annual incomes below the Canadian average (Nelson 2006; Nelson and Robinson 2002:228). For those who experience multiple barriers to employment, it is nearly impossible to determine which particular barrier was most salient in a particular instance of discrimination. Of course, these barriers may also be made more complex by the addition of discrimination on the basis of language, sexual orientation, size, age, and foreign educational credentials that are often not recognized or not accepted "on par" in Canada.

The Wage Gap

The *wage gap*—**the disparity between women's and men's earnings**—is the best-documented consequence of gender-segregated work (Reskin and Padavic 1994). No matter what group men belong to in terms of racialization or ability, they earn more than women of that same group. A wage gap persists in Canada across full- and part-time employment and in both annual income and hourly wages (Nelson 2006:227; Wilson 2001:223). The fact that women have historically been a cheaper source of labour has been one of the factors in their attractiveness to employers. In 1993, women made 72.1 percent of men's wages for full-time, full-year work (i.e., 72 cents for each male dollar earned). This was a dramatic increase from 1967, when women made 58 percent of what men made. But in 1995, women's after-tax income was only 60 percent of men's after-tax income (Status of Women Canada 1997). Statistics Canada notes that one-half the differential in the 1997 data can be explained by "male–female differences in labour market experience, education, and major field of study, occupation, job responsibilities, and industry" (1999a). This leaves one-half of the wage differential unexplained. Wilson (2001:224) notes "the unexplained portion is presumed to be due to discrimination."

The gendered wage gap also varies by age, marital status, and education, with younger workers, never-married workers, and more-educated workers having lower wage gaps. The lessened gap for younger workers may be the result of both males and females having a similar amount of work experience and the tendency for both sexes to be concentrated in entry-level jobs. For never-married individuals, it may be in part the result of more of a similarity in ability to take on similar kinds of work (i.e., work that involves travel, long hours, nonstandard shifts, and so on). More-educated workers may choose different careers than their lesser educated counterparts, with some women with higher educations pursuing careers in occupations typically held by men. For example, Adie Nelson, a sociologist specializing in gender studies, notes that "in 2000, university educated women age 25 to 29 who worked in the 10 occupations most commonly chosen by men of the same age group and qualifications earned about 89 cents for every dollar earned by their male counterparts" (2006:229). A minimal wage gap also exists for

Source: Gable, Regina Leader Post *84. Reprinted by permission of Brian Gable and the* Regina Leader Post.

unionized workers—about 30 percent of employed women and men in Canada. Unions in Canada have fought long, hard campaigns to achieve *pay equity*—**equal pay for work of equal or comparable worth**—for women, both in unions and outside unions. Interestingly, the main force driving the overall narrowing of the gendered wage gap has been the stagnation and decline of men's wages generally (Nelson and Robinson 2002; Roos and Reskin 1992; Wilson 2001).

For pay equity to occur between men and women, there has to be a broad-based commitment to *comparable worth*—**the belief that wages ought to reflect the worth of a job, not the gender or other ascribed characteristics of the worker** (Kemp 1994). To determine the comparable worth of different kinds of jobs, researchers break a specific job into components to determine (1) how much education, training, and skills are required; (2) how much responsibility a person in that position has for others' work; and, (3) what the working conditions are. Researchers then allocate points for each component to determine whether or not men and women are being paid equitably for their work (Lorber 1994). For pay equity to exist, men and women in occupations that receive the same number of points must be paid the same. However, pay equity exists for very few jobs. (See Figure 4.2 for a comparison of men's and women's earnings in selected occupations.)

Comparable worth is an important issue for men as well as women. Male workers in female-dominated jobs such as nursing, secretarial work, and elementary teaching pay an economic penalty for their choice of work. Additionally, if women were compensated fairly, an employer could not undercut men's wages by hiring women at a cheaper rate (Kessler-Harris 1990).

Sexual Harassment

Millions of men never harass women in the workplace or elsewhere, but so many men do that, sadly, it is almost impossible for women to avoid the experience (Langelan 1993). In fact, the 1993 Violence Against Women Survey, conducted by Statistics Canada, found that 87 percent of Canadian women had experienced some form of sexual harassment; just over one-half had been harassed by men they knew (Johnson 1996). Sexual harassment is a form of intentional, institutionalized gender discrimination that includes all unwelcome sexual attention affecting an employee's job conditions or

FIGURE 4.2 Women's Earnings as a Percentage of Men's across Occupational Categories, 2000

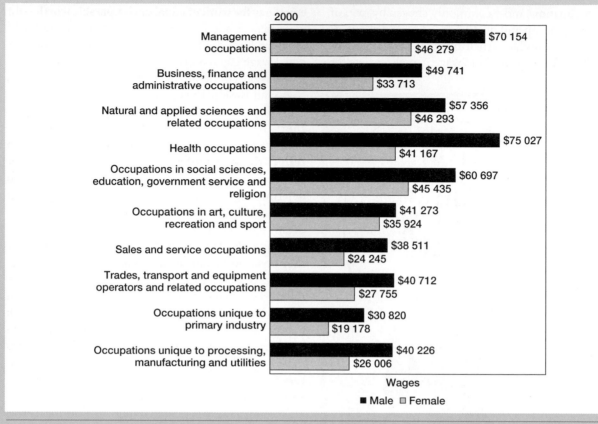

2000

Occupation	Male	Female
Management occupations	$70 154	$46 279
Business, finance and administrative occupations	$49 741	$33 713
Natural and applied sciences and related occupations	$57 356	$46 293
Health occupations	$75 027	$41 167
Occupations in social sciences, education, government service and religion	$60 697	$45 435
Occupations in art, culture, recreation and sport	$41 273	$35 924
Sales and service occupations	$38 511	$24 245
Trades, transport and equipment operators and related occupations	$40 712	$27 755
Occupations unique to primary industry	$30 820	$19 178
Occupations unique to processing, manufacturing and utilities	$40 226	$26 006

Wages
■ Male □ Female

Source: Adapted from Statistics Canada, 2001, Teacher's Kit, Activity 13: Women in the Labour Force, *Cat. no. 92F0192X (January 22, 2003).*

creating a hostile work environment. Sociologists Walter S. DeKeseredy and Ronald Hinch (1991:103) define it as "unsolicited, unreciprocated male behaviour that values a woman's sex role over her function as a worker." Sexual harassment includes verbal abuse, touching, staring at or making jokes about a woman's body, demands for sexual intercourse, and even sexual assault on the job (Benokraitis and Feagin 1995). Kemp (1994:310) distinguishes two types of sexual harassment: *quid pro quo* harassment, involving "something for something" (e.g., an explicit exchange of sex for a pay raise or better grade), or the creation of a poisoned work environment—harassment as a continuing condition of work (e.g., so-called jokes, touching, and teasing often referred to as "normal" male "on-the-job" behaviour). A recent study of female and male undergraduates found

that both sexes experienced sexual harassment but that males were generally likely to identify sexual attention from a woman (including instructors and professors) as "non-threatening," even "entertaining," ego-satisfying, and "validating of their masculinity" (Nelson 2006: 179). In contrast, a national survey of sexual harassment against employed women found that 90 percent reported at least one incidence of unwanted male sexual attention in a public place that resulted in them feeling emotionally shaken and with "the nagging, gnawing sense that something horrible *could* happen" (Smith 1993: 70).

People who are accused of sexual harassment frequently claim that their actions were merely harmless expressions of (supposedly) mutual sexual attraction. Sociologist Adie Nelson reports that "[r]esearch has indicated that behaviour that women defined as unacceptable or offensive, especially in the workplace, was viewed by men as normal and appropriate" (2006: 179). Sexual harassment is not about attraction; it is about *abuse of power*. Sexual harassment constitutes a form of intimidation and aggression: The recipient has no choice in the encounter or has reason to fear repercussions if she or he declines. Despite the fear mongering of Hollywood movies like *Single White Female*, *Fatal Attraction*, and *Disclosure*, women disproportionately experience sexual harassment at the hands of men. Some men are able to harass because they hold economic power over women (e.g., bosses, supervisors, and colleagues who have some say over promotions and raises); others are able to harass because they hold gender-based power (e.g., power rooted in cultural patterns of male dominance and backed up by the threat of violence and the ability to rape; Langelan 1993). In either case, sexual harassment serves as a means of boundary heightening between men and women in the workplace. For example, sociologist Jennifer L. Pierce (1995) found that male lawyers may exaggerate the differences between women lawyers and themselves by directing unwanted sexual invitations, attention, and behaviour at women in their firms. A recent survey conducted in Saskatchewan found that 39 percent of nurses had suffered sexual harassment, often by patients, while a recent Ontario survey found that three-quarters of female family physicians had been sexually harassed by male patients (Duffy and Cohen 2001). In the retail sales industry, where a disproportionate number of Canadian women work, a study of female retail workers and security workers employed in small outlets, mainly in Canadian malls, found that two-thirds of the retail workers reported being sexually harassed by customers (Tadic and Hughes 1998). In an interview, one woman described her experience as follows: "one guy gave me a piece of paper with his phone number on it and a condom rolled into it." Another man stared, followed her around the retail outlet, and then lay on the floor in an attempt to see up her skirt (Tadic and Hughes 1998:88). Another woman in the same study, commenting on the prevalence of unwanted touching from male customers, stated that "they'll put their arms around you or they'll put their hands on your back and rub it up and down . . . it's very uncomfortable coming into your personal space, totally unnecessary for the sales interaction" (Tadic and Hughes 1998:88). Social scientist Jocalyn Clark (1998) conducted research in a northern British

Columbia tree-planting camp, looking at health risks associated with that industry. She found that sexual harassment of female workers was central to the experience of female tree-planters, both by male co-workers and male crew supervisors. As reported by one planter:

> Certain foremen hire certain female planters based solely on the fact that they think they will be able to sleep with that person for the planting season. And when that doesn't happen, and perhaps when they see that person looking at other people, they become harder on that person, and when that person shows that they obviously have no intention of sleeping with them, in some cases I've seen them just get fired. Get really dumped on, like "Plant this shit, you're a lousy planter, what the hell is wrong with you? And why don't you just leave? I'll drive you to the bus." I've seen that happen. (quoted in Clark 1998:84)

Sexual harassment is a costly problem for women—who may lose employment opportunities, especially in today's climate where the emphasis is on "customer satisfaction"—and for their employers—who lose millions of dollars per year in low productivity, absenteeism, and employee turnover related to harassment (Basow 1992). As one woman commented, "[with] the 'customer is always right' policy, you've got to grin and bear a lot . . ." (Tadic and Hughes 1998:89). Sexual harassment and other forms of blatant and subtle discrimination in the workplace also contribute to the institutional barriers that limit women's opportunities to rise to the top positions in corporations and other occupational settings (see MacCorquodale and Jensen 1993; Rosenberg et al. 1993). Sociologist Alice Abel Kemp (1994:312) theorizes that sexual harassment serves three purposes in a patriarchal society like Canada: (1) it discourages women from participating in jobs traditionally held by men; (2) it limits women to low-wage, dead-end, female-dominated jobs; and, (3) it attributes many of women's responses to harassment (like absenteeism, job turnover, and so on) to gender stereotypes of women as "uncommitted, unreliable workers." A recent study (see Montemurro 2003) of workplace-based television sitcoms found that sexual harassment was generally likely to be depicted as a "laughing matter," a fact that has contributed to the persistence of it as a problem (Nelson 2006: 180).

TABLE 4.2 Participation In and Time Spent on Paid Work, Housework, and Other Unpaid Work

	Participants Satisfied with Work–Life Balance		Participants Not Time-Stressed		Participants Satisfied with Life Generally	
	Men	Women	Men	Women	Men	Women
	%	%	%	%	%	%
No children under 19 at home						
Less than 18 hours per day	77	74	69	51 (*)	90	85
18.0 to 21.9 hours per day	78	79	64	53	87	89
22 or more hours per day	77	66	50*	50	83	84
With children under 19 at home						
Less than 18 hours per day	80	73	61	49 (*)	95	89
18.0 to 21.9 hours per day	80	68 (*)	61	42 (*)	86	85
22 or more hours per day	71	52*(*)	49*	36*(*)	86	80

* Significantly different from couples with less than 18 hours per day and no children at the .05 level or less.

(*) Significantly different from men at the .05 level or less.

Source: Adapted from Statistics Canada, 2006, Perspectives on Labour and Income, Cat. no. 75-001 (July 19).

The Glass Ceiling and the Glass Escalator

More recently, feminist researchers have used the advancement (or lack of advancement) of women into top-tier management jobs as a litmus test for how well women are faring in the labour force as a whole. They have found that women hold only a handful of top positions. Although they are inching their way up the corporate ladder, women almost always encounter barriers when they try to enter the lucrative and prestigious top positions of their occupations. This is because of what is known as the *glass ceiling*—**the invisible institutional barrier constructed by male management that prevents women from reaching top positions in major corporations and other large-scale organizations.** Among the reasons cited for this barrier are male executives who believe that male workers will not work for women supervisors, that women workers are supposed to be in support roles only, that the prestige of the profession will decrease if women are admitted, and/or that "the ideal worker is normatively masculine" (Benokraitis and Feagin 1995; Martin 1992:220; Nelson 2006; Nelson and Robinson 2002).

The glass ceiling is particularly evident in the nation's 500 largest companies. In 1996, fewer than 3 percent of the 2400 people having titles such as chair, chief executive, vice chair, president, chief operations officer, or executive vice president, and the salary that accompanies these titles, were women. Women of colour occupy fewer than 1 percent of top management positions. According to a recent study by Catalyst (Dobrzynski 1996), a non-profit research group that studies women in upper-level management, 14 of the top 100 companies do not have a single woman among their top officers. Even if there are equivalent numbers of women and men in a workplace, a chilly climate may exist. The *chilly climate* is a concept used to draw attention to the fact that equality of access does not necessarily guarantee equality of treatment within any given institution. Nelson and Robinson (2002:234) explain the chilly climate using a quote from George Orwell's book *Animal Farm*, where a "funny sort of democracy" prevails, one where "all animals are equal, but some animals are more equal than others."

The chilly climate can be manifested as an inhospitable workplace for a person of "the wrong sex" through exclusionary, dismissive, or generally "cool" behaviours, based on cultural notions of gender-appropriate labour (Nelson and Robinson 2002). Sociologists Susan A. McDaniel and Erica van Roosmalen, citing McKinnon, concluded after their study of female university students at one Canadian campus that sexual harassment and chilly climates affect a woman by "using her employment position to coerce her sexually, while using her sexual position to coerce her economically" (cited in Nelson and Robinson 2002:237).

Overall, women are most likely to reach top positions in the service sector (for example, banking and diversified finance, publishing, retailing, food services, and entertainment), a sector in which they have traditionally been employed in great numbers. For example, Saskatchewan's LuAn Mitchell, voted Canada's Number One Female Entrepreneur by *Profit* and *Chatelaine* magazines and one of the 40 Leading Women Entrepreneurs in the World by the Star Group in 2001, took over her husband's family's 60-year-old meat-processing company after the death of her husband in 1998. Mitchell's Gourmet Foods brought in revenues of $268 million in 1999, after Mitchell formed an alliance with Schneider Foods, led expansion in Asia, and opened a new $44-million facility in Saskatoon ("Biography" n.d.).

Consistent with the idea that women who become top CEOs are most likely to reach those positions in the service sector, a glance at women CEOs of Fortune 500 companies in 2006 demonstrates that there are 10 women who run Fortune 500 companies (20 who run Fortune 1000 companies); the companies include *Sara Lee, Avon, Charming Shoppes, Ann Taylor Stores, Jack in the Box, Golden West Financial, The New York Times, Citizens Communications,* and *eBay* ("Women CEOs for Fortune 500 Companies" 2006).

Catalyst Canada, in its *Census of Women Corporate Officers and Top Earners of Canada 2004*, showed that women hold only 14.4 percent of corporate officer positions in the Financial Post 500 (the *National Post*'s list of largest Canadian companies; Tallarico and Black 2005). At this rate of growth (i.e., less than 0.5 percent since 2002), Catalyst states that "the number of women reaching the top ranks in Corporate Canada will not reach a critical mass of 25 percent until the year 2025" (Tallarico and Black 2005:1).

Women fare the worst in male-dominated businesses such as mining, crude oil, brokerages, and manufacturing. In a study of Canadian business students, psychologist R. J. Burke (1994) found that male students, more so than female students, had a negative attitude toward women in management roles generally. This, he said, may impact women in a variety of ways: (1) as colleagues, the men may not endorse career-enhancing strategies for women and/or may actively promote backlash strategies; (2) the men may not mentor women and/or may serve as poor role models to other men in their workplace relationships with women; and, (3) the men may not be supportive of the career aspirations of their own female partners or spouses (Burke 1994). In its research, Catalyst found that women who continue to bump into glass ceilings tend to leave large corporations and start their own businesses (Dobrzynski 1996).

Unlike women who enter male-dominated occupations, men who enter female-dominated occupations are apt to find little difficulty rising to the top of their occupation. In recent research on men working as registered nurses, elementary teachers, librarians, and social workers, sociologist Christine L. Williams (1995) found that they tended to rise in disproportionate numbers to administrative positions at the top of these occupations. Williams (1995:12) calls the upward movement of men in "women's professions" the *glass escalator* effect because, as she notes, "like being on an invisible 'up' escalator, men must struggle to remain in the lower (i.e., 'feminine') levels of their professions." Men also move into more "masculine" specialties within traditionally female-dominated occupations. Male librarians, for example, often move into high-technology computer information specialties and administration. In contrast, women in male-dominated occupations typically find they are bumping their heads on the glass ceiling and working a double shift.

The Double Shift

Although there have been dramatic changes in the participation of women in the labour force, the household division of labour by sex has remained unchanged in many families. While more married women now share responsibility for earning part—or all—of the family income, many married men still do not participate in routine domestic chores (Reskin and Padavic 1994). Consequently, many employed women must deal with a double workload. In the words of sociologist Arlie Hochschild (1989), women with dual responsibilities as wage earners and unpaid household workers work "the second shift" (see Table 4.2). However, the most recent data on housework and other unpaid labour demonstrates that men's participation in this type of work has increased from 72 percent in 1986 to 79 percent in 2005. Women's participation has remained steady at approximately 90 percent (Marshall 2006). Interestingly, there have been quite dramatic changes recently in the daily participation rate of what has been identified as "core housework," tasks such as meal preparation, cleaning, and laundry. Men's participation went from 40 percent in 1986 to 59 percent in 2005, while women's participation actually decreased from 88 percent to 85 percent (Marshall 2006)! There has also been an increase in women's hours per day at paid labour, from 4.5 hours to 5.4, and a corresponding decrease in hours spent doing housework. Basically, "more people today are doing some daily housework than in the past but they are spending less time at it" (Marshall 2006: 9).

While things are becoming slightly more equitable, albeit slowly, on the domestic labour front, the relative number of hours spent on housework still differs widely between women and men. Additionally, the kinds of chores men and women do also vary significantly. Women do most of the *daily* chores, such as making beds, cooking, cleaning up after meals, chauffeuring, and most of the taking care of children ("core" household work). As sociologist Adie Nelson states, "[w]omen's tasks tend to be routine, repetitive, monotonous and invisible (i.e., not noticed unless undone)" (2006:253). Men are more likely to do chores that do not have to be done every day ("non-core" work) and hence allow considerable scheduling autonomy. For example, men typically mow the lawn, repair cars or other equipment, clean out the eavestroughs, and do home improvements (Marshall 2006; Nelson 2006; Shelton 1992). Although some kinds of housework can be put off, young children's needs cannot be ignored or delayed, and daily duties in families with young children consume a great deal of time and energy. A sick child or a school event that cannot be scheduled around work causes additional stress for parents, especially mothers. Furthermore, more

and more women are becoming members of "the sandwich generation." In other words, they are caught, sandwiched, between the needs of their young children and those of older relatives for whom they are often the primary caregivers. The 1996 General Social Survey reported that among those employed for wages, 15 percent of women and 10 percent of men had additional responsibilities caring for someone with a long-term health issue (Nelson and Robinson 2002:233). In an effort to keep up with family obligations while working full- or part-time, many women spend a large portion of their earnings on fees to day-care and elder-care centres, prepared foods and meals from fast-food restaurants, and laundry services and dry-cleaning (Bergmann 1986).

When sociologists conduct research on participation in household work, both men and women state that working couples should share household responsibilities. However, when it comes down to who actually does what, most studies find that women, even those who hold full-time jobs, do most of that work. For example, in the 1996 census, 90 percent of Canadians stated that they did some unpaid household work, but the majority of this work was done by women, in terms of both the range of tasks and the number of hours contributed (Nelson 2006; Wilson 2001). This pattern remains true today. According to Arlie Hochschild

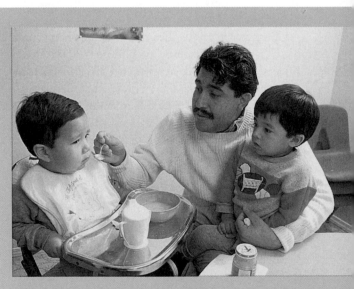

Most employed women encounter a second or even third shift when they get home from work. According to researchers, employed women still do most of the daily household chores, and most of the work involved in taking care of the children. Is this photo a hopeful sign for the future?

(1989), many women try to solve their time crunch by forgoing leisure activities and sleep. Additionally women become skilled multi-taskers. In sociologist Melody Hessing's (1993) study of employed Canadian mothers, she found that women used a variety of strategies to cope with their double shifts. They used workday lunch hours for grocery shopping, running errands, and visiting children's schools. They worked long hours and did the housecleaning in the evenings, around food preparation, laundry, and child care. They made several meals at once and prepared bag lunches ahead of time. As noted by Wilson (2001:234), "They rarely had the luxury of doing one job at a time." While the women in the study were able to cope, they did find this juggling act "stressful, physically exhausting and emotionally draining" (Wilson 2001:234).

It was not until 1996, after years of lobbying by women's groups, that the census was amended to include questions on unpaid labour. There was reluctance to measure unpaid hours of work (mainly accomplished by women) and even more resistance to attaching a dollar value to this work, work that has been carefully constructed as women's "voluntary selflessly performed 'labour of love'" (Nelson 2006:248). The census provided some interesting findings: the Vanier Institute of the Family (2000) reported that Canadians spend approximately 20 billion hours on housework annually, at least two-thirds of which is done by women, for a dollar value of more than $197 billion per year (Nelson 2006: 247). Data from the 2001 census demonstrates that the current value of unpaid housework in Canada is approximately 40 percent of Canada's GDP, conceding, as sociologist Augie Fleras points out, "the collapse of Canada's market economy without the invisible labour of women's unpaid work" (Fleras 2005:114).

The fact that women are still disproportionately responsible for unpaid household labour and child care, even while holding a full-time paid position, contributes to the pursuit of what has been dubbed by journalists as "the mommy track"—a less-pressured, lower-paid stream of employment, characterized by fewer opportunities for advancement than the typical "fast track" stream that males are expected to be on. While on the surface, the mommy track seems to provide a good compromise for those women (but not men?) who wish to combine family responsibilities with their career, it is significant that industry and business are not expected to accommodate the real needs of workers. As social critics Barbara Ehrenreich and Deirdre English (1995:215) point out, "Bumping women—or just fertile women, or married women, or whomever—off the fast track may sound smart . . . [but] it is the corporate culture itself that needs to slow down to a human pace. . . . Workloads that are incompatible with family life are. . . a kind of toxin—to men as well as women, and ultimately to businesses as well as families." Holding dual responsibilities, as women do, has resulted in many women having to make the difficult choice between family and the inferiorly compensated mommy track or no family and a career (the fast track). Because men do not have the same responsibilities for unpaid domestic labour and child care, they are free to choose both family *and* a fast-track career. For example, only approximately 40 percent of top female executives have children compared with 95 percent of top male executives (Ehrenreich and English 1995:211).

PERSPECTIVES ON GENDER INEQUALITY

Unlike functionalist and conflict perspectives, which focus on macrolevel sources of gender inequality, feminist perspectives focus on both macro structural levels and micro interactional levels. Interactionist perspectives typically focus on social constructs such as language. It is language, interactionists say, that structures our thinking and discourse about domination and subordination.

The Interactionist Perspective

Symbolic interactionists focus on the differential socialization processes that create masculinity and femininity in people. When a child is assigned a gender at birth, typically corresponding to sex, culturally appropriate gender socialization begins wholeheartedly. Children learn which attitudes, skills, behaviours, likes and dislikes, and so on are appropriate for each gender. Many people believe that socialization has changed, with fewer restrictions on the ways children are taught to act, think, and feel. It is important to recognize that many differences, where they exist at all, are class-based, with people from working classes typically enforcing more conformity to stereotypical roles. People from the middle classes often allow children more autonomy, but gender roles based on stereotypes are so entrenched and pervasive in the dominant culture that pressure to conform is enormous for most children.

Interactionists, who view society as the sum of people's interactions, view language as extremely significant in defining social realities because it provides people with shared meanings and social realities. Historically, what men have thought, written, and concluded have been the givens of our discourse (Peterson and Runyan 1993). Today, however, English and other languages are being criticized for *linguistic sexism,* that is, for words and patterns of communication that ignore, devalue, or make sex objects of women.

Linguistic sexism, some analysts believe, perpetuates traditional gender-role stereotypes and reinforces male dominance. These analysts note that the idea that women are secondary to men in importance is embedded in the English language: The masculine form (*he*) has traditionally been used to refer to human beings generally, and words such as *chairman* and *mankind* are considered to include both men and women (Miller and Swift 1991). When a woman enters a profession such as medicine or law, she is frequently referred to as a "female doctor" or "woman lawyer"; such terms linguistically protect these male-dominated professions from invasion by females (Lindsey 1994).

Language can also be used to devalue women by referring to them in terms that reinforce the notion that they are sex objects. Terms such as *fox, bitch, babe,* or *doll* further devalue women by ascribing petlike, childlike, or toylike attributes to them (Adams and Ware 1995). According to one analyst, at least 220 terms exist for sexually promiscuous women, but only 22 terms exist for sexually promiscuous men (Stanley 1972).

Research by scholars in a variety of disciplines has demonstrated not only the importance of language in patterning our thoughts but also how gender—and the hierarchy it constructs—is built into the English language (Peterson and Runyan 1993). According to sociologists Claire M. Renzetti and Daniel J. Curran (1995:151), "Given that women are denigrated, unequally defined, and often ignored by the English language, it serves not only to reflect their secondary status relative to men in our society, but also to reinforce it."

Linguist Deborah Tannen (1990) has examined how power differentials between women and men at home and in the workplace are reflected in their communication styles. According to Tannen (1990), men and women speak different *genderlects:* women are socialized to speak and hear a language of intimacy and connection, while men are socialized to speak and hear a language of status and independence. For example, women's conversations tend to focus more on relationships with others and include "rapport talk." Men's conversations are more likely to convey messages about their position in workplace or social hierarchies and include "report talk." In explanation, Tannen (1990:77) states that,

> For most women, the language of conversation is primarily a language of rapport: a way of establishing connections and negotiating relationships. Emphasis is placed on displaying similarities and matching experiences. . . . For most men, talk is primarily a means to preserve independence and negotiate and maintain status in a hierarchical social order. This is done by exhibiting knowledge and skill and by holding center stage through verbal performance such as story telling, joking, or imparting information.

Men's and women's communication styles also differ. Men have a more direct style of communication and are more likely to dominate conversations than women are. Men are taught to seek immediate solutions for problems, while women are taught to consider a variety of alternatives before reaching a decision. From this perspective, communication not only reflects women's and men's relative power in society but also perpetuates gender inequalities.

At the microlevel of interactions, we can see some of the ways that male dominance is perpetuated through non-verbal forms of communication, such as bodily movement, posture, eye contact, use of personal space, and touching. Men typically control more space than women do, whether they are sitting or standing. Men tend to invade women's personal space by standing close to them, touching them, or staring at them. Such actions are not necessarily sexual in connotation; however, when a man nudges and fondles a flight attendant or a co-worker in the office, these actions do have sexual overtones that cannot be dismissed. Recent sexual harassment cases show that women do not appreciate such acts and feel threatened by them, especially when the toucher is the employer (Lindsey 1994:79).

Although the interactionist perspective has been criticized for ignoring the larger, structural factors that perpetuate gender inequality, it is important to note that language and communication patterns are embedded in the structure of society and pass from generation to generation through the socialization process.

The Functionalist Perspective

In focusing on macrolevel issues affecting gender inequality, functionalists frequently examine employment opportunities and the wage gap between men and women.

According to such early functionalists as Talcott Parsons (1955), gender inequality is inevitable because of the biological division of labour: Men generally are physically stronger than women and have certain abilities and interests, whereas women, as the only sex able to bear and nurse children, have their own abilities and interests. Given the biological attributes, Parsons said, men find themselves more suited to *instrumental* (goal-oriented) *tasks* and women to *expressive* (emotionally oriented) *tasks*. In the home, therefore, husbands perform such instrumental tasks as providing economic support and making the most important decisions for the family, while wives perform such expressive tasks as nurturing children and providing emotional support for all family members. The division of labour by gender ensures that important societal tasks—such as procreation and the socialization of children—are fulfilled and that the family is socially and economically stable.

According to Parsons, this division of labour continues in the workplace, where women again do expressive work and men again do instrumental work. Thus, women cluster in occupations that require expressive work, such as elementary school teaching, nursing, and secretarial work, because of their interests and abilities. Women also are concentrated in specific specialties within professions such as law and medicine because of their aptitude for expressive work and their desire to spend more time with their families than men, who are in the more lucrative specialties, are able to spend. For example, many women in law specialize in family law, and many women in medicine specialize in pediatrics (infants and children), obstetrics and gynecology

(women), or family practice. In corporations, women are thought to be more adept at public relations and human resources; men are viewed as more adept at financial management.

In recent years, however, critics have rejected the dichotomy between men's instrumental work and women's expressive work set forth by functionalists (see Scott 1996). These critics have noted that the functionalist explanation of gender inequality does not take into account sex discrimination and other structural barriers that make some educational and occupational opportunities more available to men than to women. It also fails to examine the underlying power relations between women and men and does not consider the fact that society places unequal value on tasks assigned to men and women (Kemp 1994). Functionalist theories tend to justify and perpetuate gender inequities in these ways.

Other functionalist explanations of gender inequality focus on the human capital that men and women bring to the workplace. According to human capital explanations, what individuals earn is based on choices they have made, including choices about the kinds of training and experience they accumulate. For example, human capital analysts argue that women diminish their human capital when they leave the labour force to engage in child-bearing and child-care activities. While women are out of the labour force, their human capital deteriorates from non-use. When they return to paid employment, they earn lower wages than men do because they have fewer years of work experience and "atrophied human capital," that is, because their education and training may have become obsolete (Kemp 1994:70).

Critics of the human capital model note that it is based on the false assumption that all people, regardless of gender, racialization, or other attributes, are evaluated and paid fairly on the basis of their education, training, and other job-enhancing characteristics. It fails to acknowledge that White women and people of colour tend to be paid less even when they are employed in male-dominated occupations and take no time off for family duties (Lorber 1994).

Conflict Perspectives

Conflict perspectives on gender inequality are based on the assumption that social life is a continuous struggle in which members of powerful groups (males, in this case) seek to maintain control of scarce resources such as social, economic, and political superiority. By dominating individual women and commanding social institutions, men maintain positions of privilege and power. However, as conflict theorists note, not all men are equally privileged: Men in the upper classes have greater economic power because they control elite positions in corporations, universities, the mass media, and government (Richardson 1993).

Conflict theorists using a Marxist approach believe that gender inequality primarily results from capitalism and private ownership of the means of production. The gendered division of labour is seen to be inherent in capitalism and, therefore, will disappear with the demise of capitalism (Mackie 1987). With the development of private property and inheritance based upon primogeniture, women were transformed from equal, productive members of society in hunting and gathering economies into subordinate wives (and also into property or "chattel"). Further, with the institution of bourgeois marriage, women found it necessary to exchange their sexual and reproductive services for economic support (Mackie 1987). As industrialization progressed and production moved further from the home, women's skills and education became increasingly separate from those required in the paid labour force. Therefore, according to conflict theorists, the subordinate position of women is the result, not of biology, as functionalists believe, but as a result of structural and historical relations (Mooney et al. 2001).

Conflict theories have been criticized for their view that gender inequality is an inherent and inevitable feature of capitalist relations and for the simplistic and androcentric view that the liberation of women is dependent on the liberation of the working class. As sociologist Rosalind Sydie (1983:216) points out, " . . . history would take care of the 'woman question'; therefore the issue [could] be ignored and the 'proper' focus of attention—class relations—be attended to."

Feminist Perspectives

Feminist perspectives in general challenge the status quo with regard to the unequal position of females in society. Feminism, however, is far from being a unified voice. Instead, it is multifaceted, critical, and activist, seeing both the scope of the problem of gender inequality, and its solutions, differently. Basing their work on a Marxist approach, *socialist feminists* state that under capitalism, men gain control over property and over women. Thus, *capitalism* exploits women in the workplace, and *patriarchy* exploits women at home (Kemp 1994). According to this perspective, capitalists benefit from the gendered division of labour in the workplace because they can pay women lower wages and derive higher profits. Cultural ideas about the appropriateness of women in the home ensure that women return to the home after any stints in the paid labour force (for example, as a worker in the reserve army of labour required by a capitalist economy—see Chapter 2). At the same time, individual men benefit from the unpaid work women do at home by simply not having to do it and by having more leisure time. The capitalist economic system is maintained because women reproduce the next generation of workers while providing current employees (often including themselves) with food, clean clothes, and other goods and services that are necessary for those who must show up at the workplace each day (Hartmann 1976). Sociologist Marlene Mackie (1987:40) notes that "to pay women for their efforts would mean a massive redistribution of wealth." In addition, men who labour under capitalism can feel a sense of power by having a superior social position to women and may be less apt to agitate. Marxist feminist perspectives have been criticized for their emphasis on male dominance without a corresponding analysis of how men, specifically, may be oppressed by capitalism and/or patriarchy.

Unlike socialist feminists, *radical feminists* focus exclusively on *patriarchy* as the primary source of gender inequality. From this perspective, men's oppression of women is deliberate, with ideological justification provided by other institutions such as the media and religion. The subordination of women is naturalized through the assumptions inherent in patriarchy. Radical feminism challenges patriarchy and male hegemony, seeing many traditional institutions—the nuclear family in particular—as sites of female enslavement and "domestic servitude" (Fleras 2001:133). Radical feminists are criticized for their focus on patriarchy to the exclusion of other structures of domination (like class, racialization, and so on).

Liberal feminists believe that gender inequality is rooted in *gender-role socialization*, which perpetuates women's lack of equal rights and educational opportunities. This type of feminism arises out of classical liberal notions of individual freedoms or liberty. Women are seen to be unequal because they are not given access to the opportunities to make comparable wages and so on. The aim of this type of feminism, therefore, is to ensure that women are equally distributed in education and the paid labour force, alongside men. The system is seen as inherently sound and would be transformed with the removal of discriminatory barriers. Liberal feminism is criticized for its lack of focus on the structural roots of inequalities.

Black feminists, Indigenous feminists, and other feminists "of colour" believe that Indigenous women and women of colour face heightened inequalities based on the multiplicative effect of racialization, class, and gender as simultaneous forces of oppression (Andersen and Collins 1997). Oppressions are seen as intersecting patterns of subordination that cannot be viewed or treated as separate issues, but rather, that must be seen as a complex whole. Solutions to gender inequality, therefore, are inextricably linked with solutions to oppression generally. Lesbians and women with a disability experience the effects of this matrix of domination as well, in our hierarchically organized society. Feminists from the margins, those who experience multilayered oppressions, have led the much-needed critique of other feminist perspectives, advancing the incisiveness of feminist perspectives overall and strengthening activism across difference.

CAN GENDER INEQUALITY BE REDUCED?

Although the rights and working conditions of women have improved during the past 40 years, much remains to be done before gender inequality is eradicated or even significantly reduced. As for how, specifically, to go about reducing gender inequality, a point that was made in previous chapters bears repeating: How people view social problems directly affects how they think the problem should be solved. Interactionists, for example, think gender inequality can be reduced only when people redefine social realities such as linguistic sexism. In their view, language should be modified so that it no longer conveys notions of male superiority and female inferiority, which are then transmitted intergenerationally through the socialization process.

Some functionalists believe that traditional gender roles should be redefined for the well-being of individuals and society, but other functionalists suggest that women should become more aware of how their human capital is diminished by decisions they make. From this perspective, to be competitive in the workplace, women must have the same educational background and qualifications for positions that men have. Some functionalists also suggest that overt sex discrimination can be reduced by enforcing existing legislation such as the *Canadian Charter of Human Rights and Freedoms* or various provincial Human Rights Codes, which forbid discrimination on the basis of sex or gender. However, this approach would not affect covert or institutionalized discrimination, which has a negative and differential impact on White, non-White, and Indigenous women.

While some conflict theorists view elimination of sex discrimination as the primary solution for gender inequality, those using a Marxist approach believe that gender equality will occur only when capitalism is abolished. Socialist feminists agree that capitalism should be eliminated and a new economy that eliminates the gendered division of labour and the wage gap between women and men should be developed. Liberal feminists say that we could reduce gender inequality by dramatically changing gender socialization and what children learn from their families, teachers, and the media about appropriate masculine and feminine attitudes and behaviour. Radical feminists suggest that gender inequality can be reduced only when patriarchy is abolished. To achieve this goal, they say that the legal system must continue to provide relief for sex discrimination, especially sexual harassment in schools and the workplace, and that alternative institutions must be developed to replace existing gendered social institutions. For example, women's health care centres should replace male-dominated medicine, and child-care and elder-care centres should assume some of women's caregiving burdens. Finally, Black feminists and other feminists "from the margins" believe that equality will occur only when all women—regardless of racialization, class, gender, age, religion, sexual orientation, and ability or disability—are treated equitably (Andersen and Collins 1997).

Clearly, many gender issues remain unresolved. As a result of technological changes and the proliferation of service jobs, such as information clerk, nurses' aide, and fast-food restaurant worker, which often are equated with "women's work," gender-segregated jobs may increase rather than decrease. Moreover, if the number and quality of "men's jobs" shrink, many men at all class levels may become more resistant to women entering traditionally male-dominated occupations and professions (Reskin and Padavic 1994). Many analysts suggest that for a significant reduction in gender inequality to occur, women have to become more involved in the political arena and take action themselves. Again, however, this view implies that the system itself is essentially sound and that reform is possible using the tools that have been traditionally available. What do you think?

WHAT CAN YOU DO?

Gender inequality is a complex social problem that is rooted in structural sexism and that manifests itself every day in actions and in interpersonal interactions. In terms of proactive things that you can do, then, much depends on the situations you most often find yourself in, as well as what your interests are. Below are a few suggestions for social action that is either preventative or interventionist. What others can you think of?

■ Get involved in political actions in your province by joining in protests and teach-ins and by writing letters to MPPs/MLAs and the newspapers (e.g., about recent pay equity campaigns).

■ Lobby government to restore and increase core funding for women-serving organizations like women's shelters and women's centres and sexual assault centres by writing letters to government officials linking your thoughts with your vote.

■ Fundraise alone (smaller-scale effort) or with others (larger-scale effort) to support women-serving organizations in your municipality.

■ Create coalitions, along with other justice-seeking groups, to raise awareness of the gender inequality issue of interest to you.

■ Start or join a group aimed at effecting change on an issue of interest to you. (For example, in 2001, a group of men started the Men Against Sexualized Violence Group at the University of Victoria. They undertook the White Ribbon campaign, which involved them linking up with the National White Ribbon campaign, and they came to many classrooms to talk to their peers about the relationship of men to sexualized violence against women.)

■ Sign on to internet listservs and websites of groups and organizations whose interests you share as a means of keeping up to date on the issue and informing others.

■ Break the cultural taboo about wage secrecy and share information about wages as widely as possible with co-workers. Many businesses explicitly instruct employees not to discuss their wages. It is very possible that these places are paying people inequitably. You may be surprised to find where you are on the wage scale, despite what company representatives imply. If there are inequities, expose them and lobby the company to redress the situations of underpaid workers.

■ When you are being told a sexist joke (or a joke that is typically inherently sexist, like the "blonde joke"), explain to the person that the joke perpetuates harmful and derogatory stereotypes about women and that you do not find the demeaning of people amusing.

■ Be alert and open to hearing about (other) women's experiences with sexism or violence. Ask women you know what their experiences have been. Educate yourself about people's differing experiences—talk to males and females, White women and non-White women, lesbians, "trans" people, and so on. Try to hear the experience without judgment.

■ Report violence whenever you see or hear it by calling 911. Do not get involved in a situation that is unsafe physically: Call law enforcement.

■ Go to court and watch the trials of men charged with sexual assault, assaulting a women, or femicide. Critically analyze the approach of the justice system to the case. How did police handle it? How did lawyers handle it? How did the judge handle it? Write a letter to the local newspaper and/or your college/university newspaper with your analysis.

■ Think about all the words you use that are gender exclusive and/or sexist. Think of words that you can use to replace them and begin practising (don't worry about not being perfect! It takes a long time to unlearn this).

■ Educate yourself and others about "trans" issues. You may even know a "trans" person and be unaware of it. Try not to assume.

- Support "trans" people when and wherever they are. Support people's inalienable right to feel comfortable in their own skin.

- Include "trans" issues whenever you talk or write about gender. In the words of renowned feminist scholar Adrienne Rich (1984), "When someone with the authority of a teacher describes the world and you are not in it, there is a moment of psychic disequilibrium, as if you looked into a mirror and saw nothing."

- Next time you, a friend, or a relative has a child, look for gender-neutral clothing, accessories, and toys and books that promote gender equality.

- Think of any gender-stereotypical assumptions you own and challenge them.

- Consumerism is power. Begin a boycott campaign against companies that use women in narrow, stereotypical, and objectified ways in advertising. Write to the company and tell it what you are doing and why and in what ways you are planning to get your boycott message out.

- Put a sign in the window of your vehicle or on your backpack stating which local company exploits its female workers and how. (Make sure you have your facts correct.)

- Write a letter to the newspaper or advertise in some other way about companies that do have gender-equitable policies, wages, and so on. This demonstrates to all companies that the public is watching and does care.

- Report offences and breeches to the appropriate person or office (e.g., to police, ombuds offices, or anti-harassment offices on campuses). Be persistent. Get support. Be an advocate for people whose voices are marginalized in these systems. Help them to report and follow up, if appropriate.

- Volunteer for crisis lines, sexual assault centres, and women's shelters (men can volunteer in many of these places by going out and doing community education and/or fundraising, for example). It is important to demonstrate to the community that violence against women is not a women's issue: it is a community issue.

- If you witness sexual harassment in a public place, lend support to the person suffering and/or make it uncomfortable for the perpetrator to harass (again, do not take risks to your own safety).

- Think about ways in which your actions and words maintain current beauty standards. Think of ways to celebrate and support all women.

- Begin discussions with your family and friends about an issue of sexism that interests you. Inform people about some of the facts you have learned and explain why you feel that is unjust.

- Make music, make art, make word collages, make zines—whatever—that promotes the message that gender inequality is unjust and has got to go. Get that message out there!

SUMMARY

HOW DOES SEX DIFFER FROM GENDER?

Sex is the biological aspects of being male or female; gender is the socially constructed differences between females and males. In short, sex is what we (generally) are born with; gender is what we acquire through socialization. We currently operate under a two-sex, two-gender system that views the sexes/genders as binary opposites.

WHAT ARE THE PRIMARY SOCIALIZING AGENTS?

The key socializing agents are parents, peers, teachers and schools, and the media, all of which may reinforce gender stereotypes and gender-based inequalities as they attempt to teach culturally based gender-appropriate behaviour.

HOW ARE SEXISM AND PATRIARCHY RELATED?

Individual and institutional sexism are maintained and reinforced by patriarchy, a hierarchical system in which cultural, political, and economic structures are dominated by males.

WHAT ARE SOME OF THE PRIMARY CAUSES OF GENDER INEQUALITY?

Gender inequality results from economic, political, and educational discrimination against women as evidenced in gender-segregated work, which in turn results in a disparity—or wage gap—between women's and men's earnings. Even when women are employed in the same job as men, on average they do not receive the same (or comparable) pay.

WHAT IS THE SECOND SHIFT? WHY IS IT A PROBLEM FOR WOMEN?

The second shift is the unpaid household work and child care performed by employed women. Many women have a second shift because of their dual responsibilities in the workplace and at home. The typical woman in Canada who combines paid work in the labour force with parenting and housework does not have enough hours in the average day to fulfill all her responsibilities, and many men have been unwilling or unable to pick up some of the slack at home. Women, thus, employ a variety of creative strategies for coping with this problem.

HOW DO FUNCTIONALIST AND CONFLICT ANALYSTS EXPLAIN THE GENDERED DIVISION OF LABOUR?

According to functionalist analysts, women's caregiver roles in contemporary industrialized societies are crucial in ensuring that key societal tasks are fulfilled. While the husband performs the instrumental tasks of economic support and decision making, the wife assumes the expressive tasks of providing affection and emotional support for the family. According to conflict analysts, the gendered division of labour within families and the workplace results from male control and dominance over women and resources.

WHAT ARE THE MAJOR FEMINIST PERSPECTIVES? HOW DO THEY EXPLAIN GENDER INEQUALITY?

In liberal feminism, gender equality is connected to equality of opportunity. In radical feminism, male dominance is seen as the cause of oppression. According to socialist feminists, women's oppression results from capitalism and patriarchy and women's dual roles as paid and unpaid workers. Anti-racist feminism and other feminisms from the margins focus on matrices of oppression, linking gender inequality with other forms of oppression, such as class oppression, racialization, sexual orientation or preference, ability, age, and so on.

HOW DOES SYMBOLIC INTERACTIONISM EXPLAIN GENDER INEQUALITY?

Symbolic interactionists view gender inequality as the result of faulty gender role socialization, in which language use, including body language, plays a significant role. Inequality between the sexes is seen to exist and be perpetuated through the use of gender exclusive and/or sexist language and through non-verbal actions, such as male invasion of female space or males touching females in mixed-gender interactions.

KEY TERMS

androcentricity, p. 87
comparable worth, p. 105
contingent work, p. 103
gender, p. 87
gender bias, p. 97

gendered division of labour, p. 92
gender ideology, p. 92
glass ceiling, p. 108
intersexed, p. 87
patriarchy, p. 85, 102

pay equity, p. 105
pink-collar ghetto, p. 103
rape culture, p. 101
sex, p. 87

sexism, p. 85
sexual harassment, p. 98
wage gap, p. 104

QUESTIONS FOR CRITICAL THINKING

1.   Examine the various administrative offices and academic departments at your college or university. What is the gender breakdown of administrators, faculty, and staff in selected departments? Can you identify a gender-related pattern associated with women's and men's work at your school? What conclusions can you draw about the relationship between gender and employment, based on your observations? Are there any policies in place to counteract gendered inequities in that workplace? Do they work? Why or why not?

2.   Will the increasing numbers of women in higher education, the workplace, and the military, particularly in non-traditional positions or majors, tip the balance of power between men and women and result in greater gender equality in the future? Explain why or why not.

3.   What is the role of violence against women in our culture? In what ways do MuchMusic and other music-video shows perpetuate a "rape culture" and violence against women in Canada? What could be done to change this?

4.   In what ways does traditional gender socialization support capitalism?

WEBLINKS

World March of Women

www.marchemondiale.org
The World March of Women is an international feminist action network connecting about 6000 grass-roots groups in 163 countries and territories working to eliminate poverty and violence against women.

Canadian Feminist Alliance for International Action (FAFIA/AFAI)

www.fafia-afai.org
FAFIA/AFAI is a coalition of over 50 Canadian women's equality-seeking and related organizations whose mandate is to further women's equality in Canada through domestic implementation of its international human rights commitments.

Canadian Federation of University Women (CFUW)

www.cfuw.org
CFUW is a non-profit, voluntary organization of over 10 000 women graduates working to improve the socio-economic and legal situation of women. The site offers informative links, a message board, and an opportunity to join.

The History of Women and Gender in Canada

www.hartford-hwp.com/archives/44/index-eb.html
Part of the World History Archives, this page provides links to articles, essays, and information about the history of women and gender in Canada.

Canadian Research Institute for the Advancement of Women (CRIAW)

www.criaw-icref.ca

CRIAW is a national not-for-profit organization committed to advancing women's equality through research. The site gives links to a list of the organization's publications, conferences, and workshops, a database of feminist researchers, and other resources.

Match International Centre

www.matchinternational.org

Match International Centre is a nongovernmental women's organization dedicated to strengthening women's movements nationally and internationally. It was created to bring to life a feminist vision of what development work can, and should, mean.

Men for Change

www.chebucto.ns.ca/CommunitySupport/Men4Change

The site of Men for Change, a pro-feminist organization dedicating to promoting gender equality, offers information and links to those who wish to better understand and put an end to sexism and sexism-related violence.

National Clearinghouse on Family Violence (NCFV)

www.hc-sc.gc.ca/hppb/familyviolence

Health Canada's NCFV is a national resource centre providing information and research findings about violence within the family, including all aspects of its prevention and treatment.

Status of Women Canada

www.swc-cfc.gc.ca

The mandate of this federal ministry is to promote gender equality and ensure that women participate fully in the economic, social, cultural, and political landscapes of Canada. The site provides links to learning resources and tools that promote women's equality.

The 3rd WWWave

www.3rdwwwave.com

This site devoted to women's issues and Third Wave feminism provides information on and discussions of politics, sexuality, hobbies, and other topics.

5

INEQUALITY BASED ON AGE

AGEISM AS A SOCIAL PROBLEM

Age-Based Stereotypes

Social Inequality and the Life Course

Box 5.1 Social Problems in the Media: Media Ageism: Reporting on and Preferring Age Groups

Suicide and the Life Course

Death and Dying

Box 5.2 Social Problems and Social Policy: Euthanasia

PROBLEMS THOUGHT TO BE ASSOCIATED WITH AGING

Workplace Discrimination

Retirement and Changing Roles

Health, Illness, and Health Care

Victimization

Family Problems and Social Isolation

Housing Patterns and Long-Term-Care Facilities

PERSPECTIVES ON AGING AND SOCIAL INEQUALITY

The Functionalist Perspective

The Interactionist Perspective

The Conflict Perspective

The Feminist Perspective

CAN AGE-BASED INEQUALITY BE REDUCED?

WHAT CAN YOU DO?

A teacher saw my picture [in a newspaper article about 90-year-olds] in *USA Today* and had her class write to me. I got thirty lovely letters . . . . I've never been to the South, so I flew [to Decatur, Alabama] . . . . I answer any of their questions. Do you still have your own teeth? Do you have a boyfriend? I say, "No, but I'm looking for one who can cook. If you find somebody like that, let me know." They think it's funny.

They want to know how it feels to be ninety. I tell them I feel like myself. Don't you all feel like yourself? Okay, there's a difference. When I was your age, I loved to play basketball and climb mountains and slide down the other side. One thing I didn't want to do was make speeches. It was scary. Now I don't want to climb mountains and play basketball. I love to make speeches. So you see, when you're ninety, you'll do what you feel like doing. In a way, I'm telling them to value old age and respect it.

Hazel Wolf, age 95, in an interview with author Studs Terkel (1996:140)

As Hazel Wolf's statement indicates, how people of one age view people of another age is relative. Young people may view older people as "over the hill," while older people may consider the young as lacking experience. Throughout one's lifetime, age is a very important ascribed characteristic. Just consider how many times you have been asked, "How old are you?" Most of us answer this question in terms of *chronological age*—age based on date of birth. Although chronological age constitutes our "official" age, most of us view other people in terms of their *functional age*—observable individual attributes such as physical appearance, mobility, strength, coordination, and mental capacity that are used to assign people to age categories (McPherson 1990:31). A wide range of physical, psychological, and intellectual factors can influence our functional age (Chudacoff 1989). Although we may appear to be younger or older than our chronological age, there are some things that we do in life, such as driving a car or voting, that are determined by our chronological age rather than our functional age. Children—regardless of ability—are not allowed to drive and therefore eagerly look forward to the time when they will be "old enough" to drive. For the younger person, then, changes in chronological and functional age are positive. However, as some people age, they begin to lose some of the functional abilities, such as vision or hearing, that are necessary for driving. Thus, the older person may view changes in chronological and functional age negatively.

However, unless these changes can be proven to have a direct effect on one's activities, should people be forced to follow such traditional rules as mandatory retirement at age 65? Now, in some circles, retirement at age 65 is being thought of as discrimination, or *ageism*, and against the *Charter of Rights and Freedoms*. Many Canadian provinces and territories, such as Alberta, Manitoba, Quebec, PEI, New Brunswick, Yukon, Northwest Territories, and Nunavut, have banned mandatory retirement. Ontario's legislation to end mandatory retirement was passed in 2005 and came into effect on December 12, 2006.

To help us think about these and other questions related to inequalities and aging, this chapter deals with stereotypes and inequalities through the life course, with special emphasis on the elderly; suicide and the life course; death and dying and the question of euthanasia; problems of workplace discrimination and retirement; problems of health, illness, and health care; criminal victimization; and family relationships, housing, and long-term care.

The sociological perspectives are used to help explain aging problems. The chapter concludes with a discussion of ways to reduce inequality based on age and what you can do about it.

AGEISM AS A SOCIAL PROBLEM

Ageism—**prejudice and discrimination against people on the basis of age**—is a social problem that particularly stigmatizes and marginalizes older people. Gerontologist Robert Butler (1969) introduced the term *ageism* to describe how myths and misconceptions about older people produce age-based discrimination. According to Butler, just as racism and sexism perpetuate stereotyping and discrimination against people of colour and all women, ageism perpetuates stereotyping of older people and age-based discrimination. Most research has therefore focused on the negative and differential impact ageism has on older people.

Age-Based Stereotypes

There are more stereotypes about the physical and mental abilities of older people than there are about the abilities of people in any other age category. This does not mean that children and adolescents are exempt from age-based stereotypes. Comedians often refer to very young children as "crumb crunchers," "rug rats," and "little hellions." Animated television characters such as Bart and Lisa Simpson (*The Simpsons*), Beavis and Butt-Head (MTV), and young characters in many situation comedies and movies are simply stereotypic depictions of children and young adolescents.

Older people, however, are stereotyped in numerous ways. Some stereotypes depict them as slow in their thinking and movement; as living in the past and unable to change; and as cranky, sickly, and lacking in social value (Novak and Campbell 2006:7). Other stereotypes suggest that older people are "greedy geezers," living an affluent lifestyle and ignoring the needs of future generations (Toner 1995). When age-based stereotypes are accepted by many people, they can affect how people vote and what types of social policies legislators enact. Negative stereotypes of older people reinforce ageism and influence how younger people interact with older people.

Although most of us do not believe that we engage in stereotypical thinking about older people, researcher William C. Levin (1988) found that college students in his study evaluated people differently on the basis of their assumed age. Levin showed students three photographs of the same man, who had been made up to appear 25 in the first photo, 52 in the second, and 73 in the third. He then asked them to evaluate these (apparently different) men for employment purposes. Many students described the "73-year-old" as less competent, less intelligent, and less reliable than the "25-year-old" and the "52-year-old." Low ratings of the elderly are also given by older people. In a survey of older people, Ian D. Graham and Paul M. Baker (1989) found an inverted U-shaped curve of status ratings on a six-point scale: Older and younger people were rated lower than middle-aged people. Clearly our place in the social structure changes during our life course, and if we live long enough, any of us may become the target of stereotyping and discrimination directed at older people (Hooyman and Kiyak 1996).

Social Inequality and the Life Course

To study age and social inequality, many sociologists and social gerontologists focus on the *life course*—the age-based categories through which people pass as they grow older. In North America, the life course tends to be divided into infancy and childhood, adolescence and young adulthood, middle age, later maturity, and old age. The field of *gerontology* examines the biological, physical, and social aspects of the aging process. We will focus primarily on **social gerontology—the study of the social (non-physical) aspects of aging**—as we examine age classifications in Canada.

Childhood

Infants (birth to age two) and children (ages 3 to 12) are among the most powerless individuals in society. In the past, children were seen as the property of their parents, who could do with their children as they chose (Tower 1996). Although we have a more liberal attitude today, children remain vulnerable to problems such as family instability, poverty, maltreatment by relatives and other caregivers, and sexual exploitation. The Canadian Council on Social Development reports that:

- Poor children (family incomes less than $20 000) are 1.4 times more likely to engage in aggressive behaviour than children of middle- or higher income families;

- Poor children are 1.8 and 2.6 times more likely to exhibit delinquent behaviour than children from middle- and higher- income families, respectively;

- Serious health problems that affect a child's functioning, such as vision, hearing speech, or cognition, are 1.7 and 2.6 times more likely to be found in poor children than children in middle- and higher-income families; and

- Poor children are 1.8 times as likely to be registered in special education classes (Ross, Scott, and Smith 2000:2).

Non-poor children have problems also. For example, the 1998–99 cycle of the *National Longitudinal Survey of Children and Youth* (see Chapter 11 for an outline of this study) found that over one-third of children aged 2 to 11 were overweight and half of these children were obese. Obesity is now estimated to be higher among children than among adults (Statistics Canada 2002j; see Chapter 10 for more on obesity).

Relatively high rates of single parenthood, a significant increase in the divorce rate in recent decades, differing parenting styles (see Chapter 11), and the fact that many parents work several jobs in an attempt to make ends meet have caused many children to face a complex array of problems and social relationships in their families.

Adolescence

Before the 20th century, the concept of adolescence did not exist. When children grew big enough to do adult work, they were expected to fulfill adult responsibilities, such as making money to support their family (Chudacoff 1989). Today, the line between childhood and adolescence is blurred. While some researchers define adolescence as the teenage years (ages 13 to 19), others place the lower and upper ages at 15 and 24, respectively (Corr, Nabe, and Corr 1994).

Adolescents tread a narrow path between childhood and adulthood. They are not treated as children, but they are not afforded the full status of adulthood. Early teens are considered too young to drive, to drink alcohol, to stay out late, and to do other things that are considered to be adult behaviour by the media, particularly television and movies, and by members of some peer groups. Adolescents face an identity crisis in which they must figure out who they are and what they want to become. They face difficult decisions pertaining to their sexuality, their relationships with people of the same sex and the opposite sex, and fitting in with their peers. They also face educational, economic, and work problems such as

- Choosing an education for an occupation with some permanence;

- Getting high marks to enter appropriate programs, often requiring more than one degree;

- Earning money (and /or repaying loans) for tuition (see Chapter 12) and living expenses for the education necessary for the occupation; and
- Knowing that they will be surviving on low pay during the early years in the occupation.

Dealing with these or even some of these problems take its toll. The Canadian Community Health Survey (see Chapter 10) found that teenagers and young adults aged between 15 and 24 years were almost twice as likely to report symptoms of mood and anxiety disorders and substance dependencies than older adults (Statistics Canada 2003a). Support for the latter finding comes from the Canadian Addiction Survey (see Chapter 8). The researchers found that young people aged 15 to 24 years were twice as likely to be doing weekly heavy drinking (five or more drinks on one occasion) than people older than them. Moreover, young adults are less likely than older adults to use mental health resources. Only one-quarter of young adults were getting help, such as consultations with health professionals, religious advisors, group support, or telephone helplines, versus 45 percent of older adults aged 25 to 64 years (Statistics Canada 2003a). Life can be more difficult for adolescents whose families are trapped in poverty if they have neither educational nor occupational opportunity.

According to the Canadian Council on Social Development, poor adolescents are 2.5 and 4.4 times less likely to be engaged in either a school program or a job, respectively, than those in middle- or higher-income families (Ross et al. 2000:2). The resulting inactivity may leave them open to deviant behaviour. Adolescents between the ages of 12 to 17, though constituting less than 10 percent of the population, account for 21 percent of all people accused of Criminal Code offenses, excluding trafficking (see Chapter 9; Sauvé 2005:13). The problems of some young people may be intensified by today's media images of Canadian teenagers (see Box 5.1).

The problems of prolonged education, finding suitable employment, and earning a reasonable income are shown by the increasing tendency of young people to remain in the parental home. The 2001 census shows that 41 percent of young people aged 20 to 29 lived with their parents, a substantial increase from 33 percent in 1991 (Statistics Canada 2002m:7). Remaining in the parental home is likely to delay what used to be called *young adulthood*.

Young Adulthood

Typically beginning in the early to mid-20s (perhaps now in the early 30s) and lasting to about age 39, young adulthood is a period during which people acquire new roles and experience a sense of new freedom. However, many also experience problems finding their niche, particularly when it appears doubtful that they will have as high a standard of living as their parents had.

SOCIAL PROBLEMS IN THE MEDIA

BOX 5.1 Media Ageism: Reporting on and Preferring Age Groups

How are teenagers portrayed in the media? Although most research on media ageism focuses on portrayals of older people, activist groups such as Canadian Youth Rights Association (CYRA) have also examined media coverage of adolescents. According to CYRA's (1998) findings, the media perpetuate myths about teenagers in these ways:

■ The news media seldom report stories about teenagers unless they are involved in a crime or some other "deviant" behaviour. The age of the person is often used as a hook to catch readers or viewers.

■ Few news stories describe positive teenager actions, such as volunteer work.

■ While media reports refer to adults as "women" or "men" and identify them by their last names, teenagers are often referred to by their first names and described as "girls" or "boys."

■ Entertainment shows and movies typically depict teens as being self-centred, insensitive to the feelings of others, materialistic, sexually promiscuous, involved in alcohol and drug abuse, and prone toward harmful pranks and physical aggression.

What would constitute positive journalism about adolescents? Clearly, covering young people's positive endeavours, as well as their problematic activities, would be a start. To bring about real change in media portrayals, however, responsible journalists could focus on how problems in the society at large affect young people. For example, journalists could "publicize the enormous racial imbalances inherent in 'youth violence,' the fundamental sexism of the current debate over 'teen' pregnancy, the realities of millions of raped, beaten, and neglected children, the increasing rates of youth poverty imposed by ever-richer Canadian elites, and the futility of modern behaviour modification, laws and treatments aimed at forcing the young to 'adjust' to intolerable conditions" (Males 1994:5). They also could look for ways to reduce or eliminate these problems.

Whether media coverage of teenagers will change is uncertain, but one thing is apparent: Many young people are "hooked" on media (Haddock 1999). According to the Kaiser Family Foundation's recent study, which was based on a representative sampling of 3155 individuals aged 2 through 18, "children spend so much time watching television, playing video games and the like that media use could qualify as their full-time job" (Haddock 1999:A32). The typical young person spends more than five hours each day using media, and most of this time is spent watching television. What kinds of images do young people see of themselves when they watch television? Based on media coverage of teenagers, how do adults view today's adolescents?

Although media coverage of teenagers can be negative, as soon as teenagers turn 18 years of age, the media want to attract them. Advertisers want the 18- to 34-year-olds because the advertisers believe that if this segment is attracted to products, they will maintain "brand loyalty." Older segments of the population, according to the advertisers, have already made up their minds.

One of the consequences of advertisers' beliefs is that television and radio networks change or drop programs well established with the 50+ age group to appeal to younger viewers and listeners. Whereas many programs with older actors, such Angela Lansbury (*Murder She Wrote*), Andy Griffith (*Matlock*), and Betty White and the rest (*The Golden Girls*), were on prime time until the mid 1990s, and *The West Wing* until mid-2006, few shows now have older actors (MacDonald 2004).

In addition, media portrayal of seniors is degrading. At the World Congress of Gerontology, held in Vancouver in July 2001, journalist and now Senator Laurier LaPierre said, "Older people are essentially represented with ridicule" and "Older people have no life of their own beyond these media-imposed titles (bewildered grandfather or meddling mother-in-law)" (Muggeridge 2001:5). In the same article, Dolores Ewan reported on an ad from a major department store chain, which pictured the surveying of seniors. If the seniors disliked a style, that was taken as an indicator of the style being fashionable. But society does not complain about this kind of stereotyping. Ewan went on to say that if the ad had shown Blacks or Indigenous people in this light, "there would have been a hue and cry about bigotry and racism" (Muggeridge 2001:5).

What should media do about the nature of their coverage of people in different age groups? To what extent should the media, particularly public media like the CBC, organize their programming to appeal to different age groups?

The 2001 Canadian census found that young people are not doing as well as two decades ago and likely not as well as their parents a generation ago. Figure 5.1 shows that younger women were earning less that they did two decades ago. Figure 5.2 shows that younger men were doing worse off than younger men two decades ago, and relatively worse off than younger women (Statistics Canada 2003c).

Some young adults return home or perhaps do not even leave home, prolonging the practice identified in the last section. In 1996, 50 percent of unmarried women and 60 percent of unmarried men, and 4 percent of married women and 5 percent of married men aged 20 to 34, were still living with their parents (Boyd and Norris 1999:3). Perhaps the greater decline in earnings of young men than for young women is the reason for the higher percentage of young men remaining at home. Subsequent chapters examine a variety of issues affecting young adults, including alcohol and drug abuse, divorce, and employment instability. Many of these issues also concern people older than age 40.

Middle Age

Because life expectancy was lower in the past, the concept of middle age (age 40 to 65) did not exist until fairly recently. *Life expectancy*—the average length of time the members of a group of individuals will live—increased dramatically during the 20th century. Today, life expectancy at birth is approximately 80 years (see Chapter 10), compared to only 42 years at Confederation. Sociologists use an age pyramid to show the distribution of a given population by age and sex groupings at various points in time, though the figures no longer look like pyramids. As Figure 5.3 on page 128 shows, Canada is undergoing what some social analysts refer to as the *greying of the population,* the aging of the population due to an increase in life expectancy combined with a decrease in the birth rate (Chui 1996). The 2001 census showed that the median (the midpoint of the population) age of Canadians is at a record high of 37.6 years (Statistics Canada 2002m:3).

As people progress through middle age, they experience *senescence (primary aging),* which results from

FIGURE 5.1 Women Under 30 Earn Less Than They Did Two Decades Ago

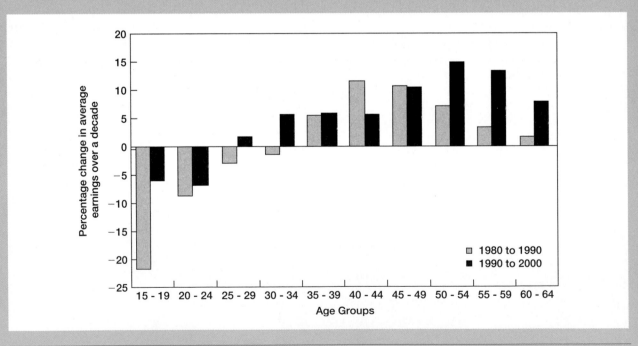

Source: Statistics Canada, 2003, Earnings of Canadians: Making a Living in the New Economy (Analysis Series), *Catalogue no. 96F0030,* March 11, 2003.

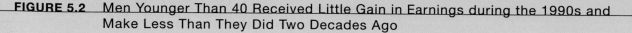

FIGURE 5.2   Men Younger Than 40 Received Little Gain in Earnings during the 1990s and Make Less Than They Did Two Decades Ago

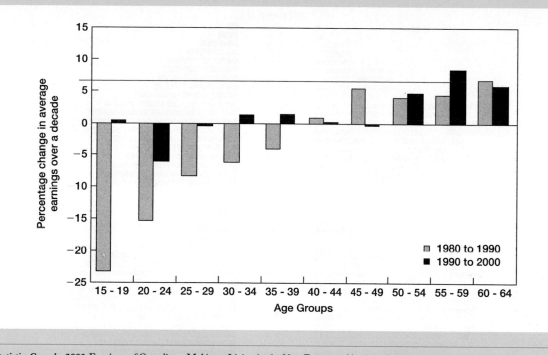

Source: Statistics Canada, 2003, Earnings of Canadians: Making a Living in the New Economy (Analysis Series), *Catalogue no. 96F0030,* March 11, 2003.

molecular and cellular changes in the body. Some signs of senescence are visible (e.g., wrinkles and grey hair); others are not (e.g., arthritis or stiffness in connective tissue joints; a gradual dulling of senses such as taste, touch, and vision; and slower reflexes). Vital systems also undergo gradual change; lung capacity diminishes, and the digestive, circulatory, and reproductive systems gradually decline in efficiency (Novak and Campbell 2006:84ff).

In addition to primary aging, people experience *secondary aging*, which has to do with environmental factors and lifestyle choices. "How you age is a question of attitude and motivation. You have to stay connected and involved . . . [some] remain interested and curious, open to new challenges even as octogenarians," says Blossom Wigdor, now emeritus professor of gerontology at the University of Toronto (quoted in Kingstone 2002:42).

Some people fight the aging process by spending billions of dollars on products such as Oil of Olay, Clairol, or Grecian Formula to hide grey hair; drugs like Viagra; and treatments like injections of Botox to eliminate wrinkles. Others have cosmetic surgery. In a recent study, one interviewee explained that she had decided to undergo liposuction (a surgical procedure in which fat is removed) because she had started to get a lot of "creepyness" in her neck, and her jowls were "coming down," owing to aging (Dull and West 1991:57). As use of these products and treatments suggest, Canada is a youth-oriented society that tends to equate beauty, stamina, and good health with youth. Because of this, many of the changes associated with growing older are viewed as something to be avoided at all costs.

While women in middle age may believe that they have become less sexually attractive than they were, middle-aged men tend to begin to realize that their physical strength and social power over others are limited, and their occupational opportunities are limited. As if to reinforce their awareness of the passage of time, many women and also men may have to face the fact that their

FIGURE 5.3 Canada's Population, 1995 and 2016

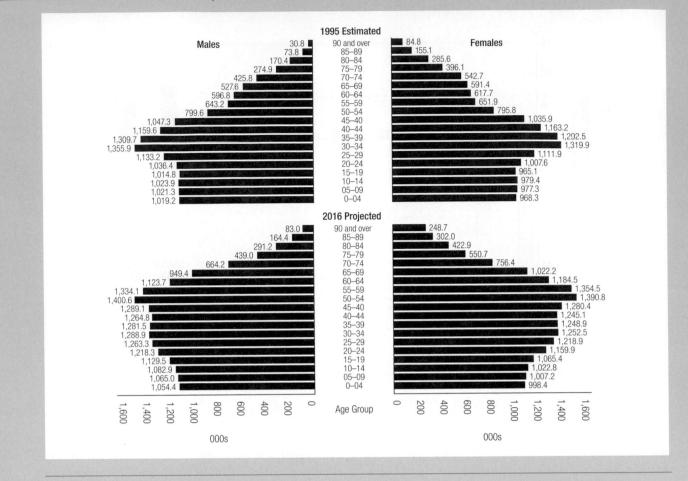

Source: Statistics Canada, 1996, "Canada's Population, 1995 and 2016," Canadian Social Trends (Autumn):3–7; Catalogue no. 11-008. Reprinted by permission.

children have grown and left home. Any of these factors might precipitate what is often referred to as a mid-life crisis. However, for some people, middle age is a time of great contentment: their income and prestige are at their peak, the problems of raising their children are behind them, they are content with their spouse of many years, and they may have grandchildren who give them a tie to the future. Even so, all middle-aged people know that their status will change significantly as they grow older.

Later Maturity and Old Age

Later maturity is usually considered to begin in the 60s. The major changes associated with this stage are social. Although many people in their 60s retain sufficient physical strength to be able to carry on an active social life, their peer groups can shrink noticeably as friends and relatives die. Many people in later maturity find themselves caring for people of their own age and older people.

Old age is usually considered to begin in the late 60s or in the 70s. Although some people continue to work past age 70, most have left paid employment by their seventieth birthday. Problems are not just social but also increasingly biological. Some physical changes, such as arteriosclerosis (the loss of elasticity in the walls of the arteries) are potentially life threatening (Belsky 1990). As bones become more porous, they become more brittle; a simple fall may result in broken bones that take longer to heal than those of a younger person. Strength, mobility, and height may decline;

Gerontologists stress that it is hard to generalize about older individuals. The stereotypes don't fit. This couple, for example, in their eighties, apparently enjoy good health—and each other.

and the abilities to see, hear, taste, touch, and smell may diminish. Because taste and smell work together to allow us to enjoy food, eating may become less pleasurable and so contribute to poor nutrition in some older adults (Belsky 1990). Although it is not true of all elderly people, the average person over age 65 does not react as rapidly (physically or mentally) as the average person who is younger than 65 (Lefrançois 1999).

The chances of heart attacks, strokes, and cancer increase along with the likelihood of some diseases that primarily affect the elderly. Alzheimer's, a degenerative disease that attacks the brain and severely impairs memory, thinking, and behaviour, may be the best-known example. People with this disease have an impaired ability to function in everyday social roles; over time, they cease to be able to recognize people they have always known, and they lose all sense of their own identity. Finally, they may revert to a speechless childishness, at which point others must feed them, dress them, sit them on the toilet, and lead them around by the hand. Alzheimer's and other dementias strike 8 percent of those over age 64, according to the 1991 Canadian Study of Health and Aging. Today, in Canada, there are likely over 350 000 people suffering from dementia, according to Burke and her colleagues (1997:25). Most of the people with dementia (78 percent) live in institutions

(Statistics Canada 1999b:63). In spite of promises for cures in the future, the disease can last 8 to 20 years, ending only with death (Lefrançois 1999).

As older people have begun to live longer, they have become an increasingly high percentage of the population. In 1998, they constituted 12 percent of the Canadian population, up 57 percent since 1981 (Statistics Canada 1999b:7). Figure 5.3 shows how the population will change from 1995 to 2016. In 2016, the largest age group in the country will be those over 50 years of age. Gerontologists have come to realize that there are significant differences among people who are now called the "young-old" (ages 65 to 74), the "middle-old" (ages 75 to 84), and the "old-old" (ages 85 and older). Although more than half of all people aged 65 and older are in the young-old category, the old-old category has grown more rapidly over the past two decades than has any other age group in Canada. In 1998, there were 380 000 people 85 years of age and older, double the numbers in 1981 (Statistics Canada 1999a:7). As with other age categories, it is difficult to make generalizations about older people. But it is not true that all old people feel lonely and lost in retirement, live in institutions, and are uniform in their health, activities, and financial situation (Novak and Campbell 2006:291).

As Bill Gleberzon, associate executive director of the Canadian Association for the Fifty-Plus (CARP [formerly using the term *retired persons*]), has said, "Competence, not age, should be the deciding criterion in any endeavour" (author's files). Or, to illustrate that some older persons do not perceive themselves as old, the co-author's then 86-year-old mother, Hilda Thompson, when asked if she had spent the money he had given her for Christmas said, "No, I'm saving it for my old age."

In some parts of the world, many older people do not have such positive feelings, and they have a high rate of suicide.

Suicide and the Life Course

Around the world, people aged 60 and above have a suicide rate that is three times the rate of younger people, aged 15 to 24 years of age (WHO 2002). Is this true for Canadians as well? Figure 5.4 shows the rate of suicide for males and females over the stages of the life course in Canada. According to Langlois and Morrison (2002:21), who studied suicide rates in Canada, few major differences in these rates occur across the life

FIGURE 5.4 Canadian Suicide Rates, by Age and Sex

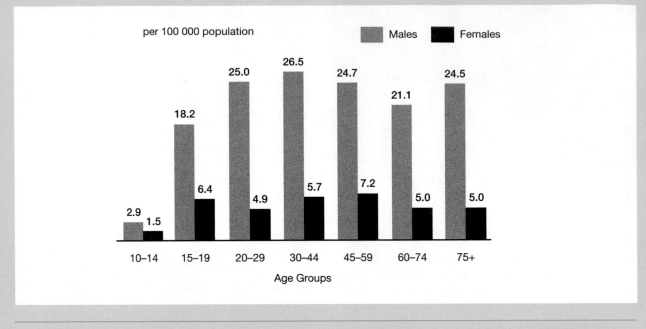

*Source: Statistics Canada, 2002, "Vital Statistics Database, 1998," **Canadian Social Trends** (Autumn):21, Catalogue no. 11–008. Reprinted with permission.*

course. For men, suicide rates rise steadily from the teenage years; they are highest for men aged 30 to 44; they decline slightly thereafter, levelling off again at ages 60 to 74, and rise slightly again for those 75 and above. Women have far lower suicide rates at each stage—the high point coming for women aged 45 to 59, with the rate declining to a low level thereafter. Overall Canadian suicide rates have remained stable over the last 20 years at an average 14 per 100 000 population, with a high point of 18 in 1983. The authors also compared Canadian rates with those of the other industrialized countries. Among industrialized countries, Canada ranks in the middle of the group, with countries like Australia and the Scandinavian countries; the U.S. has a slightly lower suicide rate, 10.5 per 100 000 population, than we do (Langlois and Morrison 2002:23). Thus, it would seem that no stage of the life course is significantly more difficult than any other for Canadians and that has been true for at least the last 20 years.

Death and Dying

In previous generations, death was a common occurrence in all stages in the life course, but today most deaths occur among older people. Because of medical advances and the increase in life expectancy, death is now viewed as an event that usually occurs in old age. According to social gerontologists, the increased association of *death* with the process of *aging* has caused many people to deny the aging process and engage in ageism as a means of denying the reality of death, particularly their own (Atchley 2000). Euphemisms such as "pass away" or "sleep" are often used to refer to death by those who are trying to avoid its reality. Researchers have found, however, that many people do not actually fear death itself as much as they fear the possibility of pain and suffering, loss of control, and the consequences of their death for survivors (Marshall and Levy 1990). Given a chance to choose, most people would choose a painless death over prolonged physical and mental deterioration and the prospect of being a burden on their families. Some researchers have also found that older people have less fear of death than younger people do (Gesser, Wong, and Reker 1986, quoted in Novak and Campbell 2006:323); others have found that education and religious beliefs are important factors in how people view death and dying (Kalish 1985).

There are three widely known frameworks for explaining how people cope with the process of dying: the stage-based approach, the dying trajectory, and the task-based approach. The *stage-based approach* was popularized by Elisabeth Kübler-Ross (1969), who proposed five stages in the dying process: (1) denial ("Not me"); (2) anger ("Why me?"); (3) bargaining and asking for divine intervention to postpone death ("Yes me, but..."); (4) depression and sense of loss; and, (5) acceptance. According to some social scientists (Kalish 1985; Marshall 1980), Kübler-Ross's study is limited because she focused primarily on the attitudes of younger people who had terminal illnesses. These scientists argue that the same stages may not apply to older people who believe that they have already lived a full life.

In contrast to Kübler-Ross's five stages, the concept of the *dying trajectory* focuses on the perceived course of dying and the expected time of death. From this perspective, not all people move toward death at the same speed and in the same way. A dying trajectory may be sudden (e.g., a heart attack) or slow (e.g., lung cancer) and is usually shaped by the condition causing death. A dying trajectory involves three phases: the *acute* phase, in which maximum anxiety or fear is expressed; the *chronic* phase, in which anxiety declines as the person confronts reality; and the *terminal* phase, in which the dying person withdraws from others (Glaser and Strauss 1968).

The *task-based approach* suggests that daily activities can still be enjoyed during the dying process and that fulfilling certain tasks makes the process of death easier, not just on the dying person, but on everyone involved. *Physical tasks* are performed to satisfy bodily needs and to minimize physical distress. *Psychological tasks* help to maximize psychological security, autonomy, and richness of experience. *Social tasks* sustain and enhance interpersonal attachments and address the social implications of dying. *Spiritual tasks* are performed to identify, develop, or reaffirm sources of spiritual energy and to foster hope (Corr et al. 1994). Most important in any approach are the rights of the dying person and the way in which care is provided.

Technological advances in medicine have helped to focus attention on the physical process of dying and, in recent years, the needs of dying patients and their families. Many people are choosing to sign a *living will*—a document stating a person's wishes about the medical circumstances under which his or her life should be allowed to end. Rejecting the idea of being kept alive by elaborate life-support systems and other forms of high-tech medicine, some people choose to die at home rather than in a hospital or nursing home. The hospice movement has provided additional options for caring for the terminally ill. ***Hospices*** **are organizations that provide a homelike facility or home-based care (or both) for persons who are terminally ill.** Some hospices have facilities where care is provided, but hospice is primarily a philosophy that affirms life, not death, and offers holistic and continuing care to the patient and family through a team of visiting nurses, on-call physicians, and counsellors. Home care enables many people to remain in familiar surroundings and maintain dignity and control over the dying process (Corr et al. 1994). Sophia Mumford summarizes the feeling of many older people about death:

> I'm afraid of one thing. I want my death to be dignified. My fear is that something will cause me to live past the point where my life has value. I don't want to live on. . . . From now on, if life says it's leaving, I'm not doing anything about it. If I get a bad pain and it's diagnosed as cancer, then I won't wait, I'll go. I'm ready, because I feel I've had a good life. (quoted in Terkel 1996:429)

Because many people want a dignified death, the topic of euthanasia will likely become very prominent in the future (see Box 5.2).

PROBLEMS THOUGHT TO BE ASSOCIATED WITH AGING

Age stratification—the inequalities, differences, segregation, or conflict between age groups—occurs throughout the life course (McPherson 1990:141–143). Age is a determinant of how education, jobs, and other scarce resources and opportunities are allocated in society. Age stratification can limit roles and opportunities. Many people automatically assume that at age 14 a person should be in school; that at age 30 a person should be married; and that at age 65 a person should retire from full-time employment. Such perceptions about age may create problems for people in all age

SOCIAL PROBLEMS AND SOCIAL POLICY

BOX 5.2 Euthanasia

According to Greek etymology, *euthanasia* means, literally, a "good death," and it comes in several types. *Passive euthanasia* means withholding or ceasing treatment of someone not likely to recover from a disease or injury. *Active euthanasia* means intervening to hasten someone's terminal illness, with, for example, a lethal dose of sedatives. *Assisted suicide* means helping someone end his or her life with, for example, drugs. Since advances in medical technology have made it possible to keep people alive longer than in the past, questions are arising about the best time and method of dying.

A number of high-profile cases, such as those of Sue Rodriguez and Robert Latimer, have highlighted the problems in this area. Sue Rodriguez was a 42-year-old woman suffering from ALS (Lou Gehrig's disease) who appealed all the way to the Supreme Court of Canada to have the legal right to have someone help her commit suicide when she wanted to die. In 1993, the Supreme Court decided against her, supporting the law prohibiting assisted suicide. Sue Rodriguez actually did die with the assistance of an unidentified doctor and Svend Robinson, an NDP MP from British Columbia. Robert Latimer is a Saskatchewan farmer who administered a lethal dose of carbon monoxide gas to his daughter, Tracy, who suffered from severe cerebral palsy. He was accused of second-degree homicide. After his first trial, at which he was found guilty, the judge imposed a two-year sentence. This sentence was appealed to the Saskatchewan Court of Appeal, which sentenced Latimer to the mandatory penalty for second-degree homicide, life

imprisonment with no chance of parole for 10 years. Later, in 2001, the Supreme Court of Canada refused to review that sentence.

An Angus Reid poll inquired about Canadians' attitude to the Latimer case and to mercy killing. This poll indicated that Canadians were very supportive of Latimer: almost three-quarters of them said that he had acted out of compassion and should have received a more lenient sentence (Sallot 1999: A5). It also found that Canadians are quite supportive of legalizing euthanasia: 41 percent said mercy killing should not be against the law under appropriate circumstances; 38 percent said it should be illegal, but perpetrators should be treated with leniency; and 18 percent said it should be treated like any other murder (2 percent had no opinion). Notably, the young (18 to 34 years of age) were slightly less lenient than older Canadians.

Some countries are making euthanasia legal. In April 2001, the Netherlands became the first country in the world to legalize euthanasia, and later that year, Belgium did the same. In Canada, much emphasis is put on individual rights, and the *Charter of Rights and Freedoms* supports this emphasis. Should we also have a right to die when and how we want to? With the increasing cost of health care, should we ever consider rationing health care so that younger people have more access to care than older people? Do you believe that Canada should legalize euthanasia? Do you think that young people might want to euthanize older relatives to make their own lives easier? If we do legalize euthanasia, what safeguards do you think should be imposed?

categories, but the problems typically are most pronounced among older people.

Workplace Discrimination

Despite the *Canadian Charter of Rights and Freedoms,* which protects all Canadians against discrimination based on many characteristics including age, many subtle forms of age discrimination in the workplace remain. Some employers prefer younger workers to older workers, whom they believe have health problems, poor motivation, and low ability. Employers may hire younger workers because they believe that they can pay them less than older workers and make more demands on their time and energy. Older employees sometimes find that

their employers have downgraded their job descriptions, failed to promote them or grant them raises, or are trying to push them out of their jobs so that cheaper workers can be hired. McMullin and Marshall (1999) found that older workers have less power and authority in the workplace just because they are thought to be old.

Despite the negative stereotypes, some employers have found it profitable to keep or hire older employees, and some older employees are able to continue working. In 1998, 6 percent of Canadians over 64 years of age had a job, mostly in agricultural and religious occupations (Statistics Canada 1999b:88). To support employers who are attempting to overcome these stereotypes, the Canadian Association for Retired People has created an award for Best Employers for 50-Plus

Canadians to recognize and reward those companies that value older workers. The 2004 recipients of this award were RBC Royal Bank; Global Banking Service Centre, Merck Frosst, The Home Depot Canada, and Avis Rent A Car (CARP 2005a).

With what appears to be the end of mandatory retirement, some of these problems will vanish. However, new ones will emerge likely around removing people who are thought not to be able to do the job.

Retirement and Changing Roles

The *retirement principle* is the "idea that at a fixed age, regardless of mental or physical ability, a person leaves work" (Novak and Campbell 2006:212). In the past, people in many occupations and professions (including tenured faculty members at universities, police officers, and fire fighters) faced mandatory retirement at age 65, regardless of their health or desire to continue working. It was simply assumed that everyone experienced a decline in physical and mental ability at a specific age. Changes in compulsory retirement laws have led many people to view retirement less as a sign of decline than as a newfound period of leisure and opportunity for adaptation, reflection, and contribution (see Peter Hare's quote at the end of this chapter). For some, however, adapting to less income, increased dependency, and the loss of roles and activities can be very difficult.

Today, women who are over 65 are less likely to have access to pension and Canada/Quebec Pension Plan (C/QPP) income in their own name than will younger women who are currently employed. Older women are usually worse off financially than men, and many senior women live in a state of poverty (Gee and McDaniel 1991). Because these women have worked part-time in traditional occupations and have experienced high rates of unemployment, the income they receive from the CPP/QPP may not be substantial (McDonald 2000). Moreover, many employed women—as well as many men—are losing out on traditional pension coverage because of changes in the economy and the workplace. Many unionized industrial jobs that once provided pension coverage have virtually disappeared, and more women than men are employed as part-time workers, who are less likely to have pension coverage than are full-time workers. In fact, companies rarely offer pension plans or health

Retirement is a time for leisure and reflection if it comes by choice and the individual is healthy and financially prepared. But for others, adapting to less income, increased dependency, and the loss of roles can be difficult.

insurance to part-time, contingent, and temporary workers.

Health, Illness, and Health Care

At age 93, Malcolm Clarke plays doubles tennis four times a week and sails his boat; he also shops and cooks for himself (Brody 1996). Although Clarke attributes his longevity and good health to "luck," studies show that many older people are not developing the disabling diseases that were common in the past, and the vast majority function quite well. Improvement in the health status of older people has been attributed, at least in part, to better education (knowing what to do and not do to stay healthy), nutrition, and public health care. As a result, most seniors living at home (78 percent) report that their health is good or very good, though 82 percent have a chronic condition like arthritis or rheumatism (Statistics Canada, 1999b:8–9). They tend to think of themselves as in good health, all things considered.

About 7 of every 10 deaths among older people are due to heart disease, cancer, or respiratory illness. Now cancer is the leading cause of death for men and women (Statistics Canada 2004h:35).

People aged 65 and older account for about one-third of all dollars spent on health care, and this figure is expected to rise dramatically with the aging of the Canadian population. Many believe the cost problems associated with health care will be further intensified by the *feminization of aging*—the formerly increasing proportion of older people who are female—because women, on average, have a greater likelihood of being poor and having no spouse to care for them (Weitz 1996). However, some researchers state that dire predictions of skyrocketing costs are greatly overstated. Robert Evans and his colleagues (2001:160) report that numerous studies show that the effects of aging on health care costs are relatively small, as a result of the "compression of morbidity" and falling needs among the elderly. Studies in British Columbia, for example, show minimal effects of population aging on health costs. Everybody—not just the elderly—is using more complex and costly services. The claims that the aging of the population will bankrupt the system, while having intuitive appeal, serve the interests of those who provide care and who wish to privatize parts of health care (Evans et al. 2001:187).

Victimization

Although older people are in fact less likely than younger people to be victims of violent crime, they fear this type of crime more than people in other age categories do. According to police-reported statistics, in 2003, female seniors were victimized at a rate of 119 per 100 000 population and male seniors at a rate of 184 (Statistics Canada 2005f:11).

However, older people are often the targets of other types of crime. Con artists frequently contact them by mail or telephone to perpetrate scams that often promise prizes or involve a "stockbroker" selling a "hot" stock or other commodity (Hays 1995). In 1998, CARP created a National Forum on Scams and Frauds, which produced recommendations such as providing more information to seniors, instituting cooling-off periods for contracts, and freezing assets of scam artists. A new brochure has been prepared with more scams to watch for, such as the Nigerian e-mail/letter asking for money promising larger sums later, and pyramid schemes (CARP 2005b). The appendix of the 1998 edition of the CARP brochure highlighted the Illinois law that makes defrauding a person of $5000 or more a more serious felony if the victim is over 60 years of age (CARP 1998). Is this a positive kind of discrimination that Canadian lawmakers should consider?

Another form of victimization is elder abuse. According to the National Clearinghouse on Family Violence (cited in Novak and Campbell 2006:310), the abuse may be physical, psychosocial, financial, and/or neglect (active or passive). E. K. Podnieks and her colleagues conducted Canada's first random sample telephone survey of elder abuse and found that in the late 1980s, 4 percent of Canadians (about 98 000) experienced abuse after turning 65 years of age (cited in Novak and Campbell 2006:310). In 2003, older women were more likely than their male counterparts to be victims of family violence. Close to 40 percent of senior female victims were assaulted by a family member, while this was the case for 20 percent of senior male victims (Statistics Canada 2005f:11).

Victims of elder abuse may be more vulnerable to complications resulting from physical violence than younger victims, since physical injuries may worsen pre-existing health problems or inhibit an older person's ability to function independently. Many analysts believe that elder abuse is under-reported because people who know of the abuse are unwilling to report it, and older people who are the victims are either too ashamed or afraid to notify authorities. Although some analysts initially believed that younger people were likely to exploit older people who were psychologically and economically dependent on them, just the opposite has often proven true: Younger people are more likely to exploit elders on whom they themselves are dependent (Novak and Campbell 2006:311).

Family Problems and Social Isolation

Older people can easily become socially isolated from their families. Younger family members who once asked for advice stop asking, perhaps because they think that their older relatives are out of touch or perhaps because of some miscommunication. Sometimes, younger family members feel unduly burdened by the concerns of their elders, which don't seem truly important to them. For one reason or another, older people can come to believe (rightly or wrongly) that they are isolated from the rest of the family.

In 1996, 29 percent of people aged 65 and above lived alone versus 9 percent of people aged 15 to 64 (Statistics Canada 1999b:31). Many older people live alone voluntarily, but others live by themselves because they are divorced, widowed, or single. The 1996 General Social Survey showed that 75 percent of Canada's widows aged 65 and older live alone (Bess 1999:2). Living alone is not the equivalent of social isolation. Many older people have networks of family and friends with whom they engage in activities. Contrary to the myth that older people are abandoned by their families, Canadian research has shown that most seniors live in a situation called "intimacy at a distance"—families usually provide much support for their older members (C. Rosenthal 1987). For those without children, many form other ties (McMullin and Marshall 1996). Many seniors also engage in volunteer work, as shown by Peter Hare's comment on page 139 and the work of Chappell (1999). To a large degree, the extent to which they associate with others has to do with social class: People with more money are able to pursue a wider array of activities and take more trips than are those with more limited resources.

Perhaps one of the saddest developments in contemporary society is the growing number of older people who are homeless. While some older homeless people have lived on the streets for many years, others have become homeless because they have been displaced from low-income housing, such as single-room occupancy (SRO) hotels. In recent years, many SROs in cities such as Vancouver and Toronto have been replaced by high-rise office buildings, retail space, and luxury condominiums. Older people who are homeless typically lack nutritious food, appropriate clothing, adequate medical care, and a social support network. They tend to die prematurely of disease, crime victimization, accidents, and weather-related crises. such as winter blizzards, when an individual without shelter can freeze to death on a park bench. Fortunately, the picture is not this bleak for many older people who remain in residences they have occupied for many years.

Housing Patterns and Long-Term-Care Facilities

Many people mistakenly assume that most older people live in long-term-care facilities such as nursing homes. In fact, however, only about 7 percent of older people live in any kind of institution. In 1996, 93 percent lived at home in a private household (Statistics Canada 1999b:30). More than people of any other age category, older people are likely to reside in the housing in which they have lived for a number of years and own free and clear of debt. Because of the high cost of utilities, insurance, taxes, and repairs and maintenance, older women, who are more

likely to live alone than are older men (58 percent of women vs. 29 percent of men 85 years of age live alone [Statistics Canada, 1999b:40]), are at a distinct disadvantage if they attempt to maintain their own homes.

Some low-income older people live in planned housing projects that are funded by federal and local government agencies or private organizations, such as religious groups. Older people with middle and upper incomes are more likely to live in retirement communities or in seniors' residences that provide amenities such as housekeeping, dining facilities, and transportation services. In recent years, religious organizations and for-profit corporations have developed *multilevel* facilities, which provide services ranging from independent living to skilled nursing care all at the same site.

Though only 7 percent of people aged 65 and older live in institutions, the percentage increases to almost 34 percent among people aged 85 and over (Statistics Canada 1999b:47). Because of their greater life expectancy, higher rates of chronic illness, and higher rates of being unmarried, older women are disproportionately represented among the people who reside in institutions (Statistics Canada 1999b:47). According to social gerontologists, the primary factors related to living in a nursing home are age (85 and over), being female, having been in the hospital recently, living in retirement housing, having no spouse at home, and having some

Although only about 7 percent of older people live in nursing homes or other long-term-care facilities in Canada, living in an institutional setting remains the only option for some older individuals. What alternative living arrangements can you suggest for older people in the future?

cognitive or physical impairment that interferes with the activities of daily living (Greene and Ondrich 1990).

While some nursing-home facilities may be excellent, others have undergone extensive media scrutiny and public criticism for violations of regulations and harmful practices such as elder abuse. As a result, many people select home care, adult day care, or assisted living for older relatives rather than institutional settings, which tend to depersonalize individuals and "reify the image of age as inevitable decline and deterioration" (Friedan 1993:516). Home care is being seen now as a way to reduce costs in the health care system. Although home care has received increased resources in the past decade, problems of getting home care still exist (Segall and Chappell 2000; and, see Chapter 10).

PERSPECTIVES ON AGING AND SOCIAL INEQUALITY

Although each of the major sociological perspectives focuses on different aspects of aging and social inequality, they all provide insights into how people view the aging process and how ageism towards the young and the old contributes to social inequality in society.

The Functionalist Perspective

According to functionalists, dramatic changes in such social institutions as the family and the economy have influenced how people look at youth and at the process of growing old. Because of these influences, both the complexity and stability of society require that people spend much time preparing for occupational roles and then leaving them at an arbitrary time, like age 65, when it is likely that they are no longer able to keep up with the role demands and jobs must be available to younger people. Encouraging older people to leave is referred to as *disengagement theory*; this theory suggests that older people want to be released from societal expectations of productivity and competitiveness. At the same time, disengagement facilitates a gradual and orderly transfer of statuses and roles from one generation to the next instead of an abrupt change, which might result in chaos. Retirement policies, then, are a means of ensuring that younger people with more up-to-date training (for example, newer computer skills) move into occupational roles while ensuring that older workers are recognized for

years of service (Williamson, Rinehart, and Blank 1992). Not allowing young people to participate in adult roles until they have many years of education is sometimes called *delayed initiation theory*. Many years of education does permit some people to be better equipped for a complex society. But an element of credentialism (see Chapter 12) also occurs, whereby employers demand more credentials than are needed for the work to reduce the line of potential recruits. Employers may also create low- (or no) income internship programs to reduce their costs and prevent being involved in long-term commitments.

Critics of this perspective object to the assumption that delayed initiation and disengagement are functional for society and say that they are dysfunctional. Among other dysfunctional consequences, young people postpone getting married and having children, and as a result, Canadian females have a total fertility rate of 1.5, which is below the replacement rate of 2.1 children per woman (Statistics Canada 2004i). Older people may not want to disengage when they are still productive and gain satisfaction from their work. Some have suggested that CPP/QPP and other pension systems will be strained by the proportionately fewer workers who are paying into the plans, which must support an increasing number of retired workers (see *dependency ratio*). As mentioned above, mandatory retirement does appear to be on the road to elimination, so pension plans will be less strained; but this does not include a shorter initiation period for young workers.

The Interactionist Perspective

Interactionist perspectives on aging and inequality focus on the relationship between life satisfaction and levels of activity. *The interactionist activity theory* is based on the assumption that people who are active are happier and better adjusted than are less-active persons. According to this theory, older people shift gears in late middle age and find meaningful substitutes for previous statuses, roles, and activities (Havighurst, Neugarten, and Tobin 1968). Those who remain active have a higher level of life satisfaction than do those who are inactive or in ill health (Havighurst et al. 1968). In contrast to disengagement theory, activity theory suggests that older people must deny the existence of old age by maintaining middle-age lifestyles for as long as possible. But some older people are themselves critiquing this idea. According to an interview study conducted by Stephen Katz, some older people object to the idea that those preferring their inner world to being active are thought to be problem people. Katz (2000) suggests that this emphasis on activity could be transformed into a means of controlling older people.

Activity theory also applies to young people. There should be meaningful ways to integrate them into society that do not involve prolonged isolation in educational institutions and limited and poorly paid internships, but that involve more cooperative education through which young people study and work for more than minimum wages in an alternating pattern of school and work.

The Conflict Perspective

In analyzing the problems of younger and older people in contemporary capitalistic societies, conflict theorists focus on the political economy of youth and aging. From this perspective, class constitutes a structural barrier to older people's access to valued resources, and dominant groups attempt to maintain their own interests by perpetuating class inequalities. According to conflict theorists, youth and aging themselves are not the social problems. The problems are rooted in societal conditions that younger and older people often face without adequate resources, such as income and housing. People who were poor and disadvantaged in their younger years become even more so in old age. Today, in Canada, a much smaller percentage of seniors live in low-income situations now than as recently as two decades ago. Whereas in 1980, 34 percent of seniors had a low income (the low income cut-off [LICO] is discussed in Chapter 2), in 1997 that percentage had declined to 19 percent (Statistics Canada 1999b:100). However, health care costs could be a greater problem in the future as programs are delisted from health care support and new, expensive drugs are not included in support plans.

In the capitalist system, many older people are set apart as a group that depends on special policies and programs. Fortunately, in Canada, seniors do not have to depend on special government programs, such as the U.S. Medicare program, for health care (see Chapter 10). Canada's health program is universal. But it is under siege by those who would like to see greater privatization of services, who claim among other things that seniors will bankrupt the system (Evans et al. 2001).

Conflict analysts draw attention to the ways that class, gender, and racialization divide older people, just as they do everyone else. The conflict perspective adds to our understanding of aging by focusing on how capitalism devalues older people, especially women. Critics assert, however, that this approach ignores the fact that industrialization and capitalism have been positive forces in society, greatly enhancing the longevity and quality of life for many older people.

The Feminist Perspective

Feminist theorists emphasize inequalities between men and women. It is well known that although women live longer than men, they are subject to higher rates of disability (see Chapter 10) and their incomes are lower. In 1997, whereas senior men's average income was $26 010, women's income was $16 070 (Statistics Canada, 1999b:95). In addition, women were more likely than men (24 percent vs. 12 percent) to be in a low-income situation (Statistics Canada, 1999b:100). What is new is that the decline in wages for young people over the past two decades has been greater for men than women (Figures 5.1 and 5.2). This is probably due to the lower wages for people in entry positions now than before, but what can be done to improve it is difficult to determine.

In addition, feminists argue that more attention should be paid to the health problems of women, as in the study done by the Ontario Women's Health Council to determine whether this difference in disability is alterable.

CAN AGE-BASED INEQUALITY BE REDUCED?

The inequality experienced by younger and older people needs to be addressed. First, the inequality experienced by the young could be reduced by increased financial support for able students from lower-income families and earlier and more progressive integration with training into complex jobs. Second, once young people are established at work and in families, accommodations must be made. In order to distribute time for family responsibilities and leisure more evenly throughout the life course, changes must occur in the workplace. Today, younger workers struggle to care for their families, without the support of employers in many cases, and leisure is associated with old age and "being put out to pasture." But people who have had no opportunity to engage in leisure activities earlier in their life are unlikely to suddenly become leisure-oriented. Employment, family responsibilities, and leisure must become less compartmentalized, and changes in technology and employment may make this possible. At present, however, it is difficult for most people to have *free time* and *money* at the same time.

For older people many dimensions must be addressed. As we have seen, technological innovations and advances in medicine have contributed to the steady increase in life expectancy in Canada. Advances in the diagnosis, prevention, and treatment of diseases associated with old age, such as Alzheimer's, may revolutionize people's feelings about growing older. Technology may bring about greater equality and freedom for older people (Novak and Campbell 2006:90–94). Home-based computer services, such as online banking and shopping, make it possible for older people to conduct their daily lives without having to leave home to obtain services. Computerized controls on appliances, lighting, and air conditioning make it possible for people with limited mobility to control their environment. Soon, sensing devices may be developed that could monitor a person's daily behaviour, such as the use of a kettle or motion, and report any deviation over the internet to a concerned relative or central office. Technology also brings recreation and education into the home. For example, Senior Net is a computer network that encourages discussion of diverse topics and provides hands-on classes in computer use. Robotics and computer systems may eventually be used by frail older people who otherwise would have either to rely on family or paid caregivers to meet their needs or move to a nursing home. However, class is again a factor: While much of home care is covered by the health care system in Canada, many of the home accessibility features are paid for by users or their families.

Economic concerns loom large in the future as baby boomers (those born between 1946 and 1964) will be retiring soon if they have not already done so, bringing about a dramatic shift in the **dependency ratio—the number of workers necessary to support youth and those over age 64.** Instead of *five* workers supporting one retiree, *three* workers will be providing support for each retiree. Some American social analysts suggest that increased age-based inequality may bring about a "war" between the generations (Toner 1995). Unlike in the American system, changes in the pension systems in Canada have brought about a decline in the number of low-income

seniors without creating many high-income seniors (Myles 2000:312–313) and, thus, fewer candidates for the epithet "greedy geezer." Moreover, the federal government has increased the pension contributions of current workers so that the plans will not go bankrupt. However, the wealth inequality could change in the future with the increased value of employment and personal (RRSP) pension plans going to the higher-income retirees. Advocates of *productive aging* suggest that instead of pitting young and old against each other, we should change our national policies and attitudes. We should encourage older people to continue or create their own roles in society, not to disengage from it. To some extent, as mentioned above, this will happen with the end of mandatory retirement. In addition, real value should be placed on unpaid volunteer and caregiving activism, and settings should be provided in which older people can use their talents more productively (Hooyman and Kiyak 1996).

Functionalists suggest that changes must occur in families and other social institutions if we are to resolve problems brought about by family diversification and increased workplace demands. Some adult children have to provide economic and emotional support for aging parents and grandparents at the same time as they are caring for their own children. These people are called the *sandwich generation.* According to the 2002 GSS, almost 3 in 10 people aged 45 to 64 years with unmarried children under 25 in the home were also caring for a senior (Statistics Canada 2004i). This is some 712 000 people in Canada. Various sacrifices made by these people included changing hours, losing income, missing promotional opportunities, and incurring medical expenses. Women tend to devote more hours than men to caring for seniors, and they tend to provide more personal care while men provide economic and transportation care. While some tax incentives are available for those taking care of seniors, given that the sandwiched generation reports generally feeling stressed, more support would certainly be welcome by them.

Other social analysts suggest that people need to rely more on themselves for their retirement and old age. Younger workers should be encouraged to save money for retirement in RRSPs. As conflict theorists have pointed out, however, many young people have loans to repay or do not have jobs or adequate income to meet their current economic needs, much less their future needs.

From the conflict perspective, age-based inequality is rooted in power differentials, and short of dramatic changes in the structure of political and economic power in society, the only way for older people to hold onto previous gains is through continued activism. Advocacy groups like CARP make presentations to government and hold forums (e.g., on scams and frauds) about policies that would benefit many older people.

According to interactionists, however, individuals who maintain strong relationships with others and remain actively involved throughout their lifetime have reason to be optimistic about life when they reach old age. An example is Peter Hare, past president of the Senior Alumni at the University of Toronto, who is doing a variety of volunteer work in his retirement:

> One topic that is important to people about to retire is the importance of continuing to be useful. I had been active in the UTAA (University of Toronto Alumni Association) and our local ratepayers association and retirement allowed me to be more active. I even added several environmental organizations. First the Metro Toronto Solid Waste Environmental Assessment Program and later the RAP (clean water issues in the Toronto area). As a matter of fact, these activities increased my sense of contributing usefully to the community as I was no longer caught up in the "administrivia" of my former employment. (author's files)

WHAT CAN YOU DO?

- Study the amount of caregiving that your elderly relatives and those of your friends require.

- Volunteer for an agency that helps seniors in your neighbourhood. Helping a senior person may be as simple as listening to one on a regular basis.

- Since this chapter is also about other stages of the life course, you might also consider helping those at another life stage. For example, Kids Help Phone is a national, bilingual, toll-free, 24-hour, confidential hotline that provides professional counselling, referrals, and internet service for children and youth. It can be reached at 1-800-668-6868 or **www.kidshelpphone.ca**. According to its website, this organization is looking for student and community ambassadors to raise funds or public awareness of its work.

- Set up a system of habits, such as exercise, recreational reading, and saving for retirement in an RRSP, to establish an activity pattern that will prepare you for later years.

- Help some seniors lobby for some improvements.

- Challenge some of the ageist stereotypes held by some young people. When one of the authors was showing a news clip about people over 80 years of age and their romantic interests, he heard sounds of disgust from the back of the classroom. You might start a discussion of ageism with questions about romantic expectations after 80. The vast majority of your age group will be there someday.

- Study the differences in problems currently faced by senior men and women. To what extent will these problems change as more women become more self-supporting?

SUMMARY

WHAT IS AGEISM? WHY IS IT CONSIDERED A SOCIAL PROBLEM?

Ageism is prejudice and discrimination against people on the basis of age. Ageism is a social problem because it perpetuates negative stereotypes and age-based discrimination, particularly against older people.

WHAT IS THE LIFE COURSE? WHY ARE DIFFERENT STAGES PROBLEMATIC FOR SOME PEOPLE?

The life course is generally divided into infancy and childhood, adolescence and young adulthood, middle age, later maturity, and old age. During infancy and childhood, we are dependent on other people and so relatively powerless in society. Adolescence is a stage in which we are not treated as children but nor are we afforded the full status of adulthood. In young adulthood, we acquire new roles and have a feeling of new freedom but also may have problems, ranging from alcohol and drug abuse to employment instability, that may make life complicated. And we may continue to live at home. During middle age, we begin to show such visible signs of aging as wrinkles and grey hair, and roles begin to change in the workplace and family as children leave home. In later maturity, we increasingly find ourselves involved in caring for people of our own age and older people. Problems of older adults vary widely because of the diverse needs of the "young-old" (ages 65 to 74), the "middle-old" (ages 75 to 84), and the "old-old" (ages 85 and older).

WHAT TYPES OF PROBLEMS DO YOUNGER PEOPLE FACE TODAY?

Younger people deal with problems of developing an identity and relationships, determining an occupation, and getting and paying for the education to achieve the occupation. Then in their early work years, low pay makes repaying students loans difficult, and many young people continue to live at home into their 30s.

WHAT TYPES OF PROBLEMS DO OLDER PEOPLE FACE TODAY?

Despite laws to the contrary, older workers may experience overt or covert discrimination in the workplace. Retirement brings about changing roles and a loss of status for those older people whose identity has been based primarily on their occupation. For some older people, low incomes, disease, and lack of health care or home care are problems. Older people may become the victims of scams by con artists and elder abuse by family members or nursing-home personnel. For some older people, moving into a nursing home represents a loss of autonomy.

KEY TERMS

ageism,   p. 122
dependency ratio,   p. 138

HOW DO PEOPLE COPE WITH THE PROCESS OF DYING?

Three explanations have been given for how people cope with dying. Kübler-Ross identified five stages that people go through: (1) denial; (2) anger; (3) bargaining; (4) depression; and, (5) acceptance. However, the dying trajectory suggests that individuals do not move toward death at the same speed and in the same way. The task-based approach suggests that daily activities can still be enjoyed during the dying process and that fulfilling certain tasks makes the process of death easier, not just on the dying person, but on everyone involved.

HOW DO FUNCTIONALIST AND INTERACTIONIST EXPLANATIONS OF AGE-BASED INEQUALITY DIFFER?

According to functionalists, disengagement of older people from their jobs and other social positions may be functional for society because it allows the smooth transfer of roles from one generation to the next. However, interactionists suggest that activity is important for older people because it provides new sources of identity and satisfaction later in life.

HOW DO CONFLICT AND FEMINIST THEORISTS EXPLAIN INEQUALITY BASED ON AGE?

According to conflict theorists, aging itself is not a social problem. The problem is rooted in societal conditions that older people often face when they have inadequate resources in a capitalist society. In the capitalist system, older people are set apart as a group that depends on special policies and programs. Feminists argue that older men tend to be in a more advantageous social and economic position than older women. Since this disadvantage for women begins much earlier, institutions such as schools and businesses should work to eliminate the inequality they generate.

hospice,   p. 131
social gerontology,   p. 123

QUESTIONS FOR CRITICAL THINKING

1. If you were responsible for reducing ageism, what measures would you suggest to bring about greater equality? What resources would be required to fulfill your plan?

2. Since we are eliminating laws regarding retirement for older people, are there laws we should consider changing or eliminating regarding young people's behaviour?

3. Does disengagement theory or activity theory more closely reflect how you plan to spend your later years? What other approaches to aging can you suggest?

4. Think of synonyms, both formal and informal, for *senior*, and look up the word *senior* in a thesaurus. How ageist are these synonyms? Make up new synonyms that are not ageist.

WEBLINKS

Health Canada Division of Aging and Seniors

www.phac-aspc.gc.ca/seniors-aines

Health Canada's site for seniors provides regular updates from its websites to help seniors locate new services, publications, news releases, and articles.

Ontario Network for the Prevention of Elder Abuse

www.onpea.org

ONPEA's mandate is to

- Educate professionals and lay persons about elder abuse and neglect.

- Promote information sharing among professionals and advocates in the field of elder abuse.

- Develop educational and training programs about elder abuse prevention and intervention for people working with the elderly.

- Advocate legislative action to meet the needs of victims, perpetrators, and their families.

- Offer services and support to victims of elder abuse and neglect.

- Be sensitive to multicultural and aboriginal issues related to elder abuse.

National Children's Agenda

http://unionsociale.gc.ca/nca_e.html

This site provides a wide variety of reports and links about children and adolescents.

Canadian Centre for Activity and Aging

www.ccaa-outreach.com

The Canadian Centre for Activity and Aging promotes an active and healthy lifestyle for Canadian adults.

Centre on Aging (University of Victoria)

www.coag.uvic.ca

The Centre on Aging at the University of Victoria is a multidisciplinary research centre. Another institute that deals with seniors and/or the life course is the **Institute for the Life Course and Aging,** www.utoronto.ca/lifecourse (University of Toronto).

Canadian Association on Gerontology

www.cagacg.ca

The Canadian Association on Gerontology is a national, multidisciplinary association designed to provide leadership in concerns related to aging.

Canadian Association for Retired Persons (CARP)

www.carp.ca

CARP is Canada's largest advocacy group for people over 50; it has over 400 000 members. It deals with a wide variety of perennial issues, such as elder abuse, workplace discrimination, poverty issues among the elderly, and health benefits. The organization is doing new work with such issues as grandparents' rights, protection of investments, scams, and pension reform.

6

INEQUALITY BASED ON SEXUAL ORIENTATION

NATURE AND EXTENT OF INEQUALITY
BASED ON SEXUAL ORIENTATION

IDEOLOGICAL BASES OF INEQUALITY
BASED ON SEXUAL ORIENTATION

Religion and Sexual Orientation

Law and Sexual Orientation

DISCRIMINATION BASED ON SEXUAL
ORIENTATION

Box 6.1 Social Problems and Social Policy:
Coming Out: Risky Business in a Homophobic
Culture

Housing Discrimination

Discrimination in Medical Care

Occupational Discrimination

Victimization and Hate Crimes

Box 6.2 Social Problems and Social Policy:
School's Out: Closing the Books on Homophobia

PERSPECTIVES ON SEXUAL
ORIENTATION AND SOCIAL INEQUALITY

Interactionist Perspectives

Functionalist and Conflict Perspectives

Feminist and Queer Perspectives

CAN INEQUALITIES BASED ON SEXUAL
ORIENTATION BE REDUCED?

WHAT CAN YOU DO?

The State has no business in the bedrooms of the nation.

Pierre Elliott Trudeau, Past Prime Minister of Canada, and Justice Minister in 1969

Ironically, where bisexuals are presumed to have access to heterosexual privilege, we are in fact contending with both externalized and internalized homophobia and heterophobia, all at the same time.

Ruby Rowan, in "Sleeping With the Enemy and Liking It: Confessions of a Bisexual Feminist," 2001

I think a lot about the qualities and designs of the public spaces that I visit regularly. I want to believe that this sensitivity to my environment, verging on an obsession, is rooted in some deep well of creativity. But my narratives of design and redesign are also part of a twentieth-century Canadian fag thing. I note escape routes from possible violence. I seek out screens for privacy and to avoid more obvious forms of hostility. I covet sites in which to have fun with my friends (new and old), natural stages on which to see and be seen. I am especially interested in the places where I find new forms of communality, which often is obscured by archaic notions of community.

Gordon Brent Ingram, in Redesigning Wreck: Beach Meets Forest as Location of Male Homoerotic Culture and Placemaking in Pacific Canada, 2001

Therefore, neither "lesbian" nor the more inclusive "queer" may be the way some choose to describe their identity or their practices, not because these terms are not plural enough to include, let's say, people of colour, but because the categories "lesbian" and "queer," when not qualified, presume a subject who is white, middle class, Euro-North American. . . in an era that demands and is engulfed by notions of globalization, categories such as "lesbian" and "queer" cannot be transposed to other nations without calling into question the very categories themselves.

Didi Khayatt, from her Addendum to Kathleen Martindale's What Makes Lesbianism Thinkable? Theorizing Lesbianism from Adrienne Rich to Queer Theory, 2001

The opening quotations give us a sample of the diversity of issues confronted by and discussed by those interested in the question of sexual orientation in our culture and beyond. This chapter will examine many issues that face us today with regard to sexual orientation. We will look at the extent of homosexuality and bisexuality and homophobia and biphobia in Canada, beginning with the definitions of various sexual orientations.

We will try to understand how and why prejudice and discrimination against people based on sexual orientation can happen in Canadian society, a society that prides itself on it high levels of "tolerance" *and* "acceptance." We will review some of the laws regarding sexual orientation and look at hate crimes, specifically, and ways they are being dealt with. Finally, we will review several theories that pertain to sexual orientation and discrimination and consider ways we can advocate for social change.

***Sexual orientation* refers to a preference for emotional–sexual relationships with individuals of the "same" sex (homosexuality), the "opposite" sex (heterosexuality), or both (bisexuality)** (Lips, 1993). The terms *homosexual* and *gay* are most often used in association with males who prefer "same"-sex relationships; the term *lesbian* is used in association with females who prefer "same"-sex relationships. Heterosexual individuals, or those who prefer "opposite"-sex relationships, are sometimes referred to as *straight* (e.g., "Have you always been straight?"). It is important to note, however, that heterosexual people are much less likely to be labelled by their sexual orientation than are people who are gay, lesbian, or bisexual, because their heterosexuality is presumed normal and is taken for granted. We will discuss this presumption of normalcy later in the chapter when we discuss heterosexual privilege. It is also important to note that although in lay terms, we talk about the "opposite" sex, there are biologically, physiologically, cognitively, and emotionally very few differences between males and females. In effect, there is no such thing as an "opposite" sex. The myth of the opposite sex is one of the most persistent and foundational binaries we adhere to in our culture.

What criteria do social scientists use to classify individuals as gay, lesbian, or bisexual? In a groundbreaking study of sexuality published in the mid-1990s, researchers at the University of Chicago established three criteria for identifying people as homosexual or bisexual: (1) *sexual attraction* to persons of one's own gender, (2) *sexual involvement* with one or more persons of one's own gender, and (3) *self-identification* as a gay man, lesbian, or bisexual (Michael et al., 1994). According to these criteria, then, engaging in a homosexual act does not necessarily classify a person as homosexual. Many participants in the Chicago study indicated that although they had *at least* one homosexual encounter when they were younger, they no longer were involved in homosexual conduct and never identified themselves as lesbians, bisexuals, or gay. In fact, self-definition plays a critical role in confounding attempts to classify people definitively. For example, many people who engage in same-sex acts, on an occasional or even regular basis, may not perceive themselves as homosexual or bisexual at all.

NATURE AND EXTENT OF INEQUALITY BASED ON SEXUAL ORIENTATION

How many homosexuals and bisexuals are there in Canada? The 2001 Canadian census was the very first Canadian census to ask questions specifically about same-sex couples. The census reports that 34 200 Canadian couples, or one-half of one percent of all couples, claim same-sex common-law status (Statistics Canada 2002p). Researchers caution, however, that these numbers may be quite low in relation to the actual number of same-sex couples in Canada—especially as they are from the first census to explore this area—and that they should be used only as a baseline: a starting point. Indeed, in the report from their recent research of Canadian lesbians, researchers for Status of Women Canada Irene Demczuk, Michele Caron, Ruth Rose, and Lynne Bouchard (2002:viii) state that "to this day, most lesbian couples still hide their sexual orientation and their conjugal situation, especially in the workplace, in order to protect themselves against the negative reactions of those around them." Jerome Ryckborst, a Vancouver writer, described the conflict that many gay and lesbian Canadians had to grapple with when faced with reporting, in essence, sexual orientation to the Canadian government: "It does feel risky . . . but the need for our community to grow up, stand up and be counted outweighs the personal concerns" (Anderssen 2002:A9). Fifty-five percent of reported same-sex

couples are male and only 3 percent of these couples had children living with them. In contrast and in keeping with gender socialization norms and typical post-divorce custody arrangements in Canada, 15 percent of the 15 200 female couples had children living with them; female couples were five times more likely than male couples to have children living with them (Statistics Canada 2002v). It will be interesting to see what the data from our most recent census (2006) demonstrate about the numbers of same-sex couples, especially given the recent change in Canadian laws allowing civil marriages between same-sex partners.

While we now have a count, however inaccurate, of same-sex common-law couples in Canada, the census has yet to count people according to their sexual orientation. Most estimates of the homosexual population state that at least 10 percent of the population engages primarily in same-sex relationships. An even higher percentage is estimated to be bisexual, as high as 25 percent of the population (Maugh 1990; Weinberg et al. 1994). There are various reasons, mainly connected with living in a homophobic culture, for why people in Canada may keep information about their homosexuality or bisexuality unannounced.

Homosexuality has existed in most, if not all, societies throughout human history. Tolerance and acceptance of homosexuality and bisexuality exist along a continuum. Most tribal societies regard some homosexual acts as socially acceptable at least some of the time. For example, some cultures, such as the Siwans, the Azande, the Dahomy, and the !Kung of Africa and the Sambians of New Guinea regard same-sex relations as a "normal" part of maturing (Blackwood 1986). In contrast, for most of the last two thousand years, there have been groups—sometimes entire societies—that considered homosexuality "a crime against nature," "an abomination," or "a sin" (Doyle 1995:224). In any case, most societies have norms pertaining to *sexuality*—**attitudes, beliefs, and practices related to sexual attraction and intimate relationships with others.** The norms are based on the assumption that some forms of attraction and sexual relationships are *normal* and *appropriate* while others are *abnormal* and *inappropriate*. In many societies, including modern North American and European societies, homosexual conduct has been classified as a form of *deviance*—**a behaviour, belief, or condition that violates social norms.** This classification may make people targets of prejudice, discrimination, and even death. Extreme prejudice toward gay men and lesbians is known as *homophobia*—**the irrational and excessive fear or intolerance of homosexuals and homosexuality.** Additionally, *biphobia* **refers to fear and intolerance of bisexuals and bisexual lifestyles.** According to sociologists, homophobia and biphobia are actually *socially determined prejudices*, not medically recognized *phobias* (Lehne 1995; Wilton 2000). Homophobia and biphobia are intensified by the ideology of *compulsory heterosexism*, a belief system that offers no options for behaviour or feelings but heterosexuality and denies, denigrates, and stigmatizes any gay, lesbian, or bisexual behaviour, identity, relationships, or community. Somewhat like institutional racism and sexism, compulsory heterosexism is embedded in a society's social structure and maintained by ideologies that are rooted in religion and law (Herek 1995). *Heterosexism* **is the belief that heterosexuality is the only normal, natural, and moral mode of relating, and hence is superior to**

homosexuality or bisexuality (Wilton 2000). What makes the following *Heterosexual Questionnaire* (see Table 6.1) humorous is that it turns the assumptions of heterosexism upside down.

IDEOLOGICAL BASES OF INEQUALITY BASED ON SEXUAL ORIENTATION

Social analysts such as Bruce Bawer (1994:81), an author and cultural critic, believe that homophobia differs significantly from other forms of bigotry:

> In a world of prejudice, there is no other prejudice quite like [homophobia]. Mainstream writers, politicians, and cultural leaders who hate Jews or blacks or Asians but who have long since accepted the unwritten rules that forbid public expression of those prejudices still denounce gays with

TABLE 6.1   The Heterosexual Questionnaire

1. What do you think caused your heterosexuality?

2. When and how did you decide you were a heterosexual?

3. Is it possible that your heterosexuality is just a phase you may grow out of?

4. Is it possible that your heterosexuality stems from a neurotic fear of others of the same sex?

5. If you have never slept with a person of the same sex, is it possible that all you need is a good gay lover?

6. Do your parents know that you are straight? Do your friends and/or roommate(s) know? How did they react?

7. Why do you insist on flaunting your heterosexuality? Can't you just be who you are and keep it quiet?

8. Why do heterosexuals place so much emphasis on sex?

9. Why do heterosexuals feel compelled to seduce others into their lifestyle?

10. A disproportionate majority of child molesters are heterosexual. Do you consider it safe to expose children to heterosexual teachers?

11. Just what do men and women do in bed together? How can they truly know how to please each other, being so anatomically different?

12. With all the societal support marriage receives, the divorce rate is spiraling. Why are there so few stable relationships among heterosexuals?

13. Statistics show that lesbians have the lowest incidence of sexually transmitted diseases. Is it really safe for a woman to maintain a heterosexual lifestyle and run the risk of disease and pregnancy?

14. How can you become a whole person if you limit yourself to compulsive, exclusive heterosexuality?

15. Considering the menace of overpopulation, how could humanity survive if everyone were heterosexual?

16. Could you trust a heterosexual therapist to be objective? Don't you feel s/he might be inclined to influence you in the direction of his/her own leanings?

17. There seem to be very few happy heterosexuals. Techniques have been developed that might enable you to change if you really want to. Have you considered trying aversion therapy?

18. Would you want your child to be heterosexual, knowing the problems that s/he would face?

Source: From "The Language of Sex: The Heterosexual Questionnaire," Changing Men (Spring 1982). Attributed to Martin Rochlin, West Hollywood, CA.

impunity. For such people, gays are the Other in a way that Jews or blacks or Asians are not. After all, they can look at Jewish or black or Asian family life and see something that, in its chief components—husband, wife, children, workplace, school, house of worship—is essentially a variation of their own lives; yet when they look at gays—or, rather, at the image of gays that has been fostered both by the mainstream culture and by the gay subculture—they see creatures whose lives seem to be different from theirs in every possible way.

According to Bawer, heterosexuals cannot identify with the daily lives of lesbians and gay men, who—unlike them—exist as identifiable categories primarily because there is such strong antigay prejudice in Canada. In fact, the stereotypical beliefs that dominant (heterosexual) group members hold about gay men and lesbians are a major impediment to achieving equal rights for gays and lesbians and reducing inequalities based on sexual orientation (Nava and Dawidoff 1994).

Stereotypical beliefs about lesbians and gay men often equate people's sexual *orientation* with sexual *practice*. For example, all gay men and lesbians—regardless of the nature and extent of their sexual activity—are stereotyped as "sex obsessed, sexually compulsive, and sexually predatory" (Nava and Dawidoff 1994:32). Media depictions tend to reinforce stereotypes of gay men as sexual exploiters or "limp-wristed sissies," while lesbians are "stomping macho soldiers" who hate men (Nava and Dawidoff 1994:32; Wilton 2000). Recently, "Top 100" movies such as *The Family Stone* and *Imagine Me and You* have attempted to demonstrate the normalcy of same-sex partnerships, while others like *Brokeback Mountain* have attempted to demonstrate some of the harms to gays and lesbians caused by living in a homophobic culture. Television shows such as *Will and Grace* and *Ellen* have sought to bring gay lifestyles into prime-time programming. Although some shows have perpetuated negative stereotypes about lesbians and gay men, others, like *Will and Grace* and *Ellen* (while it was allowed to be aired) have attempted, with limited success, to change public perceptions about issues related to sexual orientation.

Religion and Sexual Orientation

The major difference between homophobia and biphobia and other forms of discrimination such as sexism or racism is that many people believe that homosexuality or bisexuality is morally wrong. These beliefs are often, although not always, linked to religious affiliation. For example, health researcher Tamsin Wilton (2000:9) cites a strong association found by many researchers between homophobic and biphobic attitudes and strong religious beliefs. Some people use their religious affiliation as a way of reinforcing their existing prejudices against gays and lesbians while others interpret their religious doctrines as genuinely forbidding same-sex relations (Wilton 2000:9). Most of the major religions of the world—Judaism, Christianity, Islam, and Hinduism, as well as Confucianism—have historically regarded homosexuality as a sin. Indeed, the only major world religion that does not condemn homosexuality is Buddhism (Dynes 1990). This is not to suggest in any way that all or even most practising religious people are homophobic, only that most of the major religions provide justifications for homophobia, should people want them. Religious fundamentalists in particular denounce homosexual conduct as a sign of great moral decay and societal chaos. In the Judeo-Christian tradition, religious condemnation of homosexuality derives from both the Hebrew Scriptures (e.g., Genesis 19 and Leviticus 18:33) and the New Testament (e.g., Romans 1:26–27 and I Corinthians 6:9; Kosmin and Lachman 1993).

Since the early 1990s, same-sex marriages and the ordination of "practising" lesbians and gay men have been vigorously debated by various religious organizations. For example, the Vatican has directed Roman Catholic bishops in Canada and elsewhere to oppose laws that protect homosexuals, promote public acceptance of homosexual conduct, or give gay relationships equal footing with traditional, heterosexual marriage. However, many Roman Catholics disagree with the directive, stating that it is based on the faulty assumption that lesbians and gay men seek to influence the sexual orientation of children or youths with whom they live or work, that gay people are erotically attracted to every person of their own gender, and that they cannot control their sexual impulses in same-sex environments (cited in Bawer 1994). Roman Catholics are not the only religious group debating same-sex marriage and the ordination of lesbians and gay men: recently, in Toronto, the outgoing Anglican Archbishop of Canterbury stated that while it is permissible for homosexuals to be church members, it is not permissible for them to be ordained or to have their unions blessed by the Church. His views are in contrast to those of his successor, who has already ordained a practising gay priest, and of the current Anglican Bishop in Vancouver, who has been blessing the same-sex unions of his homosexual parishioners (Valpy 2002:A8). In Canada, while civil marriages are now legalized between same-sex couples, the law has stated that no religion/faith is compelled to endorse or marry same-sex couples in faith-based ceremonies.

Episcopalians have been debating for two decades whether or not "practising homosexuals" should be ordained. In 1996, an Episcopal bishop was accused of heresy for ordaining a gay deacon (Niebuhr 1996; Dunlap 1996). Some Canadian churches, like the United Church of Canada, have declared that all people, regardless of sexual orientation, are entitled to become full members of the church, including the right to become ordained ministers.

Still, increasing numbers of lesbians and gay men are carving out their own niches in religious organizations. Some gay men and lesbians have sought to bring about changes in established religious denominations; others have formed religious bodies, such as the Metropolitan Community Church, that focus on the spiritual needs of the gay community. Even so, many gay men and lesbians believe that they should not have to choose between full participation in their church and a committed same-sex relationship (Dunlap 1996).

Law and Sexual Orientation

However divided Canadians are in their opinions about how many and what kinds of rights gays and lesbians should be afforded in Canadian society, both tolerance and acceptance of homosexual and bisexual lifestyles have increased in Canada in past decades. Canadian citizens are much more tolerant of homosexual and bisexual relations than are U.S. citizens, although the vast majority of people in both countries believe that, with regard to employment, there should be no discrimination on the basis of sexual orientation. In a 1996

Gallup Poll, 60 percent of Canadians said they believed that homosexuality was an acceptable alternative lifestyle, compared with 44 percent of people in the U.S. Similarly, 64 percent of Canadians believed that consensual homosexual acts between adults should be legal, while 48 percent of people in the U.S. agreed. In April 2006, in an Angus Reid poll, homosexuality ranked third from the bottom on a list of eleven behaviours considered immoral by Canadians (see Figure 6.1). The total percentage who rated homosexuality as immoral is 31 percent—37 percent of men polled and 26 percent of women polled (Angus Reid 2006a). Clearly, Canadians are becoming increasingly accepting, or at least "tolerant," of same-sex lifestyles.

Over the past four decades, Canadians have witnessed, first, the decriminalization of sexual practices associated with same-sex relations; second, the inclusion of sexual orientation as a prohibited ground in human rights legislation; and third, the enactment of federal and provincial legislation aimed at conferring rights on same-sex couples (Demczuk et al. 2002:viii). Therefore, in Canada, discrimination on the basis of sexual orientation is prohibited everywhere. In Alberta, the provincial legislation deliberately omitted sexual orientation as a prohibited ground for discrimination; however, the Supreme Court of Canada stated in a groundbreaking April 1998 case (*Vriend v. Alberta*) that Alberta's human rights legislation would be *interpreted* as including sexual orientation as a prohibited ground for discrimination, whether the legislation specifically stated this or not, in order to bring Alberta's legislation into line with that of the rest of the provinces and territories.

These advances have been diligently pushed for and won by gay, lesbian, bisexual, and queer advocates, mainly through successful legal challenges and not, as Demczuk and colleagues (2002:viii) point out, through "the expression of any political will on the part of the federal [territorial] and provincial governments to systematically eliminate discrimination."

In the late 1960s, the Canadian government debated many much-needed reforms to the *Criminal Code,* in order to make it more reflective of current and changing Canadian values and practices. In a 1969 omnibus bill, sexual acts that were committed between consenting adults fell within the parameters of individual freedoms, and so, many sexual practices, some believed to be associated with homosexuality—for

FIGURE 6.1   Canadians Examine What Is Immoral

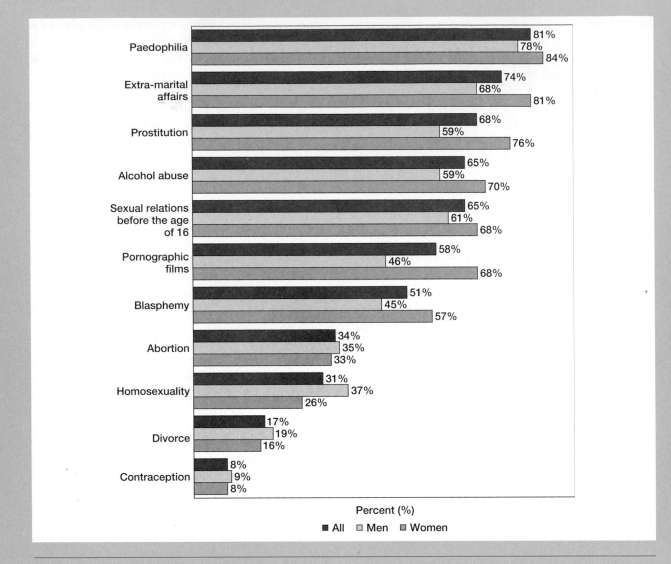

Source: 81% of the population consider pedophilia tops the list of immoral behaviours, Morality Barometer. *Reproduced with the permission of Leger Marketing, 2006 (www.legermarketing.com).*

example anal sex, or "sodomy"—were decriminalized. It still took until 1977 for the federal government to do away with the immigration regulation prohibiting homosexuals from immigrating to Canada.

> The 1969 Act . . . did not represent "a legalization of homosexuality," but rather a partial decriminalization of certain sexual practices that were not limited to homosexuals but were often associated with them. Beyond these changes to

the Criminal Code, violence, discrimination in employment, police harassment and distinctions in terms of conjugality continued to exist with impunity. (Demczuk et al. 2002:6)

In the 1960s, the United Nations adopted the *Universal Declaration of Human Rights.* As a liberal democracy, Canada was obligated to both respect this and similar declarations and to make illegal any government acts that infringe on people's individual rights. Along with the federal government, most provinces also enacted their own human rights legislation in the late 1960s and early 1970s. When Canada repatriated its Constitution in 1982, the *Canadian Charter of Rights and Freedoms* gained ascendancy, and its Section 15 provided a vehicle for disenfranchised groups to seek remedy through court challenges. Section 15(1) of the *Charter* reads,

> Every individual is equal before and under the law and has the right to the equal protection and equal benefit of the law without discrimination and, in particular, without discrimination based on race, national or ethnic origin, colour, religion, sex, age, or mental or physical disability.

In 1977, Quebec became the first province to include sexual orientation as a prohibited ground of discrimination in its provincial human rights legislation. Ontario followed 9 years later, but it still took 21 years, and the *Vriend* decision for sexual orientation to be extended as a prohibited ground in all Canadian provinces and territories.

Throughout the 1980s and 1990s, through legal challenges about pensions, bereavement leaves, alimony, and various other family-law issues, individuals pushed, with varying levels of success, for recognition of same-sex couples as analogous to heterosexual couples. Governments continued to make case by-case decisions, in several cases insisting that the decisions be non–precedent setting and that they be given more time to integrate the rights of minority groups into existing law. Finally, in the *Vriend v. Alberta* case, the Supreme Court of Canada stated,

> The need for government incrementalism was an inappropriate justification for *Charter* violations.... In my opinion, groups that have historically been the target of discrimination cannot be expected to wait patiently for the protection of their human dignity and equal rights while governments move toward reform one step at a time. If the infringement of the rights and freedoms of these groups is permitted to persist while governments fail to pursue equality diligently, then the guarantees of the *Charter* will be reduced to little more than empty words. (*Vriend v. Alberta* 1998. S.C.R. 493, paragraph 122, cited in Demczuk et al. 2002:17)

One year later, following a Supreme Court ruling that making distinctions between heterosexual couples

and homosexual couples is unconstitutional, several provincial governments amended their *Family Law Acts* to include provision for same-sex couples by changing the definition of "spouse." The first to make these changes were British Columbia, Quebec, and Ontario in 1999 and Nova Scotia in 2000. For example, in Quebec, the first Canadian province to allow same-sex partners the same benefits and responsibilities as heterosexual partners, Bill 32 committed the government to making changes to 39 provincial laws, including the Quebec Pension Plan, automobile and prescription-drug insurance, legal aid, low-cost housing, child and child-care benefits, financial assistance, student assistance programs, taxation, tax credits, RSPs, employee retirement plans, health insurance, and so on (Demczuk et al. 2002; Mooney et al. 2001). In British Columbia, through the *Definition of Spouse Amendment*, same-sex partners who have "lived and cohabitated with another person, for a period of at least two years ... in a marriage-like relationship, including a marriage-like relationship between persons of the same gender" have all the rights and responsibilities of heterosexual couples, including the right to inherit if a partner dies without a will, the right to inherit property and pensions, and the right to apply to adopt a child together (Mooney et al. 2001:292). Today, same-sex couples are usually able to adopt an unrelated child with both potential parents formally applying and being listed as parent applicants. This follows the 1999 Supreme

In a June 2006 Angus Reid poll of attitudes toward same-sex marriage, 59 percent of Canadians agreed that in principle "same-sex couples should have the same right to civil marriage as opposite-sex couples," while 33 percent disagreed (Angus Reid 2006b).

Court of Canada ruling, in *M v. H,* that opposite sex definitions of "spouse" were being read into the word "spouse" and were "unconstitutional." This ruling came into effect as of March 1, 2000, and had implications for adoption acts that stated that "spouses" could adopt children. Each province and territory in Canada oversees its own adoptions. Many same-sex couples have successfully adopted children in Canada, to date.

Same-sex couples in British Columbia, Ontario, and Quebec challenged Canada's marriage laws in 2000. Many advocates believed that until same-sex couples were granted the right to legally marry, across Canada, they would not be viewed by society as legitimate and would continue to be disenfranchised from some of the financial and many of the social benefits—such as holding hands in public, bringing one's spouse to the company picnic, having one's partnership recognized by one's parents as more than a "phase" one is going through—enjoyed by heterosexual spouses. In July 2002, two men who married in a church ceremony but were denied a marriage license by the Ontario provincial government took their case to court. Three Ontario Superior Court judges ruled that the law prohibiting same-sex marriages is unconstitutional. The Government of Canada was appealing the ruling, but on June 17th, 2003, on the recommendation of federal Justice Minister Martin Cauchon, Prime Minister Chrétien announced that the federal government would no longer engage in the legal battle and would support marriage for gays and lesbians across Canada. This marked Canada as the third country in the world to legalize same-sex marriage. The prime minister said that his government would

- Draft legislation aligned with the common-law definition of marriage that came into effect on June 10, 2003;

- Protect faith communities from having to perform any marriage that does not conform to religious values;

- Seek approval from the Supreme Court of Canada to ensure that the marriage law complies with the *Charter*, and that it is applicable to all provinces and territories; and

- Introduce the new law in Parliament's next session (September 2003) for a "free vote."

As recently as June of 1999, members of the Canadian House of Commons voted overwhelmingly to oppose same-sex marriage. However, following Chrétien's statement and, much earlier, the inclusion of sexual orientation as a protected ground in the *Canadian Charter of Rights and Freedoms,* advocates continued to challenge all provinces to expedite marriage for gay and lesbian Canadians.

As Canadians debated the issue of same-sex marriage, the courts were doing their work. On December 9, 2004, the Supreme Court of Canada ruled that Ottawa *did* have the exclusive right to determine who had the right to marry in Canada. The government's same-sex marriage bill, Bill C-38, came up for the vote in Cabinet on June 28, 2005. It passed by a 158–133 margin, with the support coming from most Liberals, the NDP, and the Bloc Québécois. Bill C-38 became law on July 20, 2005, after being passed by Senate and receiving Royal Assent. Canada is now the fourth country, after the Netherlands, Belgium, and Spain, to legalize same-sex marriage. Eighteen additional countries offer some type of legal recognition of same-sex unions (Angus Reid 2006a; "Canadians Want to Move On" 2005). As of June 2006, more than 10 000 marriage licenses have been issued to gay and lesbian couples in Canada (Angus Reid 2006b).

Not everyone was excited about Bill C-38 becoming law. Conservative leader Stephen Harper stated at the time that if his party formed the next government, he would revisit the law. He argued that "most Canadians aren't buying the final decision as most Federalist MPs are opposed to same-sex marriage" ("Harper Questions 'Legitimacy'" 2005). While Harper's Conservatives did manage to form the next government, they have been having little success in drumming up support for re-opening the same-sex marriage debate. For example, in March of 2006, the Gandalf Group in Ottawa, commissioned by Report on Business TV and *The Globe and Mail* Report on Business, conducted its quarterly *Report on Business C-Suite Survey* of the top 1000 Corporations in Canada. Chief executive officers, chief financial officers, and chief operating officers are polled to assess what they believe the most relevant issues are in Canada today. The intent of the C-Suite Survey is to inform and shape public policy and facilitate dialogue between Canadian business leaders (Gandalf Group 2006). According to survey results (see Figures 6.2 and 6.3), of all of the

FIGURE 6.2 Priorities for Canadian Business Leaders

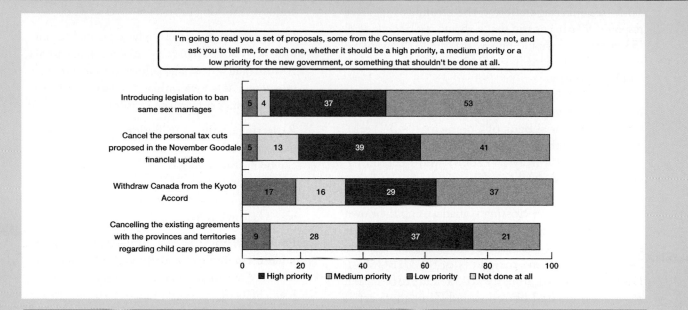

Source: C–Suite Survey Conducted by the Gandalf Group Commissioned by Report on Business, Report on Business Television, KPMG, Davies, and The Globe and Mail Report on Business.

FIGURE 6.3 Top Priorities for Canadian Business Leaders

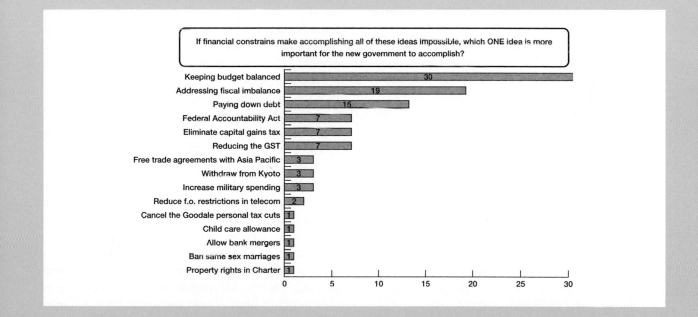

Source: C–Suite Survey Conducted by the Gandalf Group Commissioned by Report on Business, Report on Business Television, KPMG, Davies, and The Globe and Mail Report on Business.

Conservative Party's platform proposals, attempts to ban same-sex marriage elicited the strongest negative response: 90 percent said that it should not be done at all (53 percent) or should be low priority (37 percent); 4 percent felt it had medium priority and 5 percent felt it had high priority.

Beyond showing support in polls, some Canadian business leaders have gone a step further. The Canadian Imperial Bank of Commerce (CIBC) celebrated two of their employees, Kevin Bourassa and Joe Varnell, at a May 29, 2006, award ceremony. Bourassa and Varnell have the distinction of being Canada's first legally married same-sex couple, as well as the distinction of crossing Canada, using their own funds, to educate about same-sex marriage and garner support before it became legal in Canada. On May 29, the men became recipients of the CIBC 2006 Diversity Award. The award, a sculpture called *Reflecting*, created by renowned Zimbabwe artist Richard Mteki, was presented, along with the following accompanying speech by Tim Moseley, CIBC's chief compliance officer:

> Kevin and Joe are local celebrities at CIBC because they carry the distinction of being the first legally-married same-sex couple in the world. In challenging the common law definition of marriage, they brought their claim for equality to the Ontario Court of Appeal, which contributed to the Parliament of Canada's decision to legalize marriage between same-sex couples. They were both CIBC employees at the time, and have always highlighted the support they received from their employer at a time when they were making national headlines.
>
> In addition to this claim to fame, however, Kevin and Joe have also been ardent advocates of equality and diversity at CIBC. They agreed to be the keynote speakers on the topic of same sex marriage at CIBC's first-ever *Dialogue on Diversity* series. They were also founding members of the CIBC Pride Network—CIBC's first employee Affinity Group—and they have always been available to spread the message of diversity whenever they are asked to. They [spoke] to employees in CIBC's New York Offices in mid-June as part of CIBC's global celebration of Diversity Month.

> They have also served as role models for other employees seeking to be themselves at work.
>
> Kevin and Joe, the award to be presented to you tonight is entitled *Reflecting*. An important part of African (and indeed any) culture, personal reflection allows us to look within ourselves in order to cultivate inner strength and wisdom.
>
> Reflecting on the contributions the two of you have made allows us to understand that courage can be measured by a commitment to changing people's perceptions of the world around them, to creating new understandings of the struggles we all face in our lives.
>
> For your unwavering commitment to changing mindsets in the face of opposition and hatred; for reaching out to others who are struggling with issues of identity at work; and for your courage in changing the world in your own way, it is with great pleasure that we present the two of you with the 2006 CIBC Diversity Awards. (Bourassa and Varnell 2006)

In agreement with Canadian business leaders, in a June 2006 Angus Reid poll, 62 percent of Canadians stated clearly that the matter of giving same-sex couples the same right to civil marriage as opposite-sex couples was "settled" (Angus Reid 2006b). Twenty-seven percent felt the government should reopen the issue.

Further to these positions, some Canadians suggest that the inclusion of homosexual couples in definitions of "family" and "marriage" and the like will act to destabilize those definitions and categories, perhaps fundamentally and radically altering them for the betterment of all persons (Blasius 2001b; Currah 2001; Gamson 1996; Goldie 2001). This debate mirrors the debate waged between those who use the term "queer" politically—as an essentialist category, to describe themselves, to be recognized and valued for who they are, and to be included as an equal with the rest of society—and those who use the term "queer" more theoretically—as a destabilizing entity, a descriptor only in that it implies non-mainstream but refuses to define, in any essential way, what "queer" is or is not. This debate will be discussed in more detail later in the chapter.

DISCRIMINATION BASED ON SEXUAL ORIENTATION

As the campaigns for equal rights and an end to anti-gay discrimination have progressed, more people have come forward to declare that they are gay, lesbian, or bisexual and to indicate their support for gay organizations. Many lesbian or gay individuals and couples have sought the right to do all the things that heterosexual individuals and people in heterosexual relationships are permitted to do.

Housing Discrimination

Some lesbian and gay people are denied housing because they are gay; others are evicted from apartments where they have lived for some period of time, although reasons other than sexual orientation are usually given by landlords in order to avoid being the recipient of a human rights complaint. Even those who successfully rent or purchase property tend to remain targets of discrimination from some heterosexual residents, building managers, and custodial personnel, as Bruce Bawer (1994:254) explains:

> When two gay people decide to move in together, they commit themselves to insult and discrimination and attack. At one apartment building in which [a male partner] and I lived, the superintendent spit on me one day without provocation; at our next address, members of the building staff, not knowing that I understood Spanish, joked with one another in my presence about the *maricones* (faggots). Living alone, most gay people can conceal their sexuality; living together, a gay couple advertises theirs every time they step out of the house together.

SOCIAL PROBLEMS AND SOCIAL POLICY

BOX 6.1   Coming Out: Risky Business in a Homophobic Culture

In line with most social psychological models of identity formation, psychologist Jean Baker (2001:45) states that coming out is a "complex discovery process that children or adolescents go through as they gradually recognize their homosexual identity and acknowledge it to themselves and then to others." Unlike homosexuals or even bisexuals, heterosexuals have no such process to undergo. As a member of the group that is the norm, or cultural standard, they learn from a very early age what social work researcher Janet Sawyer (1989) calls "internalized dominance." Internalized dominance refers to all the messages, overt and otherwise, that signify to White people or straight people or people with no disabilities or men that they are normal; they are the standard; they are acceptable just being who they are. They are in no way "other," as people of colour or Indigenous people are; as women are; as sexual minorities are; as people with disabilities are. One of the privileges of being part of the dominant group is the privilege of never having to consider how a fundamental aspect of your self—your sexual orientation, for example—impacts on your life. Contrast this with people who belong to a marginalized group, and it is easy to see that people in marginalized groups must,

at least potentially, deal with or consider their status every day. They must consider how being openly gay or lesbian will impact their job search or apartment search or family holiday or grade in a class. Will it get them verbally or physically harassed or assaulted today?

Baker (2001:46) notes that "coming to terms with one's homosexual identity is a developmental task required of the gay child but one for which he or she receives little guidance and for which successful role models are seldom available." Taking a slightly different approach from Baker, political theorist and GLBT (gay, lesbian, bisexual, and transgender) activist Mark Blasius (2001a:155), in a discussion of an "ethos" of gay and lesbian existence, states that coming out is a multifaceted and lifelong process. Blasius believes that coming out, the goal of which is to live one's life as a lesbian or gay man, is not just about disclosure of one's gay or lesbian identity to one's self and others: "Rather than being an end-state in which one exists as an 'out' person, coming out is a process of becoming, a lifelong learning of how to become and of inventing the meaning of being a lesbian or a gay man in this historical moment." Coming out thus refers both to "an ontological recognition of the self by the self" and a "fundamental political act" (Blasius 2001a:155).

Defining oneself as gay or lesbian can have serious consequences for youth. One survey of gay youth found that 30 percent of those identifying themselves as homosexual had attempted suicide in the past year, compared with 7 percent of those identifying themselves as heterosexual (Platt 2001, in Mooney et al. 2003). One-quarter of homosexual youth drop out of school, and 40 percent report that their performance at school has been negatively affected by conflicts around sexual orientation (Mooney et al. 2003). A Calgary, Alberta, study found that gay and bisexual males were nearly 14 times more likely to have seriously attempted suicide than heterosexual males were (Mooney et al. 2003). This study also demonstrated that non-heterosexual youth of colour (lesbians, gay males, and bisexuals) were "dramatically overrepresented in the attempted-suicide statistics" (Fisher 1999, in Mooney et al. 2003). There is evidence today that gay, lesbian, and bisexual youth are coming out at earlier ages than in the past (Baker 2001).

What do you think should be done to decrease the numbers of suicides and attempted suicides among non-heterosexual youth?

This situation has contributed strongly to the creation of specific geographic spaces in major cities inhabited primarily by gay men and to some degree, lesbians, the so-called gay villages or gay ghettos. One such area, located in Toronto and called "The Gay Village," is located at the intersection of Church and Wellesley Streets. Packed with restaurants and bars, even the street signs are decorated with rainbows. Slightly less flamboyant perhaps, but no less comfortable for gays and lesbians, is Vancouver's "West End," in which Davie and Denman Streets mark the heart. Unfortunately, exposure has its costs, and there are countless reports of "gay-bashing"—physical attacks by straight men against men they perceive to be gay—in these areas over the years.

Discrimination in Medical Care

Lesbians, gay men, and bisexuals often receive substandard or intolerant health care because of their sexual orientation. Examples are ostracism, mistreatment of partners, breached confidence, and derogatory remarks (Spafford et al. 2002). In one study of 711 lesbian, gay, and bisexual doctors and medical students, 67 percent knew of patients who had received substandard care based on their sexual orientation, and 88 percent had overheard colleagues disparage their lesbian and gay patients (cited in Spafford et al. 2002).

Another form of discrimination is based on *lack* of knowledge of sexual orientation. Studies (for example, by the American Medical Association) have found that many physicians do not ask about patients' sexual orientation, and, further, that many lesbians, gay men, and bisexuals do not tell ("Health Care Needs" 1996). Heterosexuality is assumed at a high medical cost to patients: When making diagnoses, physicians may overlook diseases or medical conditions that gay men or lesbians are more prone to contract. Likewise, there are diseases or conditions that lesbians and gay men are extremely unlikely to contract and are unnecessarily tested for.

Some physicians and nurses adopt a judgmental stance when dealing with gay and lesbian patients. Many current health-care providers view homosexuality as a sin, a crime, or a disease (Spafford et al. 2002). One study of 100 nurses teaching in nursing programs found that 34 percent believed that lesbians are "disgusting," and 17 percent believed that lesbians molest children (Stevens 1992). Other physicians and nurses may provide reduced care to gays and lesbians or deny them medical care altogether ("Health Care Needs" 1996). For example, lesbians may be at risk for terminal breast or ovarian cancer because some doctors do not provide adequate information about the importance of early cancer detection through routine gynecological examinations and mammography screening (Gessen 1993).

Some of the intolerance among physicians may be traced to past views in psychiatry of homosexuality as a medicalized pathology or disorder. Aversion therapy and frontal lobotomies were used in many cases to "cure" or "adjust" a non-heterosexual (Kinsman 1996).

In fact, Karlen noted that most early writing about homosexuals by medical and legal professionals was "chiefly concerned with whether the disgusting breed of perverts could be physically identified for the courts, and whether they should be held legally responsible for their acts" (cited in Kinsman 1996:31).

Probably the most controversial topic in health care for gay men, lesbians, and bisexuals is HIV/AIDS. Although physicians, dentists, nurses, and other health professionals may learn about treating patients who are HIV-positive, many feel inadequate to deal with these patients' psychological and social needs. Since the first diagnosed case of AIDS in Canada in 1979, the numbers of those diagnosed across Canada in all risk categories (except blood product recipients) has continued to grow. By the end of 1994, 16 000 cases had been diagnosed, and by April 2004, approximately 55 000 Canadians were infected with HIV/AIDS. Frighteningly, 17 000 of these people have no idea they are HIV positive. The Canadian HIV/AIDS Information Centre for the Canadian Health Network estimates that 5000 people each year in Canada are newly infected with HIV. There remains no cure for AIDS, and to date, nearly 12 000 people in Canada have died because of it. Different people than in the past are more at risk today. Although men who have sex with other men are still the group most at risk, the proportion of cases attributable to this risk factor has been dropping each year, while heterosexual contact and illicit IV drug use are becoming increasingly high-risk factors, particularly for women (Frank 2000). Further, the median age for HIV infection has dropped dramatically from the 1980s through the 1990s, and today the proportion of new cases between ages 15 and 29 is increasing rapidly (Frank 2000; Public Health Agency of Canada 2005).

Despite the prevalence of HIV/AIDS among gay men and bisexuals in certain age groups, many medical professionals do not inform their patients about the risks associated with various types of sexual conduct and intravenous drug use, or about measures that can be taken to prevent exposure to sexually transmitted diseases and HIV. Although HIV/AIDS was often referred to in the past as "the gay disease," because heterosexuals—women in particular—are so at risk today, social analysts and medical professionals urge that it should be viewed as *everyone's* problem.

Occupational Discrimination

Fearing that they may be stigmatized or discriminated against in the workplace, many gay and lesbian people do not reveal their sexual orientation (Woods 1993). Their fears have some grounding in reality. Despite laws prohibiting employment discrimination on the basis of sexual orientation, openly lesbian and gay people often experience bias in hiring, retention, and promotion in both private- and public-sector employment. More than 100 major companies have stated that they do not discriminate on the basis of sexual orientation. Nevertheless, studies show that about two-thirds of gay employees in private-sector employment (e.g., small businesses and large corporations) have witnessed some type of hostility, harassment, or discrimination at their place of employment (Singer and Deschamps 1994). Many chief executive officers are reluctant to put a lesbian or gay man at the top of the corporate hierarchy, and some employees express concern about working around gay men and lesbians (Woods 1993). Many who do not reveal their sexual orientation to co-workers are subjected to a general disparagement of gays, as Brian, a gay executive in a large corporation, explains:

> I was in an office with the boss and another person who is my same level, and we were talking about another professional that we should probably get involved in this transaction. The person who was at the same level as me said, "Oh, he's really good, but he's a flaming faggot." What was very shocking to me was that it was an attack on this person in a professional context. You are sort of used to the way straight men sort of banter around, calling each other queer, on a social level. But it's really strange when they talk about it in a professional setting. But this person thought it was okay. I assume that he thought there were three straight men there, so he could still say these things that in mixed company he would never say. (quoted in Mead 1994:40)

Although sexual harassment occurs in the workplace, supervisors frequently do not take it seriously. Because in order to prove sexual harassment, victims must show that the harasser targeted a specific category of people, such as gay men, charges of harassment reflect the victim's sexual orientation. Victims of same-sex harassment may be blamed for causing the incident. Many fear they will lose their job if they file a grievance, even though gay rights advocates believe sexual orientation should be irrelevant in determining whether harassment has occurred (Gover 1996b).

Same-sex sexual harassment and blatant discrimination in hiring and promotion are also problems in public-sector positions at the federal and provincial government levels, as well as in local law enforcement agencies. For many years, most law enforcement agencies and police departments did not employ lesbian or gay people. Today, gay and lesbian people are employed in law enforcement agencies throughout the country because of human rights policies that preclude the agencies from asking job applicants about their sexual orientation. Despite such provisions, sociologist Stephen Leinen (a former police lieutenant) found in his study of "gay cops" that many remain "totally closeted" for fear of how other police officers and gay people will treat them. The total secrecy among lesbians and gay men in many large police departments is illustrated by one gay police officer's surprise on learning that his partner, with whom he had worked for some time, also was gay: "I was deeply shocked when he told me. We had worked together for over three years and neither of us knew about the other. He said, 'How the hell could we have worked together for so long and neither one of us knew it?'" (Leinen 1993:3).

In recent years, some gay advocates have encouraged people to "come out" (identify their sexual orientation) at work and to make the biases against people based on their sexual orientation known to the media and the general public so that demands for change will be met. As long as people remain "in the closet," the advocates argue, workplace discrimination will not be eliminated (Nava and Dawidoff 1994).

Victimization and Hate Crimes

On November 17, 2001, Aaron Webster, a 41-year-old Vancouver resident and photographer, was viciously beaten to death near Second Beach in Stanley Park by a group of three or four men. While gay bashing in Vancouver, Toronto, and other large Canadian cities is well documented, Webster's death marked the first time a person may have been charged with a hate crime in British Columbia regarding sexual orientation. In December of 2004, 22-year-old Ryan Cran was convicted of manslaughter and sentenced to six years in prison. His accomplices, young offenders at the time of the murder, were both convicted of manslaughter and sentenced to three years, two-thirds of which had to be served in closed custody ("B.C. Man Guilty in Beating Death of Gay Man" 2004). None of the three, however, ended up being charged with a hate crime, which would have resulted in harsher sentencing. In the wake of the Webster murder trial, gay advocates, along with the Webster family, protested the fact that the crime was not prosecuted as a hate crime. A concerned citizen wrote a letter in April 2005 to the Minister of Public Safety and Solicitor General, Rich Colemen, about the lack of a hate crime charge in the Webster murder. The following is an excerpt from a response letter sent May 13, by Geoff Plant, the Attorney General of British Columbia:

> When the Crown decides what charge to proceed with, they must consider all the available evidence and lay a charge which can be fairly supported by the evidence. The same is true when the Crown makes submissions to the court—they must ensure that every submission is supported by the evidence. In the case of those charged with the death of Aaron Webster, there was not sufficient evidence to charge murder; there was, however, sufficient evidence to proceed with a manslaughter charge. Further, there was no evidence that Ryan Cran's actions were motivated by hatred based on the sexual orientation of Aaron Webster. It is important to bear in mind that, after examining all the evidence, the court itself concluded the motive in this case remains obscure. . . . Because of the lack of evidence that the crime was motivated by bias, prejudice or hate based on sexual orientation, Section 718.2 was not applicable in this case. However, it is important to note that the Crown listed eleven aggravating factors to support their submission for a higher sentence. Each aggravating factor must be weighed equally and independently. All of the eleven aggravating factors were based on the evidence before the court and the court accepted many of these factors in arriving at a sentence. . . . The Reasons for Sentence are available on the Web site of the

Supreme Court of British Columbia at: http://www.courts.gov.bc.ca/jdb-txt/sc/04/16/2004bcsc1635.htm. (Plant 2005)

This incident echoed the brutal October 1998 murder of 21-year-old Matthew Shepard, the University of Wyoming student who was lured to the outskirts of town by two young men who then tied him to a fence, savagely beat him, and left him to die. He was killed because of his sexual orientation (Shephard 1999).

In Canada, under the *Criminal Code,* there is no "hate crime legislation" *per se.* Rather, under "Purposes and Principles for Sentencing," Section 718.2 states that

> a court that imposes a sentence shall also take into consideration the following principles:
>
> (*a*) a sentence should be increased or reduced to account for any relevant aggravating or mitigating circumstances relating to the offence or the offender, and, without limiting the generality of the foregoing, . . .
>
> (i) evidence that the offence was motivated by bias, prejudice or hate based on race, national or ethnic origin, language, colour, religion, sex, age, mental or physical disability, sexual orientation, or any other similar factor . . . (Department of Justice Canada 2006b)

Before the early 1990s, few acts of violence against gays and lesbians were ever reported in the media. Indeed, hate crimes against gay men and lesbians were not even acknowledged as such. Although research is finally taking place, the scope and extent of hate crimes based on sexual orientation is not known (MacMillan and Claridge 1998), but hate crimes appear to be most prevalent where homophobic attitudes and behaviours are tolerated or at least overlooked. The Webster murder was not an isolated hate crime—there are many other incidents being reported across the country every week. This is alarming, since the B.C. Hate Crimes Team estimates that only between 5 and 10 percent of all hate crimes are actually reported to police (MacMillan and Claridge 1998:2). The B.C. Hate Crimes Team, an initiative created by the B.C. Ministry of Attorney General in 1996, comprises of members of the Ministry of Attorney General, Vancouver Police Department, and the RCMP. The mandate of the Hate Crimes Team is to "ensure the effective identification, investigation, and prosecution of crimes motivated by hate, bias or prejudice" (MacMillan and Claridge 1998:7). The B.C. Hate Crimes Team reported that "based on the number of hate/bias crimes 'reported' to the police in 1997, gay males were the most victimized group in Vancouver" (MacMillan and Claridge 1998:5). The Hate Crimes Team further reported,

> a tendency for hate/bias attacks to be more vicious and severe. Research has found that victims of hate-motivated crimes are four times more likely to experience assaultive behaviour, are twice as likely to receive an injury, and are four times more likely to require hospitalization . . . . Assaults, such as gay bashings, are committed at night in poorly lit areas. Moreover, the initial attack generally comes from behind and the first blow is with a weapon or punch directed towards the victim's head in order to knock the victim to the ground. In such instances, it is very difficult for victims to identify or even see one or more attackers. Further, the majority of hate-motivated assaults are almost exclusively stranger on stranger events. (MacMillan and Claridge 1998:7 and 17)

In the United States, information gathered since the passage of the 1990 *Hate Crimes Statistics Act* shows that more than 50 percent of all reported antigay harassment and violence is perpetrated by young males age 21 or under (Comstock 1991). Further, data from Ontario show that most hate crime (95 percent) is committed by individuals who are not connected in any way to an organized hate group, despite most people's beliefs that organized hate groups such as racist groups are most often responsible for hate crime (MacMillan and Claridge 1998:6). Clearly, stronger and more pervasive measures must be taken to eliminate homophobia, biphobia, and the associated hate crimes.

PERSPECTIVES ON SEXUAL ORIENTATION AND SOCIAL INEQUALITY

Sexual orientation and social inequality can be understood from various perspectives. Biologists take one approach, and psychologists take another. Sociological

SOCIAL PROBLEMS AND SOCIAL POLICY

BOX 6.2   School's Out: Closing the Books on Homophobia

History, as taught, is devoid of gays or lesbians. Without knowing that history, it's no surprise that many consider their present-day presence strange or unnatural.

Kevin Jennings, founder of the Gay, Lesbian and Straight Education Network (in Seavor 1996:E11)

Recently, some schools have modified their curricula to incorporate information on lesbians, gays, and bisexuals. However, journalist Dan Woog (1995), author of a book on the impact of gay and lesbian issues in schools, suggests that much remains to be done. According to Woog, within the administration of each school, there should be at least one advocate to address gay issues—a person who is available to gay, lesbian, and bisexual students; who makes sure that the school complies with its responsibility to all students; and who helps with referrals to outside support groups, counselling agencies, hot lines, and organizations for family members. Woog also suggests that schools define harassment on the basis of sexual orientation and make clear that inappropriate use of language, jokes, graffiti, and vandalism based on sexual orientation is unfair, offensive, and harmful to everyone in the school community.

In the 21st century, we are still concerned about how gay men and lesbians are treated in school. The Gay, Lesbian and Straight Education Network (GLSEN) "school climate" survey, which was conducted in 1999 among nearly 500 gay, lesbian, bisexual, and transgender students, found that 91 percent of the participants had heard words like "faggot," "dyke," or "queer" used regularly at school. Sixty-nine percent stated that they had experienced direct verbal harassment; 24 percent reported incidences of physical harassment. Are other students the primary perpetrators of prejudice and discrimination? Not necessarily. The GLSEN survey found that more than one-third of the participants had heard negative remarks about sexual orientation from faculty or staff. Judy Shepard, the mother of Matthew Shepard, a university student who was brutally murdered because of his sexual orientation, decries this type of negative behaviour among teachers, administrators, and students:

I sort of get the feeling that teachers and administrators feel that they grew up with that teasing in school, and they made it through—they treat it almost as a rite of passage. "We survived it, you survive it. This is how you grow." Oh, ignorant people! Kids have scars—from being teased because they have big ears. What kind of scars do they have from being teased because they're black, or gay? (Cullen 1999:3)

What suggestions do you have for reducing the problems described in the GLSEN study? According to Judy Shepard, education is where change must begin first: "Kids go to school to learn how to behave in society . . . . And if we don't start doing that in the schools soon, it's harder to do as an adult" (Cullen 1999:2). Arguing that discrimination and violence against gays must be taken seriously in any and all settings, including schools, GLSEN and other organizations conduct teacher-training workshops in an effort to make teachers and administrators more aware of this pressing problem.

Jean Baker, a psychologist and a mother of two gay sons, conducted research with school-age gays and lesbians. In her book *How Homophobia Hurts Children: Nurturing Diversity at Home, at School, and in the Community*, she was able to report through interviews with "out" students a number of the suggestions the students had for creating safer climates for gay, lesbian, and bisexual students in schools. Among the actions schools can take are (a) improving sex education to include discussions about safe gay sex; (b) having teachers, staff, or administrators start gay/straight alliance groups or clubs in schools; (c) providing sensitivity or diversity training for school personnel and students; (d) stepping up interventions against harassment based on sexual orientation; (e) openly discussing issues of homosexuality and heterosexuality in the classrooms and including gay, lesbian, and bisexual issues in the curriculum; (f) normalizing homosexuality; (g) not making heterosexist assumptions about students or their families; (h) being role models, either as gays, lesbians, or bisexuals or as those accepting of people with diverse orientations; and (i) being aware of materials and resources that students, families, and school personnel can draw upon (Baker 2002).

What other suggestions do you have for reducing the problems described in the GLSEN study above? In what other places, besides the school system, could we introduce changes that would be beneficial in reducing homophobia?

explanations focus primarily on how sexual orientation and homophobia are associated with social learning and/or social structural factors in society. We'll look at each perspective separately.

Interactionist Perspectives

In contrast to most biological and psychological perspectives, and much like some social psychological perspectives, interactionist perspectives view heterosexual and homosexual conduct as learned behaviour and focus on the process by which individuals come to identify themselves as gay, lesbian, bisexual, or straight. According to interactionists, most people acquire the status of *heterosexual* without being consciously aware of it, because heterosexuality is the established norm and they do not have to struggle over their identity. But the same is not true of people who come to identify themselves as *homosexual* or *bisexual.* In fact, some sociologists suggest that sexual orientation is a master status for many gay men, lesbians, and bisexuals (Schur 1965). A ***master status* is the most significant status a person possesses, the one that most determines how the individual views him or herself and how he or she is treated by others.** Master status based on sexual orientation is particularly significant when it is linked to other subordinate racialized/ethnic group statuses. For example, working-class gay Latinos are more hesitant than White, middle-class gay men to come out to their families because of cultural norms pertaining to *machismo* (masculinity) and the fear that relatives will withdraw the support that is essential for surviving at the subordinate end of racialized and class hierarchies (see Almaguer 1995).

Interactionists have identified several stages in the process of accepting a lesbian, gay, or bisexual identity (Weinberg et al. 1994). First, people experience identity confusion—a situation in which they feel different from other people and struggle with admitting that they are attracted to individuals of the same sex. For example, someone who identified himself as a 14-year-old boy posted the following note on an Internet newsgroup:

> I feel like my life is over. Am I gay? God, I hope not. I walk around going, "God, I hope not." I walk around going, "Do I like him?" "Do I like her?" "How would it feel to do it with him/her?"

WHY DOES THIS HAVE TO HAPPEN TO ME!! The funny thing is, I absolutely detest everything about sex with men, and relationships with men. But somehow, I feel attracted to them anyway!! (Gabriel 1995b:1)

In the past, many gay and lesbian people had nowhere to turn in their quest for answers and support from others; today, many use the internet and other forms of global communication to connect with others who share their concerns (Gabriel 1995b). It is important to keep in mind, however, that in a more accepting and less homophobic society, young people would not need to feel their lives were "over" when experiencing feelings of attraction for those of the same sex.

The second stage in establishing a lesbian or gay identity is seeking out others who are openly lesbian or gay and perhaps engaging in sexual experimentation or making other forays into the homosexual subculture. In the third stage, people attempt to integrate their self-concept and acceptance of a label such as "homosexual," "gay," or "lesbian" by pursuing a way of life that conforms to their definition of what those labels mean (Cass 1984; Coleman 1981/2; Ponse 1978). Like most "stage" theories, however, not all people go through these stages. Even those who do may not go through each stage in the same way, and some may move back and forth between stages (Weinberg et al. 1994).

Studies on how people come to accept their sexual identity as gay, bisexual, or lesbian show the significance of labelling and how it can create barriers to full participation in Canadian society. However, these studies are typically based on a relatively narrow selection of people, which makes it difficult to generalize the findings to larger populations. That is, research participants who openly identify themselves as gay or bisexual may not be characteristic of the larger homosexual or bisexual population (Weinberg et al. 1994).

Functionalist and Conflict Perspectives

Unlike the interactionist approach, which focuses primarily on how individuals come to identify themselves as homosexual, bisexual, or heterosexual, functionalist perspectives focus on the relationship between social structure and sexual orientation. To functionalists, social norms and laws are established to preserve social institutions and maintain stability in society. From this perspective, then, many societies punish homosexual conduct because it violates the social norms established by those societies and thus undermines the stability of the societies. Sociologist David P. Aday, Jr., provides an overview of this perspective:

> Marriage and family are structural arrangements that contribute to the continuity of our contemporary society . . . . [Homosexuality undermines] arrangements that currently operate to replace societal members in an orderly way—that is, the arrangement has survival value . . . . If homosexual conduct were allowed to exist unchallenged and unpunished, then it might in time undermine norms and laws that underpin monogamous marital sex, at least some of which results in the production of offspring to repopulate the society. . . . The punishment of homosexual conduct, from ridicule and discrimination to imprisonment, reinforces expectations about heterosexual and marital sex and defines the boundaries of society. (Aday 1990:25)

The functionalist perspective explains why some people do not believe homosexual conduct or marriages between lesbian or gay couples should be protected legally. It also explains why some religious and political leaders call for a renewal of "family values" in this country. But, as pointed out by political scientist and gay rights activist Andrew Sullivan (1997:147), homosexual people are part of heterosexual families too:

> [They] are sons and daughters, brothers and sisters, even mothers and fathers, of heterosexuals. The distinction between "families" and "homosexuals" is, to begin with, empirically false; and the stability of existing families is closely linked to how homosexuals are treated within them.

As a popular bumper sticker states, "Hate is *NOT* a family value."

Critics suggest that the functionalist approach supports the status quo and ignores a need for more current definitions of marriage and family. If marriage is understood to be the decision of two people to live together in a partnership—to be a family—then the intention or the capacity to have children should not be a condition. These critics say that nothing but custom mandates that marital partners must be of different genders (Nava and Dawidoff 1994).

Whereas the functionalist approach focuses on how existing social arrangements create a balance in society, the conflict approach focuses on *tensions* in society and *differences* in interests and power among opposing groups. From this perspective, people who hold the greatest power are able to have their own attitudes, beliefs, and values—about sexual orientation, in this case—represented and enforced while others are not (Aday 1990). Therefore, norms pertaining to *compulsory heterosexuality* reflect the beliefs of dominant group members who hold high-level positions in the federal, territorial, and provincial governments and other social institutions. However, critics assert that the conflict approach fails to recognize that some people who have wealth and power are gay or lesbian yet take no action to reduce discrimination based on sexual orientation.

According to Karl Marx, conflicts over values are an essential element of social life, and less-powerful people often challenge the laws imposed on them by those in positions of power. For example, adverse decisions by provincial courts and the Supreme Court of Canada have often resulted in increased political activism by gay and lesbian rights groups. In recent years, more openly lesbian and gay people can be found in public

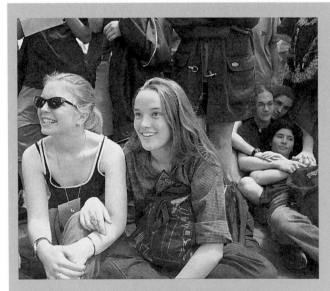

Many individuals seem to accept their identities as lesbian, gay, or bisexual in stages. Initially there is identity confusion. But seeking out others who are open about their sexual orientation and experimenting sexually can eventually lead to acceptance.

office, as elected or appointed officials; in the medical and legal professions; as educators and business leaders; and in all walks of life. However, regardless of their location in the power structure, most gay men, lesbians, and bisexuals remain acutely aware that many social barriers have not been lifted and that major shifts in people's attitudes toward homosexuality and bisexuality are still not realized.

With rapid internet communications, lesbians and gay men around the world keep informed about political decisions that may adversely affect them. Many coalitions have been formed to organize gay pride marches and protests around the world. For example, the International Lesbian and Gay Association reports that more than 400 lesbian and gay groups exist, on every continent and in more than 90 nations (Hendriks et al. 1993; International Lesbian and Gay Association 2006).

Feminist and Queer Perspectives

Feminist perspectives on sexuality have shifted considerably over the past four decades. In the late 1960s and through the 1970s, sexual orientation was mainly discussed by radical feminists who, by embracing binary and essentialist notions of males and females, claimed that women everywhere were bonded together in a sisterhood founded on their common oppression by men everywhere. As feminist writer Robin Morgan wrote in 1969, "Women have been subjugated longer than any other people on earth" (1969/1993:42). Feminist scholars Robyn Rowland and Renate Klein echoed this in 1996: "The first and fundamental theme is that women as a social group are oppressed by men as a social group and that this is the primary oppression for women" (1996:11). Along with the radical feminist theories of patriarchy came, necessarily, the analyses of compulsory heterosexuality as the cornerstone of male privilege and sexism. Feminist writer Adrienne Rich (1984), in her now famous essay "Compulsory Heterosexuality and Lesbian Existence," pointed out that heterosexuality, far from being a "natural" inclination, was, in fact, systematically imposed upon women through various means, including violence, as well as through hegemonic notions that heterosexuality was natural, inevitable, and universal. The radical feminist response to compulsory heterosexuality was varying

degrees of separatism, at least for the short term. As theorist Chris Weedon (1999:36) points out,

> a heterosexual lifestyle was often regarded as incompatible with feminism. To relate sexually to men was to consort with the enemy. This radical version of separatism implied having nothing to do with men, the first step in the process of freeing oneself from patriarchal power structures. This process involved a decolonization of patriarchally defined female consciousness, body image and ways of living. The result, it was thought, would be the discovery of a truly woman-defined womanhood.

This is not to suggest that men, gay men in particular, are not oppressed by heterosexism or compulsory heterosexuality; but sociologist Mariana Valverde (1987/2000:257) points out, "it weighs particularly heavily on women [as] men do not need female validation for their identity."

The weight of this radical feminist perspective resulted for many heterosexual feminists in feelings of guilt and confusion, estranging some from feminism altogether and reducing many to silence on the question of sexuality (Overall 2000; Valverde 2000; Weedon 1999). Recently, feminists, including radical feminists, discontented with past analyses, have again taken up the issue of sexuality, focusing on what it means to be both heterosexual and feminist. So, by the late 1980s, Valverde (1987/2000:260) made the argument that,

> Feminism asserts the right of all women to make their erotic choices, and this includes choosing men exclusively. Feminism also rejects the hierarchy of sexual practices, and so does not seek to substitute a lesbian priority for heterosexism. The goal of feminism in the area of sexuality is to establish true sexual pluralism, where no one choice is presented as "the norm."

Following on the notion of sexual pluralism, some feminist analyses focused on the possibility of being heterosexual and feminist but "conscious" of both the privileges and constraints of one's choice of heterosexuality (Overall 1990/2000). What this question brings up is the thorny issue of privilege. Therefore, women as a group may be disenfranchised. Gay men, lesbians, and bisexuals may be disenfranchised. Men have privilege.

Heterosexuals have privilege. Therefore, as sociologist Zoe Newman (2001:134) points out, "We need to map our complicity in structures of domination in order to 'move out of the subject position we claim on the margins and into the shifting and multiple subject positions of oppressed and oppressor.'" In effect, theorizing and identifying oneself as both heterosexual and feminist carries with it the discomfort of "disrupt[ing] identity posited on marginality, and reveal[ing] the coexistence of innocence and complicity" (Newman 2001:131). Despite some heterosexual feminists' claims that their relationships with men are completely egalitarian and non-oppressive,

> it nonetheless remains *possible* for the man to take advantage of his potential power. All that stands in the way of his using that power is his own good will, while he is not similarly dependent on the woman's good will. And he still benefits, however indirectly, from male hegemony, and "even the advantages that he is in a position to refuse are waiting for him if he changes his mind." (Overall 1990/2000:267)

Newman draws upon the work of theorist Michel Foucault (2001:134), stating that "even the act of shedding power is born of power; power circulates throughout our relations, it enables and it restricts." Contemporary feminists, then, with regard to the question of sexual orientation, have been focusing on the politics of difference. This is to say that because of the "hierarchization of difference in heterosexist societies," homosexuality and bisexuality continue to be hotly debated political issues within feminism, as much as they are personal ones (Weedon 1999:46).

Common ground between gay men and lesbians is discussed much more so in contemporary liberal feminist perspectives due, as Weedon (1999) points out, to the achievements of the lesbigay rights movements. For example, feminist psychologist Celia Kitzinger (1987:44) states that "the lesbian and gay man are no longer a species apart, but human beings of equal worth and dignity to heterosexuals, contributing to the rich diversity of humankind." The shift from feminist critiques of patriarchy and male power to a more inclusive politics of difference perspective accompanied the rise of postmodern thought, in particular in the form of *Queer theory.*

The quintessential feature of Queer theory is its staunch theoretical repudiation of any defining features, of any "normality" or "fixedness." Accepting the basic tenets of postmodern thought generally, those who subscribe to Queer theory or to notions of "queer" in general, allow that nothing is "normal," nothing is "natural"; everything is socially constructed and, hence, arbitrary. Queer theorists view gender and sexuality as performance and refuse to hierarchize any sex above another, any gender above another, any mode of sexual expression above another (Weedon 1999:73). Feminist psychologists Sue Wilkinson and Celia Kitzinger (1996:377) summarize one of the main thrusts of Queer theory, which is,

> . . . most popularly . . . [the] "genderfuck" . . . or "fucking with gender." The gender-fuck is supposed to "deprive the naturalizing narratives of compulsory heterosexuality of their central protagonists: 'man' and 'woman'" . . . and to illustrate the social constructedness of "sex" in all its multiple meanings.

While Queer theory seeks to subvert notions of "natural" and "normal," making any and every form of sexuality acceptable, many feminists and others find it problematic from a political or social change perspective, for a number of reasons. Queer theorists often view feminism as a "grand narrative," the assumptions and foundational propositions of which must be open to question and critique. Therefore, sexualized violence, pornography, and other heterosexually eroticized models of sexuality that are based in profoundly oppressive patriarchal relations may, within a Queer theory perspective, all be endorsed as "unimportant," "transitory," and "provisional" (Wilkinson and Kitzinger 1996:381): "Power relations within and between heterosexuality and homosexuality become invisible, allowing for a liberalism which hides oppression" (Weedon 1999:76).

Equally problematic is the widespread practice of gays and lesbians reclaiming the term "queer" as a means of self-identification, shifting the term from the pejorative to the celebratory. In doing this, they subvert the radical potential of the term "queer" by using it as an almost essentialist, but certainly bounded or fixed, category that has political value on the one hand but subverts the "mind fuck" potential on the other. From this perspective, then, a more radical use of the term may be for "straights" to begin to identify as "queer," thereby highlighting the multiplicity and arbitrariness of "queer." Indeed, many heterosexual people whose sexuality does not fit the norm for a variety of reasons do identify as queer. In this case, the value of queer as a destabilizing element is highlighted, rather than the term being used as simply a new category; as Newman (2001:129) describes it, defining one's "identity as always founded on a sense of marginality." She further points out that, used in this way, "the potential of queer seems to be that we do not come together around an assumption of sameness, but around a critique of 'the normal'" (Newman 2001:132). Sociologist Joshua Gamson (1996:396) cites queer activists Allan Bérubé and Jeffrey Escoffier saying that queer is often employed "to affirm sameness by defining a common identity on the fringes." Other critics of Queer theory note that while it may appear radical to reinterpret oneself as "queer," in terms of political activism, it is problematic. Anthropologist Max H. Kirsch (2000:97) cautions: "It is misguided as political action: it cannot generate the collective energy and organization necessary to challenge existing structures of power."

Defining oneself as queer—as "other" from a norm of heterosexuality—has concrete consequences. Some of these consequences include internalized and external oppression played out in depression, apathy, and violence. Kirsch (2000:97) notes, "We cannot simply refuse to acknowledge these facts of social life in our present society and hope that our circumstances will change." Queer theory therefore contains both the ability to be radical and destabilizing in challenging all things deemed natural or normal and, conversely, the potential to render one completely apolitical and paralyzed by apathy in the abyss of "anything goes." This is neatly summarized by political scientist Paisley Currah (2001:193–194), who also quotes feminist legal scholar Kimberlé Crenshaw (1991):

> "At this point in history, a strong case can be made that the most critical resistance strategy for disempowered groups is to occupy and defend a politics of social location rather than to vacate and destroy it." The appropriation of queer theory's useful theoretical insights by advocates of gay rights and the rights of sexual minorities requires maintaining a delicate balance between the politics of location and the politics of deconstruction.

CAN INEQUALITIES BASED ON SEXUAL ORIENTATION BE REDUCED?

As we have emphasized in previous chapters, how people view a social problem is related to how they believe the problem should be reduced or solved. Inequality based on sexual orientation is no exception. From an interactionist perspective, homosexual conduct is learned behaviour, and people go through stages in establishing a lesbian, gay, or bisexual identity. Society should, therefore, be more tolerant of people as they come to accept their sexual identity. Legal and social barriers that prevent homosexuals and bisexuals from fully participating in society should be removed, thereby making the complex psychological and social process of coming out to friends, family, and co-workers easier for those who choose to do so.

According to the functionalist perspective, social norms and laws exist to protect the family and maintain stability in society. Given this, sexual orientation becomes a social issue: Gay activists' demands for equal rights, including legal recognition of same-sex marriages, become major threats to the stability of society. With the legalization of marriage for gays and lesbians in Canada, some groups say there will be no stopping others who wish to strike down what remains of "foundational truths once thought to be self-evident" (Thomas 1996:A15).

Some advocates of this position believe that lesbians and gay men can change their sexual orientation:

> Homosexuals can and do change. My files bulge with stories of those who once engaged in sex with people of the same gender, but no longer do. They testify to the possibility of change for those who want to. The struggle to maintain what remains of the social fabric will ultimately determine whether we will continue to follow ancient Rome on the road to destruction, or come to our senses, turn around and re-enter a harbour of safety ordained by God for our own protection. (Thomas 1996:A15)

Whether gay, lesbian, and bisexual individuals can or should change their sexual orientation is the subject of widespread disagreement. However, most functionalists agree that homosexuality may be dysfunctional for society if it does not contribute to society's need for new members or if it undermines social norms and laws that preserve the family unit and maintain stability in society.

Conflict theorists believe that prejudice and discrimination against lesbians, gay men, and bisexuals are embedded in the social structure of society and are reinforced by those who hold the greatest power and thus are able to perpetuate their own attitudes, beliefs, and values about what constitutes "normal" sexual conduct. From this perspective, homophobia is similar to racism, sexism, ableism, and ageism, and the overt and covert discrimination that gay men and lesbians experience is similar to the discrimination experienced by people of colour, Indigenous peoples, all women, people with disabilities, older people, and children and youth. According to the conflict approach, the best way to reduce inequality based on sexual orientation is to continue to pass laws that ban all forms of discrimination against gay men, lesbians, and bisexuals or that represent barriers to their equality with heterosexuals. However, to gain equal rights, activism is necessary: People must continue to demand social change.

In the past, feminist theorists, using a radical critique of patriarchy, advocated separation of men and women. Lesbianism was promoted as the only rational and non-oppressive mode of relationship. This perspective led to deep divisiveness in the movement as heterosexual feminists had difficulties reconciling their sexual orientation with the political demands of the radical feminist separatists. More recently, feminists have approached questions of sexual orientation from the perspective of sexual pluralism, with the idea that all people, regardless of sexual orientation or gender, need to support one another to combat oppression. Therefore, according to contemporary feminists, to reduce inequality based on sexual orientation, people need to understand their commonalities in the face of oppression and also need to be clear about their varying positions of privilege in order to form alliances across location. In this way, everyone can fight against inequality based on sexual orientation as well as other inequalities.

Queer theorists believe that gender is a social construction and, thus, sexual orientation is also fluid. People use a queer perspective in one of two ways. Either they use the term "queer" as a descriptive category, or as a stand-in for the terms "gay," "lesbian," or

"bisexual." This use is political in that it represents a reclaiming of a term which, in most uses, has been regarded as disparaging. However, the radical potential of "queerness" as something fluid is thus subverted. From this perspective, the category or term is a means of overcoming people's homophobia by being "out," "loud," and "proud"—by demonstrating the normalcy of being outside the "norm" and raising challenging questions such as, Who defines what or who is normal? Using "queer" as a political category gives people something to rally around; it helps make collective action possible. Additionally, many people identify themselves as "queer" for a variety of reasons, and so it is a identity marker to use to provide common ground for all those who see themselves in opposition to "normal" sexuality, however that gets defined. Others use a queer perspective to refuse to define self or others, in this way enabling people to grapple with identity, subjectivity, and location. People may define themselves as queer but refuse to explain what makes them so, forcing people to engage with the questions about the importance of categorizing. From this perspective, by transgressing gender or sexuality norms (through cross-dressing, for example), people can flout the norms and demonstrate their arbitrariness and fluidity and thereby have an impact on changing or broadening norms and definitions. This is typically done on an individual basis, however, making collective actions difficult to organize.

In the 21st century, gay advocacy is perhaps the most effective means of reducing homophobia and bringing about greater equality for gay men and lesbians. In fact, it took a small riot in the United States to make the general public really aware of inequality based on sexual orientation and the need for social change. In 1969, police raided the Stonewall Inn, a bar patronized by gay men in New York City's Greenwich Village, for alleged liquor law violations. The angry response by militant gay activists caused police to stop raiding the Stonewall Inn and other gay bars and clubs on Christopher Street and ushered the Gay Liberation movement into existence (Weinberg and Williams 1975). As recently as the 1970s in Canada, the RCMP conducted raids on bars known for or suspected of patronage by gays and lesbians, and police raids on "gay bath houses" continue today. In an article describing the outcome of a February 1981 police raid on a Toronto bath house, Todd Richmond, features editor of the popular website 365gay.com, wrote that while hundreds of thousands of dollars in damage was done to the club and nearly 300 people were arrested, many of whom lost their jobs as a result, that raid marked

> the watershed moment that dates the gay liberation movement in Canada . . . . The community was galvanized for the first time. The raids, and their overkill, gave the community a sense of power that has helped lead to most of the rights enjoyed by gays and lesbians today. (Richmond 2002)

With the emergence of HIV/AIDS as a major problem in the 1980s, and with the repatriation of the Canadian Constitution and the signing into law of the *Canadian Charter of Rights and Freedoms* in 1982, many gay advocates shifted the focus of their lobbying from human rights to the need for medical research (Shilts 1988). Today, hundreds of organizations seek equal rights and protections for gay men, lesbians, and bisexuals; these groups represent a wide cross-section of the Canadian population. For example, groups like EGALE (Equality for Gays and Lesbians Everywhere) Canada, PFLAG (Parents and Friends of Lesbians and Gays) Canada, the Rainbow Coalition, and the International Lesbian and Gay Association (ILGA) serve the needs of all gay, lesbian, and bisexual people, whereas other groups serve a niche. These groups include Primetimers, specifically for older gays and lesbians; CALYPSO (Canadian Alliance Linking Young People around Sexual Orientation), for Canadian youth; Christian Lesbians, for Christians who are religiously inclined; and the Bisexual Resource Group, BiWomen of Colour, BiAdult Children of Alcoholics, and even BiStar Trekkies, which focus on the needs of some bisexual people (Gabriel 1995a; Leland 1995).

Despite some changes in the attitudes and laws pertaining to homosexuality, discrimination remains strong. According to a recent study, gay, lesbian, and bisexual sociologists who advocate gay rights are more likely than their heterosexual colleagues to encounter difficulty in obtaining academic positions, experience bias in the tenure and promotion process, and be excluded from social and professional networks (Taylor and Raeburn 1995). However, not all of the study's findings were negative: For some sociologists, being involved in gay rights issues brings professional

visibility, recognition, and opportunities for advancement (Taylor and Raeburn 1995):

> Gay rights advocates argue that gay men, lesbians, and bisexuals should not be the only ones responsible for reducing or eliminating inequality based on sexual orientation: It all comes down to this: Are people equal in this society by virtue of their citizenship, or not? If the answer is no, then we will be saying that equality does not exist . . . anymore but has been replaced by tiers of citizenship, and that what tier you occupy depends on whether people like you or not. And if we accept this, then we will have repudiated the constitutional principles of liberty and equality . . . . We believe that you will join in this cause because it is your cause, too, the cause of individual liberty and human equality. (Nava and Dawidoff 1994:167)

Some analysts suggest that people in the future will ask, What was all the fuss over gay men and lesbians (or sexual orientation) about? Valverde (1998) takes the position that 20 years in the future, it will have become as socially unacceptable to discriminate against people based on sexual orientation as today it has become to discriminate against people based on skin colour. What do you think?

WHAT CAN YOU DO?

- Reflect on the assumptions you hold about homosexuals, heterosexuals, and bisexuals, and about sexual orientation in general.

- Attend a PRIDE day or parade in your community, regardless of your sexual orientation.

- Consider voting in favour of same-sex marriages and other issues that support queer folk, in newspapers, internet, and opinion polls.

- Do not claim heterosexual privilege. Refer to your girlfriend or boyfriend or husband or wife as your "partner" or your "spouse." Keep people guessing.

- Incorporate sexual orientation issues into your relevant research papers.

- Do not refer to gay, lesbian, or bisexual friends or colleagues as "my gay friend Kim" unless you typically refer to your straight friends as "my straight friend Lee."

- Do not assume you know someone's sexual orientation. Instead, allow people to define their gender/sexuality for you.

- Write a letter to your MP asking that he or she speak against repeals of the new legislation favouring equal marriage for same-sex couples if the issue comes up in the House of Commons again, and explain why he or she should do this.

- Do not treat bisexuality as an "identity of confusion" but, rather, accept it as a real and valid (and queer) identity of its own.

- Accept public displays of affection (PDAs) between people of the same sex as natural and normal. Participate in them, to whatever degree you are comfortable (e.g., linking arms with a same-sex friend while walking down the street; hugging a same-sex friend when you meet them), in order to be in solidarity with same-sex couples and to take the heat off queer folks who are always breaking trail and feeling the brunt of it.

- If you are heterosexual and involved in an intimate partnership with a person of the other sex, try to keep this relationship "in the closet" for one week. This could involve (a) having no physical contact with the person if anyone else (friends, family, general public) is around; (b) being careful where or even if you are seen together; (c) not mentioning this person and/or the relationship to anyone; and, (d) not being seen or heard talking on the phone to this person.

SUMMARY

WHAT CRITERIA DO SOCIOLOGISTS USE TO STUDY SEXUAL ORIENTATION?

Sociologists define sexual orientation as a preference for emotional–sexual relationships with persons of the "same" sex (homosexuality), the "opposite" sex (heterosexuality), or both (bisexuality). Recent studies have used three criteria for classifying people as homosexual or bisexual: (1) sexual attraction to persons of one's own gender; (2) sexual involvement with one or more persons of one's own gender; and, (3) self-identification as a gay man, lesbian, or bisexual.

HOW DO RELIGION AND LAW INFLUENCE PEOPLE'S BELIEFS ABOUT HOMOSEXUALITY?

Most major religions, with the exception of Buddhism, regard homosexuality as a sin. Contemporary religious fundamentalists denounce homosexual conduct as a sign of great moral decay and societal chaos. Throughout Canadian history, moral and religious teachings have been intertwined with laws that criminalize homosexual conduct. While many religions do not condone homosexuality, many adherents to them do.

WHAT TYPES OF DISCRIMINATION DO GAY AND LESBIAN PEOPLE EXPERIENCE?

Although lesbians and gay men experience discrimination in most aspects of daily life, some of the principal areas are (1) housing, (2) medical care, and (3) employment. In each of these areas, gains have been made over the past three decades. However, discrimination against lesbians, gay men, and bisexuals remains among the most blatant of all forms of prejudice and discrimination experienced by members of subordinate groups.

HOW HAVE CHANGES IN THE DEFINITION OF HATE CRIMES AFFECTED GAY MEN AND LESBIANS?

Despite sexual orientation being a "protected ground" in the Charter and in most provincial and territorial human rights legislation, Canada's *Criminal Code* still does not include specific hate crime legislation, except under Section 718.2 on sentencing. Provincial hate crimes units, however, like British Columbia's, are going a long way to collect those data, perhaps influencing further and broader legislative changes in the future. Hate crimes against gays and lesbians appear to be most prevalent where homophobic attitudes are tolerated or overlooked.

HOW DO INTERACTIONISTS EXPLAIN PROBLEMS ASSOCIATED WITH SEXUAL ORIENTATION?

According to interactionists, most people acquire the status of heterosexual without being consciously aware of it. For lesbians, gay men, and bisexuals, however, sexual orientation may be a master status because it largely determines how individuals view themselves and how they are treated by others. Interactionists identify several stages in the process of accepting the identity of lesbian, gay, or bisexual: (1) experiencing identity confusion; (2) seeking out others who are openly lesbian or gay and sometimes engaging in sexual experimentation; and (3) attempting to integrate self-concept and acceptance of a label such as "homosexual," "gay," or "lesbian."

HOW DO FUNCTIONALISTS EXPLAIN PROBLEMS ASSOCIATED WITH SEXUAL ORIENTATION?

Functionalists focus on how social norms and laws are established to preserve social institutions such as the family and to maintain stability in society. They also analyze reasons why societies find it necessary to punish sexual conduct that violates social norms prohibiting non-marital sex and same-sex sexual relations. According to functionalists, homosexual conduct is punished because it undermines social institutions and jeopardizes the society.

HOW DO CONFLICT THEORISTS EXPLAIN PROBLEMS ASSOCIATED WITH SEXUAL ORIENTATION?

Conflict theorists believe that the group in power imposes its own attitudes, beliefs, and values about sexual orientation on everyone else. Thus norms enforcing compulsory heterosexuality reflect the beliefs of dominant group members in the federal and state governments, the military, and other social institutions. According to conflict theorists, social change can occur only if people demand that laws be changed to bring about greater equality for gay men and lesbians.

HOW DO FEMINIST THEORISTS EXPLAIN PROBLEMS ASSOCIATED WITH SEXUAL ORIENTATION?

Like conflict theorists, feminist theorists believe that the group in power can impose its own agenda. The group in power in this case is seen to be males, however, and notions of compulsory heterosexuality work to serve the interests of men in an unequal and gendered social system. Feminist theorists from a radical perspective first suggested that lesbianism was a rational, political choice, based on a critique of patriarchy. Today, many feminists reject the separatist stance of earlier writers on these issues and instead opt for a model that values all diversity and encourages acceptance of all people, regardless of gender, sexual orientation, and so on. Therefore, homosexuals and bisexuals need to be made equal within all institutions and facets of society.

HOW DO QUEER THEORISTS EXPLAIN PROBLEMS ASSOCIATED WITH SEXUAL ORIENTATION?

Many queer theorists believe that problems associated with sexual orientation are the result of a homophobic and biphobic culture. They advocate playing with the categories, labels, definitions, and understandings of the various genders, sexes, and sexual orientations as a way of subverting consciousness. Queer theorists believe that when people's taken-for-granted realities are disrupted, people will be enabled to see sex, gender, and sexual orientation as the social constructions they are, and thus, ease off of rigid and harmful stereotyping and actions.

HOW HAVE GAY RIGHTS ADVOCATES SOUGHT TO REDUCE INEQUALITY BASED ON SEXUAL ORIENTATION?

Beginning with the Gay Liberation movement in the 1960s, advocates have argued that lesbians and gay men are citizens and entitled to the same rights and protections that all other citizens enjoy, including the right to equal employment and housing, legally sanctioned marriage, adoption of children, and protection from harassment and hate crimes. Some analysts suggest that future social change depends on the continued vigilance of gay, lesbian, and bisexual advocacy organizations.

KEY TERMS

biphobia, p. 145
deviance, p. 144
heterosexism, p. 145
homophobia, p. 145

master status, p. 159
sexuality, p. 144
sexual orientation, p. 143

QUESTIONS FOR CRITICAL THINKING

1. Think of any assumptions you hold about homosexuals, bisexuals, and heterosexuals. What actions flow from your assumptions? What impact may your actions have on people whose sexual orientation/preference differs from your own?

2. Following a Queer theory approach, critically analyze the discomfort generated by allowing or asking people to define their gender, sex, and sexual orientation for you. What assumptions are disrupted when you do this?

3. What things can heterosexual individuals and/or couples take for granted that homosexual individuals or couples cannot?

4. The B.C. Hate Crimes Team, created by the provincial government and including members of the RCMP, reports that gays, lesbians, and bisexuals are often reluctant to report violence that is perpetrated against them. Explain why this might be so.

WEBLINKS

BiNet Canada
www.binetcanada.ca
BiNetCanada is a national volunteer organization of bisexual and sexually diverse Canadians working to raise awareness and acceptance of their issues of concern. The site gives information about regional, national, and international resources and posts up-to-date articles and press releases.

Gayscape.com
www.gayscape.com
This site is a directory that lists over 68 000 indexed sites on myriad topics of interest to gays, lesbians, and bisexuals.

Equal Marriage for Same-Sex Couples
www.samesexmarriage.ca
This site is hosted by a gay couple who worked to achieve the recognition in law that all people have the equal right to marry. It provides social and legal information and links to news items and articles.

Family Pride Canada
www.uwo.ca/pridelib/family/
Family pride is a national online resource centre focusing on the social, legal, political, educational, spiritual, and psychological issues facing lesbian, gay, bisexual, and transgender parents and their families

across Canada. Services include legal resources and informative literature.

International Lesbian and Gay Association
www.ilga.org
The International Lesbian and Gay Association is a world-wide network of national and local groups dedicated to achieving equal rights for lesbian, gay, bisexual, and transgendered (LGBT) people everywhere.

Lesbian and Gay Immigration Task Force
www.ncf.carleton.ca/legit
The Lesbian and Gay Immigration Task Force is a national organization working toward changing Canada's discriminatory immigration laws. It offers detailed information about those laws, advice, and useful links and contacts.

Parents, Families and Friends of Lesbians and Gays
www.pflag.ca
This site offers support and information to gay, lesbian, bisexual, and transgendered persons, and to their families and friends, in order to build a more

respectful and discrimination-free society. The site also provides links to other gay and lesbian organizations and a message board for discussion.

Pride Net Canada
www.pridenet.com/canada.html
The purpose of this site is to provide an intense resource centre for gays, lesbians, bisexuals, and transgenders. The information and links range from bars and restaurants to support organizations and poetry.

Pride Vision Television
www.pridevisiontv.com
PrideVision TV is the world's first GLBT television network to broadcast 24/7. The programming ranges from entertainment to current affairs and focuses on issues specifically involving the gay community.

Vancouver Island Lesbian Resources (VILR)
www.vilr.info
VILR offers emotional support, information, weblinks, message boards, and online and offline resources for lesbians from Vancouver Island seeking connection to the lesbian community.

7

THE SEX INDUSTRY IN CANADA AND BEYOND

PROSTITUTION IN HISTORICAL AND GLOBAL PERSPECTIVE

The World's Oldest Profession?

The Global Sex Industry

Box 7.1 Social Problems in Global Perspective: The Global Sex Trade—A Canadian Case

PROSTITUTION IN CANADA

Some Characteristics of Prostitution in Canada

The Extent of Prostitution in Canada

Prostitution and Age, Class, Racialization, and Ethnicity

A Closer Look at "Johns"

PERSPECTIVES ON PROSTITUTION

The Functionalist Perspective

The Interactionist Perspective

Conflict and Feminist Perspectives

PORNOGRAPHY

The Social Construction of Pornography as a Social Problem

The Nature and Extent of Pornography

Box 7.2 Social Problems and Information Technology: Canada's Role in Cracking Down on Internet Child Pornography

Research on Pornography

Pornography and Age, Gender, Class, Racialization, and Ethnicity

THE FUTURE OF PORNOGRAPHY AND THE SEX INDUSTRY

WHAT CAN YOU DO?

I just fell for it . . . I was in a vulnerable state, I lost my virginity to rape, and I was consistently abused by my mother. I was ashamed of myself, who I was, what I looked like and, when I met this man, he was the world to me. He said, "Oh you're so pretty" and I fell for it [and became a prostitute for him].

Female youth, Winnipeg, Manitoba (Kingsley and Mark 2000:54)

[People] think that all prostitutes are on heroin, or they like to be beat up. The stereotype is, "oh, they all knew what they were getting into," which they don't.

Female youth, Vancouver, B.C. (Kingsley and Mark 2000:69)

I think I would have jumped from the CN Tower a couple of times, just from being transsexual, because that's one of the things that has been so hard. Being 21, a prostitute for 10 years, being a transsexual, and just living this entire lifestyle is very hard. I've tried going home a few times, but it just doesn't work because of my sexuality. It's much easier for me to be in the city and deal with it.

Male youth, Toronto, Ontario (Kingsley and Mark 2000:28)

I got involved in the drugs because I got involved with the wrong guy and eventually the drugs just took over me. I thought I would be okay, you just start [by] running drugs for people, and they started saying "why don't you just go sleep with this guy," or "why don't you just do [these] different things" . . . I got sucked into it [the sex trade].

Female youth, Mission, B.C. (Kingsley and Mark 2000:21)

At that time [when I was working in the trade] I really wanted to die . . . I couldn't look at myself in the mirror. I couldn't accept the fact that I just thought I was a dirty bitch. Just a slut . . .

Female youth, Goose Bay, Labrador (Kingsley and Mark 2000:31)

Know those porn star shirts that say "XXX" or "Touch This" or whatever they say . . . all I can say is that you see 15-year-olds walking around in them and I'm sorry, but the first word that comes to my mind is sex. What is this? It has a lot to do with society.

Female youth, Mission, B.C. (Kingsley and Mark 2000:26)

A lot of our issues are the same, all the way across the country, whether we want to see it or not, and it all comes back to the same thing, that abuse in our families and our communities.

Female youth, Halifax, Nova Scotia (Kingsley and Mark 2000:23)

There are a multitude of reasons why people enter the sex trade, and the voices of the Canadian youth quoted above speak to some of those reasons. Unlike the young men and women portrayed here, other sex-trade workers view sex work simply as a career choice—with willing buyers and sellers, a purely economic exchange—that is no more or less degrading than any other profession (Aalbers 2005; Alexander 1987; Chapkis 1997; Doezema 1998; Kempadoo 1998, 2005; McWilliams 1996). Certainly, in this country, it is a thriving multimillion-dollar industry that includes prostitution, the film and video trade, printed pornography, escort services, massage parlours, and strip and table- and lap-dancing clubs. However, prostitution and other types of sex work have always been controversial; not all social analysts even agree on whether or not the sex industry is a social problem. To better understand the controversy over prostitution, pornography, and other sex work, we will look at each of these issues and what constitutes deviant behaviour. Looking at the way these elements of the sex trade are currently organized, as well as looking into the future, nationally and globally, will help you to decide if any of the explanations provided by various sociological and feminist perspectives clarify *your* opinions.

PROSTITUTION IN HISTORICAL AND GLOBAL PERSPECTIVE

Narrowly defined, *prostitution* **is the sale of sexual services (of oneself or another) for money or goods and without emotional attachment.** More broadly defined, systems of prostitution refer to any industry in which women's and/or children's—and sometimes men's—bodies are bought, sold, or traded for sexual use (Giobbe 1994). According to this broader definition, systems of prostitution include pornography, live sex shows, peep shows, international sexual slavery, and prostitution as more narrowly defined above. The vast majority of sex-trade workers around the globe are women and female children. Certainly, male prostitution exists, and most boys and men in the sex industry engage in sexual encounters with other males (see Browne and Minichiello 1995; Lauer et al. 2006; Leuchtag 2003; McNamara 1994; Snell 1995; Wolff and Geissel 2000).

The World's Oldest Profession?

Prostitution has been referred to as the "world's oldest profession" because references to it can be found throughout recorded history. Still, over the past 4000 years, prostitution has been neither totally accepted nor completely condemned. For example, while prostitution was widely accepted in ancient Greece, where upper-class prostitutes were admired and frequently became the companions of powerful Greek citizens, the prostitutes themselves were refused the status of wife—the ultimate affirmation of legitimacy for women in Greek society—and were negatively compared with so-called virtuous women in a "bad woman–good woman" ("Madonna–Whore") dichotomy (see Bullough and Bullough 1987; Jolin 1994; Roberts, 1992).

In other eras, attitudes and beliefs about prostitution have ranged from generally tolerant to strongly averse. Such early Christian leaders as St. Augustine and St. Thomas Aquinas argued that prostitution was evil but encouraged tolerance toward it. According to Aquinas, prostitution served a basic need that, if unmet, would result in greater harm than prostitution itself. Later Christian leaders such as Martin Luther in 16th-century Europe believed that prostitution should be abolished on moral grounds (Jolin 1994; Otis 1985).

In the 19th-century feminist movement, women for the first time voiced their opinions about prostitution. Some believed that prostitution led to promiscuity and moral degeneracy in men and should therefore be eradicated. Others believed that prostitution should be legitimized as a valid expression of female sexuality outside of marriage. Recently, some advocates have suggested that prostitution should be viewed as a legitimate career choice for women (prostitute as sex worker), but others have argued that prostitution is rooted in global gender inequality (prostitute as victim of oppression). This argument will be discussed further when we examine feminist perspectives on the issue.

In terms of prostitution being Canada's oldest profession, it is not. Sociologist Dan Allman (1999) notes that though there were some accounts of "prostitution-like" relations among Indigenous people, sex work was not actually introduced in Canada until Europeans began to settle here. Early writings about the Canadian sex trade (late 1800s to early 1900s) are limited to females who were in the public eye.

The Global Sex Industry

The past three decades have seen the industrialization, normalization, and globalization of prostitution. Although *industrialization* typically refers to the mass production of manufactured goods and services for exchange in the market, sociologist Kathleen Barry (1995:122) suggests that this term should also apply to commercialized sex manufactured within the human self. Prostitution becomes *normalized* when sex work is treated as merely a form of entertainment and there are no legal impediments to promoting it as a commodity. The *globalization* of prostitution refers to the process by which the sex industry has become increasingly global in scope (e.g., international conglomerates of hotel chains, airlines, bars, sex clubs, massage parlours, brothels, and credit card companies that have an economic interest in the global sex industry), which has occurred as people's political, economic, and cultural lives have become increasingly linked globally (Barry 1995; Davidson 1996; Matika-Tyndale, Lewis, and Street 2005). For evidence of this globalization, one has only to look at the recent increase in Canada of migrant sex workers from the former Soviet Union and Eastern Europe (see Box 7.1).

Furthermore, internet sites, such as the World Sex Guide, post listings for hundreds of cities all over the world. Would-be travellers can simply log on, click on their destination city and find out about specific women and agencies in the area, rates, services offered (e.g., if she allows "oral" on herself, if she will perform "oral" on you, how good it is, etc.), photos, laws of the particular jurisdiction, and so on. These kinds of services lend a whole new meaning to the Canadian advertising

SOCIAL PROBLEMS IN GLOBAL PERSPECTIVE

BOX 7.1   The Global Sex Trade—A Canadian Case

Many women are trafficked as domestic workers or mail-order brides. Others are trafficked for the sex trade. How many women are trafficked into Canada for involvement in the sex trade is unknown, but the demand for "exotic" and foreign-born women is well documented. An estimated one million people, mainly women, are trafficked for the sex trade worldwide and, historically, much of this traffic has involved women from various parts of Asia. Recent reports suggest that of the women who are trafficked globally, approximately 225 000 are from South East Asia, 200 000 from former Soviet republics, 150 000 from South Asia, 100 000 from Latin America and the Caribbean, 75 000 from Eastern Europe, and 50 000 from Africa (Farr 2005:4). Indications are that, today, Slavic women are the main focus of traffickers (McDonald et al. 2000:1).

The reasons for the increase in the traffic of Slavic women revolve mainly around the breakup of the Soviet Union in 1991 and the resultant economic upheaval. As Eastern Europe and the former Soviet Union struggled to make the transition from a communist economy to free-market capitalism, massive job loss and poverty ensued. Inevitably, the world over, women (and their children) have been the hardest hit by these structural economic shifts. Many women view migration to richer nations as the key to their survival or view it as a means to better their and their families' situations. Additionally, there appears to be a growing demand for women racialized as White in Europe, the Middle East, China, Thailand, Korea, and Japan (Farr 2005; Yea 2005).

Through formal means (advertisements in local newspapers, billboards, and TV) or informal means (word of mouth by friends, relatives, and co-workers), women are recruited by sex-trade traffickers to work in Canada, the United States, Asia, and Western European countries. Worldwide, Kamala Kempadoo has argued, "most 'trafficked persons' express some personal desire to migrate, and about half of women in the global sex trade appear to be conscious of the fact that they will be involved in some form of sex work prior to migration" (2005:38). While some women may be aware of the working conditions and the goals of those who recruit them for the Canadian sex trade, many appear to be ill-informed, misled, or completely deceived. Sentences for traffickers are light, as well as rare, making this a "highly profitable and enduring business" (Farr 2005:3).

In research for the *Status of Women Canada*, Lynn McDonald, Brooke Moore, and Natalya Timoshkina (2000) conducted, for the first time, an exploratory study of women migrant sex workers in Toronto who had come to Canada from Eastern Europe and the former Soviet Union. Eighteen migrant sex workers, as well as service providers and other key informants such as police officers, immigration officials, and massage parlour owners, were interviewed in order to create a comprehensive picture of these women's experiences. The researchers found that trafficking networks varied in their degree of formalization, depending on size. Large-scale networks were ones with political and economic footholds in the countries of origin and destination and were "sophisticated" in terms of producing fraudulent documents and having a "substantial infrastructure" for transit routes and destination nations (McDonald et al. 2000:5). Medium-scale networks were ones that did not sell women to others but rather recruited women from one specific country to work in their own businesses in the destination country (McDonald et al. 2000:5). The small-scale networks operated typically by fulfilling orders for one, two, or more women, perhaps from a specific region, placed by a business owner. In these operations, the traffickers recruited and then accompanied the women, ultimately delivering them to the contracting business owner (McDonald et al. 2000:5). Many women are also recruited informally, through word of mouth, by people they know who are either already here in Canada or are in the country of origin but know of contacts here.

While it would be incorrect to paint all trafficked women as innocent victims, some degree of deception is nearly always employed in recruiting them. Some women are promised legitimate employment and then forced into the sex trade, while others know they will be involved in the sex trade but are deceived about its legality in Canada, the specifics of what they are to do, the extent of their involvement, and the length of time they must be involved, as the interview comments of these Hungarian sex-trade workers in a Toronto strip-club illustrate:

I call them and I meet with them, and they said it's a babysitting job and stuff . . . and then when I come to Canada I find out here that it's not a babysitting job. And then I just find out this group in Hungary it's really organized crime. (McDonald et al. 2000:44)

The first, second, third, fourth night I didn't work at all. I said: "There is no way I'm going to dance. You can do anything with me. I'm not going to dance." On Sunday night he [owner/agent] said, "You've been here one week . . . you didn't make any money, and we are going to teach you how to make the money" . . . he sent four guys in the room so he could teach me how I have to make the money. They raped me for four days and four nights. (McDonald et al. 2000:54)

I heard that they keep the rules very strictly so I shouldn't worry about the dance. They knew I'd never danced before and that's why they said it. That nobody can ever touch me . . . always security everywhere. And so I won't have any problems with any customers, nobody can come close to me . . . The difference was that of course people tried to touch me, of course they were closer to me than I expected. There was no security where we danced. So the customers could do whatever they wanted. (McDonald et al. 2000:44–45)

McDonald, Moore, and Timoshkina (2000) found that none of the women in their study had worked in the sex-trade industry prior to being trafficked to Canada. Many believed they were coming to Canada to become legitimate chorus line–style dancers or entertainers. Most said they were aged 18 to 26, although some may have been younger than that. All had finished high school, with half the women having post-secondary certificates, degrees, and careers in their countries of origin. Most of the women were single and one-quarter of them had children. All the women came to Canada with the idea of improving their economic situations, some having other reasons in addition, such as the actuality or the threat of war in their homeland.

What many women found was that instead of making a great deal of money and living autonomous lives, their activities were often completely controlled; they found themselves living at places designated by the business owner or agent, being driven to and from work, working long hours, being videotaped or watched constantly, and earning just enough (if any) money to keep them perpetually engaged in the business, since against any earnings were charged creative fees for housing, food, the DJ's services, room rentals for sex with customers, fines for being late, and so on. Other women had more autonomy, earned decent money, and felt they could not make this kind of money elsewhere, so they remained tied to the industry due to lack of viable options (McDonald et al. 2000). Many of the women were brought into the country on visitor visas; when these expired, the owners or agents had that much more control over the women.

Many women are told they cannot leave the trade or the establishment because they will be arrested and deported, especially those women who are here on expired visas. Others have stayed in the work due to a (perceived) lack of options. Many women were expected to send money home to relatives or were trying to support families here and believed that they would not get comparably paid jobs due to language barriers and/or a lack of Canadian training or education:

In one day you can make $200. It's a big difference when you used to make $50 a day. It means you can work for two days, just close your eyes on everything and you can survive already. I signed up my girl for dancing classes, signed her up for music classes, and she paints too. And I became happier. I can help out my mother. (Russian massage parlour worker quoted in McDonald et al. 2000:61)

You know, I've been working in this business for several years, and I can tell you that all the girls have goals. But, for some reason, even older women who keep saying: "Oh, I'll just save some money and go to school" . . . You see, it is so hard to get out of it, out of this business. Mainly because of the money. It's very difficult. I tried to get out three or four times. (Moldovian massage parlour worker quoted in McDonald et al. 2000:61)

The traffic of women into Canada has serious implications for the women themselves and for all Canadians. Whether or not these women choose to remain in the sex industry, they should live in conditions free from coercion, abuse, danger, and economic insecurity. How to create the conditions for women to make free choices is a matter for policymakers and others to take up. McDonald, Moore, and Timoshkina (2000:66–68) make a number of recommendations that could have implications for the Canadian Criminal Code and for Canada's immigration laws. Some of the recommendations include:

- distributing information in countries of origin and at immigration ports, in many languages, about the realities of trafficking, the legalities of sex trade in Canada, exotic dancing, and so on;
- re-evaluating visitor's visas with a view to finding ways for women whose visas expire to avoid illegal status;
- finding ways to integrate migrant women and their partners into the core Canadian economy by offering more language classes (English/French) and by expediting the process for accreditation of immigrant professionals;
- intervening in establishments where women are working in unfavourable working conditions by having health inspectors do inspections on whole workplaces, not just the kitchens;
- developing a system of regulating sex-trade businesses to ensure basic Canadian work safety rules are followed;
- having written information posted in these businesses, in many languages, about free health and social services that are available;

■   funding agencies and organizations that work with people in the sex trade and mandating their access to these businesses; and

■   developing and funding joint initiatives for addressing organized sex-trade trafficking.

Kempadoo, using a Third World or transnational feminist perspective, notes that the sex industry is only one of several sites of global trafficking in a world increasingly dominated by globalized capitalism: "the continued demand for cheap labour by corporations, state military apparatuses, and leisure and professional classes, which are wholly complicit in sustaining conditions of economic inequality, exploitive conditions, and the criminalization of poor people, goes unfettered and unchallenged in this new crusade" (2005:51–52).

What do you think should be done about the global sex trade? In what ways is the global sex industry linked to the international division of labour and other forms of globalization?

jingle, "Be a tourist in your own hometown," as, of course, many Canadian cities are listed, along with detailed advice and reports from businessmen, long-haul truckers, and others who travel domestically.

The United Nations estimates that, worldwide, in a $7 billion-per-year enterprise, 4 million people are trafficked every year, with 50 000 brought into the United States and up to 16 000 people, mainly women, coming into Canada. The United Nations International Children's Emergency Fund (UNICEF) estimates that almost one-third of the women who are trafficked globally are "minors," many of whom are under the age of 13 (Leuchtag 2003). Over one million of the people who are trafficked are believed trafficked into the sex industry (Farr 2005). It is difficult to gain specific statistics because of the illicitness of the acts and because definitions and perceptions of "trafficking" vary. Trafficking has been defined by anti-trafficking activist Lin Lap-Chew (1999) as "all acts involved in the recruitment and transportation of a woman within and across national borders for work or services by means of violence, or threat of violence, abuse of authority or dominant position, debt bondage, deception or other forms of coercion" (in McDonald et al. 2000:8). The Solicitor General for Canada estimated that in 1998, the money involved annually in the traffic into Canada was anywhere from US$120 million to US$400 million.

Traditionally, the demand for prostitution was greatest when large numbers of men were congregated for extended periods of time in the military or on business far from home. Natural disasters or wars saw many displaced or marginalized women drawn to these areas to make a livelihood. Further, a connection between wartime rape and increased prostitution has been documented for the Vietnam War and, more recently, for the wars in El Salvador and Bosnia. Large populations of refugees and victims of rape and sexual violence tend to be exploited by networks of pimps and organized crime gangs such as the Yakuza in Japan, the Russian Mafia, and other international cartels (Leuchtag 2003; Seager 1997; Women's International Network 1995). Jyoti Sangera (1997) refers to this as the first or traditional tier of sex work. Linked to the first tier, but different from it, exists a second tier, one tied to global tourism and business. In many countries, sex tourism began with the establishment of brothels that served foreign military bases (Seager 1997). The second tier has grown up around major tourist destinations and business centres. The size of the first tier has remained relatively stable, while the size of the second tier is ever expanding providing "R and R for the corporate world workforce" (Sangera 1997:11).

In a recent case study of Windsor, Ontario, as a destination for sex tourism, Maticka-Tyndale, Lewis, and Street (2005) discuss the notion of liminal space (transitional or marginal space) as it relates to sex tourism. They suggest that people who travel to other locations are able to engage in exotic or forbidden practices because they "move into liminal space . . . [and are] 'betwixt and between,' in a socially condoned marginality, where they are bound neither by the mores of home, nor by those of the host community" (Maticka-Tyndale et al. 2005:46).

For residents of these tourist destinations, however, this is their home. Residents inhabit a space "where visitors come for the explicit purpose of violating the dominant norms and mores of Western sexuality"

(Maticka-Tyndale et al. 2005:47). How people in sex-tourism destinations deal with this varies. In Thailand, for example, sex tourism and prostitution is big business, promoted by government. Leuchtag reports that five million sex tourists visited Thailand in 1996 from the United States, Canada, Western Europe, Japan, and Australia and brought in $26.2 billion dollars, "thirteen times more than Thailand earned by building and exporting computers" (2003:96). The money earned through sex tourism assists the Thai government to pay the interest on its foreign debt, which encourages government officials to view "women as a cash crop" (Leuchtag 2003: 96). Unfortunately, with its focus on revenue generated by sex tourism, the government feels it must deny the enormous HIV epidemic sweeping Thailand.

Although recent research has indicated that the global sex industry, especially prostitution, contributes to the transmission of HIV, the virus that causes AIDS (Gil et al., 1996; Purvis, 1996), many agencies and governments have not come to grips with the problem. Moreover, the threat of HIV/AIDS may be fuelling the increased demand for children and younger, inexperienced sex workers as a "safe sex" strategy in the booming sex tourism business (Seager 1997). The Japanese Foundation for AIDS Prevention, an organization affiliated with the Japanese government, launched a poster campaign featuring a grinning, middle-aged man wearing a business suit and displaying his passport, with a caption reading, "Have a nice trip! But be careful of AIDS." The Japanese government is clearly aware that many businessmen participate in sex tourism abroad (Sachs 1994), and the poster seems to endorse this while warning them about unsafe practices. What strategies do you think these businessmen are likely to employ to avoid unsafe sex?

The picture of the global sex industry reflects the economic disparity between the poorest regions of the world—where women and children (mainly) may be bought, sold, or traded like any other commodity—and the richest regions, such as Europe and North America, where many of the global sex industry's consumers reside (see Bauerlein 1995; Davidson 1996). For example, in terms of sex tourism in the 1990s, countries that most sex tourists lived in and left from were Canada, the United States, Japan, Australia, Great Britain, France, Sweden, Germany, Norway, Saudi Arabia, China, Singapore, Malaysia, Kuwait, and Qatar. Major destinations for these tourists were Hungary, Brazil, Indonesia, Thailand, Vietnam, Kenya, Cambodia, Bangladesh, Philippines,

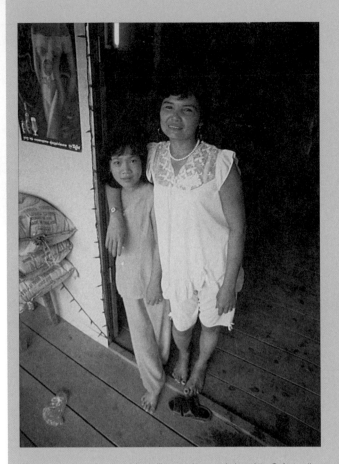

Do the two in this photo look like mother and daughter? Actually, both are employed in a Cambodian brothel. What global social and economic factors contribute to the growing number of young girls working in the sex industry?

Costa Rica, Cuba, Morocco, India, and the Dominican Republic (Seager 1997; Ward 1999). Additionally, as seen in Box 7.1, rich nations increasingly import the sexual services of people from poorer nations. As geographer and women's studies scholar Joni Seager (1997:115) notes, "As poverty deepens in Eastern Europe, it becomes a major source region for prostitutes; as wealth expands in China and Malaysia, men in those countries fuel an increased demand for the traffic in women and girls."

PROSTITUTION IN CANADA

Prostitution, among consenting adults, has never been illegal in Canada. However, sections 210–214 of the Canadian *Criminal Code* do prohibit many transactions that are quite necessary to prostitution. The activities that are illegal in Canada relating to the sex trade are communicating in a public place for the purposes of buying or selling sexual services (section 213); procuring or soliciting a person to exchange sexual services for money and living off the avails (section 212); being involved in a common bawdy house (section 210); providing direction to or transporting someone to a bawdy house (section 211); and purchasing sexual services from someone under the age of 18 years (section 214[4]; Maticka-Tyndale et al. 2005:47; Millar 2002:38; Wolff and Geissel 2000:254). These activities are considered a threat either to public decency or to public order. Those convicted of prostitution-related offences are often fined, although jail terms are possible. For example, communicating for the purposes of prostitution carries the maximum penalty of a $2000 fine or six months in jail or both. Given the economic situation of many street prostitutes, hefty fines may ensure continued sex-trade work and do not in any way act as a deterrent. As one young Saskatoon woman explains:

> [When I was arrested for prostitution] all my friends were there and it hurt so much, it made me feel much lower . . . they [the judicial system] treat you like such a bad person or that you're a slut, tramp, or whore. You're forced to go there [the streets], you were forced into that spot and if you said no, you were beat up or something worse, you could be killed. And they make it out like you're nothing, they don't try to help you, they just charge you and send you on your merry way . . . they know where you're going off to, you have to pay off your fine. (Kingsley and Mark 2000:27)

Federal laws on prostitution-related activities ensure that it is almost impossible to engage in the trade without breaking the law. Criminologist John Lowman (2000) reports that this fact adds to the already existing moral–political marginalization that sex-trade workers endure, increasing the risks of the work. Lowman (2000:1006) says our "system of quasi-criminalization,"

1. contributes to legal structures that tend to make the prostitute responsible for her [or his] own victimization, and thus reinforces the line of argument that says that, if people choose to prostitute themselves, they deserve what they get—they are "offenders" not "victims";

2. makes prostitution part of an illicit market. As such, it is left to primitive market forces and creates an environment in which brutal forms of manager-exploitation can take root;

3. encourages the convergence of prostitution with other illicit markets, particularly the drug trade. Once the price of a habit-forming, mind-altering substance is driven up by criminal prohibition, a drug like heroin can be as demanding a "pimp" as any man; and

4. alienates persons who engage in prostitution from the protective-service potential of the police. Why would prostitutes turn to police for help when police are responsible for enforcing the laws against prostitutes? . . . Criminal law sanctions institutionalize an adversarial relationship between prostitutes and police.

This may be why, instead of going to the police when they are beaten, raped, or robbed, sex-trade workers report "bad tricks" or "bad dates" to various organizations that keep, post, and monitor Bad Date Sheets. One of the first organizations in Canada to publish a Bad Date Sheet was the Alliance for Safety of Prostitutes (ASP) in 1983. Bad Date Sheets typically report the type of offence, where the offender picked the worker up, the date and time of the offence, description of and characteristics of the offender (age, racialization/ethnicity, gender, other identifying features such as tattoos, etc.) and vehicle, the type of person victimized (e.g., woman, man, transsexual, youth), and whether the person is known to be a repeat offender or not. The sheets are then circulated monthly by street and other social service workers and posted in various agencies and places prostitutes are known to go for services (Lowman and Fraser 1995). John Lowman and Laura Fraser's study (1995) *Bad Trick Reports in Vancouver, B.C. 1985–1994* shows that most "bad tricks" are Caucasian males, perceived to be in their 20s and 30s, and most victims are adult females. The most common types of bad dates were physical and sexual assaults, followed by robbery and, in a quarter of the cases, a weapon was used. Lowman and Fraser (1995) encourage us to see this violence as part of a continuum of male violence against women, not as acceptable risks associated with the job.

Many Canadian youth, women, and men are involved in the Canadian sex trade as sex workers, as "managers," or as customers, both overseas and at home. Prostitution has always been a feature of Western societies and, although some characteristics of it are changing with increasing globalization and economic disparity between more and less industrialized nations, it certainly appears to be here to stay. As this young ex-sex trade worker in British Columbia reports,

A sex worker friend of mine and I sat down one night and figured out how many tricks we'd had in our illustrious careers as street sex trade workers. We came up with about 10,000 each, so anyone who says there aren't very many men out there buying sex are just wrong (Megan in Rabinovich and Lewis 2001: 7).

FIGURE 7.1 "It Was Me: Reflections on Life as a Sex Worker," by Ally R.

It is not very often I sit and actually let myself recognize and acknowledge certain memories. Of a time that is almost mysterious to me, although I was there and it was me and I'm still me. It was me. Or some shape of me. When I think of people and times from then my first feeling is never a good one.

I can't believe most times when I look back. I see faces and fragments of scenes float through my mind.

Andrew. I think about him, my first time meeting him. Doug. Man, if I knew Doug now. But I wouldn't know him now, that's the thing. I'm no longer traveling in that circle. I don't seem to be traveling in any proverbial circles right now. Just this small one that is my daily life. But I am about to embark on expansion!

The prosecutor. The cops. I remember their faces. I wish I had known more words then. Accurate ones.

The tie man.

Ian from D. Street and how scared I became.

Howard from long ago and all the cars that drove by that day.

I don't think I'll ever remember anything I ever said.

The drummer.

The one from down the street.

The first, second and third ones. After that they're a blur.

The ones with guns when I imagined pain might be so much and so quick that I'd likely not feel it at all.

Irwin. And the snapping that took place there.

The one who liked to scream with ecstasy and madness in parking lots when he finally came. He's the one I saw other ways after we talked about how impossible it would be to ever see each other other ways

What was that one's name I'm thinking of now? Donny. That was it.

The special place in my heart I still have for Craig.

And why do some from years apart get mixed up in my mind? Why do I see them in a space of time they don't belong to?

How incredibly easy going and friendly I felt and I was. Happy. And how angry I became. The feelings I knew could belong in no other category than homicidal. Yes I could have done it. Just about did.

The total helplessness over certain things.

The Englishman.

The surprise I'd feel when one would divulge that drug or another.

When exactly was it that I lost the fear?

The cab driver.

The cab drivers.

The Turk.

Ken. Now there's a word packed with some ghastly feeling.

The day I felt my mind go in half like a snapping. Too bad I have yet to figure out how to put it back to its exact positioning.

Source: Jannit Rabinovich and Megan Lewis, 2001, Impossible, Eh? The Story of PEERS: Prostitutes Empowerment, Education and Resource Society, *Vancouver, BC: Save the Children Canada.*

All the times I slammed the door on life. And dead bolted it shut. Was it really this that I eventually wanted, or had I already been there/here?

The lying.

The doctors.

The Sister.

The Apartments.

The houses and the streets.

The actors and the directors.

The large bellied men. The small men.

The stitches in my hand.

The pink bra.

The black teddy.

The long red skirt with paisleys on it.

The pink jacket I loved so much.

The sequin bras and costumes.

The ones who always called when it was party time.

The German.

The Greek restaurant owner.

The other restaurant owners.

The Iranian restaurant owner and running through the endless park at night full of trees. Then the car and the wife.

The one from the Indy.

Thousands like them whose faces float in suspended animation somewhere in my existence. I'll see a face from then and I wonder why I am seeing it now, or ever.

The ones I started to believe because no one else was telling me anything.

The brander.

The wrestler.

The ball player.

The soccer player.

The wheelchair man.

The amputee.

The egg shaped child-like man.

The deaf man where we talked through the machine.

The dwarf.

The ones from Pennsylvania.

The one with the antique kit.

The one who had been in the Olympics, portfolio in hand, who reminded me of someone I once knew and loved.

The basements.

The waiting.

The drivers.

The murderers.

The one with all those snakes.

The one early morning sitting on a swing in his yard as dawn broke, ducks at my feet.

The farmer.

The photographer of objects.

The 2 virgins.

The ones who made me work, and the one who bought me a rose.

The travels. The journeys. The planes.

The boats.

The toys in my purse. The truck ride from North Van.

The immortality or else.

The games. The lessons.

The boat painter.

The banker with the green pendant.

The students.

The veteran who got me in the end.

The senior citizens.

The deathbeds.

The gloves.

The children.

The drunks.

(Continued)

The poets.

Garth. That was his name. I was going to call him near the end but couldn't find his number so I called the cops instead.

The pharmacist.

The widows.

The clubhouse.

The hotels and motels. The trailers.

The security men.

The names.

The rush. The timing.

The broken glass after I shattered it all.

The pillow on fire.

The fireman.

The women haters and the women.

The watch and the bracelet.

The ones I don't remember.

The snow. The rain. The wind.

The dogs.

The songs that take me to times from then. "Sentimental Journey" and play it again and again and he did and he did.

"The road to hell"

"Paint it black"

"One of these days"

The money. The credit cards. The travelers cheques. The rolls of quarters, loonies, dimes and nickels. The pennies. The bank machines.

The pleas. The excuses. The threats.

Helping that one write a letter to his son.

The one I told was right, that indeed he should kill himself.

The movies and the magazines.

The photographs.

The one who got a ride with me in the white van.

The blue Malibu and the car accident.

The codes. The questions. The clichés.

The chance encounters that were never supposed to happen. On the street. In the drug store. In 7-11. The cab ride.

That time in the liquor store. My heart ending up in my shoes.

Paul and all the loss that happened there. How it feels just to write his name down.

The exclamation.

The hardware store that was down the street.

The Flintstone skirt.

The one with the tripod.

The crates where they kept my shoe.

The million or so times I prayed please God just let him come now so I can go home. Don't these people understand I have cats that need me at home? Please and I'll never ask again.

And Lee. And Linda. And Terry. And Cheryl. I still think of Cheryl.

And Speedy.

And Steve.

And the loves of my life.

The words I remember being spoken to me.

"Move your hand."

"At least my parents loved me."

"Can I put you on my leash and walk you downtown tomorrow?"

"I'll cut you up and keep you in my cupboard", or was it "I'll chain you up and keep you in my cupboard?"

"It sounds like things are pretty out of control where you are."

"You have to have hope, Al."

"Please just tell me where you are. Don't worry about anything. Your cats will be fine."

And the words I know and can hear in my head but still can't write them down, let alone think about them.

That December of the Christmas lights and everything after.

How we approach the myriad issues raised by the sex trade (e.g., some of the associated dangers, like violence against sex-trade workers) will depend upon how we view it. In any case, it is interesting to note that while in 1985, 20 percent of Canadians identified prostitution as a pressing social problem, a decade later, fewer than 1 percent of Canadians felt it was a "very serious" social problem (Bibby 1995).

Some Characteristics of Prostitution in Canada

Clearly, not all sex-trade workers are alike: Life experiences, family backgrounds, years of formal education, locales of operation, types of customers, and methods of doing business vary widely. Even with these differences, however, sociologists have identified five levels, or tiers, of prostitution, ranging from escort workers to street prostitutes to women exchanging sex for drugs in crack houses.

Top-tier prostitutes are typically referred to as *escorts* or *call girls* and *call boys*. They are considered the upper echelon in prostitution because they tend to earn considerably higher fees and typically have more years of formal education than other prostitutes do. Many of them do not even think of themselves as prostitutes. They usually dress nicely—and often conservatively—so that they do not call undue attention to themselves at the luxury hotels, clubs, and apartment buildings they may be called to work in. Maybe most

importantly, escort sex workers have more selectivity in their working conditions and customers than do other prostitutes (Chapkis 1997; Macy 1996; Maticka-Tyndale et al. 2005). An escort worker named Terry clearly differentiates between herself and other, less fortunate workers:

> One of the reasons I think I can enjoy my work, is because I carefully screen my clients. I have no tolerance for any assholes. I'm providing a service to these men, and as far as I'm concerned, they're privileged to have it. So they have to show me the proper respect. I deserve that respect. If they don't think so then they should keep their cock in their pants and their money in their pocket. It means that I may make less money than I might otherwise, but my safety is worth it. People in more desperate circumstances have to put up with a lot more. (Chapkis 1997:100)

Escort prostitutes work "on call," going out to see customers who are referred to them by their escort service, pimp, or other procurers such as hotel concierges and taxi drivers who may receive a percentage of the prostitute's fees. (See Table 7.1 for other terminology of the sex trade.) Other escorts may "freelance," brokering their own calls and deals, advertising in local newspapers, and so on. Although their work is not as visible as that of many other sex workers, escorts generally face some of the same hazards, including abusive customers and sexually transmitted diseases.

TABLE 7.1   The Jargon of the Profession: Some Words and Phrases Commonly Used and Understood in the Canadian Sex Trade

Term	Definition
A Man	Pimp. For example, "Do you have a man?" or "You can't work here without a man."
Bad Date	Violent or abusive trick.
Bogus Call	About one in ten calls, the address can't be confirmed or it's a joke by a neighbour who is watching.
Booking On	Phoning into to an escort agency to report being available for calls.
Booking On Fee	This is a fee in order to be able to book on, which can be up to $300/month or a per shift fee of $10–$20.
Boystown	The stroll that the men and boys work.
Break	Get a customer.
Call	Trick or date sent by an escort agency.
Cancellation Fee	The $30–$100 fee charged if the date cancels because the woman is late, the driver can't find the address, or he doesn't like the look of a particular woman.
Coffee Fund	Escort agencies charge of $50–$75/month for beverages available to clients.
Date	Customer, trick, or john.

Deposit	First $100-$500 earned kept by the agency. Non-refundable.
Driver	Someone who drives women to their calls and waits. Mostly men.
Escort Service or Agency	Business where people buy time for money. They say what the two consenting adults do with their time is their business.
Exiting	Leaving, quitting the sex trade.
Experiential	People with direct, personal experience in the sex trade.
Fines	$50–$100 charged to woman by escort agency for any number of transgressions from not wearing the kind of lingerie the client wants to being late for work.
Forced Indebtedness	Period of partying which precedes entry into trade. No indication that repayment will be required and no mention of future payment. Girl is then told that she has spent thousands of dollars on drugs and someone else paid for them and repayment is demanded.
High Track	Sex trade workers who ask some of the highest prices and tend to be the "best kept" looking sex workers on the street. High track is almost always pimped.
John	Customer, date, or trick.
Keep Six	Take down the license number of cars as girls get in. Usually done by street kids for $5–$10 a car. Is also an expression for watching for the cops.
Kiddie Track	Generally 17 years old and under. Often pimped or working in partnership with other exploited youth.
Late Fine	$25 for every half hour booked on late.
Leaving Fee	Money paid to pimps or an escort agency to leave the trade. Generally a substantial amount, like $2,000–$5,000 in 1999.
Low Track	Usually in industrial areas. More of the women are older or more noticeably drug addicted and/or with mental health issues. They charge less but often make up for that in volume.
Mid Track or Renegade Stroll	Higher-end women who work without pimps or without formal pimping. Sometimes boyfriends or husbands act as pimps.
Regular	A customer that a sex trade worker sees regularly. Often have a slightly more personal relationship with one another.
Renegade	Sex worker without a pimp.
Sexually Exploited Youth	Youth in the sex trade; the term is used to differentiate them from adult sex workers or prostitutes. Sexually exploited youth are under 18 years old.
Sex Trade Worker	Adult who works in the sex trade. The term is used interchangeably with prostitute.
Spotter	Person who takes down license numbers of cars. Could be arranged by an escort agency or individual.
Square	Not in the sex trade and have never been in the trade.
Squared Up	Exited from the sex trade.
Stroll	Area where street prostitution takes place. Also called the track.
Trannie stroll	Where male-to-female transsexuals and cross-dressers work.
Trick	Customer, client. Also: John or Date.
Trick Charge	Fee some hotels charge for taking a guest to the room.
Working	Engaging in the sex trade. "I've got to go to work" as compared with mainstream employment "I have to go to my job."
Working Clothes	Clothes worn for the sex trade

Source: Jannit Rabinovich and Megan Lewis, 2001, Impossible, Eh? The Story of PEERS: Prostitutes Empowerment, Education and Resource Society, *Vancouver, BC: Save the Children Canada.*

A 1995 task force on the use of city bylaws to regulate sex work was created by the Municipal Council in Windsor, Ontario. The task was to create a bylaw that would not violate the *Criminal Code* statutes on prostitution, nor be seen as licensing sex work, but at the same time provide sex workers with safety and autonomy and the police with the ability to monitor the industry. Three factors were seen as important in the creation of a bylaw:

(a) escorts should remain integrated in their local communities and not be isolated in a red-light district; (b) escorts should be able to determine their own working conditions within the limits set by law; and (c) escorts should be provided with information that could help them conduct their work safely and contribute to their over-all well-being (Maticka-Tyndale et al. 2005:49).

Windsor escorts and agency receptionists are able to work from their own homes or to work through an agency. Escorts are licensed after meeting certain criteria such as a minimum age of 18 and a clean police record. Work must be out-calls only, and workers are required to carry and produce their licenses when asked by police. Agency personnel are required to keep records of who went where and when and to turn these records over to police if requested. By the end of 2002, there were a dozen agencies and 113 escorts licensed in Windsor. Many escorts like to maintain that their work does "not necessarily involve sexual services" (Maticka-Tyndale et al. 2005:50) and many see themselves as very different from other sex trade workers, particularly from street prostitutes.

> I'm not like them. They're disgusting, all dirty and smelly. Several of them look like they got AIDS. I'm not anything like them, no way, I'd never be a whore. (quoted in Maticka-Tyndale et al. 2005:50)

The second tier of prostitutes is comprised of hustlers, strippers, and table dancers who engage in prostitution on the side. People in this tier work primarily out of nightclubs, bars, and strip joints. The hustlers are sometimes referred to as *bar girls* or *bar boys* because they are supposed to pressure (hustle) customers to buy drinks. Most hustlers are not paid by the bar but earn their livelihood by negotiating sexual favours with bar customers, who often are lonely and want someone to talk to as well as to have sex with (Devereaux 1987).

The third tier is made up of *house girls* who work in brothels (houses of prostitution) run by a madam or a pimp, who collects approximately half of the fees earned by the women. Customers choose a "date" from women lined up in a parlour or receiving room. House prostitutes are not allowed to engage in "dirty hustling" (winking, running one's tongue over one's lips, or shaking a leg) or to turn down a customer (Devereaux 1987). Operating a bawdy house or living off the avails of prostitution is illegal in Canada, and thus houses of prostitution typically operate as body-painting studios, massage parlours, or other legal businesses. In Vancouver, although the city does not admit to licensing prostitution, criminologist John Lowman advises people to consider the fees that the city charges for different categories of business. In 1997, there were

approximately 150 distinct business categories that require annual licensing. For 115 business categories, the fee was under $200. For another 24 categories, the fee was between $201 and $500. Only a very few had annual licensing fees above $500. Lowman reports these as "pubs and cabarets . . . $556.00; a public market is $886.00; concert halls vary between $1839.00 to $2644.00 depending on seating capacity; an amusement park is $3156.00; the horse race track is $7473.00; and the Pacific National Exhibition is $10,463.00" (1997:Appendix). As for personal service type businesses, dating service agencies were charged $104 per year; health enhancement centres, $162; massage parlours, $172; escort services $802; and body rub parlours $6527 per year—the third most expensive license to procure after the PNE and the race track!

Near the bottom tier of prostitution are *streetwalkers,* who publicly solicit customers and charge by the "trick." Most street prostitutes work a specific location and many are "protected" by a pimp. Many streetwalkers derive status and some degree of protection from violent "johns" from their pimps. However, researchers have also documented the exploitative and too often violent nature of the pimp–prostitute relationship (B.C. Ministry of Attorney General 1996; Kingsley and Mark 2000; Lauer et al. 2006; Sexually Exploited Youth Committee of the Capital Regional District [SEYCCRD] 1997).

The very bottom tier of prostitution is occupied by women who are addicted to crack cocaine, heroin, or other drugs and who engage in drugs-for-sex exchanges (Fullilove et al. 1992; Kingsley and Mark 2000). Researchers have found that many crack-addicted women perform unprotected oral sex on men in crack houses in exchange for hits of crack. According to one study,

> Some men will enter a crack house, purchase enough rocks for two people for several hours, and then make it clear to every woman in the house what he has in mind . . . . [There] seems to be an expectation [in the crack house] that if a man wants to have sex with a woman, she will not oppose the offer. The expectations are implicit. Everyone involved—the house owner, the male user/customer, and the female user/prostitute are all aware of what is expected. (Inciardi et al. 1993:74–75)

In the words of one young Winnipeg woman, "I met a bunch of guys I knew, they were always giving me rock [crack] for free, I never had to do anything, except for this one guy. Then we met these guys, [and] you had to go around the whole room to get a piece [of crack from each guy]" (Kingsley and Mark 2000:21).

Although less research has been done on prostitution tiers with males, the tiers appear to be similar to those of females except that, with males, most customers are of the same gender as the sex worker. For example, in her report on escort services, journalist Marianna Macy (1996:249) found that some male escorts exist and "Men normally go see men." Most of Canada's larger cities, for example Vancouver, Toronto, and Montreal, have some form of "Boystown," where male sex workers line the stroll, on display for the primarily male customers. Some male prostitutes work as hustlers in bars and nightclubs, where they typically wear blue jeans, leather jackets, and boots, seeking to project a strong heterosexual image. Julian Marlowe, a graduate student who is putting himself through school by working as an escort, reports that "the sugar daddy of a former acquaintance of [his] once admitted he used to get a rush from picking up hustlers on his lunch break due to the sheer element of danger: the person he picked up could conceivably beat him to a pulp" (1997:141).

Sexual orientation is frequently an issue with male prostitutes, some of whom do not define themselves as gay and limit the types of sexual acts they are willing to perform. Others view sex strictly as an economic exchange and define work-related sex as "not real sex" (Browne and Minichiello 1995). Other research suggests that for hustlers who are part of gay culture, "knowing that one is attractive enough to command payment raises, rather than lowers, one's self esteem. Why would a man have low self esteem if he's being sought out and given money for his body" (Marlowe 1997:143). Most research shows that although many males are involved in the sex trade as sex workers, there are not as many boys and men as girls and women. The Department of Justice in 1993 estimated that between 10 and 33 percent of street prostitutes in Canada are male, but that at least 80 percent of situations where sex is traded for money involve women as the worker (Allman 1999). This is reinforced by the B.C. provincial study: "Sexually procured youth and adults (those who receive money for sexual services) are predominantly female. Males are less visible and tend to work primarily on a party circuit or in private residences" (B.C. Ministry of Attorney General 1996:3).

Much research in Canada has been focused on identifying the factors that bring people into the sex trade, particularly into the relatively dangerous street prostitution tier. Recent studies of youth in the sex trade in British Columbia as well as Canada-wide studies reveal that several factors are nearly always implicated in engaging youth in the sex trade. The use of the term "youth" is not accidental, as research shows that most people (96 percent) became prostitutes before age 18 (Rabinovich and Lewis 2001; Wolff and Geissel 2000). One cross-provincial study, a community consultation on prostitution in British Columbia, found that the average age of entry to prostitution in that province is 14, with some beginning as early as age 8 or 9 (B.C. Ministry of Attorney General 1996). Another study, conducted in Victoria, B.C., found the average age of entry to be 15.5 years, although some started as early as 11 (SEYCCRD 1997). Allman (1999) reported that approximately 10 to 12 percent of sex-trade workers were under 18 years of age, and most males in the trade admit to starting by age 16. There is evidence across Canada that males remain in the trade for much shorter durations than females, the average length of time being just over five years for men. Allman suggests that by the time males in the trade reach the age of 20 to 22, the youthful looks that attracted the customers are beginning to fade, so they move on to other things.

There is some evidence as well that males and females may enter the sex trade for slightly different reasons (Allman 1999). Most people involved report that the money is an enticement. A 1993 Montreal study found that prostitutes were earning anywhere from $600 to $2000 per week, with females earning considerably more than males per week (maybe due to demand; Allman 1999). Key factors leading into the sex trade for youth are generally reported to be homelessness and/or a lack of basic necessities for survival of self or of their own children (e.g., shelter, food, clothing, etc.); emotional abuse, sexual abuse/assault and/or other physical assaults at home; the development of an alcohol and/or drug addiction; a lack of satisfactory assistance with a health/mental health issue (e.g., depression, eating disorder, bipolar disorder); a lack of life skills and employment; dropping out of school; and low self-esteem (B.C. Ministry of Attorney General

1996; Kingsley and Mark 2000; Lauer et al. 2006; SEY-CCRD 1997; Wolff and Geissel 2000). As stated by a female former street worker from Thunder Bay, Ontario, "[I wouldn't have worked in the trade if] I could have had better self-esteem, I didn't have any boundaries, and I didn't care. I didn't know my worth at that time" (Kingsley and Mark 2000:31). One Ottawa-area study of youth sex-trade workers found that the "sex for survival" motif was more common for females than for males. Many homeless males were able to "couch surf," while females were expected to trade sex for food, shelter, or money (reported in Allman 1999).

The presence of several or even all of these factors does not guarantee entry into the sex trade, of course. It does, however, heighten the risk of a young person having fewer choices. As stated in one recent report, "They do not move directly from a 'normal' teenage life of home, school and extra-curricular activities to being a prostitute. Long before that, most have a long history of school problems or family problems or emotional problems or all three" (SEYCCRD 1997:4). Criminologist John Lowman reports that most female sex workers are from lower socio-economic backgrounds and are extremely dissatisfied with their home lives (1995). As clearly stated by Wolff and Geissel (2000:257), "Adolescent prostitution can be viewed as a survival behaviour." On the cover of the 1997 Report of the Sexually Exploited Youth Committee of the Capital Regional District, Victoria, British Columbia, a phony employment advertisement sums up the risk factors for youth street prostitution in Canada:

```
Wanted:
Vulnerable Youth and Children
    Preferably with no place to stay, no one
to protect them. Must be under 18; ages 12
to 15 preferred. Must be prepared to be all
things sexually to all people.
    May be required to work on demand, day
or night. Frequent sexual, physical, verbal
assaults guaranteed. Drug addiction an occu-
pational hazard.
    Pay minimal—room, board, drugs may be
included.
    High management and exit fees and beat-
ings extracted. Equal opportunity for males
and females. Preference given to those able
to withstand abuse.
```

The Extent of Prostitution in Canada

There are no reliable estimates of the extent of prostitution in Canada, for several reasons. First, the activity is quasi-legal, and hence much activity is clandestine or otherwise hidden behind massage parlours and escort services. Second, criminal charges, which are basically our only official source for quantitative data on prostitution, deal almost entirely with street prostitution. Although this is only one component of the sex trade, it is the most visible, with 95 percent of all charges in recent years being for "communicating." Further, it is not known what proportion street prostitution makes up of all sex-trade activity. Throw into all this confusion the fact that people don't always agree on how to define certain types of sex work (i.e., is it "prostitution" or not?) and the fact that people move around, change their names and addresses, and so on. Many people drift into and out of prostitution, considering it temporary work between full-time jobs or as part-time work while attending school (Allman 1999; Lowman 2000; Reynolds 1986; Potterat et al. 1990).

Prostitution and Age, Class, Racialization, and Ethnicity

Although some Canadian prostitutes are as young as 8 or 9, the vast majority is between the ages of 17 and 24. The peak earning age appears to be about 22 (Clinard and Meier 1989; DePasquale 1999). In contrast, the typical male customer is considerably older than the prostitute, White, and married, although some teenage and university-age males also hire prostitutes (National Victims Resource Center 1991). Often, the age difference between teenage prostitutes and older customers is striking, as a woman forced into prostitution at age 13 by a pimp explains:

> The men who bought me—the tricks—knew I was an adolescent. Most of them were in their 50s and 60s. They had daughters and granddaughters my age. They knew a child's face when they looked into it. . . . It was even clearer that I was sexually inexperienced. So they showed me pornography to teach me and ignored my tears as they positioned my body like the women in the pictures, and used me. (Giobbe 1993:38)

Although a small percentage of teenagers enter prostitution through coercion, most are runaways who have left home because of sexual abuse or other family problems. Some teen prostitutes are "throwaways"—thrown out of their homes by parents or other family members (Snell 1995; Vissing 1996). Regardless of their prior history, many teens become prostitutes because prostitution is the best—or only—job they can get.

Social class is directly linked to prostitution: Lower-income and poverty-level women and men are far more likely to become prostitutes than are more affluent people (Lowman 1995; Miller 1986). Some people with little formal education and few job skills view prostitution as an economic necessity. As one woman stated, "I make good money [as a prostitute]. That's why I do it; if I worked at McDonald's for minimum wage, then I'd feel degraded" (quoted in McWilliams 1996:340). However, women working for exclusive escort services are more likely to have attended college and come from the middle or upper-middle class.

Racialization is also an important factor in prostitution. Sociologist Patricia Hill Collins (1991) suggests that African-American women are affected by the widespread image of Black women as sexually promiscuous. Collins traces the roots of this stereotype to the era of slavery, when Black women—and Black men and children—were at the mercy of White male slave-owners and their sexual desires. Indigenous women are affected by similar stereotyping. Historically, First Nations women have been viewed as being sexually freer than White women (Allen 1986), a view that has, over the years, translated into the stereotype of sexual promiscuity. This stereotype has had the effect of devaluing and even dehumanizing Indigenous women and has been used as a justification for sexualized violence against them. For example, sociologists Augie Fleras and Jean Leonard Elliott (1996:148) report on the prairie practice of "squaw hopping," the "acknowledged practice for White men to harass and sexually assault native women." According to Collins (1991:175), prostitution exists within a "complex web of political and economic relationships whereby sexuality is conceptualized along intersecting axes of race and gender." Sexually-exploited-youth advocates Cherry Kingsley and Melanie Mark (2000:28–29), in their recent national consultation of sexually exploited Indigenous youth, found Indigenous women and girls overrepresented in the visible sex trade, with Indigenous youth accounting for as much as 90 percent of the visible trade in some communities. High rates of Indigenous participation in prostitution can be attributed, in part, to many young people's experiences in foster care: "Consultations with [Indigenous] youth identified their care experiences as paving the way for their commercial sexual exploitation" (Kingsley and Mark 2000:26). Today, prostitution remains linked to the ongoing economic, political, and social exploitation of people of colour and Indigenous people, particularly women.

A Closer Look at "Johns"

To date, there are few comprehensive studies conducted in Canada about the sex-trade customer or "john." This may be a reflection of the relative power of the john's social location in relation to the sex-trade worker's. Since both are, theoretically, equally liable for prosecution under Canada's communicating laws, we should have access to similar information about both groups. This power differential is well understood by one young Saskatoon sex-trade worker:

> They are always looking down on us and blaming us, but it's not only us. It's their husbands that are picking us up. Everybody is in denial: everybody pinpoints us, and blames us because we're the ones out on the street. But they're the ones that are picking us up and giving us money. They're always calling us little sluts and whores, but they never say anything about the johns . . . like they're picture perfect guys. (Kingsley and Mark 2000:25)

What little information is available indicates that most johns are men in their mid-20s to mid-40s (although older is common also), White, married, and gainfully employed (Brannigan et al. 1989; Lowman, Atchison, and Fraser 1997; National Victims Resource Center 1991). A report by the Canadian Advisory Council on the Status of Women (1984:49) notes that most observers of prostitution report that johns are "ordinary men who go to prostitutes for simple reasons," such as experiencing sexual acts they cannot have in their other relationships, experiencing sexual relationships without lasting obligations or long-term complications, engaging in "therapy" for problems like impotence, or having a good time.

This self-inking money stamp was made available by the Sex Workers Alliance of Vancouver, in 1999, to sex workers in the community. Its aim is to raise public awareness that money earned generated by the sex trade is an important part of the Canadian economy.

Source: Will Pritchard, Illustrator/Designer. Distributed by the Sex Workers Alliance of Vancouver © 1996, www.walnet.org/swav/. Reproduced with permission.

A British Columbia consultation with johns that was arranged through Sexual Addicts Anonymous provided some insights into some johns' behaviour that offer a contrast to the picture of johns as ordinary, well-adjusted men. Given the nature of the group consulted, however, these men cannot be seen to be representative of all johns (B.C. Ministry of Attorney General 1996). This consultation found that many johns reported childhood sexual abuse and believed themselves to be "addicted" to sex. The use of prostitutes resulted in the men feeling a great deal of shame, which related to their childhood experiences and caused them to act in ways that perpetuated those feelings (engaging the services of a prostitute, for example). These johns also reported that part of the attraction to cruising for prostitutes and the use of their services was the risk of getting caught, therefore indicating that "shame the johns" campaigns may in fact work counter to the stated purpose of the campaigns. The view of the men interviewed was that stopping prostitution could only be achieved by ensuring there was a treatment component inherent in the sentencing, that punishments alone would not be successful.

Other strategies aimed at customers are being tried, such as charging a john but offering the removal of the charge from the man's record if he agrees to pay a fine and attend "John School." Typically the one-day workshop will provide a legal overview, show slides of various venereal diseases, and showcase ex-sex workers who talk about how much they despised their clients. The program seems to have been moderately successful in reducing people's return to buying sex. However, most johns are repeat customers. Only a small proportion of johns limit their sex buying to one time (Lauer et al. 2006). Lowman and colleagues report that in a survey of 120 johns in the U.S., a quarter of the people said they had seen a sex worker 51 or more times, and 16 percent reported seeing a sex worker more than 100 times. Another study of 101 johns found they use the services of sex workers over several years, with two-thirds of the men reporting weekly contact with a sex worker (reported in Lauer et al. 2006:36).

In an attempt to obtain a broader picture of people who buy sexual services, the B.C. Ministry of Attorney General funded an internet survey in 1996–1997, conducted by John Lowman, Chris Atchison, and Laura

Fraser (1997). The attitudes and behaviours of 130 men worldwide who buy sex are represented in this report. As in other Canadian studies (Brannigan et al. 1989), the mean age of johns was 37, with a range from 18 to 67. Most men were married or common-law; had children; were heterosexual, White, high school graduates; and were employed full-time. Most of the men who responded online reported that their first sexual experience was with a friend or acquaintance, not with a relative or a stranger. Twenty percent reported childhood sexual abuse. We do not have comparable figures for childhood sexual abuse for men generally.

When asked about attitudes, the men who participated in this survey believed that loneliness, sexual problems at home, the desire for specific sexual acts that partners would not perform, the desire for uncomplicated sex, and a strong male sex drive were important reasons for seeking out a prostitute. Just over one-half of the participants believed that travel to a city other than one's normal residence is important for the sex-trade transaction to occur. Most men believed female sex-trade workers are "normal," hard-working women who are "just doing another job" and provid[ing] a valuable service"; most of the participants disagreed that prostitutes are the "victims of a sexist society" (Lowman et al. 1997). When asked whether prostitution should be criminalized, unsurprisingly then, most of these men believed it should not be. The exception here was that most of these men believed that sex with children under age 13, and snuff films—films where the actor, usually the female in the film, is actually killed in front of the camera—are morally reprehensible and should be prohibited. In terms of deterrents to buying sex, nearly all the men who responded stated they would buy sex even if it was completely illegal. However, when asked which strategies would be useful in preventing men from buying sex on the street, having viable off-street options was listed, as well as the fact of their spouses finding out, public exposure or public recognition by someone they know, and fear of HIV/AIDS (Lowman et al. 1997).

The way that prostitution is dealt with under the *Criminal Code of Canada* makes the prostitution-related offence, "communicating" (s. 213) a "nuisance" offence. It is the most frequently prosecuted prostitution offence but sentencing is minimal. Generally, when sentencing occurs, it is female sex trade workers who receive sentences of a few days in jail and the male customers who receive "discharges or negligible fines" (Department of

Justice Canada 1998). Procuring (s. 212), an indictable offence, is viewed as much more serious, particularly when youth are involved, and currently carries a maximum sentence of 5, 10, and 14 years' imprisonment, depending on the sub-section of the code. Keeping a bawdy house (s.210) is also an indictable offence and can result in a sentence of up to two years' imprisonment, while transporting (s. 211), not an indictable offence, can result in a summary conviction, as in s. 213.

PERSPECTIVES ON PROSTITUTION

Sociologists use a variety of perspectives to examine prostitution as a social problem. Functionalists focus on how deviance—including prostitution—serves important functions in society. Interactionists investigate microlevel concerns, such as how and why people become prostitutes or come to buy sexual services and how the stigmatization affects their self-esteem. Conflict perspectives seek to explain how the powerful enact their moral beliefs into law and how prostitution is related to capitalism and/or patriarchy, and feminist theorists focus on sex-trade work as gendered (and inequitable) labour.

The Functionalist Perspective

Functionalists believe that the presence of a certain amount of deviance in society contributes to its overall stability. According to early sociologist Emile Durkheim, deviance clarifies social norms and helps societies to maintain *social control*—**the systematic practices developed by social groups to encourage conformity and discourage deviance**—over people's behaviour. By punishing those who engage in deviant behaviour such as prostitution, the society reaffirms its commitment to its sexual norms and creates loyalty to the society, as people bind together to oppose the behaviour.

According to sociologist Kingsley Davis (1937), in societies (such as Canada) that have restrictive norms governing sexual conduct, prostitution will always exist, because it serves important functions. First, it provides quick, impersonal sexual gratification that does not require emotional attachment or a continuing relationship with another person (Freund et al. 1991).

Second, prostitution provides a sexual outlet for men who do not have ongoing sexual relationships because they are not married or have heavy work schedules. Third, prostitution provides people with the opportunity to engage in a variety of sexual practices—multiple sex partners, fellatio (oral stimulation of the male genitalia), cunnilingus (oral stimulation of the female genitalia), anal intercourse, or sadomasochism (S&M), including the use of such devices as handcuffs, whips, and chains—that regular sex partners or spouses might view as immoral or distasteful. Fourth, prostitution protects the family as a social institution by making a distinction between "bad girls" or "bad boys"—with whom one engages in promiscuous sexual behaviour—and "good girls" and "good boys"—with whom one establishes a family. Finally, prostitution benefits the economy by providing jobs for people who have limited formal education and job skills.

The Interactionist Perspective

Why do people become prostitutes? Do some prostitutes like their work? Why do people choose to pay for sex? Interactionists investigate questions such as these by using a social–psychological framework, for example, by examining people's lived experiences. Here is an excerpt from an interview with a prostitute named Dolores:

> I set my own schedule. I set my own limits and made my own rules, and I didn't have to answer to anyone. I learned a lot about myself: what I would and would not do for money, and what I was willing to do for the right amount of money . . . . I didn't have to see anyone I didn't want to see. If a man was too boring or too rough or too crude or took too much time, I didn't have to see him again. I loved it. (French 1988:180)

Dolores's remarks suggest that some people become prostitutes because it provides them with greater autonomy and more career options than they otherwise would have. These reasons fit with sociologist Howard Becker's (1963) suggestion that entering a deviant career is similar in many ways to entering any other occupation. The primary difference is the labelling that goes with a deviant career. Public labelling of people as deviant and their acceptance or rejection of that label are crucial factors in determining whether or not a person

stays in a deviant career. Some people are more willing than others to accept the label "deviant" or may believe they have no other option.

Why do men seek out prostitutes? Research by interactionists suggests that some young men seek out prostitutes to fulfill what they believe is a rite of passage from boyhood to manhood. Consider, for example, John's comments after several trips to a house of prostitution:

> We went back to school, Mike and I, after going to that first whorehouse. We were probably the only two guys in the class that had done it. We were celebrities. We had crowds around us when we'd tell them all the details, how great it was, what studs we were. . . . My reaction to all this was it wasn't really very exciting. After all the talk you hear about it, all the writing, all the pictures, all the taboos about sex, I thought, "For this? This is what it was about?" . . . It wasn't something bad; it just wasn't nearly as exciting as I thought it would be. But we thought, "This is a good chance to learn," so we went back several times. . . . I can remember up to eleven. . . . I always thought I'd keep count all my life; that was part of what being a man was all about. (quoted in Raphael 1988:74–75)

Social analysts suggest that the need of men of all ages to validate their sexual prowess or reaffirm their masculinity is an important factor in their seeking out prostitutes (Raphael 1988). Interactionist perspectives such as these highlight how people define social realities—such as the importance of sexual prowess or masculinity—in light of competing and often contradictory values they have learned through socialization.

Conflict and Feminist Perspectives

Conflict perspectives on prostitution highlight the relationship between power in society and sex work: The laws that make prostitution illegal are created by powerful dominant group members who seek to maintain cultural dominance by criminalizing sexual conduct that they consider immoral or in bad taste (Barry 1995).

Conflict analysts using a liberal feminist framework believe that prostitution should be *decriminalized*—meaning that laws making prostitution a crime should be repealed. These analysts argue that prostitution is a *victimless crime—a crime that many people believe has no real victim because it involves willing participants in an economic exchange.* Therefore, sex workers should not be harassed by police and the courts. According to Margo St. James, a former prostitute and founder of an activist group called COYOTE (Call Off Your Old Tired Ethics), "The profession itself is not abusive; it's the illegality; it's the humiliation and degradation that is dealt to them at the hands of the police" (quoted in McWilliams 1996:340). In other words, prostitution is sex work in the sex industry and should be treated as a labour issue. In a September 2004 St. John's, Newfoundland, radio broadcast Wayne Lucas, the provincial president of Canada's largest union, the Canadian Union of Public Employees, stated that sex workers should be unionized. Lucas stated that,

> Work is work. The people who work in that trade, they certainly deserve some of the benefits that other workers have traditionally received in their work fields. [They] should have access to benefits such as health care and pensions. They're people, just like your next-door neighbour. They could be a sister of ours, a mother, a cousin. They're out and they're in a dangerous field. ("Unionize Prostitutes" 2004)

Conflict perspectives using Marxist feminist and radical feminist frameworks suggest that women become prostitutes because of structural factors such as economic inequality and patriarchy (Jolin 1994). Capitalism and patriarchy foster economic inequality between women and men and force women to view their bodies as simply commodities: "When a man has bought a woman's body for his use as if it were like any other commodity . . . the sex act itself provides acknowledgment of patriarchal right. When women's bodies are on sale as commodities in the capitalist market . . . men gain public acknowledgment as women's sexual masters" (Pateman 1994:132). Summarizing a historical feminist position, the Canadian Advisory Council on the Status of Women (1984:3) in its report on prostitution in Canada pointed out that,

> Prostitution is not an exchange among equals. Men, who as a group, still hold most of the powerful positions of social, economic and political power in our society, buy services from the less

powerful: women (often poor, young and undereducated women) and male and female adolescents and children. The sellers have little or no defense against the risks of physical or sexual abuse of economic exploitation . . . The buyer . . . has the money: as a group, buyers do not depend on sellers for their income, while sellers generally do depend on buyers. This economic dependence reinforces the social vulnerability that prostitutes experience.

Feminists who hold this view believe that the exploitation involved in prostitution is an extension of the kind of exploitation women experience generally, not only with regard to economic disadvantages but also with regard to cultural standards of female attractiveness, which are bound up in youthfulness, slimness, and so on. Male customers, on the other hand, like men in general in society, are not constricted by these cultural standards, as they make up the rules and have the economic means to reinforce their desires. Many feminists believe that women who are prostitutes do not understand their exploitation and need to be saved from the "false consciousness" that traps them in these degrading occupations. However, the prostitute-as-victim stance has been challenged by many people who are advocates for and/or engaged in the sex trade, including many prostitutes and other sex-trade workers who identify as feminists. These feminists have a view of prostitution as a service for which they charge a fee, much like any other service in society. The difference, about which they are fully conscious, is that they are hiring out their bodies in ways most people may find too distasteful to engage in. They do not view themselves as exploited and encourage feminists who view them as victims to respect them, instead, as self-directed, independent, hard-working women who have made the conscious choice to be involved in the sex trade; to do what they wish with their own bodies. This debate, between feminists, on prostitution, like the debate on pornography, has been going on for decades and likely will continue. As Carol Queen, a well-known writer, lecturer, sociologist, and sex-trade worker, stated,

> Unfortunately, the exciting politics that promised me sexual freedom twenty-five years ago have veered toward dogma . . . Please . . . don't assume that you know what someone else's experience has been just because you can't imagine liking to do

it yourself. Please don't require that all people be one certain "politically correct" way. Please don't assume I can't make my own decisions, that my exhibitionism somehow makes me a victim . . . Don't tell me I don't have a soul (Queen 1997:138–141).

According to Marxist feminists, the only way to eliminate prostitution is to reduce disparities in income levels between women and men and eliminate poverty. However, radical feminists believe that prostitution will not be eliminated until patriarchy is ended.

Conflict theorists and feminists, who in examining social problems focus on the interrelationship of racialization, class, and gender, suggest that criminalizing prostitution uniquely affects poor women, especially poor women of colour and Indigenous women, who are overrepresented among street prostitutes. According to these theorists, White male supremacy—which traditionally preserves the best-paying jobs for men—makes women of colour and Indigenous women particularly vulnerable to recruitment or coercion into prostitution. Kingsley and Mark (2000:14) found, in a national consultation of commercially sexually exploited Indigenous children and youth in Canada, that "for the Aboriginal (sic) youth who participated in these consultations, economic need dictated their actions . . . [their] engagement in the sex trade."

Analysts using this framework also note that discrimination in law enforcement uniquely affects women of colour and Indigenous women, as these groups are overrepresented among prostitutes in Canada. For example, law enforcement officials target street prostitutes and other sex workers, particularly when political elites decide to crack down on "deviant" behaviour such as prostitution and pornography (Barry 1995). Lowman notes that there is a lack of political will to create safer conditions for prostitutes to ply their trade, as this would be seen as condoning prostitution, a stance Lowman (1995) calls "odd" as well as "hypocritical" given that prostitution in Canada is legal and hence already condoned. Instead, Lowman (1995) notes that crackdowns, which disproportionately affect street prostitution, occur when property-holders get up in arms about their neighbourhoods, demonstrating that "public propriety and property values heavily outweigh all other considerations."

In opposition to those feminists who view sex work as violence against women, Third World or transnational feminist analyses view sex work as a practice that emerges from the intersections of racism, patriarchy, imperialism, and capitalism. Women in this perspective are seen not simply as victims of patriarchal oppression but equally as

> agentic, self-determining, differentially positioned subjects who are capable of negotiation, complying with, as well as consciously opposing and transforming relations of power, whether these are embedded in institutions of slavery, prostitution, marriage, the household, or the labour market. (Kempadoo 2005:37)

Kempadoo concludes, therefore, that sex work or the sex trade itself is not necessarily problematic. Instead, violations to women's rights may in fact be the conditions of the work or of life, or the violence that may be part of the work or entrance into underground or informal sex trade work (2005:37).

PORNOGRAPHY

Nina Hartley (1994:176–177), founder of the Pink Ladies club, a group of women in the pornography industry, wrote of herself:

> "A feminist porno star? Right, tell me another one," I can hear some feminists saying . . . why porno? Simple—I'm an exhibitionist with a cause: to make sexually graphic (hard core) erotica, and today's porno is the only game in town . . . . As I examine my life, I uncover the myriad influences that led me to conclude that it was perfectly natural for me to choose a career in adult films . . . . I stripped once a week while getting my bachelor's degree in nursing . . . . I went into full time [adult] movie work immediately following graduation.

Pornography is the graphic depiction of sexual behaviour through pictures and/or words—including by electronic or other data retrieval systems—in a manner that is intended to be sexually arousing. Although Hartley claims to be a feminist porn star, many social analysts, as Hartley herself notes, believe that this is a contradiction in terms. Most of these analysts believe pornography is a pressing social problem.

But what kind of social problem is it? Religious groups typically construe pornography as a social problem because they say it is obscene. On the other hand, social analysts, particularly feminists, usually frame the problem in terms of patriarchy—male oppression of women—by analyzing power differentials between the actors (Leong 1991). Thus, the specific nature of pornography as a social problem is not clear-cut. Canadian sociologist Mariana Valverde (1985:124) discusses some of the difficulties with even defining what pornography is, saying that pornography "is a collection of images and texts, representations which have something in common." But what is that "something"? In noting there are no concrete ways to measure what is or is not pornography, Valverde (1985:125) explains,

> Pornography is not a natural object that can be classified, like a particular species of butterfly, but rather a complex cultural *process* . . . . Pornography does not drop from heaven onto our local corner store shelves. It is first *produced* by certain people who relate to one another via the pornography industry; it is then *consumed* by customers who buy porn in the expectation of being aroused; and finally porn derives most of its meaning and significance from the *social context* in which it exists. (italics in original)

The social context in which pornography exists is all-important (Diamond 1988; Valverde 1985). This can be demonstrated using Valverde's example of the *Playboy* centrefold. The picture, typically of a nude, young, attractive, White woman whose genitals are featured prominently, does not have much meaning in and of itself. When viewed in a North American context of sexism, racism, ableism, ageism, and so on, however, the picture is imbued with layers of meaning. She is beautiful and helpless looking and posed in such a way as to engender a specific response (arousal) in North American men: "He will not merely glance at the photo as he would at a landscape or a family photograph; he will gaze intently, stare at, and *possess* that woman with his eyes" (Valverde 1985:125–126). Further, the point of the picture is not to celebrate femaleness or the female body, but rather, in the context of capitalism, the purpose is to use the female body for profit making. Finally, besides the feelings the picture may arouse in many men, it also heightens feelings for many women;

feelings of embarrassment for the model, whose seeming naiveté is a ploy used to enhance the male viewer's pleasure in dominance. Many women may feel angry, at risk, and vulnerable. As Valverde (1985:126) concludes, "It is not the picture itself which creates these feelings. If men never raped women in real life, the same picture would not have the same power to make us feel violated." As sociologist Sara Diamond (1988:400) points out, pornography will always exist, underground or in the mainstream, until sexism is eliminated. Determining or interpreting what constitutes pornography is a difficult task.

Over time, public attitudes change regarding what should be tolerated and what should be banned because of *obscenity*—**the legal term for pornographic materials that are offensive by generally accepted standards of decency.** Who decides what is obscene? According to what criteria? A publication is deemed to be obscene according to the Canadian *Criminal Code*, Section 163, if its dominant characteristic is the "undue exploitation of sex" or is of "sex and any one or more of the following subjects, namely, crime, horror, cruelty, and violence." The fact that pornography is criminalized, at least as it pertains to children, has in part assisted in it being constructed as deviance and as a social problem.

The Social Construction of Pornography as a Social Problem

The social construction of pornography as a social problem involves both a cognitive framework and a moral framework. The cognitive framework refers to the reality or factualness of the situation that constitutes the "problem." In regard to pornographic materials, one cognitive framework might be based on the assumption that pornography *actually affects* people's actions or attitudes; an opposing cognitive framework might be based on the assumption that pornography is a fantasy mechanism that allows people to express the forbidden without actually engaging in forbidden behaviour (Kipnis 1996). The moral framework refers to arguments as to whether something is immoral or unjust. In the case of pornography, moral condemnation arises from the belief that graphic representations of sexuality are

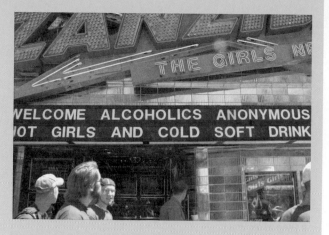

Are there any businesses like this in your community? Why do many people believe that establishments such as this not only harm individuals and their families but also the larger community?

The Nature and Extent of Pornography

As part of the multibillion-dollar sex industry, pornography is profitable to many people, including investors, filmmakers, and owners of stores that distribute such materials. *Hard-core* pornography is material that explicitly depicts sexual acts and/or genitals. In contrast, *soft-core* pornography is suggestive but does not depict actual intercourse or genitals.

Technological innovations such as digital media have greatly increased the variety of pornographic materials available as well as methods of distribution. Although some people visit live peep shows and "X-rated" adult bookstores and video arcades, sexually explicit materials are available at home or in the office through mail-order services, movies on "X-rated" cable television channels, dial-a-porn, digitized scans and striptease QuickTime movies, and private computer bulletin boards and Usenet newsgroups specializing in adult chat areas and graphics exchanges on the internet.

Hard-core pornographic films gross over $400 million a year in the United States. It is not known how much revenue is made in Canada from the pornography industry, but it is not uncommon for a small production company that shoots, manufactures, and distributes such videos to gross more than $1 million a year in the U.S. ("Despite 6-Year U.S. Campaign" 1993). However, "Ron," who works in the pornography industry, suggests that these profits, unsurprisingly, do not extend to most actors in the films:

> You'd have to go a long way to find an industry with worse labour practices. They work people very hard; they pay them very little, really, for what they do . . . . As a porn performer, you're putting up with a couple of days of hard, even abusive, behaviour that compromises your ability to do anything else in your life ever again, because the piece of evidence of your past misbehaviour continues to exist . . . . But after you've done porn films, you can't do anything else. You can't even do commercials . . . . Another thing [is that] there's an endless appetite for new faces and new bodies, which means they work [actors] to death for about six months or a year, put out twenty to thirty videos with them. And then they can't get work any more. New ones have come along. The

degrading, violent, and sinful. From this perspective, pornography is less about sex than about violating taboos in society. The moral framework often distinguishes between pornography and *erotica*—**materials that depict consensual sexual activities that are sought by and pleasurable to all parties involved.** According to sociologist Diana E. H. Russell (1993), materials can be considered erotic—rather than obscene—only if they show respect for all human beings and are free of sexism, racism, and homophobia. Contemporary erotica might include romance novels that describe two consenting adults participating in sexual intercourse (see Snitow 1994). On the other hand, materials depicting violent assault or the sexual exploitation of children would be considered pornographic or obscene. However, the distinction appears to be highly subjective, as feminist scholar Ellen Willis (1981:222) notes: "Attempts to sort out good erotica from bad porn inevitably come down to 'What turns me on is erotic: what turns you on is pornographic.'" These are issues that the Canadian justice system is continually called upon to debate; but, in the words of the report of the Special Committee on Pornography and Prostitution (the Fraser Commission; 1985:7), "Activities which threaten the physical well-being of others can find no real place in civilized society."

audience is sick of looking at the old ones and wants to see new ones. (quoted in Stoller 1991: 209–210)

According to some social analysts, pornography is a prime example of the principle of supply and demand. As long as demand remains high, pornographers will continue to market their goods and services and find new ways to use technology. According to Walter Kendrick, a scholar whose research focuses on pornography,

> Pornographers have been the most inventive and resourceful users of whatever medium comes along because they and their audience have always

wanted innovations. Pornographers are excluded from the mainstream channels, so they look around for something new, and the audience has a desire to try any innovation that gives them greater realism or immediacy. (quoted in Tierney 1994:H18)

Each new development in technology changes the meaning of pornography and brings new demands for regulation or censorship. Today, interactive media presentations and pornography on the internet are widely believed to be a far more powerful influence on people, especially children, than the printed word is (see Box 7.2).

SOCIAL PROBLEMS AND INFORMATION TECHNOLOGY

BOX 7.2 Canada's Role in Cracking Down on Internet Child Pornography

Anonymity on the internet makes it difficult to detect child pornography and to apprehend those who distribute or consume such materials (Simon 1999).

Since its inception in 1989, the internet has become the source of vast amounts of beneficial information. However, this new form of information technology has also facilitated the dissemination of child pornography. According to one legal analyst, the internet has changed the manner in which pornography can be created, distributed, and accessed:

> Prior to the invention of the Internet, consumers and distributors of child pornography had to know each other or have connections to exchange materials. Underground networks facilitated the trade of photographs or videos through the mail or in person. Currently, however, subscribers . . . can simply download graphic images through their modems to be able to view and print images.

> The anonymity available on the Internet hinders the detection of child pornography. A user can create any identity and transmit a message from [Calgary] through New Zealand, and then on to Halifax, making it impossible to determine the origin. Furthermore, "anonymous remailers" enable a user to re-route outgoing messages by removing the source address, assigning an anonymous identification code number with the remailer's address, and forwarding it to the final destination. (Simon 1999:7)

Just as the distribution of child pornography has been facilitated by the internet, sexually explicit visual depictions of children (and adults) have become much easier to create and mass produce. Scanners, video cameras, and graphics software packages are an integral part of the production of child pornography today (Simon 1999).

What social policy issues are raised by the increasing availability of pornographic materials? One major consideration is the use of children under the age of 18 in pornographic depictions. Another is the question of whether or not child pornography contributes to pedophilia (defined as an abnormal condition in which an adult has a sexual desire for children). Further complicating this issue is the fact that some child pornographers claim that the actors they use are over the age of 18 and simply appear to be younger or that the children shown are not actual children but rather computer-generated images—"virtual" actors.

This argument, however, is rendered irrelevant under Section 163.1 of the Canadian *Criminal Code*, which states that child pornography is "(a) a photographic, film, video or other visual representation, whether or not it was made by electronic or mechanical means, (i) that shows a person who is or is depicted as being under the age of eighteen years and is engaged in or is depicted as engaged in explicit sexual activity, or (ii) the dominant characteristic of which is the depiction, for a sexual purpose, of a sexual organ or the anal region of a person under the age of eighteen years; or (b) any written material or visual representation that advocates or counsels sexual activity with a person under the age of eighteen years that would be an offence under this Act."

In Canada, anything illegal off-line is illegal online. In May of 2004, the National Child Exploitation Coordination Centre (NCECC) was expanded to focus on sexual exploitation of children on the internet. Many officers within Canada's police forces have been gaining valuable internet training focused specifically on internet-based exploitation. This training includes investigative techniques for the search and seizure of illegal computer data (RCMP 2006a). Police, however, as always, are bound by the Charter and Canadian laws pertaining to protection of privacy issues.

Mystery hackers like "Citizen Tipster" are not so bound, or at least choose not to be. On June 29, 2002, the *Vancouver Sun* reported on the activities of a 21-year-old Langley, B.C., computer hacker who used a computer program he wrote to monitor the private e-mails of suspected child-porn producers and child molesters worldwide. He had read hundreds of communications each day for three years, and his tips to police resulted in the arrests of several child predators in Canada, the U.S., and Russia. His online evidence led to the arrest in 2001 of an Orange County Superior Court Judge for possession of more than 100 images of child pornography and involvement in a plot to sexually exploit young boys at a private health club. The hacker forwarded his evidence to an online organization, Predator-Hunter.com, focused on ending the exploitation of children; it, in turn, forwarded the files to the California Department of Justice. Citizen Tipster's online evidence also led to the arrest and conviction of an Alberta man who was using the internet to sell his eight-year-old daughter for sex in 1999. Police threatened Omni-Potent (the tipster's online handle) with arrest for violations of citizen's privacy, but it took them a long time to actually find him. When they finally tracked him down, via a website, they demanded his hard-drive and all his files. In the words of 21-year-old Omni-Potent, though, "Sure, a violation of privacy you must cry, but, if you have nothing hurting kids, the future of the world, then there's no reason to worry as that is all Omni-Potent protects . . . [those] who can't protect themselves" (Dimmock 2002;A14).

The vulnerability of children to online predators led to the introduction into the House of Commons on March 14, 2001, of a bill to fortify existing legislation protecting children from sexual exploitation, particularly through the internet. On June 10, 2002, the Justice Minister and Attorney General of Canada announced that "Bill C-15A, containing tough new legislation protecting children from sexual exploitation, Internet luring and child pornography" had received royal assent. Specific to child pornography, amendments to the *Criminal Code* include,

- Internet Luring and Child Pornography: It is now illegal to communicate with a child over the internet for the purpose of committing a sexual offence against that child as

well as to transmit, make available, export, and access child pornography;

- Child Sex Tourism: Amendments to the Child Sex Tourism Law (enacted in 1997) will simplify the process used to prosecute Canadians who sexually exploit children in other countries; and

- Enhanced Judicial Powers: Judges can now order both the deletion of child pornography posted on computer systems in Canada and the forfeiture of any materials and equipment used in the commission of a child pornography offence. They can keep known sex offenders away from children by using prohibition orders, long-term offender designations, and one-year peace bonds for offences relating to child pornography and the internet. (Department of Justice Canada 2002)

Following the October 2004 Speech from the Throne committing to a "crackdown on child pornography," Bill C-2, an *Act to Amend the Criminal Code* (protection of children and other vulnerable persons) and the Canada Evidence Act was passed into law in the summer of 2005. The bill includes new and tighter provisions around child pornography, new sexual exploitation offences, procedures that facilitate testimony, new voyeurism offences, and reforms to existing federal measures protecting children. The new child pornography laws were put to the test immediately in 2005. Gordon Chin of Alberta was sentenced to 18 months' probation, 100 community service hours, no computer or internet access for the duration of his probation, and his name added to a sex-offender registry for five years. His crime? Possessing anime comic books that included images of naked, tied-up children and babies being raped with pistols. Chin's investigation stemmed from customs officials seizing a package with the comic books destined for Chin's home. His sentence was viewed as "lucky" by the Crown in the case because it was handed down days before the amendment came into full effect on November 1, 2005, requiring a minimum sentence of 90 days in jail for importing or distributing child pornography ("Man Guilty of Child Porn Cartoons" 2005).

Acknowledging the global scope of the issue, the Canadian government and the RCMP are also joined by experts from 30 other nations through the Virtual Global Taskforce, and 24-hour law-enforcement points of contact have been established in order to facilitate co-operation and share information between countries of the G-8 (RCMP 2006b). Canada also launched a National Strategy to Protect Children from Exploitation on the Internet in May 2004, with $42 million in funding over the next five years. Part of that funding is for the launch of "cybertip.ca as a 24/7 public national tip line" (Department of Justice Canada 2005). Not only is the issue global, but its scope is also immense because it involves the internet. Chidley noted in 1995 that a conservative estimate of information passed on the internet equated to approximately 300 paperback pages per second.

Attempts to eliminate or censor internet child pornography may well be futile.

Certainly many people are not happy about any movement toward censorship of the internet. Jeffrey Shallit, a computer scientist at the University of Waterloo in Ontario, was also involved with an organization called Electronic Frontier Canada, which is focused on maintaining free speech in cyberspace. Shallit (cited in Chidley 1995:58) and many others believe that the issue of internet pornography has been blown way out of proportion—that it represents a minimal amount of online material. While few condone child pornography, members of online communities are nervous about where crackdowns and censorship may lead. In an open letter to the Canadian online community on the subject of "Computers and Academic Freedom," computer scientist Carl Kadie (1993) stated,

> It's a tough question—how much freedom should be given up to fight serious issues like child pornography—and are these tactics working at all? Are they harming an important resource more than they are helping fight the actual problem? Are there more effective ways to deal with the problem?

Others, such as the Coalition for Lesbian and Gay Rights in Ontario (CLGRO 1998), raise concerns about what censorship of the internet may do to advances for people with non-heterosexual sexualities, noting that with the passage of laws, "there is no reason to believe the police and courts will suddenly become less homophobic or that serious attempts will be made to educate and empower children and youth in the area of sex or encourage the autonomy of lesbian, gay and bi-sexual teens." The CLGRO also points out the inconsistency in defining people 12 and under as children in the Young Offenders Act and then defining people 18 and under as children with regard to sex-related offences (CLGRO 1998).

What social policy issues are raised by the legislation on child pornography and the internet? Some critics argue that freedom of expression involving youthful-looking adults is limited by our laws and, therefore, our laws are unconstitutional. Other critics raise the issue of privacy, asserting that people should be able to read and view whatever they want. Suppose, they say, someone else used your computer, downloaded child pornography, and then you were accused of possessing that pornography? On the other hand, supporters of the new legislation argue that these concerns are outweighed by the necessity of protecting children from being victimized by child pornographers. What do you think?

Research on Pornography

In June of 1983, the Department of Justice convened a seven-member committee to investigate and report on the then-current situation of pornography and prostitution in Canada. This resulted in the 1985 Fraser Commission report. The report concluded, with regard to pornography, that "there is agreement that the current situation is problematic [e.g., that current laws on availability and control are unsatisfactory], [but] . . . that is where consensus ends" (Special Committee on Pornography and Prostitution 1985:5). The Committee also stated that legal reform was only part of the solution, and that social policies and actions were necessary elements of any long-term strategy. Regarding its stance on pornography generally, and informing the recommendations the Committee made, were these two points:

> In essence we see two forms of harm flowing from pornography. The first is the offence which it does to members of the public who are involuntarily subjected to it. The second is the broader social harm which it causes by undermining the right to equality which is set out in section 15 of the *Charter of Rights and Freedoms*. (Special Committee on Pornography and Prostitution 1985:10)

Sociologists do not agree on the extent to which pornography that depicts excessive sex, violence, and the domination of one person by another affects behaviour. More than 80 percent of X-rated films reviewed in one study included scenes showing women dominated and exploited by men. The vast majority of these films portrayed physical aggression against women, and about half explicitly depicted rape (Cowan et al. 1988; Cowan and O'Brien 1990). Explicit violence is also part of many videos in the adult section of video stores (see Duncan 1991). Some studies have demonstrated that violent porn leads to increased aggressive attitudes toward women by men, but research has not demonstrated that attitudinal changes cause rapes or assaults on women that would otherwise have not taken place

(Valverde 1985:121). Most people therefore do not support efforts to censor adults' access to pornographic material, unless the material involves children. As Diamond (1988:396) remarks,

> The suggestion that consumers of pornographic material or other media products respond in zombie-like, imitative fashion to all-powerful images is both false and frightening.

Pornography and Age, Gender, Class, Racialization, and Ethnicity

Because viewing pornography is a secretive activity, data on the consumers of various forms are limited. Some studies have found that the typical customer of an adult bookstore is a White, relatively well-educated, married, middle-class man between the ages of 25 and 66. Other studies have found that younger and more-educated adults express more accepting attitudes toward pornography than do older, less educated adults (Lottes 1993).

Overall, men watch more sexually explicit material and hold more favourable attitudes toward it than women do. Some analysts attribute this difference to gender-role socialization. In a society in which men are socialized to be sexual initiators and often fear rejection, pornography is satisfying because it typically shows a willing female partner. In contrast, women have been socialized to respond negatively to material showing nude bodies and male pleasure that may occur at the expense of a woman's sense of safety and dignity (see Reiss 1986). However, in recent years, more women have become consumers of *Playgirl* magazine, erotic novels, and videos that are made specifically for women, such as those by Candida Royalle, a former porn star (see Lottes 1993; Macy 1996). Additionally, there is evidence that many more women are becoming involved in pornography and in the pornography industry, not only as actors, but as directors, producers, camera operators, and, of course, as consumers As writer Paula Gilovich discusses,

> Women are discovering in pornography an incredible new tool: If porn has been one of the major engines of objectification in the hands of men, it holds the potential to become an engine of subjectification in the hands of women. What better field to transmute the woman in the camera's gaze from an object to—at long, long last—the subject? Female filmmakers have begun using pornography—and female pornographers have begun using film—to challenge the relationship of sex and power. There is a transfer of ownership underway: More and more, porn now belongs to the women who make it.

> What makes this transfer of ownership so powerful is that pornography is one of the primary cultural engines of objectification. Women are most harmed through porn because they are objectified almost beyond all recognition. In porn, the female has always been the object of the male viewer's attention; she is strictly an extension of his fantasy, a tool to get him off. And this is why the feminine subversion of porn is especially feminist. We are just beginning an era when power in the porn industry is being defined by the new recognition of an old truth: there is no porn without women. (Gilovich 2002)

Historically, in general, women are more vocal than men in opposing pornography. According to sociologist Michael Kimmel (1990), men are relatively silent for several reasons: embarrassment or guilt for having enjoyed pornography, anger at women's interference in male privilege, lack of interest in what they perceive to be a non-issue, fear that speaking out will lead to questions about their masculinity, reluctance to talk openly about their sexual feelings, and confusion about "what it means to be a 'real man' in contemporary society" (Kimmel 1987:121).

According to film scholar Laura Kipnis (1996), much of the sentiment against pornography is rooted in class-based elitism: Opposition to pornography is a form of snobbery related to maintaining class distinctions in society. From this perspective, rejecting pornography amounts to rejecting all that is vulgar, trashy, and lower class. Although Kipnis does not suggest that all consumers of pornography are lower class, she believes that members of the upper classes typically view pornography consumers as lower-class people who may imitate the images they see. Similarly, women who appear in pornography or consume it are seen as brainwashed or unenlightened people who lack "class."

In another class analysis of pornography, philosopher Alan Soble (1986) linked men's use of pornography with their feelings of boredom and powerlessness, which are the result of capitalist work relations, the nature of labour, and the centralization of economics and politics. For these men, pornography becomes a diversion—a means of escaping from the dull, predictable world of work. Soble suggests that consumers of pornography use the material to construct fantasies and gain a sense of control; it gives men the opportunity—otherwise rarely available—to organize the world and conduct its events according to their own wishes and tastes. In Soble's eyes, pornography consumption is not an expression of men's power as much as it is an expression of their lack of power (Soble 1986).

In other research, sociologists Alice Mayall and Diana E. H. Russell (1993) have detailed how different racialized/ethnic groups are portrayed in pornography. Examining materials in a heterosexual pornography store, the researchers found that skin colour is a highly salient issue: White women were featured in 92 percent of the pornography, perhaps because they fulfill traditional stereotypes equating female beauty with white skin and Caucasian features (Mayall and Russell 1993).

People of colour were more likely to be found in materials featuring rape, bondage, and sadomasochism, anal sex, sex with children, and sex between women. Among women of colour, Black women were most frequently featured, followed by Asian women and Latinas. People who consume pornography have a choice of buying magazines portraying only Whites, White men with Black women, or Black men with White women. The researchers were unable to determine whether these options were based on the preferences of consumers or those of the makers of pornography (Mayall and Russell 1993). Collins (1991) suggests that racism in pornography can be traced to the oppression of Black women in slavery: African women were depicted as animals and used as sex objects for the pleasure of White men. Others have noted that, at the same time that the White man was exploiting the Black woman, he was obsessive about protecting the White woman from the Black man (Gardner 1994).

THE FUTURE OF PORNOGRAPHY AND THE SEX INDUSTRY

Public opinion polls show that people in Canada are ambivalent about pornography and other aspects of the sex industry. While they acknowledge that the sex industry may produce goods and services that serve as a "safety valve" for some, many believe that these goods and services can be a "trigger" for others. There does seem to be a consensus regarding children and pornography: Children should be shielded from some materials. At this point, however, the consensus breaks down. Who should do the shielding (the state or families?), what materials should be banned, and what is the appropriate definition of "child" with regard to sexually explicit materials?

The controversy over sexually explicit materials is particularly strong in schools, and some school boards have banned books and audiovisual materials they consider obscene, while others believe the materials to be educational and constructive to children's psycho-sexual development. For example, materials discussing or depicting homosexuality in a positive (or at least not negative) way have been banned in some schools. Many adults would also like to see children shielded from sexually explicit movies, television shows, and rock music videos—to say nothing of the sophisticated adult entertainment on child-oriented gaming platforms such as the CD-equipped Sega Genesis (Stefanac 1993). Children also have access to sexually explicit materials on the internet. The censorship wars—both online and in public life—continue to pose serious social policy questions.

All of the issues pertaining to pornography and censorship that we've discussed bring us to a point we've made in previous chapters: How people view social problems affects how they believe such problems should be solved. People seem to view pornography in one of four ways: liberal, religious conservative, antipornography feminist, and anticensorship feminist (Berger et al. 1991; Kinsman 1996; Nelson and Robinson 2002; Segal 1990; Valverde 1985). Each point of view espouses a different solution to the problem of pornography.

According to the *liberal* point of view, pornography may offend some people but brings harmless pleasure to others. It may even serve as a safety valve for those who have no other sexual outlet. Moreover, no scientific evidence links pornography to actual sexual violence or degradation of women. Therefore, the social problem is not really pornography but censorship—people attempting to impose their morals on others and thereby violating the *Canadian Charter of Rights and Freedoms* (Cottle et al. 1989).

In contrast, from a *religious conservative* point of view, pornography is a threat to the moral values of society, especially family values. Pornography encourages people to have sexual intercourse outside marriage and to engage in deviant sexual behaviour. Therefore, sexually explicit and violent materials should be censored to protect families and societal values.

Some feminist analysts are generally critical of pornography because it is sexist in its portrayal of women, reinforces gender scripts that emphasize male dominance and female submission, and encourages the valuing of women according to their ability to please men. However, not all feminists agree on what—if anything—should be done about pornography. *Antipornography feminists* believe that pornography is a primary source of male oppression of and violence against women. Viewing pornography as a form of sexual discrimination that diminishes women's opportunities in all areas of life, including employment, education, and freedom of movement, they believe it should be restricted or eliminated (see Dworkin 1988; MacKinnon 1987). In this view, pornography becomes a human rights issue, and antipornography feminists argue that communities should pass antipornography laws that would enable people who have been victimized by pornography to have legal recourse (see Russell 1993).

In contrast, *anticensorship feminists* do not believe that any single factor, such as pornography, causes women's subordination. Focusing on pornography as the primary source of sexual oppression, they say, "downplays the sexism and misogyny at work within all of our most respectable social institutions and practices, whether judicial, legal, familial, occupational, religious, scientific, or cultural" (Segal 1990:32). Therefore, pornography should not be censored because open discussions about sexuality and sexual practices promote women's sexual freedom and their right to express themselves (Kaminer 1990; Willis 1983). Instead, it is argued, we should have more breadth in the portrayal of women in sexually explicit materials. This is perhaps likely to

happen as more and more women enter the ring as pornographers in their own right.

In a world linked by the internet and other rapid sources of communication, the controversy over censorship may be rapidly becoming obsolete. In such a world, whose community standards should be applied in determining whether online materials are obscene? Should we use the standards of St. John's, Newfoundland, or those of Tokyo, Japan? Should we use the standards of the community where the image is posted, or the community where it is viewed, or both? Censorship is a very complicated proposition in an increasingly global marketplace. To restrict local access to a picture, story, or idea on the internet, access must be blocked to computer users all over the world. What are internet service providers such as CompuServe and America Online to do? For instance, German authorities asked one U.S.-based corporation in 1996 to not let German subscribers access 200 discussion groups and picture databases that allegedly violated German pornography laws. To meet this request, CompuServe had to block worldwide access to those sites. Although the ban was only temporary, it sent shock waves throughout the community of internet users, who became concerned that material deemed pornographic or obscene by people anywhere in the world could become unavailable everywhere. Among the materials Germany sought to ban were sexuality support groups for people with disabilities and a bulletin board for gay men and lesbians that provided a support network for gay youths ("A Journey of 10,000 Miles Begins with the Shoes" 1996).

In this chapter, we have focused on prostitution and materials that are defined as pornographic, obscene, and erotic. However, it is important to note that mainstream media—including magazines, movies, videos, television programming, and, specifically, music videos shown on MuchMusic and other channels—also may contribute to negative images of women and the exploitation of children. Furthermore, the mainstream media can desensitize people to sexual assault, rape, violence, and murder through repeated exposure to depictions of women as victims and sex objects and men as aggressors, rapists, and killers. What do you think is more harmful in causing violence aimed at women and children, the sex industry or the media in general?

WHAT CAN YOU DO?

- Educate yourself about the antipornography and anticensorship debates and decide which view makes the most sense for you.

- Find out what is happening regarding youth prostitution in your area and sit on an existing committee. For example, there may be a committee to establish a "safe house" for youth desiring to leave the trade.

- If your community has a safe house, volunteer at it or help educate others about the issues faced by youth attempting to leave the sex trade.

- As many youth in prostitution come from abusive homes, get involved in child-abuse prevention programs in your area.

- Put together an education/information package, with others if you wish, to send to schools so that they may include the issue of sexual exploitation in career and personal planning curricula.

- Lobby the school district to have such information available in public schools.

- Get involved in local organizations that support making the working conditions for people in the sex industry safer (e.g., Prostitutes Empowerment and Education Resource Society–PEERS).

- Get involved in international organizations to work toward ending sexual exploitation of women and children (e.g., Global Alliance Against Trafficking in Women–GAATW).

- Volunteer to teach English or French with immigrant and refugee settlement organizations.

Because cuts to funding for these programs often mean men have the first priority for language training (within certain racialized/ethnic communities and families), offer to teach women and/or youth.

- Lobby federal MPs and provincial MPPs/MLAs to have health inspectors tour entire establishments (not only kitchens) as parts of their job descriptions to ensure safer working conditions for people employed in clubs.

- Work with health care organizations to ensure that information on physical, mental, and emotional health-related issues is accurately translated into many languages and distributed in places where sex-trade workers convene.

- Write a letter to the newspaper discussing some of the issues for people in the sex trade from your point of view (e.g., Do you think prostitution should be decriminalized? Why or why not? Should johns receive counselling?).

- Lobby federal MPs and provincial MPPs/MLAs to shift the focus in prosecution from sex-trade workers onto pimps, johns, child-porn filmmakers, and so on—whomever you think should be prosecuted, if anyone.

- Work on a media awareness campaign with the goal of "deglamourizing" work in the sex trade.

- Get involved or create, with others, a public-education campaign about why young people get involved in prostitution and pornography.

- If you have been (or are) involved in the sex trade, use your knowledge to mentor others who are involved about health and safety and options.

SUMMARY

WHAT IS PROSTITUTION? HOW HAS IT CHANGED IN RECENT YEARS?

Prostitution is the sale of sexual services (one's own or another's) for money or goods and without emotional attachment. According to some social analysts, prostitution has recently become industrialized, normalized, and globalized. The industrialization of prostitution refers to commercialized sex as a product manufactured within the human self. Normalization is the process whereby sex work comes to be treated as a form of entertainment with no legal impediments to promoting it as a commodity. The globalization of prostitution refers to the process by which the sex industry has increasingly become global in scope.

WHAT LEVELS, OR TIERS, OF PROSTITUTION HAVE SOCIOLOGISTS IDENTIFIED?

Sociologists have identified several categories: Escort prostitutes (call girls or call boys) earn higher fees and can be more selective in their working conditions and customers than other prostitutes. Hustlers (bar girls or bar boys) work out of nightclubs, bars, and strip joints, where they solicit their customers. House prostitutes (house girls) work in brothels, and a substantial portion of their earnings goes to the house madam or pimp. Street prostitutes (streetwalkers) publicly solicit customers and charge by the "trick." At the very bottom of the tiers are those who exchange crack cocaine or other drugs for sex.

HOW DO FUNCTIONALISTS VIEW PROSTITUTION?

Functionalists point out that prostitution—like other forms of deviance—is functional for society. Prostitution continues because it provides people with (1) quick, impersonal sexual gratification without emotional attachment; (2) a sexual outlet for those who have no ongoing sexual relationships; (3) the opportunity to engage in non-traditional sexual practices; (4) protection for the family as a social institution; and, (5) jobs for people with few traditional job skills.

HOW DO INTERACTIONISTS VIEW PROSTITUTION?

Interactionists believe that prostitution—like other forms of deviance—is socially constructed. Entering a deviant career such as prostitution is like entering any other occupation, but public labelling—and the individual's acceptance or rejection of that label—determines whether a person stays in a deviant career.

HOW DO CONFLICT THEORISTS AND FEMINISTS VIEW PROSTITUTION?

There are several conflict perspectives on prostitution. Liberal feminists consider prostitution a victimless crime—involving a willing buyer and a willing seller—that should be decriminalized. Marxist feminists see prostitution as linked to the capitalist economy. Radical feminists trace the roots of prostitution to patriarchy in society. Conflict theorists who focus on the intersection of racialization/ethnicity, class, and gender believe that the criminalization of prostitution is a form of discrimination against poor women, particularly poor women of colour and Indigenous women. Third World or transnational feminists view sex work and trafficking as one possibility emerging from the intersections of many relations of dominance that conditions women's lives.

DOES PORNOGRAPHY DIFFER FROM OBSCENITY AND EROTICA?

Sometimes it is difficult to distinguish among these categories, but pornography usually refers to the graphic depiction of sexual behaviour through pictures and/or words—including delivery by electronic or other data retrieval systems—in a manner that is intended to be sexually arousing. Obscenity is the legal term for pornographic materials that are offensive by generally accepted standards of decency. Erotica refers to material depicting consensual sexual activities that are sought by and pleasurable to all parties involved.

HAS PORNOGRAPHY CHANGED IN RECENT YEARS?

Yes, technological innovations have greatly increased the variety of pornographic materials available as well as their methods of distribution. According to some analysts, as long as the desire for such materials is high, the multimillion-dollar pornography industry will continue to produce and market goods and services, adapting to new technologies as they become available.

DOES RESEARCH INDICATE THAT PORNOGRAPHY CONTRIBUTES TO SEXUAL VIOLENCE?

No conclusive answer has been found to this question. Some studies have found that hard-core pornography is associated with aggression in males and sexual violence in society, but other studies have found no conclusive evidence that pornography contributes to sexual violence. However, many feminist scholars suggest that pornography exploits all women and sometimes men and children. Other feminist scholars disagree.

HOW DO PEOPLE REACT TO THE CENSORSHIP OF PORNOGRAPHY?

Reactions to the censorship of pornography are varied. People with a liberal view of pornography believe that it is a safety valve for society and that censorship—not pornography—is the social problem. Religious conservatives consider pornography a threat to moral values and encourage censorship of some materials. Antipornography feminists view pornography as a primary source of male oppression and violence against women and argue for its restriction or elimination. Anticensorship feminists believe that some pornography is bad but censorship is worse because it suppresses free speech.

KEY TERMS

erotica, p. 193
obscenity, p. 192
pornography, p. 191

prostitution, p. 171
social control, p. 188
victimless crime, p. 190

QUESTIONS FOR CRITICAL THINKING

1. There have been ongoing suggestions by citizens to create "Red Light" districts in major urban centres in Canada. What arguments would you present in favour of this suggestion? What arguments would you present against it?

2. In what ways are prostitution and pornography linked to sexism, racism, homophobia, and class-based inequality?

3. In what ways does our general Canadian culture sustain and perpetuate an environment where commercial sexual exploitation of children and youth flourishes?

4. Libertarian author Peter McWilliams suggests that the problem with censorship can be summed up in two words: Who decides? Who do you think should decide what materials—if any—should be censored as pornographic or obscene? Besides deciding what's acceptable and what isn't, who should decide on the punishments for violating these standards?

WEBLINKS

John Lowman's Prostitution Research Page
http://mypage.uniserve.ca/~lowman
This page provides access to the results of several prostitution and related research projects based in British Columbia.

Factbook on Global Sexual Exploitation
www.catwinternational.org/factbook/Canada.php
The Coalition Against Trafficking in Women's *Factbook* is committed to providing facts, statistics, and information on known cases of global sexual exploitation. This page focuses on trafficking and prostitution in Canada.

The Canadian Women's Health Network
www.cwhn.ca/resources/sex_trade
The Canadian Women's Health Network is an organization committed to sharing information, resources, and strategies to better women's health. This page provides information and links about child and youth trafficking and prostitution in Canada.

Criminal Code of Canada

http://laws.justice.gc.ca/en/C-46

This site provides definitions that illustrate what would constitute "child pornography," sexual exploitation and interference, corruption of children, etc.

"Prostitution in Canada: The Invisible Menace or the Menace of Invisibility"

www.walnet.org/csis/papers/sdavis.html

A link to a thesis about Canada's defective approach to prostitution and what reforms could be implemented to improve it.

Prostitutes Empowerment, Education and Resource Society (PEERS)

www.peers.bc.ca

A link to an organization that provides support, resources, and programs for past and current sex workers—male or female—as well as help with housing, training and volunteering opportunities, advocacy and public education around sexual exploitation and the issues of adult sex work.

8

ALCOHOL AND OTHER DRUGS

DRUG USE AND ABUSE
   Defining Drug Abuse
   Drug Addiction

ALCOHOL USE AND ABUSE
   Heavy Alcohol Consumption and Gender, Age,
   Marital Status, and Class
   Alcohol-Related Social Problems
   Box 8.1 Social Problems in the Media: Maintaining a Drumbeat
   against Drunken Driving

TOBACCO (NICOTINE) USE AS A SOCIAL PROBLEM

PRESCRIPTION DRUGS, OVER-THE-COUNTER
DRUGS, AND CAFFEINE
   Prescription Drugs
   Over-the-Counter Drugs
   Caffeine

ILLEGAL DRUG USE AND ABUSE
   Marijuana
   Box 8.2 Social Problems and Social Policy: The Battle over
   Marijuana: Medicalization, Availability, Decriminalization,
   Legalization?

Stimulants
Depressants
Narcotics
Hallucinogens
Inhalants
Overall Harm from Drug Use

EXPLANATIONS OF DRUG ABUSE
   Biological Explanations
   Psychological Explanations
   The Interactionist Perspective
   The Functionalist Perspective
   The Conflict Perspective
   The Feminist Perspective

THE FUTURE OF ALCOHOL AND DRUG ABUSE
   Prevention Programs
   Treatment Programs

WHAT CAN YOU DO?

You don't know what you are talking about.

A response that Kevin, 32, a former street person, received and reported (to the author) when he tried to talk with street youth who were using drugs. Kevin, who himself had contracted both HIV and Hepatitis C from a syringe used to inject drugs, added, "The city will chew you up and spit you out."

Street people are not the only people who are affected by drugs. It is estimated that approximately 47 000 people die annually because of tobacco (37 000 people), alcohol, and other drugs (Health Canada 2006; Single, Robson, et al. 1999), and the health, economic, and social cost to Canadian society in 1992 was $18.4 billion, 2.7 percent of the gross domestic product in that year (Single et al. 1996). These costs are a combination of work-force productivity losses, transfer payments, and the costs of prevention, research, law enforcement, and health care.

In this chapter, we will examine legal drug use and abuse (e.g., alcohol, tobacco, and prescription drug); illegal drug use and abuse (e.g., marijuana, narcotics, and stimulants); explanations of drug abuse; drug prevention and treatment programs; and what you can do about drug abuse.

DRUG USE AND ABUSE

What is a drug? There are many answers to this question, so the definition is not always consistent or clear. For our purposes, a **drug is any substance—other than food or water—that, when taken into the body, alters its functioning in some way.** Drugs are used for either therapeutic or recreational purposes. *Therapeutic* use occurs when a person takes a drug for a specific purpose, such as reducing a fever or controlling an epileptic seizure. Sometimes, individuals who take prescription drugs for therapeutic purposes cross the line to drug abuse. *Recreational* drug use occurs when a person takes a drug for no other purpose than achieving some pleasurable feeling or psychological state. Alcohol and tobacco (nicotine) are *licit* (legal) drugs that are used for recreational purposes; heroin and cocaine are *illicit* (illegal) recreational drugs (Levinthal 1996). Licit drugs, which include such substances as vitamins, aspirin, alcohol, tobacco, and prescription drugs, are legal to manufacture, sell, possess, and use. Illicit drugs, such as marijuana, cocaine, heroin, and LSD (lysergic acid diethylamide), are socially defined as deviant, and using them is criminal behaviour and hence a social problem.

Defining Drug Abuse

What is drug abuse? *Drug abuse* is the excessive or inappropriate use of a drug that results in some form of physical, mental, or social impairment. A more difficult question to answer is, What constitutes drug abuse? When looked at from this perspective, drug abuse has both objective and subjective components. The *objective component* is physical, psychological, or social evidence that harm has been done to individuals, families, communities, or the entire society by the use of a drug. The *subjective component* refers to people's perceptions about the consequences of using a drug and the social action they believe should be taken to remedy the problem.

Sometimes when people talk about drug abuse, the subjective component—the perception of consequences—overrides the objective component. Consider, for example, the subjective and objective components underlying our society's view of the use of marijuana. The subjective component of marijuana use is the general belief that marijuana is harmful and therefore should not be legal, even though there is little evidence that marijuana use is detrimental to health. The subjective component of alcohol use is the general belief that it is harmless and acceptable, even though there is considerable evidence that it impairs more people and produces greater costs to individuals and society than marijuana use. Thus, the use of alcohol is legal.

Drug Addiction

The term **drug addiction (or drug dependency) refers to a psychological and/or physiological need for a drug to maintain a sense of well-being and avoid withdrawal symptoms.** Drug dependency has two essential characteristics: tolerance and withdrawal. **Tolerance occurs when larger doses of a drug are required over time to produce the same physical or psychological effect that was originally achieved by a smaller dose.** Tolerance is a matter of degree: Some drugs produce immediate and profound levels of tolerance, whereas others produce only mild tolerance. For example, when a person first drinks a five-ounce cup of coffee, containing about 100 milligrams of caffeine, the stimulant effect is usually quite pronounced. After that person drinks the same amount of coffee over a period of several days or weeks, the effect is greatly diminished, and a second or third cup of coffee (for a total of 200 to

300 milligrams of caffeine) becomes necessary to duplicate the earlier feeling (Levinthal 1996). *Withdrawal refers to a variety of physical and/or psychological symptoms that habitual drug users experience when they discontinue drug use.* For example, people who suddenly terminate their alcohol intake after long-term, heavy drinking experience various physical symptoms ranging from insomnia to DTs (*delirium tremens,* or mental confusion often accompanied by sweating and tremor) and psychological symptoms such as a reduced sense of self-worth.

ALCOHOL USE AND ABUSE

Much of the data in this section comes from the Canadian Addiction Survey (CAS), a national study of Canadians' use of alcohol and other drugs published in November 2004. The content is multidimensional, including physical, mental, and social components, and the method is in-depth telephone interviewing of over 13 000 Canadians aged 15 and older. In addition, results of a couple of the waves of the National Population Health Study (NPHS) are also reported. This study was conducted by Health Canada and Statistics Canada and consisted of in-depth interviewing of over 17 000 Canadians. It is an ongoing study to measure changes in health status of Canadians.

The use of alcohol—ranging from communion wine in religious ceremonies to beer, wine, and liquor at business and social gatherings—is considered an accepted part of the dominant culture in Canada. *Alcohol* and *alcoholic beverages* are terms that refer to the three major forms in which ethyl alcohol (ethanol) is consumed: *wine,* which is made from fermentation of fruits and contains between 12 and 14 percent ethyl alcohol; *beer,* which is brewed from grains and hops and usually contains 3 to 6 percent alcohol; and *liquor,* which includes whiskey, gin, vodka, and other distilled spirits and usually contains 40 percent (80 proof) to 50 percent (100 proof) alcohol.

According to sales data in the year ending March 2002, Canadians purchased per capita 6.5 litres of spirits, 12.2 litres of wine, and 85.0 litres of beer for a total of 103.8 litres drunk per capita. This is down from 134 litres purchased per capita in 1976 (Statistics Canada 2002c). Since some people do not drink at all, if Canada follows the American pattern this rate means 10 percent of the population could account for roughly half the total alcohol consumption (Levinthal 1996).

Many people do not think of alcohol as a drug because it can be purchased legally—and without a prescription—by adults. It is, however, a psychoactive drug that is classified as a *depressant* because it lowers the activity level of the central nervous system. The impairment of judgment and thinking associated with being drunk is the result of alcohol depressing brain functions. Alcohol also affects mood and behaviour. One to two drinks often bring a release from tensions and inhibitions. Three to four drinks affect self-control—including reaction time and coordination of hands, arms, and legs—and judgment, muddling the person's reasoning ability. Five to six drinks (binge or heavy drinking) affect sensory perception, and the person may show signs of intoxication, such as staggering, belligerence, or depression. At seven to eight drinks, the drinker is obviously intoxicated and may go into a stupor. Nine or more drinks affect vital centres, and the drinker may become comatose or even die. Of course, factors such as sex (women are more affected than men by the same amount of alcohol because they have a lower percentage of water in their bodies), body weight, physical build, and recent food and fluid consumption must be taken into account in estimating the rate of alcohol absorption in the body.

In a comprehensive discussion of the problems of drug abuse, entitled *The Dynamics of Drug Abuse*, Diana H. Fishbein and Susan E. Pease (1996) state that although negative short-term effects of drinking are usually overcome, chronic heavy drinking or alcoholism can cause permanent damage to the brain or other parts of the body. Social scientists divide long-term drinking patterns into four general categories. Social drinkers consume alcoholic beverages primarily on social occasions; they drink occasionally or even relatively frequently. Heavy drinkers are more frequent drinkers who typically consume greater quantities of alcohol when they drink and are more likely to become intoxicated. Acute alcoholics have trouble controlling their use of alcohol and plan their schedule around drinking. Chronic alcoholics have lost control over their drinking and tend to engage in compulsive behaviour such as hiding liquor bottles and sneaking drinks when they are not being observed.

Heavy Alcohol Consumption and Gender, Age, Marital Status, and Class

Since alcohol is consumed by almost 80 percent of the population, and heavy or binge drinking is considered to be a problem, the discussion of demographic factors related to alcohol consumption will focus on heavy or binge drinking (five drinks or more when alcohol is used). Table 8.1 shows that 6.2 and 25.5

TABLE 8.1   Prevalence of Weekly Heavy Drinking Among Past-Year Drinkers by Demographic Characteristics, Canada, Aged 15+, 2004

	%
Total (drinkers)	6.2
Sex	
Female (comparison group)	3.3
Male	9.2
Age Group (comparison group is previous age group)	
15–17	7.6
18–19	16.1
20–24	14.9
25–34	6.5
35–44	5.3
45–54	6.0
55–64	4.0
65–74	0.5
75+	1.5
Marital Status	
Married/partnered (comparison group)	4.6
Divorced/separated/widowed	4.9
Single/never married	10.2
Education	
Less than secondary (comparison group)	7.7
Secondary	7.3
Some post-secondary	8.0
University degree	2.4
Income Adequacy	
Lowest (comparison group)	8.7
Middle	6.0
Highest	6.7
Not stated	5.2

Source: Canadian Addiction Survey (CAS), 2005, A National Survey of Canadians' Use of Alcohol and Other Drugs: Prevalence of Use and Related Harms: Detailed Report. Ottawa: Canadian Centre on Substance Abuse.

percent of Canadians are heavy drinkers on a weekly basis. A much higher percentage of men are heavy drinkers than women (9.2 vs. 3.3 percent on a weekly basis). A higher percentage of young people than older people are heavy drinkers (approximately 15 percent vs. less than half that for older ages). Single and never-married people are much more likely to be heavy drinkers than married, partnered, divorced, separated, and widowed people (10 vs. less than 5 percent respectively). People with university degrees are much less likely to drink heavily than those with lower educational attainment (2.4 vs. 7.3 to 8.0 percent respectively). But little difference is found among those with lowest, middle, and highest income adequacy.

Alcohol-Related Social Problems

Alcohol consumption is linked to many kinds of harm, both to oneself and to others. Harms to oneself refer to harm to physical health, family and work functioning, friendships, legal problems and so on. Harms to others refer to their being insulted or humiliated, receiving verbal abuse, being in serious quarrels, family or marriage problems, or being assaulted.

According to the Canadian Addiction Survey (CAS), nearly 1 in 10 adult Canadians reported experiencing harm in the past 12 months due to their drinking. The most common harm was to physical health (5.4 percent). Smaller percentages reported harms to friendships and social life (2.7 percent) and financial position (4.7 percent). Table 8.2 shows the harm experienced because of drinking others: 32.7 percent of Canadians 18 years or older experienced one or more harms. Equal percentages of males and females experienced harm. Younger people tended to experience more harm than older people. Single and never-married people experienced more harm than married, partnered, divorced, separated, and widowed people. A higher percentage of those with some post-secondary education experienced harm than those with other levels of attainment. Experienced harm was not related to income adequacy or rural/urban status, but it was related to being a heavy drinker. Those who were heavy drinkers were much more likely to report experiencing harm than non-heavy drinkers.

TABLE 8.2 Percentage Reporting at Least One Harm During the Past Year Because of Others' Drinking, by Demographic Characteristics

	%
Total (drinkers)	32.7
Sex	
Female (comparison group)	32.6
Male	32.9
Age Group (comparison group is previous age group)	
18–19	62.6
20–24	58.3
25–34	41.9
35–44	32.7
45–54	30.4
55–64	24.8
65–74	14.9
75+	5.4
Marital Status	
Married/partnered (comparison group)	28.2
Divorced/separated/widowed	27.9
Single/never married	46.8
Education	
Less than secondary (comparison group)	25.6
Secondary	31.9
Some post-secondary	38.6
University degree	30.8
Income Adequacy	
Lowest (comparison group)	37.9
Middle	33.4
Highest	34.1
Not stated	28.1

Source: Canadian Addiction Survey (CAS), 2005, A National Survey of Canadians' Use of Alcohol and Other Drugs: Prevalence of Use and Related Harms: Detailed Report. Ottawa: Canadian Centre on Substance Abuse.

Health Problems

Although not all heavy drinkers and chronic alcohol abusers exhibit the major health problems that are typically associated with alcoholism, their risk of them is greatly increased. For alcoholics, the long-term health effects include *nutritional deficiencies* as a result of poor eating habits. Chronic heavy drinking contributes to high caloric consumption but low nutritional intake. Alcoholism is also associated with fluctuations in blood sugar levels that can cause adult-onset diabetes. Structural loss of brain tissue may produce *alcoholic*

dementia, which is characterized by difficulties in problem solving, remembering information, and organizing facts about one's identity and surroundings (Levinthal 1996).

Chronic alcohol abuse is also linked to *cardiovascular problems* such as inflammation and enlargement of the heart muscle, poor blood circulation, reduced heart contractions, fatty accumulations in the heart and arteries, high blood pressure, and cerebrovascular disorders such as stroke (Levinthal 1996). However, studies show that moderate alcohol consumption—such as a glass of wine a day—may improve body circulation, lower cholesterol levels, and reduce the risk of certain forms of heart disease.

Over time, chronic alcohol abuse also contributes to irreversible changes in the liver that are associated with *alcoholic cirrhosis*—a progressive development of scar tissue in the liver that chokes off blood vessels and destroys liver cells by interfering with their use of oxygen. Given all the possible health problems, perhaps it is not surprising that alcoholics typically have a shorter life expectancy—often by as much as 10 to 12 years—than non-drinkers or occasional drinkers who consume moderate amounts of alcohol.

Abuse of alcohol and other drugs by a pregnant woman can damage the fetus. The greatest risk of **fetal alcohol syndrome (FAS)—a condition characterized by mental retardation and craniofacial malformations that may affect the child of an alcoholic mother—**occurs during the first three months of pregnancy. Binge drinking during the third week of gestation has been linked particularly with this syndrome because that is when crucial craniofacial formation and brain growth take place in the fetus. It is estimated that approximately 100 babies per year are born in Canada with FAS and that rates are higher in remote rural and Indigenous communities (Single, Minh, et al., 1999:177). Another risk is **fetal alcohol effects (FAE)—a condition with some FAS characteristics that could include single birth defects, or developmental learning and behavioural disorders, that may not be noticed until months or years after the child's birth.** This condition is hard to identify, may be confused with other health problems, and must be diagnosed by physical examination and consideration of the health history. Thus, the rate of FAE could be substantially higher than FAS.

Alcohol in the Workplace

Productivity losses due to absenteeism, tardiness, and workplace accidents from alcohol use amounted to $4.1 billion, according to Single and his colleagues (1996:247). Excessive alcohol consumption impairs the sensorimotor skills necessary to operate machinery, heavy equipment, and motor vehicles. Numerous studies have shown a relationship between alcohol—and other drugs—and many workplace injuries or fatalities (Macdonald 1995).

Driving and Drinking

Drivers who have been drinking often do not realize how much alcohol they have consumed or what effect it has on their driving ability. As a result, many people drive dangerously even when they are not legally drunk, that is, driving with a blood alcohol level over 0.08 percent, which is referred to as *impaired driving*. Alcohol-related driving accidents occur, for example, when drivers lose control of their vehicles, fail to see a red traffic light or a car or pedestrian in the street, or miss a sharp curve in the road (Gross 1983). According to national coroner data reported in *Canada's Drug Strategy* (*CDS*), 55.6 percent of drivers aged 26 to 35 who were killed in motor vehicle accidents in 1995 had been drinking, as had 49.1 percent of those aged 36 to 45, 30.9 percent of those aged 46 to 55, and 18.8 percent of those over 55 (Health Canada 1998:22). Groups such as Mothers Against Drunk Driving (MADD) continually develop new recommendations to ensure that public interest in the issue is maintained (see Box 8.1).

Family Problems

Chronic alcohol abuse or alcoholism makes it difficult for a person to maintain social relationships and have a stable family life. According to social scientist Charles F. Levinthal (1996), for every person who has a problem with alcohol, an average of at least four other people are directly affected on a daily basis. Domestic abuse and violence in families are frequently associated with heavy drinking and alcohol abuse by one or more family members. Women whose partners consume five or more drinks at one time, compared to those whose partners never drink, are at six times the risk of violence, and abused women frequently use drugs to deal with the pain (Health Canada 1993). Growing up in a family that is affected by alcohol can have a profound impact on children. The extent to which alcohol abuse affects other family members depends on the degree of alcoholism and the type of alcoholic. Some alcoholic parents are violent and abusive; others are quiet and sullen or withdrawn. To outsiders, the family of an alcoholic may appear to be normal, but family members may feel as though they have an "elephant in the living room," as journalist Joyce Maynard (1994:80–81) explains:

> I grew up in an alcoholic household. But as difficult as it was dealing with my father's drinking, the greater pain for me was the secret keeping. Adult children of alcoholics refer to the phenomenon as "the elephant in the living room": You have a huge, inescapable fact about your life that affects everything in your home, but nobody mentions it, although everybody's behaviour is altered to accommodate or deal with it . . . . Our family squeezed past the elephant in the living room, felt his breath on our faces, and rearranged furniture to make room for him. I hid liquor bottles if a friend was coming over. To prevent my father from driving, I even stashed away the keys to his car. But I never uttered a word, and neither did the rest of my family, about what was behind those actions. . . . It wasn't until I became an adult myself that I recognized the unhealthiness of our family's conspiracy of silence.

As Maynard suggests, family members of alcoholics frequently become *enablers*—people who adjust their behaviour to accommodate an alcoholic. Enabling often takes the form of lying to cover up the alcoholic's drinking, absenteeism from work, and/or discourteous treatment of others. Enabling leads many families to develop a pattern of **codependency—a reciprocal relationship between the alcoholic and one or more non-alcoholics who unwittingly aid and abet the alcoholic's excessive drinking and resulting behaviour** (Jung 1994). When codependency occurs, the spouse or another family member takes on many of the alcoholic's responsibilities and keeps the alcoholic person from experiencing the full impact of his or her actions. Children who grow up in alcoholic families tend to have higher than normal rates of hyperactivity, antisocial behaviour, low academic achievement, and cognitive

BOX 8.1   Maintaining a Drumbeat against Drunken Driving

A selfishly drunk (BAC Blood Alcohol Concentration 240, three times the legal limit) driver took the sunshine from my life in July 1981—or was it just yesterday? That sunshine was our 19-year-old son, about to embark on his adult life: university, career, marriage. Instead, we are left with chronic emptiness: no hugs at the door on his weekends home; no daughter-in-law to love and admire; no grandchildren to be "just like so-and-so."

Helen Stauffer, former Vice President of PRIDE (People to Reduce Impaired Driving Everywhere) and its successor, MADD (Mothers Against Drunk Driving) Canada (e-mail to the author)

Like many other members of Mothers Against Drunk Driving (MADD), including Candace Lightner, who founded the organization in the United States in the early 1980s when her daughter was killed, Helen Stauffer has a personal reason for confronting the problem of drunk driving. Over the past two decades, MADD has campaigned for stricter laws against drunk driving, mounting media campaigns against drinking and driving, and promoting the idea of having a designated driver. These campaigns have been very effective. The rate of impaired driving offenses has declined from about 400 per 100 000 in 1990 to about 247 per 100 000 in 2004 (Canadian Centre for Justice Statistics 2001:11, Sauvé 2005:11).

MADD is still campaigning because people are still dying and being injured because of impaired driving. MADD uses the figures from the Traffic Injury Research Foundation to state that every two days, 9 people are killed and 230 people are injured due to drinking and driving. It is the number one cause of criminal death in Canada.

One of MADD's campaigns was to reduce the criminal code BAC level from 0.08 percent to 0.05 percent. Police are reluctant to charge people with a BAC lower than 0.10 percent because of measurement variation. The campaign to reduce the criminal code BAC led to much criticism and claims that MADD was trying to criminalize social drinking. MADD's national executive director, Andrew Murie, replied in the same press release, "A 0.05 percent BAC limit would not criminalize social drinking. What we want to stop are people who go out to drink four or five and then drive." A more recent campaign is to advocate passing a drug-impaired driving law (MADD Canada 2005)

MADD is also concerned about the influence of beer and wine advertising (distillers have informally agreed not to advertise hard spirits). Despite the fact that the annual number of alcohol-related auto accidents in this country remains high, images and fantasies associated with drinking make it seem far more exciting, romantic, and adventurous to drink than to abstain. What further policy steps do you think MADD should take to promote its message? Do you think that alcoholic beverage manufacturers have a responsibility to inform the public about the potential consequences of their products, through health facts and graphic photos on bottles like those found on cigarette packages? Why or why not?

impairment (Fishbein and Pease 1996). However, although the statistical risk of becoming an alcoholic increase if one's parent has been an alcoholic, most children of alcoholics (as many as 59 percent) do not become alcoholics themselves (Sher 1991).

TOBACCO (NICOTINE) USE AS A SOCIAL PROBLEM

The nicotine in tobacco is a toxic, dependency-producing psychoactive drug that is more addictive than heroin. It is categorized as a *stimulant* because it stimulates central nervous system receptors, activating the release of adrenaline, which raises blood pressure, speeds up the heartbeat, and gives the user a sense of alertness. Some people claim that nicotine reduces their appetite, helps them to lose weight, and produces a sense of calmness and relaxation (Akers 1992). Perhaps these physical and psychological effects of nicotine dependency help to explain why about one in every four Canadian adults over the age of 15 (25 percent of men and 22 percent of women) smoke, according to the NPHS (Statistics Canada 2001b:18). A lower percentage (19.2) of students in grades 7 to 12 are smoking cigarettes (see Table 8.4 on page 215). A promising note for the future is that the smoking rates of Canadian youth are declining. According to the Youth Smoking survey of 19 000 students in 955 classes randomly selected from Canadian schools, whereas 7 percent of those in grades 5 to 9 were smoking in 1994, now under 3 percent were smoking cigarettes (Statistics Canada 2004a).

Although the overall proportion of smokers in the general population has declined somewhat since the pioneering 1964 U.S. Surgeon General's warning that smoking is linked to cancer and other serious diseases, tobacco is still responsible for more than 37 000 deaths per year in Canada, or five times the number of deaths from car accidents, murder, suicides, and alcohol abuse combined, according to Health Canada (2006). People who smoke cigarettes, cigars, or pipes have a greater likelihood of developing lung cancer and cancer of the larynx, mouth, and esophagus than non-smokers because nicotine is ingested into the bloodstream through the lungs and soft tissues of the mouth (Akers 1992). Furthermore, many cases of bronchitis, emphysema, ulcers, and heart and circulatory disorders can be traced to nicotine consumption. When tobacco burns, it forms carbon monoxide, which disrupts the transport of oxygen from the lungs to the rest of the body and hence contributes to cardiovascular disease (Levinthal 1996).

Smoking typically shortens life expectancy. It is estimated that about half a pack (10 cigarettes) a day on average reduces a person's life expectancy by four years, and smoking more than two packs a day (40 cigarettes) reduces life expectancy by eight years. When a person uses both tobacco and alcohol, the cancer-causing effects of tobacco are exacerbated (Fishbein and Pease 1996).

Even people who never light up a cigarette are harmed by *environmental tobacco smoke*—**the smoke in the air as a result of other people's tobacco smoking** (Levinthal 1996). When someone smokes a cigarette, about 75 percent of the nicotine ends up in the air. Researchers have found that non-smokers who carpool or work with heavy smokers are more affected by environmental smoke than non-smokers who are only occasionally exposed to it. Therefore, smoking has been banned in many public and private facilities throughout the country.

Not surprisingly, cigarette smoking adversely affects infants and children. Infants born to women who smoke typically have lower than average birth weights and sometimes slower rates of physical and mental growth. When a pregnant woman smokes, blood vessels constrict, which reduces the amount of oxygen reaching the fetus. Carbon

monoxide transmitted from the mother's blood to the fetus interferes with the distribution of oxygen that does reach the fetus (DiFranza and Lew 1995). Children who grow up in households where one or both parents smoke are more apt to suffer from frequent ear infections, upper respiratory infections such as bronchitis and sinusitis, allergies, asthma, and other health problems than children whose parents do not smoke.

Why do so many people use nicotine if it is so dangerous? Several reasons have been suggested. First, nicotine creates a high level of dependency, so once a person has begun to use tobacco regularly, the withdrawal symptoms may be strong enough to make the person light up another cigarette. Some researchers have found that the majority of people who smoke recognize that smoking is bad for them and would like to quit but cannot (Fishbein and Pease 1996:213). Second, in the past, sophisticated marketing campaigns associated smoking with desirable cultural attributes such as achieving maturity, gaining wealth and happiness, or being thin and sexy. In Canada, the *Tobacco Act* of 1997 (amended in 1998 and 2000) prohibits cigarette manufacturers from advertising their products on radio or television or in magazines or newspapers; they are also prohibited from sponsoring sports and arts events. In addition, the manufacturers must print large health warnings and graphic antismoking pictures on cigarette packages and report marketing campaigns to the federal government. Finally, smoking has been used by youth as a form of rebellion and method of showing solidarity with peers. Thus, many forces combine to promote the continuation of Canada's number one public health problem.

PRESCRIPTION DRUGS, OVER-THE-COUNTER DRUGS, AND CAFFEINE

When most people think of drug abuse, they picture unscrupulous drug dealers in dark alleys selling illegal drugs. But legal drugs also may be abused. Legal drugs fall into two categories: *prescription drugs,* which are dispensed only by a registered pharmacist on the authority of a licensed physician or dentist, and *over-the-counter* (*OTC*) *drugs,* which are available off the shelf and are restricted only by the customer's ability to pay.

Prescription Drugs

According to the NPHS, in 1998, opioid analgesics (morphine-type pain relievers) were used by 4.7 percent of Canadians aged 15 or older, antidepressants by 3.6 percent, sleeping pills by 3.5 percent, tranquilizers by 2.7 percent, steroids by 0.8 percent, and diet pills by 0.5 percent (Single, Minh et al. 1999:113). Pain medication is probably the prescription drug that is most frequently abused. Though millions of people benefit from *narcotics*—natural or synthetic opiates such as morphine (brand names Duramorph and Roxanol), propoxyphene (Darvon), and codeine—that relieve pain, suppress coughing, control chronic diarrhea, and reduce heroin withdrawal symptoms, there are risks of short-term abuse and long-term psychological and physical dependence. Over time, users develop tolerance for the drug they are taking and must continue to increase dosages to obtain the same effect that was derived from the lower dose. Drug dependency that results from physician-supervised treatment for a recognized medical disorder is called *iatrogenic addiction.* Iatrogenic addiction is most likely to occur with long-term use and/or high dosages of a prescription drug; it most often affects people from the middle or upper class who have no previous history of drug abuse or addiction (Fishbein and Pease 1996).

Two widely prescribed drugs that have been the subject of controversy regarding their use and abuse are methylphenidate (Ritalin) and fluoxetine (Prozac). Ritalin is a stimulant that is prescribed for children who are diagnosed with *attention-deficit hyperactivity disorder* (ADHD). According to the American Psychiatric Association, ADHD is characterized by "emotionality, behavioural hyperactivity, short attention span, distractibility, impulsiveness, and perceptual and learning disabilities" (Fishbein and Pease 1996). Although some children are probably correctly diagnosed with this disorder, some commentators worry that Ritalin is over-prescribed in Canada. According to the continuing survey of drug use among Ontario students conducted by drug-use researchers Edward Adlaf and Angela Paglia (2003), 2.9 percent of students used the drug in 2003 (see Table 8.4 on page 215). Boys are more likely than girls to be diagnosed with ADHD and to use the drug. Advocates believe that children with normal to above-average intelligence who are performing poorly in school can benefit from Ritalin, which has proven to be safe for more than 40 years. But critics argue that many parents, doctors, and teachers see Ritalin as a quick fix for dealing with troublesome children.

One of the most abused prescription drugs for adults is Prozac, an antidepressant. Introduced in 1987 as a breakthrough medication for clinical depression, Prozac has become a cure-all for the blues, a far milder form of depression. Advocates believe that Prozac enhances the quality of life for many people, freeing them from depression and suicidal thoughts. But the long-term side effects of the drug are unknown, and there is some evidence that Prozac is associated with intense, violent suicidal thoughts in some patients. Both Prozac and Ritalin are approved by Health Canada and are considered safe and effective if taken as directed.

Over-the-Counter Drugs

A fine line exists between prescription and over-the-counter (OTC) drugs. Today, both types of drugs are advertised, in the electronic and print media, directly to the consumer, with suggestions to "ask your doctor or pharmacist about [our product] on your next visit." Some drugs are available both by prescription and over the counter, depending on their strength and dosage. For example, medication for stomach ulcers (e.g., Zantac and Tagamet) is sold over the counter in lower doses and by prescription in higher doses. Some drugs that are now sold over the counter were previously available only by prescription.

Widely used OTC drugs include analgesics, sleep aids, and cough and cold remedies. According to the NPHS, 65 percent of Canadians 12 years old and older took pain relievers; 20 percent took cold and cough remedies; and 11 percent took stomach remedies. In each case, a higher percentage of women than men took the drugs (Statistics Canada 2001b:36). Abuse of aspirin and other analgesics can cause gastric bleeding, problems with blood clotting, complications during surgery and during labour and delivery, and Reye's syndrome (a potentially life-threatening condition that can arise when children with flu, chicken pox, or other viral infections are given aspirin). Overdoses of analgesics such as acetaminophen (e.g., Tylenol and Anacin-3), aspirin, and ibuprofen (e.g., Motrin, Advil, and Midol) have been linked to cases of attempted suicide, especially by White females between the ages of 6 and 17 years. Few of these suicide attempts have resulted in death except when the analgesics were combined with alcohol or other drugs (Levinthal 1996). Like analgesics, sleep aids are dangerous when combined with alcohol or some cough and cold remedies because they are depressants that slow down the central nervous system. Even cough and cold medications alone have side effects, such as drowsiness, that can be hazardous—if, for example, users attempt to drive a car or operate heavy machinery. To counteract drowsiness, some drug companies add caffeine to their products.

Caffeine

Although it is a relatively safe drug, caffeine is a dependency-producing psychoactive stimulant (Gilbert 1986). Caffeine is an ingredient in coffee, tea, chocolate, soft drinks, and stimulants such as NoDoz and Vivarin. Coffee consumption by Canadians is higher per capita than that of either Americans or Europeans. According to Oxfam Canada, per capita we consume 402 cups per year (or 15 billion cups in total per year). Per capita, that is 77 more cups than Americans and 152 cups more than Europeans (Oxfam Canada 2005). Most people ingest caffeine because they like the feeling of mental alertness and reduced fatigue that it produces. The extent to which caffeine actually improves human performance, however, is widely debated. Caffeine may improve concentration when a person is performing boring or repetitive tasks, but it has little effect on the performance of complex tasks such as critical thinking and decision making (Curatolo and Robertson 1983; Dews 1984). The short-term effects of caffeine include dilated peripheral blood vessels, constricted blood vessels in the head, and a slightly elevated heart rate (Levinthal 1996). Long-term effects of heavy caffeine use (more than three cups of coffee or five cups of tea per day) include increased risk of heart attack and osteoporosis—the loss of bone density and increased brittleness associated with fractures and broken bones (Kiel et al. 1990).

Overall, however, the social problems associated with the abuse of caffeine and prescription and OTC drugs are relatively minor when compared with the social problems associated with illegal drugs.

ILLEGAL DRUG USE AND ABUSE

Are some drugs inherently bad and hence classified as illegal? What constitutes an illegal drug is a matter of social and legal definitions that are subject to change over time. During the 19th and early 20th centuries, people in Canada had fairly easy access to drugs that are currently illegal for general use. In the early 1800s, neither doctors nor pharmacists had to be licensed. *Patent medicines,* which sometimes contained such ingredients as opium, morphine, heroin, cocaine, and alcohol, could be purchased in stores, through mail-order advertisements, and from medicine wagons run by people who called themselves doctors and provided free entertainment to attract crowds (Young 1961). Over time, because of the rapidly growing number of narcotics addicts, prescriptions became required for some drugs. Some forms of drug use were criminalized because of their association with specific minority groups. For example, in Canada, opium could be consumed legally in cough syrup, but smoking the same amount of opium was banned by the *Opium Act* of 1908 after an investigation by Mackenzie King on the use of opium. The reason for the ban was that opium smoking was a favourite pastime of the Chinese workers building railroads in Western Canada (Small 1978). In Canada, the Division of Narcotic Control was part of the Department of Health. Its head was Col. C. H. L. Sharman, who undertook the moral entrepreneurial role against drugs in Canada that Harry Anslinger played in the United States.

The most recent legislation dealing with drugs in Canada is the *Controlled Drugs and Substances Act,* which came into effect in 1997. This legislation, according to *Canada's Drug Strategy* (Health Canada 1998:10), has enforcement measures "for the interdiction and suppression of unlawful import, export, production, distribution, and possession of controlled substances and for the forfeiture of any property used or intended to be used in the commission of such offences and profits derived from such offences." Nevertheless, drugs are still widely available. The Canadian Addiction Survey (CAS) provides an aggregate portrait of illicit drug use in Canada.

Table 8.3 shows the lifetime use by Canadians of any of the following drugs: cannabis, cocaine, speed, hallucinogens, ecstasy, and heroin, according to the CAS. Of Canadians aged 15 and over, 45.1 percent reported lifetime use of any of these six illicit drugs. A higher percentage of males than females have used them (50.6 vs. 39.9 percent respectively). A higher percentage of young than older people has used them, but with the exception of the 15 to 17 group, the percentage using

TABLE 8.3 Percentage Reporting Lifetime Use of Any of Six Illicit Drugs, by Demographic Characteristics

	%
Total	45.1
Sex	***
Female (comparison group)	39.9
Male	50.6
Age Group (comparison group is previous age group)	***
15–17	39.5
18–19	70.9
20–24	69.3
25–34	57.7
35–44	55.6
45–54	51.3
55–64	28.5
65–74	13.4
75+	3.3
Marital Status	***
Married/partnered (comparison group)	41.4
Divorced/separated/widowed	36.0
Single/never married	58.3
Education	***
Less than secondary (comparison group)	35.7
Secondary	42.9
Some post-secondary	53.0
University degree	44.7
Income Adequacy	***
Lowest (comparison group)	43.7
Middle	45.6
Highest	55.1
Not stated	35.2

Source: *Canadian Addiction Survey (CAS), 2005*, A National Survey of Canadians' Use of Alcohol and Other Drugs: Prevalence of Use and Related Harms: Detailed Report. *Ottawa: Canadian Centre on Substance Abuse.*

them remains above 50 till the age group 55 to 64 is reached. A higher percentage of people in the west than east of Canada have used them. A higher percentage of those with some post-secondary education have used them than those with other levels of education. Finally, since illicit drugs are costly, it might be expected that income level would be related to their use. A higher percentage of people with the highest income have used them than those with lower levels. If drug incidents reported in the Uniform Crime Reporting Surveys are a measure of use, then the use of illegal drugs, particularly marijuana, is increasing. In 2004 almost 100 000

reported incidents occurred, and this is an increase of 46 percent from 1994 (see Table 9.2 on page 235). The biggest increase in incidents, 120 percent is for the cultivation of marijuana or grow-ops.

To show the use of these drugs by teenagers, we turn to the continuing study by Adlaf and Paglia (OSDUS 2003) of drug use among Ontario students. This is a continuing study (since 1977) that includes students from grades 7 to 12 inclusive (aged approximately 12–17 years). Table 8.4 shows the drug use during 2003 reported by male and female students.

Marijuana

Marijuana is the most extensively used illicit drug in Canada. According to the CAS, 7.4 percent of Canadians 15 years and older used marijuana in 1993, and a higher percentage of men than women reported using it (10 percent vs. 4.9 percent) (Single, Minh, et al. 1999:144). According to the Ontario Student Drug Use Survey (OSDUS) report, 29.6 percent of students have used marijuana with little difference between the sexes. Students often laugh to hear that marijuana use is still considered deviant behaviour. In early 2005, the federal government was again considering decriminalizing possession of small quantities of marijuana (see Box 8.2).

Many teenage users report that marijuana is as easy to acquire as alcohol, and easier than cigarettes. According to one teenager, "It is so popular, so well known, it is around everywhere. Nobody is afraid of the consequences of selling it or buying it .... It is really easy to get" (quoted in Friend 1996:2A). Many young people buy the drug from friends who grow their own plants.

Marijuana is ingested by smoking it, either in a hand-rolled cigarette known as a *reefer* or *joint*, or through a pipe or other smoking implement. Potent marijuana—marijuana with high levels of the plant's primary psychoactive chemical, delta-9 tetrahydrocannabinol (THC)—has existed for many years, but potency has increased in recent years because of indoor gardens. Indoor crops have levels of THC up to four times as high as plants grown outdoors and in other nations (Navarro 1996).

Marijuana is both a central nervous system depressant and a stimulant. In low to moderate doses, the drug produces mild sedation; in high doses, it produces a sense of well-being, euphoria, and sometimes

TABLE 8.4   Percentage of Ontario Secondary Students Reporting Past Year Drug Use, by Total and Sex

	Total	Males	Females
Alcohol	66.2	68.3	64.3
Cannabis	29.6	30.9	28.3
Binge Drinking	26.5	29.4	23.8
Cigarettes	19.2	18.0	20.3
Hallucinogens	10.0	12.1	8.0
Solvents	6.1	5.9	6.3
Stimulants (NM)	5.8	4.7	6.7
Cocaine	4.8	5.4	4.3
Ecstasy (MDMA)	4.1	4.2	3.9
Methamphetamine	3.3	3.8	2.9
LSD	2.9	3.5	2.3
Ritalin (NM)	2.9	3.4	2.5
Glue	2.8	3.0	2.6
Crack	2.7	2.8	2.6
Barbiturates (NM)	2.5	2.6	2.5
PCP	2.2	2.9	1.6
Tranquillizers (NM)	2.2	2.7	1.8
Ketamine	2.2	3.0	1.6
Rohypnol	1.6	1.7	1.5
Heroin	1.4	1.9	0.9
Ice	1.2	1.3	1.0
GHB	0.7	0.8	0.6
Any Illicit, including cannabis	32.2	33.1	31.3
Any Illicit, excluding cannabis	15.3	16.6	14.2
Steroids (lifetime)	3.0	4.4	1.7

Notes: binge drinking (5+ drinks on one occasion) refers to the past 4 weeks time period; NM = non-medical use; s = estimate suppressed.

Source: Adlaf, E.M., & Paglia, A. (2003). Drug Use Among Ontario Students: Detailed OSDUS Findings, 1977-2003: (CAMH Research Document No. 13 and 14). Toronto: Centre for Addiction and Mental Health.

become apathetic and lose their motivation to perform competently or achieve long-range goals, such as completing their education. Overall, the short-term effects of marijuana are typically milder than the short-term effects of drugs such as cocaine (Fishbein and Pease 1996).

High doses of marijuana smoked during pregnancy can disrupt the development of a fetus and result in lower-than-average birth weight, congenital abnormalities, premature delivery, and neurological disturbances (Fishbein and Pease 1996). Furthermore, some studies have found an increased risk of cancer and other lung problems associated with inhaling, because marijuana smokers are believed to inhale more deeply than tobacco users.

Over the past decade, medical uses of marijuana have been widely debated. In 2001, Health Canada authorized the use of marijuana for medicinal purposes (see Box 8.2).

Stimulants

Cocaine and amphetamines are among the major stimulants that are abused in Canada. Cocaine is an extremely potent and dependency-producing drug derived from the small leaves of the coca plant, which grows in several Latin American countries. In the 19th century, cocaine was introduced as a local anesthetic in medical practice and a mood-enhancer in patent medicines (Akers 1992). It was an ingredient in Coca-Cola from the 1880s to the early 1900s (Miller 1994). Today, cocaine is the third most widely used psychoactive drug after alcohol and marijuana. Users typically sniff, or "snort," the drug into their nostrils, inject it intravenously, or smoke it in the form of crack, a potent form of cocaine that is specially processed for smoking.

According to the CADS and reported in the *Canadian Profile*, 0.7 percent of Canadians aged 15 and older had used cocaine in 1994—slightly more males than females reported using cocaine (0.8 percent vs. 0.5 percent)—and this figure has remained relatively stationary over time (Single, Minh, et al. 1999:144). Table 8.4 shows that 4.8 percent of students reported using cocaine, and more males than females (5.4 vs. 4.3 percent) used it. For some central-city residents living in poverty, with no hope of gainful employment, dealing cocaine is a major source of revenue and an entry point for other drug-related crime.

hallucinations. Marijuana slightly increases blood pressure and heart rate and greatly lowers blood glucose levels, causing extreme hunger. The human body manufactures a chemical that closely resembles THC, and specific receptors in the brain are designed to receive it. Marijuana use disrupts these receptors, impairing motor activity, concentration, and short-term memory (Cowley 1997). As a result, complex motor tasks such as driving a car or operating heavy machinery are dangerous for a person who is under the influence of marijuana. Some studies show that heavy marijuana use can impair concentration and recall in high school and college students (Wren 1996). Users

SOCIAL PROBLEMS AND SOCIAL POLICY

BOX 8.2 The Battle over Marijuana: Medicalization, Availability, Decriminalization, Legalization?

As of July 30, 2001, Canada is allowing people with medical need to use marijuana. Restrictions apply to certain types of need, such as having a terminal illness with a prognosis for a remaining lifespan of less than 12 months; having particular diseases such as multiple sclerosis, spinal cord injury, some cancers, and HIV/AIDS; and having other serious medical conditions where conventional treatments are not relieving symptoms.

In mid-2006, the Canadian AIDS Society reported that the medical marijuana program does not work. According to a CBC report ("Medical Marijuana Still Not Widely Available" 2006), "Over 85 per cent of the people we consulted who used cannabis are currently relying on illegal sources for their supply of cannabis," said Lynne Bell-Isle, who worked on the study. "Only 1.7 per cent of respondents we spoke to obtained their cannabis from the government." Few people (fewer than 200) take advantage of this program because few know of its existence or can find a doctor to support their application.

Not all doctors agree with the decision to medicalize marijuana. Both the Canadian Medical Association and the Canadian Medical Protective Association have urged physicians not to sign patients' forms, to protect the physicians against being accused of recommending an unproven treatment. In addition, Physicians for a Smoke-Free Canada say that marijuana contains many cancer-causing ingredients and more tar than tobacco and thus should not be smoked for health reasons.

Many others think the government does not go far enough to make marijuana available to the estimated thousands of sufferers who may need it. James Wakeford, a person living with AIDS, asked Health Canada to give him a safe and affordable supply of marijuana, and when it was not forthcoming, he took his case to the Ontario Court of Appeal. The court rejected the appeal on a technical ground in January 2002, saying that the governmental regulations did not have an adverse effect on Wakeford's liberty, according to his lawyer Alan Young. What should be done to help those in need now?

Given the difficulties of making marijuana available to people with a medical need, the difficulties of decriminalizing or legalizing it seem overwhelming, even though almost a majority of Canadians are in favour of this, and prominent associations support decriminalization. A Leger Marketing Survey found that 46.8 percent of Canadians were in favour of a law that would allow marijuana to be sold and used legally, and the Canadian Medical Association (in spite of the reservations about medical marijuana mentioned above) and the Canadian Association of Chiefs of Police support decriminalizing the possession of marijuana for personal use ("Canadians Evenly Split" 2001).

Advocates of *decriminalization* or *legalization* suggest that small amounts of marijuana for personal use should no longer be subject to legal control. Some U.S. states have already adopted some form of decriminalization for the possession of small amounts—usually less than one ounce or so—of marijuana. In the Netherlands, it is possible to use a variety of drugs without fear of prosecution.

According to criminologist Ronald L. Akers (1992), if marijuana were treated as a legal substance, it could be subject to restrictions on advertising, content, purchase age, and other regulations for production, distribution, and sale. But Akers (1992:160) also suggests that marijuana use "has the potential to grow to the same level as tobacco and alcohol use with basically the same magnitude of threat to health and life . . . . The benefits of legalization . . . are no more certain than are the harmful consequences of legalization." And others believe that legalizing marijuana would send the wrong message about the safety of this mind-altering drug.

In more recent developments, the Ontario Superior Court ruled in January 2003 that Ottawa's rules about the medical use of marijuana were unconstitutional because users have no legal access to the drug, and thus, patients' rights ere violated. One of the consequences of this ruling is that, if the regulations are not replaced, anyone will be legally free to possess this drug. Also in January 2003, an Ontario Court judge dismissed a marijuana possession charge because an earlier ruling had meant that it is no longer illegal for any Canadian to possess marijuana.

In April 2005, Canada was the first country to approve the sale of a cannabis-based prescription painkiller. It is being prescribed for people suffering from multiple sclerosis who have severe nerve pain (about 50 percent of the 50 000 Canadians who have MS) and those with nerve pain from other diseases ranging from cancer to shingles. The dose can be regulated more easily than smoking pot (Picard 2005). In addition, in 2005 the government was again talking of introducing legislation to decriminalize the possession of small amounts of marijuana.

What pros and cons would you give in a debate over (a) the government guaranteeing the availability of marijuana for those with medical need, or (b) the decriminalization or legalization of marijuana?

The effects of cocaine on the human body depend on how pure the dose is and what effect the user expects. Most cocaine users experience a powerful high, or "rush," in which blood pressure rises and heart rate and respiration increase dramatically. Reactions vary in length and intensity, depending on whether the drug is injected, smoked, or snorted. When the drug wears off, users become increasingly agitated and depressed. Some users become extremely depressed and suicidal; others develop such a powerful craving that they easily become addicted to the drug (Gawin and Ellinwood 1988). Occasionally, cocaine use results in sudden death by triggering an irregular heart rhythm.

People who use cocaine over extended periods of time have higher rates of infection, heart disturbance, internal bleeding, hypertension, cardiac arrest, stroke, hemorrhaging, and other neurological and cardiovascular disorders than non-users. Although these problems may develop gradually as cocaine use continues, some users experience the problems after a single dose. Intravenous cocaine users who share contaminated needles and syringes are also at risk for AIDS. The risk of contracting AIDS is especially high in crack houses, where women addicts often engage in prostitution (see Chapter 7) to acquire drugs.

Cocaine use is extremely hazardous during pregnancy. Children born to crack-addicted mothers usually suffer painful withdrawal symptoms at birth and later show deficits in cognitive skills, judgment, and behaviour controls. "Crack babies" must often be cared for at public expense in hospitals and other facilities because their mothers cannot meet their basic needs or provide nurturance. But social scientist Philippe Bourgeois suggests that blame for the problem cannot be placed on the women alone. Instead, Bourgeois blames the problem on patriarchal definitions of "family" and the dysfunctional public sector that relegates the responsibility for nurturing and supporting children almost exclusively to women. For change to occur, fathers and the larger society must share the women's burden (Bourgeois 1995).

Like cocaine, amphetamines ("uppers") stimulate the central nervous system. Amphetamines in the form of diet pills and pep formulas are legal substances when they are prescribed by a physician, but many people, believing that they cannot lose weight or have enough

Extensive media coverage of the arrest, conviction, and incarceration of film star Robert Downey, Jr., for felony drug possession called attention to the fact that drug abuse cuts across lines of racialization, class, and gender. Do you believe that media reports about Downey's prison sentence will make young people more aware of the problems associated with illicit drug use? Or does such coverage sometimes glamorize such behaviour?

energy without the pills, become physically and/or psychologically dependent on them. Speed freaks—heavy users who inject massive doses of amphetamines several times a day—often do "runs," staying awake for extended periods of time, eating very little, and engaging in bizarre behaviour such as counting cornflakes in a cereal box or pasting postage stamps on the wall before "crashing" and sleeping for several days (Goode 1989). Recent concern about amphetamine abuse has focused on a smokeable form called ICE that contains a high percentage of the pure drug and produces effects that last from 4 to 24 hours (Lauderback and Waldorf 1993).

Table 8.4 shows that 1.2 percent of Ontario students have used ICE in the past year. Chronic amphetamine abuse can result in amphetamine psychosis, which is characterized by paranoia, hallucinations, and violent tendencies that may persist for weeks after use of the drug has been discontinued. Overdosing on amphetamines can produce coma, brain damage, and even death.

Depressants

Many people who abuse stimulants also abuse depressants—drugs, including alcohol, that depress the central nervous system and may have some pain-killing properties. The most commonly used depressants are barbiturates (e.g., Nembutal and Seconal) and anti-anxiety drugs or tranquilizers (e.g., Librium, Valium, and Miltown). Table 8.4 shows that 2.5 percent and 2.2 percent of students used barbiturates and tranquilizers respectively in 2003. Relatively low oral doses of depressants produce a relaxing and mildly disinhibiting effect; higher doses result in sedation. Users may develop both physical addiction to and psychological dependence on these depressants. Users sometimes use depressants for *potentiation*—the interaction that takes place when two drugs are mixed together to produce a far greater effect than the effect of either drug administered separately. Heroin users, for example, will sometimes combine heroin and barbiturates in hopes of prolonging their high and extending their heroin supply (Fishbein and Pease 1996).

Recently, Rohypnol and GHB (gamma-hydroxybutyrate), also known as "Grievous Bodily Harm" or "Liquid X," have been topics of discussion on university and college campuses. Rohypnol is used as an anesthetic and sleep aid in other countries, but it is not approved for use in Canada. Rohypnol and GHB are popular among young people because they are inexpensive ("lunch money") drugs, and they produce a "floaty" state, a mild euphoria, increased sociability, and lowered inhibitions. Table 8.4 shows that 1.6 and 0.7 percent of students used Rohypnol and GHB respectively. For some people, Rohypnol works like a powerful sleeping pill.

Jenny Altick was a university student when she tried the drug: "I'd just pass out . . . . It seemed like a very safe thing to take. It wasn't like acid or something that was totally chemical and bad. If you're thinking about trying coke [cocaine], you've heard how bad it is. There's that little thing in your head. But this one, no one had heard about it. It was one of those new things everyone was doing" (quoted in Bonnin 1997:E1). For other users, however, the consequences are more dire. Rohypnol, a benzodiazepine, known colloquially as "roofies," is known as the "date rape drug" because a number of women have reported that they were raped after an acquaintance secretly slipped the drug into their drink. Victims, including men, become drowsy and pass out, not remembering what happened. The combination of alcohol and Rohypnol or GHB has also been linked to automobile accidents and deaths from overdoses, which occur because it is difficult to judge how much intoxication will result when depressants are mixed with alcohol (Bonnin 1997). In October 2006, the Ontario government indicated that it would bring in legislation to make it possible to carry drinks to the washrooms, thus ensuring that drinks would not be left unattended.

Narcotics

Narcotics, or opiates, are available in several forms: natural substances (e.g., opium, morphine, and codeine); opiate derivatives, which are created by making slight changes in the chemical composition of morphine (e.g., heroin and Percodan); and synthetic drugs, which produce opiate-like effects but are not chemically related to morphine (e.g., Darvon and Demerol). Because heroin is the most widely abused narcotic, we will focus primarily on its effects.

Who uses heroin? The percentage of Canadians using it is very small. The CADS combined several drugs together to report their use. The data, reported in the *Canadian Profile,* show that 1.1 percent of Canadians aged 15 and older used heroin, speed, and/or LSD in 1994, and that a higher percentage of men than women used these drugs (1.5 percent vs. 0.7 percent) (Single, Minh, et al. 1999:144). Table 8.4 shows that 3.3 percent of the students used methamphetamine, and 1.4 used heroin in 2003. Some people who try the drug have adverse side effects, such as nausea and vomiting, and never use it again; others become addicted.

What effect does heroin have on the body? Most heroin users inject the drug intravenously—a practice known as *mainlining* or *shooting*—which produces a tingling sensation and feeling of euphoria that is typically followed by a state of drowsiness or lethargy. Heroin users quickly develop a tolerance for the drug and must increase the dosage continually to achieve the same effect. Heroin and other opiates are highly addictive; users experience intense cravings for the drug and have physical symptoms such as diarrhea and dehydration if the drug is withdrawn.

What are the long-term effects of heroin? Although some users experience no long-term physical problems, there are serious risks involved in use. In high doses, heroin produces extreme respiratory depression, coma, and even death. Because the potency of street heroin is unknown, overdosing is always a possibility. Street heroin also tends to be diluted with other ingredients that produce adverse reactions in some users. Shooting up with contaminated needles can lead to hepatitis or AIDS. As well, heroin use has been linked more directly to crime than have some other types of drug use. Because hard-core users have difficulty holding a job and yet need a continual supply of the drug, they often turn to robbery, burglary, shoplifting, pimping, prostitution, or working for the underground drug industry (Johnson et al. 1985).

Hallucinogens

Hallucinogens, or psychedelics, are drugs that produce illusions and hallucinations. Mescaline (peyote), lysergic acid diethylamide (LSD), phencyclidine (PCP), and MDMA (Ecstasy) produce mild to profound psychological effects, depending on the dosage. Mescaline or peyote—the earliest hallucinogen used in North America—was consumed during ancient Native American religious celebrations.

In the 1960s, LSD became a well-known hallucinogen because of Timothy Leary's widely publicized advice, "Turn on, tune in, drop out." LSD is one of the most powerful of the psychoactive drugs; a tiny dose (10 micrograms) of the odourless, tasteless, and colourless drug can produce dramatic, highly unpredictable psychological effects for up to 12 hours. These effects are often referred to as a *psychedelic trip*, and users report experiences ranging from the beautiful (a good trip) to the frightening and extremely depressing (a bad trip). Consequently, some LSD users take the drug only with the companionship of others who

are familiar with the drug's effects. However, some studies have found that there is a possibility of *flashbacks* in which the user re-experiences the effects of the drug as much as a year after it was taken. Most long-term psychiatric problems associated with the drug involve people who were unaware that they had been given LSD, who showed unstable personality characteristics before taking the drug, or who experienced it under hostile or threatening circumstances (Levinthal 1996).

Among the most recent hallucinogens are PCP ("angel dust") and MDMA (Ecstasy). PCP can be taken orally, intravenously, or by inhalation, but it is most often smoked. Initially, PCP was used as an anesthetic in surgical procedures, but it was removed from production when patients who received it showed signs of agitation, intense anxiety, hallucinations, and disorientation. Production then went underground, and PCP became a relatively inexpensive street drug that some dealers pass off as a more expensive drug, such as LSD, to unknowing customers.

In the mid-1980s, MDMA (Ecstasy) hit the street market. Manufactured in clandestine labs by inexperienced chemists, Ecstasy, or "E," is a "designer drug" that is derived from amphetamines and has hallucinogenic effects. Users claim that it produces a state of relaxation, insight, euphoria, and heightened awareness without the side effects of LSD. Ecstasy has a high abuse potential and no recognized medical use (Milkman and Sunderwirth 1987). Table 8.4 shows that 2.9, 2.2, and 4.1 percent of students reported using LSD, PCP, and Ecstasy respectively in the past year (2003).

Inhalants

Inhalants are products that people inhale to get high. Commonly available products that are used as inhalants include gasoline, glue, paints, cleaning fluids, and toiletries. Inhalants are often called solvents because so many of them are used as inhalants. Inhalant abuse is common because inhalants are inexpensive, easy to obtain, and fast acting. They contain poisonous chemicals that can make abusers sick, damage their nerve and brain cells, and even kill them. As with many kinds of substance abuse, precise figures about use are either unavailable or questionable. However, Table 8.4

shows that 6.1 percent of students used solvents in 2003. While inhalant abuse is found in all ethnic groups in Canada, news stories suggest it is very prevalent among Indigenous children and adolescents. A study that shows a higher prevalence of inhalant use by Indigenous than White adolescents was conducted by psychologists Barbara Gfellner and John Hundleby (1995). In a survey of students (grades 7 to 12; N = 2353 White and 237 Indigenous adolescents in 1993) in a non-metropolitan centre in midwestern Canada, they found that a higher percentage of Indigenous than White adolescents sniffed glue (4.3 percent vs. 3.5 percent) and solvents (6.4 percent vs. 3.5 percent) in 1993 (Gfellner and Hundleby 1995). The usual explanation for this difference is a perception of a lack of opportunities for Indigenous adolescents.

Overall Harm from Drug Use

Table 8.5 shows the percentage of Canadians reporting harm to themselves because of illicit drug use, according to the CAS. Overall, 17.5 percent of Canadians reported harm in the past year from their drug use. Little difference was found between men and women for the last year, but a higher percentage of men reported a lifetime harm. A higher percentage of younger than older Canadians reported harm. A higher percentage of lesser-educated and lowest income adequacy reported harm.

EXPLANATIONS OF DRUG ABUSE

Why do people abuse drugs? Various explanations have been given. Some focus on biological factors; others emphasize environmental influences. Social scientists believe that drug abuse is associated with continuous and cumulative influences from the time of conception throughout the life course (Fishbein and Pease 1996). Thus, to answer the question of why people abuse drugs, we must examine the intertwining biological, psychological, and sociological factors that affect people's behaviour.

TABLE 8.5 Percentage Reporting One or More Harms from One's Own Drug Use: Past Year and Lifetime

	Past-year harm %	Lifetime harm %
Total	17.5	23.8
Sex	NS	***
Female (comparison group)	16.0	19.8
Male	18.4	27.2
Age Group (comparison group is previous age group)	***	***
15–17	29.9	37.6
18–19	30.6	43.6
20–24	18.2	29.9
25–34	13.1	25.4
35–44	15.8	22.5
45–54	10.6	18.8
55–64	3.1	16.7
65+	S	5.2
Marital Status	**	***
Married/partnered (comparison group)	11.0	18.8
Divorced/separated/widowed	16.2	22.9
Single/never married	21.7	31.5
Education	***	***
Less than secondary (comparison group)	28.5	35.5
Secondary	24.3	26.8
Some post-secondary	11.2	22.3
University degree	9.4	17.1
Income Adequacy	NS	***
Lowest (comparison group)	18.9	36.3
Middle	17.7	25.0
Highest	13.1	17.8
Not stated	22.0	24.9
Location of Household	NS	NS
Rural (comparison group)	21.3	22.1
Non-rural	17.0	24.2

Notes: For lifetime harm, percentages are of current and former drug users; for past-year harm, percentages are of current drug users; drugs used include any of the following 8: cannabis, cocaine, speed, hallucinogens, ecstasy, inhalants, heroin, and steroids.

S—estimate suppressed due to high sampling variability

Source: Canadian Addiction Survey (CAS), 2005, A National Survey of Canadians' Use of Alcohol and Other Drugs: Prevalence of Use and Related Harms: Detailed Report. Ottawa: Canadian Centre on Substance Abuse.

Biological Explanations

Some biological explanations of alcohol and other drug addiction focus on genetic factors. Some studies of alcoholism have found that children who have an alcoholic birth parent have a higher than normal risk of becoming alcoholics themselves, even if they are adopted at birth and reared by non-alcoholic parents. These studies suggest that the child of an alcoholic parent inherits a biological predisposition (or vulnerability) to problem drinking or alcoholism. For example, the child may inherit increased sensitivity to alcohol as indicated by impaired enzyme production, brain function, and physiological responsivity during alcohol intake. The child also may inherit cognitive or learning impairments (e.g., hyperactivity, attention deficit disorder, or language delay) or psychological features (e.g., impulsivity, sensation seeking, anxiety, or aggressiveness) that increase the risk of alcohol abuse by exaggerating the rewarding biological and psychological properties of alcohol (Fishbein and Pease 1996).

Other biological studies focus on the relationship between the brain and drug addiction. These studies have found convincing evidence that drugs such as alcohol, heroin, and cocaine act directly on the brain mechanisms responsible for reward and punishment. As the drugs stimulate the areas of the brain that create the sensation of pleasure and suppress the perception of pain, the user receives reinforcement to engage in further drug-taking behaviour.

According to these findings, then, drugs that provide an immediate rush or intense euphoria (e.g., cocaine and heroin) are more likely to be abused than drugs that do not. Similarly, drugs that produce pleasant but rapidly dissipating effects (e.g., alcohol) tend to encourage users to take additional doses to maintain the pleasurable effects. Biological explanations provide some insights on drug abuse, but biological factors alone do not fully explain alcoholism and other drug dependency.

PSYCHOLOGICAL EXPLANATIONS

Psychological explanations of drug abuse focus on either personality disorders or the effects of social learning and reinforcement on drug-taking behaviour. Some studies have found that personality disorders—antisocial personality, psychopathy, impulsivity, affective disorder, and anxiety, among others—are more common among drug abusers than among non-abusers (Shedler and Block 1990). Hyperactivity, learning disabilities, and behavioural disorders in childhood are also associated with a greater risk of substance abuse in adolescence or young adulthood. When people have low self-esteem or lack motivation, their desire to get away from problems is intensified, and drugs often provide the most available option for escape.

Social psychologists explain drug behaviour in terms of social learning. According to *social learning theory,* drug and alcohol use and abuse are behaviours that are acquired and sustained through a learning process. Learning takes place through instrumental conditioning (positive reinforcement or punishment) and modelling (imitation) of other people's behaviour. Every person learns attitudes, orientations, and general information about drug use from family members, friends, and significant others, so he or she comes to associate positive consequences (positive reinforcement) and negative consequences (punishment) with drug use. Therefore, whether the person abstains from, takes, or abuses drugs depends on the past, present, and anticipated rewards and punishments he or she associates with abstinence, use, or abuse. In a nutshell, the more an individual defines drug behaviour as good, or at least excusable, the more that person is likely to use drugs (Akers 1992).

The Interactionist Perspective

Like social psychologists, sociologists who use an interactionist framework believe that drug behaviour is learned behaviour that is strongly influenced by families, peers, and other people. In other words, individuals are more likely to use or abuse drugs if they have frequent, intense, and long-lasting interactions with people who use or abuse drugs. For example, some children learn to abuse alcohol or other drugs by watching their parents drink excessively or use illegal drugs. Other young people learn about drug use from their peer group. In his classic study of marijuana users, sociologist Howard S. Becker (1963) concluded that drug users learn not only how to "do" drugs from other users but also what pleasurable reactions they should expect to have from drug use.

People also are more prone to accept attitudes and behaviours favourable to drug use if they spend time with members of a *drug subculture*—**a group of people whose attitudes, beliefs, and behaviours pertaining to drug use differ significantly from those of most people in the larger society.** Over time, people in heavy-drinking or drug subcultures tend to become closer to others within their subculture and more distant from people outside the subculture. Given this, participants in hard-core drug subcultures quit taking drugs or drinking excessively only when something brings about a dramatic change in their attitudes, beliefs, and values regarding drugs. Although it is widely believed that most addicts could change their behaviour if they chose to do so, *labelling theory* suggests that it is particularly difficult for individuals to discontinue alcohol and other drug abuse once they have been labelled "alcoholics" or "drug addicts." Because of the prevailing ideology that alcoholism and drug addiction are personal problems rather than social problems, individuals tend to be held solely responsible for their behaviour.

The Functionalist Perspective

Why does the level of drug abuse remain high in Canada? Functionalists point out that there is virtually no society in which people do not use drugs of some kind (Schlaadt 1992). Drugs contribute to many rituals, like weddings and other celebrations, and some drugs, like alcohol, are often a part of daily mealtimes. Other functionalists would suggest that social institutions such as the family, education, and religion, which previously kept deviant behaviour such as excessive or illicit drug use in check, have become fragmented and somewhat disorganized. Because they have, it is now necessary to use formal mechanisms of social control to prohibit people from taking illegal drugs or driving under the influence of alcohol or other drugs. External controls in the form of law enforcement are also required to discourage people from growing, manufacturing, or importing illegal substances.

Functionalists believe that activities in society continue because they serve important societal functions. Prescription and over-the-counter drugs, for example, are functional for patients because they ease pain, cure illness, and sometimes enhance or extend life. They are functional for doctors because they provide a means for treating illness and help to justify the doctor's fee. They are functional for pharmacists because they provide a source of employment; without pills to dispense, there would be no need for pharmacists. But dysfunctions also occur with prescription drugs: Patients may experience adverse side effects or develop a psychological dependence on the drug; doctors, pharmacists, and drug companies may be sued because they manufactured, prescribed, or sold a drug that is alleged to cause bodily harm to users.

Illicit drugs also have functions and dysfunctions. On the one hand, the illicit drug trade creates and perpetuates jobs at all levels of the criminal justice system, in the federal government, in social service agencies that deal with problems of alcoholism and drug addiction, and in criminology departments. What, for example, would employees in various police services do if Canada did not have an array of illicit drugs that are defined as the "drug problem"? On the other hand, the dysfunctions of illicit drug use extend throughout society. At the individual level, addictive drugs such as heroin, cocaine, and barbiturates create severe physical and mental health problems as well as economic crises for addicts, their families, and acquaintances. At the societal level, drug abuse contributes to loss of productivity, human potential and life expectancy, and money. Hundreds of millions of dollars in taxpayers' money that might be used for education or preventive health care are spent making and enforcing drug laws and dealing with drug-related crime and the spread of AIDS by addicts who shoot up with contaminated needles. Addiction to illegal drugs, the abuse of legal drugs, and the abuse of alcohol and tobacco exacerbate the loss of human potential and undermine the stability of society.

The Conflict Perspective

According to conflict theorists, people in positions of economic and political power make the sale, use, and possession of drugs abused by the poor and the powerless illegal. We mentioned earlier that opium smoking was outlawed because it was associated with the Chinese. Restricting the drugs that members of a subordinate racialized/ethnic group use is one method of suppressing the group and limiting its ability to threaten dominant group members or gain upward mobility in

This man may be playing double jeopardy with his life. The purity of street drugs often is in doubt, and shooting up with contaminated needles is a significant source of new AIDS cases in Canada.

society (Fishbein and Pease 1996). Those who control the nation's political and legal apparatus decide whether a drug is legal or illegal.

Conflict theorists also point out that powerful corporate interests perpetuate the use and abuse of legal drugs. Corporations that manufacture, market, and sell alcohol, tobacco, and pharmaceuticals reap huge profits from products that exact a heavy toll on the personal health and well-being of abusers, their families and communities, and the larger society. Using their wealth and political clout, elites in Canadian tobacco companies have spent years vigorously fighting measures to discourage smoking. As mentioned above, tobacco companies plan to challenge the *Tobacco Act*. Since sales of tobacco products are approximately $4 billion per year, tobacco companies are not likely to give up the fight.

The Feminist Perspective

Feminist theorists point out that a significant part of the explanation of drug abuse by women has to do with women's vulnerability and disadvantaged position in society. Chapter 4, "Gender Inequality," has shown many forms of inequality, such as vulnerability to sexual and spousal abuse, the wage gap and fewer promotional opportunities, and the second shift. To deal with the feelings these forms of inequality bring about, women sometimes turn to drug abuse. "Women use drugs to cope, to deal with stress, to nurture themselves, to escape from the pain of past events or of their current status, or to continue their social roles" (Harrison 1997:230.

A feminist approach to the problem emphasizes the different types of drug abuse by males and females. Data presented above showed that males are much more likely to use alcohol and illicit drugs than females, and females are more likely to use licit, psychotherapeutic drugs than males. Several hypotheses have been suggested to account for gender differences in health behaviour. Two hypotheses that help to explain the differences in drug taking are the risk-taking behaviour of men and the willingness of women to adopt the sick role (see Chapter 10 for a discussion of the sick role). Men are socialized to take risks and women are socialized to be more cautious and take care of their health (Waldron 1997). Thus, men would engage in risky behaviour like drinking or illicit drug use to solve problems (see Table 10.1: men show a higher rate of substance dependence than women), and women would seek out medical help and use prescription drugs for problems rather than engage in risky behaviour. On the other hand, the social acceptability hypothesis suggests that women are more willing than men to admit being sick, adopt a sick role, and accept medical help such as using drugs to deal with their problems (Gee and Kimball 1987).

THE FUTURE OF ALCOHOL AND DRUG ABUSE

How to prevent abuse of alcohol and other drugs and how to treat drug-related problems after they arise are controversial issues in contemporary society. What kinds of drug abuse prevention programs are available? Will future treatment programs for alcoholics and drug addicts differ from the ones that are available today? In Canada, the federal government has developed a comprehensive strategy—*Canada's Drug Strategy* (Health Canada 1998)—to reduce both the supply of and demand for drugs. It consists of seven components: research/knowledge development; knowledge dissemination; prevention programming; treatment and rehabilitation; legislation, enforcement and control; national coordination; and international co-operation (Health Canada 1998:6).

Although most of this section will deal with prevention and treatment programming, it is important to note the other aspects of the overall strategy. First, research/knowledge development comprises undertaking and supporting literature reviews, large-scale quantitative studies, and community qualitative studies. Some of the results of that work have been presented above. Second, the dissemination of knowledge is also important; the government disseminates the results of its work and that of other national and international agencies. Third, a large part of the strategy is to prevent alcohol and drug abuse, and to this end the strategy supports direct law-enforcement procedures following the *Controlled Substances Act* that came into effect in May 1997. In addition, Canada has ratified United Nations conventions to deal with the obvious international nature of drug smuggling. According to Single and his colleagues (1996), the law enforcement costs in 1992 were $1.8 billion. However, since government estimates of the value of the illegal drug market were $7 to $10 billion (Porteous 1998), law enforcement to curtail the supply is not, alone, likely to be able to solve the drug problem.

Prevention Programs

Drug and alcohol prevention programs can be divided into three major categories: primary, secondary, and tertiary prevention. **Primary prevention refers to programs that seek to prevent drug problems before they begin.** Most primary prevention programs focus on people who have had little or no previous experience with drugs. In contrast, *secondary prevention* programs seek to limit the extent of drug abuse, prevent the spread of drug abuse to substances beyond those already experienced, and teach strategies for the responsible use of licit drugs such as alcohol (Levinthal 1996). For example, a program directed at college students who already consume alcohol might focus on how to drink responsibly by emphasizing the dangers of drinking and driving. Finally, *tertiary prevention* programs seek to limit relapses by individuals recovering from alcoholism or drug addiction. The purpose of tertiary prevention is to ensure that people who have entered treatment for

some form of drug abuse become free of drugs and remain that way.

Prevention, according to *Canada's Drug Strategy*, is best done through a combination of public awareness campaigns, educational resources, training of service providers, and community action (Health Canada 1998:7). The programs should be part of every year's school curriculum, should involve students in planning and conducting presentations, and should present honest factual material about why people use drugs and give alternatives to their use.

Scare tactics and negative-education programs do not work; they turn students off and do not achieve their desired goal. In fact, scare tactics appear to pique some students' curiosity about drugs rather than deter their use. Objective information programs often begin in kindergarten and progress through grade 12. Using texts, curriculum guides, videos, and other materials, teachers impart factual information about drugs to students, but as with scare tactics, students sometimes become more—instead of less—interested in drug experimentation. An 18-year-old student who smoked his first marijuana joint at age 13 explains why he thinks these programs are ineffective: "When someone tells you not to do it, that makes you want to do it even more" (Kolata 1996a:A12).

Comprehensive programs that include school-based and peer-conducted smoking education programs for students combined with community-based smoking cessation programs for adults are more promising than single preventive strategies. Such a comprehensive program was found to be effective in an experiment in North Karelia, Finland. After a 15-year follow-up, mean lifetime cigarette consumption was 22 percent lower among program subjects than among control subjects (Vartiainen et al. 1998).

Self-esteem enhancement and affective-education programs can be effective also. They focus on the underlying emotional and attitudinal factors that are involved in drug abuse while building character through teaching positive social values and attitudes. These programs are most effective when they, too, are incorporated into more comprehensive prevention programs.

If the purpose of prevention programs is to reduce actual drug-taking behaviour, what types of programs have the greatest likelihood of success? Many social analysts suggest that family- and school-based primary and secondary prevention programs are the most effective. Previously, some prevention programs focused on high-school students, but today elementary schools are among the first lines of attack because drug-taking behaviour now starts at younger ages. Many public schools have a program known as DARE (Drug Abuse Resistance Education), which is taught by specially trained police officers who teach children how to resist drugs. Critics suggest that police officers, whom many young people view as authority figures, are not the best people to teach adolescents that drug use is not cool. Critics also note that one-shot programs that are forced on students may not prevent drug abuse. Children who have been through the DARE program are no less likely to smoke, drink, or use other drugs than children who have not been through the program (Kolata 1996a).

Future prevention programs will be family-, school-, and community-based. They will offer alternative activities and outlets to drug use. These programs—like other drug abuse prevention efforts—will take into account issues that affect people differently depending on their racialization/ethnicity, religion, or other factors. Reaching across lines of racialization, class, and gender, the next generation of drug abuse prevention programs will use cable television channels to make people aware of the effects of drugs on the human body and how to get help in dealing with alcoholism and drug addiction. The internet will become a vital source of information. Current websites provide an array of information on drugs and offer unique features such as an online dictionary of street drug slang.

Future prevention programs provide cause for optimism, but only if social structural factors change. If illegal drugs continue to flow into Canada and television, other mass media, and advertising continues to glamorize smoking, drinking, and other drug use, the future of preventive programs is bleak. Without social change, efforts will be directed toward apprehension and incarceration of drug offenders and treatment programs for drug addicts and alcoholics, not at primary or secondary prevention strategies.

Treatment Programs

Tertiary prevention programs are programs that aim to ensure that people who have sought help for some form of drug abuse remain drug-free. It follows from the biological and social learning explanations for substance abuse and alcohol addiction that treatment must deal with the body's physiological and psychological responses. Therefore, *alcohol and drug treatment* involves the use of activities designed to eliminate physical and psychological addiction and to prevent relapse—returning to abuse and/or addiction (Fishbein and Pease 1996). Most treatment programs are based on a medical model or therapeutic community.

The Medical Treatment Model

The *medical treatment model* considers drug abuse and alcoholism to be medical problems that must be resolved through medical treatment by medical officials. Treatment may take the form of *aversion therapy* or *behavioural conditioning.* For example, drugs such as Cyclazocine and Nalozone are given to heroin and opiate addicts to prevent the euphoric feeling that they associate with taking the drugs. Supposedly, when the pleasure is gone, the person will no longer abuse the drug. Some heroin addicts also receive methadone detoxification to alleviate withdrawal symptoms associated with stopping heroin use. Over a one- to three-week period, the patient receives decreasing doses of methadone, a synthetic opium derivative that blocks the desire for heroin but does not have its negative side effects.

Antabuse is used in the treatment of alcoholism. After the person has been detoxified and no alcohol remains in the bloodstream, Antabuse is administered along with small quantities of alcohol for several consecutive days. Because this combination produces negative effects such as nausea and vomiting, the individual eventually develops an aversion to drinking, which becomes associated with uncomfortable physical symptoms. Although the medical treatment model works for some people, it is criticized for focusing on the physiological effects of alcohol and drug dependency and not dealing with the psychological and sociological aspects of dependency.

Short- and Long-Term Services and the Therapeutic Community

According to a booklet entitled *Alcohol and Drug Treatment in Ontario: A Guide for Helping Professionals,* published by the Centre for Addiction and Mental Health, many short- and long-term services (both live-at-home and live-in) are available (at no charge, except for some specialized services) for people seeking help with addictions. (The authors acknowledge that some services may not be locally available.) Short-term services include withdrawal management (detox) services, which give people a place to stay while their bodies get rid of alcohol or drugs and adapt to a drug-free state, and services that provide a place to stay for a month and insight into leading a healthy life.

When substance abusers are perceived to have an underlying psychological problem, treatment generally involves long-term services like counselling, rehabilitation, and/or the therapeutic community. Counselling often employs rehabilitated alcoholics or addicts who encourage participants to take more responsibility for their lives so that they can function better in the community. Some counselling and rehabilitation programs take place on an outpatient basis or as day treatment; others involve residential treatment. *Outpatient programs* allow drug abusers to remain at home and continue working while attending regular group and individual meetings. *Day treatment* takes place in a hospital setting where the abuser participates in day-long treatment groups and individual counselling sessions and returns home in the evening. The *therapeutic community approach* is based on the idea that drug abuse is best treated by intensive individual and group counselling in a residential setting. Residential treatment takes place in a special house or dormitory where alcoholics or drug addicts remain for periods of time ranging from several months to more than a year while they learn to rebuild their lives without alcohol or drugs.

Perhaps the best-known non-residential therapeutic communities are Alcoholics Anonymous (AA), founded in 1935, and its offshoot, Narcotics Anonymous (NA). Both AA and NA provide members with support in their efforts to overcome drug dependence and addiction. AA was established in 1935 in the United States by two alcoholics who were seeking a way of returning to sober life (Fishbein and Pease 1996). Today, the organization has more than 4800 chapters with more than 95 000 members in Canada (Alcoholics Anonymous 1998). Members use only their first names to ensure

anonymity, and recovering alcoholics serve as sponsors and counsellors for others. AA and NA are based on a 12-step program that requires members to acknowledge that they are alcoholics or drug addicts who must have the help of God and other people to remain sober or drug-free. Group support is central to success in these programs, as journalist Caroline Knapp (1996:253–254) explains:

> A few months after my one-year anniversary [of sobriety] I went to the meeting . . . on the ground floor of a church . . . . One person tells his or her story for the first half-hour, and then the meeting opens up, first to those in their first month of sobriety, then to those with three months or less, then six months or less, and so on. . . . At the end of the meeting there was a presentation for a young guy named John, who was celebrating one year without a drink. . . . He was so happy that evening, so grateful to get that one-year medallion, and so moved by the amount of support he'd gotten over the year, that his eyes welled up and his voice kept cracking. "I can't thank you all enough," he said, and his face was the picture of hope. . . . Then I had an image of every person in that room . . . getting into our beds clean and sober, another day without a drink behind us. It was a simple image but it filled me with a range of complicated feelings: appreciation for the simple presence of all those people; admiration for their courage and strength; a tinge of melancholy for the amount of pain it must have taken each and every one of them to put down the drink; affection for their humanity. I didn't realize until hours later that there was a name for that feeling. It's called love.

Various other types of testimonials are available at the Alcoholics Anonymous website, including a statement by co-founder Bill W. at **www.aa.org/ bigbookonline**.

Sociologists believe AA is successful because it gives former alcoholics the opportunity to be delabelled as stigmatized deviants and relabelled as former and repentant deviants. It should be kept in mind, however, that social class and personality factors affect people's ability to enter into the repentant role, which requires the participant to publicly admit guilt and repentance and to interact successfully with others in the program (Trice and Roman 1970).

All the approaches for reducing alcohol and drug abuse that we have discussed can help certain individuals, but none address what to do about social structural factors that contribute to the drug problem. Because drug- and alcohol-related problems and their solutions are part of deeper social issues and struggles, they cannot be dealt with in isolation, as social scientist Philippe Bourgeois (1995:319, 327) explains:

> Drugs are not the root of the problems . . . they are the expression of deeper, structural dilemmas. Self-destructive addiction is merely the medium for desperate people to internalize their frustrations, resistance, and powerlessness. . . . Instead we should focus our ethical concerns and political energies on the contradictions posed by the persistence of inner-city poverty in the midst of extraordinary opulence. . . . The economic base of the traditional working class has eroded throughout the country. Greater proportions of the population are socially marginalized. The restructuring of the world economy by multinational corporations, finance capital, and digital electronic technology, as well as the exhaustion of social democratic models for public sector intervention [e.g., welfare programs] on behalf of the poor, has escalated inequalities around class, ethnicity, and gender. . . . There is no technocratic solution. Any long-term paths out of the quagmire will have to address the structural and political-economic roots, as well as the ideological and cultural roots of social marginalization. The first step out of the impasse, however, requires a fundamental ethical and political reevaluation of basic socioeconomic models and human values.

If Canada sets out to reduce inequalities in all areas of social life, perhaps the drug problem will be alleviated

as well. What do you think it would take to make this happen?

WHAT CAN YOU DO?

- Volunteer at an agency such as Mothers Against Drunk Driving (MADD) or, if a local chapter exists, Students Against Drunk Driving (SADD). If a local chapter does not exist, contact MADD at **www.madd.ca** about founding a chapter.

- Participate in or organize a committee for challenging the various kinds of drug companies and their influence on universities. In Chapter 10, reference is made to students at the University of Toronto supporting Doctors for Research Integrity, through sponsoring an open forum. Since the influence of pharmaceutical companies on research practices is likely to be a continuing problem, much scope exists for future educational programs.

- Develop an educational program to help students stop binge drinking. Generally, the peer-initiated programs have better results. Several years ago, students at colleges in Ontario undertook a promotional campaign based on the slogan, "If you drink, don't bowl," based on the double meaning of *bowl* as a game and a place to vomit (toilet bowl). Try to devise a new catchy and effective slogan for your program. You might include some first-aid suggestions for dealing with consequences of binge drinking.

- Study the way students use prescription medicines, not only antidepressants, but also diet pills and stimulants, and study the relationship between alcohol consumption and acquaintance or date rape.

- Design a program to alert students, particularly women, to the problems of excessive body-consciousness (see also Chapter 10) as well as the need to use drugs with particular care when on dates.

SUMMARY

WHAT ARE THE MAJOR PATTERNS OF DRINKING?

Social scientists divide long-term drinking patterns into four categories: (1) *social drinkers* consume alcoholic beverages primarily on social occasions and may drink either occasionally or relatively frequently; (2) *heavy drinkers* are more frequent drinkers who typically consume greater quantities of alcohol when they drink and are more likely to become intoxicated; (3) *acute alcoholics* have trouble controlling their use of alcohol and plan their schedule around drinking; and, (4) *chronic alcoholics* have lost control over their drinking and tend to engage in compulsive behaviour.

WHAT ARE THE MAJOR HAZARDS ASSOCIATED WITH TOBACCO USE?

Nicotine is a toxic, dependency-producing drug that is responsible for about 37 000 deaths per year in Canada. People who smoke have a greater likelihood of developing cardiovascular disease, lung cancer, and/or cancer of the larynx, mouth, and esophagus. Even those who do not smoke may be subjected to the hazard of environmental tobacco smoke—the smoke in the air as a result of other people's tobacco smoking. Infants born to women who smoke typically have lower-than-average birth weights and sometimes have slower rates of physical and mental growth.

WHAT PROBLEMS ARE ASSOCIATED WITH USE OF PRESCRIPTION AND OVER-THE-COUNTER DRUGS?

Some prescription drugs have the potential for short-term abuse and long-term psychological and physical dependence. This form of dependency is known as *iatrogenic addiction*—drug dependency that results from physician-supervised treatment for a recognized medical disorder. Over-the-counter drugs, which are widely advertised and readily available, may be dangerous when combined with alcohol or other drugs.

IN CANADA, WHAT ARE THE MAJOR STIMULANT DRUGS?

Cocaine and amphetamines are the major stimulant drugs abused in Canada. Cocaine is an extremely potent and dependency-producing stimulant drug. Amphetamines can be obtained legally in the form of diet pills and pep formulas when they are prescribed by a physician.

WHAT ARE DEPRESSANTS AND WHAT HEALTH-RELATED RISK DO THEY POSE?

As the name indicates, depressants depress the central nervous system; they also may have some pain-killing properties. The most common depressants are barbiturates and anti-anxiety drugs or tranquilizers. Users may develop both physical addiction and psychological dependency on these drugs. There is also the risk of *potentiation*—the drug interaction that takes place when two drugs are mixed together and the combination produces a far greater effect than that of either drug administered separately.

HOW DO BIOLOGICAL AND PSYCHOLOGICAL PERSPECTIVES VIEW ALCOHOL AND DRUG ADDICTION?

Biological explanations of alcohol and drug addiction focus on inherited biological factors and on the effects of drugs on the human brain. Psychological explanations of drug abuse focus on personality disorders and the effects of social learning and reinforcement on people's drug-taking behaviour.

HOW DO SOCIOLOGICAL PERSPECTIVES VIEW ALCOHOL AND DRUG ADDICTION?

Interactionists believe that drug use and abuse are learned behaviours that are strongly influenced by families, peers, and others who serve as role models. People are more prone to accept attitudes and behaviours that are favourable to drug use if they spend time with members of a drug subculture. Functionalists believe that drug-related problems have increased as social institutions such as the family, schools, and religious institutions have become fragmented and somewhat disorganized. However, use of alcohol and other drugs serves important functions, even though some aspects of drug use are dysfunctional for society. According to conflict theorists, people in positions of economic and political power are responsible for making the sale, use, and possession of some drugs illegal. Conflict theorists also point out that powerful corporate interests perpetuate the use and abuse of alcohol, tobacco, and other legal drugs. Feminist theorists emphasize the vulnerability and disadvantaged position of women who abuse drugs.

WHAT IS THE PURPOSE OF PREVENTION AND TREATMENT PROGRAMS?

Primary prevention programs seek to prevent drug problems before they begin. Secondary prevention programs seek to limit the extent of drug abuse, prevent the spread of drug abuse to other substances beyond the drugs already experienced, and teach strategies for the responsible use of licit drugs such as alcohol. Tertiary prevention programs seek to limit relapses by individuals recovering from alcoholism or drug addiction. They may be based either on a medical model or the therapeutic community. The best-known therapeutic community is Alcoholics Anonymous (AA).

WHAT OTHER FACTORS MUST BE TAKEN INTO ACCOUNT IN EFFORTS TO REDUCE THE DRUG PROBLEM?

Alcoholism and drug abuse are intertwined with other social problems, such as dramatic changes in the economic and technological bases of society, the growing gap between the rich and poor, and inequalities based on racialization/ethnicity and gender.

KEY TERMS

codependency, p. 209
drug, p. 205
drug addiction (drug dependency), p. 205
drug subculture, p. 222
environmental tobacco smoke, p. 211

fetal alcohol effects (FAE), p. 208
fetal alcohol syndrome (FAS), p. 208
primary prevention, p. 224
tolerance, p. 205
withdrawal, p. 206

QUESTIONS FOR CRITICAL THINKING

1. Does public tolerance of alcohol and tobacco lead to increased use of these drugs? Why do many people view the use of alcohol and tobacco differently from the use of illicit drugs?

2. If stimulants, depressants, hallucinogens, and inhalants have such potentially hazardous side effects, why do so many people use these drugs? If drug enforcement policies were more stringently enforced, would there be less drug abuse in this country?

3. As a sociologist, how would you propose to deal with the drug problem in Canada? If you were called upon to revamp existing drug laws and policies, what, if any, changes would you make in them?

4. How have changes in technology affected the problem of alcohol and drug abuse over the past century? How have changes in the global economy affected drug-related problems in this country and others?

WEBLINKS

Alcoholics Anonymous

www.alcoholics-anonymous.org

Alcoholics Anonymous is a self-help group with chapters throughout the world to help people and their friends and relatives addicted to alcohol.

Canadian Centre on Substance Abuse

www.ccsa.ca

This non-profit organization works to minimize the harm associated with the use of alcohol, tobacco, and other drugs. Available from the home page are links to current topics, resources, statistics, and networks.

Centre for Addiction and Mental Health

www.camh.net

The Centre for Addiction and Mental Health is a public hospital providing direct patient care for people with mental-health and addiction problems. The centre is also a research facility (**www.camh.net/Research/ index.html**), an education centre (**www.camh.net/ ets/index.html**), and a community organization providing health promotion and prevention services, and it is a collaborator with world health bodies.

Health Canada: Drug Strategy and Controlled Substances

www.hc-sc.gc.ca/ahc-asc/branch-dirgen/ hecs-dgsesc/dscsp-psasc/index_e.html

Health Canada's Drug Strategy and Controlled Substances Program regulates controlled substances and promotes initiatives that reduce or prevent the harm associated with these substances and alcohol. The program also provides expert advice and drug analysis services to law enforcement agencies across the country. A link is also available for tobacco control.

Medical Marijuana in Canada

www.hc-sc.gc.ca/dhp-mps/marihuana/ index_e.html

Health Canada's site for information, such as how to apply, law enforcement issues, ongoing research, Health Canada's supply and stakeholders statistics.

Mothers Against Drunk Driving (MADD)

www.madd.ca

This site presents information about MADD and its programs, its library, and ways you can help.

Narcotics Anonymous

www.na.org

Narcotics Anonymous is a world service to help people learn about and control their addiction to narcotics.

9

CRIME AND CRIMINAL JUSTICE

CRIME AS A SOCIAL PROBLEM
    Problems with Official Statistics
    Defining Crime and Delinquency

TYPES OF CRIMES
    Violent Crime
    Property Crime
    Crime Comparisons between Canada and the United States
    Occupational (White-Collar) Crime
    Corporate Crime
    Organized Crime
    Box 9.1 Social Problems in Global Perspective: Organized Crime: The Global Empire
    Youth Crime

WHO COMMITS CRIMES AND WHO IS VICTIMIZED?

BIOLOGICAL AND PSYCHOLOGICAL EXPLANATIONS OF CRIME

Biological Explanations
Psychological Explanations

SOCIOLOGICAL EXPLANATIONS OF CRIME
    The Functionalist Perspective
    The Conflict Perspective
    The Interactionist Perspective
    Feminist Perspectives

THE CRIMINAL JUSTICE SYSTEM
    The Police
    The Courts
    Punishment and the Prisons
    Box 9.2: Social Problems and Social Policy: Plea Bargains and Later Restrictions: The Case of Karla Homolka
    Restorative Justice
    The Death Penalty
    Box 9.3 Social Problems and Social Policy: To Collect or Not Collect Racialization and Ethnicity Statistics

WHAT CAN YOU DO?

The video surveillance of public streets that the RCMP is carrying out in Kelowna is not necessary. There is no evidence that it is effective or is likely to be effective.

Privacy Commissioner George Radwanski, who launched a lawsuit in the Supreme Court of British Columbia, believed the cameras violated the Charter's guarantee of the right to privacy (quoted in Lunman 2002:A1)

The RCMP continually seeks to find appropriate means to ensure and increase public safety and security, be that through police or community-based initiatives.

RCMP Sergeant Paul Marsh, in reply to Privacy Commissioner George Radwanski (quoted in Lunman 2002:A8)

After the discovery of the images of four alleged suicide bombers before and on the day of the bombings, July 7, 2005, London's Police Chief Sir Ian Blair said that Britain's four million closed-circuit TVs' results speak for themselves (Byrne 2005:A9).

The placing of cameras in what criminologists call "hot spots" (Sherman et al. 1989) is a way of deterring *routine activities crime*, **crime that occurs when a motivated offender finds a suitable target in the absence of suitable guardianship.** Some researchers suggest that crime that would be deterred by the cameras would, like street prostitution, just move to another location. In early August 2005, Canadians were asked in a Globe CTV poll conducted by the Strategic Counsel if they would support having video cameras in public places: 72 percent supported or strongly supported it and 25 percent opposed or strongly opposed it ("Do Canadians Feel Secure?" 2004). What do you think? Would you feel safer with surveillance cameras in public places?

In this chapter you will learn about the problem of defining crime and measuring crime with official statistics or victimization surveys; the level of various kinds of crime (e.g., violent, property, and youth crime) and how the levels of some of these crimes in Canada compare to those in the United States. You will also learn about the nature of occupational and organized crime; why people commit crimes (the biological, psychological, and sociological explanations of crime); and the nature of the criminal justice system. The chapter concludes with some suggestions for ways you might help deal with the problem of crime.

CRIME AS A SOCIAL PROBLEM

Many people in Canada fear crime and are somewhat obsessed with it even though they have no direct daily exposure to criminal behaviour. Their information about crime comes from the media (Chermak 1995) and sometimes from watching real-crime dramas such as *America's Most Wanted* (sightings by Canadians have led to the arrest of a few of the suspects). They are also influenced by fictionalized crime stories on television, such as *DaVinci's Inquest*. Media coverage of crime is extensive, but it is not because crime is increasing.

With the exception of the rate of serious and violent crime, which has continued to fall during the last 10 years, crime rates have remained relatively stable over the past two decades. That is not to say that crime isn't a problem. Crime statistics tell only part of the story. Crime *is* a significant social problem because it endangers people's lives, property, and sense of well-being. In 1999, about 25 percent of Canadians over the age of 15 were victims of at least one crime, for a total of 8.3 million incidents (Besserer and Trainor 2000:1). Since approximately $10 billion, or three cents of every tax dollar, was spent on police, courts, corrections, legal aid, and criminal prosecutions (figures for 1994–95 [CCJS 1999:3]), individuals who are not directly victimized by crime are harmed because they have to pay taxes to fight it.

Problems with Official Statistics

Over the past two decades, sophisticated computer-based information systems have not only improved rates of detection, apprehension, and conviction of offenders but also provided immediate access to millions of bits of information about crime, suspects, and offenders (Barlow 1996). The leading source of information on crimes reported in Canada is the *Uniform Crime Report* (UCR). The UCR was developed by Statistics Canada with the co-operation and assistance of the Canadian Association of Chiefs of Police. The survey became operational in 1962 and collects crime and traffic statistics reported by all police agencies in Canada. UCR data is based on reported crime substantiated by police investigation. It is made available by the Canadian Centre for Justice Statistics (CCJS) in its periodical *Juristat* (Logan 2001:13) for use in presentations such as this chapter. Since 1988, the UCR has been using an incident-based reporting system (collecting data on each criminal event, offender, and victim) instead of an aggregate system. It is thus providing a more complex portrait of crime in Canada. The crime rate reported here includes offences like homicide, assault, sexual assault, break and enter, robbery, theft, motor vehicle theft, and fraud. It does not include other violations, such as traffic and drug offences. In total, police reported 2.6 million of these types of criminal incidents in 2004 (see Table 9.2; Sauvé 2005:3).

How accurate are these crime statistics? Any answer to this question must take into account the fact that the statistics reflect only crimes that are reported to law enforcement agencies or that police officers see occur. According to the UCR, overall rates of crime (number of crimes per 100 000 people), which increased from the early 1960s to 1991, have decreased since then (see Figure 9.1).

This downward trend probably reflects several factors, including increasing job opportunities and a shift in population (see Chapter 5). The percentage of the Canadian population under age 26—the age group most likely to commit crimes—began to decline in 1992.

Because the number of crimes *reported* is not necessarily the number of crimes *committed,* Statistics Canada conducts victimization surveys, for example in the General Social Survey (GSS) of 2004, which surveyed 24 000 randomly selected households to identify victims of personal crimes (e.g., theft of personal property, break and enter, assault, sexual assault, robbery, motor vehicle theft, and hate), and to determine whether the crime was reported or not (see Chapter 1). These surveys indicate that the number of crimes committed is substantially higher than the number reported. Table 9.1 shows that the percentage of crimes reported to police ranged from less than 10 percent for sexual assault to over 50 percent for break and enter. The main reason given for not reporting crimes to police was that the incident was not considered significant enough. Victims of sexual assault reported seeking help from social services and support centres.

However, the GSS has limitations, too:

1. Responses are based on recall, and some people don't remember specifically when a crime occurred. (They are supposed to report on the previous 12 months.)

2. For various reasons, respondents may not be truthful.

3. The surveys focus on theft and assault and do not measure workplace crimes, such as embezzlement or bribery, and organized crime.

Defining Crime and Delinquency

Crime **is behaviour that violates the criminal law and is punishable by fine, jail term, or other negative sanctions.** There are two components to every crime: the act itself, and *criminal intent*—expressed in the concept of *mens rea*, meaning "guilty mind." An individual's intent in committing a crime may range from willful conduct (hiring someone to kill one's spouse) to an unintentional act of negligence that is defined as a crime (leaving a small child unattended in a locked automobile in extremely hot weather, resulting in the child's death).

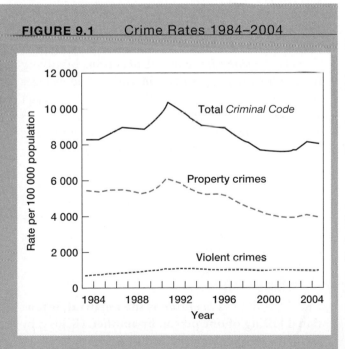

FIGURE 9.1   Crime Rates 1984–2004

Source: Statistics Canada, 2005, Juristat, *Catalogue Vol. 25, No. 5,* Crime Statistics in Canada, *July 21.*

TABLE 9.1   Self-Reported Victimization Incidents Reported to the Police, 2004[1,2]

	Total No. of Incidents	Incidents Reported to the Police[3]		Incidents Not Reported to the Police		Don't Know/ Not Stated	
	x 1000	x 1000	%	x 1000	%	x 1000	%
Total	7723	2613	34	4962	64	148	2
Total violent	2109	687	33	1381	66	41[E]	1[E]
Sexual assault	512	42[E]	8[E]	448	88	F	F
Robbery	274	127	46	144	53	F	F
Physical assault	1323	519	39	789	60	16[E]	1[E]
Total household	3206	1188	37	1958	61	59	2
Break and enter	505	275	54	223	44	7	1
Motor vehicle/parts theft	571	281	49	285	50	5	1
Theft household property	1136	330	29	786	69	20	2
Vandalism	993	303	31	664	67	26	3
Theft personal property	2408	738	31	1623	67	47[E]	2[E]

[E] Use with caution.

[F] Too unreliable to be published.

[1] Figures may not add to total due to rounding.

[2] Spousal violence incidents are excluded.

[3] Includes incidents reported by the victim or by someone else.

Source: Statistics Canada, 2005, "General Social Survey: Criminal Victimization," The Daily, *Catalogue 11-001, November 20.*

Criminal law is divided into two major categories: summary and indictable offences. ***Summary conviction offences* are relatively minor crimes that are punishable by a fine or less than a year in jail.** Examples include public unlawful assembly, theft ($5000 and under), and traffic violations. ***Indictable offences* are more serious crimes, such as murder or aggravated assault, that are punishable by more than a year's imprisonment.** Adolescents (12 to 17 years of age) who commit illegal or antisocial acts usually are adjudicated as *delinquent* or *youth crime* by a Youth Court Judge.

TYPES OF CRIMES

To make the study of crime—a large and complex subject—manageable, sociologists and criminologists categorize types of crime. In this section, we will look at six categories of crime: violent crime, property crime, occupational crime, corporate crime, organized crime, and youth crime. Table 9.2 shows the rate of particular crimes in 2004 and the percentage change since 1994.

Violent Crime

While it is well known to occur frequently in the United States, violent crime occurs much less frequently in Canada. ***Violent crime* consists of actions involving force or the threat of force against others** and includes homicide, attempted homicide, the three levels of assault and sexual assault, robbery, and other violent offences like criminal negligence causing death. Violent crimes are committed against people; non-violent crimes are usually committed against property. People tend to fear violent crime more than other kinds of crime because victims are often physically injured or even killed and because violent crime receives the most sustained attention from law enforcement officials and the media (see Parker 1995; Warr 1995).

Homicide

The *UCR* defines ***homicide* as the unlawful, intentional killing of one person by another.** (Killing by accident, in self-defence, or during wartime is not homicide.) By this definition, murder involves not only an unlawful act but also *malice aforethought*—the

TABLE 9.2   Crime Rates for Selected Offences, Canada, 2004

	Number of Crimes (2004)	Rate per 100 000 Population (2004)	% Change 2003–2004	% Change 1994–2004
Homicide	622	2	12.3	−5.3
Attempted murder	717	2	0.5	−29.4
Assaults (levels 1, 2, 3)	233 774	732	−2.2	−4.5
Other assaults	12 873	40	1.8	−18.1
Sexual assaults (levels 1, 2, 3)	23 534	74	−0.8	−32.6
Other sexual offences	2 625	8	1.4	−37.6
Abduction	635	2	12.6	−48.9
Robbery	27 477	86	−4.2	−14.0
Violent crime: Total	**302 257**	**946**	**−2.0**	**−9.7**
Break and enter	274 717	860	−4.4	−35.7
Motor vehicle theft	169 544	531	−3.5	−3.5
Theft over $5000	17 294	54	−11.7	−40.8
Theft $5000 and under	680 885	2 131	−3.7	−23.4
Possession of stolen goods	35 400	111	5.8	6.7
Fraud	97 091	304	3.5	−14.6
Property crime: Total	**1 274 931**	**3 991**	**−3.2**	**−24.1**
Mischief	353 661	1 107	−2.0	−19.1
Counterfeiting currency	159 889	500	13.8	333.5
Bail violations	104 334	327	2.3	43.6
Disturbing the peace	117 022	366	12.7	107.4
Offensive weapons	18 002	56	1.2	−13.5
Prostitution	6 493	20	13.1	5.7
Arson	13 148	41	6.1	−11.7
Other	222 123	695	−4.4	−13.2
Other Criminal Code: Total	**994 672**	**3 114**	**1.8**	**10.4**
Criminal Code: Total: Excluding traffic (crime rate)	**2 571 860**	**8 051**	**−1.2**	**−11.8**
Cannabis: Total	**67 832**	**212**	**10.0**	**52.0**
Possession	48 052	150	15.3	53.8
Trafficking	10 470	33	−1.4	16.9
Cultivation	8 328	26	−4.0	120.1
Importation	982	3	45.0	55.8
Cocaine	16 837	53	17.3	23.9
Heroin	792	2	19.5	−55.3
Other drugs	11 674	37	6.9	85.6
Drugs: Total	**97 135**	**304**	**10.9**	**46.6**

Source: Statistics Canada, 2005, "Crime Statistics in Canada," Juristat, *Catalogue Vol. 25, No. 5, July 21.*

intention of doing a wrongful act. A person who buys a gun, makes a plan to kill someone, and carries out the plan has probably committed homicide. In contrast, *manslaughter* is the unlawful, *unintentional* killing of one person by another. An intoxicated person who shoots a gun into the air probably holds no malice toward the bystander who is killed by a stray bullet. Sometimes a person's intentions are clear, but many times they are not, and the lines between intentional, unintentional, and accidental homicides are blurred. As Table 9.2 shows, the homicide rate, two victims per 100 000 population, has declined over the past 10 years, though it was up slightly from 2003 to 2004.

***Mass murder* is the killing of four or more people at one time and in one place by the same person.** Fortunately, the examples of mass murder in Canada are few. Marc Lepine's killing of 14 women in 1989 in the École Polytechnique in Montreal is an example of mass murder.

According to criminologists, mass murderers tend to kill in the areas where they live. They are likely to be male, problem drinkers, and collectors of firearms and other weapons, which they often hide (Dietz 1986). Some recent mass murderers have been disgruntled employees or former employees who seek out supervisors and co-workers in the workplace. An example of this kind of mass murder was the 1992 killing of four faculty members by Valery Fabrikant, a professor of engineering, at Concordia University in Montreal. In the U.S., a number of these violent eruptions have occurred in post offices, hence the term "going postal."

Serial murder **is the killing of three or more people over more than a month by the same person.** Serial murders account for few homicides, but receive extensive media coverage. In Canada, Clifford Olson, who killed 11 boys and girls and was sentenced to life imprisonment in 1982, and Michael Wayne McGray, who pleaded guilty to 6 murders in 1998, are examples of a serial killer. The finding of many bodies at the pig farm owned by Robert Pickton in Port Coquitlam, a suburb of Vancouver, would appear to indicate another example of serial murder. In mid-2005 he was charged with the murder of 27 people.

It is difficult to characterize serial killers, outside of the fact that the best-known ones are White males. Some travel extensively to locate their victims; others kill near where they live. One study identified four basic types of serial killers: (1) *visionaries,* who kill because they hear a voice or have a vision that commands them to commit the murderous acts; (2) *missionaries,* who take it on themselves to rid the community or the world of what they believe is an undesirable type of person; (3) *hedonists,* who obtain personal or sexual gratification from violence; and, (4) *power/control seekers,* who achieve gratification from the complete possession of the victim (Holmes 1988).

Characteristics of Victims and Accused

Statistics on homicide are among the most accurate official crime statistics available. Homicides rarely go unreported, and suspects are usually apprehended and charged. Although annual rates vary slightly, murder follows certain patterns in terms of gender, age, racialization, and region of the country, as analyses from earlier years shows. Men make up the vast majority of murder victims and offenders. Of the 622 homicides reported in 2004, two-thirds of the victims were male, and 90 percent of the offenders were male (Dauvergne 2005:1).

Age and sex patterns are clearly evident in murder rates. The rate of accused and victimized males peaked at 18 to 24 years of age and declined thereafter; but the rate of accused females was constant from 18 to 39 years of age, and the rate of victimized females was fairly constant from 18 to 49 years of age (Dauvergne 2005:12).

In Canada, unlike the U.S., homicide is not an urban phenomenon. In 2004, the homicide rate for the Census Metropolitan Areas (CMAs) with populations less than 100 000 had homicide rates slightly higher than larger CMAs (2.03 vs. 1.51; Dauvergne 2005:4). Regarding regional differences, homicide is more likely to occur in Western than Eastern Canada (Dauvergne 2005:4).

In the past, most murder victims knew their killers, but this pattern seems to be gradually changing somewhat. In 2004, half of all homicides were committed by an acquaintance, 35 percent by a family member, and 15 percent by a stranger (Dauvergne 2005:7). Among spousal victims, the homicide rate was five times greater for females than for males (0.71 vs. 0.14 per 100 000 (Dauvergne 2005:10)

Across the nation, in 2004, firearms were used in approximately 28 percent of all homicides, a rate similar to the last 10 years (33 percent died by stabbings and 22 percent were beaten to death; Dauvergne 2005:4)—a fact that leads to ongoing political debate over gun control, especially of handguns.

Sexual Assault

Many people think of *sexual assault* (the term "rape" is no longer used in criminal law) as a sexually motivated crime, but it is actually **an act of violence in which sex is used as a weapon against a powerless victim** (Vito and Holmes 1994). Both men and women can be victimized by sexual assault. In Canada, it is classified into three levels:

- Level 1 includes touching, grabbing, kissing—the category of least physical harm to the victim.

- Level 2 includes assault with a weapon, threats to use a weapon, or causing bodily harm.

- Level 3, or aggravated assault, includes wounding, maiming, or endangering the life of the victim.

Date rape is forcible sexual activity that meets the legal definition of sexual assault and involves people who first meet in a social setting (Sanday 1996). This definition is preferred by some scholars because it encompasses dates and casual acquaintances but excludes spouses (marital rape) and relatives (incest). The phrase was coined to distinguish forced, non-consensual sex between people who know one another from forced, non-consensual sex between strangers—but both are against the law. Date rape is often associated with alcohol or other drug consumption (see "roofies" on page 218 in Chapter 8), especially among college students. We probably know much less about the actual number of date rapes than we do about the number of stranger assaults, because victims are less likely to report sexual attacks by people they know.

On university or college campuses, date or acquaintance rape sometimes takes the form of gang or party rape. Unlike individual acquaintance rape, gang rape is used as a reinforcing mechanism for membership in a group of men (Warshaw 1994). In fact, men who rape in groups might never commit individual rape. As they participate in gang rape, they experience a special bonding with each other and use rape to prove their sexual ability to other group members and thereby enhance their status among members.

Characteristics of Victims and Accused

Statistics on sexual assault are misleading at best because it is often not reported. According to the 1993 Violence Against Women Survey, which interviewed 12 300 women about their experiences of sexual and physical assault, 39 percent reported at least one incident of sexual assault since the age of 16 (CCJS 1999:278). According to the 1999 GSS, the sexual assault rate is 21 per 1000—up from 16 per 1000 in 1993 (Besserer and Trainor 2000:5). According to UCR data for 2004 (see Table 9.2), sexual assaults constituted less than 10 percent of violent crime and declined by about a third since 1994. Some women may not report that they have been assaulted because they believe that nothing will be done about it or that the attacker may try to get even. It should be noted that not only were sex offenders more likely than violent offenders overall to be incarcerated, but they were also more likely to be sent to prison for longer periods of time. Whereas in 1997–98, 14 percent of the violent offenders received terms exceeding one year, 37 percent of the sex offenders received terms exceeding one year (CCJS 1999:273)

Like homicide, sexual assault follows certain patterns in terms of gender, age, racialization, and education. With the proviso that inmates of correctional institutions may not fully represent the population that commits these crimes, we can gain much information from a major inmate survey by consultant David Robinson and his colleagues (1999:275). According to the census of inmates conducted on October 5, 1996, incarcerated sexual offenders were male (99 percent), older than other violent offenders (35 vs. 31 years of age), slightly more likely to be of Indigenous status than other violent offenders (23 vs. 19 percent), and less educated (having grade 9 or less) than the rest of the population (41 vs. 19 percent).

In most sexual assaults, according to the Violence Against Women Survey of 1993, the victim is young (18 percent for women aged 18 to 24 vs. 1 percent for women aged 45 and over). Single and separated/divorced women were six times more likely to report sexual assault than women married or living common-law (CCJS 1999:278).

Gang Violence

Gang violence includes homicide, sexual assault, robbery, and aggravated assault. But actually defining a "gang" is difficult. Police define gangs so broadly— "two or more persons engaged in antisocial behaviour who form an allegiance for a common criminal purpose and who individually or collectively are creating an atmosphere of fear and intimidation within a community" (quoted in Abbate 1998:A10)—that to identify violence as gang violence using this definition is too inclusive. Criminologist Robert M. Gordon (2000:48) has identified six types of gangs in Vancouver:

1. youth movements, like skinheads and punks who perpetrate hate crimes;

2. youth groups, youth who hang out together in public places, like malls;

3. criminal groups, small groups who band together for a short time for illegal financial gain;

4. "wanna-be" groups, loosely structured groups, frequently substitute families, that indulge in impulsive criminal behaviour;

5. street gangs, young adults who plan criminal behaviour; and

6. criminal business organizations, older, well-established groups, sometimes with ethnic membership, like the Lotus, Flying Dragons, Hells Angels, and Bandidos.

Typically, gangs are composed primarily of young males of the same ethnicity. Some gangs are basically peer groups that hang out together, seeking a sense of belonging, like a family, but others are well organized and violent. In recent years, gang activity and gang-related violence have increased significantly not only in large metropolitan areas but also in smaller cities and suburbs. In Canada, gang-related killings tripled between 1995 and 2000, rising from 21 in 1995 to 71 in 2000. The deaths were due primarily to fighting over drug trafficking, and over half occurred in Quebec (Fedorowycz 2001:6).

Some analysts have suggested that gang violence may be exacerbated by socialization of males for male dominance and by patriarchal social structures. Sociologist Martín Sánchez Jankowski (1991) suggests that violence attributed to gangs is often committed by gang members acting as *individuals* rather than as agents of the organization. According to Jankowski, most gang members do not like violence and fear that they may be injured or killed in violent encounters. As a result, gang members engage in collective violence only to accomplish specific objectives, such as asserting authority or punishing violations by their own members who are incompetent or who break the gang's code. Violence against other gangs occurs primarily when a gang feels threatened or needs to maintain or expand its operations in a certain area. In general, according to Jankowski, collective violence is used to achieve the goals of gang membership (proving masculinity and toughness, providing excitement, and maintaining reputation), mainly when gang members are provoked by others or when they are fearful.

Sociologists Jack Levin and Jack McDevitt (1993) suggest that some gangs look for opportunities to violently attack "outgroup" members because they are seeking a thrill and view their victims as vulnerable. When violent attacks are made because of a person's racialization, religion, skin colour, disability, sexual orientation, national origin, or ancestry, they are considered to be hate crimes (see Chapter 1) and are

likely performed by the "youth movements" in Robert Gordon's typology.

Intervention by law enforcement officials and the criminal justice system has had only limited success. But in the spring of 2002, "Mom" Boucher, the closest thing to a godfather in the Hells Angels in Quebec, was convicted on several counts of homicide; and police arrested 36 members of the Bandidos, the second largest biker gang.

Hate Crimes

Hate crimes are crimes that are motivated by the offender's hatred of certain characteristics of the victim, e.g., national or ethnic origin, language, colour, religion, gender, age, mental or physical disability, or other similar factor. In the GSS victimization survey, people were asked if the crime they reported could be a hate crime. Four percent of 273 000 incidents were

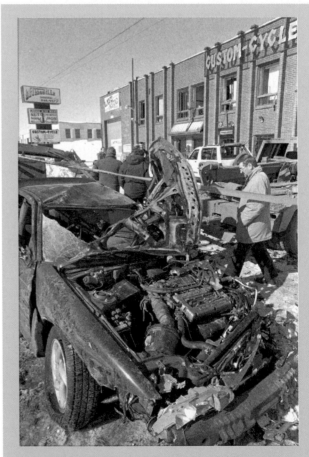

Biker violence includes vandalizing clubs and killing people in their homes and cars.

reported as hate crimes, and the most frequently cited characteristic was the victim's ethnicity, cited by 43 percent of the victims; the culture, by 18 percent; and the gender, by 18 percent (Besserer and Trainor 2000:180). The Hate Crime Pilot Study collected recorded incidents from 12 participating police departments for 2002 and 2003. Police classified 928 incidents as criminal hate incidents. Whereas race/ethnicity was the most frequent motive among the incidents (race/ethnicity, 57 percent; religion, 43 percent; and sexual orientation, 10 percent), the largest group of targets identified in this study were Jewish people or institutions (Jews, 25 percent; Blacks, 17 percent; and Muslims, 11 percent; Silver, Mihorean, and Taylor-Butts 2004:8).

Property Crime

Property crime is the taking of money or property from another without force, the threat of force, or the destruction of property. Breaking and entering, possession of stolen goods, theft, motor vehicle theft, and fraud are examples of property crimes. Table 9.2 shows that over one million property crimes were reported in 2004. Overall, property crime has fallen by a quarter since 1994. According to victimization surveys, the most frequent property crime is *breaking and entering*—the unlawful or forcible entry or attempted entry of a residence or business with the intent to commit a serious crime. Breaking and entering usually involves theft—the burglar illegally enters by, for example, breaking a window or slashing a screen (forcible entry) or through an open window or unlocked door (unlawful entry). Although breaking and entering is normally a crime against property, it is more serious than most non-violent crimes because it carries the possibility of violent confrontation and the psychological sense of intrusion that is associated with violent crime. To fully grasp the possibility of violent confrontation, consider the following explanations by two burglars of the pressures—both internal and external—that motivate them to commit breaking and entering:

> Usually what I'll do is a [break and enter], maybe two or three if I have to, and then this will help me get over the rough spot. . . . Once I get it straightened out, I just go with the flow . . . the only time I would go and commit a burglary is if

I needed the money at that point in time. That would be strictly to pay the light bill, gas bill, rent. (Dan Whiting, quoted in Wright and Decker 1994:37)

> You ever had an urge before? Maybe a cigarette urge or a food urge, where you eat that and you got to have more and more? That's how that crack is. You smoke it and it hits you [in the back of the throat] and you got to have more. I'll smoke that sixteenth up and get through, it's like I never had none. I got to have more. Therefore, I gots to go do another burglary and gets some more money. (Richard Jackson, quoted in Wright and Decker 1994:39)

According to victimization surveys, the young have a higher risk of being subject to property crime than older people. Risk of victimization is also much higher for families with incomes under $15 000 living in rental property or in inner-city areas. In contrast, people who live in well-maintained residences with security systems on well-lit streets or cul-de-sacs are less likely to be victimized (Logan 2001:1). The UCR likely does not accurately represent the number of burglaries committed because people tend to report them only when very valuable, insured goods are taken.

The most frequently reported crime is called *theft $5000 and under*—unlawfully taking or attempting to take property from another person. This kind of theft includes purse snatching and pickpocketing. Table 9.2 shows that in 2004, 53.4 percent of the reported property crimes were theft $5000 and under; 21.5 percent were breaking and entering, 13.2 percent were motor vehicle theft, and 7.6 percent were fraud.

Statistics on auto theft are more accurate than those for many other crimes because insurance companies require claimants to report the theft to police. Analysts have identified four basic motives for auto theft:

1. Joyriding—the vehicle is stolen for the fun of riding around in it and perhaps showing off to friends.

2. Transportation—the vehicle is stolen for personal use.

3. Crime—the vehicle is used as an aid in the commission of another crime.

4. Profit—the vehicle is sold or taken to a "chop shop," where it is dismantled for parts, which are then sold separately (H.D. Barlow 1996).

Property crimes such as this one occur far more frequently than violent crime, yet the media give far greater coverage to violence than to acts like auto burglary. Should the media's motto be "If it bleeds, it leads"? Why, or why not?

Shoplifting accounts for billions of dollars in losses to retail businesses each year. For some stores, the annual loss can be as high as 2 to 5 percent of the total value of inventory (Vito and Holmes 1994). Early criminologists thought that shoplifters fell into three categories: the *snitch*—someone with no criminal record who systematically pilfers goods for personal use or to sell; the *booster* or *heel*—the professional criminal who steals goods to sell to *fences* (people who receive and dispose of stolen property) or pawnshops; and the *kleptomaniac*—someone who steals for reasons other than monetary gain (e.g., for sexual arousal; Holmes 1983). Most experts think that shoplifting is committed primarily by amateurs across lines of racialization, class, gender, and age (Barlow 1996).

Credit card fraud—using a credit card or account number to obtain property, services, or money under false pretences—has increased sharply with the increase in the availability of cards and the decrease in the use of cheques. Despite the security measures taken by banks and other credit card issuers, credit card fraud is perpetrated in many ways. A lost or stolen wallet or purse can provide a potential offender with all the identification necessary to open up charge accounts in the victim's name and run up large bills before the individual becomes aware of what has happened. Sometimes credit cards are obtained by pickpockets, purse-snatchers, robbers, burglars, and sometimes by prostitutes who go through their customers' pockets. There are companies using the internet to sell personal information—such

as a person's Social Insurance Number and mother's maiden name—that can be used to apply for and activate some credit cards (Hansell 1996). Credit card information can also be stolen by people who have legitimate access to personal data (e.g., airline or hotel reservationists or department or grocery store personnel) or by computer hackers. Table 9.2 shows that fraud has declined by almost a quarter since 1994.

The crime whose rate has increased most dramatically—333.5 percent since 1994 (see Table 9.2)—is counterfeiting currency, presumably due to the high quality and low cost of colour printers and the increased detection of such printing. Sauvé reported that the Bank of Canada estimated the value of counterfeit bills to be $13 billion (2005:10).

Crime Comparisons between Canada and the United States

Canadians absorb much of their crime information from the U.S. media. It is therefore worthwhile to show the differences in crime rates in Canada and the U.S. so that we do not automatically assume that their crime problem is our crime problem. Over the past 20 years, Canada has had a much lower violent crime rate than the U.S. In 2000, the U.S. homicide rate was three times our rate (5.5 vs. 1.8 per 100 000), and this difference is maintained in 2003–2004 (Dauvergne 2005:3); the aggravated assault rate was two times our rate (324 vs. 143 per 100 000); and the robbery rate was 1.65 times our rate. On the other hand, over the 1990s our property crime rate was higher than their rate, though it was converging toward theirs at the end of the decade. Our break-and-enter rate in comparison to their rate was 954 vs. 728 per 100 000, and our motor vehicle theft in comparison to their rate was 515 vs. 414 per 100 000.

Sociologist Marc Ouimet (1999:403) analyzed these differences and found that they were not uniform throughout the country. For example, homicide rate differences were nine times greater in the U.S. than Canada for cities with populations of 1 million or more. Ouimet (1999:402) suggested that these differences occur because U.S. cities are much more dangerous than Canadian cities. Unlike U.S. cities, Canadian cities do not contain ghettos, where people are very poor, are disproportionately members of visible minorities, suffer many social problems, and have guns. Whereas two-thirds of U.S. homicides involve firearms, less than one-third of Canadian homicides do (Statistics Canada 2001a). Ouimet refers to Jan van Dijk and his colleagues' international study (1990), which showed that whereas less than 5 percent of Canadian households have a gun, 29 percent of American households have a gun. Ouimet (1999:401) went on to suggest that this lack of guns might also help explain Canada's higher property crime rate. Canadian burglars might be encouraged to commit more break-and-enters than their American counterparts since they have less chance of facing an armed householder.

Another possible explanation for the different patterns could be the reporting of crimes by victims. The study by van Dijk and his colleagues (1990) shows that reporting differences are minimal. Whereas 80.6 percent of Canadian victims reported a robbery, 78.9 percent of U.S. victims did; and whereas 56.5 percent of Canadians reported a break and enter, 59.5 percent of U.S. victims did.

Occupational (White-Collar) Crime

Occupational (white-collar) crime **refers to illegal activities committed by people in the course of their employment or normal business activity.** When sociologist Edwin H. Sutherland (1949) first introduced the term *white-collar crime*, he was referring to such acts as employee theft, fraud (obtaining money or property under false pretences), embezzlement (theft from an employer), and soliciting bribes or kickbacks. With the advent of personal computers, some white-collar crimes have become easier to commit, and some criminals have developed new types of crime based on computer technology. One type of white-collar crime that has been in the news lately is *insider trading* of securities: An offender buys or sells stocks on the basis of information that isn't publicly known and that he or she obtained only as a corporate insider. A recent high-profile example of this was the case of Michael Cowpland, former president of Corel Corporation. In 1997 he sold $20.4 million worth of Corel stock a month before Corel reported a big loss. The agreement with the Ontario Securities Commission was that Cowpland's holding company was to pay a $1 million fine after pleading guilty to one count of insider trading, and he has to pay a $575 000 fine and cannot sit on

a board of publicly traded firms for two years. For individual investors without insider knowledge, the losses from the decline in the value of Corel stock might have been in the thousands of dollars. For institutional investors, like pension funds, losses could have been much higher.

Corporate Crime

Some white-collar offenders engage in *corporate crime*—**illegal acts committed by corporate employees on behalf of the corporation and with its support.** Examples include acts injurious to the public or employees; pollution; manufacturing of defective products; antitrust violations (seeking an illegal advantage over competitors); deceptive advertising; infringements on patents, copyrights, and trademarks; unlawful labour practices involving the exploitation or surveillance of employees; price fixing; and financial fraud. These crimes arise from deliberate decisions by corporate personnel to profit at the expense of competitors, consumers, employees, and the general public. A striking Canadian example of economic effects of corporate crime was the case of the gold-mining company Bre-X Minerals Ltd. A company geologist, Michael de Guzman, added gold to survey samples, making the results look like those of a great gold mine. When the adding was discovered in 1997, the company and its stock became worthless, wiping out millions of dollars from various portfolios, including pension funds, and de Guzman apparently committed suicide. Other examples are found in the crimes of multinational companies such as Arthur Andersen—convicted in the spring of 2002 of obstructing justice—that have consequences for the companies' branches and accounting practices in Canada.

Recently, some quite severe penalties have been given to those executives convicted of fraud. For example, in mid-July 2005, Alberta native Bernie Ebbers was given a sentence of 25 years for WorldCom's $11 billion accounting fraud, and Timothy and John Rigas were given sentences of 20 and 15 years respectively for looting the U.S. cable company Adelphia communications earlier in 2005. The upcoming trials of Conrad Black will also be worth watching.

Corporate crime has huge direct and indirect injurious as well as economic effects. Direct injury and death from corporate crime are immense in comparison to crime rates of murder and manslaughter. Sociologist John L. McMullan reports that before the mid-1980s in Canada, the corporate death rate was more than six times greater than the street crime rate of murder and manslaughter (1992: 24). A notable example of lethal corporate crime is Nova Scotia's Westray mine, whose failure to follow good safety procedures resulted in the deaths of 26 workers in 1992. The top executives were not prosecuted for this disaster.

Organized Crime

***Organized crime* is a business operation that supplies illegal goods and services for profit.** These illegal enterprises include drug trafficking, prostitution, gambling, loan sharking, money laundering, and large-scale theft such as truck hijacking (Simon 1996). No single entity controls the entire range of corrupt and illegal enterprises (Chambliss 1988). Instead, there are many groups—syndicated crime networks, including biker gangs—that can thrive because there is great demand for illegal goods and services. Criminologist Margaret Beare (1996) suggests that groups vary according to their dependence on organized crime. Whereas some groups are organized to carry out organized crime activities (e.g., Russian and Nigerian groups and Colombian cartels), other groups have other goals and use organized-crime activities to support them (e.g., terrorist groups and motorcycle gangs). Sometimes these groups form alliances with businesspeople, law enforcement officials, and politicians.

In its annual report on organized crime in Canada for 2004, the Canadian Intelligence Service Canada identified several organized groups that are priorities for them:

■ Asian-based groups are found in British Columbia and greater Toronto, but they have significant influence in other areas and supply drugs to other groups. The Vietnamese-based groups are involved in residential marijuana grow operations.

■ Eastern European-based groups operate nationally and are involved in numerous enterprises.

■ The Hells Angels remains the largest and most powerful outlaw motorcycle gang in Canada (see "Gang Violence" on page 237). (The Outlaws and Bandidos are a lesser threat.) They are found in British Columbia and Ontario, but are currently

being prosecuted by the authorities. New organized-gang legislation now permits courts to link individual criminals with identifiable criminal groups, and thus, assign stiffer penalties.

■ Italian-based or traditional organized crime is centred in Montreal, Toronto, Hamilton, and the Niagara Region. These groups continue in the illicit drug trade and white-collar crime.

■ Aboriginal-based groups take advantage of some reserves on or near the Canada–U.S. border to conduct smuggling operations.

All groups are involved in illicit firearms activities. Street gangs are involved in assaults and/or homicide and may also be connected to organized crime groups. Technological advances are facilitating the availability of child pornography, and online criminal networks are distributing it. Illicit drugs smuggling and growing, fraud, violence, and so on create a variety of destructive impacts on Canadian society (Criminal Intelligence Service Canada 2004:1–4). Syndicated crime networks operate at all levels of society and even globally (see Box 9.1).

Youth Crime

***Youth crime* involves a violation of law or the commission of a status offence by a young person 12 to 17 years of age.** Many behaviours that are identified as youth crime or juvenile delinquency are not criminal acts per se but *status offences*—acts that are illegal because of the age of the offender—such as cutting school, buying and consuming alcoholic beverages, or running away from home. But measuring youth crime is difficult because youth who come into contact with the law can be charged or cleared by a variety of other means, such as a warning or an extrajudicial sanctions program, or the complainant decided not to lay a charge. The *Youth Criminal Justice Act* (YCJA; 2003) recognizes that effective responses to youth crime may be outside the courts. Figure 9.2 shows not only a decline in total youth crime since the early 1990s but also a recent increase in the cleared otherwise rate, resulting in a steady decline in charging youth. The YCJA appears to be effective, at least initially, in diverting youth from courts.

The statistics for youth crime are still high. Whereas people aged 12 to 17 constitute less than 10 percent of the Canadian population, they account for 20

SOCIAL PROBLEMS IN GLOBAL PERSPECTIVE

BOX 9.1   Organized Crime: The Global Empire

Fifty people were arrested Monday in Europe and Canada in an Italian-led operation against money laundering by the Russian Mafia, Italian authorities said. Police also seized real estate, luxury cars and bank accounts for hundreds of millions of dollars, said Francesco Gratteri, the head of the police unit which led the operation.

Authorities said 20 people were arrested in Italy, 13 in France and others in Austria, Switzerland, Monte Carlo and Canada. More than half of them were Russian nationals. They have been charged with criminal association with the intent to launder money . . .

The money was allegedly coming from the Mafia's illicit activities, such as drug and arms trafficking and the smuggling of human beings, said Gratteri.

Pierluigi Vigna, Italy's anti-Mafia prosecutor, said the operation shows how deeply the Russian Mafia had infiltrated Italian and European economies. ("Fifty People Arrested" 2002)

This is one of the many reports of international organized crime, some of which involves Canada. *Money laundering* is the process of converting or cleansing money, knowing that it comes

from serious crime, for the purpose of disguising its origin. Estimates of the amount of money that is laundered in Canada vary. In 1997, the RCMP estimated $5 to $10 billion, the Canadian Chiefs of Police estimated $7 to $14 billion, and Interpol estimated $17 billion (Sambugaro 2000:10). Canada is considered a good location for money laundering because of light justice sanctions, a strong economy, closeness to the United States, many ethnic communities, and international airports. While money laundering is big business in Canada, other places, such as the Cayman Islands, the Bahamas, Liechtenstein, Panama, and Russia, are considered major havens.

Globally, seven or eight crime syndicates often operate in collusion. In addition to the Russian syndicate and the Sicilian Mafia, other organized-crime groups allegedly include the Colombian cocaine cartels, which have operations in Spain, and ethnic Chinese from East and Southeast Asia, who have overseas bases in Rotterdam and London. At a lower level, the transport and marketing of drugs and other contraband are managed by syndicates of Nigerians, Moroccans, Pakistanis, Lebanese, Albanians, and others (Viviano 1995).

What can Canada do about global organized crime? Can any one nation or organization—such as the United Nations—reduce international money laundering and drug trafficking? What do you think?

percent of all persons charged in Canada with *Criminal Code* offenses, excluding traffic (Sauvé 2005:13). Forty percent of youth crimes are related to property, and the majority of these (e.g., motor vehicle theft and break-ins) declined in 2004 (Sauvé 2005:13). However, the youth violent crime rate has remained stable over the last few years, as seen in Figure 9.3, though most categories of youth violent crime, (e.g., homicide and robbery) have declined. What has declined is the charge rate due to the increase in cases being cleared otherwise. While we hear about higher rates of female violent crime, of the 40 youth accused of homicide, 37 were male and 3 were female. Both these numbers were lower than the previous 10-year average. While the rates vary from year to year, the 10-year average male rate is over

five times the female rate of homicide (Dauvergne 2005:13, 26).

Juveniles who are apprehended are processed by the youth court system, which is based on the assumption that young people can do better if they are placed in the right setting and receive guidance. Thus, of the two-thirds of cases that end in conviction, most youth dispositions are served in the community (Hendrick 1999:90). Custody sentences are ordered in one-third of the cases with convictions (Hendrick 1999:91). Unfortunately, most juvenile correction facilities or "training schools" hold large numbers of young people in overcrowded conditions and provide only limited counselling and educational opportunities for rehabilitation (Donziger 1996).

FIGURE 9.2   Youth Crime Rate Decreased in 2004

FIGURE 9.3   Youth Violent Crime Stable

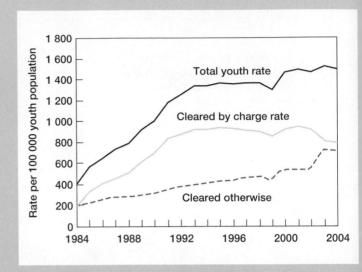

Source: Statistics Canada, 2005, "Crime Statistics in Canada," Juristat, Catalogue Vol. 25, No. 5, July 21.

Source: Statistics Canada, 2005, "Crime Statistics in Canada," Juristat, Catalogue Vol. 25, No. 5, July 21.

BIOLOGICAL AND PSYCHOLOGICAL EXPLANATIONS OF CRIME

As with other social problems, crime and delinquency have been explained in biological, psychological, and sociological terms. Most biological and psychological explanations assume that criminal behaviour is an inherent or acquired individual trait with genetic, biological, or psychological roots. Sociological perspectives, in contrast, focus on external factors.

Biological Explanations

One of the earliest biological explanations of criminality came from the *positivist school*, which created physical typologies that were used to classify and study criminals (Barlow 1996). The biological approach of Cesare Lombroso, a 19th-century Italian physicist, is probably the best known. Lombroso suggested that some people were born criminals or *atavists*—biological throwbacks to an earlier stage of evolution—and could be recognized by their low foreheads and smaller than normal human cranial capacities. A later theory, also

based on physical traits, which received some attention for a time was proposed by physician William Sheldon (1949). According to Sheldon's *somatotype theory, mesomorphs*—people who are muscular, gregarious, aggressive, and assertive—are more prone to delinquency and criminal behaviour than are *endomorphs*—people who are fat, soft, round, and extroverted—or *ectomorphs*—people who are thin, wiry, sensitive, and introverted.

Contemporary biological approaches based on genetics have attempted to link higher rates of aggression in men to levels of testosterone or chromosomal abnormality (an extra Y chromosome). But this research has produced no consistent findings, and social scientists argue that the differences in aggression may be due to gender-role socialization of men and women rather than to biological factors (Katz and Chambliss 1995).

Other contemporary biological approaches suggest that violence is a natural and inevitable part of human behaviour that can be controlled only by social organization. Some scientists, however, say that violence is neither natural nor inevitable but the result of traumatic brain injury or some combination of brain injury and other factors. Although most people with brain injuries are not violent, injuries to certain parts of the brain or injuries in combination with an abusive childhood or psychotic symptoms (e.g., paranoia) can affect an individual's ability to conform to societal norms.

The cortex of the brain—particularly the frontal lobes—is most closely associated with violent behaviour. It is the cortex that modifies impulses, allowing us to use good judgment, make decisions, and organize behaviour; it also facilitates learning and adherence to rules of conduct (Gladwell 1997). Using various neurological and psychiatric examinations, medical experts try to determine whether violent offenders have frontal-lobe impairment, were abused as children, or have any psychological disorders. These factors, especially in combination, make people prone to violent behaviour.

Psychological Explanations

Like biological explanations of delinquency and crime, psychological explanations focus on individual characteristics. Some researchers have used personality inventories in hopes of identifying abnormal personality traits in individuals who have committed crimes or engaged in delinquent behaviour. Other researchers have investigated the effects of social learning and positive reinforcement (e.g., rewards such as money or special attention) and negative reinforcement (e.g., the withdrawal of reward or lack of attention) on delinquent and criminal behaviour.

The most enduring psychological explanations of delinquency and crime seem to be the ones that bridge the biological explanations by linking intelligence and crime. Since the introduction of IQ (intelligence quotient) tests in the early 1900s, some analysts have suggested that people with lower intelligence scores are more likely to commit crimes than are people with higher intelligence scores. However, both the validity of IQ tests and the assertion that low intelligence causes delinquency or crime have come under great scrutiny and much criticism (see Hirschi and Hindelang 1977).

Of course, some social analysts do acknowledge the possibility of a relationship between low intelligence and delinquency or crime. These analysts note that low intelligence may indirectly promote delinquency because it affects school performance. As mentioned above, differences are present between those who commit crimes and those who go to jail; for

example, the less intelligent may be more likely to become inmates. People with grade 9 or less are greatly overrepresented in prison: Whereas 19 percent of Canada's population has grade 9 or less, 36 percent of inmates have grade 9 or less, according to the one-day survey of inmates in Canada's adult correctional facilities conducted by Robinson and his colleagues (1999:57).

One psychological explanation of violent crime focuses on *aggression*—behaviour intended to hurt someone, either physically or verbally—that results from frustration (Weiten and Lloyd 1994). According to the *frustration–aggression hypothesis,* people who are frustrated in their efforts to achieve a highly desired goal become aggressive toward others (Dollard et al. 1939). The object of the aggression becomes a **scapegoat— a substitute for the actual source of frustration— who can be blamed, especially if that person or group is incapable of resisting the hostility or aggression.**

Explaining violence in biological and/or psychological terms suggests responses based on some type of psychiatric or other medical intervention. After all, if violent behaviour is associated with specific neurological problems, it can be diagnosed like any other neurological illness and treated with drugs, including, possibly, anticonvulsants, antidepressants, and antihypertensive medications that act on the cortex to moderate violent behaviour.

SOCIOLOGICAL EXPLANATIONS OF CRIME

Unlike biological and psychological explanations that focus on individual behaviour, sociological explanations focus on those aspects of society that may contribute to delinquent or criminal behaviour.

The Functionalist Perspective

Although there are numerous functionalist perspectives on crime and delinquency, we will focus on two: strain theory and control theory, as illustrated in social bond theory.

Functionalist explanations for why people commit crimes can be traced to Emile Durkheim, who believed that the macrolevel structure of a society produces social pressures that result in high rates of deviance and crime. Durkheim introduced the concept of *anomie* to describe a social condition that engenders feelings of futility in people because of weak, absent, or conflicting social norms. According to Durkheim (1895/1964), deviance and crime are most likely to occur when anomie is present in a society. On the basis of Durkheim's theory, sociologist Robert Merton (1938, 1968) developed strain theory to explain why some people conform to group norms while others do not. **Strain theory states that people feel strain when they are exposed to cultural goals that they cannot reach because they do not have access to a culturally approved means of achieving those goals.** When some people are denied legitimate access to cultural goals such as success, money, or other material possessions, they seek to acquire these things through deviant—and sometimes criminal—means. This lack of legitimate access is typical of many of Canada's inmates. According to Robinson and his colleagues, the one-day snapshot of inmates shows that criminals are much more likely to be unemployed than the general population (52 percent vs. 7 percent). A more recent study of crime patterns over a 40-year period (from 1962 to 2003) found that economic factors were associated with some kinds of crime. For example, periods of inflation like the 1970s were associated with

robbery, breaking and entering, and motor vehicle theft and unemployment is associated with homicide (Statistics Canada 2005i).

Merton identified five ways in which people respond to cultural goals: conformity, innovation, ritualism, retreatism, and rebellion (see Table 9.3).

- *Conformity* occurs when people accept the culturally approved goals and pursue them through the approved means. People who choose conformity work hard and save their money to achieve success. Someone who is blocked from achieving a high level of education or a lucrative career typically conforms by taking a lower-paying job and attending school part-time, joining the military, or trying alternative (but legal) avenues, such as playing the lottery.

- *Innovation* occurs when people accept society's goals but use illegitimate means to achieve them. Innovations for acquiring material possessions include shoplifting, theft, burglary, cheating on income taxes, embezzling money, and other kinds of occupational crime.

- *Ritualism* occurs when people give up on societal goals but still adhere to socially approved means for achieving them. People who cannot obtain expensive material possessions or wealth seek to

TABLE 9.3 Merton's Strain Theory

Mode of Adaptation	Method of Adaptation	Agrees with Cultural Goal	Follows Institutional Means
Conformity	Accepts culturally approved goals; pursues them through culturally approved means	Yes	Yes
Innovation	Accepts culturally approved goals; adopts disapproved means of achieving them	Yes	No
Ritualism	Abandons society's goals but continues to conform to approved means	No	Yes
Retreatism	Abandons both approved goals and the approved means to achieve them	No	No
Rebellion	Challenges both the approved goals and the approved means to achieve them	No—seeks to replace	No—seeks replace to

Source: Adapted from Robert King Merton, 1968, **Social Theory and Social Structure,** *New York: Free Press.*

maintain the respect of others by being "hard workers" or "good citizens" to an extreme degree.

- *Retreatism* occurs when people abandon both the approved goals and the approved means of achieving them. Retreatists include hard-core drug addicts and some middle- or upper-income people who reject conventional trappings of success and the means to acquire them, choosing to "drop out" instead.

- *Rebellion* occurs when people reject both the approved goals and the approved means for achieving them and advocate an alternative set of goals and means. Rebels may use violence (such as vandalism or rioting) or non-violent tactics (such as civil disobedience) to change society and its cultural beliefs. Or they may withdraw from mainstream society, like the Amish, to live their own life.

Another functionalist perspective—*control theory*—seeks to answer the question, Why do people *not* engage in deviant behaviour? According to control theory, people are constantly pulled and pushed toward deviant behaviour. Environmental factors (pulls), such as adverse living conditions, poverty, and lack of educational opportunity, draw people toward criminal behaviour while, at the same time, internal pressures (pushes), such as feelings of hostility or aggressiveness, make people not want to act according to dominant values and norms (Reckless 1967). If this is true, why doesn't everyone who is poor or has a limited education commit crimes? According to control theorists, people who do not turn to crime or delinquent behaviour have *outer containments*—supportive family and friends, reasonable social expectations, and supervision by others—or *inner containments*—self-control, a sense of responsibility, and resistance to diversions. This lack of outer and inner containments is found among Canada's inmates. According to Robinson and his colleagues, inmates are much more likely to be unmarried than the general adult population (31 percent vs. 63 percent; 1999:57) and have high levels of crime-causing needs, like personal and emotional problems, substance abuse, and problems functioning in the community (1999:66).

The best-known control theory is **social bond theory**—the proposition that criminal behaviour is most likely to occur when a person's ties to society are weakened or broken. According to criminologist Travis Hirschi (1969), who proposed this theory, social bonding consists of (1) *attachment* to other people, (2) *commitment* to conformity, (3) *involvement* in conventional activities, and (4) *belief* in the legitimacy of conventional values and norms. When a person's social bonds are weak and when peers promote antisocial values and violent behaviour, the probability of delinquency and crime increases (Massey and Krohn 1986).

When analyzing violent crime, some functionalists believe that a sense of anomie is the root cause. Others believe that violence increases when social institutions such as the family, schools, and religious organizations weaken and the primary mechanisms of social control in people's everyday lives become external—law enforcement and the criminal justice system. Others accept the **subculture of violence hypothesis, that violence is part of the normative expectations governing everyday behaviour among young males in the lower classes** (Wolfgang and Ferracuti 1967). These violent subcultures are most likely to develop when young people, particularly males, have few legitimate opportunities available in their segment of society and when subcultural values accept and encourage violent behaviour.

Another functionalist perspective on violence, discussed in Chapter 1, is the *lifestyle–routine activity approach*, which holds that the patterns and timing of people's daily movements and activities as they go about obtaining the necessities of life—such as food, shelter, companionship, and entertainment—are the keys to understanding violent personal crimes and other types of crime in our society (Cohen and Felson 1979). In other words, changes in social institutions, such as more families in which both parents (or the sole parent) work outside the home or extension of shopping hours into the night, put some people at greater risk than others of being victims of violent crime (Parker 1995).

Functionalist explanations contribute to our understanding of crime by emphasizing that individuals who engage in such behaviour are not biologically or psychologically impaired but are responding to social and economic conditions in society. However, functionalists are not without their critics. Strain theory may point out that people from low-income and poverty-level backgrounds are prevented from achieving success goals through legitimate channels, but it is still criticized for focusing almost exclusively on crimes committed by the lower classes and ignoring crimes committed by people in the middle and upper classes. Critics of social bond theory say that it is limited in its ability to explain more serious forms of delinquency and crime (Krohn 1995).

The Conflict Perspective

Conflict theorists explain criminal behaviour in terms of power differentials and/or economic inequality in society. One approach focuses on how authority and power relations can contribute to some people—but not others—becoming criminals. According to sociologist Austin Turk (1966, 1971), crime is not a *behaviour* but a *status* that is acquired when people with the authority to create and enforce legal rules apply those rules to others.

A second conflict approach focuses on the relationship between economic inequality and crime. Having roots in the work of Karl Marx, the *radical critical-conflict approach* argues that social institutions (such as law, politics, and education) create a superstructure that legitimizes the class structure and maintains capitalists' superior position. In fact, say these theorists, the crimes people commit are based on their class position. Thus, crimes committed by low-income people typically involve taking things by force or physical stealth, while white-collar crime usually involves nonphysical means, such as paper transactions or computer fraud. Some critical theorists believe that affluent people commit crimes because they are greedy and continually want more than they have, whereas poor people commit street crimes such as robbery and theft to survive (Bonger 1916/1969).

In sum, the conflict approach is useful for pointing out how inequalities of power, class, and racialization can contribute to criminal or delinquent behaviour. Nevertheless, critics say that conflict theorists have not shown that powerful political and economic elites manipulate law making and enforcement for their own benefit. Rather, say these critics, people of all classes share a consensus that acts such as homicide, sexual assault, and armed robbery are bad (Klockars 1979).

The Interactionist Perspective

Interactionists emphasize that criminal behaviour is learned through everyday interaction with others. We will examine two major interactionist theories: differential association theory and labelling theory. ***Differential association theory*** **states that individuals have a greater tendency to deviate from societal norms when they frequently associate with people who tend toward deviance rather than conformity.** According to sociologist Edwin Sutherland (1939), who formulated this theory, people learn not only the techniques of deviant behaviour from people with whom they associate but also the motives, drives, rationalizations, and attitudes. Former gang member Nathan McCall (1994:93–94) describes such a learning process in his own life:

> Sometimes I picked up hustling ideas at the 7-Eleven, which was like a criminal union hall: Crapshooters, shoplifters, stickup men, burglars, everybody stopped off at the store from time to time. While hanging up there one day, I ran into Holt.... He had a pocketful of cash, even though he had quit school and was unemployed. I asked him, "Yo, man, what you been into?" "Me and my partner kick in cribs and make a killin'. You oughta come go with us sometimes...." I hooked school one day, went with them, and pulled my first B&E [breaking and entering].... After I learned the ropes, Shell Shock [another gang member] and I branched out, doing B and Es on our own. We learned to get in and out of houses in no time flat.

As McCall's description indicates, criminal activity often occurs within the context of frequent, intense, and long-lasting interactions with people who violate the law. When more factors favour violating the law than not, the person is likely to become a criminal. Although differential association theory contributes to our knowledge of how deviant behaviour reflects the individual's learned techniques, values, attitudes, motives, and rationalizations, critics note that many individuals who are regularly exposed to people who break the law still conform most of the time. Many critics think that the theory does not adequately take into account possible connections between social inequality and criminal behaviour.

Labelling theory, which was mentioned briefly in Chapter 1, takes quite a different approach from differential association theory. According to ***labelling theory***, **delinquents and criminals are people who have been successfully labelled as such by others.** No behaviour is inherently delinquent or criminal; it is defined as such by a social audience (Erikson 1962). According to sociologist Howard Becker (1963), labelling is often done by *moral entrepreneurs*—people who use their own views of right and wrong to establish rules and label others "deviant." Furthermore, the process of labelling is directly related to the power and status of the people who do the labelling and those who are being labelled. In support of this theory, one study of juvenile offenders has found that youths from lower-income families were more likely to be arrested and indicted than were middle-class juveniles who did the same things (Sampson 1986). Sociologists have also noted that the criminal justice system generally considers such factors as the offender's family life, educational achievement (or lack thereof), and social class in determining how to deal with juvenile offenders. According to one study, the individuals who are most likely to be apprehended, labelled delinquent, and prosecuted are people of colour who are young, male, unemployed, and undereducated and who live in urban high-crime areas (Vito and Holmes 1994).

Sociologist Edwin Lemert (1951) expanded labelling theory by distinguishing between primary and secondary deviance. **Primary deviance is the initial act of rule breaking** in which the individual does not internalize the delinquent or criminal self-concept. **Secondary deviance occurs when a person who has been labelled a deviant accepts that new identity and continues the deviant behaviour.** The concept of secondary deviance is important to labelling theory because it suggests that when people accept a negative label or stigma that has been applied to them, the label may actually contribute to the behaviour it was meant to control. In other words, secondary deviance occurs if a person is labelled a juvenile delinquent, accepts that label, and then continues to engage in delinquent behaviour. Labelling theory is useful for making us aware of how social control and personal identity are intertwined. Critics, however, do not think that labelling theory explains what causes the original acts that constitute primary deviance, nor do they think that it adequately explains why some people accept deviant labels and others do not (Cavender 1995).

In 1843, Daniel M'Naughton was acquitted of attempting to kill the British prime minister and shooting an official by reason of insanity. This was the beginning of the plea of insanity, but it did not provide any clear definition or measure of irrational behaviour. Since that time, a wide variety of defences involving a loss of self-control by the accused due to medical problems have been advocated by defence attorneys. The process has been called the ***medicalization of crime*, the converting of criminal behaviour to a medical condition or disease.** It is parallel to the medicalization of deviance—the converting of deviance, such as alcoholism, to a medical condition. Given the current and likely future development of our understanding about the influence of biological factors on serious violent crime, questions about the definition of personal responsibility versus medical conditions for irrational behaviour will be central to many future criminal proceedings.

Feminist Perspectives

Feminist scholarship focuses on why women commit crimes or engage in delinquent behaviour. We have already noted the differences in victimization rates for men and women. Criminologist Elizabeth Cormack (1999) reminds us that studies of offenders in prison often find that the women have experienced physical and/or sexual abuse. Scholars who use a *liberal feminist* framework believe that women's delinquency or crime is a rational response to gender discrimination in society. They attribute crimes such as prostitution and shoplifting to women's lack of educational and job opportunities and to stereotypical expectations about roles women should have in society (Daly and Chesney-Lind 1988). Scholars who espouse *radical feminism* believe that patriarchy contributes to crimes such as prostitution because, according to society's sexual double standard, it is acceptable for a man to pay for sex but unacceptable for a woman to accept money for such services. A third school of feminist thought, *socialist feminism*, believes that women are exploited by capitalism and patriarchy. Because most females have relatively low-wage jobs and few economic resources, crimes such as prostitution and shoplifting become a means of earning money and acquiring consumer products. Feminist scholars of colour, and other feminist scholars who wish to broaden the perspective of criminology beyond the patriarchy, suggest that consideration be given to "the complex and diverse ways in which patriarchal (along with class and racialization) privilege and power invade people's subjectivities and experiences" (Cormack 1999:166).

Another approach that focuses on differences in males' and females' crime behaviour, specifically on the higher rates of male versus female youth crime, is the power-control theory of sociologist John Hagan and his colleagues (1987). This theory emphasizes the structure of the family and socialization, rating families from "unbalanced," or highly patriarchal, to "balanced," or egalitarian, in the exercise of power by husbands and wives and according to their traditional versus egalitarian socialization of their sons and daughters. In a study in Toronto, Hagan and his colleagues found that gender differences in crime were greater in unbalanced than balanced families. Girls from families where girls were highly controlled and boys were freer committed fewer crimes relative to boys than girls from families with more egalitarian socialization (Hagan et al. 1987).

THE CRIMINAL JUSTICE SYSTEM

The term *criminal justice system* is misleading because it implies that law enforcement agencies and courts constitute one large, integrated system when actually they are a collection of somewhat interrelated, semi-autonomous bureaucracies (Sheley 1995). The **criminal justice system is the network of organizations, including the police, courts, criminal prosecutions, and corrections, involved in law enforcement and the administration of justice** (CCJS 1999:4). Originally, the criminal justice system was created to help solve the problem of social disorder and crime. Today, however, some social analysts wonder whether the criminal justice system is part of the problem. Most cite two reasons for concern: (1) the criminal justice system fails in its mission to prevent, control, or rehabilitate offenders; and (2) unequal justice occurs because officials discriminate against people on the basis of racialization, class, gender, age, sexual orientation, or other devalued characteristics. We'll examine both issues in greater depth. First, though, let's look at each component of the justice system, starting with the police.

The Police

The police are the most visible link in the criminal justice system because they determine how to apply the law to control crime and maintain order. The police

reported 2.8 million *Criminal Code* incidents in 1996 and cleared, or solved, 22 percent of them with a charge (CCJS 1999:xiii). Four factors seem to influence the occurrence of an arrest:

1. the nature of the alleged offence or problem;

2. the quality of available evidence;

3. the age, racialization, and gender of the alleged offender; and

4. the level of deference shown to police officers. (Mastrofski 1995)

Given these factors, law enforcement officials have fairly wide *discretion*—use of personal judgment regarding whether and how to proceed in a given situation—in deciding who will be stopped and searched and which homes and businesses will be entered and for what purposes (Donziger 1996). Sociologist Jerome Skolnick (1975) argues that because police officers must often make these decisions in a dangerous environment, they develop a sense of suspicion, social isolation, and solidarity.

Most officers feel that they must demand respect on the streets, but they also know that they must answer to their superiors, who expect them to handle situations "by the book." But police officers' lives are often on the line in confrontations with suspects, and sometimes the officers have less firepower than the individuals they are attempting to apprehend.

In Canada in June 2001, there were 57 000 police officers—184 officers per 100 000 population. This number is lower than the comparable U.S. figure of 247 per 100 000 in 1998. Among the largest Canadian metropolitan areas, Thunder Bay had 195 officers per 100 000, and Regina and Toronto had 181 per 100 000. In 1998, there were 8300 women officers, representing 15 percent of all officers. In the past, women were largely excluded from law enforcement because of stereotypical beliefs that they were not physically and psychologically strong enough for the work. The total cost of policing in 2000 was $6.8 billion (Statistics Canada 2002k).

How can police departments become more effective in reducing crime as a social problem? According to some analysts, police departments with entrenched problems must first reform their own agencies and win the respect of the communities they serve. One way to do this is to be sure that police departments reflect the racialized and ethnic composition of these communities. It is difficult for an all-White police force to build trust in a primarily Indigenous area. In Canada in 1996, 3.0 percent of police officers were Indigenous, slightly higher than the 2.3 percent Indigenous people constitute of the Canadian population 15 years and older (Swol 1999:23). Visible minorities do not yet appear as police officers in numbers similar to their participation in the work force. In 1996, whereas members of visible minorities composed 10 percent of the work force, they composed only 3 percent of police officers (Swol 1999:21). When women, Indigenous peoples, and members of other visible minorities gain greater representation in police departments, a wide range of complaints against police regarding profiling, domestic violence, and violence against minorities should be reduced.

In addition to hiring members of minority groups, police officers must have an opportunity to speak out about problems such as profiling, and programs must be set up to change behaviour. After the Toronto Police Service was in a continuing controversy about profiling, then chief Julian Fantino asked Black officers for an assessment of this problem in 2003. The report was not made public, but documents were obtained by the *Toronto Star* in 2005 that stated, among other issues, that

- the officers described "differential enforcement activities";
- the stereotype that Black motorists in expensive cars and neighbourhoods were given extra attention was true; and
- a majority of the officers felt they had been stopped for improper reasons while off duty (Mascoll and Rankin 2005:A20).

Some police departments have begun *community policing* as a way of reducing crime. Community policing involves integrating officers into the communities they serve—getting them out of their patrol cars and into a proactive role, recognizing problems and working with neighbourhood citizens to find solutions. In cities where community policing has been implemented, crime rates appear to have dropped; however, it should be noted that there has also been a general trend toward fewer crimes, especially violent crimes, in some cities where community policing is not employed (Sacco and Kennedy 1998:356ff).

The Courts

Criminal courts are responsible for determining the guilt or innocence of people who have been accused of committing a crime. In theory, justice is determined in an adversarial process: A prosecutor (an attorney who represents the state) argues that the accused is guilty and a defence attorney argues that the accused is innocent. In reality, judges have a great deal of discretion. Working with prosecutors, they decide who will be released, who will be held for further hearings, and—in many instances—what sentences will be imposed on people who are convicted.

Because courts have the capacity to try only a small fraction of criminal cases, an attrition process occurs. This process begins with the police, who clear about a third of all offences reported to them. The police clear a fifth of all reports with a charge. About 15 percent of the total reports result in conviction, and 4 percent of the reports result in a sentence to custody (CCJS 1999:xiii). This attrition process has been called a "crime funnel" (Silverman et al. 1996, cited in Sacco and Kennedy 1998:205). In 2000–2001, 375 486 cases were heard in seven Canadian provinces and Yukon, involving 816 449 charges; 61 percent of the cases resulted in a conviction (Thomas 2002:1). Many cases are resolved by *plea bargaining*—**a process whereby the Crown attorney negotiates with a defence attorney for a guilty plea for a less serious crime.** In other words, defendants (especially those who are poor and cannot afford to pay an attorney) plead guilty to a lesser crime in return for not being tried for the more serious crime for which they were arrested. As cases are sifted and sorted through the legal machinery, steady attrition occurs. At each stage, various officials determine what alternatives will be available for the cases that remain in the system (Hills 1971).

Sometimes plea bargaining occurs to get a conviction in a high-profile case when no other avenue seems available. A notorious example was the case of the sentencing of Karla Homolka to 12 years in prison in return for her testimony and evidence (tapes missed in the search by police, recording the homicides of two girls) to convict Paul Bernardo of the girls' homicide (see Box 9.2).

SOCIAL PROBLEMS AND SOCIAL POLICY

In 1993 Paul Bernardo and Karla Homolka were convicted of abducting, torturing, and killing Leslie Mahaffy and Kristen French, and drugging and sexually assaulting Karla Homolka's younger sister Tammy, who died as a result. Paul Bernardo received a life sentence, but Karla Homolka received a 12-year plea-bargained sentence for admitting guilt, providing testimony against Paul Bernardo, including telling the police of videotapes of the torture and killings. Many Canadians thought she received too light a sentence for such horrific acts and called it "a deal with the devil," but police thought they did not have sufficient evidence for a clear conviction. In prison, Homolka appeared to be a model prisoner, even earning a BA.

In 2005, just before Homolka was scheduled to be released, the question was raised whether post-jail conditions should be imposed on her. Imposing such restrictions is very controversial, and the law governing this was passed only after her sentencing.

A judge imposed 14 restrictions, including

- Notifying police of address, job, and names of people she lives with
- Reporting to the police monthly and notifying them of a move
- Advising police of any change of name
- Notifying police of trips of more than 48 hours, who she is travelling with, and length of stay,
- Not communicating with convicted criminals or Mr. Bernardo, and
- No non-medically prescribed drugs, or employment authority over people less than 16 years of age (Peritz 2005:A6).

Such restrictions are usually for those who are a continuing danger to society. Her lawyer argued that she committed the crimes under the influence of Bernardo and is no longer a danger to society. But Homolka did stand up to Bernardo to protect her dog, though not the two teens, and was in correspondence with the convicted killer of a young woman while in prison. In addition, some concern has been raised that without

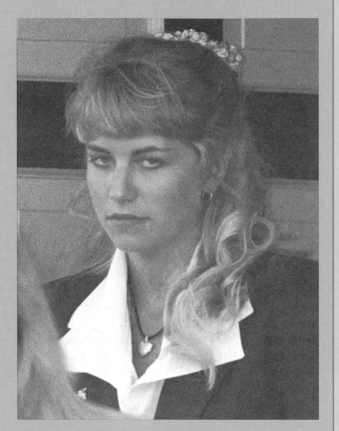

Karla Homolka, 1993

restrictions, someone may try to seek vengeance on her. Internet searches showed a number of references to Homolka, including a website of a death pool inviting people to guess when she will die. Is it possible that these restrictions, which are not onerous, might help to protect her? In late November 2005, a judge lifted the restrictions, reasoning that she did not represent a real and imminent danger to the community. Should there be a law restricting people after they have served their time? If you were a judge, would you put restrictions on her and if so, what kinds?

Punishment and the Prisons

Punishment **is any action designed to deprive a person of** **things of value (including liberty) because of an offence** **the person is thought to have committed** (Barlow 1996). Punishment is seen as serving four functions:

1. *Retribution* imposes a penalty on the offender. Retribution is based on the premise that the punishment should fit the crime: The greater the degree of social harm, the more the offender should be punished. An individual who murders, for example, should be punished more severely than one who steals an automobile.

2. *Social protection* results from restricting offenders so that they cannot continue to commit crimes.

3. *Rehabilitation* seeks to return offenders to the community as law-abiding citizens. However, the few rehabilitation programs that exist in prisons are seriously understaffed and underfunded. Often, the job skills (such as agricultural work) that are taught in prison do not transfer to the outside world, and offenders are not given help in finding work that fits the skills they might have once they are released.

4. *Deterrence* seeks to reduce criminal activity by instilling a fear of punishment. Criminologists debate, though, whether imprisonment has a deterrent effect, given that 30 to 50 percent of those who are released from prison commit further crimes.

In 1999–2000, about 31 600 people were in custody in Canada (Lommo 2001:3). An incarceration rate of 115 per 100 000 population is not the highest rate of incarceration in relation to population in a high-income country. That distinction belongs to the U.S., which has a rate of over 600 in prison per 100 000 population. However, Canada's rate is higher than that of most European countries: England and Wales at 100, France at 95, and Germany at 90 per 100 000 population (CCJS 1999:ix).

Jail and prison conditions often do little to rehabilitate offenders. In fact, three out of four inmates are housed in such overcrowded facilities that two people often live in a space only slightly larger than a walk-in closet. Some inmates suffer physical abuse by prison officials or other inmates.

Because of plea bargains, credit for "good time" served, and overcrowded prison conditions, most convicted criminals do not serve their full sentences. They are released on conditional sentences, including probation (close supervision of their everyday lives in lieu of serving time), parole (early release from prison), or statutory release, where inmates serve the last third of their custodial sentence in the community. About 121 000 people (79 percent of the total) are on supervision (Lommo 2001:3). If offenders violate the conditions of their probation or parole, they may be returned to prison to serve their full sentence. Conditional sentencing can occur if several conditions are met. The judge, after imposing a term of less than two years, may order the offender to serve the prison sentence in the community, under supervision. The judge may impose further conditions, like attendance at a treatment program. If these conditions are not followed, the offender will return to court and may be sent to custody.

Recently the numbers of people sentenced to custody has declined. This is due to such factors as increased use of conditional sentences and to the decrease in the crime rate. Despite the decline, certain problems remain. For example, there is an overrepresentation of Indigenous people in prison. Whereas Indigenous people are 3 percent of the adult population, they are 18.73 percent of the federal prison population, according to a report by Howard Sapers, correctional investigator, in October 2006 ("It's Alarming How Many Aboriginals Are in Prison" 2006). Incarcerating Indigenous people for crimes like drunkenness, vagrancy, and so on, crimes for which Whites are less likely to be incarcerated, has been a longstanding feature of our justice system. In Box 9.4, this fact and the overrepresentation of Black people is noted in the discussion of whether to use racialization-based statistics.

The decline in the incarceration rate also helps keep the cost of correctional services low. In 1999–2000, the cost of housing per prisoner averaged $183.66 per day in federal custody and $128.10 per day in provincial custody, or almost $2.4 billion for all correctional services per year (Lommo 2001:14).

Restorative Justice

In Canada, Europe, Australia, and New Zealand, the concept of restorative justice comprises diverse practices, including conferencing, sentencing circles, and

SOCIAL PROBLEMS AND SOCIAL POLICY

BOX 9.3 To Collect or Not Collect Racialization and Ethnicity Statistics

Unlike the crime statistics in the United States, those in Canada do not report on ethnic background of victim and accused. We do have information about backgrounds in the Canadian correctional system where, for example, as mentioned above, Indigenous people (3 percent of the population) constitute 18.73 percent of the federal prison population. And the policy question is whether to include racialization/ethnicity information at other levels of the system.

Criminologist Scot Wortley (1999) presents arguments for both sides. Arguments opposed to collecting racialization/ethnicity-based data include

- the risk of publishing inaccurate information due to the problems of official statistics and measuring racialization/ethnicity; and

- the support provided for racist theories.

Arguments in favour of collecting the data include

- the opportunity to learn whether minorities are receiving differential treatment at any level of the system (e.g., to what extent does profiling occur?). In late May 2005, Kingston, Ontario, Chief of Police Bill Closs released data reporting that whereas Blacks were 0.6 percent of the Kingston community, they constituted 2.2 percent of those stopped for questioning and were 9.6 percent of people arrested or charged. But Asians were half as likely to be stopped, and Blacks were seen in higher proportions at the malls, at nightspots, and so on than other groups. So does this constitute profiling or reflect other kinds of behaviour? The *Toronto Star* and the *Globe and Mail* disagree on the results (*Globe and Mail* 2005: A24). What do you think?

- the identification of crimes that are of particular concern to a minority. While it is well known that homicide is primarily an intraracial problem in the U.S., Blacks killing Blacks is also a problem for Canadians. Some Black community leaders, like Dudley Laws in Toronto, have spoken out against publishing racialization-based crime statistics. However, in 2001, the Black Action Defence Committee, of which Laws is the executive director, launched a campaign supported by many other associations to stop the killings of Black youths by other Black youths. From 1996 to 2001, over 100 Black youths were killed by other Black youths, and the agencies were appealing to "society in general to address this very urgent problem" (*Metro Today,* August 17, 2001:9). And the killing continues. As shown in this example, members of a minority group may feel comfortable publishing data about their own group but not wish to see it compared to the data for other groups, for fear that the data will be used to label rather than address inequities faced by members of their group;

- a ban on such data does not prevent the spread of racist theories (racialization-based distortions are widely available, for example, on the internet).

Do you think racialization/ethnicity-based crime statistics should be published as readily as racialization/ethnicity education and income data (see Chapters 3 and 12), or should there be no collection of these kinds of data? Or should the collection be limited to certain situations? What situations would they be? Or should the decision be left with the minority group themselves? Would this last approach cause any problems?

victim–offender mediation. ***Restorative justice* focuses on repairing the harm caused by crime by holding moderated meetings of crime victims, offenders, and others affected by crime, which can be used at different sites in the justice system,** for example, as a diversion from court, a pre-sentencing option, and after the release from prison.

Current applications of the idea began to emerge in the 1970s in North America, beginning with a victim–offender reconciliation program in Ontario in 1974. A recent example was the Indigenous sentencing circle created to deal with the bullying situation that resulted in the suicide death of Dawn-Marie Wesley in British Columbia (see also Chapter 12 for more on bullying). According to a report in *The National Post* by Ian Bailey (2002), the mother of Dawn-Marie hugged the girl convicted of criminally harassing her daughter and accepted her apology. The girl also received a sentence of 18 months' probation, a six-month cell-phone ban (the instrument of the harassing), and an assignment of writing a 750-word essay on bullying and doing 20 hours of community work that could include speaking about bullying. Another example is the response of the parents of Reena Virk, killed in 1997, and one convicted killer, Warren Glowatski (see Box 1.2 in Chapter 1). In the fall of 2005 in a church in Mission, B.C., and in the summer of 2006, they hugged each other during an Aboriginal healing circle that was part of his parole hearing (Mason 2006:A3). The Virks hugged him, they said, to release some of the anger that had built up inside them and to help him to not "carry a heavy heart around with him for the rest of his life" (Mason 2006:A3).

Sentencing circles are not common—they are primarily an Indigenous peoples' cultural practice; the concept of restorative justice is integral to many Indigenous cultures. One sentencing circle consisted of the participants speaking of the victim, the offender, and the nature of the tragedy over a period of five hours. The mother of the victim argued against a jail term for the offender and said she was satisfied with the sentence because it allowed her to speak to the offender in a way that might not have been possible in a "White man's" court. She also felt that her daughter participated in the circle and was "at peace with the way it was handled." Many people are optimistic about the value of sentencing circles and are satisfied with the results. However, the people who participate in circles are biased, because only those who accept responsibility for their crime are allowed to participate. Restorative justice may not work for all kinds of crime and enforcement may be a problem, but it does hold promise for youth offenders and other situations where restoration is possible.

The Death Penalty

Although in Canada capital punishment was abolished in 1976, and a 2001 Ipsos-Reid poll indicated that support for it has fallen to a low of 52 percent (Freeze 2001:A1), the death penalty can still affect Canadians. In 2001, United States authorities wanted to extradite two Canadians to stand trial for murdering three people in the state of Washington. The Supreme Court of Canada, condemning the use of the death penalty, ruled that the two could be extradited only if the U.S. authorities would guarantee that they would not face the death penalty. The U.S. authorities did provide such assurances and the two were extradited. Americans

themselves are showing less support for the death penalty, and a couple of states have halted executions because of the racist bias in death rows.

Is the solution to our "crime problem" to build more prisons and execute more people? Only about 20 percent of all crimes result in a charge, only half of these lead to a conviction, and fewer than 4 percent of convictions result in a jail term. The "lock 'em up and throw away the key" approach has little chance of succeeding. As for individuals who commit occupational and corporate crime, the percentage that enters the criminal justice system is so minimal that prison is relatively useless as a deterrent to others. Furthermore, the high rate of recidivism strongly suggests that the rehabilitative efforts of our existing correctional facilities are sadly lacking. One thing is clear: The existing criminal justice system cannot solve the crime problem.

Is equal justice under the law possible? As long as social problems exist in our society, equal justice under the law may not be possible for all people; however, that does not keep it from being a goal that citizens and the criminal justice system should strive to reach.

WHAT CAN YOU DO?

- Seek out a community/police liaison committee in your neighbourhood and learn about local problems and what people are trying to do about them.

- Seek out an advocacy group and participate in one of its activities. For example, in Ontario, an organization called Justice for Children and Youth challenged the Ontario law banning squeegee kids' solicitations and various kinds of begging (e.g., while intoxicated). This organization seeks participation on its Youth Advisory Committee to help it deal with the problems of young people. It is located in Toronto (tel. 416-920-1633).

- Organize seminars to discuss or debate ideas like the publication of racialization/ethnicity data for crime or the value of restorative justice.

- Work with campus groups to alert female students to the problem of date rape.

SUMMARY

WHY IS IT DIFFICULT TO STUDY CRIME AND YOUTH CRIME?

Studying crime, criminals, and youth crime is difficult because it involves complex human behaviour, and many criminals and victims hide their involvement. There also are problems inherent in using official sources of data, such as the *Uniform Crime Report*, because they reflect crimes that are reported rather than crimes that are committed, and they do not provide detailed information about offenders.

HOW DOES VIOLENT CRIME DIFFER FROM PROPERTY CRIME?

Violent crime consists of actions involving force or the threat of force against others and includes homicide, sexual assault, robbery, and aggravated assault. Property crime consists of taking money or property from another without force, the threat of force, or the destruction of property.

WHY IS SEXUAL ASSAULT AS A VIOLENT CRIME NOT WELL UNDERSTOOD? HOW IS THIS LACK OF UNDERSTANDING REFLECTED IN OUR SOCIAL RESPONSE TO SEXUAL ASSAULT?

First, many people think that sexual assault is a sexually motivated crime, but it is actually an act of violence in which sex is used as a weapon against a powerless victim. Moreover, statistics on sexual assault are misleading at best because sexual assault is often not reported. Many reasons keep victims from coming forward. Some victims may be so traumatized that they just want to forget about it. Others fear the attacker will try to get even. Many also fear how they may be treated by the police and, in the event of a trial, by Crown attorneys.

WHAT IS OCCUPATIONAL CRIME?

Occupational (white-collar) crime refers to illegal activities committed by people in the course of their employment or normal business activity. Occupational crime includes crimes such as employee theft, fraud (obtaining money or property under false pretences), embezzlement (theft from an employer), soliciting bribes or kickbacks, and insider trading of securities.

HOW DOES OCCUPATIONAL CRIME DIFFER FROM CORPORATE CRIME?

Occupational crimes are illegal activities committed by people in the course of their employment or normal business activity. Corporate crimes are illegal acts committed by corporate employees on behalf of the corporation and with its support.

WHAT IS ORGANIZED CRIME AND WHY DOES IT FLOURISH IN CANADA?

Organized crime is a business operation that supplies illegal goods and services for profit. These illegal enterprises include drug trafficking, prostitution, gambling, loan sharking, money laundering, and large-scale theft. Organized crime thrives because there is great demand for illegal goods and services.

HOW DOES YOUTH CRIME DIFFER FROM ADULT CRIME?

Youth crime refers to a violation of law or the commission of a status offence by people who are younger than a specific age. Many behaviours that are identified as juvenile delinquency are not criminal acts per se but status offences—acts that are illegal because of the age of the offender—such as cutting school or purchasing and consuming alcoholic beverages. Juvenile hearings take place in juvenile courts or before juvenile judges, whereas adult offenders are tried in criminal courts.

WHO IS MOST LIKELY TO BE ARRESTED FOR A CRIME IN CANADA?

Men are more likely to be arrested than women. Teenagers and young adults are most likely to be arrested for serious crimes such as homicide, sexual assault, and robbery. Although individuals from all social classes commit crimes, people from lower socioeconomic backgrounds are more likely to be arrested for violent and property crimes, whereas people from the upper classes generally commit white-collar or corporate crimes. Indigenous people and Blacks are overrepresented in arrest data.

HOW DO FUNCTIONALISTS EXPLAIN CRIME?

Functionalists use several theories to explain crime. According to strain theory, people are socialized to desire cultural goals, but many people do not have institutionalized means to achieve the goals and therefore engage in criminal activity. Control perspectives, such as social bond theory, suggest that delinquency and crime are most likely to occur when a person's ties to society are weakened or broken.

HOW DO CONFLICT THEORISTS EXPLAIN CRIME?

Conflict theorists explain criminal behaviour in terms of power differentials and/or economic inequality in society. One approach focuses on the relationship between authority and power and crime; another focuses on the relationship between economic inequality and crime.

HOW DO INTERACTIONISTS EXPLAIN CRIME?

Interactionists emphasize that criminal behaviour is learned through everyday interaction with others. According to differential association theory, individuals have a greater tendency to deviate from societal norms when they frequently associate with people who are more likely to deviate than conform. Labelling theory says that delinquents and criminals are those people who have been successfully labelled by others as such.

HOW DO FEMINIST THEORISTS EXPLAIN CRIME?

Feminist approaches offer several explanations of why women commit crimes: gender discrimination, patriarchy, a combination of capitalism and patriarchy, and a combination of family structure and socialization.

WHAT ARE THE COMPONENTS OF THE CRIMINAL JUSTICE SYSTEM?

The criminal justice system is a network of organizations involved in law enforcement, including the police, the courts, and the prisons. The police are the most visible link in the criminal justice system because they are responsible for initially arresting and jailing people. Criminal courts are responsible for determining the guilt or innocence of people who have been accused of committing a crime.

Imprisonment, conditional sentences, probation, and parole are mechanisms of punishment based on retribution, social protection, rehabilitation, and deterrence.

KEY TERMS

corporate crime, p. 241
crime, p. 233
criminal justice system, p. 250
date rape, p. 237
differential association theory, p. 248
homicide, p. 234
indictable offence, p. 234
labelling theory, p. 248
mass murder, p. 235

medicalization of crime, p. 249
occupational (white-collar) crime, p. 241
organized crime, p. 242
plea bargaining, p. 251
primary deviance, p. 249
property crime, p. 239
punishment, p. 253
restorative justice, p. 254
routine activities crime, p. 232

scapegoat, p. 245
secondary deviance, p. 249
serial murder, p. 236
sexual assault, p. 236
social bond theory, p. 247

strain theory, p. 246
subculture of violence hypothesis, p. 247
summary conviction offence, p. 234
violent crime, p. 234
youth crime, p. 242

QUESTIONS FOR CRITICAL THINKING

1. Do you think that putting surveillance cameras in public places to monitor people and their possible deviant behaviour is a good idea? Why, or why not?

2. How would sociologists argue with the claim that crime is committed by disturbed people?

3. Does the functionalist, conflict, or interactionist perspective best explain why people commit corporate crimes? Organized crimes? Explain your answer.

4. How would you reorganize the criminal justice system so that it would deal more equitably with all people in this country and prevent problems like profiling?

WEBLINKS

Crime Prevention through Social Development
www.ccsd.ca/cpsd/ccsd/index.htm
This site provides information on how social interventions in housing, education, and health can prevent crime, and is especially helpful in preventing youth crime. Interventions have been shown to reduce crime by 25 to 50 percent in 10 years.

Centre for Restorative Justice
www.sfu.ca/crj
This site contains a variety of resources for restorative justice.

Nathanson Centre for Study of Organized Crime and Corruption
www.yorku.ca/nathanson/Links/links.htm
The Nathanson Centre for Study of Organized Crime and Corruption advances the study and discussion of this topic in Canada.

National Crime Prevention Strategy
www.psepc-sppcc.gc.ca/prg/cp/ncps-en.asp
The National Crime Prevention Strategy aims to reduce crime and victimization by tackling crime before it happens. The strategy is based on the principle that the surest way to reduce crime is to focus on the factors that put individuals at risk, such as family violence, school problems, and drug abuse.

Statistics Canada Justice Trend Tables
www40.statcan.ca/l01/ind01/l2_2693.htm
Data at this location are devoted to a wide variety of subjects, such as correctional services, police services, crimes and offences, and so on.

Cecil E. Greek's Criminal Justice Links
www.criminology.fsu.edu/cjlinks
Criminologist Cecil E. Greek has created a site with a huge set of links to crime and justice sites, primarily in the U.S., but also in Canada. These links facilitate the comparison of American and Canadian data.

10

HEALTH, ILLNESS, AND HEALTH CARE AS SOCIAL PROBLEMS

The Terry Fox Run

HEALTH AND ILLNESS AS SOCIAL PROBLEMS

Acute and Chronic Diseases and Disability

Sex and Gender, Class, and Indigenous Status

Obesily

Box 10.1 Social Problems in Global Perspective: HIV/AIDS Worldwide

MENTAL ILLNESS AS A SOCIAL PROBLEM

Treatment of Mental Illness

THE "CRISIS" IN CANADIAN HEALTH CARE

Development of the National Health Care System

Current Issues in the Health Care System

Box 10.2 Social Problems and Social Policy: Health Care: The American Model

PERSPECTIVES ON ILLNESS AND HEALTH CARE PROBLEMS

The Functionalist Perspective

The Conflict Perspective

The Interactionist Perspective

The Feminist Perspective

WHAT CAN YOU DO?

When you get $520 per month and pay $400 for rent, how can you live on $120?

Richard, aged 46, an engineer now on welfare, speaking of the difficulty of purchasing nutritious food on his allowance (author's files).

How many women have that amount of money lying around?

Diana Brynlee, quoted in the Globe and Mail, *March 10, 2001:A2, speaking of her ability to pay for a diagnostic test that can detect cancer early.*

I believe it is a far greater perversion of Canadian values to accept a system where money, rather than need, determines who gets access to care.

Roy Romanow, quoted in the Globe and Mail, *November 29, 2002:A1, as he delivered his report on Canada's health care system.*

Since unreasonable wait times for treatment that pose a risk to patients are an infringement of Charter rights to "life liberty, and security of person," Quebec patients should be able to pay for insurance to cover treatments already provided by medicare to avoid a long wait.

Supreme Court of Canada ruling June 9, 2005, allows people to prevent long waits.

Richard, quoted above, was speaking to the author at a dinner provided by Street Health, a downtown Toronto agency providing a variety of health and social services to recovering addicts and homeless and poor people. Diana Brynlee made her statement after paying to obtain a PET scan (positron emission tomography takes internal pictures of people to diagnose disease). If she had not had the money to pay for it, she would have had to wait longer for a test and missed the opportunity that early diagnosis afforded. She was wondering about the consequences for people who could not afford the test. Roy Romanow disagrees with those such as Don Mazankowski, also the author of a health care report, who think it is a perversion of Canadian values that they cannot use their own money to speed up their diagnosis and treatment. Mazankowski holds that since our health care system was not designed to do all that it is doing now (Mahoney 2002:A3), the system must diversify its revenue stream with more private options and initiatives, such as private clinics. And now the Supreme Court of Canada agrees with Mr. Mazankowski.

The health situations faced by Richard and Diana Brynlee tend to be viewed as *personal problems*, but lack of access to nutritious food and expensive diagnostic tests is also a *social problem*. For one thing, it affects many people; for another, it is a problem that cannot be reduced or eliminated without a significant social response, such as willingness to devote more money to health and social services. Despite their differing viewpoints, both Romanow and Mazankowski agree on the need for more money and/or different options for payment for the health care system. This chapter examines health, illness—including both physical and mental illness—and health care problems and current issues in providing health services in this country.

This chapter also draws attention to inequalities regarding disease and disability for people of different sex, gender, class, and racialization or ethnicity; recent problems like HIV/AIDS and obesity; mental illness as a social problem; and the crisis faced by the Canadian health care system and recommendations to improve it. The sociological perspectives are used to explain health problems, and the chapter concludes with suggestions for what you can do to improve your health and the health of others.

HEALTH AND ILLNESS AS SOCIAL PROBLEMS

According to the World Health Organization (WHO; 1946:3), *health* is a state of complete physical, mental, and social well-being. In other words, health is not only a biological issue, but also a social issue. After all, physical and mental health are intertwined: Physical illness can cause emotional problems; mental illness can produce physical symptoms. Many people think there is a positive relationship between the amount of money a society spends on health care and the overall physical, mental, and social well-being of its people—that spending a great deal of money on health care should result in physical, mental, and social well-being. But if this were true, people in the United States would be the healthiest and most fit in the world, and they are not.

While physical, mental, and social well-being are difficult to measure, *life expectancy*, **an estimate of the average lifetime of people born in a specific year,** is relatively easy to measure. If we use this widely accepted measure of the effectiveness of the health care system, we find the relationship between health expenditure and health of the population is not strong. The U.S. spends the equivalent of more than OECD$4000 (Organisation for Economic Co-operation and Development dollars, adjusted for differences in prices in different countries) per person and Canada spends less than OECD$2500 per person on health care each year (Canadian Institute for Health Information [CIHI] 2001:Figure 64). The health service industry accounts for almost 14 percent of the gross domestic product in the U.S. and 9 percent in Canada, yet Canadians live longer. Whereas U.S. females born in 2000 can expect to live 79.9 years and males can expect to live 74.2 years (U.S. Bureau of the Census 2001), Canadian females born in 2001 can expect to live 82.2 years and males can expect to live 77.1 years (Statistics Canada 2004a:35).

Unfortunately, this high overall life expectancy of almost 80 years does not hold for all the members of Canadian society: A gap of 6 years exists between the life expectancy of Indigenous people and that of the general population (Frideres 2002:155). Besides life expectancy, another widely used measure of the effectiveness of the health care system is the *infant mortality rate*, **the number of deaths of infants under 1 year of age per 1000 live births in a given year.** During the last century, Canada's infant mortality rate has decreased greatly. In 2001, the infant mortality rate (per 1000 live births) for Canada was 5.2 (Statistics Canada 2004a:35). The infant mortality rate is an important indication of a society's level of preventive (prenatal) medical care, maternal nutrition, childbirth procedures, and care for infants. For all our expenditures in health care and use of high-tech equipment, however, infant mortality among Indigenous people is still high, 12.0 in 1997, or more than twice the rate for Canada as a whole (Frideres 2002:155).

Acute and Chronic Diseases and Disability

Life expectancy in Canada and other developed nations has increased largely because vaccinations and improved nutrition, sanitation, and personal hygiene have virtually eliminated many acute diseases, including measles, polio, cholera, tetanus, typhoid, and malaria. *Acute diseases*

are illnesses that strike suddenly and cause dramatic incapacitation and sometimes death (Weitz 1996). Acute diseases that are still common in Canada are chicken pox and influenza. Recently, too, multi–drug-resistant strains of tuberculosis, Lyme disease, and HIV (the virus that causes AIDS)—and now SARS—have become pressing health problems, problems exacerbated by global trade, which has increased 1000 percent since World War II, and the worldwide movement of 1.5 billion airplane passengers per year (Donnelly 2003). (See Box 10.1.)

With the overall decline in death from acute illnesses in high-income nations, however, has come a corresponding increase in *chronic diseases*, **illnesses that are long term or lifelong and that develop gradually or are present from birth** (Weitz 1996). Chronic diseases are caused by various biological, social, and environmental factors. In Chapter 8, we discussed two of the most common sources of chronic disease and premature death: tobacco use, which increases mortality among both smokers and people who breathe the tobacco smoke of others; and alcohol abuse. According to some social analysts, we can attribute many chronic diseases in our society to the *manufacturers of illness*, groups that promote illness-causing behaviour and social conditions, such as smoking (McKinlay 1994). The effect of chronic diseases on life expectancy varies because some chronic diseases are progressive (e.g., emphysema worsens over time), whereas others are constant (e.g., paralysis after a stroke); also, some are fatal (lung cancer), but others are not (arthritis and sinusitis). Because of the combination of longer life expectancies and the disabling consequences of some diseases, new terms have been coined—for example, "active" life or health expectancy and "disability-free" life expectancy. These terms emphasize good health rather than ill health and death. In Canada, from 1995 to 1997, *disability-free life expectancy*, **the number of years of life that can be expected to be free of activity limitation**, was 68.7 years for females and 65.5 years for males, which when subtracted from the life expectancies mentioned above indicate more than 13 years of disability for females and 11 years of disability for males (Statistics Canada 2001b:42)

Some chronic diseases produce disabilities that significantly increase health care costs for individuals and for society. *Disability* can be defined in several ways. Medical professionals tend to define it in terms of

SOCIAL PROBLEMS IN GLOBAL PERSPECTIVE

BOX 10.1   HIV/AIDS Worldwide

Although chronic diseases have replaced infectious diseases as the major cause of death in Canada, infectious diseases are still a problem here and a problem of epidemic proportions in the developing world. Certainly the most widely publicized of these diseases is HIV/AIDS. In Canada, 56 000 people are living with HIV/AIDS, but in the rest of the world, 39.4 million, including 3.2 million children, are living with HIV/AIDS. In 2004 alone, 4.9 million people, including 800 000 children, were newly infected with HIV (UNAIDS 2005). Map 10.1 shows the distribution of HIV/AIDS around the world. Note the huge number of 25.4 million people living with HIV/AIDS in Sub-Saharan Africa. Over 20 million people are thought to have died of AIDS, but this figure is difficult to confirm.

MAP 10.1   A Global View of HIV/AIDS

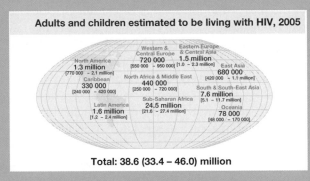

Source: *UNAIDS 2005. Reproduced with permission of UNAIDS.*

In different parts of the world, different approaches have been taken to prevent and treat HIV/AIDS. In Canada and in the Western world generally, since the early 1980s, the approach has been an aggressive educational campaign. A dramatic example of this was the advertising campaign of the AIDS Committee of Toronto urging the use of condoms. These advertisements, called "Condom Country," mimicked Marlborough cigarette advertisements with pictures of rugged cowboys in a Western setting.

Action has also been vigorous in some developing countries. Thailand confronted the problem in 1991 by distributing condoms, shutting down brothels that didn't use them, and requiring radio stations to broadcast HIV/AIDS prevention information hourly. These actions have been effective. In 1990 in Thailand, there were 215 000 new cases of HIV/AIDS; by the early 2000s, the number of new cases was expected to be down to about 90 000 (Shenon 1996).

The story is different in India, where HIV/AIDS appeared in 1991, 10 years after it was recognized as a new disease (Altman 1996). The number of people with HIV/AIDS is exploding in India, and the World Health Organization projects that the country will soon be the world centre of the disease, with one-quarter of all infected people (Burns 1996). One immediate source of the problem is India's truck drivers, who often have long layovers with nothing to do, and the many prostitutes available along the roadsides, flying gaily coloured scarves to identify themselves. Drivers who pick up the disease carry it to other prostitutes in previously uninfected regions as well as home to their wives and future children. The red-light districts of Mumbai, Calcutta, and New Delhi are another source of the growing epidemic. An estimated 52 percent of the brothel "cage girls" (enslaved child prostitutes who are kept in cages during the day so they don't escape) in Mumbai are infected with HIV/AIDS (Burns 1996).

Fighting HIV/AIDS in India means fighting more than the disease. It means fighting the caste system, because prostitutes and those with HIV/AIDS are discriminated against. It means fighting social taboos against talking about sex. It means fighting poverty, because prostitutes who use condoms lose clients and starve. And it means fighting the denial of the problem by political leaders; only $35 million of a five-year $100 million HIV/AIDS prevention program had been spent in four years (Burns 1996).

In many parts of sub-Saharan Africa, the situation is even worse. While this area contains 10 percent of the world's population, it has 70 percent of its HIV/AIDS cases. All governments are undertaking prevention programs, such as the provision of drugs to rape victims and measures to prevent mother-to-child transmission of HIV/AIDS (South Africa reversed its policy of not providing drugs in April 2002).

There is hope, however. In early 2001, after vigorous lobbying by HIV/AIDS activists, the United Nations, and governments of developing countries, five drug companies (Boehringer Ingelheim, Bristol-Myers Squibb, F. Hoffman-LaRoche, GlaxoSmithKline, and Merck) agreed to reduce the price of HIV/AIDS drugs such as antiretrovirals, and generic versions of these drugs are now being produced at costs far below Western prices (UNDP 2001:22). In June 2001, Stephen Lewis, a former UN Ambassador for Canada, was appointed to coordinate efforts for the UN fight against HIV/AIDS in Africa, and a budget of $10 billion was sought for the program. In 2005 much is being pledged to help Africa by the G8 countries, but little money has so far appeared.

How do you think Canada can best contribute to this program?

organically based impairments—that is, the problem is entirely within the body (Albrecht 1992). However, disability rights advocates believe that disability is a physical or health condition that stigmatizes or causes discrimination. Perhaps the best way to define disability is, as medical sociologist Rose Weitz (1996:428) has said, in terms of both physical and social factors: ***Disability*** **is a restricted or total lack of ability to perform certain activities as a result of physical or mental limitations or the interplay of these limitations, social responses, and the social environment.** In Canada in 2001, an estimated 3.4 million people aged 15 and over, or 15 percent of the adult population, had one or more physical or mental disabilities. Older people have more disabilities than younger; women have more severe disabilities than men; and many kinds of disabilities exist. Figure 10.1 shows the mobility and pain-related disabilities that are most prevalent among those aged 15 and over by sex. Mobility is the prime disability experienced by 12.2 percent of women and 8.6 of men. Women experience most other disabilities more than men. Men experience more hearing, learning, and speech problems. (Statistics Canada 2004g:16).

Disabilities are an important social problem because people with disabilities have higher unemployment rates and lower incomes than those without disabilities. Among those 25 to 64 years of age in 2001, 10.7 percent of the disabled were unemployed versus 5.9 percent of the non-disabled. Among those 25 to 54 years of age in 2001, 47 percent of the disabled had incomes below $15 000 versus 25 percent of the non-disabled (Statistics Canada 2004g:18). In addition, many disabled people need specialized equipment like wheelchairs (some motorized), hearing aids, and so on, and some need help with everyday tasks (Statistics Canada 2004g:17).

The number of disabled people continues to increase for several reasons. First, with advances in medical technology, many people who in the past would have died from an accident or illness now survive with impairment. Second, as people live longer, they are more likely to experience chronic diseases (such as arthritis) that may have disabling consequences (Albrecht 1992). Third, people born with serious disabilities are more likely to survive infancy because of medical technology. (However, only a small percentage

FIGURE 10.1   Mobility and Pain-Related Disabilities

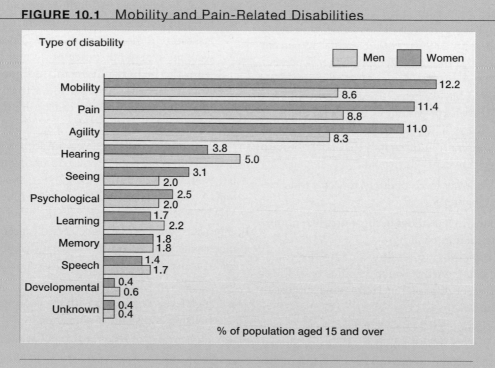

Source: Statistics Canada, 2004, Canadian Social Trends, *Catalogue no. 11-008 (Spring):16.*

of people with a disability today were born with it; accidents, disease, and violence account for most disabilities in this country.) Many people with a chronic illness or disability will not live out the full life expectancy for people in their age category.

Sex and Gender, Class, and Indigenous Status

Chronic diseases vary substantially by major demographic variables. Non-fatal diseases or conditions are more common among females. In this chapter, much data comes from the National Population Health Survey (NPHS). The NPHS was conducted by Health Canada and Statistics Canada to measure the health status of adult, non-Indigenous Canadians and to monitor changes over time. (Children and Indigenous adults [i.e., adults with "Aboriginal status"] were surveyed separately.) The content is multidimensional, including physical, mental, and social components, and the method is in-depth interviewing. The first wave of data collection occurred in 1994–95 and consisted of a sample of 17 626 Canadians, and subsequent waves were undertaken in 1996–97 and 1998–99.

According to the 1998–99 NPHS, larger percentages of females than males aged 12 and over reported having arthritis (19 percent vs. 11 percent), high blood pressure (13 percent vs. 9 percent), migraine (13 percent vs. 4 percent), and bronchitis/emphysema (3 percent vs. 2 percent). A higher percentage of males than females reported having heart disease (5 percent vs. 4 percent) and diabetes (4 percent vs. 3 percent; Statistics Canada 2001b:25). The reasons for these differences could be a combination of factors that contribute to females' longer life expectancies, such as

- consuming lower levels of drugs, tobacco, and alcohol (see Chapter 8);

- not working in hazardous occupations, like mining and construction; and

- having biological protection during the childbearing years, during which females have lower levels of heart disease, but later, being subject to more disease.

Class, measured by income, is related to longevity. According to the National Population Health Survey, people in lower-income groups in 1994–95 had a higher mortality rate than those in upper-income groups (Statistics Canada 1998a). Class, measured by income and education, is also related to chronic conditions. According to the Joint Canada/United States Survey of Health, Canadians (and Americans) who were in the poorest income quintile were much more likely than those in the richest quintile to report fair/poor health status (23 vs. 4 percent; see Figure 10.4). As well, smaller percentages of people with university degrees than people with elementary or less education reported having heart disease (2.7 percent vs. 11.1 percent) and having functional disability (5.5 percent vs. 24.3 percent; Segall and Chappell 2000:162–163). The reasons for these differences are likely a combination of people with lower levels of education

- being unable to afford nutritious food (Richard's opening quote is telling, but evidence also comes from a study of welfare incomes and expenses in Toronto: Given the cost of housing, welfare did not cover housing and the cost of food for a single-person household, a two-parent two-child family, and a single-parent two-child family [Vozoris et al. 2002]);

- engaging in risky health behaviour like smoking, drinking, and drug use (see Chapter 8);

- working in dangerous industries; and

- living in some areas, like the North, far from medical care. (In the Yukon and NWT, in 1993, people were an average distance of 23.6 and 155.2 km from the nearest physician, and population per physician was much higher than in the 10 provinces, according to a chart from the Canadian Medical Association (Hewa 2002:66).

Indigenous status is a very important predictor of illness, both acute and chronic. According to sociologist James Frideres (2002:156–157), Indigenous people have higher rates of infectious diseases, like tuberculosis and HIV/AIDS, than the general Canadian population; chronic conditions, like diabetes and cancer, are likewise increasing. The reasons for these differences are similar to those for class-related differences in health, including:

- high levels of poverty, with the accompanying poor housing and sanitary conditions;

- higher rates of risky health behaviour, and

- being distant from medical care in Nunavut, Yukon, and Northwest Territories.

Besides sex and gender, class, and Indigenous status, many other structural variables, like marital status, social support, and neighbourhood, and inequality of income in society, affect the health of people. Determining the relative influence of these variables and the health behaviour variables identified in Chapter 8 is not an easy task. With the comprehensive set of questions about health behaviour and social structural variables in the National Population Health Survey, it is possible to begin this analysis. Using the NPHS data, sociologists Margaret Denton and Vivienne Walters (1999) studied the relative influence of health variables—like smoking, drinking, physical activity and weight—and structural variables—like family structure, education, occupation, income, and social support—on subjective health status and functional health status data from the Health Utilities Index (in the NPHS), which inquires into vision, hearing, speech, mobility, cognition, emotion, and so on. They discovered that the social structural variables had a greater effect on health than the health variables. This finding confirms that health and illness are social problems and suggests that changing social conditions would be more helpful than health promotion in improving health. Denton and Walters also found differences between males and females. Females' health was determined more by structural variables (e.g., being in the highest income bracket, working full-time, caring for a family, and having social support) than males' health. Regarding the influence of risky health behaviour, males' health was determined more by smoking and drinking, and females' health was determined more by exercise and weight.

For both men and women, a non-heterosexual sexual orientation can also be a factor in health, due to ignorance and discrimination on the part of doctors and other health care professionals. This issue and related health issues for persons living with HIV/AIDS are discussed in Chapter 6.

Obesity

A relatively new health risk—being overweight—is now affecting about half the Canadian population. Excess weight is linked to heart disease, Type II diabetes, back problems, certain forms of cancer, and stroke. A healthy weight-range is indicated by the body mass index (BMI), which is calculated by dividing weight in kilograms (kg) by height in metres squared (m^2). A person with a BMI

of less than 18.5 is considered underweight; with a BMI of 18.6 to 24.9, of normal weight; with a BMI of 25.0 to 29.9, overweight; and with a BMI of 30.0+, obese.

According to the latest report of the Canadian Community Health Survey (CCHS) in 2004, 2.7 percent of Canadians aged 15 and older were underweight; 46.7 percent were of normal weight; one-third were overweight; and 14.9 percent were obese. Whereas 15.9 percent of men were obese, 13.9 percent of women were obese. (Statistics Canada 2004a). These figures were based on self-reports. In 2005 the CCHS released figures obtained with actual measurements and found not only higher rates of obesity (23 percent for Canadian adults), but also big increases for some age groups in comparisons with figures obtained in 1978–79. Figure 10.2 shows big increases in obesity for the age groups 12 to 17 (from 3 to 9 percent), 25 to

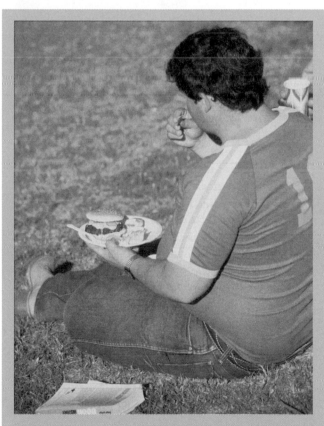

According to a recent Canadian Community Health Survey, 23 percent of adult Canadians are obese. What kinds of problems does this increasing trend present for the health care system in the future?

FIGURE 10.2 Obesity Rates More than Doubled for Some Age Groups

Source: Statistics Canada, 2005, "Canadian Community Health Survey: Obesity among Children and Adults," The Daily, July 6, Catalogue no. 11-001.

34 (from 9 to 21 percent), and 75+ (from 11 to 24 percent) over the past 25 years (Statistics Canada 2005b)

A curvilinear pattern was found for age, with middle-aged people being the most likely to be obese. Region of the country is also important. People in Newfoundland and Labrador and New Brunswick were found to have higher rates of obesity than people in the rest of the country.

Obesity is not just a problem for Canadians; it is a problem worldwide. Although data are difficult to confirm, as of 2000, the World Health Organization estimates the number of obese adults to be over 300 million worldwide. And obesity is not limited to Western societies. The WHO estimates that over 115 million people in developing countries also suffer from obesity-related problems (WHO 2003). If the proportion of overweight to obese people found in Canada were true of the rest of the developed world, nearly 1 billion people would be overweight or obese.

How can we reduce the overweight/obesity problem? Besides the usual suggestions for self-help groups, increased physical activity, and better diets, suggestions now include putting health warnings, like those found on cigarette packages, on packages of junk food, as well as adding a tax to junk food to discourage consumption. Would you be discouraged from eating junk food by graphic pictures of health consequences? Would you buy as much junk food if it were taxed like cigarettes?

MENTAL ILLNESS AS A SOCIAL PROBLEM

Mental illness is a social problem because of the number of people it affects, the difficulty of defining and identifying mental disorders, and the ways in which mental illness is treated. Although most social scientists use the terms *mental illness* and *mental disorder* interchangeably, many medical professionals distinguish between a *mental disorder*—a condition that makes it difficult or impossible for a person to cope with everyday life—and *mental illness*—a condition that requires extensive treatment with medication, psychotherapy, and sometimes hospitalization.

The most widely accepted classification of mental disorders is the American Psychiatric Association's (1994) *Diagnostic and Statistical Manual of Mental Disorders IV (DSM-IV)*. (See Figure 10.3.) The *DSM* is now in its fourth edition, and with each revision, its list of disorders has changed and grown. Listings change partly because of new scientific findings, which permit more precise descriptions that are more useful than broad terms covering a wide range of behaviours, and partly because of changes in how we view mental disorders culturally (at one time, for example, homosexuality was considered a mental disorder). Despite these changes, some social analysts still question the extent to which mental health professionals can accurately detect and treat mental disorders.

How many people are affected by mental illness? According to the Canadian Community Health Survey, as shown in Table 10.1, some 4 percent of people interviewed reported having experienced symptoms or feelings associated with major depression, almost 5 percent experienced anxiety, and when substance dependence is included, 1 in 10 Canadians aged 15 and over experienced mental problems at some time within 12 months of the interview.

FIGURE 10.3   Mental Disorders Identified by the American Psychiatric Association

1. Disorders first evident in infancy, childhood, or adolescence	These disorders include mental retardation, attention-deficit hyperactivity, anorexia nervosa, bulimia nervosa, and stuttering.
2. Organic mental disorders	Psychological or behavioural disorders associated with dysfunctions of the brain caused by aging, disease, or brain damage.
3. Substance-related disorders	Disorders resulting from abuse of alcohol and/or other drugs, such as barbiturates, cocaine, or amphetamines.
4. Schizophrenia and other psychotic disorders	Disorders with symptoms such as delusions or hallucinations.
5. Mood disorders	Emotional disorders such as major depression and bipolar (manic-depressive) disorder.
6. Anxiety disorders	Disorders characterized by anxiety that is manifest in phobias, panic attacks, or obsessive-compulsive disorder.
7. Somatoform disorders	Psychological problems that present themselves as symptoms of physical disease such as hypochondria.
8. Dissociative disorders	Problems involving a splitting or dissociation of normal consciousness, such as amnesia and multiple personality.
9. Eating or sleeping disorders	Includes such problems as anorexia and bulimia or insomnia and other problems associated with sleep.
10. Impulse control disorders	Symptoms include the inability to control undesirable impulses, such as kleptomania, pyromania, and pathological gambling.
11. Personality disorders	Maladaptive personality traits that are generally resistant to treatment, such as paranoid and antisocial personality types.

Source: Adapted from American Psychiatric Association, 1994, Diagnostic and Statistical Manual of Mental Disorders IV, *Washington, DC: American Psychiatric Association.*

Rates of mental illness are affected by gender, age, class, and Indigenous status. It is often thought that females have higher rates of mental illness, including depression and episodes that cause distress, than males; however, when alcohol and substance dependence are included, the researchers found little difference in prevalence (11 percent for females vs. 10 percent for men). The same study found that youth aged 15 to 24 were more likely than other age groups to suffer from mental disorder or substance abuse problems. About 18 percent of them reported experiencing symptoms or feelings consistent with the disorders or substance dependence People in lower social classes have higher rates of mental disorders than people in upper classes. But according to sociologist Harley Dickinson (2002), this relationship could be explained by the "downward

TABLE 10.1 Measured Mental Disorders or Substance Dependence in the Past 12 Months (as total number and percentage of the Canadian population)

	Total		Males		Females	
	Number	%	Number	%	Number	%
Major depression	1 120 000	4.5	420 000	3.4	700 000	5.5
Mania disorder	190 000	0.8	90 000	0.7	100 000	0.8
Any mood disorder	**1 210 000**	**4.9**	**460 000**	**3.8**	**750 000**	**5.9**
Panic disorder	400 000	1.6	130 000	1.1	270 000	2.1
Agoraphobia	180 000	0.7	40 000	0.4	140 000	1.1
Social anxiety disorder (Social phobia)	750 000	3.0	310 000	2.6	430 000	3.4
Any anxiety disorder	**1 180 000**	**4.7**	**440 000**	**3.6**	**740 000**	**5.8**
Alcohol dependence	640 000	2.6	470 000	3.8	170 000	1.3
Illicit drugs dependence	170 000	0.7	120 000	1.0	50 000	0.4
Substance dependence	**740 000**	**3.0**	**540 000**	**4.4**	**200 000**	**1.6**
Total - Any measured disorder or substance dependence	**2 600 000**	**10.4**	**1 190 000**	**9.7**	**1 410 000**	**11**

Source: Statistics Canada, 2003, "Canadian Community Health Survey: Mental Health and Well-being," The Daily, *September 3,* Catalogue no. 11-001.

drift hypothesis"—that people with mental illnesses are unable to function properly, neither getting an education nor keeping a job. Thus, they slip into the lower classes (Dickinson 2002:376). Frideres (2002:157) states that, compared with the rest of the Canadian population, for Indigenous people the suicide rate is three times higher (six times for the 15 to 24 age group), the homicide rates are twice as high, and the rate of violent death is three times higher. Reasons for these differences are attributed to significant differences in living conditions, as mentioned above, and lack of opportunities.

Treatment of Mental Illness

People who seek professional help for mental illness are treated with medication and psychotherapy, to help them understand the underlying reasons for their problem. Because medication is used so routinely today, we tend to forget that institutionalization used to be the most common treatment for severe mental illness. In fact, it was the development of psychoactive drugs that made possible the deinstitutionalization movement of the 1960s.

Deinstitutionalization **is the practice of discharging patients from mental hospitals into the community.** Although deinstitutionalization was originally devised as a solution for the problem of warehousing mentally ill patients in large, prison-like mental hospitals in the first half of the 20th century, many social scientists now view deinstitutionalization as a problem. To understand how this solution evolved into a problem, one must understand the state of mental health care in Canada during the 1950s and 1960s. The practice of *involuntary commitment* (i.e., without a patient's consent) allowed many patients to be warehoused in mental hospitals for extended periods of time, with only minimal and sometimes abusive custodial care. According to sociologist Erving Goffman (1961), a mental hospital is a classic example of a *total institution*—**a place where people are isolated from the rest of society for a period of time and come under the complete control of the officials who run the institution.** Patients are stripped of their individual identities—or depersonalized—by being required to wear institutional clothing and follow a strict regimen of activities, meals, and sleeping hours; sometimes they are referred to impersonally, as a "CMI" (a person who is chronically mentally ill; see Grobe 1995). The deinstitutionalization movement sought to release patients from mental

Although there are many causes of homelessness, ranging from lack of affordable housing to drug dependency, some analysts believe that the deinstitutionalization of patients from mental hospitals has significantly increased the number of people living on the streets in Canada. What other alternatives can you suggest for dealing with mental illness?

hospitals so that they could live at home and go about their daily activities. Professionals believed that the patients' mental disorders could be controlled with medication and treatment through community-based mental health services. Other advocates hoped that deinstitutionalization would remove the stigma attached to hospitalization for mental illness.

Deinstitutionalization did occur in a substantial way in Canada. Between 1960 and 1976, the number of beds in mental hospitals declined from 47 633 to 15 011, although the number of beds in psychiatric wards in general hospitals increased from 844 to 5836 (Cochrane et al. 1997:1).

Although deinstitutionalization had worthwhile goals—protection of civil rights, more humane and less costly treatment—in too many cases, it simply moved

people out of mental hospitals into the streets and jails. Today, critics of deinstitutionalization argue that it exacerbated long-term problems associated with treating mental illness.

If schizophrenia and other serious mental illnesses do not lead to jail, they often result in homelessness. One study concluded that as many as 30 percent of homeless people were previously patients in mental hospitals, and about 80 percent have some diagnosable mental disorder (Searight and Searight 1988). However, it is difficult to determine which came first—the mental disorder or homelessness. If you were homeless, for instance, what are the chances that you might develop mental health problems if you tried to survive on the streets or in and out of shelters and city jails? In any case, social scientists and homeless advocates agree that most homeless shelters and other community services cannot adequately meet the needs of people known as "the homeless mentally ill" (see Torrey 1988).

Although involuntary commitment to mental hospitals has always been controversial, it remains the primary method by which police officers, judges, social workers, and other officials deal with people—particularly the homeless—whom they have reason to believe are mentally ill and imminently dangerous to themselves and others (Monahan 1992). However, it should be recognized that involuntary commitment is a social control mechanism, used to keep people with a history of mental illness off the streets so that they cannot engage in violent crime. It does little—if anything—to treat the medical and social conditions that contribute to mental disorders (Catalano and McConnell 1996). Given this, mental hospitals tend to function as revolving doors to poverty-level board-and-care homes, nursing homes, or life on the street. Patients who can pay private psychiatric facilities through private insurance coverage or public health care are not part of this cycle (Brown 1985).

THE "CRISIS" IN CANADIAN HEALTH CARE

We hear so often that the Canadian health care system is in a state of crisis. In this section, we will outline the development of the system, and its current issues. We will also look at the American model of health care.

Development of the National Health Care System

While the idea of universal health care had been circulating for some time, and Saskatchewan had pioneered its major features, the features of the national health care system emerged with the following pieces of federal legislation and recent changes in funding:

- The *Hospital Insurance and Diagnostic Service Act* 1957 provided insurance for hospital and diagnostic services.

- The *Medical Care Act* 1966 provided insurance for medical services, to which all the provinces agreed by 1972, emphasizing five principles: universality—all Canadians should be covered; accessibility—reasonable access must be unimpeded by financial or other barriers; comprehensiveness—all medically necessary services should be guaranteed; portability—Canadians should be able to have their benefits transferable to other provinces or other countries; and public administration—the system to be operated by a public body on a non-profit basis.

- The *Canada Health Act* 1984 confirmed the five principles and prohibited private charges or extra billing by doctors or hospitals.

- The federal government substantially reduced its contributions to the provinces in the mid-1990s to 26 percent or less of the total cost.

- The federal government increased its contributions to the provinces in 1999, but not to the 50 percent level established at the beginning.

- A federal–provincial agreement in February 2003 saw the federal government state that it will inject almost $35 billion into the health care system over the next five years. This was increased to $41 billion in the 2005 budget.

The many health care changes, such as reductions in the size, number, and functions of hospitals; increased use of drugs and home care; increased knowledge of health by patients and consultation of alternate health practitioners; and new technological developments for diagnosis and treatment, have brought about many issues that must be addressed.

Current Issues in the Health Care System

Coverage of Care

Since much of contemporary health care is neither hospital-based nor delivered by physicians, coverage of care is an issue. With the restructuring of hospitals, closing of hospital beds, and increase of out-patient procedures, the need for home care has grown. Home care ranges from visits just after hospital discharge to long-term help in maintaining independence. Not all such care is covered by the public health care system, especially the long-term general support. Although ministers of health have increased support for home care, demand seems to exceed supply. The cost of drugs can also be a problem for those in home care. During the last 25 years, the use and effectiveness of drugs has greatly increased, so that drugs now constitute double the percentage of health care costs that they did in 1975 (CIHI 2001:Figure 69). Drugs taken outside the hospitals are not covered by the publicly funded system. Because not everyone, especially those among the poor, has an insurance plan to cover him or her, the need for "pharmacare," or government support of drug purchases, has increased. Several provinces have created plans where citizens pay a yearly fee after which the government pays for the drugs. An example of such a program is the British Columbia plan. In 1995, the B.C. government established its reference-based program where, for each class of drugs, a low-priced (not necessary the lowest priced), effective drug is selected and the program will pay for it. If a higher-priced drug is desired, but no medical benefit is present, the individual pays the difference (Segall and Chappell 2000:252). Needs for other kinds of care, like long-term care, palliative care, and dental care, are great and will likely increase as well as the population ages.

Accessibility

A second issue is accessibility. People complain of waiting lists for treatment. According to Statistics Canada, a significant increase in unmet health care needs occurred between 1994–95 and 2000–2001. Self-reported unmet needs rose from 4.2 percent to 12.5 percent of the population—an estimated 3.2 million people. Respondents gave a variety of reasons for unmet needs, the most prominent being waiting time. The percentage that gave waiting time as the reason rose from 23 percent in 1998–99 to 30 percent in 2000–2001. The percentage who indicated availability of services as the reason remained stable at 14 percent, and those who presented personal circumstances, such as being too busy, as the reason declined somewhat (Statistics Canada 2002b). The distance some people in Canada need to travel for medical health, especially in the North, has already been noted.

In Canada, a major factor affecting access to health care is region. Region can be defined in several ways. In Canada, provinces are frequently used as the measure for region. A better measure of region for health purposes is the "health region." In Canada, 119 health regions have been designated. The advantage of using this measure is that variation within provinces can be identified. Access to health care both between and within provinces can thus be addressed. For the past four years, *Maclean's* has been ranking health regions in Canada according to indicators such as life expectancy, low birth weight, incidence of pneumonia and flu, preventable hospital admissions, physicians and specialists per capita, and 10 other indicators. The "Fourth Annual Ranking" covers 54 of the 119 regions (those with populations over 125 000) and captures 87 percent of the national population (Hawaleshka 2002:23). The ranking of health regions can be criticized for

- choosing these particular indicators—no mention of cancer outcomes is made;

- weighting the indicators—outcomes have a weighting of 2 and resources a weighting of 1;

- ranking individual indicators instead of presenting actual rates (differences in ranking could reflect greatly or insignificantly different rates); and

- combining the indicators in an overall score when regions have high and low rankings for different indicators.

However, the "Fourth Annual Ranking" shows definite variation in Canada, where comprehensive health services are supposed to be accessible for all citizens. The ranking also seems to be reliable; a comparison with the "Third Annual Ranking" shows the same geographical differences in access to care (Marshall 2001).

As expected, communities with medical schools (and thus, with teaching hospitals) appear among those with the best scores. Edmonton leads the list (as in the "Second" and "Third" rankings), followed by Hamilton,

Saskatoon, Ottawa, and Toronto. Thirteen of 15 "Communities with Medical Schools" appear in the top half of the ranking. The next group, "Other Major Communities," which includes wealthy suburbs like North and West Vancouver, and Mississauga, Brampton, and Burlington (Ontario), demonstrates that communities close to major centres profit from the proximity of medical centres and people's ability to afford the quality services available. These two regions stood first and fourth in the ranking overall. The third group, "Largely Rural Communities," tends to fall in the lower half of the rankings, with the notable exceptions of Kelowna, B.C.; Nanaimo, B.C.; Lethbridge, Alberta; Lévis, Quebec; and Moncton, New Brunswick. The top scorer in this group and the fifth overall, Kelowna, has developed programs to help residents stay healthy; for example, an outreach program teaches coronary-risk patients healthy habits, and a retirement community encourages residents to do as much as possible for themselves to prevent "learned helplessness" (Marshall 2001).

Costs and Payment Methods

The overall costs of the health care system and the way they are paid is increasingly an issue. While the overall costs of the health care system have risen, they have been contained: Health care costs were only 9 percent of the GDP in 1998, a figure very similar to that in the late 1980s. Although Canada has a single-payer, public method of financing health care, a private segment now exists in our system—for cosmetic surgery, dental practice, eyeglasses, drugs outside hospitals, and other out-patient aids. It amounts to 30 percent of the total health care expenditures in 1998 (CIHI 2001:Figure 64). While this private-care figure is high relative to that of some European countries, it is well below the United States' comparable figure of 55 percent (CIHI 2001:Figure 64). See Box 10.2 for a discussion of how Americans pay for health care.

In some countries with universal health care, people have an opportunity to pay for their own operations and thereby jump the public queue. The two-tier system of health care, with both public and private funding and delivery of health care, results in differential access—poorer access for those who cannot afford to pay. Pressure groups in the private sector are advocating that private clinics and services be made available for people

SOCIAL PROBLEMS AND SOCIAL POLICY

BOX 10.2 Health Care: The American Model

The United States spends more on health care than any other high-income country, and it is well known for health care facilities like the Mayo Clinic and its many medical discoveries, such as drugs and diagnostic tools. Yet many people in the United States go without health care because it is too expensive. An estimated 41.2 million people in the United States had no health insurance in 2001 (Goldstein 2002). About one-quarter of those not covered by health insurance are children.

Access to health care is often limited by racialization, class, or sex and gender. Do people have a *right* to health care? No, say some; it is unfortunate that some people suffer illness or disability, but it is not up to society to make the world a fair place (Engelhardt 1996). On the contrary, say others, health care is a right, not a privilege or a choice, because the choice is ultimately between life and death, and every individual has inherent worth (Rawls 1971). So far, the nays have it in the United States; but among developed nations, only the United States and the Union of South Africa stand together: all others provide universal health coverage for their citizens.

The United States, too, is concerned about containing health care costs. Several models are in place to deal with this cost. Many insurance companies have established an option known as *preferred provider organizations* (PPOs), with such names as HealthSelect (a Blue Cross/Blue Shield entity). In a PPO, doctors work out of their own offices on a fee-for-service basis, but contract with an insurance company to provide care for insured patients. The doctors agree to charge set fees (set by the insurance company) for particular services; these fees may be higher or lower than those for other patients who are not covered by the PPO. This model of health care delivery shares certain commonalities with the health maintenance organization (HMO) and managed care models.

Like other private insurance plans, HMOs emerged during the Great Depression as a means of providing workers with health coverage at a reasonable rate by keeping costs down. A **health maintenance organization provides, for a fixed monthly fee, total heath care with an emphasis on prevention to avoid costly treatment later.** The doctors do not work on a fee-for-service basis, and patients are encouraged to get regular checkups and to practise good health habits (exercise and diet). As long as patients use only the doctors and hospitals that are affiliated with their HMO, they pay no fees, or only small co-payments beyond their insurance premium (Anders 1996). Believing that the HMO model could be a source of high profits because of its emphasis on prevention, many for-profit corporations moved into the HMO business in the 1980s (Anders 1996). However,

research has shown that preventive care is good for the individual's health but does not necessarily save money.

Early detection of HIV infection, diabetes, or high cholesterol, for example, often means a lifetime of costly treatments and drugs. Indeed, some health experts have suggested that for-profit HMOs are unlikely to provide top-notch early detection and prevention programs because of the costs—especially future costs—involved (Rosenthal 1997). Some critics have even charged that some HMOs require their physicians to withhold vital information from their patients if it is going to cost the HMO money to provide the needed procedure or hospitalization (Gray 1996). Recently, some HMOs have responded to such criticism (and threats of lawsuits) by allowing doctors and patients greater participation in the HMO's process of determining treatment.

Another approach to controlling health care costs is known as *managed care*—a term that is used to refer to any system of cost containment that closely monitors and controls health care providers' decisions about medical procedures, diagnostic tests, and other services provided to patients (Weitz 1996). In most managed care programs, patients choose a primary-care physician from a list of participating doctors. When patients need medical services, they first contact the primary-care physician; then, if a specialist is needed for treatment, the primary-care physician refers the patient to a specialist who participates in the program. Doctors must get approval before they perform certain procedures or admit a patient to the hospital. If they do not, the insurance company has the prerogative of not covering part of the cost.

Today, of the total U.S. health care bill, patients pay slightly less than 25 percent; insurance companies pay about 33 percent, and the government pays more than 40 percent (Pear 1996). Although private health insurance companies were well established by the 1950s, and almost all working people and their immediate families had hospitalization insurance, those who did not work—the elderly and the poor—were often uninsured. Federal legislation extending health care coverage to the elderly and the poor was not passed until the 1960s. Two kinds of public insurance are available in the United States: Medicare and Medicaid. Medicare is public health insurance for people age 65 and over and is funded by Social Security payments. Although Medicare provides coverage for many older people who otherwise would have no health insurance, there are large gaps in its coverage, and elderly near-poor individuals often find it difficult to pay the required deductibles (an initial specified amount that the patient pays before the insurance begins payments) and co-payments (shared costs). Also, Medicare provides only limited coverage for costly and sometimes long-term expenses, such as post-hospital nursing services, home health care, nursing homes, and hospice services (Toner and Pear 1995). Unlike Medicare coverage, which is based primarily on age, Medicaid provides medical, hospital, and long-term care for people who are poor *and* either aged, vision-impaired, pregnant, or have a disability. Also, whereas Medicare is funded by people's payments into the Social Security system, Medicaid is funded by the federal and state governments. As a result, many people view Medicaid as a welfare program and Medicare as an entitlement program—Medicare recipients are assumed to have earned medical coverage through years of hard work and paying into the system. Both programs are considered costly to the public because there are no incentives to keep costs down.

Comparisons of how healthy Canadians and Americans feel according to their income quintile, and thus, the contribution of our respective systems to the most vulnerable members of society (from the Joint Canada/United States Survey of Health conducted from November 2002 to June 2003) can be found in Figure 10.4. The richest people in both countries are less likely to report fair/poor health than those who are poorer. But differences become very pronounced among the poorest people. Whereas 23 percent of Canadians in the poorest group reported fair/poor health, 31 percent of Americans reported fair/poor health (Statistics Canada 2004c). The lack of health insurance by the lowest income earners in the U.S. may explain the difference.

Some have suggested that the 2005 Supreme Court of Canada ruling on the right to pay for private health coverage, discussed below, will put us on the path to an American system. Others have suggested that some European countries, such as Britain, have this dual system, and their public health system has not been mortally wounded. Given what you know now

Figure 10.4   Fair/Poor Health by Households Income Quintile, Canada and the United States, 2002–2003

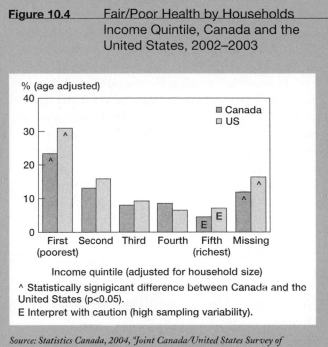

^ Statistically signigicant difference between Canada and the United States (p<0.05).
E Interpret with caution (high sampling variability).

Source: Statistics Canada, 2004, "Joint Canada/United States Survey of Health," The Daily, June 2, Catalogue no. 11–001.

about the consequences of this ruling, to what extent is our system like the U.S. system, and is this good for the health of Canadians?

The United States' health care system is frequently thought of as a model of financing and delivery of care. Do you think it provides any solutions for the Canadian system?

who can afford to pay for them. But many others fear that allowing two tiers in the health system will reduce overall support for the public system.

However, the Supreme Court of Canada made a historic ruling in June 2005 that may significantly alter our health care system. In a battle that originated in Quebec and that pitted two institutions (the public health care system and the *Charter of Rights and Freedoms*) that Canadians hold in high esteem against each other, the Supreme Court of Canada ruled that the Quebec government cannot prevent people from paying for private insurance for procedures covered under the public system. Unreasonable wait times pose

a threat to our rights to "life, liberty, and security of the person." While this ruling was for the province of Quebec, it has implications for the rest of the country. The case was brought by an individual who was waiting almost a year for hip surgery and also involved a doctor who was trying to set up a private hospital in Quebec. How this ruling will affect the health care system is difficult to determine now. While people may decide to pay for reasonably inexpensive elective surgery, like hip replacement and cataract surgery, to get it quickly, they likely would not be able to pay for cancer care that reaches hundreds of thousands of dollars in some cases.

An idea that combines public and private insurance also comes from Quebec. In July 2005, Quebec Health Minister Philippe Couillard responded to a report about the rising costs of health care by suggesting that the province use more privately delivered health care, financed and regulated by the public and paid for by an old-age insurance scheme, to cover the health problems of an aging population. Under this plan, all taxpayers would pay premiums into the plan and receive money during times of illness in their old age, and they could use premiums as they wish for public or private care, such as nursing homes or private care. He stressed that this is not a tax, but a program in which "you pay for guaranteed service to yourself" (Séguin 2005:A6).

How has the public/private mix changed in Canada during the last few years? How do you expect it to change in the future?

Supply and Demand of Health Care Professionals

How can we ensure that we have enough health care professionals? Are health care networks an efficient operating model, and if so, how should practitioners be paid? After laying off nurses in the mid-1990s as a cost-cutting measure and after reducing positions in medical schools because of a fear of a surplus of doctors, Canada's provinces now face the looming possibility of a severe shortage of nurses and doctors. The Canadian Registered Nurses Association suggested in 2002 that by 2011, we will need 60 000 nurses, about 25 percent of the current nursing labour force; and a survey by the College of Family Physicians predicts a shortage of 6000 family physicians (a shortfall of around 10 percent) by 2011 (Galt 2002:A5). Even if the need is exaggerated in this report, many more of both professional groups will likely be needed to deal with an aging population and retirement of current professionals.

Not only is there a need for more professionals, but also their payment and organization of work are concerns. Doctors have seen their salaries fall somewhat in the last 30 years, and nurses have experienced several pay freezes in that time. Doctors are paid on a fee-for-service basis and have been criticized for "churning," or having patients return for multiple visits for a problem. They have also been criticized for trying to see too many in a single day. More imaginative methods of payment, like *roster*, or *capitation*—payment per patient in the care of a small network of doctors, nurses, and other health workers, where the incentive is to keep people well and reduce the care they require—should be offered. Local community health centres were formed in Quebec in the 1970s. In Ontario, some health centres offering a variety of health and social services exist. Recently, in Ontario, the Ministry of Health asked doctors if they would be interested in setting up family health networks consisting of at least five doctors and some nurses. The doctors would work normal hours, and a nurse triage system (organizing patients according to the severity of their problems) would be available after hours, so that patients would have 24/7 coverage. In questionnaires sent to general practitioners, a small percentage of doctors responded positively, but others were not interested in changing their pattern of fee-for-service, perhaps because they were offered only $97 per person per year for the care (Smith 2002:A8). The results suggest that a wider variety of options are likely needed if networks are to gain more support.

The Use of Alternative Health Care

Over the last decade, the interest in and the consultation of alternate health practitioners has increased. The NPHS has studied this behaviour, asking respondents, "In the past 12 months, have you seen or talked to an alternate health care provider such as an acupuncturist, naturopath, homeopath or massage therapist about your physical, emotional or mental health?" (Millar 2001:14). Chiropractors were not on this list, but were included by respondents to a question about contact with health care providers. Chiropractors were the most consulted alternative practitioner (Millar 2001:14).

The researchers found an increase in the consultation of alternate health care providers over its three waves. In 1998–99, 17 percent of Canadians consulted them, up from 15 percent in 1994–95 (Millar 2001:12). Factors significantly related to consultation were sex, region, age, and experience of chronic pain:

- Women consulted them more than men (19 vs. 14 percent);
- Westerners consulted them more than Easterners (25 and 22 percent for B.C. and Alberta respectively vs. less than 10 percent for each of the Atlantic provinces);

- Working age people (25 to 64 years of age) consulted them more than younger or older people (19 vs. 11 percent); and
- People who experienced chronic pain consulted them more than those experiencing no pain (26 vs. 15 percent; Millar 2001:13).

In addition, those who believed in self-care and followed more proactive health behaviour, like taking vitamins and avoiding foods with a high fat or sugar content, and those who thought that the traditional system was not meeting their needs were more likely to consult alternative providers than others who did not report this behaviour or perception (Millar 2001:17). Millar concluded that people were "supplementing, not rejecting, conventional health care" (2001:19) and suggested that as the population ages and more multiple chronic diseases emerge with accompanying pain that "the demand for alternate therapies could increase even further." (2001:20) Given the extensive use of alternative health providers, the willingness of some doctors to recommend their use, and the willingness of some private insurance plans to pay for their use, the integration of alternate and traditional health providers is an important issue to be addressed.

Quality of Care

Two measures of our quality of care are (a) Canadians' rating of the system; and (b) reports of different patterns of medical practice, including different rates of procedures, such as surgical operations, that might be expected to have close-to-uniform rates across the country. Although Canadians' rating of their recent experience with doctors and general treatment by the system is high, the percentage rating the overall system excellent has declined substantially. According to the Conference Board of Canada, whereas 60 percent of the population rated the system as excellent or very good in 1991, only one-quarter rated it that highly in 2000 (CIHI 2001:Table 6).

A study by sociologists Noralou P. Roos and L. L. Roos (1994) found these problems with medical intervention:

- physicians vary in their patterns of medical practice;
- evidence of benefit does not exist for certain procedures, such as for many Caesarian sections;
- a significant amount of care provided is inappropriate; and

- application of practice guidelines does not guarantee lower surgical rates.

Reports about significant variation in surgical rates in different parts of Canada regularly appear. For example, a study of data from 2000 reported regional variations on these procedures:

- hip replacements: an overall rate of 59.7 per 100 000 population, but a rate in Newfoundland of 35.5 per 100 000, and in Nova Scotia, 76.4 per 100 000;
- knee replacements: an overall rate of 67.2 per 100 000 population, but a rate in Quebec of 34.4 per 100 000, and in Manitoba, 94.8 per 100 000; and
- hysterectomies: an overall rate of 484 per 100 000 population, but a rate in Ontario of 476 per 100 000, and in Newfoundland, 750 per 100 000 (Statistics Canada 2002b).

This variation suggests the discretionary nature of medicine and that greater attention should be given to the study of the effectiveness of surgical and other procedures.

Use of Technology

Large flows of information take place among providers of traditional, alternative, and robotic care (e.g., surgical procedures at a distance). How will we integrate this information with e-health and with other forms of learning? Patients must be notified in advance about how their information is to be used and must give their permission. They must also have the opportunity to opt out of projects (e.g., drug promotions). Besides improved ways of maintaining connections among providers, the system needs a better means of keeping track, across a variety of locations and data bases, of the treatment of individual patients, drugs prescribed, and so on. One controversial suggestion is that a chip be placed on the health card, so that doctors will have a record of the patient's history and thus be able to provide better care.

These are some of the major issues faced by our health care system. Not only do others exist, but more will also emerge with the social and technological developments that are continuously taking place.

PERSPECTIVES ON ILLNESS AND HEALTH CARE PROBLEMS

What are the primary causes of health care problems in Canada? How can health care be improved? The answers that social scientists give to these questions depend on their theoretical framework. Analysts approaching these questions from a functionalist perspective focus on how illness affects the smooth operation of society and how medicine serves as a social institution. Some sociologists, using a conflict perspective, focus on how a capitalist economy affects health and health care delivery. Those who use an interactionist framework look at the social and cultural factors affecting communication between doctors and patients. Finally, feminist theorists look at inequalities of racialization, class, and sex and gender.

The Functionalist Perspective

The functionalist perspective views illness as a threat to a smoothly functioning society, which depends on all people fulfilling their appropriate social roles. According to this view, when people become ill, they cannot fulfill their everyday responsibilities to family, employer, or the larger society and instead adopt the *sick role*—patterns of behaviour expected from individuals who are ill. Sociologist Talcott Parsons (1951) identified four role expectations of the sick role:

1. Sick people are not responsible for their incapacity;

2. They are exempted from their usual role and task obligations;

3. They must want to leave the sick role and get well; and

4. They are obligated to seek and comply with the advice of a medical professional.

In other words, illness is a form of deviance that must be controlled. According to Parsons, physicians are the logical agents of social control. By certifying that a person is physically or mentally ill and by specifying how the ill person should behave, doctors use their professional authority to monitor people with illnesses, thereby granting them only a temporary reprieve from their usual social roles and responsibilities. Today, however, the dramatic increase in chronic illness and disorganization in the delivery system for medical services mean that many people have less access to doctors, and doctors have less control over those aspects of patients' lives that can increase their chances of becoming ill. Acknowledging these major changes, sociologist Alexander Segall has modified the original conception of the sick role by identifying six expectations. The rights of sick people comprise

- making decisions about health-related matters;

- being exempt from performing usual well roles; and

- making use of social support and depending on others outside the medical profession;

and the duties of sick people comprise

- maintaining health and managing illness;

- engaging in routine self-health management; and

- making use of available health care resources. (Segall and Chappell 2000:2)

These changes take into account both the increase in chronic conditions and the need for a more active rather than passive role for the sick person.

Functionalists believe that the problems in Canadian health care are due to macrolevel changes, such as the development of high-tech medicine and drugs; restructuring of the system, including the reduction of the hospital sector; and increased demand for health care by consumers. As a result of these changes, the equilibrium of the system has been greatly affected, and procedures must be implemented to restore the equilibrium. Some observers, writing in a functionalist manner, state that incremental changes will solve the problems. For example, C. David Naylor, then dean of the Faculty of Medicine and now president of the University of Toronto, suggests that incremental changes—such as strengthened home care services, provision of a more equitable coverage of prescription drugs, wider adoption of blended compensation mechanisms (e.g., salary, roster, and fee-for-service) for physicians, primary-care reform, integrated regional services, quality improvement initiatives, and better information gathering—are the best ways for the health care system to "be rendered more accountable, integrated, and sustainable in the next millennium" (Naylor 1999:24).

The Conflict Perspective

The conflict approach is based on the assumption that problems in health care delivery are rooted in the capitalist economy, which views medicine as a commodity produced and sold by the medical–industrial complex. The *medical–industrial complex* **encompasses both local physicians and hospitals as well as global health-related industries such as the pharmaceutical and medical supply companies that deliver health care** (Relman 1992). Although this expression was coined to typify the U.S. health care system, it applies in part to the Canadian system also. For example, the pharmaceutical companies have been well known to put profits first, as outlined by physician Joel Lexchin (2002). Lexchin (2002:402) argues that when profit and health considerations come into conflict—in the examples of Lilly's anti-arthritis drug, benoxaprofen, and Bristol-Myers Squibb's statin drug, Pravachol (pravastatin)—then profit wins.

Another disturbing example of the influence of pharmaceutical companies is the treatment of Dr. Nancy Olivieri in 1997 because of her publishing research about the problems of a drug, deferiprone. The research was supported by the drug's manufacturer, Apotex, and Apotex threatened her with legal action because she broke a confidentiality agreement by publishing the research. Olivieri alleged that at first, the Hospital for Sick Children and the University of Toronto, where she held appointments, did not support her in her case. She was ultimately supported by a report commissioned by the Canadian Association of University Teachers that stated that she "should be given redress for the unfair treatment she received" (Thompson 2001:15) and that the "Hospital for Sick Children and the University of Toronto could and should have effectively supported Dr. Olivieri" (Thompson 2001:14). After a five-year legal battle, a deal was announced on November 12, 2002, by Olivieri, the Hospital for Sick Children, and the University of Toronto, resolving all outstanding disputes.

Radical conflict theorists say that only when inequalities based on sex and gender, class, and racialization/ethnicity—and on occupation, neighbourhood, and region—are reduced and a system based on a different treatment model is developed will inequalities in health outcomes be reduced. For example, observers such as sociologists Pat Armstrong and Hugh Armstrong (1996:227) want to see a system that is oriented to a care model and not to a medical model like the present one. They advocate applying the four determinants of health identified in the Lalonde Report (by the then federal minister of health, Marc Lalonde [1974])—human biology, lifestyle, environment, and health care—to the provision of services: emphasizing health maintenance and promotion; improving occupational and income opportunities; and improving the physical and social environment. As long as variable societal conditions—environmental pollution, lack of affordable housing, high levels of stress associated with working conditions or unemployment, inadequate nutrition, lack of early diagnosis for diseases such as breast cancer and heart disease, and kind of available health model—affect people, health outcomes will be unequal.

Some conflict theorists also call attention to the unintended negative effects of doctors and suggest that the doctor–patient relationship should be demystified. An early theorist of the negative effects of doctors and the system was Ivan Illich, who coined the term *iatrogenesis,* **problems caused by doctors and the health care system.** These problems are of three types. *Clinical iatrogenesis* occurs when pain, sickness, and death result from medical care. The term used in Canada is "adverse effects." A study of 2000–2001 hospital records in Canada found that adverse effects, such as the wrong medication or dose, infection, adverse transfusion reactions, and in-hospital hip fractures, occurred in 7.5 percent of hospital admissions; and of these, 36.9 percent were preventable and 20.8 percent resulted in death (Baker et al. 2004). Projected to Canada's 2.5 million annual admissions, this study suggests that 185 000 adverse effects occur annually, and 70 000 of these are preventable. *Social iatrogenesis* occurs when the health care system creates dependency and ill health, for example, by discouraging home births. *Cultural iatrogenesis* occurs when the system undermines the ability of people to care for themselves (Illich 1975:165). Conflict theorists argue that if patients were given the information and resources they need for prevention, self-treatment, and home care, the need and demand for expensive medical care would be greatly reduced (Stewart 1995). And some of these theorists are doctors themselves. The Medical Reform Group is a Toronto-based voluntary association of physicians and medical students who believe that the medical profession must look to the social, economic, and political forces shaping health and health care in Canada. They believe that health care is a right and that today's health care is too hierarchical, giving too much power to doctors and not enough to patients. (The Medical Reform Group website is **www.hwcn.org/link/mrg/**.)

Another group that challenges accepted thinking in the area of health is the disability rights organizations. They are especially concerned with the public's support of euthanasia, or mercy killing, of people with disabilities who cannot speak for themselves. A recent example of this is the Tracy Latimer story (see also Box 5.2 on page 132). Latimer was a 12-year-old girl with severe cerebral palsy. Her father asphyxiated her, was tried and convicted of her killing, and was sentenced to prison. Disability rights advocates argue that it would not be a problem to have a disability, if persons with disabilities were not discriminated against and oppressed. In the United States, a rights group that campaigns against euthanasia is called Not Dead Yet (from the film, *Monty Python and the Holy Grail*, in which someone about to be put on a cart of plague victims says, "I'm not dead yet"). Its website is **www.notdeadyet.org**.

In the past, most patients relied on doctors for heath-related information. Today, many people receive medical information from the media and the internet. Many thousands of websites are devoted to health and medical information, ranging from potentially life-saving research in top medical journals to alternative therapies such as herbal preparations and colon irrigation (Fisher 1996; Kolata 1996b). Many computer bulletin boards, chat groups, and Usenet newsgroups have emerged to support people with conditions such as HIV/AIDS and multiple sclerosis (Kantrowitz 1993). Some U.S. corporations have online ventures that offer not only research on any health care topic but also information on physicians, nurses, hospitals, HMOs, and preferred provider organizations—in the United States, fees come from the providers, not from users viewing the pages (Fisher 1996). Because of the proliferation of medical information on the internet, Health Canada is working to provide guidance to the consumer. Whether or not this proliferation of information helps to demystify doctor–patient relationships remains to be seen.

The Interactionist Perspective

Interactionists believe that many problems pertaining to health and illness in our society are linked to social factors that influence how people define our health care system. According to interactionists, we socially construct notions of crisis according to our desire to promote political objectives. Some past provincial premiers, like Ralph Klein and Mike Harris, have described our system as being in a state of crisis. As noted at the beginning of this chapter, Don Mazankowski has declared, in a report for the Alberta government, that in its present form the system is unsustainable. On the other hand, Roy Romanow, who led a health care commission for the federal government, says that it is not in a state of crisis.

On February 5, 2003, the provincial premiers and Prime Minister Jean Chrétien (but not the territorial leaders) agreed to a new deal to pay for new programs to address some of the issues mentioned above. These new programs include increased home care, relief from high drug costs (a form of pharmacare), and reduced waiting times for high-tech diagnostic tests. The deal also encourages the formation of networks or group clinics of family physicians and the creation of a database that will be able to link doctors', hospitals', and governments' databases. In addition, a health council was created to report on how the money is spent and to determine whether the provinces are meeting targets for the programs specified in the federal–provincial agreement. Money was also to be made available to support existing services such as hospitals and more health programs for Indigenous people. Although the new federal money offered was substantial, $12 billion in new funds for the next three years and upwards of $35 million over five years ($41 million according to the 2005 budget), it was less than the recommendation in the final report of the Romanow Commission.

Interactionists are also interested in using telecommunications to promote health. A relatively new method being tried is Telehealth, a toll-free, confidential telecare service. For example, Telehealth Ontario, a program recently introduced in Ontario that follows models in other parts of the country, is a free, confidential telephone service anyone can call to get health advice or general health information from a registered nurse. Available 24 hours a day, 7 days a week, it provides information on symptoms, illness, medications, nutrition and health, help for teens, and so on, but does not provide prescriptions or specific doctor referrals, and it is not a substitute for emergency (911) calls.

Interactionists also examine how individuals can construct their own health, to be producers rather than consumers of health. Writing in the interactionist manner, K. Green (1985) introduced the concept of self-health management, which recommends that people engage in practices to promote their own health—from following good health behaviour guidelines, to seeking alternative care, to seeking comfort from a friend. *Self-health management* **includes self-care practices, mutual aid, and membership in self-help groups** (Segall and Chappell 2000:131). While the last two items are self-explanatory, the notion of self-care requires some expansion. This concept originated with Ivan Barofsky (1978) and has been developed by Alexander Segall (Segall and Chappell 2000:135–138). Self-care comprises four components:

- *regulatory* self-care consists of daily habits that affect health, like eating a balanced diet, getting rest, and exercising;

- *preventive* self-care consists of deliberate actions taken to reduce the risk of illness, such as brushing and flossing teeth;

- *reactive* self-care consists of determining what to do when one feels ill and may involve seeking over-the-counter remedies as well as seeking advice from friends or experts; and

- *restorative* self-care consists of compliance with treatments and medications prescribed by professionals, or part compliance, according to self-determination.

Self-care emphasizes lay control over health decision making and health maintenance.

The Feminist Perspective

Feminist theorists examine the extent to which women are treated in a disadvantageous manner in health or health care through processes like medicalization. *Medicalization* **is the treating of a person's condition as an illness.** This topic is of particular concern to women because many of women's natural conditions have been treated as physical or psychological illnesses. Deborah Findlay and Leslie Miller (2002) have written on the medicalization of women's bodies and women's lives. They begin by describing the rise of the medical profession, showing how healing became "men's work" and women's bodies "offered a lucrative new territory for

profit-making" (Findlay and Miller 2002:188). First, mothering, child rearing, and childbirth were defined as medical problems; then, disorders suffered by women—anorexia nervosa, for example—were defined as diseases. Findlay and Miller (2002:202) suggest that, in light of medical talk of "manopause" to typify such youth-seeking behaviour as undergoing cosmetic surgery, buying a sports car, and dating much younger women, men may now be about to experience the same process. Another concern of feminists is the treatment of women in research studies.

Adequate funding for research on women's health issues and diseases is lacking, and women have been excluded from most experimental drug trials, which are conducted to determine the positive and negative effects that a specific drug has on a given category of patients (Laurence and Weinhouse 1994). Many clinical studies virtually ignore women. For example, although women are the group with the most rapidly increasing incidence of HIV/AIDS, very little HIV/AIDS research relating to women is being conducted (Nechas and Foley 1994). Similarly, in a widely reported study on the effects of aspirin on heart disease, all of the patients were men, even though heart disease is the leading cause of death for both women and men (Steering Committee of the Physicians' Health Group Study 1989).

The failure to include women in research contributes to their differential treatment for certain kinds of medical problems. For example, women with the same symptoms of kidney failure as men are much less likely to receive an organ transplant (Steingart et al. 1991). Similarly, far fewer women than men with an abnormal heart scan are referred for a procedure known as cardiac catheterization to remedy the problem. Without adequate studies, diseases in women may go unrecognized, be misdiagnosed, or be attributed to a non-physical factor.

A third concern of feminists has been the presence and treatment of women in the medical profession itself. It is well known that until recently it was not easy for women to enroll in medical faculties, and thus not easy to become a doctor. With the increase of women in medical schools came the corresponding increase in women in medicine and related health professions. In 2000, women made up more than half (53 percent) of all doctors and dentists in Canada, according to Statistics Canada's *Women in Canada: Work Chapter Updates* (2001h:8).

WHAT CAN YOU DO?

- Volunteer at an agency, like Street Health, that deals with people who are on welfare, are homeless, are recovering addicts, or are recently released from prison. Among the sociological insights you will get is an appreciation of how their health is affected by their social status. You may also make a difference in the life of a participant.

- Some students on your own campus may not be able to afford nutritious meals, especially at the end of term when meal cards and money run out. Students at York University organized a program called Food 4 Thought, a food bank for students. The bank gets funds from grants and student fees, gets workers from student volunteers, and gives food to students who can no longer afford it. Unused food is given to community organizations (its website is **www.yorku.ca/food**). Other post-secondary schools have done the same. If your college or university has not created a food bank, you might see if such a need exists and, if so, help to fill it.

- Participate in or organize a committee for research integrity at your college. Nancy Olivieri and David Healy—a professor whose offer of employment was originally cancelled at the University of Toronto (though later partially reinstated), possibly because of his criticism of Prozac—spoke at a fundraiser for Doctors for Research Integrity at the University of Toronto, sponsored by the Students' Administrative Council, to discuss the problems of the influence of commercial interests at universities. Since this is likely to be a continuing problem, much scope exists for future educational programs.

- Develop a self-care management program for yourself. Consider how you could make use of mutual aid and the self-help groups that are available on university and college campuses, and how you could follow the four types of self-care to maintain your health.

- Study the way women, and men too, are exploited for profit in cosmetic surgery and other health-related ways. Develop a seminar on body consciousness. You might start with the work of Tovée and associates (1997), who compare the BMIs (see above) of post-secondary female students, glamour and fashion models, and anorexic females. Fashion models (BMI=17.6) are halfway between the female students (a normal BMI=21.6) and anorexic females (BMI=14.7).

- If you plan to do research in this area in the future, apply for a grant from the recently formed Canadian Institute of Health Research. As one of its four directions, it plans to improve the health status of vulnerable populations and create institutes for specific populations, such as Indigenous peoples, and children and youth. Included in this list is the Institute of Gender and Health, which supports research about how sex and gender interact with other health factors, leading to different risk factors and interventions for women and for men. Of particular interest is research on gender inequalities.

SUMMARY

WHY ARE ILLNESS AND HEALTH CARE SOCIAL PROBLEMS?

Health care is a social issue because, according to the World Health Organization, health is a state of complete physical, mental, and social well-being. Although people in Canada pay less for health services than people in the United States, our measures of health show better outcomes than theirs. Thus, high expenditures do not translate into improved life expectancy for everyone.

HOW HAVE HEALTH CARE PROBLEMS CHANGED OVER THE LAST CENTURY?

Since acute illnesses (e.g., measles, polio) are largely under control with vaccinations and improved public health practices, most health problems today are chronic diseases (e.g., arthritis, diabetes, heart disease) or disabilities (e.g., back injuries, hearing or vision problems, brain injuries), which require long-term treatment. Medical advances mean that many people born with serious disabilities survive, as do many who would have died from acute illnesses or accidents in earlier times. As more people survive and live longer, more are likely to experience chronic illnesses and disabilities.

WHY IS OBESITY A SOCIAL PROBLEM?

Close to half of Canadians over 15 years of age are overweight/obese. Being overweight is related to a number of diseases, such as heart disease and Type II diabetes. People in rural Canada are more likely to be overweight than people in urban Canada. The problem exists worldwide, even in developing countries. Suggestions to reduce this problem are similar to those suggested to reduce smoking, such as warnings on packages and taxes on junk food.

WHY IS MENTAL ILLNESS A SOCIAL PROBLEM?

Mental illness is a social problem because of the number of people it affects, the difficulty in defining and identifying mental disorders, and the ways in which it is treated. Deinstitutionalization—discharging mental patients from hospitals into the community—was considered a solution to the problem of warehousing patients, but it has created new problems.

HOW DO SEX AND GENDER, CLASS, AND INDIGENOUS STATUS AFFECT PHYSICAL AND MENTAL HEALTH?

Men, the poor, and Indigenous people have lower life expectancies than women, the rich, and non-Indigenous people. Although women report more chronic conditions and disabilities than men, they do have higher disability-free life expectancies than men. The poor and elementary-educated report more disability and poorer health than the rich and highly educated. Although women report more mental illness than men, when addictive behaviour is included, men have higher rates of mental illness. Indigenous people have higher rates of suicide than non-Indigenous people.

WHAT ARE THE FIVE CHARACTERISTICS OF THE CANADIAN HEALTH CARE SYSTEM?

Our system is universal—covering all Canadians; accessible—unimpeded by financial and other barriers; and comprehensive—providing service on the basis of need. It is portable across provinces. Lastly, it is publicly managed and funded.

WHY IS HEALTH CARE CONSIDERED A PROBLEM?

With the restructuring and closing of hospitals and the capping of doctors' fees, waiting periods for care are longer, especially in emergency rooms. As well, many people have unmet health needs and use alternate health providers. Other components of care, like home care, pharmacare, and access to diagnostic equipment will become part of the system, due to the recent agreement among the premiers and prime minister. Issues of quality of care and organization of doctors and other health professionals are more problematic.

WHAT ARE THE SOCIOLOGICAL EXPLANATIONS FOR HEALTH CARE PROBLEMS?

Functionalists consider the sick role a form of deviance that medicine as an institution controlled until recently. Some functionalists believe that the whole health system must be reorganized; others believe that incremental change is the best answer. Some conflict theorists believe that our health problems are rooted in capitalism and the medical–industrial complex. Some, like Ivan Illich, criticize the control of the system and would like to see people take more responsibility for their own health. Others, including some doctors, believe that only when sex and gender-, class-, and Indigenous status–based inequalities are reduced will inequalities in health care be reduced. Interactionists believe that communication problems between politicians and advocates create much of our concern about the health care system, but that these problems can be resolved through negotiation. They believe that people must become more involved in self-health management and health care reform. Feminists believe that women have been treated in a disadvantageous manner regarding their bodies and health, the distribution of money to diseases that affect them, and their participation in medical careers.

KEY TERMS

acute diseases, p. 261
chronic diseases, p. 261
deinstitutionalization, p. 268
disability, p. 263
disability-free life expectancy, p. 261
health maintenance organization (HMO), p. 272
iatrogenesis, p. 277

infant mortality rate, p. 261
life expectancy, p. 260
managed care, p. 272
medical–industrial complex, p. 277
medicalization, p. 279
self-health management, p. 279
total institution, p. 268

QUESTIONS FOR CRITICAL THINKING

1. Because Canadians take pride in their high level of life expectancy, they are usually surprised to learn that the infant mortality rate of Indigenous people is double the rate of Canadians generally. Why is this, and what do you think individuals can do at the community level to save these young lives?

2. In what ways are sex and gender, class, and Indigenous status intertwined with physical and mental illness? Consider causes and treatments.

3. Do you know people with mental illness? What do you think would help them function better in our society?

4. Now that our health care system will get additional funding for home care, pharmacare, better diagnostic services, and money for health care professionals, what would you propose next to reform the system?

WEBLINKS

Canadian Health Network (CHN)
www.canadian-health-network.ca
CHN is a national, non-profit, bilingual, Web-based health information service. Its goal is to help Canadians find the information they are seeking on how to stay healthy and prevent disease. This network of health information providers includes Health Canada and national/provincial/territorial non-profit organizations, universities, hospitals, libraries, and community organizations. Links to over 10 000 resources are available, covering almost any health problem.

Commission on the Future of Health Care in Canada (The Romanow Commission)

www.hc-sc.gc.ca/english/care/romanow/index1.html

Building on Values: The Future of Health Care in Canada, the final report of the Romanow Commission, is available for downloading. While some years have gone by since its release, it is probably the best discussion of our health care system and its problems.

Health Care Information Resources

http://hsl.mcmaster.ca/tomflem/top.html

Health Care Information Resources contains medical and health care resources for patients, family and friends, and health care workers.

Health Canada Online

www.hc-sc.gc.ca/english/

Health Canada Online provides an overview of health care in Canada, up-to-date information on health topics, headlines, governments' negotiations, information about diseases, etc., and links to frequently asked questions.

Medical Reform Group

www.hwcn.org/link/mrg/

The Medical Reform Group is an organization of physicians, medical students, and others committed to ensuring access to high-quality health care for all Canadians. Access links to a newsletter, briefs, and other like-minded health, social, and environmental organizations.

Overeaters Anonymous

www.oa.org

This program, like the other anonymous programs mentioned in Chapter 8, is a 12-step recovery program for compulsive overeating. It is not just about weight loss, but also addresses physical, emotional, and spiritual well-being. It does not promote any particular diet and is not a religious organization. It claims to have 7000 groups in 52 countries.

11

THE CHANGING FAMILY

THE NATURE OF FAMILIES

Changing Family Structure and Patterns

Are Canadian Families in Decline?

Box 11.1 Social Problems in Global Perspective: The Changing Family around the World

Changing Views on Marriage and Families

PERSPECTIVES ON FAMILY-RELATED PROBLEMS

The Functionalist Perspective

The Conflict Perspective

The Feminist Perspective

The Interactionist Perspective

DIVERSITY IN INTIMATE RELATIONSHIPS AND FAMILIES

Singlehood

Postponing Marriage

Common-Law, Cohabitation, and Domestic Partnerships

Dual-Earner Marriages

Comparing Two-Parent and One-Parent Households

CHILD-RELATED FAMILY ISSUES

Reproductive Freedom, Contraception, and Abortion

Infertility and New Reproductive Technologies

Adoption

Parenting Style

Teen Pregnancies and Unmarried Motherhood

Same-Sex Parenting

DIVORCE AND REMARRIAGE

DOMESTIC VIOLENCE

Child Abuse

Box 11.2 Social Problems in the Media: Speaking Out on Incest

Box 11.3 Social Problems and Social Policy: Should Spanking Be Permitted?

Spouse Abuse

Social Responses to Domestic Violence

FAMILY-RELATED PROBLEMS IN THE 21ST CENTURY

WHAT CAN YOU DO?

I don't need a knight in shining armour to rescue me.

A university student (author's files)

It's difficult to expect people to live together for such a long time.

Another university student (author's files)

I was working from six-thirty in the morning to seven at night without breaks. I wasn't eating. I was irritable. I couldn't deal with anybody. I was fighting with my wife all the time. We were breaking apart. I wasn't communicating anymore. The job took control of me. I was possessed. I didn't feel patient with my daughter anymore. It was taking a big toll on me, and I didn't like it at all. I decided it wasn't worth it and the only way to stop it was to leave.

Ernie, a physical therapist, explaining that he resigned from a managerial position in a large corporation when he discovered that his job was damaging his family relationships (Gerson 1993:145)

Since the divorce what's been hard is worrying about paying the bills   having enough money for food for my son, I don't even get to think about buying him new sneakers.

A 35-year-old secretary, who was married for 16 years and had one child (Kurz 1995:90)

I never had a chance to be young . . . In high school when they were saying, 'Let's move to first base and kiss boys,' I was doing things with my father.

Jeannie Hilton (see Box 11.2)

Many people today experience the problems described by these individuals: women wanting equality, worries about long-term commitment, the family–work dilemma, economic hardship after divorce, and sexual abuse. Although most sociologists believe that the family as a social institution will endure in one form or another, they also acknowledge that family-related problems are a challenge not only to individuals but also to our entire society.

THE NATURE OF FAMILIES

What is a family? According to sociologist Robin Wolf (1996), that question generates heated debate: Some say that any definition of the family must emphasize tradition and stability; others argue that any useful definition must take into account diversity and social change. Traditionally, *family* has been defined as a group of people who are related to one another by blood, marriage, or adoption and who live together, form an economic unit, and bear and raise children (Benokraitis 1993). Today, however, the traditional definition of family is often modified to incorporate diverse living arrangements and relationships such as single-parent households, cohabiting unmarried couples, domestic partnerships of lesbian or gay couples, and several generations of family members (grandparent, parent, and child) living under the same roof. To encompass all these arrangements, we will use the following definition as we look at family-related social problems: A **family is a relationship in which people live together with commitment, form an economic unit and care for any young, and consider the group critical to their identity** (Benokraitis 1993; Lamanna and Riedmann 1994).

Changing Family Structure and Patterns

The basis of the traditional family structure is **kinship, a social network of people based on common ancestry, marriage, or adoption.** Kinship is very important in pre-industrial societies because it serves as an efficient means of producing and distributing food and goods (clothing, materials for building shelter) and transferring property and power from one generation to the next. In many pre-industrial societies the primary kinship unit is the **extended family, a family unit composed of relatives in addition to parents and children, all of whom live in the same household.** Extended families typically include grandparents, uncles, aunts, or other relatives in addition to parents and children. When the growing and harvesting of crops is the basis of economic production, extended families mean that large numbers of people participate in food production, which can be essential to survival. Living together also enables family members to share other resources, such as shelter and transportation. Though extended families are not common in Canada, except in some immigrant communities, they are in some countries in Latin America, Africa, Asia, and parts of Eastern and Southern Europe (Busch 1990).

With industrialization, other social institutions begin to fulfill kinship-system functions. The production and distribution of goods and services, for example, largely shifts to the economic sector. The form of kinship that is most typical in industrialized nations is the ***nuclear family,*** **a family unit composed of one or two parents and her/his/their dependent children who live apart from other relatives.** The nuclear family in an industrialized society functions primarily to regulate sexual activity, socialize children, and provide family members with affection and companionship.

Table 11.1 shows the change in different types of families over 70 years.

Although many people view the two-parent nuclear family as the ideal family, in the 1960s a higher percentage of Canadian families consisted of a married couple and one or more children aged 24 and under, and a much lower percentage of lone parents occurred than in either 1931 or 2001 (common-law couples were first included in the census in 1981; Statistics Canada 2002l). Sociologists attribute the current decrease of couples with children to a greater number of births among unmarried women, a trend toward postponing or forgoing marriage and childbearing, and high rates of separation and divorce. Note the high number of lone parents in the past. This could have occurred because of the death of one of the parents.

Are Canadian Families in Decline?

Will the family as a social institution disappear in the future? Social analysts answer this question differently, depending on whether they adopt a traditional definition of the family or a modified definition. Sociologist David Popenoe (1988, 1996) uses a traditional definition and believes that three trends mark the coming end of the traditional nuclear family:

- The divorce rate has increased sharply (it currently is 2.3 per 1000 people in Canada (Statistics Canada 2002e), and parents increasingly decide to forgo marriage, so a sizable number of children are being raised in single-parent households apart from other relatives.

- Large numbers of married women have left the role of full-time mother and housewife to go into the labour market, and not all the functions of the former role are being fulfilled.

- The focus of many families has shifted away from childbearing to the needs of the adult members. Increasingly, even when parents have young children to raise, they break up if their psychological and self-development needs are unmet in the marriage relationship (Popenoe 1995:16).

TABLE 11.1   Census Families Time Series

Census year	Married couples with children at home %	Common-law couples with children at home %	Lone parents %	Married couples without children at home %	Common-law couples without children at home %
1931	55.4	n/a	13.6	31.0	n/a
1941	56.6	n/a	12.2	31.2	n/a
1951	57.6	n/a	9.9	32.5	n/a
1956	n/a	n/a	8.6	n/a	n/a
1961	62.3	n/a	8.4	29.3	n/a
1966	62.9	n/a	8.2	28.9	n/a
1971	60.1	n/a	9.4	30.5	n/a
1976	60.1	n/a	9.8	30.1	n/a
1981	55.0	1.9	11.3	28.1	3.7
1986	51.9	2.7	12.7	28.2	4.5
1991	48.1	4.0	13.0	29.2	5.8
1996	45.1	5.5	14.5	28.6	6.2
2001	41.5	6.3	15.7	29.1	7.5

Source: Statistics Canada, 2002, Profile of Canadian Families and Households: Diversification Continues, 2001 Census, *October 22, Catalogue no. 96F0030.*

Some sociologists have suggested that if marriage and the family weaken enough and no satisfactory substitute for marriage emerges, industrial societies will not survive (Davis and Grossbard-Shechtman 1985).

According to some analysts, research has shown that the structure of the family is undergoing profound changes around the world, in both rich and poor nations (see Box 11.1). These analysts say the family isn't declining, it's simply changing. From this social-change perspective, families are becoming more complex and diverse; they are not in a state of irreversible decline (Cherlin 1992; Skolnick 1991). In fact, according to

SOCIAL PROBLEMS IN GLOBAL PERSPECTIVE

BOX 11.1   The Changing Family around the World

Yelena Polyakovskaya lives with her 6-month-old baby, relying on friends and babysitters to watch Aleksandr when she is at work. The father, an unmarried journalist, has never seen his child. Her 6-year-old son, Simeon, is being raised by his grandmother and great-grandmother in Kiev. Polyakovskaya says she hopes to bring him to Moscow, but cannot even afford train fare to visit him.

She loves her job covering music and ballet, but it is ill paid. In her bare one-room apartment, she sleeps on a tiny, fold-out couch next to the baby's crib. An ironing board serves as a desk. But like many women raising children alone, she said she does not want to marry again.

"My life is difficult," she said, "but God, if I had to come home from work and clean, cook and iron for a husband who keeps telling me I am doing it wrong, it would be even worse."

Yelena Polyakovskaya, age 32, a television reporter in Russia (Stanley 1995)

Yelena Polyakovskaya is one of a growing number of women in Russia raising her family without a husband. Approximately 15 to 20 percent of Russian families are single-parent households. This is similar to Canada, but in Russia, single mothers span all social strata; in Canada, single-parent households are much more likely to be poor (Ross et al. 2000:145). In Japan, single-parenthood because of abandonment or divorce is rare, but a practice called *tanshin hunin* has the same effect. When middle managers are transferred, they go without their families so that their children don't have to change schools. When possible, the fathers commute home on weekends, but the mothers are essentially single parents (O'Connell 1994).

Increasing single-parenthood is just one worldwide trend. According to Judith Bruce, author of a report published by the Population Council, a non-profit group in New York, "trends like unwed motherhood, rising divorce rates, smaller households and the feminization of poverty are not unique to America, but are occurring worldwide" (Lewin 1995). Among the report's findings are the following:

- Divorce rates are rising. In many developed countries, the divorce rates doubled between 1970 and 1990; in less developed countries, about one-quarter of first marriages end by the time women are in their 40s.

- Unwed motherhood is increasing virtually everywhere.

- Children in single-parent households are more likely to be poor than are children in two-parent households, especially when the parent is the mother (often termed the feminization of poverty).

Though the reason varies from country to country, more women are entering the work force and taking increasing economic responsibility for children. For example, in Bangladesh, older husbands frequently take young wives. When a husband dies, the wife must find work to support her children. In Asia, if a father who migrates for better work opportunities stops sending money, the mother must support the family herself. In sub-Saharan Africa, a woman's husband may go on to another polygamous marriage and support those children instead (Lewin 1995).

The fact that families around the world are changing in similar ways shows that there is nothing inevitable about the form of the family or the roles of women and men even within a single society (O'Connell 1994). The fact of so much change in the most basic unit of society also poses important questions for the 21st century. Is the basic problem really inequality between women and men? Would shared responsibilities in the home and equal opportunities in the workplace create better families? Can some general principles for social policies be developed, given vastly different societal conditions? What do you think?

sociologist Andrew Cherlin (1992), the family will last as a social institution precisely because it can adapt to social change and modify its form. However, Cherlin goes on to say that the best way to minimize the costs of change in the family unit is to modify the other social institutions of daily life—such as the economy and workplace.

Changing Views on Marriage and Families

The term *marriage* refers to a legally recognized and/or socially approved arrangement between two individuals that carries certain rights and obligations and usually involves sexual activity. In Canada, the only legal form of marriage is **monogamy, a marriage between one woman and one man.** The marriage rate (number of marriages per 1000 population) in Canada is about 4.7, down from 9.2 in 1972 (Statistics Canada 2004h:35; Milan 2000:6).

Figure 11.1 shows that over 140 000 marriages were performed in 2002, down from 200 000 in the early 1970s.

Marriage was once a cultural imperative. There was "something wrong" with a person who didn't marry. But since the 1970s, people's attitudes toward marriage and the family have changed as other aspects of society have changed. Cultural guidelines on marriage and childbearing have grown weaker as our society has experienced a broader cultural shift toward autonomy and personal growth. In the 1970s, according to Cherlin (1992:127), "family life became a matter of personal choice in which individuals made decisions based on a calculus of self-interest and self-fulfillment. Marriage was still desirable, but no one any longer had to be married to be a proper member of society." Marriage also became much less of an economic necessity for women in the 1970s because of new job opportunities and rising incomes. Although women's wages remained low in comparison to men's during this time, their wages rose in absolute terms (Cherlin 1992).

Still, marriage is a persistent preference for most people today. In a national survey conducted by Angus Reid, two-thirds of Canadian adults strongly agreed that their families were the greatest joy in their lives (Angus Reid 1994, cited in Milan 2000:5). According to the 1995 General Social Survey (GSS), 98 percent of those in marriages and 96 percent of those in common-law

FIGURE 11.1   Number of Marriages and Divorces in Canada, 1921 to 2002

Source: Statistics Canada, 2004, "Divorces 2001 and 2002," The Daily, *May 4, Catalogue no. 11-001.*

unions feel that a long-term relationship is important for their happiness (quoted in Milan 2000:5).

On June 28, 2005, the same-sex legislation, Bill C-38, was passed by the House of Commons (and by the Senate in July). Canada was about to become a place where gay and lesbian marriage could take place. Up to that time it was possible for gays and lesbians to marry in some provinces, but it is now possible anywhere in the country. According to the 2001 census, 34 200 couples, or 0.5 percent of all couples in Canada, are same-sex couples (Statistics Canada 2002l:4). In the future it will be possible to count same-sex marriages and cohabitations.

The divorce rate (number of divorces per 1000 population) in Canada during the 20th century has varied from being almost nonexistent in the early 1900s to an all-time high of 3.6 in 1987; by 2000 it had declined to 2.3 (Milan 2000:7 and Statistics Canada 2002e). Figure 11.1 shows that over 70 000 divorces were finalized in 2002, down from 96 000 in 1987. Though many believe marriage should last "until death do us part," others feel marriage is a commitment "for as long as love allows." Through a pattern of marriage, divorce, and remarriage, many people reaffirm their belief in the institution of marriage but not to the individual they initially married. This pattern of successive marriages, in which a person has several spouses over a lifetime but is legally married to only one partner at a time, is referred to as *serial monogamy*. Some social analysts consider serial monogamy a natural adaptation to other social changes in society; others think it is detrimental to individuals and to society and serves as further evidence of the decline of the family (see Popenoe 1996). Who is right? As with other social problems we have examined, the view of causes, effects, and possible solutions for family-related problems depends on the theoretical framework the analyst uses.

PERSPECTIVES ON FAMILY-RELATED PROBLEMS

What purposes do families serve in contemporary societies? Do families create problems for society or solve them? The latter, say functionalists, who believe that the family fulfills important functions for individuals at the microlevel and for the entire society at the macrolevel. Conflict and feminist theorists, on the other hand, consider families a primary source of inequality—and sometimes abuse and violence—in society. Taking a microlevel approach, interactionists analyze family-related social problems in terms of socialization and social interactions among family members.

The Functionalist Perspective

Functionalists emphasize the importance of the family in maintaining the stability of society and the well-being of individuals. According to Emile Durkheim, marriage is a microcosmic replica of the larger society; both marriage and society involve a mental and moral fusion of physically distinct individuals (Lehmann 1994). Durkheim also believed that a division of labour contributed to greater efficiency in marriage and families (and in all areas of life). In his study of family life in the United States, sociologist Talcott Parsons (1955) also viewed a division of labour as important. He saw the husband in an ideal nuclear family as fulfilling an *instrumental role*—meeting the family's economic needs, making important decisions, and providing leadership—and the wife as fulfilling an *expressive role*—running the household, caring for children, and meeting family members' emotional needs.

Using Durkheim's and Parsons's work as a basis for their model of the family, contemporary functionalists believe that a division of labour makes it possible for families to fulfill a number of functions that no other social institution in high-income nations can perform as efficiently and effectively:

1. Regulate sexual behaviour and reproduction: Families are expected to regulate the sexual activity of their members and thus control reproduction so that it occurs within specific boundaries. Sexual regulation of family members by the family is supposed to protect the *principle of legitimacy*—the belief that all children should have a socially and legally recognized father (Malinowski 1964).

2. Socialize and educate children: Parents and other relatives are responsible for teaching children the values and norms of their culture.

3. Provide economic and psychological support: Families are responsible for providing for their members' physical (food, shelter) and emotional needs.

4. Provide social status: Families confer social status on their members, including *ascribed statuses* such as racialization, ethnicity, nationality, class, and religious affiliation, although some of these statuses may change later in life.

Considering their view of the family, functionalists believe that problems in the family are a social crisis. The functional family provides both social order and economic stability by providing for the survival and development of children; the physical and emotional health of adults; and the care of those who are sick, injured, elderly, and have disabilities. The family is also the front line for reinforcing society's norms and values. Functionalists consider the family to be part of the solution to many problems faced by people in contemporary societies. In this view, dysfunctions in families are problems that threaten the well-being of individuals, groups, and nations.

Functionalists believe that changes in other social institutions, such as the economy, religion, education, law, medicine, and the government, contribute to family-related problems. For example, some functionalists think that changing the law to recognize no-fault divorce contributes to higher rates of divorce and dramatically increases single-parent households, which do not provide children with the nurture and guidance they get in a two-parent home (Popenoe 1996).

The Conflict Perspective

Most conflict analysts believe that functionalist views on family problems are idealized and inadequate. Rather than operating harmoniously and for the benefit of all members, families, these analysts say, are sources of social inequality and conflict over values, goals, and access to resources and power.

Conflict theorists who focus on class relations in capitalist economies compare family members to workers in a factory, emphasizing the inequality in each institution. Women are dominated by men in the home just as workers are dominated by managers and capitalists in factories (Engels 1972). As wives and mothers, women contribute to capitalism by producing the next generation of workers and providing the existing labour force with food, clean clothes, and emotional support. Women's work in the family not only benefits the capitalist class but also reinforces women's subordination because the work is unpaid and often devalued. This unpaid work has received much attention in research on the family in Canada. According to Statistics Canada, in 1992 adult Canadians spent 25 billion hours on unpaid work, or 1164 hours per adult, and women spent 78 percent more time on unpaid work than men. Meal preparation and cleaning were the most time-consuming activities, but childcare and other caregiving, volunteer work, and home maintenance were also time consuming. Using the replacement-cost method of valuing work, a wage rate paid to people who do similar work, the value of unpaid work totalled about $11 000 per adult in 1992. In total, these activities were worth $235 billion, or approximately one-third of the GDP (Jackson 1996: 29).

The Feminist Perspective

Many feminist theorists think that male dominance and female subordination began long before capitalism and the private ownership of property arose as an economic system (Mann 1994). They see women's subordination as rooted in patriarchy, particularly in men's control over women's labour power. At the same time that women's labour in the home is directed by men, it is undervalued, which allows men to benefit from their status as the family breadwinner (Firestone 1970; Goode 1982). In a more recent study, sociologist Jane Riblett Wilkie (1993) found that most men are reluctant to relinquish their status as family breadwinner. Although only 15 percent of the families in Canada are supported solely by a male breadwinner, many men continue to construct their ideal of masculinity based on this role. It is acceptable for wives to enter the paid work force if their role is simply to earn money; they should not, however, challenge the ideal roles of male breadwinner and female homemaker.

Like conflict theorists, feminist theorists argue that family problems derive from inequality—not just within the family, but in the political, social, and economic arenas of the larger society as well (Aulette 1994). In fact, pervasive societal inequality leads to one of the most tragic family problems: wife battering. According to feminist theorists, wife battering and other forms of domestic violence may even be conscious strategies that men use to control women and perpetuate gender inequality (Kurz 1989). Fortunately, the rates seem to be declining with the general crime rates, but the rate of women being killed in domestic violence is vastly greater than the rate of men being killed. According to the 2006 edition of the report *Family Violence in Canada: A Statistical Profile* (Statistics Canada 2006a:52), from 1974 to 2004, the rate of female victims of spousal homicide dropped 57 percent from 16.5 per million women in spousal relationships to 7.1, and the rate of male victims dropped 68 percent from 4.4 to 1.4. (The rates of overall spousal violence are mentioned below.)

According to feminist theorists, family-related problems, including domestic violence and wife battering, can be solved only if all social institutions work to eliminate the subordination of women in society. Increased educational and occupational opportunities for women over the last quarter-century may be contributing to a reduction in domestic violence. Related to increased opportunities for women, the increase in the age of first marriage may be another contributing factor (see "Postponing Marriage") to the decline in violence.

The Interactionist Perspective

Some interactionists view the family communication process as integral to understanding the diverse roles that family members play; therefore these analysts examine how husbands, wives, and children act out their roles and react to the parts played by others. Although societies differ widely on the rules and norms that should shape family and kin relationships, people are socialized to accept their society's form of the family as the acceptable norm. According to sociologists Peter Berger and Hansfried Kellner (1964), marital partners develop a shared reality through their interactions with each other. Although newlyweds bring separate identities to a marriage, over time they construct a shared reality as a couple. In the process, the partners redefine their past identities to be consistent with their new realities. Interactionists say that the process of developing a shared reality is continuous and occurs not only in the family but in any group in which the couple participates together. In cases of separation and divorce, the process is reversed: Couples may start with a shared reality but once again become individuals with separate realities in the process of uncoupling their relationship.

How do interactionists explain problems in a family? Some look at the subjective meanings and interpretations people give to their everyday lives. According to sociologists Charles Jones, Lorna Marsden, and Lorne Tepperman (1990), over the past few decades, women have gained more choice and opportunities in life. Women have become more "individualized." One of the consequences of this dramatic change is that women have few role models to follow; as a result, new expectations about work and child rearing could cause problems for the family. Obviously, men would also be uncertain about how to behave with these changed expectations. According to sociologist Jessie Bernard (1982), women and men experience marriage differently. While the husband may see *his marriage* very positively, the wife may feel less positive about *her marriage*. The reverse may also be true. Evidence for the different realities of marriage comes from research that shows that husbands and wives often give very different accounts of the same event (Safilios-Rothschild 1969).

Still other interactionists view family problems in terms of partners' unrealistic expectations about love and marriage, which can lead to marital dissatisfaction and, sometimes, divorce. These analysts note that our culture emphasizes *romantic love*—a deep and vital emotion based on significant need satisfaction, caring for and acceptance of another person, and the development of an intimate relationship (Lamanna and Riedmann 1994). Indeed, most couples in Canada get married because they are in love, but being a "nation of lovers" doesn't mean that men and women have the same ideas about what constitutes romantic love. According to sociologist Francesca Cancian (1990), women tend to express their feelings verbally, whereas men tend to express their love through such non-verbal actions as preparing dinner or doing household repairs. Women may not always interpret these actions as signs of love. One man complained (Rubin 1976:146), "What does she want? Proof? She's got it, hasn't she? Would I be knocking myself out to get things for her—like to keep up this house—if I didn't love her? Why does a man do things like that if not because he loves his wife and kids? I swear, I can't figure what she wants." His wife replied, "It's not enough that he supports us and takes care of us. I appreciate that, but I want him to share things with me. I need for him to tell me his feelings."

Whatever their different viewpoints on marriage and family, most social theorists agree on one fact: Three decades ago, the nuclear family was the most common family form, and today it is only one of many patterns.

DIVERSITY IN INTIMATE RELATIONSHIPS AND FAMILIES

Greater diversity in intimate relationships and families in Canada has come about because of dramatic increases in (1) singlehood, (2) postponed marriage, (3) living together without marriage (called common-law, cohabitation, or domestic partnerships), (4) dual-earner marriages, and (5) one-parent families.

Singlehood

Although some young singles will eventually marry, 10 percent of the population will remain single for their lives. When this figure is combined with those who have been widowed, separated, or divorced, the proportion of the Canadian population that lives in one- or single-person households is 25 percent, according to the 2001 census (Statistics Canada 2002l:5). Some people choose singlehood over marriage because it means greater freedom from commitments to another person. Others choose it because of increased career opportunities (especially for women), the availability of sexual partners without marriage, the belief that the single lifestyle is full of excitement, or the desire for self-sufficiency and freedom to change and experiment (Stein 1976, 1981). Though some analysts think that individuals who prefer to remain single hold more individualistic values and are less family-oriented than are people who choose to marry, sociologist Peter Stein (1981) has found otherwise: Many singles still feel a strong need for intimacy, sharing, and continuity and, as a result, develop relationships with other singles, valuing friends and personal growth more highly than marriage and children (Alwin et al. 1985; Cargan and Melko 1982).

Some people are single not by choice but by necessity. Because of structural changes in the economy, many young working-class people cannot afford to marry and set up their own households. Indeed, some college graduates have found that they cannot earn enough money to set up households separate from those of their parents (Boyd and Norris 1999).

Postponing Marriage

Young people today are less eager to get married than they were two decades ago; many are remaining single into their late 20s. In 1997, the average age at which men first married was 29.5 years, and the average age for women was 27.4 years (Milan 2000:6). Although the age at which people marry for the first time has been rising steadily since the 1950s, it has accelerated since the 1970s. Between 1970 and today, the proportion of women aged 25 to 29 who have never married has tripled.

Why are more people postponing first marriages? Although some reasons are the same as those for staying single, sociologist Robin Wolf (1996) suggests four key factors: (1) economic uncertainty due to the changing job structure in Western societies; (2) women's increasing participation in the labour force; (3) the sexual revolution of the 1970s that made sexual relationships outside marriage more socially acceptable; and, (4) the rising divorce rate—young people watching their parents divorce may be less anxious to jump into marriage themselves. Other analysts suggest that a significant increase in cohabitation and domestic partnerships also contributes to the percentage of people who are counted as single or postponing marriage.

Common-Law, Cohabitation, and Domestic Partnerships

The popularity of cohabitation has increased in the past two decades. **Common-law, or *cohabitation*, is two unmarried adults living together in a sexual relationship without being legally married.** According to the 2001 census (see Table 11.1), 1.158 million couples—14 percent of all couples—were living common-law, up from 5.6 percent in 1981. Now almost 40 percent of men and women aged 30 to 39 are expected to choose common-law as their first union (Statistics Canada 2002d:3). The proportion of cohabiting couples still varies significantly by language spoken. In Quebec, 30 percent of all couples were living common-law in 2001 (Statistics Canada 2002l:5). This seems counter-intuitive in a predominantly Roman Catholic province. What do you think?

For some couples, cohabitation is a form of trial marriage and constitutes an intermediate stage between dating and marriage. According to anthropologist Margaret Mead (1966), dating patterns do not adequately prepare people for marriage and parenting responsibilities. Mead proposed a two-stage marriage process, each with its own ceremony and responsibilities. In the first stage, the individual marriage, two people would make a serious commitment to each other but agree not to have children during this stage. In the second stage, the parental marriage, the couple would decide to have children and to share responsibility for their upbringing. Many people today seem to be following this pattern, though without intention, and with different partners. Divorce in the first couple of years of marriage is quite common, and the break-up of a common-law relationship is even more likely. *American Demographics* editor Pamela Paul, having been through an early divorce herself, interviewed 60 other young, divorced couples and wrote a book about what she called a "starter marriage." She claimed that most of her sample had not given marriage much thought before getting married; they had developed "matrimania" due to a marriage-oriented culture (Paul 2002).

For other couples, cohabitation is not necessarily a first step toward marriage. In one study, researchers found that slightly more than 50 percent of cohabitation relationships eventually culminated in marriage, whereas 37 percent broke up and 10 percent were still ongoing at the time of the study (London 1991).

Does cohabitation contribute to marital success? The evidence is mixed. Some studies show that cohabitation has little or no effect on marital adjustment, emotional closeness, satisfaction, and intimacy (Watson and DeMeo 1987). Other studies indicate that couples who cohabit first are more likely to divorce than those who do not (Bennett et al. 1988). Apparently, partners in this study who had cohabited were less satisfied with their marriage and less committed to the institution of marriage than were those who had not lived together before marrying. The researchers theorized that cohabitation may contribute to people's individualistic attitudes and values, while making them more aware that alternatives to marriage exist (Axinn and Thornton 1992; Thomson and Colella 1992).

Dual-Earner Marriages

More than 60 percent of all marriages in Canada are *dual-earner marriages,* **marriages in which both spouses are in the labour force.** Over half of all employed women hold full-time, year-round jobs, and in a change from the past, there are more married women with young children in the paid labour force today than ever before.

Many married women who are employed outside the household face hours of domestic work and childcare when they get home. Sociologist Arlie Hochschild (1989) refers to the later half of women's dual workdays as the *second shift*—**the domestic work that many employed women perform at home after completing their workday on the job.** According to Hochschild, the unpaid housework that women do on the *second shift* (see Chapter 4) amounts to an extra month of work each year. In households with small children or many children, the amount of housework increases (Hartmann 1981). Across racialization and class lines, numerous studies confirm that domestic work remains primarily women's work (Gerstel and Gross 1995).

In recent years, more husbands have been sharing some of the household and childcare responsibilities, especially when the wife's earnings are essential to family finances (Perry-Jenkins and Crouter 1990). But even when husbands assume some of the household responsibilities, they typically spend much less time in these activities than do their wives (see Coverman 1989). Women and men perform different household tasks, and the deadlines for their work vary widely.

Recurring tasks that have specific times for completion (such as bathing a child or cooking a meal) tend to be the women's responsibility, whereas men are more likely to do the periodic tasks that have no highly structured schedule (such as mowing the lawn or changing the oil in the car; Hochschild 1989).

Couples with more egalitarian ideas about women's and men's roles tend to share more equally in food preparation, housework, and childcare (Wright et al. 1992). An *egalitarian family* is one in which the partners share power and authority equally. As women have gained new educational and employment opportunities, a trend toward more egalitarian relationships has become evident in Canada. Some degree of economic independence makes it possible for women to delay marriage or to terminate a problematic marriage (O'Connell 1994). For some men, the shift to a more egalitarian household occurs gradually, as the following quotation indicates:

> It was me taking the initiative, and also Connie pushing, saying, "Gee, there's so much that has to be done." At first I said, "But I'm supposed to be the breadwinner," not realizing she's also the breadwinner. I was being a little blind to what was going on, but I got tired of waiting for my wife to come home to start cooking, so one day I surprised the

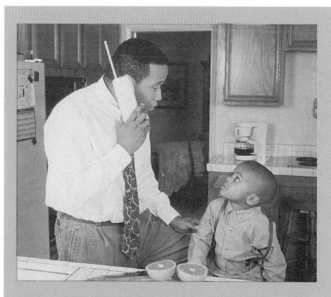

In the age of dual-earner marriages, it has become increasingly important for fathers to assume childcare and household duties. How does this photo show the competing demands faced by many employed parents?

hell out [of] her and myself and the kids, and I had supper waiting on the table for her. (Gerson 1993:170)

Problems associated with providing economic support for the family and rearing children are even more pressing in many one-parent households.

Comparing Two-Parent and One-Parent Households

When the mother and father in a two-parent household truly share parenting, children have the benefit of two primary caregivers. Some researchers have found that when fathers take an active part in raising the children, the effect is beneficial for all family members. Fathers find that increased contact with their children provides more opportunities for personal and emotional gratification (Coltrane 1989).

However, living in a two-parent family does not guarantee children a happy childhood. Children whose parents argue constantly, abuse them, or are alcoholics have a worse family experience than do children in a single-parent family where there is a supportive environment. Women who are employed full-time and are single parents probably have the greatest burden of all. These women must fulfill their paid employment duties and meet the needs of their children and the household, often with little help from ex-husbands or relatives.

How prevalent are one-parent households? The past two decades have seen a significant increase in one-parent households due to divorce, death of a parent, and births outside of marriage. In 2001, lone-parent families made up 16 percent of the total families in Canada (Statistics Canada 2002l:3). Who heads most one-parent households? Today, 83 percent of all one-parent families are headed by single mothers. Men are heads of about 17 percent of one-parent families (Statistics Canada 2002o:27); a study of one-parent households headed by fathers found that most of the men had very positive relationships with their children (Risman 1987).

What effect does a one-parent household have on children? According to one study based on six nationally representative data sets of more than 25 000 children from various racialized and social-class backgrounds in the United States, children growing up with only one biological parent are at risk of serious problems, including poor academic achievement, dropping

out of school, drug and alcohol abuse, teen pregnancy, early marriage, and divorce (McLanahan and Sandefur 1994). Obviously, living in a one-parent family does not necessarily cause these problems. Factors such as poverty, discrimination, unsafe neighbourhoods, and high crime rates must also be considered. (See also the section below on parenting styles, for another important factor.) In fact, other researchers have found some benefits to growing up in a one-parent family (Lauer and Lauer 1991). For example, children in one-parent families are often less pressured to conform to rigid gender roles. Rather than having chores assigned by gender, as is common in two-parent families, single-parent children typically take on a wider variety of tasks and activities. Many single-parent children also show high levels of maturity and self-sufficiency earlier because they have to help out at a younger age than do children in other families (Lauer and Lauer 1991).

What about the fathers of children in one-parent households headed by women? Although some fathers remain involved in their children's lives, others only occasionally take their children out for recreational activities or buy them presents on birthdays and holidays. Personal choice, workplace demands on time and energy, location of the ex-wife's residence, and limitations placed on visitation by custody arrangements are all factors that affect how often absentee fathers visit their children. Increasingly, parents are receiving joint custody of their children, and it appears that joint custody can minimize the disruption of divorce in a child's life, if the ex-spouses cooperate with each other and live in relatively close geographical proximity. Ex-spouses who constantly argue or live far away from each other can create serious problems for "commuter" children, as author David Sheff (1995:64) describes:

My son began commuting between his two homes at age 4. . . . The commuter flights. . . were the only times a parent wasn't lording over him, so he was able to order Coca-Cola, verboten [forbidden] at home. . . . But such benefits were insignificant when contrasted with his preflight nightmares about plane crashes. . . . Like so many divorcing couples, we divided the china and art and our young son. . . . For the eight years since, he has been one of the thousands of American children with two homes, two beds, two sets of clothes and toys, and two toothbrushes.

The transition from a two-parent family to a one-parent family is only one of many child-related family issues that many people today must deal with, as we discuss in the next section.

CHILD-RELATED FAMILY ISSUES

One of the major issues facing many individuals and families today is reproductive freedom, a term that implies both the desire *to have* and the desire *not to have* a child. As sociologists Leslie King and Madonna Harrington Meyer (1997:8) explain,

> The average woman is fertile, and therefore must attempt to control her reproductivity, for one-half of her life. For most women, it is the preoccupation with preventing births that consumes their health care dollars and energies; for a small minority, it is the preoccupation with achieving a birth that dominates. The ability to control fertility is, to a great extent, linked to access to various forms of reproductive health services, including contraceptives and infertility treatments.

Reproductive Freedom, Contraception, and Abortion

Reproductive freedom has been a controversial issue throughout much of Canadian history. In 1869, the Canadian government banned abortion. It was not until 100 years later that a bill was passed making it possible for a woman to get an abortion, with the judgment of three doctors in a hospital that a women's life or health was in danger. That bill, introduced in 1967 by then Justice Minister and future Prime Minister Pierre Elliott Trudeau with the famous expression "The state has no business in the bedrooms of the nation!" also legalized homosexuality and contraception. Earlier in the 1960s the "Pill" was introduced, and public opinion about women's reproductive freedom began to change. By 1971, the "Pill" was the most popular form of contraception in Canada (Bélanger 1998:17). Many women spend about 90 percent of their fertile years trying to avoid pregnancy (Gold and Richards 1994).

Over the last 25 years, the methods of contraception have changed greatly. According to the General Social Survey of 1995, the use of contraceptive sterilization doubled in that time. Whereas in 1976, 30.5 percent of couples used sterilization, by 1995, 56.1 percent of couples, mostly older couples with two or more children, were using sterilization (e.g., tubal ligation or vasectomy; Bélanger 1998:17). Since 1976, there has also been a decline in the use of the pill and an increase in the use of condoms. Perhaps this is because of the cost. For example, at Shoppers' Drug Mart, different types of oral contraceptives cost about $170 to $300 per year, and one dose of an after-pill to prevent pregnancy costs almost $30. Perhaps men are willing to take more responsibility for contraception and are more concerned about the spread of sexually transmitted diseases (Bélanger 1998:19).

Although the 1967 law permitted abortion, it was not always easy to obtain one. Some provinces were not sympathetic to abortions, and some hospitals did not set up committees to judge the situations. Because he felt that women had a basic right to abortions, Dr. Henry Morgentaler started to perform abortions in a clinic in Montreal. Since he was breaking the law, he was tried three times, but no jury would convict him. He took his case to the Supreme Court of Canada and won. The law permitting abortions under strict circumstances was declared unconstitutional in 1988. The next year, the federal government tried once again to pass an abortion bill, but it was defeated in the Senate. No provincial government has tried to pass a bill on abortion since that time, and opportunities for abortion did increase in the 1990s. However, policy on abortion varied among the provinces:

- Prince Edward Island refused to provide any abortion services;
- New Brunswick and Manitoba refused to fund abortions; and
- Nova Scotia and Quebec provided only partial payment for abortions.

To provide direct and immediate help, Morgentaler set up clinics in several Canadian cities, but not without a struggle: in 1992, his clinic in Toronto was bombed.

Opposition to abortion was strong into the mid-1990s. In 1994, a doctor who performed abortions, Garson Romalis, was shot in Vancouver, British Columbia. Two other anti-abortion shootings took place, one in Ontario in 1995, and one in Manitoba in 1997. While protesting at clinics has continued, no

For a number of decades, there have been intense public confrontations between abortion rights advocates and members of the anti-abortion movement. Demonstrators are a familiar sight outside abortion clinics, hospitals, and government buildings.

further serious attacks have occurred. This may be due to a decline in the number of abortions being performed. In 2003, 103 768 abortions were performed for Canadian women, a decrease of 1 percent from 2002. Now there is less than one abortion for every three live births in Canada (Statistics Canada 2006d).

At the microlevel, abortion is a solution for some pregnant women and their families but a problem for others, particularly when they face religious or family opposition. At the macrolevel, abortion is both a problem and a solution when activists try to influence the making and enforcement of laws pertaining to women's reproductive rights and the control of new reproductive technologies.

Infertility and New Reproductive Technologies

Infertility is defined as an inability to conceive after a year of unprotected sexual relations. In 40 percent of

the cases, the woman is infertile, and in another 40 percent, the man is infertile; 20 percent of the time, the cause is impossible to determine (Gabriel 1996).

Sexually transmitted diseases are a leading cause of infertility: Each year, many women become infertile as a result of a sexually transmitted disease that develops into pelvic inflammatory disease (Gold and Richards 1994). There are also some women—both married and unmarried—who would like to have a child but cannot because of disabilities. Some analysts point out that a growing number of prospective parents delay childbearing into their 30s and 40s, by which time it may be more difficult for them to conceive.

About 50 percent of infertile couples who seek treatment can be helped by conventional, low-tech treatments such as fertility drugs, artificial insemination, and surgery to unblock fallopian tubes. The other 50 percent require advanced technology, sometimes called assisted reproductive technology (ART). Many middle- and upper-income couples, for example, receive in vitro fertilization (IVF), which, according to the Infertility Awareness Association of Canada, costs a minimum of $7000 and up to $10 000 (with travel and drugs) per attempt (see Table 11.2). Despite the popularity of such treatments and the growth of fertility clinics (from 30 slightly over a decade ago to more than 300 today), only one in five couples who receive ART actually become parents (Gabriel 1996). In Canada, the Ontario Hospital Insurance Plan (OHIP) will cover only up to three cycles of treatment and even then, only if the fallopian tubes are completely blocked. Typically, very few private insurance plans will cover this procedure because it is perceived to be too expensive. (Infertility Awareness Association of Canada 2003).

For couples like Michael and Stephanie Plaut, who spent three years and thousands of dollars trying to have a baby through IVF and other procedures, every unsuccessful attempt is traumatic. Journalist Felicia Lee (1996:A1) has documented the trauma the couple undergoes: "Michael Plaut answered the telephone . . . [and the] call confirmed his worst fear: the pregnancy test was negative. The Plauts sobbed, held each other and then had a glass of Scotch. 'It's like we're in a period of mourning,' Mrs. Plaut said.' You just get to the point where you want this to be over.'" Couples like the Plauts who have their hopes raised by the new reproductive technologies only to find that they do not work for them often form support groups. Many couples finally decide to remain childless, but some adopt one or more children.

Adoption

Adoption is a legal process through which the rights and duties of parenting are transferred from a child's biological and/or legal parents to new legal parents. The adopted child has all the rights of a biological child. In long past adoptions, a new birth certificate was issued, and the child had no further contact with the biological parents, although more recently agencies have been arranging for people to meet their biological parents or children with mutual consent. Now some provincial acts have made disclosure a right. For example, Ontario passed the *Adoption Information Disclosure Act* in 2005 to give all adopted children who have reached the age of 18 full access to their birth records. This act will be fully proclaimed and in force in September 2007.

Matching children who are available for adoption with prospective adoptive parents can be difficult. The children often have specific needs, and prospective parents often specify the kind of children they want to adopt. Because many prospective parents do not want to adopt children who are non-White (most prospective parents are White), older, or have disabilities or diseases, many children available for adoption are not chosen, and instead move from foster home to foster home (Zelizer 1985).

Prospective parents frequently want infants, but fewer infants are available for adoption than in the past because contraception and abortion are more readily

TABLE 11.2   Forms of Assisted Reproductive Technology

Name	Description
In vitro fertilization (IVF)	Eggs that were produced as a result of administering fertility drugs are removed from the woman's body and fertilized by sperm in a laboratory dish. The embryos that result from this process are transferred to the woman's uterus.
Micromanipulation	Viewing the process through a microscope, a specialist manipulates egg and sperm in a laboratory dish to improve the chances of a pregnancy.
Cryopreserved embryo transfer (CPE)	Embryos that were frozen after a previous assisted reproductive technology procedure are thawed and then transferred to the uterus.
Egg donation	Eggs are removed from a donor's uterus, fertilized in a laboratory dish, and transferred to an infertile woman's uterus
Surrogacy	An embryo is implanted in the uterus of a woman who is paid to carry the fetus until birth. The egg may come from either the legal or the surrogate mother, and the sperm may come either from the legal father or a donor.

Source: Trip Gabriel, 1996, "High-Tech Pregnancies Test Hope's Limit," New York Times, *January 7:1, 10–11.*

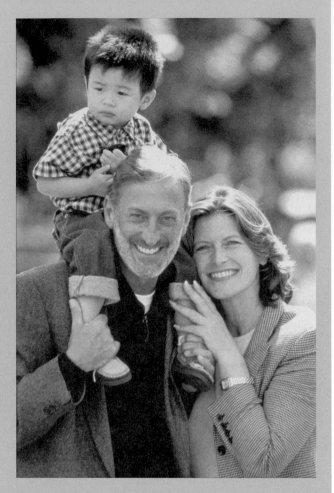

Many parents who adopt one or more children also add to the racialized/ethnic diversity of their household. What can children and adolescents learn from growing up with others whose background is not identical to their own?

themselves. I think that I'm really doing a favour to my baby, although I'm always going to wonder what it looks like and what it's doing. (Luker 1996:163)

Because fewer infants are available for adoption, some Canadians are adopting through a private agency or from a foreign country (e.g., Romania, Russia, and China).

Parenting Style

Besides the influence of factors like low income and family structure, other factors, like the way parents treat their children, affect children's development. To study the effect of parenting styles on child development, a massive study was begun in 1994. The National Longitudinal Survey of Children and Youth (NLSCY) is a study of 23 000 families that is investigating a wide variety of variables, like income, family structure, and parenting style, on child development. Parenting style is based on responses to questions about being

- rational (e.g., How often do you think that the kind of punishment you give him/her depends on your mood?);
- responsive (e.g., How often do you praise?);
- reasoning (e.g., When your child breaks the rules . . . do you: (a) calmly discuss the matter? And (b) describe alternative ways of behaving . . . ?); and
- firm (e.g., When you give him/her a command to do something, what proportion of the time do you make sure that he/she has done it?).

Based on answers to questions like these, the parents are divided into four groups ranging from positive (warm and nurturing) to ineffective (very intolerant and erratic). Among the first findings the researchers made was that parenting style had more effect on behavioural problems than family structure or income. Children living with two parents with poor parenting skills were five times more likely to have such developmental problems as aggression, hyperactivity, and depression than children living with a single but effective parent; this is also a wider gap than one due to income differences (Statistics Canada 1998b).

However, if the parenting environment changed from punitive to non-punitive over the ages 2/3 to 8/9 years, then aggressive behaviour will decline (Statistics Canada 2004f). Figure 11.2 shows the

available, and more unmarried teenage parents are deciding to keep their babies. Some teenagers, however, believe that adoption is the best way to solve the problem of early childbearing. Christina, one of many teenagers facing the realities of an early pregnancy and lack of resources to meet the child's needs, explained her decision this way:

> I know I can't keep my baby. I can't give it all the things a baby needs and I sure can't dump it on my parents because they can't afford to take care of their own family. I've decided to give it up for adoption. I think it's better for the baby to give it up to parents who can't have a baby

FIGURE 11.2   Children's Aggressive Behaviour Linked with Current Punitive Parenting

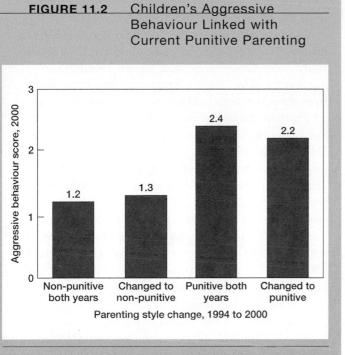

Source: *Statistics Canada, 2004, "Parenting Style and Children's Aggressive Behaviour, 1994 to 2000,"* The Daily, *October 25, Catalogue no. 11-001.*

children's behaviour change to the level of the children in the non-punitive environment if the parent's punitive behaviour changes to non-punitive. Note that the reverse is possible too. Why do you think this occurs?

Teen Pregnancies and Unmarried Motherhood

The birth rate among teenagers has declined substantially over the last few decades. From the early 1970s to the 1990s, the proportion of births to teenagers declined from 11 to 6 percent of all births (Milan 2000:7). However between 1961 and 1991, the birth rate per 1000 unmarried teenagers rose from about 11 to 19 (Belle and McQuillan 1994:17).

Although a popular myth claims that most births to unmarried women occur in the central cities of large urban areas, the greatest proportion of unmarried women giving birth occurs in Quebec, Newfoundland and Labrador, and Saskatchewan (Belle and McQuillan 1994:17). Two of the key factors behind this statistic are poverty and lack of employment opportunity.

According to social analysts, the outcome of teen pregnancies is problematic because teenage mothers are typically unskilled at parenting, are likely to drop out of school, and have no social support other than relatives (Chase-Lansdale et al. 1992). Family support is extremely important to unmarried pregnant teens because emotional and financial support from the fathers of their children is often lacking (Nath et al. 1991). Without this support, teen mothers rely on their own mothers and grandmothers to help with child rearing. As a result, many unmarried teenage mothers do not make the same transition from the family of orientation to the family of procreation that most people make when they become parents. The ***family of orientation*** **is the family into which a person is born and in which early socialization takes place.** When teenage mothers and their children live with their grandmothers or other relatives, they do not establish the separate family unit known as a ***family of procreation***—**the family that married or cohabiting couples create by having or adopting children.** The picture for the children of teenage mothers without parental support is especially bleak because few of these mothers have adequate parenting skills or knowledge of child development. Children of unwed teenage mothers tend to have severely limited educational and employment opportunities and a high likelihood of living in poverty (Benokraitis 1993). Teenagers are not the only ones having children without getting married. Since 1961 the birth rate for unmarried women between the ages of 25 to 29, and 30 to 34, has doubled. It now accounts for 27 and 15 percent respectively of births to unmarried women in 1991 (in comparison with 14 and 8 percent respectively in 1961) (Belle and McQuillan 1994:15). Third and fourth births outside marriage are also occurring, most commonly in Quebec, Saskatchewan, and Manitoba (Belle and McQuillan 1994:16). According to demographer Charles Westoff, these rates reflect "the declining significance of marriage as a social obligation or a social necessity for reproduction. Increasing proportions of White women who have not been married are deciding that having a child is more important than any kind of disapproval they might face" (quoted in Connell 1995). With less of a social stigma attached to unmarried pregnancy, fewer women seem to be seeking abortion and are deciding instead to raise the child themselves, whether the pregnancy was planned or not.

Same-Sex Parenting

Over the last 20 years, same-sex parenting has become a topic of public attention. Many individual accounts have appeared, discussing choosing parenthood, defining the family, raising children, reflecting on identity, and examining gay and lesbian parenting and the law (e.g., Arnup 1995). However, few studies have appeared in Canada exploring these topics. The 2001 census inquired not only about same-sex cohabitation but also about the presence of children. More female than male same-sex couples have children (15 percent vs. 3 percent; Statistics Canada 2002l:4).

Various alternatives make it possible for same-sex couples to obtain their baby. An obvious method is one of the partners leaving a heterosexual relationship with his or her child(ren), another method is surrogacy where a person pays a woman to bear the child, a third method is co-parenting where a gay and lesbian couple arrange for artificial insemination and agree to bring up the child(ren) together, and a final method is adoption. In 1996 British Columbia became the first jurisdiction in the world to pass legislation that allowed same-sex spouses to adopt children as couples, with the same rights as heterosexual couples (Philip 2003:F4). In the first seven years, 20 children were placed with same-sex couples; and from 2000 to 2003, the Children's Aid Society of Toronto placed 23 children with same-sex couples (Philip 2003:F4).

Regarding same-sex couple interaction, a study that focuses on reproductive decision making, mothering, and family life from the perspective of the mother was conducted by Fiona Nelson (1996). She interviewed 30 lesbian women in Alberta cities. Fifteen women already had children from a previous heterosexual relationship and thus created blended families with their partners. Others became pregnant by means of donor insemination. One of her interesting findings was the difference in the role of the non-biological mother in the blended and donor-inseminated (D.I.) families. Whereas in the D.I. family, each woman regards herself as the mother with equal division of authority and responsibilities, in the blended family, the non-biological mother is a step-parent and is rarely allowed to be a "mother" (Nelson 1996:134). Nelson (1996:137) suggests that as more women pursue the D.I. means of family formation, it will become more visible and accepted, and "the educative effect may be such that *all* mothers will come to rethink what it means to be a mother" (emphasis in original).

Among the topics that Nelson was unable to explore was the perspectives of children. One small study from Arnup's collection reports research showing that the older children have not suffered excessively from their mother's lesbianism. They may even have grown more mature through coping with examples of homophobia, since they are frequently teased at school (McLaughlin 1995:249). One student wrote a letter to his teacher, who was beginning a unit on the family, complaining that as "a son of a lesbian mother, when I looked on the list for a description of my family and it wasn't there, I felt like my type of family wasn't considered 'real.'" And he signed his letter " *Someone who is proud of his mom!*" (emphasis in original) (McLaughlin 1995:248). The growing prominence of lesbian and gay parenting should lead to much rethinking of the nature of families and parenting.

In contrast to these studies of lesbian motherhood, James Miller (1996:132) presents a personal statement of his own family, which he calls an "out family" because of "its openness to homosexual membership; its opposition to *heterosexist* conformity (the prejudicial assumption of heterosexuality as normal and proper); and its overtones within the contemporary lesbian and gay movement" (emphasis in original). In a comprehensive article, Miller

- outlines various problems experienced by his children and partner;
- provides critiques of a CBC documentary about the domestic struggles of a gay father and his son, and "learning-to-read" books; and
- portrays, schematically, the relationships of family and friends.

DIVORCE AND REMARRIAGE

Divorce is the legal process of dissolving a marriage, which allows former spouses to remarry if they so choose. Have you heard such statements as "Almost one out of every two marriages ends in divorce"? Statistics might initially appear to bear out this statement, but consider the following: Most sociologists use a statistic called the *refined divorce rate* to calculate the incidence of divorce. The number of divorces in a year is divided by the total number of marriages in that year. In Canada, (see Figure 11.1) there were over 140 000 marriages and over 70 000 divorces in 2002 (Statistics Canada 2004b). However, it is misleading to compare the number of marriages with the number of divorces from year to year and say that the divorce rate is 50 percent, because couples who divorce in any given year are very unlikely to have come from the group that married that year. Also, some people go through several marriages and divorces, which skews the divorce rate because the likelihood of divorce goes up with each subsequent marriage.

Why does divorce occur? A number of factors contribute to a couple's statistical likelihood of becoming divorced, including

- getting married during the teenage years (Balakrishnan et al. 1993);
- getting married after only a short acquaintanceship (Goode 1976);
- having relatives and friends disapprove of the marriage (Goode 1976);
- having limited economic resources and earning low wages (Spanier and Glick 1981);
- both partners having a high-school education or less (Houseknecht et al. 1984);
- having parents who were divorced or who had unhappy marriages (Goode 1976); and
- having children present at the beginning of the marriage (Rankin and Maneker 1985; Morgan et al. 1988; Martin and Bumpass 1989).

Because these factors are interrelated with such other factors as class, racialization, and age, determining the likelihood of divorce is very complicated. For example, age is intertwined with economic resources, and people from low-income families typically marry earlier than do people from more affluent families; but if divorce occurs, which factor—age or economic resources—is more closely associated with it?

Religion may affect the divorce rate of some. People who attend religious services weekly are much more likely to want to keep the family together and place more importance on home life than non-attenders, according to the 1995 GSS (Clark 1998).

Divorce laws in Canada once required the partner seeking the divorce to prove misconduct on the part of the other spouse. Under today's *no-fault divorce laws,* however, proof of blameworthiness is no longer necessary, and most divorces are granted on the grounds of *irreconcilable differences,* which means that a breakdown has occurred in the marital relationship and neither partner is to be specifically blamed.

With or without blame, divorce usually has a dramatic economic and emotional impact on family members. An estimated 60 percent of divorcing couples have one or more children. Indeed, some children experience more than one divorce during their childhood because one or both of their parents may remarry and subsequently divorce again. Although we do not know how many Canadians have experienced multiple divorces, we do know about multiple disruptions (including death and/or remarriage of a parent) of the family and their effects on childhood happiness. The 1995 GSS asked about family disruptions and their effects on children's feelings of well-being and closeness to parents. According to Statistics Canada analyst Cara Williams (2001:3), 8 percent of Canadians (1.9 million people) aged 15 and older experienced one change in parental structure, 800 000 Canadians experienced two, and 200 000 experienced three or more. Disruptions do affect childhood happiness. Whereas 92 percent of those without disruptions reported having a happy childhood, only 50 percent of those with three or more disruptions reported having happiness (Williams 2001:4). Those with one or more disruptions also reported being less close to their mother and father than those without disruptions (Williams 2001:4). The topic of the consequences of divorce quickly brings out strong debate, ranging from those like researcher Anne-Marie Ambert (1998), who say that divorce has negative effects, to those like independent researcher Judith Harris (1998), who dismiss its negative effects. Cherlin (1999) suggests that neither extreme gives a clear portrait of growing up after divorce, because his studies showed that children whose parents would later divorce already showed more emotional problems at age seven than children from families that would remain intact. Although the effects can be overstated, disruptions do tend to have negative effects on childhood happiness and on relationships with parents.

Divorce changes relationships not only for the couple and children involved but also for other relatives. Some grandparents feel that they are the big losers.

Grandparents who wish to see their grandchildren have to keep in touch with the parent who has custody; but if the grandparents are in-laws, they are less likely to be welcomed and may be seen as taking the "other side" simply because they are the parents of the ex-spouse. Recently, some grandparents have sued for custody of minor grandchildren. For the most part, these suits have not been successful except when there has been some question about the emotional stability of the biological parents or the suitability of a foster-care arrangement.

Most people who divorce remarry. In 1997, in more than 34 percent of all marriages, either the bride, the groom, or both had previously been married (Milan 2000:8). Of individuals who divorce before age 35, about half remarry within three years of their first divorce (Bumpass et al. 1990). Most divorced people marry others who have been divorced (London and Wilson 1988), though remarriage rates vary by gender and age. At all ages, a greater proportion of men than women remarry, often relatively soon after the divorce. Among women, the older a woman is at the time of divorce, the lower her likelihood of remarrying (Wallerstein and Blakeslee 1989). Women who have not graduated from high school and have young children tend to remarry relatively quickly. Women with a college degree and without children are less likely to remarry (Glick and Lin 1986).

Divorce followed by remarriage often creates complex family relationships. A **blended family consists of a husband and wife or a same-sex couple, children from previous marriages, and children (if any) from the new marriage.** At least initially, stress in blended families may be fairly high because of rivalry among the children and hostilities directed toward step-parents or babies born into the family. The NLSCY found that nearly 9 percent of Canadian children under age 12 were living in a blended family. These children were more likely than children from intact families to say they lacked emotional support from their parents and to report difficulties in getting along with siblings and parents (Milan 2000:9). In some cases, when parents divorce and marry other partners, the children become part of a *binuclear family,* living with one biological parent and a step-parent part of the time and with the other biological parent and another step-parent the rest of the time.

As Cherlin (1992) points out, the norms governing divorce and remarriage are ambiguous, so people must make decisions about family life (such as who should be invited to a birthday celebration or a wedding) on the basis of their own feelings about the people involved. But in spite of the problems, many blended families succeed.

DOMESTIC VIOLENCE

The term *domestic violence* obscures the fact that most victims of domestic violence are women and children. Women are more likely to be assaulted, injured, or raped by their male partners than by any other type of assailant. Children are extremely vulnerable to abuse and violence because of their age and economic and social dependence on their parents or other adult caregivers.

Child Abuse

In 2001, Nico Trocmé and his colleagues published the Canadian Incidence Study of Reported Child Abuse and Neglect (CIS), the first nation-wide study to examine the incidence of reported child maltreatment and the characteristics of children and families investigated by Canadian child welfare services. Most of us, when we hear the words *child abuse,* think in terms of physical injury or sexual abuse, but the most frequent form of child maltreatment, according to the CIS, is *child neglect*—not meeting a child's basic needs for emotional warmth and security, adequate shelter, food, health care, education, clothing, and protection (Trocmé et al. 2001:xv). We will focus primarily on physical injury and sexual abuse because these actions are classified as violent personal crimes.

In the past, children in Canada were considered the property of their parents and could be punished or ignored as the parents wished. Now, despite legislation protecting children, through child welfare services in the provinces and territories, many physical injuries to children are intentionally inflicted by parents and other caregivers (see Trocmé et al. 2001:4–5). Parental violence can, in fact, lead to the *battered child syndrome,* a psychological disorder in which a child experiences low self-esteem and sometimes clinical depression associated with former or current abuse by a biological or custodial parent (Kempe et al. 1962).

The CIS identified four kinds of maltreatment: physical abuse, sexual abuse, neglect, and emotional maltreatment. In 1998, 135 573 cases of maltreatment were investigated and 45 percent were substantiated (22 percent were suspected and 33 percent were unsubstantiated) (Trocmé et al. 2001:xiv). Regarding the kinds of maltreatment,

- 31 percent were physical abuse (34 percent substantiated);

- 10 percent were sexual abuse (38 percent substantiated);

- 40 percent were neglect (43 percent substantiated); and

- 19 percent were emotional maltreatment (54 percent substantiated). (Trocmé et al. 2001:xv)

The physical abuse of children in Canada is a serious social problem that remains largely hidden unless an incident results in the death or serious injury of a child. According to the CIS, some form of physical harm was found in 13 percent of the investigations, and in 3 percent, the harm was sufficiently severe to require treatment (Trocmé et al. 2001:xvi). Some researchers have found that children are most likely to be assaulted in their own homes if their parents were abused, neglected, or deprived as children, and if their parents are socially isolated as adults. Parents who lack a support network and suddenly face a crisis tend to make their children the targets of their frustration and sometimes their aggression (Kempe and Kempe 1978). Other researchers have found that abusive parents characteristically feel unloved and unworthy and totally unprepared to cope with their circumstances (Tower 1996).

The signs of physical abuse include bruises, particularly on the back of the legs, upper arms and chest, neck, head, or genitals. Fractures in infants under 12 months of age are a strong indication of abuse, as are head injuries and burns, especially cigarette burns. Most physicians and emergency room personnel are specially trained to identify signs of child abuse so that parents or guardians can be reported to the appropriate authorities. In fact, reporting of suspected child abuse has improved significantly in recent years because of increased training, awareness, and legislation, which established that reports of suspected abuse would be investigated promptly and fully. In the past,

even when physicians suspected abuse, they often chose to treat the child but not to report the incident, believing that abuse would be too difficult to prove (Tower 1996).

Besides physical harm, instances of emotional harm were noted in 24 percent of investigations, and in 15 percent of the cases, the harm was sufficiently severe to require treatment (Trocmé et al. 2001:xvii). Examples of emotional harm included changes in development (e.g., withdrawal), disruption of sleep patterns, and crying and clinging. Problems in overall functioning were also noted in 44 percent of the investigations. The five most often indicated problems were behavioural problems, depression or anxiety, negative peer involvement, irregular school attendance, and developmental delay (Trocmé et al. 2001:xxiv).

One of the most disturbing forms of maltreatment of children is sexual abuse. Unfortunately, there is a lack of consensus on how to define *sexual abuse*. In the CIS, *sexual abuse* was defined in seven categories: sexual activity attempted, sexual activity completed, touching/fondling genitals, adult exposing genitals, sexual exploitation (e.g., prostitution), sexual harassment, and voyeurism (Trocmé et al. 2001:33).

According to the CIS, the incidence of sexual abuse investigated was 2.48 per 1000 children, with 38 percent of the investigations being substantiated (Trocmé et al. 2001:33). Two-thirds of the sexual abuse cases involved female children and one-third involved males (Trocmé et al. 2001:65). Regarding the prevalence of sexual abuse, it appears that between 10 and 15 percent of girls and boys experience some form of sexual contact as children (Finkelhor 1984). While the overall rate of investigations was similar for boys and girls at all ages, females are more likely than males to be victims of sexual abuse as well as *incest,* or sexual relations between individuals so closely related that they are forbidden to marry by law (Trocmé et al. 2001:66). Box 11.2 looks at incest.

The vast majority (93 percent) of the perpetrators of maltreatment are parents and relatives (Trocmé et al. 2001:49). The alleged perpetrators of physical abuse are almost evenly divided between biological mothers (47 percent) and fathers (42 percent) and of sexual abuse are mostly male, both biological fathers (15 percent) and other relatives (28 percent) (Trocmé et al. 2001:49).

BOX 11.2   Speaking Out on Incest

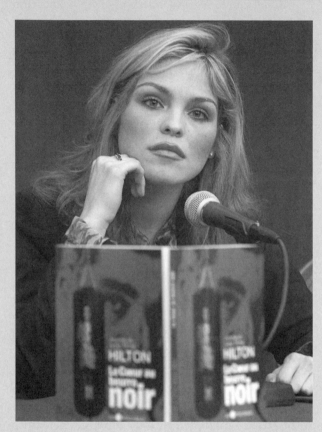

Jeannie Hilton, 2004

In the fall of 2004, Jeannie Hilton published a book detailing the five years of abuse suffered by her and her younger sister Anne Marie. Originally written in French, the book was entitled *Le coeur au beurre noir,* translated to *A Heart with a Black Eye.* Their father, Dave Hilton, Jr., is a former world-champion boxer who was convicted in 2001 of sex-related charges and received a seven-year sentence. According to a newspaper article by T. T. Ha, the father, like his brothers raised to be a fighter, led a chaotic life, drinking until bars closed and solving disputes with insults and punches.

He began molesting his daughters at age 11, first forcing them to perform oral sex and then taking their virginity through intercourse (Ha 2004:A9). Jeannie Hilton is quoted as saying in the book, "I never had a chance to be young . . . In high school when they were saying, 'Let's move to first base and kiss boys,' I was doing things with my father." But she also affirmed, "You have to talk about it. If you don't, it'll eat at you . . . There is no way out of it." (Ha 2004:A9).

Do you feel this is the best way to deal with such a horrendous experience? Are there other alternatives worth considering?

According to the 2006 edition of the report *Family Violence in Canada: A Statistical Profile,* police reports from 2004 showed that children and youth were more likely than adults to be physically or sexually assaulted (775 vs. 631 per 100 000 population; Statistics Canada 2006a:29–30). Child and youth victims were likely to know their aggressor. Of the 775 per 100 000 population, 196 assaulters were family members and 376 were known, but not family (30). Rates of family violence were higher for girls than boys (31). Family-related sex assault rates were highest for preteen and teenage girls and for young boys (32).

A usually less severe form of punishment, used by most parents, is spanking. Some people consider this abuse. Box 11.3 presents a discussion of this topic and reference to cases featured in the media.

SOCIAL PROBLEMS AND SOCIAL POLICY

BOX 11.3   Should Spanking Be Permitted?

Every schoolteacher, parent or person standing in the place of a parent is justified in using force by way of correction toward a pupil or child, as the case may be, who is under his care, if the force does not exceed what is reasonable under the circumstances.

Criminal Code, Section 43

In 2000, children's rights advocates appealed to the Ontario Superior Court to have this law declared unconstitutional. Judge David McCombs ruled in July 2000 that spanking does not violate the constitutional rights of children. He agreed with the advocates that corporal punishment should not involve a slap to the head or cause injury, which would be a case of child abuse, and noted that public attitudes to corporal punishment of children are changing. But he also said that parents should have a protected sphere in which to raise children, and reasonable force should be used only with the best interests of the children.

When this decision was appealed to the Ontario Court of Appeal, it ruled in January 2002 that parents and teachers are free to spank children for disciplinary purposes, but only if the force they use is reasonable. The judges acknowledged that many people who were acquitted of abuse before would not be acquitted today. They also suggested such guidelines as not hitting a teenager or a child under two, not using an object such as a belt or ruler, and not hitting or slapping the head of a child (Makin 2002:A8).

In July 2001, six children, 6 to 14 years of age, were taken from their home in Aylmer, Ontario, because their parents would not promise not to hit them with switches if they disobeyed. The parents are members of a Mennonite church whose members believe in the literal truth of the Bible, which states in the King James version, "He that spareth his rod hateth his son: but he that loveth him chasteneth him betimes" (Proverbs 13:24). The family's pastor, Mr. Hillebrandt, indicated that following the Bible does not mean injuring the child; the children were examined for injuries—none were found. But he does believe that corporal punishment "works in our time to do just like it's written" (quoted in Saunders 2001:A7). Steve Bailey, the executive director of Family and Children's Services of St. Thomas and Elgin, said while they believed that spanking "per se is not child abuse . . . We would look at whether there's any use of inanimate objects such as belts or cords or sticks" (quoted in Saunders 2001:A7). The children were originally taken into foster care and then released. In the summer of 2002, a trial took place in which the authorities sought to allow the children to remain at home, but only under a year-long supervision order which will see them subject to regular monitoring.

In their chapter "Should Johnny Be Spanked?" Tepperman and Blain (2006:36–37) identify some of the negative consequences of corporal punishment—from immediate depression, anxiety, lower grades, and slower physical development to crime, racism, and violence as adults. While acknowledging that though a majority of people are spanked, only a minority become abusive or criminal. They conclude that "parents should not spank their children if they want to reduce misbehaviour; it doesn't work. Alternative methods, like reasoning with the child and withholding rewards, are more successful if the parents are consistent." The National Longitudinal Study of Children and Youth also showed that aversive parenting was very often related to behavioural problems.

What do you think about the Criminal Code section? Do you think it should be repealed or amended? Do you believe in the parent's right to spank a child? What do you think about the case of the six children? Should the family be monitored for any length of time?

Another kind of abuse that deserves attention is parental abuse. This is not elder abuse (see Chapter 5), but abuse of middle-aged people by their teenaged offspring. Types of parental abuse include physical, psychological, and financial (stealing or damaging the home or possessions). Some children who abuse may have a disorder or condition like ADHD. Mothers are the most frequent victims of parent abuse, but fathers are susceptible too. Although this abuse can occur in any class or family structure, abused mothers are often single parents (Cottrell 2001).

Spouse Abuse

From the days of early Rome to current times, spouse abuse has been acknowledged to exist, but until recently, it was largely ignored or tolerated. Fortunately, the rates of abuse seem to be declining in step with the decline of crime generally. According to the 2006 edition of the report *Family Violence in Canada: A Statistical Profile* (Statistics Canada 2006a:13), female victim rates dropped 14 percent from the peak of 377 per 100 000 females in 2000, to 323 per 100 000 in 2004. Male rates showed a smaller decrease of 8 percent, from the peak of 67 per 100 000 male victims in 2000 to 62 per 100 000 in 2004. However, the suffering and such other harmful consequences as needing medication are experienced much more strongly by the woman. Unfortunately, some of these abused women end up victims of homicide. As noted above in the section on the feminist perspective, women are more than seven times as likely as men to be killed by their spouses or intimate partners. Fortunately, a substantial decline in spousal homicide is occurring for both sexes (see above).

Social Responses to Domestic Violence

Although every few months we read in the papers about extreme domestic violence, such as a murder (of a woman) and suicide (by a man), many people who are aware of domestic abuse don't do anything about it, feeling that they do not want to become involved in a "private matter."

Historically, in Canada, an *ideology of nonintervention*—a strong reluctance on the part of outsiders to interfere in family matters—has led people and police officers to ignore or tolerate domestic violence (Lauer 1995). Unfortunately, the pattern of violence that ultimately results in a homicide is eerily similar in many cases of domestic abuse, and in most of those cases, death might have been prevented by earlier intervention. Positive changes in how law enforcement officials handle domestic violence calls are now being made—changes that are long overdue.

FAMILY-RELATED PROBLEMS IN THE 21st CENTURY

As we have seen, families and intimate relationships changed dramatically during the 20th century. Because of these changes, some people believe that the family as we know it is doomed; others think that returning to traditional family values can save this important social institution and create a more stable society. Another point of view, however, comes from sociologist Lillian Rubin (1994), who suggests that clinging to a traditional image of families is hypocritical in light of our society's failure to support the family, whether through family allowances or decent public-sponsored childcare facilities. Some laws even hurt children whose families do not fit the traditional model. Welfare cuts, like those by the Progressive Conservative government in Ontario in 1995, for example, affect children as well as the adults who are trying to provide for them.

For the family to remain a viable and effective social institution, a macrolevel societal commitment is needed, as sociologist Demie Kurz (1995:232) states:

> As a society we should make a commitment to helping all families—traditional nuclear families, two-parent, two-earner families, and single-parent families—and to providing adequately for their members, particularly their children. To help families we must reduce female and male poverty, making special efforts to end institutionalized discrimination against minorities. We must also promote equality between men and women in the family. This includes creating new conceptions of what it means to be a father and what it means to be a partner in a marriage and share family life and household work. It also means taking decisive steps to end violence toward women and children. While the costs of creating humane and just social policies are high, the cost of failing to promote the welfare of family members is far higher.

WHAT CAN YOU DO?

- Investigate if any shelters for women could use any help in your community. Volunteer at the shelter; help is always needed.

- Analyze who does what unpaid domestic labour in your household, or suggest that a tutorial be devoted to discussing who should do what unpaid domestic labour in a relationship.

- Find out what family concerns feminist groups on campus have and help them address them.

- Look further into the topic of Canadian parenting styles by studying recommendations of parenting magazines and websites and thinking of new variables or situations for this research topic.

SUMMARY

WHAT IS A FAMILY?

A family is a relationship in which people live together with commitment, form an economic unit, care for any young, and consider the group critical to their identity. This definition modifies the traditional definition to account for today's greater diversity in living arrangements and relationships in families.

ARE CANADIAN FAMILIES IN DECLINE?

Not at all, say analysts who take a social change perspective. Families are becoming more complex and diverse, adapting to other changes in society. For one thing, marriage is no longer a cultural imperative; for another, many people reaffirm their belief in the institution through serial monogamy, a succession of marriages over a lifetime.

WHAT ARE THE SOCIOLOGICAL PERSPECTIVES ON FAMILY-RELATED PROBLEMS?

Functionalists believe that the family provides social order and economic stability; the family is the solution to many societal problems, and dysfunctional families threaten the well-being of individuals and the whole of society.

Conflict theorists see the family as a problem in society, not a solution; they believe that the family is a major source of inequality in society brought on by capitalism.

Feminist theorists see women's subordination as rooted in the patriarchal system, coming long before capitalism.

Interactionists view the family first in terms of socialization. Some speak of the shared reality of marriage; some view family problems in terms of the subjective meanings that people give to their everyday lives; and some cite partners' unrealistic expectations about love and marriage.

WHAT CHARACTERIZES SINGLEHOOD IN CANADA TODAY?

The proportion of the Canadian population that has never married has continued to grow since the 1960s to about 10 percent of adults. Some people remain single by choice, others by necessity; many working-class young people cannot afford to marry and set up a household.

WHY DO YOUNG PEOPLE POSTPONE MARRIAGE TODAY?

Four factors are important: Changing job structures in Canada lead to economic uncertainty; more women are in the labour force; sexual relationships outside of marriage are more socially acceptable than before; and young people observing the rising divorce rate may be cautious about jumping into marriage.

DOES COMMON-LAW OR COHABITATION USUALLY LEAD TO A SUCCESSFUL MARRIAGE? WHAT IS A DOMESTIC PARTNERSHIP?

According to one recent study, only about 50 percent of cohabiting couples marry, and evidence on the success of those marriages is mixed. Some studies show little or no effect; others show that partners who cohabit are more likely to divorce than partners who do not. A domestic partnership is a partnership in which an unmarried couple lives together in a committed relationship and is granted many of the same legal rights and benefits accorded to a married couple.

WHAT DOES RESEARCH SHOW ABOUT DUAL-EARNER MARRIAGES?

More than 60 percent of all marriages in Canada are dual-earner marriages, that is, marriages in which both spouses are in the labour force. Many women in these marriages do the domestic work at home after completing their workday jobs, though there seems to be a gradual trend toward more egalitarian division of labour.

IS A TWO-PARENT FAMILY ALWAYS PREFERABLE TO A ONE-PARENT FAMILY?

If the parents argue constantly, abuse the children, or are alcoholics, a supportive single-parent family would be preferable. However, a child growing up in a single-parent household faces serious risks that are complicated by other factors, such as poverty, discrimination, unsafe neighbourhoods, and high crime rates.

WHY IS REPRODUCTIVE FREEDOM SUCH A CONTROVERSIAL ISSUE?

Reproductive freedom implies the option to have or not to have a child. The roles that religious organizations, physicians, and society (through the legal system) should (and should not) play in controlling a woman's fertility continue to be debated. Contraception, abortion, and the new reproductive technologies all raise personal and societal issues.

WHICH IS MORE IMPORTANT, PARENTING STYLE OR INCOME?

A continuing national study has found that parenting styles ranging from positive to ineffective had more influence on behavioural problems than family income or structure.

ARE NON-MARITAL PREGNANCIES INCREASING OR DECLINING?

Births to teenagers, as a percentage of all births, have decreased over the past 30 years, but the birth rate is higher for unmarried teenagers than in the past. In addition, the proportion of births to unmarried women aged 25 to 34 has greatly increased.

WHAT PERCENTAGE OF CANADIAN HOUSEHOLDS REPORT BEING IN SAME-SEX RELATIONSHIPS? ARE MEN OR WOMEN MORE LIKELY TO UNDERTAKE SAME-SEX PARENTING?

According to the 2001 census, 0.5 percent of couples are same-sex, and female same-sex couples are much more likely to have children than male same-sex couples. Studies of the experiences of both groups are starting to accumulate.

WHO GETS DIVORCED? DO MOST PEOPLE REMARRY?

Many factors affect who gets divorced (e.g., marrying during the teen years or having limited economic resources), and these factors are interrelated with class, racialization, and age, so it is very difficult to determine any kind of statistical likelihood of divorce. Most people do remarry, and divorce followed by remarriage leads to complex family relationships, such as blended families.

KEY TERMS

blended family,   p. 302
common-law and cohabitation,   p. 292
dual-earner marriages,   p. 293
extended family,   p. 285
family,   p. 285
family of orientation,   p. 299

family of procreation,   p. 299
kinship,   p. 285
monogamy,   p. 288
nuclear family,   p. 286
second shift,   p. 293

QUESTIONS FOR CRITICAL THINKING

1.   Sociologist Andrew Cherlin says that the family is a highly adaptable social institution, but we can minimize the costs of change in the family unit by modifying other social institutions of daily life, such as the economy and workplace. What specific suggestions can you give for modifications in work–family arrangements?

2.   What do you think of Margaret Mead's proposal of a two-stage marriage? What problems, such as reducing "starter marriages," might it forestall? Would it create any new ones?

3.   What suggestions can you offer to help offset the potentially detrimental effects of single-parent households, especially when the parent is a woman who is employed full-time?

4.   Why do you think more lesbian couples have children than do gay couples? Do you think this will change in the future?

WEBLINKS

2001 Census: Family and Household Website (Statistics Canada)
www12.statcan.ca/english/census01/Products/
Analytic/companion/fam/contents.cfm
A summary of and links to a wide variety of resources, including tables and maps.

National Clearinghouse on Family Violence
www.phac-aspc.gc.ca/ncfv-cnivf/
familyviolence/index.html
The NCFV is Canada's resource centre for information on violence within relationships of kinship,

intimacy, dependency, or trust. It contains information about resources and services that are available to be downloaded, and the usual links and FAQs.

Canadian Families Project
http://web.uvic.ca/hrd/cfp/
This interdisciplinary research project, based in Victoria, B.C., studies the family in Canada.

Families and Work Institute
www.familiesandwork.org
Tips for managing work and family issues.

National Clearinghouse on Family Violence
www.phac-aspc.gc.ca/ncfv-cnivf/
familyviolence/index.html
The NCFV collects, develops, and disseminates information on family violence, including abuse of children, older people, and men and women, across the country and abroad. The site also contains links to videos, a library, and other resources.

Canadian Equal Parenting Groups Directory
www.canadianequalparentinggroups.ca
This site provides links for a wide variety of parenting problems by province (though some provinces lack entries).

Statistics Canada Social Conditions Tables
www40.statcan.ca/l01/ind01/l2_75.htm
Data is available on a wide variety of subjects, such as families, households, housing, and support groups.

PROBLEMS IN EDUCATION

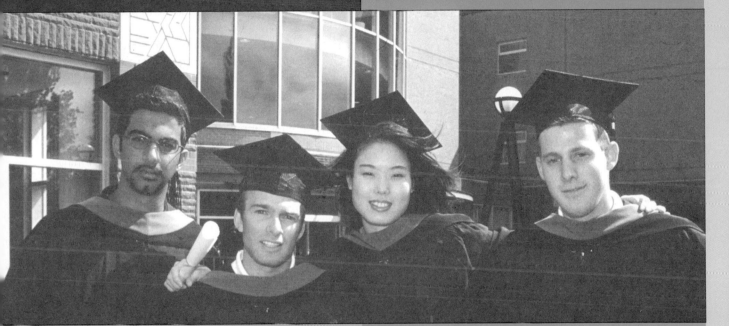

PERSPECTIVES ON EDUCATION

Functionalist Perspectives

Box 12.1 Social Problems in Global Perspective: Change in Education in Japan: Becoming More Like Us?

Conflict Perspectives

Interactionist Perspectives

Box 12.2 Social Problems in the Media: Students Challenge the Ghetto Image

Feminist Perspectives

PROBLEMS IN CANADIAN EDUCATION

What Can Be Done about Illiteracy?

Educational Problems of Immigrants

Educational Opportunities and Ascribed Statuses

Bullying and School Violence

Residential Schools

PROBLEMS IN FINANCING EDUCATION

Elementary and Secondary Education

Post-secondary Education

Commercialization of Post-secondary Education

EDUCATIONAL PROBLEMS IN THE 21ST CENTURY

WHAT CAN YOU DO?

Students should have a say in who they are [and] should not be limited by their background.

Ainsworth Morgan, a teacher at Nelson Mandela Park School, an inner-city Toronto school, who encourages students to challenge stereotypes of the "ghetto"

It's the basic tenet of the education system that you've got to try and give everyone a chance to succeed and provide them with what they need. It's why we have special education. It's why we're supposed to be there helping people succeed. And the lack of curriculum and the lack of a separate literacy test means we're setting them [students in the applied stream] up to fail right from the very beginning.

Annie Kidder, member of People for Education, quoted in the Globe and Mail *(June 24, 2002)*

It's as if we're saying to students, technology is not important and working in tech jobs is somehow a second class occupation. For many students these programs keep them interested, keep them in school and provide a pathway to success in secondary school.

Elena Aleinikov, principal of Lord Lansdowne Senior Elementary School, talked about the loss of the Design and Technology program and its effect on students at a press conference to release the eighth annual study by People for Education, June 21, 2005.

Annie Kidder was shocked to learn that in Ontario, 70 percent of students in the vocational stream, which prepares students for the work force rather than college or university, had failed a mandatory grade 10 literacy test for getting a high-school diploma. The students had failed a test that 80 percent of the students in the stream for college and university had passed. Devising separate streams, also known as *tracking*—**assigning students to specific courses and educational programs on the basis of their test scores, previous grades, or both**—can have a positive effect on achievement of some students, but a negative effect on students not in the post-secondary stream, especially if they are asked to perform at the level of students in the post-secondary stream. The harm isn't intentional. The people who authorized the test want all students to perform well so that they will be able to thrive in a complex, changing environment. It is possible for inner-city students to do well with the right encouragement, like that from teachers like Ainsworth Morgan (see his story at the end of the chapter).

Canada and other industrialized nations highly value *education*—**the social institution responsible for transmitting knowledge, skills, and cultural values in a formally organized structure.** But a wide gap exists between the ideals of Canadian education and the realities of daily life in many schools. As a result, business and political leaders, parents, teachers, and the general public tend to complain about the state of education in this country, even as many parents report feeling relatively positive about the schools their children attend.

In this chapter you will learn about the problems of low-level literacy; educational problems of immigrants; opportunities for both high-school completion and post-secondary education available to people from differing family structures, socio-economic backgrounds, racialized/ethnic backgrounds, gender, and regions; school violence and bullying; residential schools for Indigenous children; financing for elementary, secondary, and post-secondary education and the commercialization of post-secondary education; the future of educational problems; and what you can do about them.

First, the sociological perspectives—functionalist, conflict, interactionist, and feminist—on education will be outlined to help us understand the problems and to show how educational problems are often intertwined with other problems.

PERSPECTIVES ON EDUCATION

The way a sociologist studies education depends on the theoretical perspective he or she takes. Functionalists, for example, believe that schools should promote good citizenship and upward mobility and that problems in education are related to social disorganization, rapid social change, and the organizational structure of schools. Conflict theorists believe that schools perpetuate inequality and that problems in education are the result of bias based on racialization, class, and gender. Meanwhile, interactionists focus on microlevel problems in schools, such as how communication and teachers' expectations affect students' levels of achievement and dropout rates. Lastly, feminist theorists focus on the differences of male and female performance in, and responses to, the educational system.

Functionalist Perspectives

Functionalists believe that education is one of the most important social institutions because it contributes to the smooth functioning of society and provides individuals with opportunities for personal fulfillment and upward social mobility. According to functionalists, when problems occur, they can usually be traced to the failure of educational institutions—schools, universities, colleges—to fulfill one of their manifest functions. ***Manifest functions* are open, stated, and intended goals or consequences of activities within an organization or institution.** While the most obvious manifest function of education is the teaching of academic subjects (reading, writing, mathematics, science, and history), education has at least five major manifest functions in society:

1. *Socialization:* From kindergarten through college, schools teach students the student role, specific academic subjects, and political socialization. In kindergarten, children learn the attitudes and behaviour generally considered appropriate for a student (Ballantine 1997). In primary and secondary schools, ideally, students are taught specific subject matter that is appropriate to their age, skill level, and previous educational experience. At the college level, students expand their knowledge and seek out new areas of study. Throughout, students learn the democratic process.

2. *Transmission of culture:* Schools transmit cultural norms and values to each new generation and play a major role in *assimilation*, the process whereby recent immigrants learn dominant cultural values, attitudes, and behaviour so that they can be productive members of society.

3. *Social control:* Although controversy exists over whose values should be taught, schools are responsible for teaching values such as discipline, respect, obedience, punctuality, and perseverance. Schools teach conformity by encouraging young people to be good students, conscientious future workers, and law-abiding citizens.

4. *Social placement:* Schools are responsible for identifying the most qualified people to fill available positions in society. Students are often channelled into programs on the basis of their perceived individual ability and academic achievement.

Graduates receive credentials generally required for entering the paid labour force.

5. *Change and innovation:* Schools are a source of change and innovation. To meet the needs of student populations at particular times, new programs—such as HIV/AIDS education, computer education, and multicultural studies—are created. University faculty members are expected to conduct research and publish new knowledge that benefits the overall society. A major goal of change and innovation in education is to reduce social problems.

In addition to these manifest functions, education fulfills a number of ***latent functions*—hidden, unstated, and sometimes unintended consequences of activities in an organization or institution.** Consider, for example, these latent functions of education: Compulsory school attendance keeps children and teenagers off the streets (and, by implication, out of trouble) and out of the full-time job market for a number of years (controlling the flow of workers). High schools, colleges, and universities serve as matchmaking institutions where people often meet future marriage partners. By bringing people of similar ages, racialized/ethnic groups, and social-class backgrounds together, schools establish social networks.

Functionalists acknowledge many *dysfunctions* in education, but to many, one seems overriding: Our public schools are not adequately preparing students for jobs and global competition. In comparative rankings of students across countries on standardized reading, mathematics, and science tests, Canadian students were lagging. For example, in the 1996 International Mathematics and Science Study, a comprehensive study of science and math achievement by students in 41 countries, Canadian students ranked slightly above average in math and science (Bagby 1997). Among the nine countries that outperformed Canada in math was Singapore, where all students are tracked individually and expected to perform well, and Japan, where students used to attend regular schools for one more day per week than their Canadian counterparts and, in addition, may even attend cram schools (see Box 12.1). However, in the most recent international assessment sponsored by the Organisation for Economic Co-operation and Development (OECD), in 2000, Canadian students made a substantial improvement, placing sixth in mathematics and fifth in science (still behind Singapore and Japan) and second in reading (behind Finland; Statistics Canada 2001c). And Canadian students' high-ranking continued into 2003 (Statistics Canada 2004d). If these scores are maintained in future tests, it will show that significant change can occur in the educational system.

Other dysfunctions include the fact that our schools not preparing students for their political responsibilities as citizens of a democracy (to think and question and be well informed). In addition, due to increasing class sizes, constantly changing curriculums, and loss of teacher-preparation time in primary and secondary public schools, actual teaching—as opposed to caretaking—is increasingly devolving onto parents and private tutors, leaving those children (predominantly lower-class) whose parents can't teach them, due to their own lack of education or lack of time because they must work long hours, with little in the way of an education. Yet the solutions to many social problems depend to a large degree on the education system reaching those very children. In post-secondary education, the former undergraduate experience of professor–student contact is lost in class sizes of 500+ and evaluation consisting of multiple-choice questions. Moreover, tuition is sky-rocketing.

SOCIAL PROBLEMS IN GLOBAL PERSPECTIVE

BOX 12.1   Change in Education in Japan: Becoming More Like Us?

Until recently, the education system was very uniform, producing children like manufactured goods.

Michiro Iida, a teacher at Shingakai Educational Institute, a nationwide chain of cram schools in Japan (WuDunn 1996)

In Canada, education is a local enterprise. Provinces and local school districts decide on standards, set curricula, and assess—or do not assess—students' achievement. This system may seem to be just fine, except that in international math and science tests, Canada used to rank low in comparison to other modern, industrialized countries and still ranks lower than Japan and Singapore. Critics say that we need higher standards, perhaps national standards backed up by a common nationwide curriculum that culminates in standardized achievement tests.

Countries that rank highest in international pupil achievement tests have national standards. Japan, for example, boasts nearly universal literacy and high-school students who can solve complicated math problems. In Japan, at age three, sometimes earlier, children prepare for preschool entrance exams by entering the first of a series of cram schools—called *juku*. Some *juku* are national chains; others are held in small neighbourhood apartments. The best are known only by word of mouth and charge more than $9000 a year (WuDunn 1996); but the discipline and thinking skills they teach set students on the path to a first-rate future. In Japan, the job one gets depends on the university one attended, which depends on the high school one went to, which in turn depends on one's elementary school, which, finally, depends on where one went to preschool.

Thus, the sooner a child begins cramming, the better. The following excerpt describes a scene from Keiokai Educational Institute, where three- and four-year-olds sit at little desks in a 90-minute class designed to improve performance on IQ tests (WuDunn 1996).

The children followed the teacher's instructions: first, string as many coloured beads as possible within two minutes; second, string only six beads or ten beads; third, string coloured beads without letting two beads of the same colour touch.

Then the teacher pinned pictures of fruits on the blackboard, arranging them in a line. Which fruit is in the middle? Which is second from the left? Second from the right? Then the fruits were rearranged vertically and the exercise was repeated. To a U.S. student, a cram school for 3-year-olds may sound cruel, but many students enjoy the classes. That is not to say the system is perfect: Some Japanese parents and educators feel students become "trained seals"—mechanical thinkers—and there is a movement today to nurture more individuality and independent thinking.

Another problem comes from the competition for elite schools: "Preparation for entrance exams makes students turn everyone into rivals, so they come to find pleasure in another's failure," says one Japanese headmaster. "What is most important for human society [compassion] is not nurtured in Japan" (WuDunn 1996).

Then there are the children who cannot function in the Japanese system. These are the "school refusers"—children as young as eight or nine who will not go to school. They cannot handle the academic pressure, rigid dress and hairstyle codes, and corporal punishment during the day followed by cram school at night. Truancy is a growing problem, especially among junior high-school students (Pollack 1996). Traditionally, truants have been considered psychologically ill and sent to strict private schools that teach discipline or to mental hospitals. With 210 beds, Tokyo Metropolitan Umegaoka Hospital is the world's largest psychiatric hospital devoted solely to treating truant students.

Today, though, the Japanese Ministry of Education acknowledges that the school system itself may play a role in the problem of truancy. In April 2002, it introduced measures to make education less pressured. Students will be encouraged to be creative and to learn independently, both for themselves and for the needs of the global economy. According to a report by foreign correspondent Geoffrey York (2002:A12), Saturday classes were eliminated, and the mathematics, science, and language programs were cut by 30 percent and replaced by field trips and general studies. Many parents and politicians, thinking "hardship builds character," are worried that students will do less well on exams. Some wealthy parents will still send their children to *jukus* and other private schools. Assuming that such students will get higher marks, some critics feel that the new approach will result in advantage to the middle class and the wealthy (York 2002:A12).

Although Japan's economy did very well in the 1970s and 1980s, it was in recession during the 1990s. Although Canadians are concerned that, formerly, our students had poor results in mathematics and science, our economy has done well during the last two decades. Is it possible that a more open and flexible school system has contributed substantially to that development? Do you think that Japan's recent move is a step in the right direction, even if the mathematics and science scores slide? What do you think is the best way to encourage individual creativity and prepare young people for the global economy?

Conflict Perspectives

Sociologists using a conflict framework for analyzing problems in education believe that schools—which are supposed to reduce social inequalities in society—actually perpetuate inequalities based on class, racialization, and gender (Apple 1982). In fact, conflict theorists such as French sociologist Pierre Bourdieu argue that education *reproduces* existing class relationships (see Bourdieu and Passeron 1990). According to Bourdieu, students have differing amounts of *cultural capital* that they learn at home and bring with them to the classroom (see Chapter 2). Children from middle- and upper-income homes have considerable cultural capital because their parents have taught them about books, art, music, and other forms of culture. According to Bourdieu, children from low-income and poverty-level families have not had the same opportunities to acquire cultural capital. Some social analysts believe it is students' cultural capital—rather than their "natural" intelligence or aptitude—that is measured on the standardized tests used for tracking. Thus, test results may unfairly limit some students' academic choices and career opportunities (Oakes 1985).

Other sociologists using the conflict framework focus on problems associated with the hidden curriculum, a term coined by sociologist John C. Holt (1964) in his study of why children fail. The **hidden curriculum refers to how certain cultural values and attitudes, such as conformity and obedience to authority, are transmitted through implied demands in the everyday rules and routines of schools** (Snyder 1971). These conflict theorists, such as sociologists Samuel Bowles and Herbert Gintis (1976), suggest that elites use a hidden curriculum that teaches students to be obedient and patriotic—values that uphold the status quo in society and turn students into compliant workers—to manipulate the masses and maintain the elite's power in society. An update by Bowles and Gintis (2002) showing that genetic inheritance of cognitive skill explains only a small part of the persistence of status levels among families further supports this finding.

Although students from all social classes experience the hidden curriculum to some degree, working-class and poverty-level students are the most adversely affected (Ballantine 1997). When middle-class teachers teach students from lower-class backgrounds, for example, the classrooms are very structured and the teachers have low expectations about the students' academic achievement (Alexander et al. 1987). In one study of five elementary schools with students from different class backgrounds, researchers found significant differences in how knowledge was transmitted despite similar curricula (Anyon 1980). Schools for working-class students emphasize rules and rote memorization without much decision making, choice, or explanation of why something is done a particular way. In contrast, schools for middle-class students stress the processes that are involved in getting the right answer. Elite schools develop students' analytical powers and critical-thinking skills, teaching them how to apply abstract principles to problem solving. Elite schools also emphasize creative activities so that students can express their own ideas and apply them to different areas of study. Compare the following comments from students in high-track and low-track classes who were asked what they learned in a particular class (Oakes 1985:86–89):

> I want to be a lawyer and debate has taught me to dig for answers and get involved. I can express myself.
>
> —*High-track English student*

> To understand concepts and ideas and experiment with them. Also to work independently.
>
> —*High-track Science student*

> To behave in class.
>
> —*Low-track English student*

> To be a better listener in class.
>
> —*Low-track English student*

> I have learned that I should do my questions from the book when he asks me to.
>
> —*Low-track Science student*

As these comments show, the hidden curriculum teaches working-class and poverty-level students that they are expected to arrive on time, follow bureaucratic rules, take orders from others, and experience high levels of boredom without complaining (Ballantine 1997). The limitations on what and how these students are taught mean that many of them do not get any higher education and therefore never receive the credentials to enter high-paying professions (Bowles and Gintis 1976). Our society emphasizes *credentialism*—a process of social selection that gives class advantage and social status to people who possess academic qualifications (Collins 1979). Credentialism is closely related to *meritocracy*—a social system in which status is acquired

through individual ability and effort (Young 1994). People who acquire the appropriate credentials for a job are assumed to have gained the position through what they know, not who they are or whom they know. According to conflict theorists, however, the hidden curriculum determines in advance that credentials, at least at the higher levels, will stay in the hands of the elites, so Canada is not a meritocracy even if it calls itself one.

Interactionist Perspectives

Whereas functionalists examine the relationship between the functions of education and problems in schools, and conflict theorists focus on how education perpetuates inequality, interactionists study classroom dynamics and how practices such as labelling affect students' self-concept and aspirations.

Interactionists believe that education is an integral part of the socialization process. Through the formal structure of schools and interpersonal relationships with peers and teachers, students develop a concept of self that lasts long beyond their schooling. Overall, social interactions in school can be either positive or negative. When students learn, develop, and function effectively, their experience is positive. For many students, however, the school environment and peer group interactions leave them discouraged and unhappy. When students who might do better with some assistance from teachers and peers are instead labelled "losers," they may come to view themselves as losers and thus set the stage for self-fulfilling prophecies. As noted in Chapter 1, a *self-fulfilling prophecy* occurs when a false definition of a situation evokes a new behaviour that makes the original false conception come true. On the other hand, the students can challenge "loser" thinking as students in a downtown Toronto school did when they criticized Ghetto Dolls for their stereotypical images (see Box 12.2).

Standardized tests can also lead to labelling, self-fulfilling prophecies, and low self-esteem.

According to interactionists, labels such as *learning disabled* stigmatize students and *marginalize* them—put them at the lower or outer limits of a group—in their interactions with parents, teachers, and other students. Such labelling leads to self-fulfilling prophecies (Carrier 1986; Coles 1987). To counteract this possibility, many of these students have been reintegrated into regular classes over the last decade.

SOCIAL PROBLEMS IN THE MEDIA

BOX 12.2   Students Challenge the Ghetto Image

Shortly after teachers Ainsworth Morgan and Barbara Schwartz challenged their grade 7 and 8 students in Nelson Mandela Park School in downtown Toronto to think about the term "ghetto" in a non-derogatory way, an article appeared in the *Toronto Star* (February 7, 2002) about a new line of dolls— Ghetto Dolls. Ghetto Dolls, appearing in different dilapidated clothes and ethnicities, were modelled after Cabbage Patch Dolls and included, in the package, a garbage can and extreme stories about surviving addicted, incarcerated, or slain parents, thus appearing to pander to stereotypes. These stories are now online at **www.ghettokidshood.com**.

The G.H.E.T.T.O. Project was originally designed to help students challenge the stereotype of the ghetto by, among other things, writing acrostic poetry using the letters of ghetto, such as Great Hearts Express The Truth Openly and Giving Help Especially To Those Oppressed. As an additional component of the project, the students decided to write letters to both the *Toronto Star* and Teddi's Toys, the dolls' manufacturer, expressing their concerns about the image these toys were portraying.

Excerpts from some of the letters to the company follow. Not all responses were negative. Students envisioned parents buying a doll for their children and tried to think about how the parents could discuss the doll with their children:

I think by purchasing a doll it would be a bad influence on younger children because the stories may influence the children to do bad things. . . . From my point of view I think that the dolls are not realistic. Why should the dolls have smiles if the dolls have complicated and difficult lives? . . . They're also not realistic because of their skin tones, they all have different backgrounds and they're all the same colour.

—*Khadra, Grade 7*

What I think is that the Ghetto Dolls are a really good thing for kids and adults. They teach kids and show them examples (their histories) of what you are going to be if you behave like the Ghetto Dolls parents . . . Kids would talk to their parents about the Ghetto Dolls history no one would want to be like that. . . . My opinion is to buy these dolls and learn something from it and then to teach your kids and they would teach their own and everybody can learn something.

—*Nasim, Grade 7*

The Ghetto dolls are a good influence for children because the dolls' life is based on real life experiences that children can learn more. . . . It will help your child to be prepared for what will come in the future in their lives, but there are some areas that the company could have improved on. For example, all the dolls look happy and have the same smile but they had bad lives. Their clothes are new and clean and have no sign of different backgrounds or cultures.

—*Sami, Grade 8*

Both companies responded. The *Toronto Star's* editor of the Letters to the Editor section came to the school on his day off to praise the students and to teach them about journalism. A representative of the company in Chicago replied, saying the students had addressed some important concerns and suggested that future dolls' stories might incorporate some of the students' suggestions. He also said that he would like to visit the school.

In May, the students were invited to visit the *Toronto Star* building, and afterward, almost all had decided they wanted to work for a newspaper. The guide at the *Star* suggested that some mentorships might be created with the students in the next year. In sum, Ainsworth Morgan felt that this project "helped alleviate the emphasis on stereotypical ideas and move it [the focus] toward pre-adolescents exploring and defining their identities and finding ways to approach common experiences that are challenging." He also hopes this project can be continued next year despite budget cuts.

Source: Thanks to the staff and students at Nelson Mandela Park School. A special note of thanks to Room 36, Mr. Morgan and Ms. Schwartz.

At the opposite end of the spectrum, labelling students *gifted* and *talented* may also result in self-fulfilling prophecies. Students who are identified as having above-average intellectual ability, academic aptitude, creative or productive thinking, or leadership skills may achieve at a higher level because of the label. However, this is not always the case. Girls who are identified as gifted may deny their intelligence because of cultural norms about the proper roles of women and men (see Eder 1985; Eder and Parker 1987). Afraid that their academic achievement will make them unpopular, high-achieving girls, and sometimes boys, can become victims of *anti-intellectualism*—hostility toward people who are assumed to have great mental ability or toward subject matter that is thought to require significant intellectual ability or knowledge (see discussion of the Horizons Project, below, which attempts to counteract this problem). White students are overrepresented in gifted-and-talented programs, whereas students of colour are underrepresented. As one social scientist puts it, if students are not given equal opportunities for gifted education, it is "a mythology that schools represent the great equalizing force in society . . . [and] . . . every child has an equal chance at success and achievement" (Sapon-Shevin 1993:43–44).

Feminist Perspectives

Feminist theorists and researchers traditionally emphasized the extent to which girls and women were disadvantaged by receiving less attention in mathematics and science classes, as shown in a study by the American Association of University Women (1992; see also Chapter 4). Recent work has shown that it is no longer easy to show which gender is the more disadvantaged. As noted below in the section on educational opportunity, women have higher rates of educational attainment than men except at the doctoral and some professional (e.g., engineering) degree levels, and women are doing better in mathematics and science at the secondary level. As psychologist Carol Tavris (2002:B7) has said in the *Chronicle*,

> Who is having more trouble in schools: girls, more likely to be overlooked, or boys, who have more learning disabilities? Who has the greater self-esteem problem: girls, who feel insecure and fall silent, or boys, who feel insecure and brag? Who has the greater bullying problem: girls, who do it verbally, or boys, who do it physically? Who has

the eating and body-image disorders: White middle-class girls, with their familiar problems of anorexia and bulimia, or teenage boys, many of whom are taking dangerous amounts of steroids and pumping themselves up to meet a cultural ideal no less damaging than gauntness is for girls?

Some feminists are studying boys and speaking up for their problems, as Carol Gilligan did by giving a keynote address at a recent international conference on educating boys. She said she had "seen some public schools switching over to single-sex classes as a way to boost concentration, reduce distractions and even enhance student performance" (Owens 2002). Feminists have traditionally emphasized the disadvantaged situation of women and girls. In the future, we may find them not looking at men as the opposition, but rather conducting programs and research to help anyone at a disadvantage, no matter which gender.

PROBLEMS IN CANADIAN EDUCATION

Although we have already identified a variety of problems in education, other issues must be addressed in planning for the future of this country. These issues

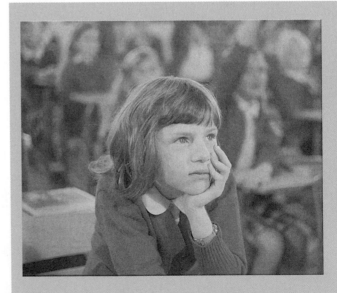

To overcome gender bias in schools, some parents are now enrolling their children in same-sex schools, such as this private school that enrolls only girls.

include the problem of illiteracy; the impact of high rates of immigration on educational systems; racialized, class, and gender inequalities in educational opportunities; and growing concerns about violence in schools.

What Can Be Done about Illiteracy?

From time to time, reports emerge suggesting that a high percentage of Canadians are *functionally illiterate*—**unable to read and/or write at the skill necessary for carrying out everyday tasks.** Even more startling, as we learned in November 2005, celebrated people like former Montreal Canadiens Stanley Cup–winning head coach Jacques Demers could neither read nor write. To determine the extent of illiteracy in many industrialized countries, including Canada and the United States, the International Adult Literacy Survey was conducted in 1994–95 and replicated in 2003. Four types of literacy were surveyed in the 2003 version:

- prose: understanding and responding to instructions;
- document: understanding maps, graphs, or timetables;
- quantitative: calculating costs of various items; and
- problem solving.

Five levels of each type of literacy were created. For example, Level 1 of prose involved applying instructions on a medicine bottle and Level 5 involved answering a question from a personnel department in terms not used in the question. In Canada, 5660 people aged 16 to 65 were surveyed, and the majority had adequate literacy skills, measured as being at Level 3 or higher for the three types of literacy (Clark 1996:28). Little difference was found between males and females (women scored slightly higher in prose, and men scored slightly higher in quantitative literacy). Younger people scored higher than older people (Clark 1996:30). People who were more highly educated and people who read frequently scored predictably higher than those who had not completed high school and did not read newspapers and books (Clark 1996:33). Another analysis of the data showed that whereas anglophones scored higher than francophones, the difference in scores was almost entirely due to education, not language differences. In Canada, until recently, anglophones tended to have higher educational attainment than francophones (Corbeil 1998:6).

Although the majority of Canadians are quite literate, a sizable proportion, one in six people, had literacy skills at Level 1. In 2003, after testing over 23 000 Canadians, the researchers found that this proportion had improved, though not substantially, to one in seven (Statistics Canada 2005a). Perhaps, instead of "functionally illiterate," a new term, such as *low-level literate,* should be used to identify **those who can maintain their current occupation but have minimal skills for adapting to a more complex occupation.** The problem is that in a complex and rapidly changing world, Canadians need to be functioning at higher levels of literacy to adapt to new challenges. The follow-up survey showed that those with the lowest levels of document literacy have lower levels of employment. Figure 12.1 shows that in every part of Canada, those with lower levels of literacy have lower levels of employment and, as might be predicted, those with higher levels were earning more than those with lower levels (Statistics Canada 2005g).

FIGURE 12.1   Employment Rate at the Highest and Lowest Levels of Document Proficiency

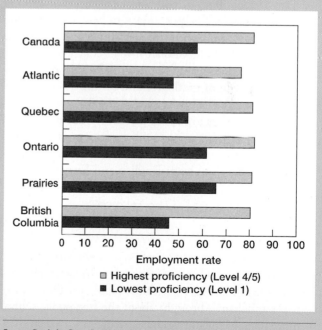

Source: Statistics Canada, 2005, "International Adult Literacy and Skills Survey: Building Our Competencies," The Daily, November 20, Catalogue no. 11-001.

Volunteers and trained professionals are an important link in reducing adult illiteracy. How can we make it easier for people to learn to read without experiencing embarrassment?

One ray of hope comes from the general increase in years of schooling, or educational attainment, among younger people. The percentage of people completing secondary school is now almost 90 percent. Thus, the proportion of people who are low-level literate might be expected to decrease in the future. Only 10 percent of secondary-school graduates and no university graduates function at Level 1 (Clark 1996:33).

Some critics argue that the illiteracy problem is largely an immigration problem. Recent immigrants to this country may continue to speak their own languages rather than learn English and French.

Educational Problems of Immigrants

Debates over the role of schools in educating immigrants for life in Canada are not new. In fact, high rates of immigration—along with the rapid growth of industrial capitalism—brought about the free public school movement. Many immigrants arriving in Canadian cities around the beginning of the last century spoke no English and could neither read nor write. But workers needed basic reading, writing, and arithmetic skills to

get jobs in factories and offices. Initially, a grade 8 education was considered sufficient for many jobs, but soon a high-school diploma became a prerequisite for most jobs above the level of the manual labourer. Schooling during this era was designed primarily to give people the means to become self-supporting. Educational systems were supposed to turn out workers with the knowledge and skills needed to enter the labour market and produce profits for managers and owners.

In the second half of the 20th century, this country is again experiencing high rates of immigration from many nations around the world, and many of the newcomers are school-age children. Although some of the recent groups of immigrants, including many Chinese and Asian Indians, are well educated, most others have limited formal education and few job skills. Immigrant parents are likely to have either lower or higher levels of education than Canadian-born parents (Statistics Canada 2001d), and their children likely speak neither English nor French.

How best to educate children of recent immigrants with lower levels of education and income is a pressing problem in such cities as Toronto, Vancouver, and Montreal, which have high levels of immigration.

Preliminary studies of newcomer programs show that children learn English and Canadian culture rather quickly. According to the National Longitudinal Study of Children and Youth (see Chapter 11), while children (whether or not born in Canada) of immigrant parents start school with more than 20 percent less developed reading, writing, and mathematics skills than do classmates of Canadian-born parents, by the time they are age 10 or 11, they have caught up and in some cases surpassed their classmates. Where the language spoken at home was not English or French, the children were at a greater disadvantage. But children whose parents had more education had less of a disadvantage (Statistics Canada 2001d).

Educational Opportunities and Ascribed Statuses

Table 12.1 shows the overall improvement in educational attainment for Canadians aged 25 and over. The percentage of people with college and university graduation increased from 27.6 to 36.2 percent of the adult population. For those in the 25 to 34 age group, the increase was from 34.9 to 48.5 percent. Now close to half that age group now has post-secondary graduation.

TABLE 12.1   Educational Attainment in the Population Aged 25 and Over, by Age Groups, Canada, 1991 and 2001

1991

Age group	Population 25 and Over	Less Than High School	High School	Trades	College	University
	Number			Percentage		
25 to 34	4 840 335	23.0	28.3	13.8	17.2	17.7
35 to 44	4 353 580	24.9	26.7	13.6	15.0	19.9
45 to 54	2 960 445	37.2	21.5	13.4	11.5	16.5
55 to 64	2 385 240	53.5	18.0	11.1	7.6	9.8
65 and over	2 932 320	64.4	16.0	7.4	5.2	7.0
Population aged 25 and over	17 471 920	37.0	23.3	12.2	12.4	15.2

2001

Age group	Population 25 and Over	Less Than High School	High School	Trades	College	University
	Number			Percentage		
25 to 34	3 973 075	15.2	24.3	12.0	20.9	27.6
35 to 44	5 074 090	19.6	25.1	13.7	19.7	21.9
45 to 54	4 393 180	23.4	24.8	13.0	16.7	22.1
55 to 64	2 847 955	37.6	20.1	12.4	12.4	17.5
65 and over	3 624 850	57.3	16.9	8.8	7.5	9.5
Population aged 25 and over	19 913 150	29.0	22.7	12.1	16.0	20.2

Source: Statistics Canada, 2003, Education in Canada: Raising the Standard, 2001 Census, Catologue no. 96F0030 (March 11).

(Differences in this table from what appears below have to do with ages of people included in the discussion.)

We have long known that ascribed statuses—such as family structure and socioeconomic status, children's gender or racialized/ethnic status, and geographic region lived in—have a significant affect on educational outcomes. The following sections look at a variety of ascribed statuses and their influence on children's educational outcomes.

Secondary Education

The findings of the 1994 General Social Survey provide an opportunity to study the influence of family structure on the likelihood that children will complete high school. According to a study by Statistics Canada analyst Judith Frederick and sociologist Monica Boyd (1998:13), children from families living with both biological parents are more likely to complete high school than children from either blended or lone-parent families. Whereas over 80 percent of children living with both biological parents completed high school, slightly less than 70 percent of the children from blended families and slightly more than 70 percent of the children from lone-parent families completed high school. However, if the lone-parent had high-school or higher educational attainment, then the chances of the adolescents completing high school increased greatly; about 85 percent of these children completed high school, in comparison with 94 percent of the adolescents from two-parent families completing high school (Frederick and Boyd 1998:14). Thus, whereas family structure does affect educational outcomes, parents' education appears be even more influential.

The results of an analysis by Statistics Canada analyst Patrice de Broucker and consultant Laval Lavallée (1998:13) of Canadian data from the previously noted International Adult Literacy Study also show that parents' education does count and continues to count (Statistics Canada 2005g). The probability of earning a diploma or degree is highest for young adults whose parents also have post-secondary education. Whereas over 60 percent of young adults whose parents have post-secondary completion earn a diploma or degree, only about a quarter of young adults whose parents have not completed high school have post-secondary completion. In the replicated study of literacy, young adults whose parents had completed 12 years of schooling scored 24 points higher than young people whose parents completed only eight years (Statistics Canada 2005a).

The social class of the parents is also crucial. De Broucker and Lavallée (1998:13) also discovered that the socioeconomic status (SES—composed of measures of the workers' income and education, and the percentage of women among the workers) of the parents' occupations was related to the educational attainment of the young adults. The higher the SES score of the father, the higher the child's educational level. Even fathers without high-school education but with a higher SES occupation can provide an environment and resources to help their children attain a post-secondary degree. Regarding performance in individual subjects, in an OECD study of reading, mathematics, and science, students from high SES backgrounds outperformed students from low SES backgrounds (Statistics Canada 2001c).

As regards high-school completion, women are doing very well. According to Statistics Canada's Youth Transition survey (Statistics Canada 2002s), only 9 percent of women dropped out of high school in 1999, as measured by the percentage of 20-year-olds who had not completed high school and were no longer in school. This is an important improvement over 1991, when 14 percent dropped out. A higher though decreasing percentage of men are dropping out: 15 percent of men in 1999 in comparison to 22 percent in 1991. The results of this study also underlined the influence of family structure noted above. Although

the majority of both high-school graduates and dropouts lived in a two-parent family during high school, a greater percentage of dropouts than graduates (32 percent vs. 16 percent) lived with a single parent. Dropouts were also three times as likely as graduates to have parents who had not finished high school (27 percent vs. 9 percent).

As a result of concern that the dropout rate was trending up in 2005, the Ontario government has decided to make attendance at school compulsory to age 18 (or graduation). New Brunswick has already made attendance to 18 compulsory, but is not enforcing it, so the dropout rate has not changed. Ontario plans to enforce attendance by denying driving licences to those who drop out. Perhaps a better approach would be to support programs like Pathways to Education, a downtown Toronto program that provides tutoring to inner-city secondary school students and a $1000 per year scholarship toward post-secondary education.

For particular subjects, like mathematics and science, a large number of past studies have shown what amounted to gender bias; girls were discouraged from doing well in these subjects or even pursuing them. Now, however, girls are now doing much better in these courses, as shown in recent national test results. According to the OECD study, in which Canadians scored very high, no significant differences between girls and boys were found in science test scores. Scores for reading were significantly higher for girls, and scores for mathematics were significantly higher for boys, but by a slimmer difference than for reading (Statistics Canada 2001c).

Unfortunately, data on the influence of racialization/ethnicity on high-school completion are not as recent as other data seen here. A study by sociologists Jason Z. Lian and David Ralph Matthews (1998:467), using data from the 1991 census, showed that whereas 30 percent of all Canadians had not completed high school, 60 percent of those reporting Portuguese ancestry, 44 percent of those reporting Greek, and 41 percent of those reporting Vietnamese had not completed high school. Those reporting British or French ancestry were at the overall average; 30 percent had not completed high school. Blacks were not far off that figure: 31 percent had not completed high school. A comparison of 1986 and 1996 census data showed that the percentage of Indigenous men and women with less than high-school completion had fallen. Whereas 62 percent of men and 59 percent of women had not completed high school in 1986, those percentages had declined to 48 and 42 respectively (Tait 1999). But Indigenous people are still at a disadvantage, since they are still 2.6 times as likely to be without high-school completion as non-Indigenous people. In conclusion, given the present low percentage of 20-year-olds who have not graduated from high school, the 2001 census should show much lower percentages of people from all racialized/ethnic groups who have not completed high school.

Although no clear differences are found among the large regions of Canada for completing high school, Quebec and Prince Edward Island were the provinces with the highest percentages (16 percent) of dropouts, and New Brunswick and Saskatchewan were the provinces with the lowest percentages (8 percent) of dropouts.

Post-secondary Education

Many educators had hoped that, with the expansion of the higher-education sector in the1960s and 1970s, the influence of ascribed statuses such as racialization/ethnicity, class, gender, and region would be eliminated. Indeed, a large percentage of the 1960s cohort did go to university and 19 percent of the cohort achieved a baccalaureate degree (Wanner 1999). During the last decades of the 20th century, it was obvious that a very high percentage of women and francophones were going to university. But were class factors being reduced also? To answer this question, Wanner studied data from the 1973 Canadian Mobility Study and the 1986 and 1994 General Social Surveys. He found that in recent cohorts the influence of gender and language (francophone in Quebec) were negligible. He also found, however, that class was still a factor, though less so than previously. As noted above, parents' education is related to that of the children. If parents did not complete high school, a good chance exists that, because of lack of resources or learning environment, the children will not go on to university.

Although a relatively high percentage of Canadians have completed university, this is not true for all ethnic groups. According to the study by Lian and Matthews (1998:467), whereas in 1991, 16.7 percent of all Canadians had completed university, only 11.9 percent

of Black, 4.5 percent of Portuguese, and 4.2 percent of Indigenous Canadians had completed university.

The Youth Transition Study also showed that Eastern and Central Canadians were slightly more likely to attend post-secondary school than Western Canadians, but the differences were minimal (Statistics Canada 2002s). A more telling measure of the influence of region is commuting distance to university. It has a significant effect on university attendance. High-school students who lived beyond commuting distance of a university (beyond 80 km) were far less likely to attend university than those living within commuting distance (within 40 km). To compound the problem, commuting distance had a much greater negative impact on university access for students with lower family incomes (Statistics Canada 2002d).

Bullying and School Violence

In the past 10 years, one student—Reena Virk of Victoria, B.C.—has been killed and three students—Dawn-Marie Wesley and Hamed Nastoh, also of British Columbia, and Emmet Fraslick of Halifax—have committed suicide because of bullying. But in June 2002, two other students, David Knight and his sister Katharine Knight, in Burlington, Ontario, took a very different approach to this problem. They sued their current and former high-school principals and vice-principals for failing to protect them from a group of bullies. They are also suing the ringleaders for harassment (Malarek 2002:A4). Because of incidents like these, bullying has become a very prominent social problem in the last few years.

Bullying is common at schools. In a fact sheet prepared for the National Crime Prevention Council, psychologists Debra Pepler, Wendy Craig, and Jennifer Connelly (1997:2) state that in a Canadian survey of elementary-school children, 6 percent admitted bullying others "more than once or twice" in the past six weeks and 15 percent of the children reported being victimized at the same rate. They also note that these data are similar to other surveys. As a result of its prominence, questions about bullying, defined as "when one or more people tease, hurt, or upset a weaker person on purpose," were added by drug use researchers Edward Adlaf and his colleagues (2002:46) to their continuing survey of drug use by older students in Ontario. They found for the year 2001 that 31.8 percent of students in grades 7 through OAC (grade 13, now abolished) reported bullying others at school and 24.6 percent reported being bullied, with 5.7 percent being bullied daily or weekly. That a higher percentage of people report bullying than being bullied may be due to group bullying or the reluctance of people to admit being a victim. As is commonly the case, males reported both bullying and being bullied more than girls, and younger students reported both bullying and being bullied more than older students (Adlaf et al. 2002:46).

Although bullying has been prominent recently, school violence has been a concern for much longer. In his study of officials from 260 school boards and 250 police chiefs across the country, criminologist Thomas Gabor (1995) found that 80 percent of both groups felt that violence and intimidation had grown from the mid-1980s to the mid-1990s. Studying weapons use in Canadian schools, S. G. Walker (1994) found that weapons use increased from the late-1980s to the mid-1990s. Adlaf and colleagues (2002:43), in their study, found that 12.3 percent of the students surveyed had assaulted someone in the past year, and 10.4 percent admitted carrying a weapon at school. In both cases, a higher percentage of males reported the offence, but no significant grade or age differences occurred. This study was one of the continuing biennial (since 1977) surveys of Ontario students' drug use by the Centre for Addiction and Mental Health (formerly the Addiction Research Foundation). Previous waves of this study of drug use had asked students in grades 7, 9, 11, and OAC about committing assault and carrying weapons. Comparing only these grades, the researchers found that the incidence of assault peaked in 1997, with 20.4 percent of the students reporting it, and then declined to 11.5 percent in 2001; carrying weapons peaked in 1993, with 15.4 percent of the students reporting it, and then declined to 9.0 percent in 2001 (Adlaf et al. 2002:43).

Dealing with bullying and violence is a major challenge. Some places in the United States have chosen to rebuild schools. Today, some school buildings look like fortresses or prisons, with high fences, bright spotlights at night, and armed security guards. Many schools have installed metal detectors at entrances, and some schools search students for weapons, drugs, and other contraband as they enter. Consider this journalist's description of how one school district is attempting to reduce violence (Applebome 1995a:A1):

The sprawling new brick building next to the Dallas County Probation Department has 37 surveillance cameras, six metal detectors, five full-time police officers and a security-conscious configuration based on the principles of crime prevention through environmental design. It is not the Big House. It is a schoolhouse: Dallas's $41 million state-of-the-art Townview Magnet Center.

Most educational analysts acknowledge that technology alone will not rid schools of violence and crime. In Canada, a wide variety of programs has been developed—from zero tolerance of violence (e.g., Scarborough, a former suburb of Toronto, Board of Education), to Alberta's Safe and Caring School Project, to the creation of the Canadian Safe Schools Network (CSSN), a grassroots organization dedicated to reducing youth violence and making schools and communities safer (**www.canadiansafeschools.com**). In September 2002, the CSSN launched the Empowered Student Partnerships (EPS) program to empower students to plan, organize, and execute safe-school programs in the Toronto area. Organizations involved include the Toronto Police Service; City Council; ProAction, a concerned business association; and the Toronto School Board. The CSSN has also created a CD-ROM of six bullying incidents and interventions, which can be viewed from the perspective of the victim, perpetrator, and bystander.

Some educators have advocated the use of school uniforms because young people are less likely to be attacked for a pair of sneakers or for jewellery or designer clothes if all students are required to dress alike (Mathis 1996). We do not know yet whether the positive effects of school uniforms outweigh the negative consequences—such as the embarrassment of poor families who cannot purchase the uniforms (Mathis 1996; Muto 1995).

Ensuring safety at school for students and teachers alike is another challenge facing school districts that are burdened with shrinking budgets, decaying buildings, and heightened demands for services.

Residential Schools

Residential schools for Indigenous youth to help them assimilate into the Euro-Canadian culture began in the late 19th century and grew in number to a total of 80 schools by 1930 (Miller 2002). By then, the Roman Catholic Church operated 60 percent of these schools, and the remainder was divided between the Anglican and United Churches. Generally the Indigenous students experienced more misery than benefit from poor facilities, poor teaching methods, frequent corporal punishment, and sexual abuse. In addition, Indigenous languages were forbidden in the school, Indigenous ways were disparaged, and the Euro-Canadian values were considered superior (Miller 2002).

After many years of protest by Indigenous people and the realization that the schools were at best ineffective and at worst very damaging, in 1969 it was decided to close the residential schools. Now, Indigenous people's groups are suing the churches and government for compensation for the consequences of the maltreatment. The churches have said that settling these suits could bankrupt them. In November 2005, the federal government announced a two billion dollar residential schools agreement to settle this racist issue. This settlement could provide up to $30 000 per student.

PROBLEMS IN FINANCING EDUCATION

Elementary and Secondary Education

It is well known that governments have been cutting back on school budgets. Although support for elementary and secondary education in Canada is among the highest in the developed world, the contribution by governments per pupil has declined since the mid-1990s. Recently the Canadian Centre for Policy Alternatives released a study showing this decline for Ontario. The author of the study, researcher Hugh Mackenzie (2002), said that the general legislative grants (GLG) for 2002–2003, announced by the government on May 21, 2002, were presented as providing the relief school boards needed. But an analysis of the funding announcement revealed that when cost increases and enrolment changes were taken into account, the grants to school boards were at least $144 million short of what would be needed to avoid further cuts in programs for 2002–2003. Analysis of school board funding for 2002–2003 showed that funding for elementary and secondary education on a real, per-student basis had

been cut by between $2.2 and $2.5 billion since 1995. Adjusting for enrolment change and cost increases, 2002–2003 funding would have to be increased by at least $2.2 billion to match the 1994 level. In general, the cuts were concentrated in large, urban public boards in southern Ontario. In 2000–2001, total board operating deficits amounted to $37 million. For 2001–2002, the Ontario Public School Boards Association estimated that half the boards in the province would complete the year in deficit. On a per-student basis, funding increased by $349 from 1994 before adjusting for costs. After adjusting for costs, funding per student was down by $581 from 1994.

Post-secondary Education

Like the other levels of education, the post-secondary level has seen substantial decline in governmental support. In order to make up the shortfall, universities and colleges increased tuition substantially during the last 15 years.

Figure 12.2 shows the great increase in fees, on average from $1464 in 1990–91 to $4172 in 2004–2005. Fees are highest in Nova Scotia (almost $6000) and lowest in Quebec (almost $1700; Statistics Canada 2004j). Moreover, according to the Global Higher Educational Rankings of 2005, Canada ranked eleventh out of 16 countries in the affordability of university education (continental European countries having more affordable tuition, and English-speaking countries and Japan having less affordable education; Mascoll 2005:A16).

The provincial governments also deregulated fees for certain courses so that the universities and colleges could charge increased tuition for professional and graduate education. As a result in 2004–2005, average graduate education tuition was $5475, medicine was $9977, and law was $6471. Although student loans were available for paying tuition and expenses, an obvious consequence was that the number of graduating students with large debts increased. Even before the most recent big hikes, students were having difficulties. According to the National Graduates Surveys of 2002, just under 50 percent of the 2000 graduates owed money; on average, graduates of universities owed $19 500 and graduates of colleges owed $12 600 (Statistics Canada 2004e). This compares with the amounts owed in 1997 by 1995 graduates: $9600 by college students and $13 300 by university students.

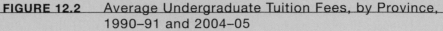

FIGURE 12.2 Average Undergraduate Tuition Fees, by Province, 1990–91 and 2004–05

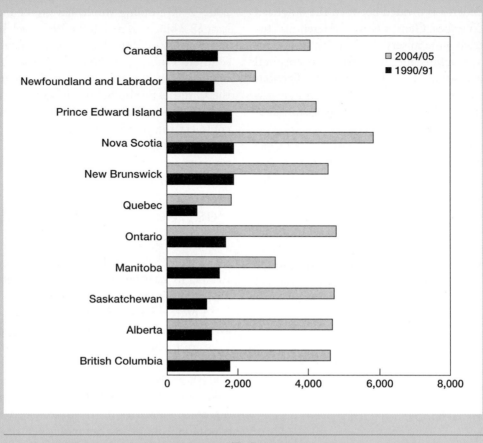

Source: Statistics Canada, 2004, "University Tuition Fees," The Daily, September 2, Catalogue no. 11-001.

Because earnings did not keep pace with repayment demands, students experienced difficulties, and by 1997, 1 in 20 students had defaulted (Clark 1998:28). Now, 5 percent of the graduating class of University of Toronto leaves school with the maximum Ontario Student Assistance Program (OSAP) debt ($28 000), according to President Robert Birgeneau (2002:5). He went on to say, "Such high debt is unacceptable in my view, and we must work with the province and our students to reduce this burden." To protest these increases in tuition, students from across the country held a National Day of Action on February 6, 2002.

A more extreme example of tuition increase is that for studying law at the University of Toronto, where the Faculty of Law plans to increase tuition to $22 000 over the next few years. In defence of the increase, Dean Ronald J. Daniels (2002:A15) wrote in the *Globe and Mail*, "We're pursuing an ideal by offering a challenging intellectual experience steeped in Canadian law and legal institutions that also takes account of broader international experience." He also said the faculty was offering expanded ranks of professors, reduced class sizes, and new courses. Finally, he noted that it was offering increased financial aid and compared the increased tuition to that at top U.S. schools, which charge $27 500 even for in-state students. The Black Law Students Association of Canada was very critical of the tuition hike and asked the Ontario Human Rights Commission to investigate the increase, saying that it would discriminate against minority and low-income students. According to the Association, the average annual income for Black families in Toronto is $25 000. Louise James, a member of the Association, quoted in the *Varsity,* the student newspaper of the University of Toronto, said that the faculty, "don't address the problem that is going to be posed by the tuition hike, in terms of attracting more students of diverse backgrounds and improving their experience at law school" (Holloway 2002:1).

Commercialization of Post-secondary Education

Another important aspect of school financing is commercialization. The commercialization of universities and colleges takes many forms—for example, the obvious increase in corporate advertisements in washrooms and corridors and the greater numbers of soft-drink machines and fast-food franchises, such as Tim Hortons. The machines are on almost every floor, and the franchises are in almost every building with classrooms on campus. Another form of commercialization is the opportunity for corporations to name buildings and classrooms. Individual bricks are available for the names of individual donors. As a speaker at a retirement party for a university president suggested, "Only the doorknobs remain." As a result, the fundraising arm of universities—called by a succession of euphemisms, such as external relations, advancement, and development—has gained in importance and its vice-president is sometimes the highest-paid official at the university. These forms of commercialization are found at both colleges and universities, but a third form of commercialization is more problematic for universities.

Universities are being encouraged to form partnerships with corporations. These relationships are intended to provide research facilities and funding as government funding declines. From the access to university researchers, businesses feel they can be at the cutting-edge of their industry. The university can enhance its image if it can contribute innovative products—from drugs to software. For example, the University of Waterloo is well known for its innovative contributions to computer technology and generating of companies like OpenText. Finally, students can gain because the collaborations can help them find co-op assignments and future employment.

However, there are problems with these collaborations. For example, in Chapter 10, we have already seen an example of such conflict. Despite an agreement

of confidentiality, a medical researcher, Dr. Nancy Olivieri, because of ethical concerns, published results about the harmful effects of a drug she was testing for Apotex, a pharmaceutical company. At the same time, the University of Toronto was negotiating with Apotex for a substantial grant for the university. Although the problems have been resolved now, Olivieri did not receive immediate support from the university. In their book *No Place to Learn: Why Universities Aren't Working,* political scientists Tom Pocklington and Allan Tupper (2002:148) discuss the close links between universities and corporations and conclude that universities

> may knowingly or unwittingly link themselves with corporations and thereby operate in ways contrary to other legitimate interests and groups in society. In this way, universities can seriously overextend their mandates as educational institutions. Their priorities can be badly distorted as a result.

EDUCATIONAL PROBLEMS IN THE 21st CENTURY

Many problems remain unsolved in Canadian education. Rates of low-level literacy are worrisome, especially when many people feel complacent about their being at that level. Perhaps the best way to give the greatest number of people the opportunity to learn how to read and thus more opportunities in society is to address illiteracy at both the national and local levels.

What about the issue of Canadian students traditionally not achieving, in reading, science, and mathematics, at the levels of students in other high-income nations? Although recent results suggest that a significant improvement has been made, only when these results have been confirmed by trend data can we be confident that we are moving in the right direction.

Several years ago, the United States set national goals to be met by the year 2000:

1. All children in the United States will start school ready to learn.

2. The high-school graduation rate will be 90 percent or higher.

3. Students will leave Grades 4, 8, and 12 showing competency in challenging subject matter.

4. American students will be the best in the world in mathematics and science.

5. Every adult in the United States will be literate.

6. Schools will be free of drugs, guns, and violence.

7. Schools will promote partnerships with parents.

8. Teachers will have the means for professional development. (Kendall 2001:267–268)

Because education is a provincial matter, Canadians do not set national educational goals. We have come very close to achieving Goal 2 and reasonably close to Goal 4. The United States is far from achieving any of the goals. Do you think it is a good idea to set goals like these? Do you think it is discouraging to set goals so lofty that they are unlikely to be met?

Some parents are avoiding the problems of school safety and quality by home schooling their children. Home schooling has become a popular option for some Canadian families, especially in the West. Home schooling occurs when a student participates in his or her schooling at home rather than attending a public, private, or other type of school (Luffman 1998). Since the early 1990s, the numbers receiving home schooling have grown from 0.1 percent of school-aged children to over 0.4 percent—17 000 students in 1995–96. Parents who teach their children at home are generally dissatisfied with the public system or believe that parents should be the educators. The majority of home-schoolers are at the elementary level. But with the internet providing greater access to information, and the opportunity to follow a blended approach of taking some courses at home and some at school, students may continue home schooling to higher levels. Such students can sometimes be admitted to university by passing entrance examinations, but not having a full transcript from a high school may make admission very difficult (Luffman 1998).

Some provinces have charter schools. A charter school is an autonomous public school. The school has full authority and is freed from the bureaucracy of a larger school district. Some charter schools have a special emphasis, such as science or special education; others offer the same curricula as other public schools but in an "improved," more creative version. Some charter schools are found in Alberta. They are popular with parents, and students seem to be doing as well in these schools as students in the public system (Bosetti et al. 2000). However, many people believe charter schools create more problems than they solve because they take money away from already financially strapped, conventional public schools (Wallis 1994).

Another approach is sending children to private schools. In 1998–99, 5.6 percent of elementary and high school students, almost 300 000 students, went to private schools of all types (Statistics Canada 2001f). Although private-school students tend to come from upper-income groups, they are found in all income groups, with the highest percentage, 29 percent, from households earning $50 000 to $74 000 per year. Quebec and British Columbia have the highest percentages (9.2 and 8.8, respectively) of students attending these schools; very few in the Atlantic provinces attend private schools. The low rate of 4.3 percent for Ontario students was expected to rise with the introduction of a tax credit for private-school fees (deferred for a year in June 2002).

In the United States, some for-profit companies have been hired to operate public schools on a contract basis. The Edison Project took over management of schools in Boston, Massachusetts; Mount Clemens, Michigan; Sherman, Texas; and Wichita, Kansas. Initially, the project was hailed as a rousing success because academic performance improved and students received such extras as home computers. But whether improvement can be maintained is uncertain. Some argue that demands from investors for increased profits are likely to result in cost-cutting measures and lack of public accountability (Applebome 1996). Although Canada does not yet have a privately run educational system, we do have many private tutoring services. For example, some parents hire tutors or send their children to private tutoring schools like Kumon, Oxford Learning Centre, and Sylvan Learning Centre. According to sociologist Scott Davies and his colleagues (2002:37), these franchises have grown 60 percent in Ontario in the past decade and have "hundreds of sites across Canada." These franchises develop their own methods of assessment, pedagogy, and evaluation. Besides providing tutoring in mathematics and language to school-age students, they also provide tutoring in time management and preschool education. Davies and colleagues (2002:38) believe that private tutoring businesses and learning centres are "part of a burgeoning industry that may alter the landscape of Canadian education."

During the 21st century, we must not underestimate the importance of education as a social institution. It is a powerful and influential force that imparts the values, beliefs, and knowledge necessary for the social reproduction of individual personalities and entire cultures (Bourdieu and Passeron 1990). But in what direction should this tremendous social force move? Some educators, parents, and political leaders believe that we should continue to focus on delivering a core curriculum and instilling discipline in students. We must also provide safety and order in our public schools (Loury 1997).

Others argue that education must prepare students for today's high-tech living. They believe learning how to use the computer and how to access information on the internet and the World Wide Web are perhaps the most important skills schools can teach contemporary students. Almost all Canadians, 97 percent, believe that computer technology and the internet are key to Canada's ability to compete in the global economy in the future. Therefore, they think it is important for today's students to have access to computers and the internet in the schools. A small percentage (less than 10 percent) feel that computers are used too much at elementary, secondary, and university levels (Ipsos-Reid 2002). But will computers, the internet, and the World Wide Web improve education? The internet can make doing assignments easier for those who prefer to cut and paste information rather than think in an ordered or comprehensive manner. Here is what author Clifford Stoll (1996:E15) says about technology and learning:

> What's most important in a classroom? A good teacher interacting with motivated students. Anything that separates them—filmstrips, instructional videos, multimedia displays, e-mail, TV sets, interactive computers—is of questionable education value . . . . Yes, kids love these high-tech devices and play happily with them for hours. But just because children do something willingly doesn't mean that it engages their minds. Indeed, most software for children turns lessons into games. The popular arithmetic program Math Blaster simulates an arcade shoot-'em-down, complete with enemy flying saucers. Such instant gratification keeps the kids clicking icons while discouraging any sense of studiousness or sustained mental effort . . . . For decades, we've welcomed each new technology . . . as a way to improve teaching. Each has promised better students and easier learning. None has succeeded. Except that it is even more expensive, I suspect that classroom computing isn't much different.

The importance of a good teacher is exemplified in the philosophy and work of Ainsworth Morgan, mentioned in Box 12.2 as one of the developers of a project to challenge the ghetto image among inner-city students. He is actually a graduate of the school where he teaches, the first graduate to return to teach there in the school's 150 years. He says that his inspiration comes from his mother, who created, first, an atmosphere of respect at home, believing that "love comes later." With this inspiration, hard work, and considerable athletic ability, he obtained his bachelor's degree in the U.S. on an athletic scholarship. Then, he returned to Canada to play wide receiver for the Toronto Argonauts and Saskatchewan Roughriders. Realizing his true calling was teaching, he then took teacher training at the University of Toronto and obtained a job teaching science and core grades 7 and 8 at his "alma mater."

Ainsworth's philosophy is similar to his mother's; he creates an atmosphere of respect and emphasizes that "Students should have a say in who they are" and "should not be limited by their postal code." He works closely with the students, frequently staying till six o'clock to help them with projects, like the G.H.E.T.T.O. Project. (When one of the authors visited his class at the end of the school day, he saw a student preparing to storm out of the class. After Ainsworth's quiet request for an explanation for leaving and an expression of interest in her, she returned and was still working when the author left.)

His dedication to inner-city students extends into the summer. The Horizons Project, which takes place in Upper Canada College, a private boarding and day school in Toronto, brings together urban youth who show academic potential, from situations where academic achievement is not celebrated because local peer culture discourages it (see above the section on labelling). That potential is nurtured and celebrated in an open and caring environment. The students are taught mathematics, science, history, and language for three years beginning in grade 6. Discovering that it is possible to do well and being supported by peers should help the youth do well in high school.

In co-operation with others, Ainsworth has developed a complex mentorship/life-skills training program called G.H.E.T.T.O. Movement (Gaining Higher Education To Teach Others).

The school where Ainsworth teaches has recently been renamed after Nelson Mandela. Ainsworth has adopted an African proverb that Nelson Mandela lives by, "People are people through other people." Ainsworth Morgan's philosophy and work is a vivid example of that adage. Pursuing such an ideal and widely replicating this program would certainly help remedy some of the problems in Canadian schools.

Another excellent example of local activism in education is JUMP (Junior Undiscovered Math Prodigies), a Toronto-based charitable program founded in 1998 by mathematician and writer John Mighton and eight volunteers, which provides free tutoring, by volunteer tutors from many disciplines and backgrounds, to students having difficulty succeeding in mathematics. JUMP coordinates its program with dedicated educators at partnering elementary schools across the city and specifically targets children and schools in low-income areas (JUMP 2002).

Working with 11 partner schools across Toronto, JUMP recruits, trains, and schedules volunteer tutors to work with elementary-level students in need, identified and referred to the program by their teacher or school administrator. In 2002–2003, JUMP had over 200 volunteer tutors working with hundreds of individual students across Toronto; a pilot program in 10 Toronto District School Board classrooms; and a pilot program with the York Detention Centre, a secure custody and detention facility located in downtown Toronto that serves youth from ages 12 to 15.

In line with the findings of accumulating research in early childhood education, JUMP believes that children, with very few exceptions, are born capable of learning anything, and that when any student fails a test, it should be seen as a failure of the education system. With its innovative teaching program and one-on-one approach, JUMP is adding to the evidence.

When JUMP began, its initial four students were in remedial grade 6 classes. This past year, having been in the program for three years, they were enrolled in academic grade 9 math classes. In fall 2002, at Queen Victoria Public School, 30 JUMP students were given numeracy tests by a special education teacher. After five months of tutoring with JUMP, they had all advanced by one to four grade levels, with many advancing at least two grades. Similar results are being seen throughout the program, and parents and teachers are astounded at the changes they are seeing, not just in the children's math abilities, but in their overall confidence and self-esteem (JUMP 2002). But Mighton (2002) argues that the students are not the only ones to benefit:

> Though the developed countries of the world presently have the resources to feed and educate everyone on earth, more than half the world's children still live in abject poverty. In affluent countries, violence, over-consumption, and the destruction of the environment continue at the same pace. JUMP was founded in reaction to the institutionalized apathy and ignorance that underlie these problems. If children grow up frustrated and insecure—meeting only a fraction of their potential, unable to reason clearly or weigh the consequences of their actions, and having witnessed few models of effective charity, they will be easily exploited and misled by corporations and politicians seeking gain. Until educated people devote themselves to breaking this cycle of ignorance, no amount of political action is likely to improve our condition. The profound love parents feel for their children, and the money and time they lavish on their families, have not, to this day, been sufficient to change the world. Until we reach beyond our families, to children in need, we will continue to neglect the needs of the children closest to us, by passing on a world that is unfit for them to inherit.

WHAT CAN YOU DO?

- See if your college or university has a co-operative program with a local elementary or high school to provide mathematics, English, or other kinds of tutoring. If not, you might volunteer your services to a local principal or guidance counsellor.

- Find out if your student government has a program to educate students about the skyrocketing cost of tuition. You might help with the education program or organize a protest.

- Check out if your college or university has a peer-mediator program to help settle disputes, or if a local, or your former, elementary or high school needs help with their programs to deal with bullying. If they do not have such programs, you might introduce them to the programs of the Canadian

Safe School Network (see above) and help them organize a program.

- Familiarize yourself with the wide variety of ways in which girls and boys, and women and men, do poorly or feel at a disadvantage in schools and do some research to determine what approach can help overcome these problems.

- As a way of following all perspectives, you might consider becoming a teacher, like Ainsworth Morgan and John Mighton, to help students have a say in who they are and not be limited by their backgrounds.

SUMMARY

WHAT IS EDUCATION?

Education is the social institution responsible for transmitting knowledge, skills, and cultural values in a formally organized structure.

WHAT IS THE FUNCTIONALIST PERSPECTIVE ON EDUCATION?

Functionalists believe that education contributes to the smooth functioning of society when it fulfills its manifest functions. Education has at least five major manifest functions: socialization, transmission of culture, social control, social placement, and change and innovation. Schools also fulfill a number of latent functions—hidden, unstated, and sometimes unintended consequences of its activities—like matchmaking and networking.

WHAT IS THE CONFLICT PERSPECTIVE ON EDUCATION?

Conflict theorists believe that schools, which are supposed to reduce inequality in society, actually perpetuate inequalities based on class, racialization, and gender.

The sociologist Pierre Bourdieu, for example, says that children from low-income and poverty-level families come to school with less cultural capital (values, beliefs, attitudes, and competencies in language and culture) than middle- and upper-income children. Conflict theorists also think that elites manipulate the masses and maintain their power in society through a hidden curriculum that teaches students to be obedient and patriotic and thus perpetuates the status quo in society.

WHAT IS THE INTERACTIONIST PERSPECTIVE ON EDUCATION?

Interactionists study classroom dynamics and the ways in which practices such as labelling affect students' self-concept and aspirations. If students are labelled "learning disabled," for example, the label may become a self-fulfilling prophecy, that is, an unsubstantiated or erroneous belief that results in behaviour that makes the false belief come true. A student who is erroneously labelled "learning disabled" may stop trying, and teachers may lower their expectations, with the result that the student doesn't succeed in the long run.

WHAT IS THE FEMINIST PERSPECTIVE ON EDUCATION?

Feminists were traditionally concerned that girls were not getting equal attention in class with boys, especially for such courses as science and mathematics. Now, girls are performing almost as well as boys on international science and mathematics tests at the secondary level, and women are surpassing men in academic attainment at university, except for engineering and doctoral programs. As a result, some feminists are concerned that boys are at a disadvantage, with higher levels of learning disabilities, lower reading scores on the same international tests, and lower high-school completion rates than girls.

WHAT IS ILLITERACY? WHAT CAN BE DONE ABOUT IT?

Functional illiteracy is the inability to read and/or write at the skill level necessary for carrying out everyday tasks. Today, one in six adults in Canada has low-level literacy, with higher proportions among lesser-educated and older people. Many of those with test scores at the lowest level of literacy feel that their abilities are good enough for their jobs. To be able to adapt to a modern economy, people need to have a high level of literacy. Perhaps with increasing percentages of people graduating from high school, there will be fewer with low-level literacy. But perhaps extra effort will be required to help people prepare to adapt.

ARE HIGH RATES OF IMMIGRATION A PROBLEM FOR CANADIAN SCHOOLS?

Though some immigrants are well educated, most have limited formal education and few job skills. Also, many immigrants are children, so schools must cope with language differences among students. Upon entering school, children of immigrant parents are at a disadvantage in reading, writing, and mathematics. But with the help of a variety of programs, such children have generally overcome these problems by the end of elementary school.

HOW DO ASCRIBED STATUSES LIKE FAMILY STRUCTURE, CLASS, RACIALIZATION/ETHNICITY, GENDER, AND REGION AFFECT EDUCATIONAL OPPORTUNITIES IN SECONDARY AND POST-SECONDARY SCHOOLS?

Children from lone-parent families, from families with parents having low SES scores, from some racialized/ethnic groups (e.g., Black, Portuguese, and Indigenous), and from some provinces are less likely to graduate from high school than others. Rates of high school completion are also higher for girls than boys. As concerns post-secondary education and thus graduation, the above factors also apply, as well as how far away from college or university the students live.

HOW HAVE BULLYING AND VIOLENCE AFFECTED OUR SCHOOLS?

Suicides of students who were bullied have highlighted bullying as a significant factor at school. Among grade 7 to OAC students in Ontario, a quarter report being bullied and almost a third report bullying someone in the past year. Although assault and weapon carrying seems to be declining, it is still at an unacceptably high level. In Ontario, 1 in 8 students report assaulting someone in the past year, and 1 in 10 report carrying a weapon to school.

WHAT IS THE CRISIS IN SCHOOL FINANCING?

Most educational funds for elementary and secondary education come from provincial and local taxes. Ontario government grants have not kept up with inflation and increasing enrolment. The per-student grant is lower now than in the mid-1990s. Government funds for post-secondary schools have also been reduced, and tuition fees have been increased by over 100 percent in the past decade. Since fees for professional and graduate schools have been deregulated, some fees have skyrocketed. An extreme example is the University of Toronto Faculty of Law's plan to increase annual tuition to $22 000. As a result of past increases, some students have high levels of debt. With poor employment prospects, some students have had to default on their loans.

WHAT ARE THE MAJOR PROBLEMS IN HIGHER EDUCATION?

The soaring cost of a post-secondary education is a major problem because, say conflict theorists, it reproduces the existing class system: Those who attend university or college are stratified according to their ability to pay. Should racialization, ethnicity, and gender be taken into consideration for admissions, financial aid, scholarships, and faculty hiring?

WHAT ARE THE URGENT EDUCATIONAL PROBLEMS OF THE 21st CENTURY?

To compete in the global economy, Canada must come to terms with illiteracy in our adult population, and we must provide *all* children with safe, high-quality education. Some parents deal with issues of school safety and quality by home schooling their children, starting charter schools, or sending the children to private schools. Other innovative approaches are being tried by individuals and groups across the country.

KEY TERMS

education,   p. 312
functionally illiterate,   p. 319
hidden curriculum,   p. 315
latent functions,   p. 313

low-level literate,   p. 319
manifest functions,   p. 313
tracking,   p. 312

QUESTIONS FOR CRITICAL THINKING

1.   Are you for or against support of schooling outside the public system (e.g., home, private, or charter schooling)? Why?

2.   What would the effect be on public education if the curriculum were not subject to political agendas that can change every few years; if, for example, it were managed by an arm's length education council?

3.   If you separate the caretaking function (need for child care all day so parents can work) from the educational functions of school, what different options become possible for improving the quality of education? (For example, classes of half the size could attend school for half a day instead of a full day.) And what else in society would have to change to make this work (e.g., the length of the standard work-week, more flex-time, a minimum wage that meant one income—or two half-incomes—could support a family, and so on)?

WEBLINKS

Canadian Education on the Web
www.oise.utoronto.ca/canedweb
This site brings together everything about education in Canada to the web.

Canadian Federation of Students
www.cfs-fcee.ca/index_fl.html
The Canadian Federation of Students represents over 450 000 students in 70 colleges and universities. Besides offering information about student concerns, like tuition hikes, it has links about health care, travel, and work abroad.

Departments of Education Across Canada
www.edu.gov.on.ca/eng/relsites/oth_prov.html
This site features education links for all the provinces and territories.

Canadian Children's Rights Council: Bullying
www.canadiancrc.com/Bullying.htm
This site provides links to a comprehensive set of resources for information and support on bullying, including cyberbullying.

Statistics Canada Education Tables
www40.statcan.ca/l01/ind01/l2_1821.htm
Data is available on a wide variety of subjects, such as attainment, institutions, enrolment, and graduates.

CanLearn
www.canlearn.ca
This is a one-stop information centre to explore post-secondary learning and educational opportunities, research occupations, develop learning strategies, and create financial plans to achieve your educational goals.

13

POPULATION, URBANIZATION, AND THE ENVIRONMENTAL CRISIS

GLOBAL POPULATION PROBLEMS

CONTROLLING FERTILITY

IMMIGRATION AND ITS CONSEQUENCES

CHANGES IN CANADIAN CITIES

URBAN PROBLEMS IN CANADA

PROBLEMS IN GLOBAL CITIES

PERSPECTIVES ON URBAN PROBLEMS

Please see Contents for detailed chapter breakdown.

URBAN PROBLEMS IN THE FUTURE

ENVIRONMENTAL PROBLEMS

PERSPECTIVES ON POPULATION AND THE ENVIRONMENT

POPULATION AND THE ENVIRONMENT IN THE FUTURE

WHAT CAN YOU DO?

You see, there are only nine cabins in the steamer launch which comes from Dhaka to Patuakhali. In the nine cabins only 18 people can travel. The ticket is expensive, so only the rich people travel in the cabins. The rest of the common passengers travel in the deck. The latrine facility [restroom] is provided only for the cabin passengers. But sometimes the passengers from the deck want to use the latrines. The cabin passengers allow them to use the latrine because they are afraid that if the poor deck passengers get angry then they might go down and make a hole in the launch. Then the launch will sink; they will die no doubt but the rich cabin passengers will not survive either. So, my dear sisters, do not give birth to more children as they cause a problem for the cabin passengers.

Writer Farida Ahkter recalls the story she heard one family-planning officer tell a group of poor and illiterate women in a remote village in Bangladesh (The Ecologist 1993:143)

Johannesburg [the World Summit on Sustainable Development, August, 2002] aims to put equal emphasis on the twin aspirations of sustainable development . . . to show that we take this challenge seriously and ultimately to exercise greater responsibility, for one another as well as for the earth on which our progress and well-being depend.

UN Secretary General Kofi Annan writing about challenges for the World Summit and humanity (2002)

Given the already established centrality of cities to the current and future prosperity of the country, then all great social policy questions of the day—education, health, poverty, housing and immigration—become urban policy questions.

Meric S. Gertler, Goldring Chair in Canadian Studies at the University of Toronto (2001:128)

A vibrant city depends on communities of mixed incomes and uses.

Pam McConnell, Toronto City Councillor (statement to author)

I am noting the same thing as several other heads of state all around the world, which is to say that the international community won't attain the objectives of the Kyoto Protocol.

Prime Minister Stephen Harper, on April 6, 2006

Global population control and environment policies are the subject of international controversy. Although some people believe that government policies are essential for curbing overpopulation and protecting the environment, others argue that government policies are a means by which dominant group members decide "*who* will be born, *how* many will be born, and of *what* race, class, sex and 'quality' they will be" (*The Ecologist* 1993:143) or whether resources will go to protecting the envirnment. On the other hand, the concern of ***sustainable development*—meeting the needs of the present generations without compromising the ability of future generations to meet their needs,** as pursued by past Secretary General Kofi Annan and the United Nations—should contribute to both the development of people and the preservation of the environment.

In this chapter, you will learn about the causes of population growth—fertility, mortality, and migration; the impact of population growth and the consequences for world hunger; suggestions for controlling population growth; immigration and its consequences; environmental degradation and various kinds of pollution, such as air and water pollution and including global warming; problems of soil erosion, deforestation, and solid and toxic wastes; and how sociologists study these problems using the functionalist, conflict, interactionist, and feminist perspectives. We will also discuss what the earth's population and the environment will be like in the future, and what you can do about it.

In this chapter, we also examine some of the most pressing urban problems in Canada and the rest of the world. You will learn about the growth of cities in Canada over the last 100 years; urban problems, such as fiscal crises, health care, housing (and homelessness), and spatial separation of the poor and visible minorities; the great growth of global cities and the formation of megalopolises; how sociological perspectives, functionalist, conflict, interactionist, and feminist, help us understand these problems; and future urban problems and what you can do about them.

GLOBAL POPULATION PROBLEMS

During the past 55 years, the world's population has more than doubled, growing from 2.5 billion in 1950 to over 6.5 billion today. And it is projected to go above 9 billion by mid-century. Even today, more than 1 billion of the world's people do not have enough food and lack basic health care (Hauchler and Kennedy 1994). Will the earth's resources be able to support such a population? This is an urgent question and one for which we need answers.

Population Growth

Growth rates vary among nations; high-income nations (for example, Canada and the United States) have a lower population growth rate than low-income nations, especially those in Africa, Asia, and Latin America. A *population* is all the people living in a specified geographic area. In some nations, the population growth rate is negative; that is, fewer people are added to the population through birth and immigration than are lost through death and emigration. Current estimates suggest that countries such as Italy, Romania, Russia, and Spain will shrink in population over the next 50 years (Sanger 2000).

Demography **is the study of the size, composition, and distribution of populations.** Global population changes are important because they have a powerful influence on social, economic, and political structures both within societies and between societies. For example, the population growth imbalance between high-income and middle- and low-income nations is a potential source of global conflict, particularly if world hunger and environmental destruction increase. Three primary factors affect the rate of population growth in any nation or area: fertility (births), mortality (deaths), and migration (movement between geographic areas). We'll look at each in turn.

Fertility

Fertility **refers to the number of children born to an individual or a population.** The most basic measure of fertility is the *crude birth rate*—the number of live births per 1000 people in a population in a given year. In 2004, Canada had a crude birth rate of 10.5 per 1000 (Statistics Canada 2005h:27). The crude birth rate is used to gauge fertility because it is based on the entire population and does not take into account the variables that affect fertility, such as age, marital status, and racialization/ethnicity.

The level of fertility in a society is associated with social as well as biological factors. For example, countries that have high rates of infant and child mortality often have high birth rates. By having many children, parents in these nations are more likely to see a few of them survive to adulthood. In nations without social

security systems to provide old-age insurance, parents may view children as an "insurance plan" for their old age. In patriarchal societies, having many children—especially sons—is proof of manliness. Finally, in cultures in which religion dictates that children are God-given and family planning is forbidden because it "interferes with God's will," many more children are usually born (Hauchler and Kennedy 1994).

Although men are obviously important in the reproductive process, the measure of fertility focuses on women, because pregnancy and childbirth are more easily quantified than biological fatherhood. One factor in determining how many children will be born in a given year is the number of women of childbearing age (usually between the ages of 15 and 45) who live in the society. Other biological factors that affect fertility include the general health and nutrition level of women of childbearing age. However, on the basis of biological capability alone, most women could produce 20 or more children during their childbearing years. In industrialized nations, therefore, many people limit their biological capabilities by practising abstinence, refraining from sexual intercourse before a certain age, using contraceptives, being sterilized, or having one or more abortions over the course of their reproductive years. Fertility rates also are affected by the number of partners available for sex and/or marriage, the number of women of childbearing age in the work force, and government policies regarding families. China, for example, had a one-child policy, so abortion or sterilization can be required by the government when there is an unauthorized pregnancy (Mosher 1994).

Mortality

Birth rates are one factor in population growth; another is a decline in *mortality*—**the number of deaths that occur in a specific population.** The simplest measure of mortality is the *crude death rate*—the number of deaths per 1000 people in a population in a given year. In 2004, Canada had a crude death rate of 7.3 per 1000 (Statistics Canada 2005h:27). In many nations, mortality rates have declined dramatically as diseases such as malaria, polio, cholera, tetanus, typhoid, and measles have been virtually eliminated by vaccinations and improved sanitation and personal hygiene (Weeks 1998).

In addition to measuring the crude death rate, demographers often measure the *infant mortality rate*—the number of deaths of infants under one year of age per

1000 live births in a given year. In general, infant mortality has declined worldwide over the past two decades because many major childhood and communicable diseases are now under control. Still, infant mortality rates vary widely between nations. In high-income nations, the average was 6 deaths per 1000 live births in 1997 (Japan had a low of 4 deaths per 1000 live births), in sharp contrast to about 72 deaths per 1000 live births in southern Asia and about 105 deaths per 1000 live births in sub-Saharan Africa (UNDP 1999).

In any nation, the infant mortality rate is an important reflection of a society's level of preventive (prenatal) medical care, maternal nutrition, childbirth procedures, and neonatal care for infants. In Canada, differential levels of access to these services are reflected in the gap between infant mortality rates for Indigenous and non-Indigenous people. As we saw in Chapter 10, in 1997, for example, mortality for Indigenous infants was 12 deaths per 1000 live births (Frideres 2002:155), compared to 5.5 per 1000 live births for the total Canadian population (Statistics Canada 2001e:25).

Demographers also study *life expectancy,* the estimated average lifetime of people born in a specific year. For example, in 1998, the life expectancy at birth for a person born in Canada was 78.4 years, compared to 80.0 years in Japan and less than 50.0 years in the African nations of Burundi, Chad, Rwanda, and Uganda (Statistics Canada 2001b:42; U.S. Bureau of the Census 1998). In fact, the estimated life expectancy for people in Uganda and Zambia has dropped significantly over the past two decades. In Uganda, life expectancy has dropped from 48 to 43 years for women and from 45 to 41 years for men (United Nations 1995). Life expectancy varies not only by nation but also by sex. Females born in Canada now have a life expectancy of about 81 years, whereas males born now have a life expectancy of about 75 years. Life expectancy also varies by racialization and ethnicity. Indigenous people have a life expectancy that is six years less than non-Indigenous people (Frideres 2002:155).

Migration

Migration is the movement of people from one geographic area to another for the purpose of changing residency. Migration takes two forms: *immigration*—the movement of people *into* a geographic area to take up residency—and *emigration*—the movement of people *out of* a geographic area to take up residency elsewhere. Today, more than 23 million people live outside their countries of origin (Kane 1995).

In the mid-1990s, about 250 000 people were entering Canada each year, but this number has decreased to 200 000 and will likely decrease further because of more restrictive immigration policies and stricter enforcement. This is still a large number of people for a country the size of Canada. The number is about equal to the natural increase (births minus deaths) in the country (Bourne and Rose 2001:110). However, it should be noted that official immigration statistics do not reflect the actual number of immigrants who arrive in this country. Canadian immigration authorities record only legal immigration based on entry visas and change-of-immigration-status forms. Some people who enter the country as temporary visitors, coming for pleasure or business, as students, or as temporary workers or trainees, do not leave when their stated purpose has been achieved and their permits expire.

Approximately 20 000 refugees are also admitted to this country annually as permanent residents. According to the 1951 United Nations Convention on Refugees, the term *refugee* applies solely to those who leave their countries because of persecution for reasons of racialization, religion, nationality, membership in a particular social group, or political opinion (Kane 1995). People who leave home to escape famine or to improve their economic position, for example, do not officially qualify as refugees.

Although some immigrants enter illegally, it is impossible to estimate their number or how many are still in Canada, since many come to Canada to gain access into the United States. Occasionally we learn of large numbers of illegal immigrants because of problems with the boats that were transporting them.

To determine the effects of immigration and emigration, demographers compute the *crude net migration rate*—the net number of migrants (total immigrants minus total emigrants) per 1000 people in a population in a given year. Currently, the net migration rate in Canada is about 5.9 per 1000 population (Statistics Canada 2005h:27).

Many nations face the challenges and opportunities offered by the migration of people worldwide (see Box 13.1).

SOCIAL PROBLEMS IN GLOBAL PERSPECTIVE

BOX 13.1   Challenges and Opportunities Presented by Worldwide Migration

These countries in Europe will face the wall. They either bring in migrants, or they are going to decline in size. The model that the United States has—and Canada and Australia—is increasingly becoming attractive to some of the thinkers in those countries.

Joseph Chamie, director of the United Nations population division (Crossette 2000:WK1)

For years, many nations have had strictly limited immigration. Canada had limited immigration, especially of non-Whites; for example, there was a head tax on Chinese between 1885 and 1923; the *Chinese Immigration Act* of 1923 banned almost all Chinese; and refugees, notably Jews before and during WWII, have been refused entry. However, with the introduction of the point system in 1967, nationality and racialization/ethnicity were removed from the selection process. Now, according to the 2001 census, the proportion of Canada's population that was born outside the country has reached its highest level in 70 years (Statistics Canada 2003b). On Census Day, 2001, 5.4 million people, or 18.4 percent of the total population, were born outside Canada and, the "People's Republic of China was the leading country of birth among individuals who immigrated to Canada in the 1990s" (Statistics Canada 2003b). And the three largest visible minority groups in 2001, Chinese, South Asians, and Blacks, accounted for two-thirds of the visible minority population (Statistics Canada 2003b).

According to the United Nations, because of the inequality between the rich and the poor in the world, numerous countries can expect large migrations. More than 900 000 Turkish "guest workers" have moved to Germany and the Scandinavian countries to work; nearly 3 million Mexicans live in the United States; and more than 1 million immigrants work in Saudi Arabia (Kane 1995; U.S. Bureau of the Census 2001). Migrants follow the flow of jobs, and in countries with severely shrunken labour forces and increasing ranks of older retirees, immigrants may be part of the solution to population concerns rather than part of the "problem," as they have been perceived to be in the past.

Today, many European countries (as well as Canada, the United States, and Japan) are faced with populations that will soon have more older people and fewer babies than ever before. If these nations want to maintain the social services and economic structures that many residents have become accustomed to, it will be necessary for them to "lower their borders" and accept a change in the racialized/ethnic composition of their populations (Crossette 2000). According to some demographers, Italy will have to add about 9 million immigrants by 2025, at a rate of about 300 000 a year, to maintain its population at its 1995 level; Germany will need to import an additional 14 million people, or 500 000 a year; and France will need to add 2 million. Overall, the European Union will need to allow the immigration of about 35 million people to maintain the population at the level of the 1990s (Crossette 2000). By comparison, Canada will need to admit 250 000 immigrants per year after 2020 just to prevent population decline (Bourne and Rose 2001:117).

As the pressure from overpopulation builds in some nations, and given that Canada, the United States, and some European countries have increasingly "aging" populations, demographers believe that the flow of migrant workers will increase dramatically around the world. Many challenges remain, however.

First, in some European nations, cultural homogeneity has led to anti-immigration sentiment and hate crimes perpetrated against people on the basis of perceptions about their racialization, ethnicity, or nationality. In Scandinavia and Central and Eastern Europe, racist violence has erupted on various occasions against non-Europeans. Second, migration of university graduates from low-income countries, especially the smaller ones, means that those countries are losing people who could help them develop.

It is estimated that more than half of known graduates from the world's poorest nations are living abroad. About one-third of R&D professionals from developing countries are estimated to be residing in OECD countries. From Africa, some 300,000 professionals live and work in Europe and North America. (Chamie 2005)

What other issues are important to consider regarding global migration?

The Impact of Population Growth

What is the effect of population growth on a society? Population growth affects *population composition*—**the biological and social characteristics of a population, including such attributes as age, sex, racialization, marital status, education, occupation, income, and size of household.** In Canada, for example, the age distribution of the population is associated with the demand for community resources such as elementary and secondary schools, libraries, health care and recreational facilities, employment opportunities, and age-appropriate housing.

What are the effects of rapid population growth on individuals? According to Population Action International's *Human Suffering Index* (HSI), the countries that have the highest rates of growth also have the most human suffering. For example, 20 of the 27 countries listed in the "extreme human suffering" category are in Africa, the fastest-growing region in the world (Population Action International 1992). The HSI also shows that while many people in poverty-stricken regions die from hunger and malnutrition each year, people in the high-income nations spend billions of dollars annually on diet products and exercise gear because they think they are overfed and overweight.

What are the consequences of global population growth? Not all social analysts agree on the answer to this question. As you will discover in the sections that follow, some analysts warn that the earth is a finite system that cannot support its rapidly growing population. Others believe that capitalism—if freed from government intervention—could develop innovative solutions to such problems as hunger and pollution. Still others argue that capitalism is part of the problem, not part of the solution.

Starving children in nations such as Somalia raise important questions about Malthusian and neo-Malthusian perspectives. Is world hunger primarily a consequence of overpopulation, or are other political and economic factors also important?

The Malthusian Perspective

Rapid population growth and overpopulation are not new problems. Causes and solutions have been debated for over two centuries. In 1798, for example, Thomas Malthus, an English clergyman and economist, published *An Essay on Population.* Malthus (1798/1965) argued that the global population, if left unchecked, would exceed the available food supply. The population would increase in a geometric (exponential) progression (2, 4, 8, 16, . . .), but the food supply would increase only by an arithmetic progression (1, 2, 3, 4, . . .). Thus, the population would surpass the food supply, ending population growth and perhaps eliminating the world population (Weeks 1998). Disaster, according to Malthus, could be averted only by positive checks (e.g., famine, disease, and war) or preventive checks (e.g., sexual abstinence before marriage and postponement of marriage for as long as possible) to limit people's fertility.

The Neo-Malthusian Perspective

Today, *neo-Malthusians* (or "new Malthusians") speak of the "population explosion" and "population bomb" to emphasize the urgent need to reduce global population growth. Among the best known neo-Malthusians are biologists Paul Ehrlich and Anne H. Ehrlich, who believe that world population growth is following the exponential growth pattern that Malthus described (Ehrlich and Ehrlich 1991:15):

> Exponential growth occurs in populations because children . . . remain in the population and themselves have children. A key feature of exponential growth is that it often seems to start slow and finish fast. A classic example . . . is the pond weed that doubles each day . . . to cover the entire pond in thirty days. The question is, how much of the pond will be covered in twenty-nine days? The answer, of course, is that just half of the pond will be covered in twenty-nine days. The weed will then double once more and cover the entire pond the next day. As this example indicates, exponential growth contains the potential for big surprises.

To neo-Malthusians, the earth is a dying planet with too many people in relation to the available food supply. Overpopulation and rapid population growth exacerbate global environmental problems ranging from global warming and rainforest destruction to famine and epidemics such as AIDS.

Demographic Transition Theory

According to **demographic transition theory, societies move from high birth and death rates to relatively low birth and death rates as a result of technological development.** The demographic transition takes place in four stages. The *preindustrial stage* is characterized by little population growth: High birth rates are offset by high death rates. This period is followed by the *transitional* or *early industrial stage,* which is characterized by significant population growth as the birth rate remains high but the death rate declines because of new technologies that improve health, sanitation, and nutrition. Today, large parts of Africa, Asia, and Latin America are in this second stage. The third stage is *advanced industrialization and urbanization*: The birth rate declines as people control their fertility with various forms of contraception, and the death rate declines as medicine and other health care technologies control acute and chronic diseases. Finally, in the *postindustrial stage*, the population grows very slowly, if at all. In this stage, a decreasing birth rate is coupled with a stable death rate.

Proponents of demographic transition theory believe that technology can overcome the dire predictions of

Malthus and the neo-Malthusians. Critics point out that not all nations go through all the stages or in the manner outlined. They think that demographic transition theory explains development in Western societies but not necessarily in others. As an example they cite China, which was in the process of significantly reducing its birth rate but only because of the government's mandated one-child-per-family policy, not because of technological advances or urbanization (Weeks 1998).

World Hunger

Food shortages, chronic hunger, and malnutrition are the consequences of rapid population growth, particularly in low-income nations. Approximately 800 million people in the world experience *chronic malnourishment—*inadequate food to provide the minimum energy necessary for doing light work over a period of time (FAO 1995). Chronic malnourishment contributes to childhood health problems such as anemia (a blood condition that produces weakness and a lack of energy and can result in child mortality or impaired mental functioning), stunting (impaired physical growth or development), and being underweight (United Nations 1995). In pregnant women, malnutrition increases the risk of anemia, infection, birth complications, and lack of breast milk (see Figure 13.1). In contrast, improvements in nutrition significantly reduce health risks and the spread of some communicable illnesses (Hauchler and Kennedy 1994).

What efforts are being made to reduce global food shortages and world hunger? Organizations such as the United Nations, the World Health Organization, and the International Red Cross have programs in place, but the most far-reaching initiatives are known as the green revolution and the biotechnological revolution.

The Green Revolution

The *green revolution* refers to dramatic increases in agricultural production that have been made possible by high-yield "miracle" crops, pesticides, fertilizers, and good farm management. In the 1940s, researchers at the International Maize and Wheat Improvement Center started the green revolution by developing high-yield varieties of wheat, which increased world grain production. The new dwarf-type wheat, which produces more stalks, has dramatically increased the wheat yield in countries such as India and Pakistan since the 1960s.

FIGURE 13.1 The Circle of Malnutrition

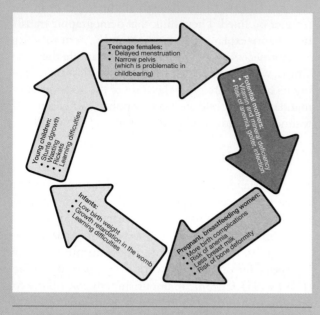

Source: Based on United Nations, 1995, The World's Women 1995: Trends and Statistics, *New York: United Nations.*

Researchers have also developed a high-yield dwarf rice with twice as many grains per plant, greatly improving the rice output in India, Pakistan, the Philippines, Indonesia, and Vietnam (Weeks 1998).

How successful has the green revolution been in reducing world hunger? During the 1970s, the green revolution helped to increase the global food supply at a somewhat faster pace than the global population grew; but in the 1980s and 1990s, agricultural production slowed considerably. Also, while the new miracle crops have increased food production in Latin America and Asia, they have not really benefited Africa (Kennedy 1993).

They have not done so for several reasons. For one thing, the fertilizers, pesticides, and irrigation systems needed to produce these new crops are very costly and beyond the budgets of most middle- and low-income nations. Furthermore, the fertilizers and pesticides often constitute health hazards and become a source of surface water and groundwater pollution (Weeks 1998). Moreover, for the green revolution to eliminate hunger and malnutrition, the social organization of life in many middle- and low-income nations would have to change significantly. People would have to adopt the Western methods of farming on which the green revolution was built, and they would have to be willing to produce a single crop in very high volume. But reliance on a single crop can lead to nutritional deficiencies if other varieties of food are not available. Even with these drawbacks, however, the green revolution continues. Researchers recently developed high-yield sorghum, yams, and other crops that can be grown successfully in the nations of Africa where some of the greatest food shortages exist (Weeks 1998).

The Biotechnological Revolution

A second approach to reducing global food shortages, known as the *biotechnological revolution,* encompasses any technique for improving plants or animals or using microorganisms in innovative ways. Developing pest-resistant crops, thus reducing the need for pesticides, is one technique. Using growth hormone to increase milk output in cows is another technique. Scientists are also exploring ways to genetically alter the reproductive cells of fish, poultry, sheep, and pigs to speed up conventional breeding times (Kennedy 1993). Scientists have already genetically altered micro-organisms in several ways. Soon, for example, it should be possible to spray frost-sensitive plants, such as strawberries, with a strain of bacteria that will protect the plants against up to 95 percent of frost damage.

Some scientists believe that the biotechnological revolution can close the gap between worldwide food production and rapid population growth, but the new technology is not without problems. First, giving growth hormones to animals can make their meat unfit for human consumption. Hogs that get growth hormones are prone to gastric ulcers, arthritis, dermatitis, and other diseases (Kennedy 1993). Second, the cost of biotechnological innovations is beyond the budgets of most middle- and low-income nations. Third, the new biotechnologies are developed for use with conventional (Western) farming methods (Hauchler and Kennedy 1994). Fourth, genetic erosion (by breeding or gene manipulation) may eventually make the people of the world reliant on only a few varieties of plants and animals for their entire food supply and thus vulnerable to famine as the result of a single pest or disease. Finally, environmental accidents, such as the unintentional release of genetically manipulated micro-organisms, pose a potential hazard.

Increasing the food supply is one way of coping with a rapidly growing world population, but hardly the only way. Some people believe that we can forestall the problem by controlling fertility.

TABLE 13.1   The Measure of the 20th Century

Item	Increase Factor, 1890s to 1990s
World population	4
Urban proportion of world population	3
Total world urban population	13
World economy	14
Industrial output	40
Energy use	16
Coal production	7
Air pollution	~5
Carbon dioxide emissions	17
Sulfur dioxide emissions	13
Lead emissions to the atmosphere	~8
Water use	9
Marine fish catch	35
Cattle population	4
Pig population	9
Horse population	1.1
Blue whale population (Southern Ocean only)	0.0025 (99.75% decrease)
Fin whale population	0.03 (97% decrease)
Bird and mammal species	0.99 (1% decrease)
Irrigated area	5
Forest area	0.8 (20% decrease)
Cropland	2

Note: Some of the numbers are more trustworthy than others. Comments on their reliability appear in the source from which they are drawn.

Source: From Something New Under the Sun *by J. R. McNeill. Copyright © 2000 by J. R. McNeill. Used by permission of W.W. Norton & Company, Inc.*

CONTROLLING FERTILITY

The global population increase in the 20th century has been unprecedented. As Table 13.1 shows, the global population has increased by a factor of four.

Although demographers know that limiting fertility is the best way to slow down population growth, they also know that the issue is fraught with controversy. Consider the three preconditions that demographer Ansley Coale (1973) believes are necessary before there can be a sustained decline in a society's fertility:

1. People must accept calculated choice as a valid element in marital fertility. If people believe a supernatural power controls human reproduction, it is unlikely that they will risk offending that deity by trying to limit fertility. On the other hand, the more worldly wise people are, the more likely they are to believe they have the right to control reproduction.

2. People must see advantages to reduced fertility. People must have some reason to want to limit fertility. In some places, children become workers for the family and support parents in their old age. Without incentives to reduce fertility, natural attraction could lead to unprotected sexual intercourse and perhaps numerous children.

3. People must know about and master effective techniques of birth control. The means for limiting family size must be available, and people must know how to use them successfully.

Although Coale believes that all three preconditions must be met to limit fertility effectively, most government policies in the developing world focus only on the third: family planning measures (Weeks 1998).

Some analysts believe that China's one-child policy devalued female infants. What long-term effects might such a policy have on the sex ratio (number of males in relation to number of females) in that country? Could this influence the number of females and males available for marriage and parenting in the future?

Family Planning

Family planning programs in the developing world provide birth control information, contraceptive devices, sometimes sterilization and abortion procedures, and health services. The earliest programs were based on the assumption that women have large families because they do not know how to prevent pregnancy or they lack access to birth control devices. Though we know today that women may have large families for many other reasons, most programs are still based on this assumption. Such programs do little, for example, to reduce a couple's desire to have children, and they ignore the reality that, in some middle-and low-income nations, women are not free to make their own decisions about reproduction. There is overwhelming evidence that women want only the number of children that they can care for adequately (United Nations 1995).

Some critics of family planning programs argue that most policies are developed by political leaders in high-income nations who are motivated by racialization and class issues rather than by a genuine concern about world hunger or overpopulation. They say that high-income nations—such as England, France, and the United States—encourage births among middle-and upper-income women in their own countries but advocate depopulation policies in low-income regions such as sub-Saharan Africa (O'Connell 1994). For example, the French government is promoting larger families because of a rapidly aging population, a low fertility rate, and a national concern that the country is losing its identity because of high immigration rates (Weeks 1998).

Zero Population Growth

With *zero population growth,* **there is a totally stable population, one that neither grows nor decreases from year to year because births, deaths, and migration are in perfect balance** (Weeks 1998). For example, the population growth rate would be zero if a nation had no immigration or emigration and the birth rate and the death rate were the same (Ehrlich and Ehrlich 1991).

Canada is nearing zero population growth because of several factors:

1. A high proportion of women and men in the labour force find satisfaction and rewards outside of family life;

2. Birth control is inexpensive and readily available;

3. The trend is toward later marriage (see Chapter 11);

4. The cost of raising a child from birth to adulthood is rising rapidly; and

5. Schools and public service campaigns make teenagers more aware of how to control fertility (United Nations 1995).

Near-zero population growth is one characteristic of the Canadian population; another is a rapidly changing population.

IMMIGRATION AND ITS CONSEQUENCES

High rates of immigration are changing the composition of the Canadian population. Today, according to the 2001 census, over 5.4 million people—or 18 percent of the total Canadian population—have come here from other nations. In fact, most Canadians are immigrants or first-generation descendents of immigrants. On a global basis, immigration and internal migration are causing urban populations to grow faster than the total population (see Map 13.1, and note that, according to the 2001 census, about 80 percent of Canada's population is now urban; see also Map 13.2 for recent growth in urban centres). Because most cities do not have the capacity to deal with existing residents, much less with significant increases in the number of those residents—especially those with limited education and economic resources—immigration and internal migration often lead to patterns of urban squalor and high levels of stress in daily living.

What are the consequences of today's high rate of immigration to Canada as a whole? Not all social analysts agree on the answer to this question. Some believe that immigrants cost taxpayers millions of dollars each year in adjustment and education (teaching English or French as a second language) costs. But we also know that immigrants contribute as workers and consumers to the economy. American economist James P. Smith sums this up for the U.S. (Pear 1997:1, 15):

> It's true that some Americans are now paying more taxes because of immigration, and native-born

MAP 13.1   Urban Population as a Percentage of Total National Population

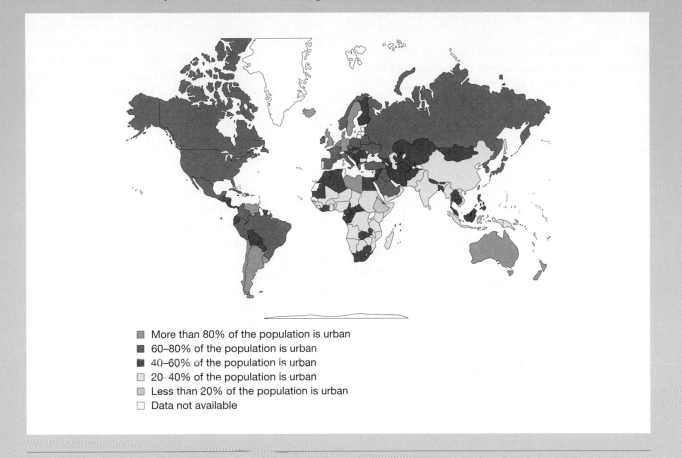

■ More than 80% of the population is urban
■ 60–80% of the population is urban
■ 40–60% of the population is urban
□ 20–40% of the population is urban
■ Less than 20% of the population is urban
□ Data not available

Source: From Statistical Abstract of the United States, 2001 *(118th ed.), U.S. Bureau of the Census, 2001, Washington, DC: U.S. Government Printing Office.*

Americans without a high school education have seen their wages fall slightly because of the competition sparked by lower-skilled, newly arrived immigrants. But the vast majority of Americans are enjoying a healthier economy as a result of the increased supply of labour and lower prices that result from immigration.

Richard Florida (2002:T8), a professor of regional development at Carnegie Mellon University, goes further, to suggest that major cities' and Canada's economic future depends on immigration, which helps to create and nourish a Creative Class (see also later in this chapter).

However, although the economic future depends in part on immigrants, recent immigrants do not seem to be sharing in the opportunities as quickly as did their predecessors. According to sociologists Abdolmohammed Kazemipur and Shiva S. Halli (2001:235), recent immigrants have a poorer economic record, including lower salaries and more unemployment, than previous cohorts, and it is not because they do not have good education or language skills. In addition, since it is the immigrant men who are likely to have the jobs, immigrant women are unlikely to get an appropriate return on their education (Kazemipur and Halli 2001:236).

Besides being undesirable, stemming the flow of immigrants appears to be a virtually impossible task for any one nation. When immigrants come to Canada now they settle in cities, and it is to cities and urbanization to which we now turn our attention.

CHANGES IN CANADIAN CITIES

Cities are obviously important to Canada. But over the last decade, the increased services our cities have had to provide—as a result of provincial downloading of hundreds of millions of dollars in new responsibilities with no increase in taxing powers—have put overwhelming strains on their capacity to provide support for Canada's new economy. Can Canadian cities recover from this situation?

Urban problems in Canada are closely associated with the profound socioeconomic, political, and spatial changes that have taken place since the Industrial Revolution. Over one hundred years ago, many people (about two-thirds of Canadians) lived in rural areas. Early in the 21st century, about 80 percent of the Canadian population lives in urban areas, and many of these people live in cities that did not exist 200 years ago (Statistics Canada 2002n).

Early Urban Growth and Social Problems

According to sociologists, a *city* is a relatively dense and permanent settlement of people who secure their livelihood primarily through non-agricultural activities (Weeks 1998). Although cities existed long before the Industrial Revolution, the birth of the factory system brought about rapid *urbanization,* which we defined in Chapter 1 as the process by which an increasing proportion of a population lives in cities rather than in rural areas. Canada industrialized after World War I, and the shift toward urban living is shown in home-ownership rates. Today, two-thirds of Canadian households own their homes, but in 1931, although over three-quarters of rural families owned their own home, less than half of urban families did (Kremarik 2000:18).

Contemporary Urban Growth

The growth of suburbs and outlying areas after WWII forever changed the nature of city life in this country. Suburban areas existed immediately adjacent to many central cities in the 1920s; but after the late 1940s, these communities began to grow in earnest because of the automobile and families wanting their own homes in which to bring up what is now called the "baby boom" generation. They were referred to as "bedroom communities" because most of the residents were there on nights and weekends but went into the central city for jobs, entertainment, and major shopping. Most suburban dwellers drove to work each day, except where public transit was convenient, establishing a pattern that would result, decades later, in traffic congestion and air pollution, problems that have drastically worsened in the past decade.

To reduce the housing shortage, the federal government subsidized what became a mass exodus from the central city to outlying suburbs. The federal government established the Central (now Canada) Mortgage and Housing Corporation to grant and insure mortgages. Between 1945 and 1951, the CMHC was responsible for the construction of half a million houses (Kremarik 2000:19). Other factors also contributed to the postwar suburban boom, including the availability of inexpensive land, low-cost mass construction methods for building tract houses, new federally and provincially financed highway systems, inexpensive gasoline, and consumers' pent-up demands, after the depression and war, for single-family homes on individually owned lots. By 1971, 60 percent of Canadian households owned their own home, and although they had their dream, more than half had a mortgage (Kremarik 2000:19).

Although early suburbanization provided many families with affordable housing, good schools and parks, and other amenities not found in the central city, the shift away from central cities set up an economic division of interests between cities and suburbs that remains in place even today (Flanagan 1995). While many people in the suburbs still rely on the central city for employment, entertainment, or other services, they pay taxes to their local governments and school districts. As a result, suburban police and fire departments, schools, libraries, and recreational facilities are usually well funded and well staffed, with up-to-date equipment. Suburbs also have newer infrastructures (such as roads, sewers, and water treatment plants) and money to maintain them. In contrast, many central cities have aging, dilapidated schools and lack funds for essential government services (see Chapter 12).

MAP 13.2 Canada's Population Change, 1996 to 2001, by 2001 Census Division

Source: Adapted from map produced by Statistics Canada, Geography Division, 2002, from http://geodepot.statcan.ca/Diss/Highlights/Maps_e.pdf. Reproduced with permission.

Today, edge cities are springing up beyond the central cities and existing suburbs. An *edge city* **is a middle-to upper-middle-class area that has complete living, working, shopping, and leisure activities so that it is not dependent on the central city or other suburbs** (Garreau 1991). Map 13.2, presenting the Canadian population change between the 1996 and 2001 censuses, shows examples of edge cities around Toronto, Montreal, Vancouver, and from Calgary to Edmonton. These four areas grew 7.6 percent, compared with virtually no growth (0.5 percent) in the rest of the country. In 2001, 51 percent of Canada's population lived in these four areas (Statistics Canada 2002n).

Edge cities begin as residential areas; then retail establishments and office parks move into the adjacent area, creating an unincorporated edge city. Automobiles are the primary source of transportation in many edge cities, and pedestrian traffic is discouraged—and even dangerous—because streets are laid out to facilitate high-volume automobile traffic, not walkers or bicyclists. Edge cities may not have a governing body, so they drain taxes from central cities and older suburbs. Many businesses and industries move their physical plants—and tax dollars—to these areas because land is cheaper, workers are better educated, and utility rates and property taxes are lower than those in the city. As a result, many jobs move away from poor, visible minority racialized/ethnic workers in central cities, creating structural unemployment.

Over time, large-scale metropolitan growth produces a *megalopolis*—**a continuous concentration of two or more cities and their suburbs that have grown until they form an interconnected urban area.** The East Coast of the United States, for example, is a megalopolis, with Boston, Providence, Hartford, and their suburbs merging into New York City and its suburbs, which in turn, merge southward into Newark, Philadelphia, Baltimore, and Washington, D.C., and their suburbs. It is almost impossible to tell where one metropolitan area ends and another begins. When metropolitan areas merge into a megalopolis, there are big population changes that can bring about or exacerbate social problems and inequalities based on racialization, class, and gender. In Map 13.2, the beginning of megalopolises can be seen in the west, Surrey-Delta-Vancouver, and in the centre, Hamilton-Toronto-Oshawa. In the future, that concentration could extend to Montreal and beyond.

URBAN PROBLEMS IN CANADA

While we have traditionally thought that Canadian cities did not have the magnitude of the problems of poverty, crime, racism, homelessness, drug abuse, and inadequate school systems that cities in the United States experience because of years of neglect and deterioration, now "the rebirth of American cities is putting Canada's urban landscapes to shame" according to David Crombie (2001:A15), Toronto's former mayor. Intertwined with and exacerbating these problems in many older central cities are periodic fiscal crises.

Fiscal Crisis in Cities

It has traditionally been thought that Canadian cities were in better fiscal shape than U.S. cities. No major Canadian city went into financial default like Cleveland in 1978 or to the edge of collapse like New York in 1975. Nor did our cities experience the flight to the suburbs or the major *deindustrialization*—**the process by which capital is diverted from investment in basic industries (in the form of economic resources, plants, and equipment) to business practices such as mergers and acquisitions and foreign investment**—that left so many blighted areas in the centres of U.S. cities. However, today the tables have turned. Federal and provincial government cutbacks have left Canadian cities, with their limited sources of revenue—primarily property taxes—in desperate financial straits. Out of every $1.00 of taxes collected, $0.07 goes to municipalities, and the federal and provincial governments receive $0.51 and $0.42, respectively (Moloney 2002:A9). In the Toronto Dominion Bank's recent report, *A Choice Between Investing in Canada's Cities or Disinvesting in Canada's Future* (2002), the bank calls for the revitalization of cities and notes that, between 1995 and 2001, local government revenues increased by 14 percent and the federal and provincial government revenues increased by 38 percent and 30 percent respectively. U.S. cities, with additional sources of revenue such as income and sales taxes and greater support from federal and state governments and business, are spending more per person than Canadian cities are. Jack Layton, former president of the Federation of Canadian Municipalities and now leader of the NDP, stated that Canadian municipalities spend US$785 per person, whereas their U.S. counterparts spend US$1652 per person (Moloney 2002:A9). Many groups, like the TD Bank, the Prime Minister's Task Force on Urban Issues, and the Conference Board of Canada, have called for a revitalization of Canadian cities with the help of more stable and ongoing revenue and business partnerships (see Box 13.2 for more discussion about saving our cities).

SOCIAL PROBLEMS AND SOCIAL POLICY

BOX 13.2 Saving Our Cities

A wide variety of policies are being recommended to save Canadian cities. Implicitly following a functional perspective, some politicians and advocates have recommended amalgamation of cities and their suburbs and edge cities, or at least, regional thinking. Rob MacIssac (2002:T3), mayor of Burlington, part of the "905" (named after the telephone exchange) edge city of Toronto and a member of the Ontario government's Smart Growth Panel, states that "we need to be thinking about the connectedness of the entire Golden Horseshoe from Oshawa to Barrie to St. Catharines—one continuous area with its own economy." He says that infrastructure to deal with such problems as pollution, congestion, and land use must be planned and maintained over 25- or 50-year horizons, and politicians must be willing to cut services or raise taxes or user fees. He concludes that because Ontario's and Canada's futures are depending on it, we should "insist on the creation of a city-region we deserve" (MacIssac 2002:T3). However, MacIssac does acknowledge that co-operation between cities and edge cities is difficult, because the main city's politicians do not always think about the region, and edge cities' politicians fear being taken over by the main city (MacIssac 2002:T3).

Second, implicitly following a conflict perspective, many politicians and advocates would like to see a redistribution of income among the federal, provincial, and municipal governments. Gaining income primarily from property taxes, cities get less than 10 percent of the taxes raised in Canada, and property taxes have increased less than other forms of taxes during the 1990s. Thus, advocates would like to see a more definite revenue stream, perhaps coming from a tax source like the GST or a percentage of federal and provincial taxes. In recent years, some federal cabinet ministers, such as David Collenette (2002:T3), have suggested that "the federal government has an obligation to relieve urban congestion, to remove impediments to trade and productivity, to ensure air and water quality to improve the health of Canadians, and to help provide shelter for those less fortunate." However, Collenette did go on to state that "there can be no issuing of blank cheques," implying that no new sources of income will be designated for cities. A key problem is that in Canada, cities are the responsibilities of provinces, so the federal government has to work with the provincial governments to provide help for the cities. For the federal government to be able to fund cities separately, a fundamental change in the nature of Canadian federalism would be needed.

Third, implicitly following the interactionist perspective, some advocates recommend promoting the creativity and dynamism of the city by attracting creative people. Richard Florida has written about the importance of the availability of technology, talent, and tolerance to attract creative people to promote economic development. It is not usually possible for cities to grow just with technology and world-class universities, as London, Ontario, a smaller city, has. Cities also have to be sufficiently tolerant and open-minded to attract and retain top creative talent (Florida 2002:T8).

Besides being tolerant and open to diversity, cities should welcome immigrants, build participatory features like bike paths and waterfronts, and cut back on big generic shopping malls. Creating comprehensive transit plans—including express bus service around the city, new or shoulder bus lanes for highways, and expanded park and ride lots, as recently recommended by the Central Ontario Smart Growth Panel (Brennan 2002:A1)—would also help people mix and participate in city life. Such plans could have very beneficial results, but they can also be stalled by lack of resources and political will.

Obviously, many major proposals as well as proposals to encourage individual participation exist to help us save our cities. What do you think should be done, and how can you see yourself contributing?

One plan to help the cities is to build homes on sites of abandoned factories. In Toronto, Massey-Ferguson, a major maker of farm machinery, and Inglis, a maker of stoves, closed their factories and left land vacant for a decade. Now, houses are being built on the land, and condominium lofts are being built in the 120-year-old Massey-Ferguson headquarters. The first residents moved in five years ago, and now there are a dozen condominium complexes and hundreds of houses, which will be home to over 5000 people. City planners say that this community, called King West Village, is a good example of the kind of redevelopment that they want to promote. With projects like this, planners hope to house up to a million more residents over the next 30 years (Immem 2002:A10).

The Crisis in Urban Health Care

As Meric Gertler (2001) indicates in the opening quotation, most of our social problems are urban problems. This is also true for health care. Although *Maclean's* magazine's Fourth Annual Ranking of Canadian health centres found that most of the major cities (except Montreal) ranked in the top 10 regions, they were helped by having medical schools in their area (Hawaleshka 2002:24; and see Chapter 10). However, overall scores may mask some problems, particularly with disadvantaged populations. We also know from Chapter 10 that disadvantaged people have greater rates of disease, disability, and death. A study of hospital use in a downtown neighbourhood in Toronto showed that while those from poor neighbourhoods were not discriminated against regarding admission, they had high admission and readmission rates (Glazier et al. 2000). As a result, the costs of care are about 50 percent greater for poor than for wealthy neighbourhoods. These added costs put greater burdens on hospital emergency, admitting, billing, and discharge departments (Glazier et al., 2000:272). The authors conclude (2000:272) that "Canadian policy makers should take account of the income levels of the neighbourhood when deciding on resource allocation for public health, ambulatory care, community services and hospitals." If hospitals in downtown neighbourhoods do not get additional resources, they will not be able to continue to provide appropriate help to the often disadvantaged people they serve.

The growing homeless population in major urban areas has simply added to the cost of providing health care.

Housing Problems

Many regions in Canada lack affordable housing for low-income individuals and families (see Chapter 2). Over the last 10 years, there has been a significant increase in homelessness, especially among families with children. Each year, we are made aware of the plight of homeless people through extensive media coverage during the Christmas holiday season and after winter deaths on the street. During the rest of the year, many people view the homeless with less compassion.

The Housing Shortage

Two-thirds of Canadian households own their homes (Statistics Canada 2002g). And since the rent for a two-bedroom apartment in a major city like Toronto equals the costs of carrying a median-priced townhouse of over $250 000, a good chance exists that the percentage of households that realize their dream of owning their home will increase. But housing is still an income issue, because only 40 percent of people in the lowest income quintile (see Chapter 2) own their homes. In addition, although 86 percent of Canadian households are suitably housed (measured by the homes not needing major repairs and being large enough for their needs), 20 percent of those in the lowest income quintile and 23 percent of female lone-parents are not suitably housed (Statistics Canada 2002g).

Although Canadian cities do not have the blighted neighbourhoods and abandoned buildings found in U.S. cities, they do have pockets of poverty. With the reduction in the building of social housing due to government cutbacks, a big increase has occurred in the percentage of people paying 50 percent or more of their income on rent. According to the Federation of Canadian Municipalities, the completion of social housing units went from a high point of 19 621 in 1992 to 1439 in 1998 (Layton 2000:212).

Governments in recent years have begun again to realize the importance of social housing; in spring 2002, the federal government created a $680 million national program to build 27 000 affordable apartments and townhouses across Canada. This program requires matching grants from the provinces. In Ontario, the Harris government withdrew from social housing in 1998, but in the 2003 election campaign, the Liberals promised to provide 20 000 units of affordable housing, using the existing federal–Ontario housing agreement. According to Municipal Affairs and Housing Minister John Gerretsen, about 6500 units are in place, either occupied or in planning or construction stage (Gillespie 2006:A6). As a result of the earlier stoppage in building and the current federal–Ontario disagreement about how much money will be available, about 122 000 households in Ontario are on a waiting list to get an affordable home (Gillespie 2006:A6).

Some cities are encouraging developers to create housing on these sites, as in the Toronto example mentioned earlier. But this kind of housing is not likely to help the homeless or the people who need subsidized housing.

Many of the most successful recent initiatives for replacing substandard housing and building lower-cost housing for poor and lower-income families have come from community groups and volunteer organizations. One of the best known of these, in the U.S., is Habitat for Humanity, which has received extensive press coverage because of former U.S. President Jimmy Carter's participation. This organization also operates in Canada and, according to its fundraising letter, its volunteers had built, by November 2005, 1000 homes across Canada for needy families.

In an effort to replace substandard housing and build lower-cost housing for poor and lower-income families, groups such as Habitat for Humanity continually build houses in communities across the country. Would you be willing to volunteer to build low-income housing for others like these volunteers are doing?

Perhaps the Pruitt-Igoe project in St. Louis, Missouri, is the all-time worst example of public housing projects. Built as a monolithic high-rise, the building immediately had structural problems, high rates of crime, inadequate maintenance, and poor management. Pruitt-Igoe received media attention and was the subject of sociological research, but finding a solution to the building's many problems was virtually impossible, and it was demolished in the 1970s. Although little high-rise social housing has been built in Canada, St. James Town, in Toronto, is a similar project. It was developed in the 1960s by the private sector and consists of 18 high-rise apartment buildings with 7000 units for 12 000 people. It is one of the most densely populated residential areas in Canada (cited in Hulchanski 1990:16). While it is still standing, this now somewhat shabby development never became the model neighbourhood its proponents claimed it would become.

But another large development *has* become a neighbourhood. The St. Lawrence neighbourhood in downtown Toronto is a good example of a large development that is socially mixed. This neighbourhood was conceived in the mid-1970s, with first occupancy in mid-1979. Although it is a large development of 3500 units, it has become a neighbourhood because people

who wanted to live there were involved in the planning. St. Lawrence was begun, planned, and implemented by the municipal government (the former City of Toronto) in co-operation with other levels of government, the private sector, and community organizations (such as housing co-operatives and non-profit societies; Hulchanski 1990:4). The neighbourhood is

- socially mixed, including people of different ages, income, and household size (Hulchanski 1990:13);

- tenure mixed, including 39 percent condominium apartments, 30 percent non-profit co-operatives and non-profit rentals, 27 percent municipal non-profit rental, and 4 percent ownership of townhouses (Hulchanski 1990:15); and

- 57 percent non-market, or social, housing (Hulchanski 1990:3). "St. Lawrence demonstrates that public planning of large development projects in an open and democratic fashion can be successful and that desirable high density socially mixed neighbourhoods can be developed by a municipality" (Hulchanski 1990:17).

Plans are underway to tear down Toronto's Regent Park, the first subsidized housing project in Canada. With increased housing (and no reduction in subsidized housing), multiple family structures, roads, and commercial development, it is expected to create another St. Lawrence neighbourhood (see Box 13.3 on page 359).

Since the 1970s, some middle- and upper-middle-class families and developers have re-entered central city areas and gentrified properties. **Gentrification is the process by which people renovate or restore properties in central cities.** Some people view gentrification as the way to revitalize the central city. Others think that it further depletes the stock of affordable housing for the poor and pushes low-income people out of an area where they had previously lived (Flanagan 1995; Palen and London 1984; and see below, "The Spatial Separation of the Poor and Visible Minorities").

Homelessness

The worst outcome of the housing shortage has been a significant increase in the number of homeless people in Canada. Accurate data about the actual number of homeless people in Canada is unavailable. It is extremely difficult to count the number of homeless people because most avoid interviews with census-takers and social scientists. The 2001 census did try to identify one group of homeless people by counting those in shelters for persons lacking a fixed address. On May 14, 2001, 14 145 people were counted in such shelters (Statistics Canada 2002p). This count does not identify all the homeless people, since many others may have been in other accommodations or on the street. A more comprehensive study of the number of homeless people in a major metropolitan area, Toronto, is found in *The Report of the Mayor's Homelessness Action Task Force* (sometimes called the Golden Report, after its head, Anne Golden). The researchers found that:

- The fastest-growing groups of homeless people using hostels are youth under 18 and families with children. Families were 46 percent of the people using Toronto hostels in 1996.

- Nearly 26 000 different people used hostels in that year. There were about 3200 on any given night in 1996, and the number was much higher in the winter. (Now an estimated 6000 people seek emergency shelter each night in Toronto.)

- There were 5300 children living in hostels in 1996.

- Between 30 percent and 35 percent of homeless people are living with mental illness. The estimates are higher for some groups. For example, 75 percent of homeless single women have mental illness.

- 4400 people (17 percent of hostel users in 1996) stayed in the hostel system for a year or more. This group of "chronic hostel users" takes up about 46 percent of the beds and services.

- 170 000 different people used shelters between 1988 and 1996.
- At least 47 percent of hostel users come from outside Toronto. (Golden et al. 1999:4)

According to social scientists, studies that focus exclusively on personal problems of the homeless, such as mental illness or substance abuse, may result in *specialism*—the assumption that individual characteristics of poor people cause their homeless condition and that, therefore, the only way to alleviate homelessness is to cure the individual's personal problems (Wagner 1993). This approach downplays the

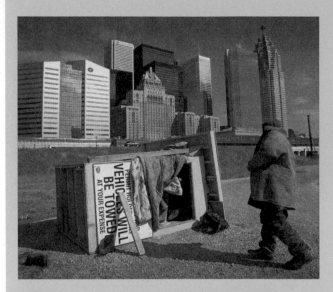

Because of the lack of affordable housing in major Canadian cities, homeless people rely on homeless shelters for food and protection at night, or resort to constructing their own form of shelter in unused city lots or buildings. In 2002, this tent city erected by a number of homeless people in Toronto was ordered destroyed and its residents evicted without notice.

significance of structural factors such as the unavailability of low-income housing and mental-health care, which are the most important determinants of homelessness.

Realizing the importance of structural change, Golden and her colleagues made many recommendations to deal with the problem of homelessness, including:

- a shelter allowance for the working poor;
- supportive housing for people with mental illness and/or addictions;
- new affordable housing;
- a plan to preserve existing housing;
- incentives for prevention including preparing people to leave hostels and providing follow-up support after leaving;
- service planning for key subgroups, such as youth and families; and
- a homeless services information system with a database of services and a 24-hour information telephone line (Golden et al. 1999:8–10).

In late 1999, the *Let's Build* program was launched in Toronto to help create some affordable housing. In 2002, 304 housing units in six projects are underway, and it is anticipated that with the help of other programs, 700 to 1000 units a year could be generated (Guslits 2002:24).

Spatial Separation of the Poor and Visible Minorities

Although it is generally acknowledged that Canada does not have the segregation of poor—especially racialized poor—and non-poor found in the U.S., the increasing immigration of racialized/ethnic minorities to our cities leaves open the possibility that the U.S. segregation problems could occur here. Residential segregation in the U.S., according to sociologists Douglas S. Massey and Nancy Denton, is associated with many other problems.

The 2001 census shows that the proportion of visible minorities has grown in Canadian cities. Table 13.2 shows the growth in the proportion of visible minorities in the Census Metropolitan Areas (CMAs) in Canada from 1991 to 2001. At the top of the list, visible minorities constitute 36.9 percent and 36.8 percent of the populations of Vancouver and Toronto respectively. And in just about every other major CMA, the proportion of visible minorities has grown substantially. However, the proportion of visible minorities in a CMA does not indicate the extent of segregation in that area. The 2001 census release does provide maps of the major CMAs showing the concentration of visible minorities by individual census tracts. It is not possible to include maps for every major city in Canada in this textbook, but you can see the concentration of visible minorities in the CMAs by going to the website **http://geodepot.statcan.ca/Diss/Maps/ThematicMaps/Ethnocultural_e.cfm**. According to these maps, the concentration of visible minorities seems greater in Montreal than in Toronto or Vancouver, where they are more evenly distributed. This segregation may help account for the findings of a report that shows that, in Montreal, Blacks had a higher unemployment rate than in the rest of Canada (26.5 vs. 19.3 percent) and a much higher

TABLE 13.2   Proportion of Visible Minorities, Census Metropolitan Areas, 2001, 1996, and 1991

	2001	1996	1991
	%	%	%
Canada	**13.4**	**11.2**	**9.4**
Vancouver	36.9	31.1	24.0
Toronto	36.8	31.6	25.8
Abbotsford	17.8	12.9	10.6
Calgary	17.5	15.6	13.7
Edmonton	14.6	13.5	12.7
Ottawa-Hull[1]	14.1	11.7	10.2
Ontario part	17.3	14.5	12.3
Quebec part	4.3	3.1	3.7
Montreal	13.6	12.2	11.0
Windsor	12.9	9.8	8.9
Winnipeg	12.5	11.1	10.5
Kitchener	10.7	8.9	8.4
Hamilton	9.8	7.9	7.1
London	9.0	7.4	6.6
Victoria	8.9	7.6	7.1
Halifax	7.0	6.6	6.2
Oshawa	7.0	6.0	5.9
Saskatoon	5.6	5.2	4.7
Regina	5.2	5.4	5.1
Kingston	4.7	4.5	4.0
St. Catharines–Niagara	4.5	3.7	3.3
Saint John	2.6	2.1	2.3
Sherbrooke	2.6	2.1	2.3
Thunder Bay	2.2	2.1	2.1
Greater Sudbury	2.0	1.7	2.0
Quebec	1.6	1.5	1.4
St. John's	1.4	1.4	1.4
Trois-Rivières	0.9	0.9	0.8
Chicoutimi-Jonquière[2]	0.6	0.4	0.5

[1]Now known as Ottawa-Gatineau

[2]Now known as Saguenay

Source: Adapted from Statistics Canada, 2003, Canada's Ethnocultural Portrait: The Changing Mosaic, p. 59, Catalogue no. 96F0030.

rate than non-Blacks (26.5 vs. 9.9 percent; Solyom 2001:A14).

To determine the extent of spatial separation of visible minorities in Canada, Hou and Picot studied the extent to which minority group members are exposed only to one another (isolation index) in their neighbourhoods (census tracts in Toronto, Montreal, and Vancouver) from the 1981 to 2001 censuses. In tracing the composition of the population over the 20 years, they discovered that the mass immigration of visible minorities has created more visible minority neighbourhoods. The number of visible minority neighbourhoods increased in these cities from 6 in 1981 to 254 in 2001. The majority of these neighbourhoods were Chinese (60 percent), followed by South Asian (about 33 percent; Hou and Picot 2004:11). Few (13) Black neighbourhoods exist, perhaps because Blacks have been in Canada for many generations and they come from several places. Toronto and Vancouver have many more visible minority neighbourhoods (135 and 111 respectively) than Montreal (8; Hou and Picot 2004:11). As the above table shows, far fewer visible minority immigrants go to Montreal than the other two cities. Whether the increase in visible minority neighbourhoods is a good or bad thing is debatable. On the plus side, these neighbourhoods can provide a wide variety of support and services for the immigrant and help promote ethnic identity. On the negative side, immigrants may become socially isolated and be slow to learn the host area language and take advantage of available educational and occupational opportunities. These neighbourhoods also have the tendency to have high unemployment and low income rates. This is probably because a third of the population are recent immigrants, and recent immigrants are doing less well than earlier immigrants upon arrival (see Kazemipur and Halli 2001).

Figures from the 1996 census showed that the poor population of metropolitan areas was growing at a much greater rate than the population as a whole. Whereas the metropolitan population grew by 6.9 percent, the poor population in the same areas grew by 33.8 percent (Lee 2000). Moreover, the poor population tended to be in the centre of the cities. For example, the percentage of poor in the centre of Toronto was 27.5 (Lee 2000:91). In 2000, the Canadian Council for Social Development (CCSD) and the United Way of Greater Toronto (UWGT) wrote a report to identify the current problems. Among their key findings were:

■ Income gaps also grew in the 1990s between the poor and non-poor neighbourhoods in the city. The median income in Toronto's 12 poorest neighbourhoods fell from $43 600 in 1990 to $36 800 in 1999 (in 1999 constant dollars), or a loss of $6800 in real income in the decade.

■ The rate of poverty for all persons in Toronto rose from 22.6 percent in 1995 to 23.3 percent in 1999—a 0.7 percent increase. By comparison, poverty grew by 1.9 percent within the 12 neighbourhoods with the highest rates of poverty.

■ Although there are some very distressed neighbourhoods in Toronto and pockets of poverty where more than one-third of the population is poor, poverty is still quite widely dispersed across the city. In both 1995 and 1999, the 12 lowest-income neighbourhoods contained about 13 percent of the city's population, but over 18 percent of the population living in poverty. These bottom 12 neighbourhoods had poverty rates of 29 percent or higher in 1999, but another 72 neighbourhoods had poverty rates between 12 percent and 29 percent (CCSD and UNGT 2000).

PROBLEMS IN GLOBAL CITIES

Although people have lived in cities for thousands of years, the time is rapidly approaching when more people worldwide will live in or near a city than live in a rural area. In 1900, only 1 person out of 10 lived in a city; by 2007, 1 person out of 2 will live in a city (Chamie, 2005). In 1950, New York was the only mega-city with 10 million or more inhabitants. Now there are 19 mega-cities (Chamie, 2005). By 2015, no European or U.S. city will be among the 10 most populous in the world (see Table 13.3).

Rapid global population growth is producing a wide variety of urban problems, including overcrowding, environmental pollution, and the disappearance of farmland. In fact, many cities in middle- and low-income nations are quickly reaching the point at which food, housing, and basic public services are available to only a limited segment of the population (Crossette 1996c). With urban populations growing at a rate of 170 000 people a day in 1996, cities such as Cairo, Lagos, Dhaka, Beijing, and São Paulo

TABLE 13.3   Populations of the World's 10 Largest Cities

(In Millions, Estimated)

1996		2015	
Tokyo, Japan	26.8	Tokyo, Japan	28.7
São Paulo, Brazil	16.4	Mumbai, India	27.4
New York City, U.S.A.	16.3	Lagos, Nigeria	24.4
Mexico City, Mexico	15.6	Shanghai, China	23.4
Bombay, India	15.1	Jakarta, Indonesia	21.2
Shanghai, China	15.1	São Paulo, Brazil	20.8
Los Angeles, U.S.A.	12.4	Karachi, Pakistan	20.6
Beijing, China	12.4	Beijing, China	19.4
Calcutta, India	11.7	Dhaka, Bangladesh	19.0
Seoul, South Korea	11.6	Mexico City, Mexico	18.8

Source: "The Megacity Summit," 1996, New York Times, April 8, A14.

are likely to soon have acute water shortages; Mexico City is already experiencing a chronic water shortage ("The Megacity Summit" 1996).

Natural increases in population (higher birth rates than death rates) account for two-thirds of new urban growth, and rural-to-urban migration accounts for the rest. Some people move from rural areas to urban areas because they have been displaced from their land. Others move because they are looking for a better life. No matter what the reason, migration has caused rapid growth in cities in sub-Saharan Africa, India, Algeria, and Egypt. At the same time that the population is growing rapidly, the amount of farmland available for growing crops to feed people is decreasing. In Egypt, for example, land that was previously used for growing crops is now used for petroleum refineries, food-processing plants, and other factories (Kaplan 1996). Some analysts believe that the United Nations should encourage governments to concentrate on rural development; otherwise, acute food shortages brought about by unchecked rural-to-urban migration may lead to riots (Kaplan 1996).

As global urbanization has increased over the past three decades, differences in urban areas based on economic development at the national level have become apparent. According to sociologist Immanuel Wallerstein (1984), nations occupy one of three positions in the global economy: core, semi-peripheral, and peripheral. *Core nations* **are dominant capitalist centres characterized by high levels of industrialization and urbanization.**

The United States, Japan, and Germany, among others, are core nations. Some cities in core nations are referred to as *global cities*—interconnected urban areas that are centres of political, economic, and cultural activity. New York, Tokyo, and London are generally considered the largest global cities. They are also considered postindustrial cities because their economic base has shifted largely from heavy manufacturing to information technologies and services such as accounting, marketing, finance, mergers and acquisitions, telecommunications, and other highly specialized fields (Friedmann 1995). Global cities are the sites of new and innovative product development and marketing, and they often are the "command posts" for the world economy (Sassen 1995). But economic prosperity is not shared equally by all people in the core nation global cities. Growing numbers of poor people work in low-wage service sector jobs or in assembly production, in which they are paid by the item (piecework) for what they produce, without employment benefits or job security. Sometimes the living conditions of these workers more closely resemble the living conditions of workers in semiperipheral nations than those of middle-class workers in their own country.

Most African countries and many countries in South America and the Caribbean are *peripheral nations*—**nations that depend on core nations for capital, have little or no industrialization (other than what may be brought in by core nations), and have uneven patterns of urbanization.** According to

Wallerstein (1984), the wealthy in peripheral nations support the exploitation of poor workers by core nation capitalists in return for maintaining their own wealth and position. Poverty is thus perpetuated, and the problems worsen because of the unprecedented population growth in these countries.

Between the core and the peripheral nations are the *semiperipheral nations,* **which are more developed than peripheral nations but less developed than core nations.** Only a few global cities are located in semiperipheral nations: São Paulo, Brazil; the centre of the Brazilian economy, Bangalore, India, the centre of the Indian high-tech industry; Beijing, China, the manufacturing capital of the world; and the city-state of Singapore, the economic centre for a multicountry region in Southeast Asia. Like peripheral nations, semiperipheral nations—such as China, India, Iran, and Mexico—are confronted with unprecedented population growth. In addition, a steady flow of rural migrants to large cities is creating enormous urban problems. Semiperipheral nations exploit peripheral nations, just as the core nations exploit both the semiperipheral and the peripheral nations.

According to Wallerstein, it is very difficult—if not impossible—for peripheral and semiperipheral nations to ever occupy anything but their marginal positions in the class-like structure of the world economy because of their exploitation by the core nations (Wallerstein 1984). Capital investment by core nations results in uneven economic growth, and in the process, the disparity between the rich and the poor in the major cities increases. Such economic disparity and urban growth is obvious at the U.S.–Mexican border, where transnational corporations have built *maquiladora plants,* factories where goods are assembled by low-wage workers—on the Mexican side—to keep production costs down. The demand for workers in these plants has caused thousands of people to move from the rural areas of Mexico to urban areas along the border in hope of earning higher wages. The influx has pushed already overcrowded cities far beyond their capacity. Because their wages are low and affordable housing is nonexistent, many people live in central city slums or at the edge of cities in *shantytowns,* where houses are made from discarded materials. There have been some gains in wages and working conditions in recent years, but the workers now must compete with the still cheaper wages in China. (Rosenberg 2006).

Not all analysts agree with Wallerstein's (1984) hierarchy. However, most scholars acknowledge that nations throughout the world are influenced by a relatively small number of cities (e.g., the financial giants, New York and London) as well as by transnational corporations that have brought about a shift from an international to a more global economy (see Knox and Taylor 1995; Wilson 1997). In middle- and low-income nations, all social problems are "incubated and magnified in cities" (Crossette 1996c:A3).

PERSPECTIVES ON URBAN PROBLEMS

Throughout the 20th century, sociologists analyzed urban problems to determine the causes and consequences of rapid industrialization and urbanization for people's daily lives and the structure of society. The conclusions they reach about the underlying problems and possible solutions depend on the framework they apply.

Overcrowded living conditions are a way of life for people residing in this area of Mumbai. How will rapid population growth in the future affect urban areas in global cities?

The Functionalist Perspective

In examining urban problems, most functionalists focus on three processes that have contributed to social disorganization and the disruption of social institutions. First, mass migration from rural areas to urban areas during the industrializing of Canada contributed to social disorganization by weakening personal ties in family, religion, education, and other institutions. Second, large-scale immigration in the late 19th and early 20th centuries was more than most cities could absorb, and many individuals were never fully assimilated into the cultural mainstream. With larger numbers of strangers living close together in central cities, symptoms of social disorganization, such as high rates of crime, mental illness, and suicide, grew more pronounced. According to Durkheim (1893/1933), urban life changes people's relationships. Rural areas are characterized by *mechanical solidarity*—**social bonds based on shared religious beliefs and a simple division of labour**—but these bonds are changed with urbanization. Urban areas are characterized by *organic solidarity*—**social bonds based on interdependence and an elaborate division of labour (specialization).** Although Durkheim was optimistic that urbanization could be positive, he also thought that some things were lost in the process. Third, mass suburbanization created additional social disorganization, and many central cities in the U.S., though less so in Canada, have been unable to reach an equilibrium since the mass exodus to the suburbs following World War II. According to urban ecologist Amos Hawley (1950, 1981), new technologies, such as commuter railways and automobiles, have led to the decentralization of city life and the movement of industry from the central city to the suburbs, with disastrous results for some people. Although urbanization, mass immigration, and suburbanization have had functional consequences—including citizenship, job opportunities, and home ownership—for many people, they have also created problems, particularly for people who are left behind in rapidly declining parts of central cities and people who experience discrimination.

Besides emphasizing processes, functionalists also emphasize systems. Sociologist Talcott Parsons (1966:28) identified four systems that interact with each other in urban areas: the cultural system, social system, personality system, and behavioural organism. William Michelson (1976:24) has drawn attention to a fifth system, the environmental system, in particular the human-made physical, or built, environment, most fully illustrated by the urban environment. He suggested that the effects of the phenomena in the built environment on the other systems, and vice versa, should be studied. Michelson also developed the concept of *congruence* to indicate that some states of variables in one system may coexist with some states of variables in another system better than with others. Mismatches of states of variables constitute incongruence. An example of incongruence is the building of economically efficient high-rise subsidized housing for families with small children, like the Pruitt-Igoe project in St. Louis mentioned above; mothers living in such projects are not able to follow their children to other floors and ground level to supervise or protect them (Michelson 1976:26). High-rise public housing has also had problems with property damage and bullying because of lack of supervision.

The Conflict Perspective

Conflict analysts do not believe that cities grow or decline by chance. Members of the capitalist class and political elites make far-reaching decisions about land use and urban development that benefit some people at the expense of others (Castells 1977; Feagin and Parker 1990). According to conflict theorists, the upper classes have successfully maintained class-based and sometimes racialized segregation (in the United States) through political control and legal strategies such as municipal incorporation, defensive annexation, restrictive covenants, and zoning regulations (Feagin and Parker 1990; Higley 1995). But where do these practices leave everyone else? Marx suggested that cities are the arenas in which the intertwined processes of class conflict and capital accumulation take place; class consciousness and worker revolt are more likely to develop when workers are concentrated in urban areas (Flanagan 1995).

Contemporary conflict theorists Joe R. Feagin and Robert Parker (1990) speak of a *political economy model*, believing that both economic and political factors affect patterns of urban growth and decline. Urban growth, they say, is influenced by capital investment decisions, power and resource inequality, class and class conflict, and government subsidy programs. Members of the capitalist class choose corporate locations, decide on sites for shopping centres and factories, and spread the population that can afford to purchase homes into sprawling suburbs located exactly where the capitalists think they should be located (Feagin and Parker 1990). In this view, a few hundred financial institutions and developers finance and construct most major and many smaller urban development projects, including skyscrapers, shopping malls, and suburban housing projects. These decision makers can make housing more affordable or totally unaffordable for many people. Ultimately, their motivation rests not in benefiting the community, but rather in making a profit, and the cities they produce reflect this mindset (Feagin and Parker 1990).

The concept of *uneven development*—the tendency of some neighbourhoods, cities, or regions to grow and prosper while others stagnate and decline—is a by-product of the political economy model of urban development (Perry and Watkins 1977). Conflict theorists argue that uneven development reflects inequalities of wealth and power in society. Uneven development not only affects areas in decline but also produces external costs that are paid by the entire community. Among these costs are increased pollution, traffic congestion, and rising rates of crime and violence. According to sociologist Mark Gottdiener (1985:214), these costs are "intrinsic to the very core of capitalism, and those who profit the most from development are not called upon to remedy its side effects." One advantage of the political economy framework is that it can be used to study cities in middle- and low-income nations as well as high-income nations (see Jaffee 1990; Knox and Taylor 1995; Wilson 1997).

Uneven development does not occur in the same way in Canadian cities as it does in U.S. cities. Canadian city governments are more actively involved in land-use management and are committed more strongly than U.S. city governments to public services, including transit, parks, and libraries. Canadian cities also are characterized by more equal distribution of public services than the more politically fragmented U.S. cities (Ley and Bourne 1993). Thus, the land and property values in the Canadian central city remain highly competitive despite a substantial rate of suburban development.

This difference in uneven development does not mean that corporate capitalism does not have an effect on major cities in Canada. For example, Gertler (2001:123) notes that Toronto's share of the top 500 Canadian firms declined from 40 percent to 35 percent from 1989 to 1999 (pre– and post–North American Free Trade Agreement) due primarily to a decline in foreign-based Canadian subsidiaries, from 105 to 85. He suggests that a worldwide concentration of corporate control is likely occurring. However, since then, Toronto's share of headquarters of Canadian firms has increased slightly, from 89 to 91. Other centres, like Calgary, Vancouver, and Ottawa, have seen substantial growth in headquarters placement from both Canadian and foreign firms (Gertler 2001:123). This movement could have harmful effects for workers and their families and merchants in the older downtowns of Toronto and Montreal unless other projects, like in-fill housing (for example, the King West Village mentioned earlier) is developed to fill the void of the former headquarters.

The Interactionist Perspective

Interactionists examine urban problems from the standpoint of people's *experience* of urban life and how they subjectively define the reality of city living. How does city life affect the people who live in a city? According to early German sociologist Georg Simmel (1950), urban life is so highly stimulating that people have no choice but to become somewhat insensitive to events and individuals around them. Urban residents generally avoid emotional involvement with one another and try to ignore the events—including, possibly, violence and crime—that take place nearby. They are wary of other people, looking at others as strangers; some people act reserved to cloak deeper feelings of distrust or dislike toward others. At the same time, Simmel thought that urban living could be liberating because it gives people opportunities for individualism and autonomy (Flanagan 1995).

On the basis of Simmel's observations of social relations in the city, early University of Chicago sociologist Louis Wirth (1938) suggested that urbanism is a "way of life" that increases the incidence of both social and personality disorders in individuals. *Urbanism* refers to the distinctive social and psychological patterns of life that are typically found in the city. According to Wirth, the size, density, and heterogeneity of urban populations result in an elaborate division of labour and in spatial segregation of people by racialization/ethnicity, social class, religion, and/or lifestyle. The division of labour and spatial segregation produce feelings of alienation, powerlessness, and loneliness.

In contrast to Wirth's gloomy analysis of urban life, sociologist Herbert Gans (1962/1982) believed that not everyone experiences the city in the same way. On the basis of research in the West End of Boston in the late 1950s, Gans concluded that many residents develop strong loyalties and a sense of community in central city areas that outsiders often view negatively. According to Gans, in large urban areas, personal behaviour is shaped by the type of neighbourhood a person lives in. For example, *cosmopolites*—students, artists, writers, musicians, entertainers, and professionals—view the city as a place where they can be close to cultural facilities and people with whom they share common interests. *Unmarried people* and *childless couples* live in the city because they want to be close to work and entertainment. *Ethnic villagers* live in ethnically segregated neighbourhoods because they feel most comfortable within their own group. The *deprived* and the *trapped* live in the city because they believe they have no other alternatives. Gans concluded that the city is a pleasure and a challenge for some urban dwellers and an urban nightmare for others.

According to interactionists, the deprived and the trapped contribute to a social construction of reality that stereotypes city dwellers as poor, down-and-out, and sometimes dangerous, whereas most city dwellers are not this way at all. Because of the U.S. movies and television shows seen by Canadians, and, particularly, because of extensive media coverage of crime or racialized unrest in the largest metropolitan areas of the U.S., which presents a very negative image of cities, an anti-urban bias remains strong among many non-urban dwellers. Even urban dwellers can have negative stereotypes of parts of cities. Box 13.3 shows that a social housing plan for poor people can change over several decades to become an object of media vilification, but that even when new plans are developed to improve the area, strong sentiments about the area still remain.

On the other hand, Richard Florida, a professor of regional development, like Gans, believes that cities can be pleasurable and tolerant, and thus attract the kind of creative people (what he calls the Creative Class) that will hold the key to Canada's economic future. With Canadian collaborator Meric Gertler, he compiled, a Bohemian Index, a measure of talent that looks at Canadian cities' per capita population of artists, poets, novelists, and various entertainers using the 1996 census. Florida and Gertler concluded that Vancouver had 12.85 bohemians per 1000 population and, slightly behind it, Toronto had 12 bohemians per 1000 (or about 50 000 people). In comparison with American cities, the two Canadian cities rank below but close to San Francisco, New York, Los Angeles, Seattle, and Washington D.C. (Florida 2002:T8).

SOCIAL PROBLEMS IN THE MEDIA

BOX 13.3   Different Perceptions about Regent Park

Regent Park in downtown Toronto was Canada's first experiment in social housing. It was developed in the middle 1940s and built from 1948 to 1957. It consisted mostly of low- and high-rise apartments and was designed to be set apart from the city with no commercial buildings or stores and no through streets to limit traffic and make the inner areas recreational. However, this plan resulted in making many areas vulnerable to crime, including drugs, prostitution, and vandalism. In 2001, over 11 000 people lived in the development, in which

- almost 60 percent of the people were born outside the country;
- almost 20 percent of the people were unemployed (over double the national average); and

- people had incomes of about 60 percent of the Toronto average (Rusk and Boffa 2005).

As a result it became a much-vilified development.

However, a $1-billion building plan has begun, after years of consultation with the residents, to intensify the development with streets, stores, and town houses and higher-rise buildings—with no reduction in subsidized units. The doubling of housing units should create more of a mix of incomes, ethnicities, and family structures, like the St. Lawrence area.

Still, some residents find the demolition sad, since so many memories are wrapped up in what people called home. A grade seven student from Lord Dufferin Public School wrote the following realistic, yet ultimately optimistic, poem about Regent Park.

In Regent Park

In Regent Park
where silence is not generous even in the dead of night
and music blares from left and right
a place with one face beautiful, the other disfigured
gangs roam the streets,
but peacekeepers hold them back
one man hates the life he has,
another gives him the happiness he lacks
a woman, blind to the truth are her eyes
another takes away the lies
a homeless, misery rings in his heart
another gives him a new start.

In Regent Park
a playground for people from different places
a party letting you meet different faces
a person from Pakistan, another from Sudan
a person from Nigeria another from Iran
From around the world they come here
to settle and make a home.

In Regent Park
where the summers are brutal
and the winters, unforgiving
the snow builds up making it impossible for living
as others do.
The summer's sun is unmerciful
and the heat, blinding
making it impossible to have enough energy to go finding
where you put your last school essay.

In Regent Park
where there is both good and bad
where there are people happy, others sad,
we live like a family
singing the same melody.
Though through differences we are sometimes separated
causing pain and tears and hatred,
we come together once more
facing, together, what life has in store.

Source: Courtesy of Samar Haouas, Valedictorian 2006, Lord Dufferin Public School.

Finally, cities are also known for problems of loneliness and alienation. Some interactionists propose that people who live in large metropolitan areas develop subcultural ties to help them feel a sense of community and identity. A ***subculture* is a group of people who share a distinctive set of cultural beliefs and behaviours that set them apart from the larger society.** Joining an interest group—from bowling with friends from the office to volunteering in a literacy program—is one way of feeling connected. Ethnic neighbourhoods are an example of subcultures; some are tightly knit, whereas others have little influence on residents' daily lives. Interactionists note that members of subcultures, especially those based on racialization, ethnicity, or religion, sometimes come into conflict with each other. These conflicts can result in verbal exchanges, hate crimes, or other physical violence, or they can cause the individuals to withdraw almost entirely from the larger community and become more intensely involved with the subculture. (See Chapter 12, Box 12.2, to discover how some teachers and students are challenging subcultural stereotypes.)

The Feminist Perspective

In the same way that great social policy issues are urban policy issues, feminist analyses are germane to virtually every aspect of city life. Many of these analyses have been dealt with in other chapters; here are just a couple of examples of feminism's application to urban problems. Some feminist theorists emphasize the occupational opportunities, freedom, convenience, and stimulation for women present in cities but not available in smaller centres or suburbs—Betty Freidan (1963) and, more recently, Margrit Eichler (1995) have been very critical of the lack of stimulation and the oppressiveness of women's lives in low-density suburbs. In cities, women have the chance to participate in a variety of occupations, and they are very well represented in the (usually lowly paid) jobs that constitute the Bohemian Index (e.g., artists and entertainers). Moreover, in cities, women do not have to worry about what the neighbours will think of their behaviour. They can choose to interact with their neighbours, or not. Lastly, women who live in a city instead of a suburb and have the dual roles of worker and mother will usually have a shorter commute to their jobs and more locally available services. Thus, they may feel less stress in fulfilling their responsibilities and have more time for themselves. On the other hand, some feminists have been so concerned about the threats to women at night in cities that they have organized "Take Back the Night" marches in most major cities.

URBAN PROBLEMS IN THE FUTURE

In a best-case scenario, Canada would convert to regional governments to provide water, wastewater (sewage), transportation, schools, parks, hospitals, and other public services. In this scenario, revenues would be shared among central cities, affluent suburbs, and edge cities, since everyone would benefit from the improved quality of life. Cities would get a permanent source of taxation, besides property taxes; and, they would create a tolerant and creative climate. Meanwhile, as we wait and hope for solutions to the problems of urbanization at the macrolevel, we can—as citizens, neighbours, tenants, property owners, workers, employers, and users of public and private services throughout the city—exercise some

degree of control over the quality of life in our own communities. There is increasing impetus to take control because one thing is certain: As the world population continues to grow in this century, urban problems will intensify, and this will affect us all.

ENVIRONMENTAL PROBLEMS

The environment provides us with the means to survive and thrive (see Table 13.4).

Although it is popularly believed that most environmental problems arise from rapid growth in middle- and low-income nations, this is not entirely the case. Many scientists believe that high-income nations present a much greater threat to the earth's ecosystems (Ehrlich and Ehrlich 1991). An *ecosystem* is "all the populations of plants and animal species that live and interact in a given area at a particular time, as well as the chemical and physical factors that make up the nonliving environment" (Cable and Cable 1995:124). Thus, an ocean is an ecosystem; a tropical rainforest is an ecosystem; and, on a much

TABLE 13.4   <u>What the Natural World Does for Us (If We Don't Mess It Up Too Much)</u>

Food production	Produces fish, game, and crops—even without our help
Raw materials	Produces (without our help) the raw materials from which humans create things.
Genetic resources	On its own, creates the ability for crops, vegetation, and animals to survive.
Pollination	Without our help, plants and animals naturally reproduce
Biological control	Somehow, most species of plants and animals survive for millions of years without our help.
Climate regulation	Unless we mess it up, nature has created an ozone layer that protects all plants and animal life from the sun's ultraviolet radiation.
Water regulation	If we don't mess with it, the world's water supply keeps reproducing and distributing itself.
Gas regulation	If we don't mess it up too badly, nature keeps carbon dioxide and oxygen in balance—a balance necessary for life.
Recreation	Just think of the wonderful sights and recreation that nature has created.

Source: From William K. Stevens, 1997, "How Much Is Nature Worth? For you, $33 Trillion," New York Times, *May 20, B7, B9.*

smaller scale, a house on a lot is an ecosystem. When all of the earth's ecosystems are put together, they make up the *biosphere*.

Ecosystems do not have an infinite ability to support either population growth or environmental depletion or destruction. In fact, some scientists believe that many of the world's ecosystems have already exceeded their *carrying capacity*—the maximum population that an ecosystem can support without eventually being degraded or destroyed (Cable and Cable 1995). According to Ehrlich and Ehrlich (1991), a baby born in a country like the U.S., and to a lesser extent Canada, will have two times the destructive impact on the earth's ecosystems and services as a baby born in Sweden; 100 times the impact of a baby born in Bangladesh or Kenya; and over 200 times the impact of a baby born in Chad, Rwanda, Haiti, or Nepal. How did the Ehrlichs reach such a conclusion? They developed a formula for determining the impact that human beings have on their environment: $I = P \times A \times T$, or Impact = Population × Affluence × Technology. Thus the size of the population, its level of affluence, and the technology available in the society are major contributing factors to ***environmental degradation*—disruptions to the environment that have negative consequences for ecosystems** (Cable and Cable 1995). Environmental degradation involves both removing natural resources from the environment and adding to environmental problems through pollution.

In Canada, environmental degradation increases as people try to maintain the high levels of wealth and material comfort to which they have become accustomed. They consume the earth's resources and pollute its environment with automobiles, airplanes, speedboats, computers, television sets and VCRs, year-round air conditioning and heating, and other amenities that are far beyond the grasp of most of the world's people. Although these products are made possible by high levels of industrial production and economic growth, economic growth often depletes and destroys the environment.

Economic Growth and Environmental Degradation

During most of the 20th century, economic growth in Canada and the world was based on increased output in the manufacturing sector (see Table 13.1 for the increase in industrial output in the 20th century). The environment is affected at all phases of the manufacturing process, from mining and transportation to manufacturing and waste disposal. Industrial production involves extracting raw materials—natural resources—from the environment, usually through mining. Mining depletes mineral resources and fossil fuel reserves—coal, oil, and natural gas. Mining also disturbs ecosystems; this is particularly true of surface mining, which strips bare the land, destroying natural vegetation and wildlife habitats. Other problems typically follow, including erosion of the land by wind and water and runoff of acids, silt, and toxic substances into nearby surface water and groundwater; this leads to the pollution of rivers and streams with toxic compounds that kill fish and other aquatic life (Cable and Cable, 1995).

Table 13.1 provides some indication of the enormous effects humanity's activity has had on our planet during the last 100 years. This chart ignores huge expansions that took place after 1900, like automobiles—in Canada, from zero to 14 million by the end of the century—and huge declines of natural resources of special interest to Canadians, such as the 99 percent decrease in the cod fishery, which has not returned and may never return to 1980s levels despite more than a 10-year moratorium on fishing.

The environmental impact of mining doesn't stop when the raw materials have been mined. Now the raw materials must be transported to a plant or factory, where workers will transform them into manufactured products. Transporting requires the use of energy—particularly the burning of fossil fuels—which contributes to air pollution because motor vehicles produce carbon monoxide, nitrogen oxides, and photochemical pollutants. Each of these pollutants is associated with various illnesses, including heart and respiratory disease and cancer. The manufacturing process further depletes the supply of fossil fuels and contributes to air pollution. (See Table 13.1 for the amount of various kinds of pollution produced in the 20th century.) People who work in or live near facilities that pollute the environment are often harmed by the solid or toxic wastes resulting from the manufacturing process.

Many analysts believe that we cannot continue this pattern of environmental degradation. They believe future economic development—in Canada and globally—will require drastic changes in the structure of industry, especially in the energy, transportation, chemical, and agricultural sectors of the economy. If we don't make changes, environmental degradation—of our air, water, soil, and forests—constitutes a major threat to the well-being of all human beings and ecosystems on the earth.

Air Pollution and Smog

Nature performs many *ecosystem services*—valuable, practical functions that help to preserve ecosystems. For example, if the atmosphere is not overburdened, it can maintain a proper balance between carbon dioxide and oxygen, as well as provide ozone for protection against ultraviolet radiation (see Table 13.4). However, air pollution interferes with many ecosystem services. The carbon dioxide that pollutes the air we breathe keeps the sun's heat from radiating back into space, thereby causing the earth to heat up (the greenhouse effect, discussed in the next section).

The drastic increase in air pollution during the 20th century has placed an undue burden on the atmosphere's ecosystem services (Stevens 1997). Beginning with the Industrial Revolution in the late 19th and early 20th centuries, more and more pollutants have been emitted into the atmosphere by households, industries, and automobile traffic. Though these three sources have become more fuel-efficient, constantly increasing amounts of carbon dioxide, carbon monoxide, nitrogen oxide, and sulphur oxide, as well as such heavy metals as lead, zinc, and copper still pollute our air (Hauchler and Kennedy 1994). In 1998, 85 percent of the air pollution in urban areas could attributed to the internal combustion engine used in automobiles and other vehicles, like sports utility vehicles (SUVs; U.S. Bureau of the Census 1998).

Air pollution affects all life and ecosystems on the planet. Air pollution in the form of acid rain destroys forests, streams and lakes, and other ecosystems. *Acid rain is rainfall containing large concentrations of sulphuric and nitric acids (primarily from the burning of fuel and car and truck exhausts).* Canadian efforts to reduce acid rain from the United States have been blocked by the automobile industry; companies that mine, haul, and sell high-sulphur coal; and coal miners. Fortunately, new industries are less dependent on burning coal than are older factories in the industrial northeast and midwest states (Petersen 1994).

The word *smog* is a combination of the words "smoke" and "fog." Smog is the most visible form of air pollution. According to the North American Commission for Environmental Cooperation (CEC; 2001), Ontario is the most polluted area in Canada and the fifth most polluted area in North America, after Ohio, Texas, Michigan, and Indiana. Since the Atlantic provinces, followed by British Columbia and Alberta, are among the cleanest of 63 North American areas studied, and Quebec is 24th, this discussion will concentrate on Ontario. Ontario has half of the top 10 polluters in Canada, such as Ontario Power Generation's Nanticoke Generating Station and the Inco Ltd. Copper Cliff Smelter Complex (North American CEC 2001).

To monitor air pollution in Ontario, the Air Quality Index (AQI) was devised to measure ground level ozone, nitrogen dioxide, carbon monoxide, sulphur dioxide, sulphur compounds, and fine suspended particles. An AQI of 50+ may cause eye irritation, breathing difficulties, and even lung damage to those physically active. Since the inception of the AQI in 1993, the number of smog alerts has been growing. In 2001 in southern Ontario, 33 smog alerts were made, and in 2005, up to early October, 15 smog alerts totalling 53 days were made (obtained from the Ontario Ministry of Environment on October 12, 2005). And smog is not limited to southern Ontario, though across the country, provincial data are not comparable. While BC is one of the cleanest provinces, smog can be so bad in the summer in Vancouver that it can eliminate Mt. Baker from view when the polluted air is trapped against the mountains.

Showing relationships between long-term exposure to air pollution and mortality has been difficult because of a wide variety of confounding variables and the problems of measuring air pollution consistently. A Toronto Public Health publication by research consultant Ronald Macfarlane and his colleagues (2000:5) states that air pollution in Toronto is linked to about 1000 early deaths, and 5500 hospital visits are linked to heart and lung diseases every year, based on 1995 data. But this is only one centre. A study that followed 1.2 million adults in more than 150 cities in the United States since 1982 confirmed the health hazards of air pollutants. The results of this study, by economist C. Arden Pope III and colleagues (2002), among whom were Canadian colleagues, showed fine particulate and sulphur oxide were associated with all-cause lung cancer and cardiopulmonary mortality. Furthermore, they showed that elevations in the amount of pollutants were associated with definite percentage increases in mortality. The Public Health Department of the City of Toronto conducted a retrospective study for the period 1954–2000 to determine the relative influence of hot and cold weather and air pollution on mortality. The analysis showed an annual excess of 822 deaths due to air pollution for that period of time. If current global warming trends continue, it is projected that the annual mortality will rise to 1070 per year in 2080 (McKeown 2005:iii). For Ontario, it is estimated that air pollution costs the province $9.6 billion in health and environmental damage and is associated with 4881 premature deaths per year, and more than half of the costs is due to transboundary pollution from over 20 states (Campbell 2005:A7).

In the past, air pollution in middle- and low-income nations was attributed primarily to the fight for survival and economic development, whereas most air pollution in high-income nations was attributed to relatively luxurious lifestyles. However, distinctions between air pollution in high-income and middle- and low-income nations are growing weaker, even though Western industrial nations

account for about 68 percent of the carbon monoxide in the atmosphere (World Resources Institute 1992). Automobile ownership, once considered a luxury, is rising rapidly in urban centres in middle-income nations such as Mexico, Brazil, Taiwan, Indonesia, and China (Bradsher 1997). In 1997, for example, São Paulo, Brazil, had approximately 4.5 million cars on its streets (Bradsher 1997). That is about one-third of all the cars, almost 14 million, in Canada (Kremarik 2000:18). Mexico City, known as the smog capital of the world, has only 37 days a year when the air quality measures as "satisfactory" (S. L. Walker 1994). Affluent Mexican residents buy bottled oxygen at the drug store; the less affluent buy quick shots of oxygen at street-corner kiosks (Cleeland 1991). Cities such as Mumbai, Shanghai, and Jakarta have also seen a significant increase in the number of automobiles, bringing a corresponding rise in air pollution and traffic problems (Bradsher 1997). In the summer of 2002, southern and lower eastern Asia was suffering from a "brown cloud," a three-kilometre-thick haze, from combustion of wood and fossil fuels.

But there are some hopeful signs that we are curbing fossil fuel pollution. In Canada, antipollution laws have brought about changes in how automobiles are made and the fuels they consume. Cars are now equipped with catalytic converters and other antipollution devices, and leaded gasoline (a major offender) has been phased out. However, while some middle-income nations are requiring antipollution devices on new vehicles, many leaded-gas-burning cars—often used cars from Canada and the United States—are still a significant source of air pollution. In October 2006, the federal government introduced its *Clean Air Act* to fight air pollution (see Box 13.4). Given that its mandatory standards come in the future, it is difficult to know how much of an impact the Act will have.

The Greenhouse Effect

Emissions from traffic and industry not only add to general air pollution but also contribute to the enhanced *greenhouse effect*—**an environmental condition caused by excessive quantities of carbon dioxide, methane, and nitrous oxide in the atmosphere.** When carbon dioxide molecules build up in the earth's atmosphere, they act like the glass roof of

Air pollution is a pressing problem in many nations, but nowhere more so than in Mexico City, where daylight hours often look like they do in this photo. How is air pollution related to people's health and life expectancy?

MAP 13.3   Climate Change Across the Country

British Columbia - Of greatest concern are "debris flows" — watery slurries of mud, gravel, and boulders that travel at high speeds down steep mountain stream courses during heavy rains. Warmer winters may increase insect pests while wetter springs may delay planting.

Western Arctic - Thawing of permafrost, or permanently frozen ground, could impact buildings and roads constructed for those solid conditions. Meanwhile, seasonal forest fire danger levels are predicted to increase in the Yukon and Northwest Territories.
Nunavut - Summer melting of glaciers may lead to wide-scale flooding. The Greenland Ice Sheet contains enough ice to raise the global sea level by six to seven metres if it melts.

Climate Change ACROSS the COUNTRY...

The North

West Coast

Atlantic - Highly sensitive to the effects of sea-level rise, this portion of Canada will experience such effects as increased erosion, rapid migration of beaches, and flooding of coastal freshwater marshes.

Prairies - Hotter and longer summers result in increased evaporation, and less surface water is available for use. Forty percent of the rural population of Saskatchewan relies on groundwater.

Prairies

Quebec

Atlantic

Ontario

Quebec - The freshwater portion of the St. Lawrence River may see a deterioration in water quality, loss of wetland habitats and reduction in biodiversity. Droughts would mean less water available for consumption, agriculture, and recreation and more conflicts over use.

Ontario - A warmer climate and longer frost-free seasons may permit the spread of new diseases from warmer climates, such as Lyme disease, malaria, and West Nile virus.

Visit www.climatechange.gc.ca for more info.

Source: Environment Canada, 2006. Reproduced with the permission of the Minister of Public Works and Government Services.

a greenhouse, allowing sunlight to reach the earth's surface but preventing the escape of infrared radiation back into space. The radiation that cannot escape is reradiated as heat, causing the earth's surface temperature to rise (Weiner 1990). Scientists believe that the earth will have a temperature increase of from 1.5 to as much as 5 degrees over the next hundred years. In fact, if current rates of emission into the atmosphere remain unchanged, temperature increases might eventually bring about catastrophic consequences.

One consequence could be significant changes in weather patterns and climate. Changes in weather patterns could bring increased evaporation, creating new deserts and decreasing regional water reserves. Changes in air circulation and climatic conditions could also result in more frequent and intense storms, hurricanes, flooding, and droughts. Vegetation zones could shift, and forests in the northern hemisphere might die off (see Map 13.3 for the possible consequences of climate change in different parts of Canada).

Not all scientists believe that the greenhouse effect exists or that its effects will be this disastrous (Lomborg 2001; and see the interactionist perspective below). However, studies show a marked retreat of glaciers and the beginning of a shift in vegetation, and one possible cause is the greenhouse effect (Hauchler and Kennedy 1994). To reduce greenhouse gases, the Kyoto Protocol was developed (see Box 13.4).

SOCIAL PROBLEMS AND SOCIAL POLICY

BOX 13.4 The Ratification of the Kyoto Protocol

The problem of global warming has the highest profile of any of the environmental problems we face. According to most scientists, a major contributor to global warming is our fossil fuel, or CO2, emissions. In an attempt to reduce CO2 emissions, 150 nations met in Kyoto, Japan, in 1997 and agreed to a plan, called the Kyoto Protocol, to reduce the amount of emissions expected in the year 2012 by 20 to 30 percent. This reduction required the industrialized countries to reduce their emissions to about 6 percent below their 1990 level. (The non-industrialized countries were not required to reduce their CO2 emissions in this round, the belief being that the faster they industrialized, the faster their rates of emissions would decline, as the industrialized world's CO2 emissions have over the last 50 years. In December 2005 at a follow-up conference for the years after 2012, many other nations pledged to reduce their greenhouse gas emissions.) The Kyoto Protocol was ratified by enough nations for it to become binding. Canada ratified it in December 2002.

After the general agreement, individual nations still had to ratify the protocol. Since the agreement, Japan and the 15 European Union countries have ratified it, and the United States has said it will not ratify it. On December 10, 2002, the Canadian Parliament voted to ratify the protocol. The federal budget, tabled on February 18, 2003, allocated $2 billion to meeting Canada's commitments under the protocol. Technically, we have until 2008, when the first cutbacks are supposed to take place. Although the vast majority of Canadians—93 percent, according to a Decima Research Inc. poll reported in the *Globe and Mail* (Middlestaedt 2001:A4)—believe the government should do more to reduce pollution that causes climate change, many businesspeople, the premier of Alberta, and some outside commentators, like Bjorn Lomborg, have publicly opposed ratification in favour of other methods. He recommended that, in 2005, a small percentage of the GDP be devoted to alternate energy research. Businesspeople are concerned about the cost of reducing emissions, especially when their principal competitors in the U.S. will not have these costs. The premier of Alberta is concerned because the province is an energy producer, and with this production comes CO2 emissions. For example, a large amount of energy is required to separate the sand from oil in the tar sands. Alberta claims that it is not opposed to taking action on climate change, just to this protocol. Estimates of the costs of ratifying Kyoto range from the Alberta government estimate of $30 to $40 billion and the loss of 450 000

jobs, to the federal government estimate of $300 million to $3 billion, or a 0.5 percent reduction in the expected growth of 31 percent in GDP by 2010. As part of the strategy to keep costs low, the federal government (a) has sought a reduction in the 6 percent below the 1990 standard to 3.5 percent; (b) has sought consideration for producing and exporting emission-free hydroelectricity; (c) has offered to cap, at $15 a tonne, the cost of greenhouse gas emissions to corporations; and, (d) is expecting to buy emission credits from industries and areas (e.g., Eastern Europe) that surpass their reduction goals. The selling of emission credits is often considered to be a licence to pollute, but it makes sense from an economic point of view of rewarding the reducers and increasing costs to the lesser reducers. As of the end of 2003, Canada was not doing so well at reducing greenhouse gasses. Between 1990 and 2003, according to Environment Canada, Canada had actually increased its emissions by 24 percent so that we are now 32 percent above our target (Statistics Canada 2005c).

The Liberal government ratified the Kyoto Protocol in 2002. In 2006, after Prime Minister Harper acknowledged that Canada would not meet its greenhouse gas emissions target on time (see the quotation at the beginning of this chapter), the Conservative government took an entirely different approach. In mid-October 2006, they introduced the *Clean Air Act,* which calls for the reduction in intensity of emissions, not an absolute reduction in emissions, and makes no mention of the Kyoto Protocol. The act's proposals include

- in 2007 limiting emissions from vehicles and products including motorcycles and personal watercraft and tighter standards for appliances;

- in 2011 making mandatory fuel-efficiency standards for new cars and trucks sold in Canada and fixed caps on emissions by industrial polluters;

- in 2025 putting a cap on greenhouse gas emissions through national targets for smog and ozone levels; and

- in 2050, the target year to reduce greenhouse gas emissions, reducing 2003 levels by 45 to 65 percent (Curry 2006:A4)

Unless the Liberals return to govern and uphold the Kyoto Protocol, it seems as though we will repudiate an international treaty. How important is it that we maintain our international treaty obligations, and how much would you be willing to sacrifice to do so?

Depletion of the Ozone Layer

There is some indication that the ozone layer of the atmosphere has been endangered by air pollution. In 1992, a hole the size of North America was reported in the ozone layer over Antarctica, and scientists have concluded that the ozone layer was thinning out at a rate of 6 percent a year in the 1990s (Hauchler and Kennedy 1994). Ozone is vital to life on earth because it is the only gas in the atmosphere that can absorb the sun's dangerous ultraviolet radiation. A thinning ozone layer increases risk of skin cancer, damages marine life, and lowers crop yields. It is important to note that the ozone shrinkage that scientists are currently measuring is the result of emissions in the early 1980s. Thus, the emissions we produce today will exert their destructive effects in the future (Hauchler and Kennedy 1994). Many countries, hoping to control damage to this delicate ecosystem in the future, are now phasing out products that contain CFCs, which damage the ozone layer and do not break down quickly. In 1987, 49 countries signed the Montreal Protocol to cut CFC production and consumption by 50 percent by the year 2000 (Harper 2001:131). As a result of this protocol, world CFC production was reduced greatly, from over 1 000 000 ozone-depleting tonnes in 1986 to less than 150 000 ozone-depleting tonnes in 1999 (Sheehan 2002:55). New information from autumn 2005 suggests that the hole has been shrinking since 2003. It appears that the cooperative effort has worked. However climate change could stall the shrinking of the hole. (ABC News Online 2005)

Toxic Air Pollutants

Toxic air pollutants refer to a wide variety of chemicals found in the air in low but sufficient concentrations to be associated with a lifetime cancer risk greater than one in a million. A study commissioned by Toronto Public Health assessed the potential for exposure to 10 key carcinogens, including asbestos, benzene, and polycyclic aromatic hydrocarbons (PAHs), in Toronto workplaces and environments. The results showed that Toronto residents are routinely exposed to a variety of carcinogenic chemicals in the environment and "many of these people are exposed to additional and even higher levels of carcinogens at work" (Basrur 2002:iii). The report also recommends finding ways to determine people's actual exposure to these chemicals and reduce the releasing of them.

Problems with Water, Soil, and Forests

Water, soil, and forests (vegetation) are interdependent, crucial resources that face increasing degradation or destruction because of pollution. As a result of climate changes, waste, pollution, and rapid depletion, the earth's drinking water is endangered and its fertile land is being lost.

Water Shortages and Pollution

Water depletion and pollution are serious problems. A shocking example occurred in 2000 in the small town of Walkerton, in southern Ontario. Seven people died and about 2300 became ill as a result of E. coli contamination in the water. The primary source of the contamination was manure that had been spread on a farm near a major well. This well had not been monitored appropriately by the water utility operators. In the end, Ontario Premier Mike Harris was forced to admit that he and his government were, in part, responsible for the tragedy: Despite ongoing strong public support for environmental protection, they had slashed funding for environmental programs (along with funding for welfare, education, and health); at the same time, they had devolved responsibility in many areas—including water testing and manure management—to the municipalities, which had neither

In our delicate ecosystem, water pollution has a disastrous effect on all forms of life—not just on human life. What measures might we implement to reduce water pollution like this?

the money nor the knowledge needed to handle these responsibilities.

Obviously, such problems are not limited to Canada. Although approximately 70 percent of the earth's surface is covered by water, most water is not drinkable: 97 percent is saltwater, 2 percent is in ice caps and glaciers, and most of the remaining 1 percent is so far underground that it is beyond human reach (Petersen 1994). The primary sources of water for use and consumption are rainfall, streams, lakes, rivers, and aquifers (accessible underground water supplies). Canada is often thought to be a source of limitless fresh water, but according to the Water Quickfacts website of Environment Canada (2002), we have only 7 percent of the world's renewable, or flowing, freshwater, as opposed to the stationary freshwater in lakes; moreover 60 percent of our fresh water runs north.

Because of the current rate of world population growth and existing climatic conditions, water scarcity is increasing throughout the world. According to the *UN World Water Development Report,* the first global assessment of the world's fresh water supply, about seven billion people, two-thirds of the world's population in the middle of this century, will likely face water scarcity. Areas that already experience water shortages, like India, Pakistan, the Middle East, and sub-Saharan Africa, will experience the most severe problems (UNEP 2003).

Where does the water go? The largest amount (about 70 percent) is used for crop irrigation; in some African and Asian countries, as much as 85 percent of the available water is used in agriculture. The second largest use of water is in industry (23 to 25 percent). Industrial use of water depends on the level of development in a country and the structure of its economy. For example, high-income nations use as much as 60 percent of their water for industry, whereas a middle- or low-income nation may use less than 10 percent. A mere 8 percent of all available water is used for domestic or private household use. Over the past 100 years, global use of water has gone from 1000 to 2000 litres per day (Lomborg 2001:151), with affluent people in high-income nations using far more water than do families living in African villages, where water must often be carried several kilometres (about 2 to 5 litres is the physical minimum needed per person per day). Medical analysts believe that about 80 percent of all illnesses in developing nations are partly due to insufficient water supplies (Petersen 1994). According to the *UN World Water Development Report,* about 6000 people die daily due to water-borne diseases

(UNEP 2003). Overall, water pollution killed tens of millions of people in the 20th century, making it humanity's most costly pollution problem (McNeill 2000:147).

Water pollution seriously diminishes the available supply of water. Water may be polluted in a variety of ways. Most often, though, the cause is unpurified or insufficiently treated sewage from households and industry discharged into groundwater, or surface water, or pesticides and mineral fertilizers leached from farmland (Hauchler and Kennedy 1994). The pollutants range from nitrates and phosphates to metals, salts, and disease-causing micro-organisms.

Environment Canada studied 345 southern Canadian freshwater sites from 2001 to 2003 and found that less than half was rated good or excellent for meeting guidelines that set limits for pollutant levels, a third were rated as fair, and a quarter as marginal or poor. It is estimated that 100 000 tonnes of toxic pollutants are discharged into surface waters in 2003 (Statistics Canada 2005c).

Soil Depletion and Desertification

About 11 percent of the earth's surface is used for growing crops, 32 percent is forest, and 24 percent is used to graze animals. Each year, however, many acres of usable land are lost through erosion and contamination. *Deforestation*—excessive removal of trees—usually results in serious erosion. Since the 1992 Earth Summit in Rio de Janeiro, high-income nations have made an effort to protect forests. Unfortunately, prior industrialization in Canada and other high-income nations has already taken a serious toll on forests, and the pattern is continuing in some middle- and low-income nations as they become more industrialized. In Canada, especially in the Pacific Northwest, logging is an issue. Environmentalists say that logging, besides destroying old-growth forests, increases landslides, floods, and changes in rivers and streams, which devastate fish stocks (Goldberg 1997). Furthermore, when road building, which is necessary to get to the trees in the forest, is combined with cutting all the timber in an area (clear-cutting), the damage is even greater. More water flows down slopes, and when roads wash out, rocks and soil fall onto lower slopes and into streambeds (Goldberg 1997).

Today, many regions are losing an increasing amount of useable land as a result of *desertification*— **the process by which usable land is turned into desert because of overgrazing, harmful agricultural practices, or deforestation.** It is estimated that desertification destroys as many as 6 million hectares (15 million acres) of land a year. An additional 20 million hectares (50 million acres) of crop and pasture land become inefficient each year because of excessive application of herbicides and pesticides, insufficient crop rotation, and intensified agricultural production (UNEP 1992).

In Canada's Prairies, according to the North American Commission for Environmental Cooperation (2002), in the mid-1990s, soil loss through erosion is thought to have amounted to about 177 million tonnes annually, despite successful efforts to reduce loss by the planting of winter cover crops and windbreaks. Although soil erosion has declined, more soil is being lost than is being regenerated naturally, because heavy use of chemical fertilizers has harmed soil structure.

Although desertification takes place in both high-income and middle- and low-income nations, its effects are particularly devastating in middle- and low-income nations. When a country is already hard hit by rapid population growth, virtually any loss of land or crops is potentially devastating to large numbers of people (UNEP 1992). The United Nations and other international organizations have therefore tried to make protection of the environment an integral part of all economic development policy. However, environmental protection specialists say that to translate policy into action, conservation programs must be supported by the people, and the major sources of the problem—population and poverty—must also be addressed (UNEP 1992).

Solid, Toxic, and Nuclear Wastes

Even with a rapidly growing world population and ongoing economic development in industrialized nations, the planet might be able to sustain life for a long time if it weren't for all the solid and toxic chemical waste that is dumped into the environment.

Solid Waste

In Canada and some other high-income nations, people consume a vast array of products and—in these *disposable societies*—throw away huge quantities of paper, plastic, metal, and other materials. *Solid waste* is any and all unwanted and discarded materials that are not liquids or gases. For example, in 2000, each person in Canada disposed of about 0.75 tonnes of waste (Statistics Canada

2002h), of which only 30 percent was recycled—reused resources that would otherwise be discarded. In comparison, earth sciences reporter Alanna Mitchell (2000:F4) found that the Dutch recycle 91 percent of their glass, 70 percent of their paper and cartons, 86 percent of their car wrecks, and 50 percent of their packaging.

Toxic Waste

At the same time that technology has brought about improvements in the quality and length of life, it has created the potential for new disasters. One source of a potential disaster is *toxic waste*, the hazardous chemical by-products of industrial processes. Perhaps the most widely known U.S. case of toxic waste is Love Canal. In the late 1970s, residents of Niagara Falls, New York, learned that their children were attending a school that had been built on top of a toxic landfill (Gibbs 1982). After large numbers of children became ill and the smell and appearance of the chemicals permeated the entire area, many people mobilized against Hooker Chemical Company, which had dumped tons of chemicals there (Gibbs 1982). Eventually, the federal government bought many of the houses, moved the residents out, and removed as much of the toxic waste as possible. Today, families again live in the area, but they have a highly visible neighbour: a 16-hectare grassy landfill, 9.14 metres high at the centre, with a 2.4-metre-high chainlink fence surrounding it. The landfill contains 20 000 tonnes of toxic chemical waste and the remains of 239 contaminated houses (Hoffman 1994). A lesser-known Canadian example of chemical discharge, by Uniroyal Chemical, permanently contaminated the water supply in Elmira, Ontario, with a "toxic soup of cancer-causing chemicals." In 1989, the Ontario Ministry of the Environment ordered Uniroyal to cease the discharge and clean up the local environment (Cameron 1995:298).

Government regulates the disposal of toxic wastes, but some hazardous wastes are not covered by regulations, and some corporations avoid the regulations by locating their factories in other countries (see also Chapter 2). In addition, there is often nowhere to safely dispose of the chemicals. Many people take a "not in my backyard" attitude toward toxic chemical waste dumps (Dunlap 1992; Freudenberg and Steinsapir 1992).

According to a report by the North American Commission for Environmental Cooperation, Canada is a dumping ground for hazardous waste. Representatives from three environmental groups—the Texas Center for

Policy Studies, the Canadian Institute for Environmental Law and Policy, and La Neta: Proyecto Emisiones—prepared a joint report that they presented at the CEC's North American Symposium on Understanding the Linkages Between Trade and Environment, in October 2000. Their findings (North American CEC 2002) were disturbing:

■ Exports of hazardous waste from the United States to Canada grew by nearly 400 percent between 1994 and 1999, with Quebec and Ontario receiving the bulk of it. In 1999, Quebec disposed of more than 333 000 tonnes of American toxic waste and Ontario more than 325 000 tonnes.

■ The largest increase in American waste exports to Canada occurred in 1994, the year that the U.S. adopted tough new laws for treatment and disposal. In that year alone, Ontario's share of U.S. toxic waste surged by 414 percent.

Nuclear Waste

Nuclear, or radioactive, wastes are the most dangerous of all toxic wastes. Radioactive waste in Canada comes primarily from nuclear power plants, which provide enough electricity in Canada to power 6 million homes (Canadian Nuclear Association 2002). In addition, small amounts of waste are by-products of certain medical procedures. According to the *Harper's* Index, citing an Organization for Economic Co-operation and Development Report, Canada generates more grams of nuclear waste per capita than either Britain or the U.S. (50 vs. 15 and 7 respectively; "Harper's Index" 2002). Nuclear waste remains deadly for prolonged periods of time. For example, uranium waste from nuclear power plants (an estimated 50 000 tonnes by the early 2000s) will remain dangerously radioactive for the next 10 000 years, and plutonium waste for the next 240 000 years (Petersen 1994). Although there are many problems with nuclear power, some environmentalists are reconsidering its value, because it does have the advantage of not producing any CO_2 emissions.

Technological Disasters

Technological disasters, such as the 1986 meltdown and radiation leak at the Chernobyl nuclear power plant in Ukraine, have increased global awareness of the problems associated with radioactive waste. However, despite the disaster, the former Soviet Union was still using 19 similar reactors in 1994 (Petersen 1994). Sociologist Kai T. Erikson (1991:15) sees the world facing a new species of trouble today:

> [Environmental problems] contaminate rather than merely damage . . . they pollute, befoul, taint, rather than just create wreckage . . . they penetrate human tissue indirectly rather than just wound the surfaces by assaults of a more straightforward kind. . . . And the evidence is growing that they scare human beings in new and special ways, that they elicit an uncanny fear in us.

The chaos that Erikson (1994:141) describes is the result of *technological disasters*—"meaning everything that can go wrong when systems fail, humans err, designs prove faulty, engines misfire, and so on." Chernobyl, Love Canal, and Elmira were technological disasters, as were radiation leakage at the Three Mile Island nuclear power plant in Pennsylvania in 1979 and the leakage of lethal gases at the pesticide plant in Bhopal, India, which killed over 3000 people in 1984. In the worst-case scenario, technological disasters kill tens of thousands of people; in the best-case scenario, they place tremendous stress on the world's ecosystems and greatly diminish the quality of life for everyone.

PERSPECTIVES ON POPULATION AND THE ENVIRONMENT

As sociologists have examined how human behaviour affects population and environmental problems, the subdiscipline of environmental sociology has emerged. According to Cable and Cable (1995:5), " *environmental sociology* examines people's beliefs about their environment, their behaviour toward it, and the ways in which the structure of society influences them and contributes to the persistent abuse of the environment." Like all sociologists, environmental sociologists—as well as demographers—approach their study from one or another perspective.

The Functionalist Perspective

Some functionalists focus on the relationship between social structure, technological change, and environmental problems. On the one hand, they say, technological innovation serves important functions in society. For example, automation and mass production have made a wide array of goods—from automobiles and computers to McDonald's burgers—available to many people. On the other hand, technological innovation has latent dysfunctions; automation and mass production, for example, create air pollution, overuse and depletion of natural resources, and excessive solid waste. From this point of view, some environmental problems are the price a society pays for technological progress. If this is true, the best way to alleviate the problem is to develop new technologies. This is what happened, some functionalists note, when the catalytic converter and other antipollution devices were developed for automobiles.

Other functionalists take a neo-Malthusian perspective and believe that to reduce food shortages and environmental problems, population must be controlled. In other words, the more people there are alive, the greater are the overuse of finite resources and degradation of soil, water, and land.

No matter which view functionalist environmental sociologists take, they believe that solutions to overpopulation and environmental degradation lie in social institutions such as education, the government, and business. Educators can encourage population control by teaching people about the limits to agriculture and the difficulty of feeding rapidly increasing populations. Government leaders and international organizations such as the United Nations can co-operate to find far-reaching and innovative solutions and develop understandings about more equitable use of the world's resources (Ehrlich and Ehrlich 1991). Although the Conservative government said Canada will not meet the standards of the Kyoto Protocol, it did introduce a *Clean Air Act* which the government claims will reduce air pollution (see Box 13.4).

Business can be helpful by becoming "greener"— applying environmentally friendly principles to its buildings and operations, putting gardens on plant roofs, using alternative energy sources to coal and oil, sequestering greenhouse gases in underground storage, and cutting waste. Business can also develop environmentally friendly products like cars powered by a hybrid of gasoline-powered engines and electric motors (e.g., Toyota's Prius, Honda Insight, Ford Escape, and others) and solar- and wind-powered devices.

The concept of sustainable development, mentioned at the opening of this chapter, summarizes the ideal of cooperation of these major institutions. Recently an Environmental Sustainable Index has been developed to identify the countries that are more and less environmentally sustainable (Esty et al. 2005). The index consists of 74 variables organized into five dimensions:

- environmental systems, e.g., air and water quality;
- stress reduction, e.g., reducing air pollution, water, waste, and consumption stresses, and natural resource management;
- reduction of human vulnerability, e.g., promoting environmental health;
- social and institutional capacity, e.g., environmental governance, private sector responsiveness, and eco-efficiency; and
- global stewardship, e.g., international collaboration and reducing transboundary environmental pressures.

Most of these variables have been compiled for most of the countries in the world, and a map of sustainability has been developed (see Map 13.4). The darker the shade, the more environmentally sustainable the country. Canada's rank in the world is sixth overall (the U.S. ranks 45th). While this can provide some comfort, we are still very deficient in reducing greenhouse gases and do not yet have interim targets and timelines for meeting our commitment to the Kyoto Protocol.

The Conflict Perspective

Analysts using a conflict framework believe that population and environmental problems have less to do with overpopulation and shortages of resources than with power differentials in societies and in the larger global economy. For example, early conflict theorists, such as Karl Marx and Friedrich Engels (1848/1976), did not think that the food supply was threatened by overpopulation because agricultural technology (even in their era) could meet the food needs of the growing world population, if it were not for poverty. According to Marx and Engels (1848/1976), poverty exists because workers are exploited by capitalists. They argued, for example, that poverty existed in England because the capitalists skimmed off some of the workers' wages as profits. Thus, the labour of the working classes was used by capitalists to earn profits, which, in turn, were used to purchase machinery that could replace the workers rather than supply food. From this classical Marxist point of

MAP 13.4 Environmental Sustainability Index (ESI) 2005

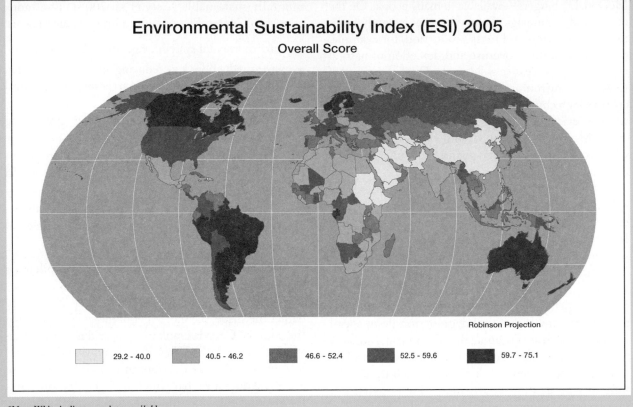

Environmental Sustainability Index (ESI) 2005
Overall Score

Robinson Projection

29.2 - 40.0	40.5 - 46.2	46.6 - 52.4	52.5 - 59.6	59.7 - 75.1

Note: White indicates no data available.

Source: Daniel C. Esty, Marc Levy, Tanja Srebotnjak, and Alexander de Sherbinin, 2005, 2005 Environmental Sustainability Index: Benchmarking National Environmental Stewardship, New Haven: Yale Center for Environmental Law & Policy.

view, population growth is encouraged by capitalists who use unemployed workers (the industrial reserve army) to keep other workers from demanding higher wages or better working conditions.

According to contemporary conflict theorists, corporations and the government are the two main power institutions in society. As a result, when economic decisions made by members of the capitalist class and elite political leaders lead to environmental problems, the costs are externalized, or passed along to the people (Cable and Cable 1995:13):

> [The externalization of environmental costs of production] . . . means that the costs of production's negative impact on the environment (for example,

the expense of cleaning polluted water to make it suitable for drinking) are not included in the price of the product. The company neither pays for the privilege of polluting the water nor cleans it; it saves the cost of proper waste disposal and makes environmentally conscious competition impossible. Not even the consumer of the product pays the environmental costs of production directly. Rather, the public at large essentially subsidizes the company, by either paying for the cleanup of the environment or enduring degraded environmental quality.

Another conflict approach uses an *environmental justice framework,* examining how racialization and class intersect in the struggle for scarce environmental resources. Of particular interest to these theorists is *environmental racism*—**the belief that a disproportionate number of hazardous facilities are placed in areas populated primarily by poor people and people of colour** (Bullard and Wright 1992). Hazardous facilities include waste disposal and treatment plants and chemical plants (Schneider 1993). A 1987 study by the U.S. Commission for Racial Justice concluded, "Race was the most potent variable in predicting the location of uncontrolled (abandoned) and commercial toxic waste sites in the United States" (Bullard and Wright 1992:41). A possible example of environmental racism occurred in Halifax, Nova Scotia, in 2002. According to *Maclean's* magazine (DeMont 2002), a proposal to build a water treatment plant to prevent the dumping of sewage into the ocean elicited a complaint to the Nova Scotia Human Rights Commission stating that the placement of the plant discriminates on the basis of class and colour against the local population, which includes a large Black population. According to local authorities, repositioning the plant would cost $11 million and the concerns about noise and odour are misplaced, as the plant is built to a state-of-the-art design.

The Interactionist Perspective

Since interactionists take a microlevel approach, viewing society as the sum of all people's interactions, they look at environmental problems in terms of individuals' social construction of reality.

According to sociologist John A. Hannigan (1995), environmental claims-makers assemble, present, and contest the claims they make about various environmental problems. To gain public attention and support, the claims must be newsworthy, have scientific credibility, and get past various interests. It is helpful to have

- supporters who span science and media, such as David Suzuki, the award-winning scientist (the UN Environmental Medal and many honourary degrees), host of the CBC program, *The Nature of Things*, and author of many books concerned with the environment;

- incentives for change, such as better health; and

- sustaining support by major international organizations, such as the United Nations. (Hannigan 1995)

Having institutional support can lead to the creation of international protocols, like the Kyoto Protocol

for global warming (see Box 13.4), though it cannot guarantee full international co-operation.

Although few would argue that the concerns raised by environmentalists are groundless, some feel the dangers may be exaggerated. For example, in *The Skeptical Environmentalist* (2001), Bjorn Lomborg, an associate professor of statistics in Denmark, challenges claims about natural resources running out, a growing population depleting the food supply, the relative value of the Kyoto Protocol versus helping "Third World" countries develop, and great quantities of species becoming extinct (Harvard University entomologist E. O. Wilson, in contrast, suggests 50 percent of species will be extinct by the end of the century). Though Lomborg is not an environmental researcher, he has been concerned about the environment for a long time and is a former member of Greenpeace (2000:xix). Lomborg and his work were severely criticized in *Scientific American* (January 2002), and he was not given an opportunity to respond. (His response does appear on his website: **www.lomborg.org**.) If some claims of environmental degradation were to turn out to have been exaggerated for effect, would that undermine the environmental movement? Which picture, a scientifically accurate or a dramatically exaggerated one, will better solve environmental problems?

The social construction approach also helps us understand people's accounts of the estimation of environmental risk and their response to different kinds of communication. McMaster University researchers John Eyles and his colleagues (1993) studied the effects of the tire fire in 1990 in Hagersville, Ontario—a fire broke out on a site on which 13 to 14 million tires were located and burned for 17 days before being extinguished. When the fire broke out, 300 households were evacuated. Eyles and his colleagues conducted in-depth interviews among a small sample of those who experienced the evacuation and were helped by local groups. The researchers found (1993: 287) that although the effects of the fire were short-lived, many residents had anxieties about future problems such as their children's health, toxic water runoff, and the value of their property. Eyles and colleagues (1993:287) also found that the authorities did not do a good job of communicating with people about the evacuation, the de-evacuation, the clean up, and compensation for loss. Since perceived risk is increased when the threat is uncontrollable, involuntary, and problematic for future generations, the researchers "conclude that the nature of the message is as important as information itself" (Eyles et al. 1993:288). For the authorities to communicate better with people, they must "recognize and cater to ways in which lay publics act, think and talk" (Eyles et al. 1993:288).

Feminist Perspectives

Two strands of feminist theorizing in population and the environment are *women's agency* and *ecofeminism.* Regarding overpopulation, the relationship between women's literacy and fertility is well established. Higher-educated women have fewer children, not only in developed countries, but also in developing countries. While the fertility rate in India is over 3.0, the rate in Kerala, a state in which women are well educated and participate in the labour force, is below replacement level at 1.7 (Sen 1999:199). Thus, encouraging women's education and participation in the labour force would contribute to both women's well-being and the reduction of fertility rates.

The term *ecofeminism* was coined by French writer Françoise d'Eaubonne, who thought that men's oppression of women and of the environment were two components of the same phenomenon (Eckersley 2001). Ecofeminists believe that women are more nurturing, co-operative, and conservation-minded than men and point to the term "Mother Nature" to support the general acceptance of women as being closer to nature. The viewpoint that women have a unique capacity to construct a new approach to the environment and the viewpoint is combined with activism (Mies and Shiva 1993). Women have the opportunity to take on a bigger share of social and environmental decision making. Equally, men could assume a bigger share of domestic, social, and environmental responsibility as part of a more equitable division of labour in the home and community. These goals should be part of a much broader ecofeminist protest against what British ecofeminist Mary Mellor (1997) has called " *parasitical transcendence.*" This concept draws attention to the gross asymmetries in the size of the ecological and social "footprints," at term coined by William Rees, a Canadian ecologist, left behind by certain classes, social groups, and nations relative to others. It argues that any form of "parasitism" (living off the back of others, benefiting from the unacknowledged work, social marginalization, or suffering of others) or transcendence (attempting to deny and live beyond our human biological and ecological means) cannot be supportable (Mellor 1997). Sociologist Melody Hessing (1995:254) also believes in expanding the issues to include reviews of taxation of child-support payments, assessment of habitat loss for endangered species, and reduction of poverty for sole-support mothers. This scenario would "increase values of life support, caring, co-operation, and well-being."

POPULATION AND THE ENVIRONMENT IN THE FUTURE

The problems we have considered in this section include some of the greatest challenges that humans face in the 21st century. Global overpopulation and environmental depletion and devastation have irreversible consequences, and actions taken—or not taken—today will be with us far into the future. Futurists believe that we must use a wide-angle lens to examine population and environmental concerns (Peterson 1994). We must see the world and our role in it in a much different way than we did in the past. We must understand that environmental issues are *security* issues—as much as a terrorist threat or a missile or bomb (Peterson 1994). Once we understand that, we will think of environmental problems in a completely different light. For example, to eliminate the global threats posed by overpopulation and environmental degradation, all societies can make the following changes (based on Petersen 1994:109):

- Reduce the use of energy.
- Shift from fossil fuels to solar-based energy systems or other energy-efficient systems such as water power, wind power, or geothermal energy.
- Develop new transportation networks and city designs that reduce automobile use.
- Work for redistribution of land and wealth so that the poor will not be exploited by increasing concentration of farming.

- Push for equality between women and men in all nations, emphasizing literacy training, educational opportunities, and health care (including reproduction and contraception information) for women.

- Effect a rapid transition to smaller families.

- Co-operate internationally to reduce the consumption of resources by the wealthy nations and bring higher living standards to poorer nations.

Are these changes likely to occur? Not if people in high- and middle-income nations adhere to their current belief systems. Some social analysts think that it will take a threatening event—a drastic change in the earth's weather patterns or a sudden increase in natural disasters—to capture the attention of enough of the earth's people and convince political leaders that a serious change in direction is required if the planet is to continue to support human life (Petersen 1994). We can only hope that people will not wait until it's too late.

WHAT CAN YOU DO?

For this cause, there is no shortage of opportunities to do something. Here are a few places to start for the environment:

- Visit the Youth website of the federal government, which describes just about every opportunity imaginable, at **www.ec.gc.ca/youth/index_e.cfm**. At this site, one is invited to apply for a Youth Round Table on the Environment (for youth up to 26 years of age) to increase involvement in Environment Canada program and policy development and act as an advisor to the minister. Links are available to environmental jobs and internships and community volunteer efforts, such as monitoring plant and frog populations in your area. You can find out about events and conferences such as the yearly Sustainable Campuses Conference for groups promoting environmentally friendly and sustainable campuses. There are also links to issues like Sustaining the Environment, where you find more opportunities to learn about sustainable development and what you can do to contribute to it. You will find an EnviroZine to read, and a

mailing list to join to learn what is new. Finally, it is possible to contact the ministry with questions and concerns. This site provides a great range of possibilities for participation.

- Reduce energy consumption (e.g., by driving less, having a fuel-efficient car, not idling the car engine, and, at home, reducing heating fuel use through proper insulation, lowering water and air heating, etc.); reduce waste (e.g., recycling, and composting); and reduce consumption—you know what we mean.

- Lobby Members of Parliament, by yourself or with others, to encourage them to take action to promote a sustainable environment.

- Join with others to change energy use (e.g., urge people idling their cars to stop, as students in Mississauga, Ontario, are doing as part of an environmental internship program with City Council and their Environmental Studies Program at University of Toronto).

Here are some things you can do for cities:

- If you live in a city, you might join your local residents' association. These associations are always looking for volunteer help for committees: to undertake liaison with the police, to have representatives for every street in the area, to keep track of problems like drug dealing and prostitution, and to undertake social projects. Be aware that some of the members of some of these groups are more concerned with enhancing the value of their properties than with solving social problems in the area and may seek to reduce local shelters and social agencies.

- If you are searching for a place to live and like the idea of working with your neighbours, try cooperative housing. You will gain a great experience working with others.

- Join a group lobbying for the homeless. Public Interest Research Groups are found on many university and college campuses, and they sometimes, like the Ontario Public Interest Research Group in Toronto, support action to help the homeless.

- Participate in irregular programs to plant trees or clean up your neighbourhood.

- Sit in on a city council meeting so you can learn more about the activities and governance of a city and meet other interested citizens and lobby your councilor or mayor.

SUMMARY

WHAT IS THE GLOBAL POPULATION? WHY IS POPULATION GROWTH A PROBLEM?

The world's population was more than 6 billion in 2003; it doubled in the last 50 years and, if this trend continues, will double again in the next 50 years. Can the earth's resources support this rapid population growth?

WHAT ARE THE PRIMARY FACTORS THAT AFFECT POPULATION GROWTH?

Three factors affect population growth: fertility, the actual number of children born to an individual or population; mortality, the number of deaths that occur in a specific population; and migration, the movement of people from one geographic area to another for the purpose of changing residency.

HOW DOES POPULATION GROWTH AFFECT A SOCIETY?

Population growth affects population composition—the biological and social characteristics of a population, including such attributes as age, sex, racialization, marital status, education, occupation, income, and size of household. In Canada, for example, the age distribution of the population affects the need for schools, employment opportunities, health care, and age-appropriate housing.

WHAT ARE THE MAJOR THEORETICAL PERSPECTIVES ON OVERPOPULATION?

According to the Malthusian perspective, population expands geometrically while the food supply increases arithmetically; disaster can be averted through positive checks (e.g., famine, disease, war) or preventive checks (e.g., sexual abstinence, delayed marriage). The neo-Malthusians believe that the earth is a ticking bomb because population problems exacerbate environmental problems. The third perspective is more hopeful. According to demographic transition theory, societies move from high birth and death rates to low birth and death rates as a result of technological development. However, critics say that demographic transition theory applies chiefly to Western societies.

WHAT SOLUTIONS DO WE HAVE TO WORLD HUNGER?

Two of the most far-reaching initiatives are the green revolution (the growing of high-yield "miracle" crops) and the biotechnological revolution, which involves "improving" plants or animals or using microorganisms in innovative ways. However, some social analysts believe that the solution is not to produce more food but to control fertility.

HOW IS IMMIGRATION CHANGING THE POPULATION COMPOSITION OF CANADA?

Today, the proportion of Canadian immigrants in the population is about 18 percent. If immigration continues at the present rate, it will account for half of the expected population growth in the next 50 years. (Canada is otherwise below zero population growth—a stable population.) Immigration could lead to higher taxes, but it also brings substantial economic and cultural benefits.

HOW DID URBANIZATION COME ABOUT?

Urbanization—the process by which an increasing proportion of a population lives in cities rather than rural areas—began with industrialization. Before the Industrial Revolution, most people lived in sparsely populated rural areas, where they farmed. Industrialization led to the growth of cities; and urbanization brought about profound changes in societies and spawned new social problems, such as housing shortages, overcrowding, unsanitary conditions, environmental pollution, and crime.

HOW DID MASS SUBURBANIZATION OCCUR? WHAT WERE THE RESULTS?

Mass suburbanization began with government efforts to correct the housing shortage that followed World

War II. The Central (now Canada) Mortgage and Housing Corporation contributed to the building of half a million homes between 1946 and 1951 by granting mortgages. Other factors included the availability of inexpensive land, low-cost mass construction methods, new federally financed highway systems, inexpensive gasoline, and consumer demand for single-family homes on individually owned lots. Mass suburbanization brought about a dramatic shift in the distribution of the Canadian population and set up an ongoing economic division of interests between cities and suburbs.

WHY ARE MANY CITIES IN FISCAL CRISIS?

Large numbers of middle- and upper-income people have moved out of the central cities to the suburbs; and more recently, many retail businesses and corporations have also moved to the suburbs or moved their operations abroad. The shrinking central cities have been left with greatly reduced sources of revenue. Many of the remaining central city residents are poor, unemployed, or older people living on fixed incomes, who cannot afford to pay higher taxes. At the same time, city governments must still provide city services for them. Moreover, suburbanites who regularly use city services do not pay taxes to the city to keep up these services.

WHY IS THERE A HOUSING SHORTAGE IN CANADA? WHAT IS BEING DONE ABOUT IT?

A major reason for the housing shortage is that Canada has yet to find a way to provide safe, livable, low-income housing. In addition, as part of governmental cutbacks in the mid-1990s, the federal and provincial governments stopped building social housing. Some non-governmental groups have been doing good work. One of the most successful initiatives for creating affordable housing is the volunteer organization Habitat for Humanity.

HOW GREAT A PROBLEM IS HOMELESSNESS? ARE THERE ANY SOLUTIONS?

Accurate data on the actual number of the homeless are extremely difficult to get because homeless people avoid interviews with census takers and social researchers. The Golden Report showed that the fastest-growing segment of the homeless population is families and children. Most experts agree that any long-term, successful solution to homelessness must take structural factors into account, especially low-income housing and mental-health care.

DOES RESIDENTIAL RACIALIZED OR ETHNIC SEGREGATION EXIST?

Spatial separation of the poor and non-poor is greater than separation of racialized/ethnic groups. While, in contrast to in U.S. cities, there are no extensive areas of blight, decay, or abandoned housing in Canadian cities, there are pockets of poor racialized/ethnic groups coexisting beside upscale neighbourhoods.

WHAT ARE THE MAJOR PROBLEMS IN GLOBAL CITIES?

In 2007, one out of every two people in the world lives in a city. Increasing population accounts for two-thirds of the new urban growth, and rural-to-urban migration accounts for the rest. Rapid urban growth brings a wide variety of problems, including overcrowding, environmental pollution, and the disappearance of farmland. The exploitation of semiperipheral nations by core nations and of peripheral nations by both semiperipheral and core nations serves to increase the urban problems in these nations. Core nations are dominant capitalist centres characterized by high levels of industrialization and urbanization. Peripheral nations depend on core nations for capital, have little or no industrialization (other than what is brought in by core nations), and have uneven patterns of urbanization. Semiperipheral nations are more developed than peripheral nations but less developed than core nations.

WHAT IS THE FUNCTIONALIST PERSPECTIVE ON URBAN PROBLEMS?

Functionalists believe that today's urban problems are the result of mass migration from rural areas during the Industrial Revolution, large-scale immigration in the late 19th and early 20th centuries, and mass suburbanization. One solution is to create regional governments.

WHAT IS THE CONFLICT PERSPECTIVE ON URBAN PROBLEMS?

Conflict theorists believe that cities grow or decline according to decisions made by capitalists and the political elite. In other words, these theorists use a political economy model. Urban problems can be reduced through political activism and organized resistance to oppressive conditions.

WHAT IS THE INTERACTIONIST PERSPECTIVE ON URBAN PROBLEMS?

Interactionists look at how people subjectively experience urban life. According to German sociologist Georg Simmel, urban life is so stimulating that people have no choice but to become somewhat insensitive to people and events around them. On the other hand, urban living gives people opportunities for individualism and autonomy. Sociologist Louis Wirth expanded on Simmel's ideas, saying that urbanism produces feelings of alienation and powerlessness. Herbert Gans concluded from his research that city life is a pleasure for some and a nightmare for others. Commenting on Toronto and Vancouver, Richard Florida states these cities have a high rate of Creative Class people because of the stimulation and tolerance in these cities, and this is a key to a bright economic future. A way to avoid the nightmare of alienation is to develop subcultural ties.

WHAT IS THE FEMINIST PERSPECTIVE ON URBAN PROBLEMS?

Feminist theorists emphasize the occupational opportunities, the freedom from scrutiny, and the convenience of short distances between work and home that allows fulfillment of multiple roles for women.

WHAT IS ENVIRONMENTAL DEGRADATION? WHAT ARE ITS CAUSES?

Environmental degradation is caused by disruptions to the environment that have negative consequences for ecosystems. Human beings, particularly as they pursue economic development and growth, cause environmental degradation.

WHAT IS THE MAJOR SOURCE OF AIR POLLUTION? WHAT ARE ITS EFFECTS?

The major source is fossil fuel pollution, especially from vehicles but somewhat from industry. One of the most serious consequences of air pollution is the greenhouse effect, an environmental condition caused by excessive quantities of carbon dioxide, methane, and nitrous oxide in the atmosphere, leading to global warming. Another is depletion of the ozone layer, the part of the earth's atmosphere that absorbs dangerous ultraviolet radiation from the sun. Although restrictions on the use of CFCs may prevent serious depletion, the already present CFCs will continue to adversely affect the ozone layer.

WHAT WATER, SOIL, AND FOREST PROBLEMS DO WE FACE?

Water is increasingly scarce throughout the world, and water pollution further diminishes the available water supply. About 177 million tonnes of soil are lost each year on the Canadian prairies. However, desertification is greatest in middle- and low-income nations.

WHY ARE SOLID, TOXIC, AND NUCLEAR WASTES A PROBLEM?

High-income nations are running out of space for the amount of solid waste produced by their "disposable societies." Toxic waste (hazardous chemical by-products of industry) causes death and disease if it is not disposed of properly. Canada has become a significant importer of toxic waste. Nuclear, or radioactive, waste is a problem because of the length of time it remains deadly.

WHAT IS THE FUNCTIONALIST PERSPECTIVE ON POPULATION AND THE ENVIRONMENT?

Functionalists say that the latent dysfunctions of technology cause environmental problems but that new technologies can solve these problems. Most functionalists take a neo-Malthusian perspective on population but believe that social institutions, especially education and the government, can co-operate to solve population and environmental problems.

WHAT IS THE CONFLICT PERSPECTIVE ON POPULATION AND THE ENVIRONMENT?

In the classical Marxist view, there would be enough food for all people if poverty were alleviated; poverty exists because capitalists skim workers' wages for profits. Contemporary conflict theorists believe that the two main power institutions in society—corporations and the government—make economic decisions that result in environmental problems.

WHAT IS THE INTERACTIONIST PERSPECTIVE ON POPULATION AND ENVIRONMENT?

Interactionists see population and environment problems in microlevel—individual—terms. Social constructionists show how environmental claims-makers assemble, present, and contest the claims they make about various environmental problems. Sometimes scary scenarios are created, and those who challenge this definition of reality are dismissed as wishful thinkers. Social contructionists can also help us understand people's estimation of environmental risk.

WHAT IS THE FEMINIST PERSPECTIVE ON POPULATION AND THE ENVIRONMENT?

Feminists emphasize the importance of promoting women's literacy and participation in the labour force to help control fertility. Ecofeminism emphasizes that the patriarchy is the root cause of the oppression of women and of nature. Living off the backs of others and living beyond ecological means are both unsupportable.

KEY TERMS

acid rain, p. 363
core nations, p. 355
deindustrialization, p. 348
demographic transition theory, p. 341
demography, p. 337
desertification, p. 368
edge city, p. 347
environmental degradation, p. 362
environmental racism, p. 373
fertility, p. 337
gentrification, p. 351
greenhouse effect, p. 364

mechanical solidarity, p. 357
megalopolis, p. 348
migration, p. 338
mortality, p. 337
organic solidarity, p. 357
peripheral nations, p. 355
population composition, p. 340
semiperipheral nations, p. 356
subculture, p. 360
sustainable development, p. 336
zero population growth, p. 344

QUESTIONS FOR CRITICAL THINKING

1.   Which perspective on population growth do you favour—neo-Malthusian or demographic transition theory—and why?

2.   Where do you live—in the core central city, an edge city, a suburb, or a megalopolis? What examples from your everyday life can you give that relate to the problems described in this chapter? Which sociological perspective do you think best explains the urban problems you observe?

3.   The government has so far failed to provide adequate low-income and poverty-level housing. What new initiatives can you suggest?

4.   The 2001 census releases have included maps of the distribution of visible minorities in the Census Metropolitan Areas. They are available at **http://geodepot.statcan.ca/Diss/Maps/ThematicMaps/Ethnocultural_e.cfm**. Study the map of your area and compare it to maps of other cities. How segregated

are racialized/ethnic groups? What do you think can be done to ensure that Canadian cities do not have the segregation that causes so many problems in the U.S.?

5. If you had to focus on a single aspect of environmental degradation—air pollution; water, soil, or forest problems; or, solid, toxic, or nuclear waste disposal—which would it be, and why? What would you do to make people aware of the seriousness of the problem? What new solutions could you propose?

6. Explore how people use the term *sustainable development*. Do you think this is a good term for the effort to help a variety of institutions become more protective of the environment?

7. Is it possible to have development without environmental degradation?

WEBLINKS

2001 Census: Ethnocultural Portrait of Canada

www12.statcan.ca/english/census01/release/release5.cfm

This site introduces two 2001 census releases, Canada's ethnocultural portrait, and information about immigration and citizenship, both with discussion, tables, and maps.

Teaching and Learning About Canada

www.canadainfolink.ca/cities.htm

This site provides information about the 30 largest metropolitan/urban centres in Canada based on the 2001 census data, with links to cities and provinces.

Environment Canada: The Green Lane

www.ec.gc.ca/envhome.html

Visit this site for a general introduction to environmental problems, to find out what Environment Canada does, and to find out what you can do to help the environment.

Environmental Defence Canada

www.environmentaldefence.ca

This organization hosts information-awareness programs and watches for air, food, and pollution.

Population Reference Bureau

www.prb.org

This site contains introductory notes linked to articles, datasheets, and reports on the environment, HIV/AIDS, population trends, and reproductive health. It deals with a wide variety of other topics, like aging, gender, health, and poverty, for all regions of the world. It also highlights interesting data about world population.

United Nations Environment Programme (UNEP)

www.unep.net

The UNEP provides a wide variety of information accessed from thematic portals dealing with climate change, fresh water, and socio-economic topics and regional portals for the Arctic, Latin America, and Europe (with more to come).

Worldwatch Institute

www.worldwatch.org

Worldwatch works to inform policy-makers and the public about emerging global problems and trends and the complex links between the world economy and its environmental support systems.

HOW CAN SOCIAL PROBLEMS BE SOLVED?

The___Hotel here is a favorite watering hole of the well-heeled and is known for its fantastic views of the city. . . . Just across the street in___Park, homeless people, more concentrated here than in most parts of the city, spend the day sipping from half-empty juice boxes and picking through the garbage discarded by children using the playground. . . . The gap between rich and poor . . . is widening, spurred by economic and social change.

Stephanie Strom (2000:A1)

Does this scenario describe Vancouver? Regina? Montreal? Another large urban centre in Canada? No, this is a reporter's description of what's going on in Tokyo, Japan, as the 21st century begins. Although the similarity of patterns associated with such social problems as poverty and homelessness in Canada and Japan leaves us concerned about their persistence, we are also hopeful that we may be able to find ways to reduce or alleviate some of these problems—across cities, provinces, and nations—in the 21st century. However, as social analysts have said, solving social problems is a far more complex undertaking than simply identifying them and pinpointing their social locations:

> Identifying social problems and calling for action are quite different matters from actually designing and implementing programs to solve them. Calling attention to the problem, for example, can often be accomplished relatively quickly and easily. Trying to actually carry out a solution, by contrast, involves innumerable obstacles, delays, and frustrations, and demands immense dedication and perseverance. (Weinberg et al. 1981:6)

Perhaps the first obstacle that we face in trying to solve social problems is the difference between ideal solutions and "do-able" solutions. As sociologists Martin S. Weinberg, Earl Rubington, and Sue Kiefer Hammersmith (1981:6) have stated, "There is usually considerable conflict between what the *ideal* solution would be and what a *workable* solution might be." Sometimes, for example, the ideal solution to a problem entails high costs that governments may be unwilling to pay. Sometimes there is little or no agreement about what the problem *is* and what efforts should be made to reduce or eliminate it. After all, the people and organizations involved in the problem-defining stage of a

social problem generally are not the same people and organizations involved in the problem-solving stage. Social problems are often identified and defined by political or social activists, journalists, social scientists, and religious leaders. In contrast, the problem-solving stage usually involves elected officials and/or people working in agencies and governmental bureaucracies. Moreover, sometimes a proposed solution to a problem only gives rise to a whole new set of unforeseen problems (Weinberg et al. 1981). In this chapter, we will review several approaches for dealing with social problems and reiterate a pressing question: What are you willing to do to reduce or eliminate social problems?

The underlying theoretical assumptions that we hold regarding social problems often have a profound influence on what we feel may be the best solution for a specific problem. Do we believe society is based on stability, or conflict? Is conflict good for society or bad for society? Each of the four sociological perspectives summarized below suggests ways in which social problems may be reduced. In doing so, they produce divergent views on social changes that might reduce or eliminate social problems.

According to the functionalist perspective, a society is a stable, orderly system that is composed of a number of interrelated parts, each of which performs a function that contributes to the overall stability of the society. From the functionalist perspective, social problems arise when social institutions do not fulfill the functions they are supposed to or when dysfunctions (undesirable consequences of an activity or social process that inhibit a society's ability to adapt or adjust) occur. Dysfunctions create social disorganization, which in turn causes a breakdown in the traditional values and norms that serve as social control mechanisms. As shown in Table E.1, the social disorganization approach of functionalists traces the causes of social problems to any social change that leaves existing rules inadequate for current conditions. In societies undergoing social change—for example, retrenchment of social programs, high rates of immigration, rapid changes in technology, and increasingly complex patterns of social life—social disorganization produces stress at the individual level and inefficiency and confusion at the institutional and societal levels (Weinberg et al. 1981). Thus, the functionalist approach to reducing social problems has as central factors the prevention of rapid social changes, the maintenance of the status quo, and the restoration of order.

TABLE E.1   Perceived Problems and Possible Solutions

Perspective	Causes	Possible Solutions
Functionalist:		
Social disorganization	Social change; inadequacy of existing social rules	Development and implementation of social rules that are explicit, workable, and consistent
Conflict:		
Value conflict	Conflict between different groups' values; economic, social, and cultural diversity	Group action involving confrontation of opponents for lasting changes in policy or legislation
Critical-conflict (Marxist)	Relations of domination and subordination are reinforced by the global capitalist economy and political leaders who put other priorities ahead of the good of the people	Changing the nature of society, particularly inequalities that grow more pronounced as the wealthy grow richer and the poor worldwide become increasingly impoverished
Interactionist:		
Deviant behaviour	Inappropriate socialization within primary groups	Resocialize or rehabilitate individuals so that they will conform
Labelling	How people label behaviour, how they respond to it, and the consequences of their responses	Changing the definitions through discriminalization; limit labelling
Feminist:		
Interlocking oppressions	Patriarchy, capitalism, and other hierarchical systems that cause competition between groups and place value on one group over another	Consider the ways that oppressions are interconnected; educate oneself and others about inequities; change one's own behaviours; join with others to create models of change and visions of co-operative society; help to alleviate the suffering of individuals and groups who experience discrimination while simultaneously working to make broad-based and foundational social and political change.

Source: Based on The Solution of Social Problems: Five Perspectives (2nd ed.), Martin S. Weinberg, Earl Rubington, and Sue Kiefer Hammersmith, 1981, New York: Oxford University Press; and Social Problems: A Critical-Conflict Perspective (5th ed.), Joe R. Feagin and Clairece Booher Feagin, 1997, Upper Saddle River, NJ: Prentice Hall.

In contrast, the conflict perspective assumes that conflict is natural and inevitable in society. Value conflict approaches focus on conflict between the values held by members of divergent groups. These approaches also highlight the ways in which cultural, economic, and social diversity may contribute to misunderstandings and problems. According to Marxist, or critical-conflict, theorists, groups are engaged in a continuous struggle for control of scarce resources. As a result of the unjust use of political, economic, or social power, certain groups of people are privileged while others are disadvantaged. Thus, for critical-conflict theorists, social problems arise out of major contradictions that are inherent in the ways in which

societies are organized. When this approach is used, the root causes of social problems—capitalism and spending priorities that place corporate tax breaks and military spending ahead of social services, for example—must be radically altered or eliminated altogether. Focusing on the political economy, one critical-conflict approach states that the capitalist economy, which is now global, maintains and reinforces domination and subordination in social relations. This approach also examines how political leaders may put their own interests ahead of any common good that might exist (Feagin and Feagin 1997). Clearly, any solutions to social problems proposed by this approach would require radical changes in society and thus are not always viewed positively in societies in which economic prosperity based on individual attributes rather than collective activities is considered a mark of personal and social achievement. This is particularly problematic, conflict theorists point out, when elites maintain power through hegemony. Change can only be achieved, then, through counter-hegemonic means.

Operating at the microlevel, the interactionist perspective focuses on how people act toward one another and make sense of their daily lives. From this perspective, society is the sum of the interactions of individuals and groups. Thus, interactionists often study social problems by analyzing the process whereby a behaviour is defined as a social problem and how individuals and groups then come to engage in activities that a significant number of people view as major social concerns. Interactionist theories of deviance note that inadequate socialization or interacting with the "wrong" people may contribute to deviant behaviour and crime and, hence, to some social problems. Similarly, interactionists who use the labelling framework for their analysis of social problems study how people label behaviour, how they respond to people engaged in such behaviour, and the consequences of their responses (Weinberg et al. 1981).

Feminist theorists concentrate analyses at both macro and micro levels of interaction. Social problems are therefore examined on the basis of power in individual relations and in ideologies and structures, in particular looking at gender as a key component. Society is seen as a matrix of oppression, organized according to specific relations of domination–subordination. Sexism, along with other forms of oppression, such as classism, homophobia, biphobia or transphobia, racism, ableism, and so on, are examined in terms of the ways they privilege and disadvantage whole groups of people as well as the ways that these forms of oppression work in tandem to reinforce a paradigm of oppression, competition, and hierarchy. Feminist theorists who look at social problems look at the roles people play in resisting and/or perpetuating oppressions and at the locations or standpoints people come from. The inequalities and harm stemming from interlocking systems of oppression and domination are viewed as central to social problems. The solutions for reducing or eliminating social problems are, therefore, multifaceted: Pivotal is the push

for a paradigm shift that holds the values of cooperation, diversity, and power sharing in highest regard; also key is changing the unequal dynamics embedded in current racialized/ethnic, class, and gender relations and in relationships between individuals that get played out within these contexts. Paradigm shifts require dramatic changes in the ways we view society and the ways we interact with one another, individually and collectively. Further, paradigm shifts require us to retrain ourselves so that our behaviours fall into line with our new ways of thinking. This takes a great deal of commitment and hard work and is one of our challenges in the new millennium.

Will the internet open up new possibilities for activists to get information to those they would like to mobilize? Clearly, given the number of websites now open, a large number of individuals and organizations believe that this may be the case. Many sites serve as national and international mobilizing vehicles for groups seeking avenues to foster social change. Through news groups, bulletin boards, and other similar vehicles, people are able to learn from each other and share information about social problems. They are also able to join in collective action or encourage others to take some specific action.

Do you follow the news about social issues? If so, do you get your information primarily from television, radio, the internet, or other sources? Based on the information you receive from various media sources, are you motivated to participate in organizations or actions that endeavour to bring about social change?

According to some analysts, we need to develop a human agenda that focuses on the needs of people and offsets the corporate agenda that is currently taking precedence over other issues and concerns. Social activists Jeremy Brecher and Tim Costello suggest that any proposed human agenda should

- improve the lives of the great majority of the world's people;
- correspond to widely held common interests as well as integrate the interests of people worldwide;
- provide opportunities for action at a variety of levels;
- include elements that can be implemented independently, at least in part, but that are compatible or mutually reinforcing;

- make it easier to solve social problems such as environmental protection; and,
- grow out of social movements and coalitions that have developed in response to the needs of diverse peoples.

So, the question remains, can social problems be solved? It seems they can; after all, what has been created can be re-created. So what do we need to recreate, a more just world? Foundationally, we need social analysis, for as Swift, Davies, Clarke, and Czerny (2003:202) state in their book *Getting Started on Social Analysis in Canada*, "the very activity of social analysis . . . helps to 'lift the fog' and overcome ideological confusion. . . . It can also lead directly into effective action." Take the quiz in Figure E.1 and evaluate your tendency toward social analysis.

FIGURE E.1   Social Paralysis Quiz

5	4	3	2	1
strongly agree	agree	don't know	disagree	strongly disagree

☐ Canadian society is too complicated for me to understand.

☐ In Canada there's a premium on authority and obedience: the prudent thing, whenever there's social tension, is to stay out of it.

☐ Things are always getting worse and I feel the news is too awful to take in.

☐ If the experts cannot agree among themselves on any social problem, much less the solution, I haven't a chance.

☐ Faced with issues too big and complicated for me, I feel overwhelmed–it's better not to start.

☐ Because decisions about social issues are very personal, I feel alone and isolated in facing the social world.

☐ There are too many facts to absorb, and it's like I'm drowning in a deluge of information.

☐ I have no control over the important decisions that shape life in Canada.

☐ Economics is a science so mysterious that even economists can't understand how the Canadian economy works.

☐ We will never reach a perfectly just society, because human greed and the lust for power will always reassert themselves, so why bother?

☐ I want to live a well-ordered life–I keep my world quite small.

☐ Social analysis might work in a Third World country, where the inequities are obvious, but it's nearly impossible to analyze a free society like Canada, with its complex issues.

☐ People used to understand the world from the viewpoint of the community they lived in all their lives, but now things are moving too fast for us to understand.

☐ There are tendencies towards evil built into human nature, and until individual hearts are changed there's no point in tampering with social structures.

☐ Political decisions are too weighty for most citizens to grasp.

☐ Total score

This quiz tests people's disposition towards social analysis. The higher you score, the more you have to struggle against social complacency or paralysis–the tendency to leave social concerns to experts, professionals, or activists. A lower score suggests that people believe they can understand their society and hope to have some impact on it.

In a group, everyone's scores could be averaged to see if they tend towards a belief that they have the power to change society for the better, or towards paralysis and disbelief. There could be a discussion of the items that group members tended to score on the pessimistic side.

Source: Jamie Swift, Jacqueline M. Davies, Robert G Clarke, and Michael Czerny S.J., 2003, Getting Started on Social Analysis in Canada, *4th ed., Toronto: Between the Lines, p. 8.*

We need a shared vision and shared values. In their book on globalization and social problems, Peterson, Wunder, and Mueller (1999:414) provide an example of shared visioning and collective values using a statement derived from the 1993 Parliament of the World's Religions called *Toward a Global Ethic*. Some of the values stated in this document include equality between men and women; the dignity and worth of all humans, regardless of ethnicity, gender, language, religion, ability, and so on; generosity, compassion, and caring for one another; economic and social justice; respect for the environment and human rights, truthfulness and honesty, moderation and modesty, loyalty, freedom as long as it does not impose on others, safety, security, and so on. The ability to participate freely and fully in social life is at the core of these values, so, lastly, we need participation. Many of us feel paralyzed by the idea that social problems are big, and we are small. Even small changes, however, can create critical mass, turning "seemingly impossible change into an inevitable one" (Swift et al. 2003:203).

What kind of world you hope for? What kind of world are you willing to participate to (re)create? What values do you hold that may propel you toward that participation? What answers has your social analysis brought you? What questions? As we conclude this book and our time together, won't you join sociologists, social activists, and others who seek to use these tools to face up to one of the greatest challenges of the 21st century: bringing peace, justice, and greater social equality to all?

QUESTIONS FOR CRITICAL THINKING

1. What is most useful about applying a sociological perspective to the study of social problems? What is least useful about a sociological approach? How can you contribute to a better understanding of the causes, effects, and possible solutions to social problems?

2. Do governments at all levels in Canada listen to their constituents about social issues? What evidence can you find to support that they do or do not? Why is the situation the way it is?

GLOSSARY

absolute poverty a condition that exists when people do not have the means to secure the most basic necessities of life (food, clothing, and shelter).

acid rain rainfall containing large concentrations of sulphuric and nitric acids (primarily from the burning of fuel and car and truck exhausts).

acute diseases illnesses that strike suddenly and cause dramatic incapacitation and sometimes death.

ageism prejudice and discrimination against people on the basis of age.

amalgamation a process in which the cultural attributes of diverse racialized or ethnic groups are blended together to form a new society incorporating the unique contributions of each group.

androcentricity putting males at the centre.

Anglo-conformity model a pattern of assimilation whereby members of subordinate racialized/ethnic groups are expected to conform to the culture of the dominant (white) Anglo-Saxon population.

anti-Semitism prejudice and discriminatory behaviour directed at Jews.

assimilation the process by which members of subordinate racialized and ethnic groups become absorbed into the dominant culture.

biphobia fear and intolerance of bisexuals and bisexual lifestyles.

blaming the victim a practice used by people who view a social problem as emanating from within the individual who exhibits the problem.

blended family a family that consists of a husband and wife, or a same-sex couple, children from previous marriages, and children (if any) from the new marriage.

capitalism an economic system characterized by private ownership of the means of production, from which personal profits can be derived through market competition and without government intervention.

chronic diseases illnesses that are long-term or lifelong and that develop gradually or are present from birth.

civil disobedience non-violent action that seeks to change a policy or law by refusing to comply with it.

class system a system of social inequality based on the ownership and control of resources and on the type of work people do.

codependency a reciprocal relationship between the alcoholic and one or more non-alcoholics who unwittingly aid and abet the alcoholic's excessive drinking and resulting behaviour.

collective behaviour voluntary, often spontaneous activity that is engaged in by a large number of people and typically violates dominant group norms and values.

common law, or cohabitation two adults living together in a sexual relationship without being legally married.

comparable worth the belief that wages ought to reflect the worth of a job, not the gender or other ascribed characteristics of the worker.

conflict perspective a framework for viewing society that is based on the assumption that groups in society are engaged in a continuous power struggle for control of scarce resources.

contingent work part-time work, temporary work, and subcontracted work that offers advantages to employers but can be detrimental to workers' welfare.

core nations dominant capitalist centres characterized by high levels of industrialization and urbanization.

corporate crime illegal acts committed by corporate employees on behalf of the corporation and with its support.

crime a behaviour that violates criminal law and is punishable by a fine, a jail term, or other negative sanctions.

criminal justice system the network of organizations, including the police, courts, criminal prosecutions, and corrections, involved in law enforcement and the administration of justice.

cultural capital social assets, such as values, beliefs, attitudes, and competencies in language and culture, that are learned at home and required for success and social advancement.

date rape forcible sexual activity that meets the legal definition of *sexual assault* and involves people who first meet in a social setting.

deindustrialization the process by which capital is diverted from investment in basic industries (in the form of economic resources, plants, and equipment) to business practices such as mergers and acquisitions and foreign investment.

deinstitutionalization the practice of discharging patients from mental hospitals into the community.

demographic transition theory the theory that societies move from high birth and death rates to relatively low birth and death rates as a result of technological development.

demography the study of the size, composition, and distribution of populations.

dependency ratio the number of workers necessary to support youth and those over age 64.

desertification the process by which usable land is turned into desert because of overgrazing, harmful agricultural practices, or deforestation.

deviance a behaviour, belief, or condition that violates social norms.

differential association theory the belief that individuals have a greater tendency to deviate from societal norms when they frequently associate with people who tend toward deviance rather than conformity.

disability a restricted or total lack of ability to perform certain activities as a result of physical or mental limitations or the interplay of these limitations, social responses, and the social environment.

disability-free life expectancy the number of years of life that can be expected to be free of activity limitation.

discrimination actions or practices of dominant group members (or their representatives) that have a harmful impact on members of subordinate groups.

dominant group the group whose members are disproportionately at the top of the hierarchy, "with maximal access to society's power resources, particularly political authority and control of the means of economic production" (Marger 1999: 273). (see also *majority (dominant) group*)

drug any substance—other than food or water—that, when taken into the body, alters its functioning in some way.

drug addiction (or drug dependency) a psychological and/or physiological need for a drug to maintain a sense of well-being and avoid withdrawal symptoms.

drug subculture a group of people whose attitudes, beliefs, and behaviours pertaining to drug use differ significantly from those of most people in the larger society.

dual-earner marriages marriages in which both spouses are in the labour force.

edge city a middle- to upper-middle-class area that has complete living, working, shopping, and leisure activities so that it is not dependent on the central city or other suburbs.

education the social institution responsible for transmitting knowledge, skills, and cultural values in a formally organized structure.

environmental degradation disruptions to the environment that have negative consequences for ecosystems.

environmental racism the belief that a disproportionate number of hazardous facilities are placed in areas populated primarily by poor people and people of colour.

environmental tobacco smoke the smoke in the air as a result of other people's tobacco smoking.

erotica materials that depict consensual sexual activities that are sought by and pleasurable to all parties involved.

ethnic group a category of people who are distinguished, by others or by themselves, on the basis of cultural or nationality characteristics. These can include language, country of origin, and adherence to culture.

ethnic pluralism the coexistence of diverse racialized/ethnic groups with separate identities and cultures within a society.

ethnocentrism the assumption that one's own group and way of life are superior to all others.

extended family a family unit composed of relatives in addition to parents and children, all of whom live in the same household.

family a relationship in which people live together with commitment, form an economic unit and care for any young, and consider the group critical to their identity.

family of orientation the family into which a person is born and in which early socialization takes place.

family of procreation the family that married or cohabiting couples create by having or adopting children.

feminization of poverty the trend whereby women are disproportionately represented among individuals living in poverty.

fertility the number of children born to an individual or a population.

fetal alcohol effects (FAE) a condition with some FAS characteristics that could include single birth defects, or developmental learning and behavioural disorders, that may not be noticed until months or years after the child's birth.

fetal alcohol syndrome (FAS) a condition characterized by mental retardation and craniofacial malformations that may affect the child of an alcoholic mother.

functionalist perspective a framework for viewing society as a stable, orderly system composed of a number of interrelated parts, each of which performs a function that contributes to the overall stability of society.

functionally illiterate being unable to read and/or write at the skill level necessary for carrying out everyday tasks.

gender culturally and socially constructed differences between females and males that are based on meanings, beliefs, and practices that a group or society associates with femininity or masculinity.

gender bias a situation in which favouritism is shown toward one gender.

gender ideology ideas of masculinity and femininity that are held to be valid in a given society at a specific historical time.

gendered division of labour the process whereby productive tasks are separated on the basis on gender.

gendered racism the interactive effect of racism and sexism in exploiting Indigenous and visible minority women.

genocide the deliberate, systematic killing of an entire people or nation.

gentrification the process by which people renovate or restore properties in central cities.

glass ceiling the invisible institutional barrier constructed by male management that prevents women from reaching top positions in major corporations and other large-scale organizations.

grassroots groups organizations started by ordinary people who work in concert to change a perceived problem in their neighbourhood, city, province or territory, or nation.

greenhouse effect an environmental condition caused by excessive quantities of carbon dioxide, methane, and nitrous oxide in the atmosphere.

hate crime an act of violence motivated by prejudice against people on the basis of racialized identity, ethnicity, religion, gender, or sexual orientation. This can include the dissemination of materials intended to incite hatred.

health maintenance organization (HMO) an organization that provides, for a fixed monthly fee, total health care with an emphasis on prevention to avoid costly treatment later.

heterosexism the belief that heterosexuality is the only normal, natural, and moral mode of relating, and hence is superior to homosexuality or bisexuality.

hidden curriculum how certain cultural values and attitudes, such as conformity and obedience to authority, are transmitted through implied demands in the everyday rules and routines of schools.

high-income nations countries with highly industrialized economies; technologically advanced industrial, administrative, and service occupations; and relatively high levels of national and per capita (per person) income.

homicide the unlawful, intentional killing of one person by another

homophobia the irrational and excessive fear or intolerance of homosexuals and homosexuality.

hospice an organization that provides a homelike facility or home-based care (or both) for people who are terminally ill.

iatrogenesis problems caused by doctors and the health care system.

income the economic gain derived from wages, salaries, income transfers (governmental aid, such as income assistance [welfare], or ownership of property).

indictable offence a more serious crime, such as murder, rape, or aggravated assault, that is punishable by more than a year's imprisonment or even death.

individual discrimination one-on-one acts by members of the dominant group that harm members of the subordinate group or their property.

industrialization the process by which societies are transformed from a dependence on agriculture and handmade products to an emphasis on manufacturing and related industries.

infant mortality rate the number of deaths of infants under one year of age per 1000 live births in a given year.

institutional discrimination the day-to-day practices of organizations and institutions that have a harmful impact on members of subordinate groups.

interactionist perspective a framework that views society as the sum of the interactions of individuals and groups.

internal colonialism a process that occurs when members of a racialized/ethnic group are conquered or colonized and forcibly placed under the economic and political control of the dominant group.

internalized dominance all the ways that White people learn they are normal, feel included, and do not think of themselves as "other" or "different."

intersectionality when people experience oppression in more than one aspect of their lives (e.g., sexism plus racism plus homophobia), the resulting oppression is greater than the sum of these oppressions.

intersexed having either unrecognizably male or female genitalia, or having both male and female genitalia

kinship a social network of people based on common ancestry, marriage, or adoption.

labelling theory the proposition that delinquents and criminals are those people who have been successfully labelled as such by others.

latent functions hidden, unstated, and sometimes unintended consequences of activities in an organization or institution.

life chances the extent to which individuals have access to important societal resources such as food, clothing, shelter, education, and health care.

life expectancy an estimate of the average lifetime of people born in a specific year.

lifestyle–routine activity approach the belief that the patterns and timing of people's daily movements and activities as they go about obtaining the necessities of life—such as food, shelter, companionship, and entertainment—are the keys to understanding violent personal crimes and other types of crime in our society.

low-income nations primarily countries with agrarian economies, little industrialization, and low levels of national and personal income.

low-level literate those who can maintain their current occupation but have minimal skills for adapting to a more complex occupation.

macrolevel analysis focuses on social processes occurring at the societal level, especially in large-scale organizations and major social institutions such as politics, government, and the economy.

majority (or dominant) group a group that is advantaged and has superior resources and rights in a society.

managed care any system of cost containment that closely monitors and controls health care providers' decisions about medical procedures, diagnostic tests, and other services that should be provided to patients.

manifest functions open, stated, and intended goals or consequences of activities within an organization or institution.

mass murder the killing of four or more people at one time and in one place by the same person.

master status the most significant status a person possesses because it largely determines how individuals view themselves and how they are treated by others.

mechanical solidarity social bonds based on shared religious beliefs and a simple division of labour.

medical–industrial complex encompasses both local physicians and hospitals as well as global health-related industries such as the pharmaceutical and medical supply companies that deliver health care.

medicalization the treating of a person's condition as an illness.

medicalization of crime the converting of criminal behaviour to a medical condition or disease.

megalopolis a continuous concentration of two or more cities and their suburbs that have grown until they form an interconnected urban area.

meritocracy a nation where the best person can rise to the top in any situation, despite his or her antecedents.

microlevel analysis focuses on small-group relations and social interaction among individuals.

middle-income nations countries undergoing transformation from agrarian to industrial economies.

migration the movement of people from one geographic area to another for the purpose of changing residency.

minority (or subordinate) group a group whose members, because of physical or cultural characteristics, are disadvantaged and subjected to negative discriminatory treatment by the majority group and regard themselves as objects of collective discrimination.

monogamy a marriage between one woman and one man.

monopoly a situation that exists when a single firm controls an industry and accounts for all sales in a specific market.

mortality the number of deaths that occur in a specific population.

norms established rules of behaviour or standards of conduct.

nuclear family a family unit composed of one or two parents and her/his/their dependent children who live apart from other relatives.

obscenity the legal term for pornographic materials that are offensive by generally accepted standards of decency.

occupational (white-collar) crime illegal activities committed by people in the course of their employment or normal business activity.

organic solidarity social bonds based on interdependence and an elaborate division of labour (specialization).

organized crime a business operation that supplies illegal goods and services for profit.

patriarchy a hierarchical system of social organization in which cultural, political, and economic structures are controlled by men.

pay equity equal pay for work of equal or comparable worth

peripheral nations nations that depend on core nations for capital, have little or no industrialization (other than what may be brought in by core nations), and have uneven patterns of urbanization.

perspective an overall approach or viewpoint toward some subject.

pink-collar ghetto where the jobs primarily held by women are relatively low-paying, non-manual, semiskilled.

plea bargaining a process whereby the Crown attorney negotiates with a defence attorney a reduced sentence in exchange for a guilty plea.

population composition the biological and social characteristics of a population, including such attributes as age, sex, racialization, marital status, education, occupation, income, and size of household.

pornography the graphic depiction of sexual behaviour though pictures and/or words—including by electronic or other data retrieval systems—in a manner that is intended to be sexually arousing.

poverty rate the proportion of the population whose income falls below the government's official poverty line—the level of income below which a family of a given size is considered to be poor.

power the ability of people to achieve their goals despite opposition from others.

prejudice a negative attitude about people based on such characteristics as racialization, gender, age, religion, or sexual orientation.

prestige the respect, esteem, or regard accorded to an individual or group by others.

primary deviance the initial act of rule breaking.

primary groups small, less-specialized groups (see *secondary groups*) in which members engage in face-to-face, emotion-based interactions over an extended period of time.

primary prevention programs that seek to prevent drug problems before they begin.

property crime the taking of money or property from another without force, the threat of force, or the destruction of property.

prostitution the sale of sexual services (of oneself or another) for money or goods and without emotional attachment.

punishment any action designed to deprive a person of things of value (including liberty) because of an offence the person is thought to have committed.

racialized group a category of people who have been singled out, by others or themselves, as inferior or superior, on the basis of subjectively selected physical characteristics such as skin colour, hair texture, and eye shape.

racism a set of attitudes, beliefs, and practices used to justify the superior treatment of one racialized or ethnic group and the inferior treatment of another racialized or ethnic group.

rape culture the pervasive system of cultural values, attitudes, and practices that support and perpetuate sexualized violence against women

relative poverty a condition that exists when people may be able to afford basic necessities, such as food, clothing, and shelter, but cannot maintain an average standard of living in comparison to that of other members of their society or group.

restorative justice the focus on repairing the harm caused by crime by holding moderated meetings of crime victims, offenders, and others affected by crime; restorative justice practices can be used at different sites in the justice system.

routine activities crime crime that occurs when a motivated offender finds a suitable target in the absence of suitable guardianship.

scapegoat a person or group that is blamed for some problem causing frustration and is therefore subjected to hostility or aggression by others.

second shift the domestic work that many employed women perform at home after completing their workday on the job.

secondary deviance the process that occurs when a person who has been labelled a deviant accepts that new identity and continues the deviant behaviour.

secondary groups larger, more-specialized groups (see *primary groups*) in which members engage in impersonal, goal-oriented relationships for a limited period of time.

segregation the spatial and social separation of categories of people by racialization, ethnicity, class, gender, religion, or other social characteristics.

self-fulfilling prophecy the process by which a false definition of a situation results in new behaviour that makes the original false conception become true.

self-health management includes self-care practices, mutual aid, and membership in self-help groups.

semiperipheral nations nations that are more developed than peripheral nations but less developed than core nations.

serial murder the killing of three or more people over more than a month by the same person.

sex the biological differences between females and males.

sexism the subordination of one sex, female, based on the assumed superiority of the other sex, male.

sexual assault an act of violence in which sex is used as a weapon against a powerless victim.

sexual harassment unwanted sexual advances, requests for sexual favours, or other verbal or physical conduct of a sexual nature.

sexual orientation a preference for emotional–sexual relationships with individuals of the "same" sex (homosexuality), the "opposite" sex (heterosexuality), or both (bisexuality).

sexuality attitudes, beliefs, and practices related to sexual attraction and intimate relationships with others.

situational approach the belief that violence results from a specific interaction process, termed a "situational transaction."

social bond theory the proposition that criminal behaviour is most likely to occur when a person's ties to society are weakened or broken.

social change the alteration, modification, or transformation of public policy, culture, or social institutions over time.

social construct a classification of people based on social and political values—rather than a biological given.

social control the systematic practices developed by social groups to encourage conformity and discourage deviance.

social disorganization the conditions in society that undermine the ability of traditional social institutions to govern human behaviour.

social gerontology the study of the social (non-physical) aspects of aging.

social movement an organized group that acts collectively to promote or resist change through collective action.

social problem a social condition (such as poverty) or a pattern of behaviour (such as violence against women) that people believe warrants public concern and collective action to bring about change.

social stratification the hierarchical arrangement of large social groups on the basis of their control over basic resources.

society a large number of individuals who share the same geographical territory and are subject to the same political authority and dominant cultural expectations.

sociological imagination the ability to see the relationship between individual experiences and the larger society in which they are contextualized.

sociology the academic and scholarly discipline that engages in systematic study of human society and social interactions.

stereotypes overgeneralizations about the appearance, behaviour, or other characteristics of all members of a group.

strain theory the proposition that people feel strain when they are exposed to cultural goals that they cannot reach because they do not have access to culturally approved means of achieving those goals.

subculture a group of people who share a distinctive set of cultural beliefs and behaviours that set them apart from the larger society.

subculture of violence hypothesis the hypothesis that violence is part of the normative expectations governing everyday behaviour among young males in the lower classes.

subordinate group a group whose members, in relation to the dominant group (or groups), do not occupy positions of power (see also *minority group,* above).

summary offence a relatively minor crime that is punishable by a fine or less than a year in jail.

sustainable development meeting the needs of the present generations without compromising the ability of future generations to meet their needs.

theory a set of logically related statements that attempt to describe, explain, or predict social events.

theory of racial formation a theory that states that the government substantially defines racialized and ethnic relations.

tolerance a condition that occurs when larger doses of a drug are required over time to produce the same physical or psychological effect that was originally achieved by a smaller dose.

total institution a place where people are isolated from the rest of society for a period of time and come under the complete control of the officials who run the institution.

tracking assigning students to specific courses and educational programs on the basis of their test scores, previous grades, or both.

urbanization the process by which an increasing proportion of a population lives in cities rather than in rural areas.

values collective ideas about what is right or wrong, good or bad, and desirable or undesirable in a specific society.

victimless crime a crime that many people believe has no real victim because it involves willing participants in an economic exchange.

violence the use of physical force to cause pain, injury, or death or damage to property.

violent crime actions involving force or the threat of force against others.

wage gap the disparity between women's and men's earnings.

wealth the value of all economic assets, including income and savings, personal property, and income-producing property, minus one's liabilities or debts.

welfare state a nation in which the government intervenes in the welfare of its citizens through various social policies, programs, standards, and regulations.

withdrawal a variety of physical and/or psychological symptoms that habitual drug users experience when they discontinue drug use.

youth crime a violation of law or the commission of a status offence by a young person 12 to 17 years of age.

zero population growth a situation in which a population is totally stable, neither growing nor decreasing from year to year because births, deaths, and migration are in perfect balance.

REFERENCES

Aalbers, Manuel B. 2005. "Big Sister is Watching You: Gender Interaction and the Unwritten Rules of the Amsterdam Red-Light District." *The Journal of Sex Research* 42:54–62.

Abbate, Gay. 1998. "Gangs Small But Growing Roots: Police Hope to Arrest Development." *Globe and Mail,* November 20, A10.

ABC News Online. 2005. "Shrinking ozone hole 'proves pacts work.'" Retrieved Nov. 25, 2006 (HYPERLINK "http://www.abc.net.au/news/newsitems/200510/s148537.htm" http://www.abc.net.au/news/newsitems/200510/s1485373.htm).

Abella, Irving. 1989. *A Coat of Many Colours: Two Centuries of Jewish Life in Canada.* Toronto: Lester and Orpen Dennys.

Abella, Irving, and Harold Troper. 1991. *None Is Too Many: Canada and the Jews in Europe 1933–1948* (3rd ed.). Toronto: Lester and Orpen Dennys.

Abu-Laban, Sharon McIrvin and Susan A. McDaniel. 2001. "Beauty, Status, and Aging." In Nancy Mandell (Ed.), *Feminist Issues: Race, Class, and Sexuality* (3rd ed.). Toronto: Pearson, pp. 108–133.

Adams, Karen L., and Norma C. Ware. 1995. "Sexism and the English Language: The Linguistic Implications of Being a Woman." In Jo Freeman (Ed.), *Women: A Feminist Perspective* (5th ed.). Mountain View, CA: Mayfield Publishing, pp. 331–346.

Adams, Tom. 1991. *Grass Roots: How Ordinary People Are Changing America.* New York: Citadel Press.

Aday, David P., Jr. 1990. *Social Control at the Margins: Toward a General Understanding of Deviance.* Belmont, CA: Wadsworth.

Adlaf, Edward M. and Angela Paglia. 2003. *Drug Use Among Ontario Students: ODUS Highlights, 1977–2003.* (CAMH Research Documents No. 14). Toronto: Centre for Addiction and Mental Health.

Adlaf, Edward M., Angela Paglia, and Joseph H. Beitchman. 2002. *The Mental Health and Well-Being of Ontario Students 1991–2001: Findings from the OSDUS.* Toronto: Centre for Addiction and Mental Health.

Adler, Patricia A., Steven J. Kless, and Peter Adler. 1995. "Socialization to Gender Roles: Popularity Amongst Elementary School Boys and Girls." In E.D. Nelson and B.W. Robinson (Eds.), *Gender in the 1990s: Images, Realities and Issues.* Toronto: Nelson, pp. 119–141.

A Commitment to Training and Employment for Women (ACTEW). 1998. "ACTEW's Top 8 Reasons Why Workfare Won't Work." In Luciana Ricciutelli, June Larkin, and Eimear O'Neill (Eds.), *Confronting the Cuts: A Sourcebook for Women in Ontario.* Toronto: Inanna, pp. 96–97.

Akers, Ronald L. 1992. *Drugs, Alcohol, and Society: Social Structure, Process, and Policy.* Belmont, CA: Wadsworth.

Albrecht, Gary L. 1992. *The Disability Business: Rehabilitation in America.* Newbury Park, CA: Sage.

Alcoholics Anonymous. 1998. *A.A. Fact File.* Retrieved July 18, 2005 (http://www.alcoholics-anonymous.org).

Alexander, Karl L., Doris Entwisle, and Maxine Thompson. 1987. "School Performance, Status Relations, and the Structure of Sentiment: Bringing the Teacher Back In." *American Sociological Review,* 52:665–682.

Alexander, Priscilla. 1987. "Prostitution: A Difficult Issue for Feminists?" In Frederique Delacoste and Priscilla Alexander (Eds.), *Sex Work: Writings by Women in the Sex Industry.* San Francisco: Cleis Press, pp. 184–214.

Alfred, Taiaiake. 1999. *Peace, Power, Righteousness: An Indigenous Manifesto.* Don Mills, ON: Oxford University Press.

Allen, Paula Gunn. 1986. *The Sacred Hoop: Recovering the Feminine in American Indian Traditions.* Boston: Beacon Press.

Allman, Dan. 1999. *M is for Mutual, A is for Acts: Male Sex Work and AIDS in Canada.* Co-published with Health Canada; AIDS Vancouver; The HIV, Social, Behavioural, and Epidemiological Studies Unit, Faculty of Medicine, University of Toronto; and the Sex Workers Alliance of Vancouver. (http://www.walnet.org/members/dan_allman/mutualacts/index.html).

Allport, Gordon. 1958. *The Nature of Prejudice* (abridged ed.). New York: Doubleday/Anchor.

Almaguer, Tomás. 1995. "Chicano Men: A Cartography of Homosexual Identity and Behavior." In Michael S. Kimmel and Michael A. Messner (Eds.), *Men's Lives* (3rd ed.). Boston: Allyn and Bacon, pp. 418–431.

Altman, Lawrence K. 1996. "India Quickly Leads in H.I.V. Cases, AIDS Meeting Hears." *New York Times* (July 8):A8.

Alvi, Shahid, Walter DeKeseredy, and Desmond Ellis. 2000. *Contemporary Social Problems in North American Society.* Don Mills, ON: Addison-Wesley.

Alwin, Duane, Philip Converse, and Steven Martin. 1985. "Living Arrangements and Social Integration." *Journal of Marriage and the Family*, 47:319–334.

Ambert, Anne-Marie. 1998. *Divorce: Facts, Figures, and Consequences.* Ottawa: Vanier Institute of the Family.

American Association of University Women (AAUW). 1992. *The AAUW Report: How Schools Short-Change Girls.* Washington, DC: The AAUW Educational Foundation and National Educational Association.

American Psychiatric Association. 1994. *Diagnostic and Statistical Manual of Mental Disorders IV.* Washington, DC: American Psychiatric Association.

Amott, Teresa, and Julie Matthaei. 1991. *Race, Gender, and Work: A Multicultural Economic History of Women in the United States.* Boston: South End Press.

Anders, George. 1996. *Health against Wealth: HMOs and the Breakdown of Medical Trust.* Boston: Houghton Mifflin.

Andersen, Margaret L., and Patricia Hill Collins (Eds.). 1997. *Race, Class, and Gender: An Anthology* (3rd ed.). Belmont, CA: Wadsworth.

Anderssen, Erin. 2002. "Same-Sex Census Numbers Due Today." *Globe and Mail* (October 22):A9.

Angus Reid. 2006a. "Canadians Examine What Is Immoral." *Angus Reid Global Monitor: Polls & Research* (June 15). Retrieved October 4, 2006 (http://www.angus-reid.com/polls/index.cfm/fuseaction/viewItem/itemID/12241).

Angus Reid. 2006b. "Same-Sex Marriage Issue Settled, Say Canadians." *Angus Reid Global Monitor: Polls & Research* (June 21). Retrieved October 4, 2006 (http://www.angus-reid.com/polls/index.cfm/fuseaction/viewItem/itemID/12288).

Angus Reid. 2006c. "Irish Ponder Same-Sex Unions, Adoption." *Angus Reid Global Monitor: Polls & Research* (February 22). Retrieved October 23, 2006 (http://www.angus-reid.com/polls/index.cfm/fuseaction/viewItem/itemID/10964).

Annan, Kofi. 2002. "Beyond the Horizon." *Time* (August 26):46–47.

Anyon, Jean. 1980. "Social Class and the Hidden Curriculum of Work." *Journal of Education*, 162:67–92.

Appelbe, Alison. 2001. "Culture War: Trans-Sexual Fights for Right to Counsel Rape Victims." *CNS News* (April 17). (http://www.cnsnews.com/culture/archive/200104/CUL200 10417c.html).

Apple, Michael W. 1982. *Education and Power: Reproduction and Contradiction in Education.* London: Routledge & Kegan Paul.

Applebome, Peter. 1995. "For the Ultimate Safe School, Official Eyes Turn to Dallas." *New York Times* (September 20): A1, B8.

Applebome, Peter. 1996. "Grading For-Profit Schools: So Far, So Good." *New York Times* (June 26):A1, A13.

Aristophanes. 2003. *Lysistrata.* Adapted by Adam Webster (orig. published in 1996). Retrieved March 2, 2003 (http://www.lysistrataproject.com).

Armstrong, Pat, and Hugh Armstrong. 1996. *Wasting Away: The Undermining of Canadian Health Care.* Don Mills, ON: Oxford University Press.

Arnup, Katherine (Ed.). 1995. *Lesbian Parenting: Living with Pride and Prejudice.* Charlettetown, PEI: gynergy books.

Ash, Roberta. 1972. *Social Movements in America.* Chicago: Markham.

Atchley, Robert C. 2000. *Social Forces and Aging: An Introduction to Social Gerontology* (9th ed.). Belmont, CA: Wadsworth.

Aulette, Judy Root. 1994. *Changing Families.* Belmont, CA: Wadsworth.

Axinn, William G., and Arland Thornton. 1992. "The Relationship between Cohabitation and Divorce: Selectivity or Casual Influence?" *Demography*, 29(3):357–374.

Bagby, Meredith (Ed.). 1997. *Annual Report of the United States of America 1997.* New York: McGraw-Hill.

Bailey, Ian. 2002. "Dead Girl's Mother Hugs Bullying B.C. Teenager." *National Post* [online] (May 15).

Baker, G. Ross, Peter C. Norton, Virginia Flintoft et al. 2004. "The Canadian Adverse Effects Study: The Incidence of Adverse Effects in Canadian Hospitals." *Canadian Medical Association Journal*, 170 (11):1678–1686.

Baker, Jean M. 2002. *How Homophobia Hurts Children: Nurturing Diversity at Home, at School, and in the Community.* London: Harrington Park Press.

Balakrishnan, T.R., Evelyn Lapiere-Adamoyk, and Karol J. Krotk. 1993. *Family and Childbearing in Canada: A Demographic Analysis.* Toronto: University of Toronto Press.

Ballantine, Jeanne H. 1997. *The Sociology of Education: A Systematic Analysis* (4th ed.). Englewood Cliffs, NJ: Prentice-Hall.

Bandura, Albert. 1973. *Aggression: A Social Learning Analysis.* Englewood Cliffs, NJ: Prentice-Hall.

Bane, Mary Jo, and David T. Ellwood. 1994. *Welfare Realities: From Rhetoric to Reform.* Cambridge, MA: Harvard University Press.

Bannerji, Himani. 1995. *Thinking Through: Essays on Feminism, Marxism and Anti-Racism.* Toronto: Women's Press.

Barlow, Hugh D. 1996. *Introduction to Criminology* (7th ed.). New York: HarperCollins.

Barofsky, I. 1978. "Compliance, Adherence and the Therapeutic Alliance: Steps in the Development of Self-Care." *Social Science and Medicine*, 12:369–376.

Barrett, Stanley R. 1991. "White Supremists and Neo-Fascists: Laboratories for the Analysis of Racism in Wider Society."

In Ormond McKague (Ed.), *Racism in Canada*. Saskatoon: Fifth House, pp. 85–99.

Barry, Kathleen. 1995. *The Prostitution of Sexuality*. New York: New York University Press.

Basow, Susan A. 1992. *Gender Stereotypes and Roles* (3rd ed.). Pacific Grove, CA: Brooks/Cole.

Basrur, Sheila V. 2002. *Ten Key Carcinogens in Toronto Workplaces and Environment: Assessing the Potential for Exposure*. Toronto: Toronto Public Health.

Bauerlein, Monika. 1995. "The Borderless Bordello." *Utne Reader* (November–December):30–32.

Bawer, Bruce. 1994. *A Place at the Table: The Gay Individual in American Society*. New York: Touchstone.

"B.C. Man Guilty in Beating Death of Gay Man." 2004. *CTV News,* December 11. Retrieved October 23, 2006 (http://www.ctv.ca/scrvlct/ArticleNews/story/CTVNews/1102715020316_56/?hub=).

Beare, Margaret E. 1996. *Criminal Conspiracies.* Scarborough, ON: Nelson.

Becker, Howard S. 1963. *Outsiders: Studies in the Sociology of Deviance*. New York: Free Press.

Bedard, Gabriel. 2000. "Deconstructing Whiteness: Pedagogical Implications for Anti-Racism Education." In George J. Sefa-Dei and Agnes Calliste (Eds.), *Power, Knowledge and Anti-Racism Edication: A Critical Reader*. Halifax: Fernwood, pp. 41–56.

Beeghley, Leonard. 1989. *The Structure of Social Stratification in the United States*. Boston: Allyn and Bacon.

Beitel, Ashley H. and Ross D. Parke. 1998. "Parental Involvement in Infancy: The Role of Maternal and Paternal Attitudes." *Journal of Family Psychology,* 12(2):268–288.

Bélanger, Alain. 1998. "Trends in Contraceptive Sterilization." *Canadian Social Trends,* (Autumn):16–19.

Belle, Marilyn, and Kevin McQuillan. 1994. "Births Outside Marriage: A Growing Alternative." *Canadian Social Trends,* (Summer):14–17.

Belsky, Janet. 1990. *The Psychology of Aging: Theory, Research, and Interventions* (2nd ed.). Pacific Grove, CA: Brooks/Cole.

Bem, S.L. 1974. "The Measurement of Psychological Androgyny." *Journal of Consulting and Clinical Psychology,* 42:155–162.

Bennett, Niel G., Ann Klimas Blanc, and David E. Bloom. 1988. "Commitment and the Modern Union: Assessing the Link between Premarital Cohabitation and Subsequent Marital Stability." *American Sociological Review,* 53:127–138.

Benoit, Cecilia M. 2000. *Women, Work, and Social Rights: Canada in Historical and Comparative Perspective*. Scarborough, ON: Prentice Hall/Allyn and Bacon.

Benokraitis, Nijole V. 1993. *Marriage and Families: Changes, Choices, and Constraints*. Englewood Cliffs, NJ: Prentice-Hall.

Benokraitis, Nijole V., and Joe R. Feagin. 1995. *Modern Sexism: Blatant, Subtle, and Covert Discrimination*. Englewood Cliffs, NJ: Prentice-Hall.

Berger, Peter. 1963. *Invitation to Sociology: A Humanistic Perspective*. New York: Anchor.

Berger, Peter, and Hansfried Kellner. 1964. "Marriage and the Construction of Reality." *Diogenes,* 46:1–32.

Berger, Peter, and Thomas Luckmann. 1967. *The Social Construction of Reality: A Treatise in the Sociology of Knowledge*. Garden City, NY: Anchor Books.

Berger, Ronald J., Patricia Searles, and Charles E. Cottle. 1991. *Feminism and Pornography*. Westport, CT: Praeger.

Bergmann, Barbara R. 1986. *The Economic Emergence of Women*. New York: Basic Books.

Bernard, Jessie. 1982. *The Future of Marriage*. New Haven, CT: Yale University Press.

Bess, Irwin. 1999. "Widows Living Alone." *Canadian Social Trends,* (Summer):2–5.

Besserer, Sandra, and Catherine Trainor. 2000. "Criminal Victimization in Canada, 1999." *Juristat,* 20(10).

Best, P. 1995. "Women, Men and Work." *Canadian Social Trends,* 36(Spring):30–33.

Bibby, Reginald. 1995. *The Bibby Report: Social Trends Canadian Style*. Toronto: Stoddart.

Bibby, Reginald W., and Donald C. Posterski. 1985. *The Emerging Generation: An Inside Look at Canada's Teenagers*. Toronto: Irwin.

Bibby, Reginald W., and Donald C. Posterski. 1992. *Teen Trends Canadian Style*. Toronto: Stoddart.

"Biography." n.d. LuAnn Mitchell-Halter Website. Retrieved October 19, 2006 (http://www.luanmitchell.com/biography/index.php).

Birgeneau, Robert J. 2002. "The Noise about Rising Tuition." *The University of Toronto Magazine,* (Summer).

Bishop, Anne. 2002. *Becoming an Ally: Breaking the Cycle of Oppression in People* (2nd ed.). Halifax: Fernwood.

Blackwood, E. 1986. "Breaking the Mirror: The Social Construction of Lesbianism and the Anthropological Discourse on Homosexuality." In *The Many Faces of Homosexuality: Anthropological Approaches to Homosexual Behavior*. New York: Harrington Park Press, pp. 1–17.

Blasius, Mark. 2001a. "An Ethos of Lesbian and Gay Existence." In Mark Blasius (Ed.), *Sexual Identities—Queer Politics*. Princeton, NJ: Princeton University Press, pp. 143–177.

Blasius, Mark. 2001b. "Sexual Identities, Queer Politics, and the Status of Knowledge." In Mark Blasius (Ed.), *Sexual Identities—Queer Politics*. Princeton, NJ: Princeton University Press, pp. 3–19.

Blauner, Robert. 1972. *Racial Oppression in America*. New York: Harper & Row.

Bluestone, Barry, and Bennett Harrison. 1982. *The Deindustrialization of America: Plant Closings, Community Abandonment, and the Dismantling of Basic Industry*. New York: Basic Books.

Bonacich, Edna. 1972. "A Theory of Ethnic Antagonism: The Split Labor Market." *American Sociological Review,* 37:547–549.

Bonacich, Edna. 1976. "Advanced Capitalism and Black–White Relations in the United States: A Split Labor Market Interpretation." *American Sociological Review,* 41:34–51.

Bonger, Willem. 1969. *Criminality and Economic Conditions* (abridged ed.). Bloomington, IN: Indiana University Press (orig. published in 1916).

Bonnin, Julie. 1997. "Knockout Drugs." *Austin American-Statesman* (February 2):E1, E12.

Bosetti, Lynn, et al. 2000. *Canadian Charter Schools at the Crossroads: Executive Summary.* Kelowna, BC: Society for the Advancement of Excellence in Education.

Bourassa, Kevin, and Joe Varnell. 2006. "First Gay Marriage Was Supported by CIBC." Equal Marriage for Same-Sex Couples (July 19). Retrieved October 4, 2006 (http://www.samesexmarriage.ca/advocacy/CIB190706.htm).

Bourdieu, Pierre, and Jean-Claude Passeron. 1990. *Reproduction in Education, Society, and Culture.* Newbury Park, CA: Sage.

Bourgeois, Philippe. 1995. *In Search of Respect: Selling Crack in el Barrio.* New York: Cambridge University Press.

Bourne, Larry S., and Damian Rose. 2001. "The Changing Face of Canada: The Uneven Geographies of Population and Social Change." *Canadian Geographer,* 45(1):105–119.

Bowles, Samuel, and Herbert Gintis. 1976. *Schooling in Capitalist America: Education and the Contradictions of Economic Life.* New York: Basic Books.

Bowles, Samuel, and Herbert Gintis. 2002. "Schooling in Capitalist America Revisited." *Sociology of Education,* 75(1):1–18.

Boyd, Monica. 2004. "Gender Inequality: Economic and Political Aspects." In Robert J. Brym (Ed.), *New Society: Sociology for the 21st Century,* (4th ed.). Toronto: Thomson Nelson, pp. 214–243 .

Boyd, Monica, and Doug Norris. 1999. "The Crowded Nest: Young Adults at Home." *Canadian Social Trends* (Spring):2–5.

Bradsher, Keith. 1997. "In the Biggest, Booming Cities, a Car Population Problem." *New York Times* (May 11):E4.

Brannigan, Augustine, Louis Knafla, and Christopher Levy. 1989. *Street Prostitution: Assessing the Impact of the Law—Calgary, Regina, Winnipeg.* Ottawa: Department of Justice Canada.

Brecher, Jeremy, and Tim Costello. 1998. *Global Village or Global Pillage: Economic Reconstruction From the Bottom Up* (2nd ed.). Cambridge, MA: South End Press.

Brennan, Richard. 2002. "Leave the Car, Take the Bus." *Toronto Star* (August 15):A1.

British Columbia (B.C.) Ministry of Attorney General. 1996. *Community Consultation on Prostitution in British Columbia: Overview of Results.* Victoria, BC: Ministry of Attorney General, Government of British Columbia.

British Columbia Ministry of Community Services, Women's Services. 2006. *A Minute of Silence: Statistics on Violence Against Women.* Retrieved July 31, 2006 (http://www.mcaws.gov.bc.ca/womens_services/a-minute-of-silence/weq_print.htm).

Brody, Jane E. 1996. "Good Habits Outweigh Genes as Key to a Healthy Old Age." *New York Times* (February 28):B9.

Brown, Phil. 1985. *The Transfer of Care: Psychiatric Deinstitutionalization and Its Aftermath.* Boston: Routledge & Kegan Paul.

Browne, Jan, and Victor Minichiello. 1995. "The Social Meanings Behind Male Sex Work: Implications for Sexual Interactions." *British Journal of Sociology,* 46(4):598–623.

Buechler, Steven M. 2000. *Social Movements in Advanced Capitalism: The Political Economy and Cultural Construction of Social Activism.* New York: Oxford University Press.

Bullard, Robert D., and Beverly H. Wright. 1992. "The Quest for Environmental Equity: Mobilizing the African-American Community for Social Change." In Riley E. Dunlap and Angela G. Mertig (Eds.), *American Environmentalism: The U.S. Environmental Movement, 1970–1990.* New York: Taylor & Francis, pp. 39–50.

Bullough, Vern, and Bonnie Bullough. 1987. *Women and Prostitution: A Social History.* Buffalo, NY: Prometheus.

Bumpass, Larry, James E. Sweet, and Teresa Castro Martin. 1990. "Changing Patterns of Remarriage." *Journal of Marriage and the Family,* 52:747–756.

Burke, Mary Anne, Joan Lindsay, Ian McDonald, and Gerry Hill. 1997. "Dementia among Seniors." *Canadian Social Trends,* (Summer):24–27.

Burke, R.J. 1994. "Canadian Business Students' Attitudes toward Women as Managers." *Psychological Reports,* 75:1123–1129.

Burns, John F. 1996. "Denial and Taboo Blinding India to the Horror of Its AIDS Scourge." *New York Times* (September 22):A1.

Busch, Ruth C. 1990. *Family Systems: Comparative Study of the Family.* New York: P. Lang.

Butler, Robert N. 1969. "Ageism: Another Form of Bigotry." *The Gerontologist,* 9:243–246.

Byrne, Caroline. 2005. "CCTV Helps Police Close in on Suspects." *Globe and Mail* (July 28): A9.

Cable, Sherry, and Charles Cable. 1995. *Environmental Problems, Grassroots Solutions: The Politics of Grassroots Environmental Conflict.* New York: St. Martin's Press.

Cameron, David. 1995. "The Making of a Polluter: A Social History of Uniroyal Chemical in Elmira." In Michael D. Mehta and Eric Ouellet (Eds.), *Environmental Sociology Theory and Practice.* North York, ON: Captus Press, pp. 297–320.

Campbell, Murray. 2005. "U.S. Pollution Is Killing Ontarians, Report Finds." *Globe and Mail* (June 17):A7.

Canadian Advisory Council on the Status of Women. 1984. *Prostitution in Canada.* Ottawa: Canadian Advisory Council on the Status of Women.

Canadian Association of Food Banks. 2002. *Hunger Count 2002—Eating Their Words: Government Failure on Food Security.* Prepared by Beth Wilson and Emily Tsoa. Toronto: Canadian Association of Food Banks.

Canadian Association of Food Banks. 2005. *Time for Action: Hungercount 2005*. Toronto, ON: Canadian Association of Foodbanks.

Canadian Centre for Justice Statistics (CCJS) (Ed.). 1999. *The Juristat Reader: A Statistical Overview of the Canadian Justice System*. Toronto: Thompson.

Canadian Centre for Justice Statistics (CCJS). 2001. "Canadian Crime Statistics, 2000." *Juristat,* 21(8).

Canadian Centre for Justice Statistics (CCJS). 2004. *Family Violence in Canada: A Statistical Profile, 2004.* Ottawa, ON: Statistics Canada. Catalogue NO. 85-224-XIE. Edited by Jodi-Anne Brzozowski.

Canadian Council on Social Development (CCSD) and the United Way of Greater Toronto (UWGT). 2000. *A Decade of Decline.* (http://www.uwgt.org/who_we_help/Decade_in_Decline/Poverty_Report.htm#key_findings).

Canadian Human Rights Commission. 2003. *Annual Report 2001: The Health of Human Rights in Canada.* Retrieved (http://www.chrc-ccdp.ca/ar-ra/RapportAnnuel2001/AR01RA/annualReport_1_rapportAnnuel.asp?l=e).

Canadian Institute for Health Information. 2001. *Health Care in Canada 2001.* Retrieved January 15, 2003 (http://secure.cihi.ca/cihiweb/dispPage.jsp?cw_page=AR_43_E&cw_topic=43).

Canadian Labour Congress. 2006. *Report Card 2005: Is Your Work Working for You?* Ottawa, ON: Canadian Labour Congress. (http://www.canadianlabour.ca).

Canadian Nuclear Association. 2002. July 30, 2002 (http://www.cna.ca).

Canadian Youth Rights Association (CYRA). 1998. "Media Ageism." Retrieved November 11, 1999 (http://www.cyra.org/media/shtml).

Canadian Taxpayers Federation. 2003. (http://www.taxpayer.com).

"Canadians Evenly Split on Legalizing Pot." 2001. *Globe and Mail* (June 25):A4.

"Canadians Want to Move On from Same-Sex Debate: PM." 2005. *CBC News.* Retrieved October 23, 2006 (http://www.cbc.ca/canada/story/2005/06/29/pm-samesex050629.html).

Cancian, Francesca M. 1990. "The Feminization of Love." In C. Carlson (Ed.), *Perspectives on the Family: History, Class, and Feminism.* Belmont, CA: Wadsworth, pp. 171–185.

Capponi, Pat. 1999. *The War at Home: An Intimate Portrait of Canada's Poor.* Toronto: Viking/Penguin.

Cargan, Leonard, and Matthew Melko. 1982. *Singles: Myths and Realities.* Newbury Park, CA: Sage.

Carmichael, Stokely, and Charles V. Hamilton. 1967. *Black Power: The Politics of Liberation in America.* New York: Vintage.

CARP. 1998. *CARP's National Forum on Scams and Frauds.* Toronto: CARP.

CARP. 2005a. "CARP Announces Canada's Best Employers for the 50+." Retrieved October 3, 2006 (http://www.carp.ca/display.cfm?DocumentID=1490&cabinetID=304&libraryID=70).

CARP. 2005b. *CARP's Fight Against Scams and Frauds.* Toronto: CARP.

Carrier, James G. 1986. *Social Class and the Construction of Inequality in American Education.* New York: Greenwood Press.

Carroll, William K. 1997. "Social Movements and Counterhegemony: Canadian Contexts and Social Theories." In William K. Carroll (Ed.), *Organizing Dissent: Contemporary Social Movements in Theory and Practice.* Toronto: Garamond Press, pp. 3–38.

Cass, Vivien C. 1984. "Homosexual Identity Formation: Testing a Theoretical Model." *Journal of Sex Research,* 20:143–167.

Castells, Manuel. 1977. *The Urban Question.* London: Edward Arnold.

Catalano, Ralph A., and William McConnell. 1996. "A Time-Series Test of the Quarantine Theory of Involuntary Commitment." *Journal of Health and Social Behavior,* 37:381–387.

Cavender, Gray. 1995. "Alternative Approaches: Labeling and Critical Perspectives." In Joseph F. Sheley (Ed.), *Criminology: A Contemporary Handbook* (2nd ed.). Belmont, CA: Wadsworth, pp. 349–367.

CBC TV. 1999. *Peacekeeping: The Invisible Wounds.*

Chambliss, William J. 1988. *Exploring Criminology.* New York: Macmillan.

Chaimie, Joseph. 2005. "21st Century Demographics: Highs and Lows." *The Globalist,* July 14. Retrieved July 14, 2005 (http://www.theglobalist.com/DBWeb/StoryId.aspx?StoryId=4629).

Chapkis, Wendy. 1997. *Live Sex Acts: Women Performing Erotic Labour.* New York: Routledge.

Chappell, Neena L. 1999. *Volunteering and Healthy Aging: What We Know.* Report for Volunteer Canada, Ottawa: Manulife Financial and Health Canada.

Chase-Lansdale, P. Lindsay, Jeanne Brooks-Gunn, and Roberta L. Palkoff. 1992. "Research and Programs for Adolescent Mothers: Missing Links and Future Promises." *Family Relations,* 40(4):396–403.

Cherlin, Andrew J. 1992. *Marriage, Divorce, and Remarriage* (rev. and enlarged ed.). Cambridge, MA: Harvard University Press.

Cherlin, Andrew J. 1999. "Going to Extremes: Family Structure, Children's Well-Being, and Social Science." *Demography,* 36(4):421–428.

Chermak, Steven M. 1995. *Victims in the News: Crime and the American News Media.* Boulder, CO: Westview.

Chidley, Joe. 1995. "Red Light District... From S & M to Bestiality, Porn Flourishes on the Internet." *Maclean's* (May 22):58.

Children Now. 1999. "Children Now Annual Report 1999 Highlights." (http://www.childrennow.org/annual-reports/annual-report-1999.htm).

Chudacoff, Howard P. 1989. *How Old Are You? Age Consciousness in American Culture.* Princeton, NJ: Princeton University Press.

Chui, Tina. 1996. "Canada's Population: Charting into the 21st century." *Canadian Social Trends,* (Autumn): 3–7.

Clark, Jocalyn. 1998. "The More Lady You Are, the More They Treat You Like a Lady: Sexual Harassment and Health Risk for Young Women in a Male-Dominated Work Setting." *Canadian Women's Studies,* 18(1):82–85.

Clark, Warren. 1996. "Adult Literacy in Canada, the United States, and Germany." *Canadian Social Trends* (Winter):27–33.

Clark, Warren. 1998. "Religious Observance, Marriage and the Family." *Canadian Social Trends,* (Autumn):2–7.

Cleeland, N. 1991. "Gasping in Smoggy Mexico City Oxygen Kiosk May Prove Helpful." *San Diego Union* (March 9). (Cited in Michael P. Soroka and George J. Bryjak. 1995. *Social Problems: A World at Risk.* Boston: Allyn and Bacon, p. 116.)

Clinard, Marshall B., and R. F. Meier. 1989. *Sociology of Deviant Behavior* (7th ed.). Fort Worth, TX: Holt, Rinehart and Winston.

Coale, Ansley. 1973. "The Demographic Transition." Proceedings of the International Population Conference, Liege. Vol. 1, pp. 53–72. (Cited in Weeks, 1992.)

Coalition for Lesbian and Gay Rights in Ontario (CLGRO). 1998. *Young People and Sex.* Pamphlet [online]. (May). (http://www.web.net/~clgro/consent/htm).

Cochrane, J., J. Durbin, and P. Goering. 1997. *Best Practices in Mental Health Reform.* Discussion paper prepared for the Federal/Provincial/Territorial Advisory Network on Mental Health. Ottawa: Health Canada.

Cohen, Lawrence E., and Marcus Felson. 1979. "Social Change and Crime Rate Trends: A Routine Activity Approach." *American Sociological Review,* 44:588–608.

Coleman, Eli. 1981/2. "Developmental Stages of the Coming Out Process." *Journal of Homosexuality,* 7:31–43.

Coles, Gerald. 1987. *The Learning Mystique: A Critical Look at "Learning Disabilities."* New York: Pantheon.

Collenette, David. 2002. "Where Ottawa Stands." *Globe and Mail* (June 24):T3.

Collins, Patricia Hill. 1991. *Black Feminist Thought: Knowledge, Consciousness, and the Politics of Empowerment.* New York: Routledge.

Collins, Randall. 1979. *The Credential Society: An Historical Sociology of Education.* New York: Academic Press.

Coltrane, Scott. 1989. "Household Labor and the Routine Production of Gender." *Social Problems,* 36:473–490.

Community Childhood Hunger Identification Project. 1995. *A Survey of Childhood Hunger in the United States.* Washington, DC: Food Research and Action Committee (July).

Comstock, Gary David. 1991. *Violence against Lesbians and Gay Men.* New York: Columbia University Press.

Connell, Christopher. 1995. "Birth Rate for Unmarried Women Surges." *Austin American-Statesman* (June 7):A18.

Corbeil, Jean-Pierre. 1998. "Literacy: Does Language Make a Difference?" *Canadian Social Trends,* (Winter):2–6.

Cormack, Elizabeth. 1999. "New Possibilities for a Feminism 'in' Criminology." *Canadian Journal of Criminology,* 41(2):161–170.

Corr, Charles A., Clyde M. Nabe, and Donna M. Corr. 1994. *Death and Dying, Life and Living.* Pacific Grove, CA: Brooks/Cole.

Cottle, Charles E., Patricia Searles, Ronald J. Berger, and Beth Ann Pierce. 1989. "Conflicting Ideologies and the Politics of Pornography." *Gender and Society,* 3:303–333.

Cottrell, Barbara. 2001. *Parent Abuse: The Abuse of Parents by Their Teenage Children.* Family Violence Prevention Unit, Ottawa: Health Canada. Cat. no. H72-21/180-2000E. Retrieved October 25, 2006 (http://www.phac-aspc.gc.ca/ncfv-cnivf/familyviolence/html/fvparentsabu_e.html).

Council of Canadians. 1999. "Trade and Investment Must Serve...." Retrieved March 7, 2003 (http://www.canadians.org/display_document.htm?COC_token=1@@465cb4da239ed216035817807630876d&id=332&isdoc=1&catid=133).

Coverman, Shelley. 1989. "Women's Work Is Never Done: The Division of Domestic Labor." In Jo Freeman (Ed.), *Women: A Feminist Perspective* (4th ed.). Mountain View, CA: Mayfield, pp. 356–368.

Cowan, Gloria, C. Lee, D. Levy, and D. Snyder. 1988. "Domination and Inequality in X-Rated Videocassettes." *Psychology of Women Quarterly,* 12:299–311.

Cowan, Gloria, and Margaret O'Brien. 1990. "Gender and Survival vs. Death in Slasher Films: A Content Analysis." *Sex Roles,* 23:187–196.

Cowley, Geoffrey. 1997. "Can Marijuana Be Medicine?" *Newsweek* (February 3):22–27.

Cox, Oliver C. 1948. *Caste, Class, and Race.* Garden City, NY: Doubleday.

Criminal Intelligence Service Canada. 2004. *Annual Report on Organized Crime in Canada.* Ottawa.

Crombie, David. 2001. "Grow Smart or Grow Worse." *Globe and Mail* (April 4):A15.

Crossette, Barbara. 1996a. "Agency Sees Risk in Drug to Temper Child Behavior: Worldwide Survey Cites Overuse of Ritalin." *New York Times* (February 29):A7.

Crossette, Barbara. 1996b. "U.N. Survey Finds World Rich-Poor Gap Widening." *New York Times* (July 15):A3.

Crossette, Barbara. 1996c. "Hope, and Pragmatism, for U.S. Cities Conference." *New York Times* (June 3):A3.

Crossette, Barbara. 2000. "Europe Stares at a Future Built by Immigrants." *New York Times* (January 2):WK1, 4.

CTV. 1995. *Hearts of Hate: The Battle For Young Minds.* Toronto: Investigative Productions.

Cullen, Dave. 1999. "The Reluctant Activist." *Salon* (October 15):1–4. Retrieved November 15, 1999 (http://www.salon.com/news/feature/1999/10/15/laramie/index.html).

Curatolo, Peter W., and David Robertson. 1983. "The Health Consequences of Caffeine." *Annals of Internal Medicine,* 98:641–653. (Cited in Levinthal, 1996.)

Currah, Paisley. 2001. "Queer Theory, Lesbian and Gay Rights, and Transsexual Marriages." In Mark Blasius (Ed.), *Sexual Identities—Queer Politics*. Princeton, NJ: Princeton University Press, pp. 178–199.

Curry, Bill. 2006. "Critics Blast Ottawa's 'Shameful' Green Plan." *Globe and Mail* (October 20):A1, A4.

Dagg, Anne Innis, and Patricia J. Thompson. 1988. *MisEducation: Women and Canadian Universities*. Toronto: OISE Press.

Daly, Kathleen, and Meda Chesney-Lind. 1988. "Feminism and Criminology." *Justice Quarterly,* 5:497–533.

Daniels, Ronald J. 2002. "Let's Reach for the Gold in Higher Education." *Globe and Mail* (March 1).

Danziger, Sheldon, and Peter Gottschalk. 1995. *America Unequal*. Cambridge, MA: Harvard University Press.

Dauvergne, Mia. 2005. "Homicide in Canada, 2004." *Juristat,* 25(6).

Dauvergne, Mia and Holly Johnson. 2001. "Children Witnessing Family Violence." *Juristat,* 21(6).

Davidson, Julia O'Connell. 1996. "Sex Tourism in Cuba." *Race and Class,* 38(1):39–49.

Davies, Scott, Janice Aurini, and Linda Quirke. 2002. "New Markets for Private Education in Canada." *Education Canada,* (Fall):36–38.

Davis, Kingsley. 1937. "The Sociology of Prostitution." *American Sociological Review,* 2:744–755.

Davis, Kingsley, and Amyra Grossbard-Shechtman (Eds.). 1985. *Contemporary Marriage: Comparative Perspectives on a Changing Institution*. New York: Russell Sage Foundation.

de Broucher, Patrice, and Laval Lavallée. 1998. "Getting Ahead in Life: Does Education Count?" *Canadian Social Trend,* (Summer):11–15.

DeKeseredy, Walter S., and Ronald Hinch. 1991. *Woman Abuse: Sociological Perspectives*. Toronto: Thompson.

Delk, J.L., R.B. Madden, M. Livingston, and T.T. Ryan. 1986. "Adult Perceptions of the Infant as a Function of Gender Labeling and Observer Gender." *Sex Roles,* 15:527–534.

Demczuk, Irene, Michele Caron, Ruth Rose, and Lyne Bouchard. 2002. *Recognition of Lesbian Couples: An Inalienable Right*. Ottawa: Status of Women Canada.

DeMont, John. 2002. "Cleaning Up the Harbour Has a Downside." *Maclean's* (July 29):19.

Denis, Angele. 2001. "Corridors: Language as Trap and Meeting Ground." In Carl E. James and Adrienne Shadd (Eds.), *Talking About Identity: Encounters in Race, Ethnicity and Language*. Toronto: Between the Lines, pp. 133–145.

Denton, M., and V. Walters. 1999. "Gender Differences in Structural and Behavioural Determinants of Health: An Analysis of Social Production of Health." *Social Science and Medicine,* 48:1221–1235.

Department of Justice, Canada. 2002. "Stronger Child Pornography Laws Receive Royal Assent" (June 10). Retrieved October 16, 2006 (http://canada.justice.gc.ca/en/news/nr/2002/doc_30529.html).

Department of Justice, Canada. 2006a. "Highlights of Bill C-2 Amendments to Protect Children and Other Vulnerable Persons: Backgrounder." *Newsroom* (March 31).

Department of Justice, Canada. 2006b. *Criminal Code*: Part XXII, Sentencing. Retrieved July 21, 2006 (http://laws.justice.gc.ca/en/c-46/268353.html).

Department of Justice, Canada. 2006c. *The Youth Criminal Justice Act: Summary and Background*. Retrieved September 20, 2006 (http://www.justice.gc.ca/en/ps/yj/ycja/explan.html).

DePasquale, Katherine M. 1999. "The Effects of Prostitution." Retrieved December 3, 1999 (http://www.feminista.com/v1n5/depasquale.html).

de Silva, Rex. 1980. "Developing the Third World." *World Press Review* (May):48.

"Despite 6-Year U.S. Campaign, Pornography Industry Thrives." 1993. *New York Times,* July 4, 10.

Devereaux, Anna. 1987. "Diary of a Prostitute." *Cosmopolitan* (October 1987):164, 166.

Devor, Aaron. 2003. Interview with Aaron Devor, Dean of Graduate Studies, University of Victoria, by Vicki Nygaard, February 20, 2003. See also Devor's website for more information and additional publications (web.uvic.ca/~ahdevor/).

Devor, Holly. 1989. *Gender Blending: Confronting the Limits of Duality*. Bloomington: Indiana University Press.

Devor, Holly. 1997. *FTM: Female to Male Transsexuals in Society*. Bloomington: Indiana University Press.

Dews, Peter B. 1984. "Behavioral Effects of Caffeine." In Peter B. Dews (Ed.), *Caffeine: Perspectives from Recent Research*. Berlin: Springer-Verlag, pp. 86–103. (Cited in Levinthal, 1996.)

Diamond, Jared. 2000. "The Greening of Corporate America." *New York Times* (January 8):A31.

Diamond, Sara. 1986. "Childhood's End: Some Comments on Pornography and the Fraser Committee." In J. Lowman, M.A. Jackson, T.S. Palys, and S. Gavigan (Eds.), *Regulating Sex: An anthology of Commentaries on the Findings of the Badgley and Fraser Reports*. Vancouver: School of Criminology, Simon Fraser University, pp. 143–158.

Diamond, Sara. 1988. "Pornography: Image and Reality." In Arlene Tigar McLaren (Ed.), *Gender and Society: Creating a Canadian Women's Sociology*. Mississauga, ON: Copp Clark Pitman, pp. 390–404.

Dickinson, Harley D. 2000. "Work and Unemployment as Social Issues." In B. Singh Bolaria (Ed.), *Social Issues and Contradictions in Canadian Society* (3rd ed.). Toronto: Harcourt Brace, pp. 26–50.

Dickinson, Harley D. 2002. "Mental Health Policy in Canada: What's the Problem?" In B. Singh Bolaria and Harley

D. Dickinson. (Eds.), *Health, Illness, and Health Care in Canada* (3rd ed.). Scarborough, ON: Nelson.

Dietz, P. 1986. "Mass, Serial and Sensational Homicide." *Bulletin of the New England Medical Society,* 62:477–491.

DiFranza, Joseph R., and Robert A. Lew. 1995. "Effect of Maternal Cigarette Smoking on Pregnancy Complications and Sudden Infant Death Syndrome." *The Journal of Family Practice,* 40:385–394.

Dimmock, Gary. 2002. "The Secret Life of a Teenage Cyber Informant." *Vancouver Sun* (June 29):A1, A14.

Dobrzynski, Judith H. 1996. "Study Finds Few Women in Five Highest Company Jobs." *New York Times* (October 16):C3.

"Do Canadians Feel Secure?" 2005. Editorial. *Globe and Mail* (August 11):A5.

Doezema, Jo. 1998. "Forced to Choose: Beyond the Voluntary v. Forced Prostitution Dichotomy." In Kamala Kempadoo and Jo Doezema (Eds.), *Global Sex Workers: Rights, Resistance and Redefinition.* New York: Routledge, pp. 34–50.

Dollard, John, Neal E. Miller, Leonard W. Doob, O. H. Mowrer, and Robert R. Sears. 1939. *Frustration and Aggression.* New Haven, CT: Yale University Press.

Donavon, Tina. 2001. "Being Transgender and Older: A First Person Account." *Journal of Gay and Lesbian Social Services: Issues in Practice, Policy and Research,* 13(4):19–22.

Donnelly, John. 2003. "CIA Had Idea of Contagion, and of Governments' Reactions." *Boston Globe.* Retrieved April 26, 2003 (http://www.boston.com/dailyglobe2/117/nation/).

Donziger, Steven R. (Ed.). 1996. *The Real War on Crime: The Report of the National Criminal Justice Commission.* New York: HarperPerennial.

Doob, Anthony N. and Jane B. Sprott. 2006. "Punishing Youth Crime in Canada: The Blind Men and the Elephant." *Punishment and Society,* 8(2):223–233.

Doyle, James A. 1995. *The Male Experience* (3rd ed.). Madison, WI: Brown and Benchmark.

Dua, Enakshi. 1999. "Canadian Anti-Racist Feminist Thought: Scratching the Surface of Racism." In Enakshi Dua and Angela Robertson (Eds.), *Scratching the Surface: Canadian Anti-Racist Feminist Thought.* Toronto: Women's Press, pp. 7–31.

Dubois, Julie. 2006. *Trends in Student Borrowing and Pathways: Evidences from the 1990, 1995 and 2000 Classes.* Human Resources and Skills Development Canada, Cat. No.: HS28-39/2006E-PDF. Retrieved September 25, 2006 (http://www11.hrsdc.gc.ca/en/cs/sp/hrsdc/lp/publicatios/2006-002850/page01.shtml)

Duffy, Anne, and Rina Cohen. 2001. "Violence Against Women: The Struggle Persists." In Nancy Mandell (Ed.), *Feminist Issues: Race, Class, and Sexuality* (3rd ed.). Toronto: Pearson, pp. 134–165.

Duffy, Ann, and Nancy Mandell. 2001. "The Growth in Poverty and Social Inequality: Losing Faith in Social Justice" in *Canadian Society: Meeting the Challenges of the 21st Century.* Don Mills, ON: Oxford University Press, pp. 77–116.

Dull, Diana, and Candace West. 1991. "Accounting for Cosmetic Surgery: The Accomplishments of Gender." *Social Problems,* 38(1):54–70.

Duncan, David F. 1991. "Violence and Degradation as Themes in 'Adult' Videos." *Psychology Reports,* 69(1):239–240.

Dunlap, David W. 1996. "Role of Openly Gay Episcopalians Causes a Rift in the Church." *New York Times* (March 21):A8.

Dunlap, Riley E. 1992. "Trends in Public Opinion toward Environmental Issues: 1965–1990." In Riley E. Dunlap and Angela G. Mertig (Eds.), *American Environmentalism: The U.S. Environmental Movement, 1970–1990.* New York: Taylor & Francis, pp. 89–113.

Durkheim, Emile. 1933. *Division of Labor in Society.* George Simpson. (Trans.) New York: Free Press (orig. published in 1893).

Durkheim, Emile. 1964. *The Rules of Sociological Method.* Sarah A. Solovay and John H. Mueller. (Trans.) New York: Free Press (orig. published in 1895).

Dworkin, Andrea. 1988. *Letters to a War Zone.* New York: Dutton/New America Library.

Dynes, Wayne R. (Ed.). 1990. *Encyclopedia of Homosexuality.* New York: Garland.

Eckersley, Robyn. 2001. "Ecofeminism and Environmental Democracy: Exploring the Connections." *Women & Environments International Magazine,* 52/53(Fall):23–26.

The Ecologist. 1993. *Whose Common Future? Reclaiming the Commons.* Philadelphia: New Society Publishers.

Ecumenical Coalition for Economic Justice. 1996. *Promises to Keep: Miles to Go: An Examination of Canada's Record in the International Year for the Eradication of Poverty.* Toronto: Ecumenical Coalition for Economic Justice.

Eder, Donna. 1985. "The Cycle of Popularity: Interpersonal Relations among Female Adolescents." *Sociology of Education,* 58(July):154–165.

Eder, Donna, and Stephen Parker. 1987. "The Cultural Production and Reproduction of Gender: The Effect of Extracurricular Activities on Peer Group Culture." *Sociology of Education,* 60:200–213.

Ehrenreich, Barbara, and Deirdre English. 1995. "Blowing the Whistle on the 'Mommy Track.'" In E.D. Nelson and B.W. Robinson (Eds.), *Gender in the 1990s: Images, Realities and Issues.* Toronto: Nelson, pp. 211–215.

Ehrlich, Paul R., and Anne H. Ehrlich. 1991. *The Population Explosion.* New York: Touchstone/Simon & Schuster.

Eichler, Margrit (Ed.). 1995. *Change of Plans: Towards a Non-Sexist City.* Toronto: Garamond Press.

Engelhardt, H. Tristan, Jr. 1996. *Foundations of Bioethics.* New York: Oxford University Press.

Engels, Friedrich. 1972. *The Origin of the Family, Private Property and the State.* New York: Pathfinder. (orig. published in 1884).

Environment Canada. 2002. "Quick Facts." Freshwater Website. Retrieved August 15, 2002 (http://www.ec.gc.ca/water/en/e_quickfacts.htm).

Epstein, Cynthia Fuchs. 1988. *Deceptive Distinctions: Sex, Gender, and the Social Order.* New Haven, CT: Yale University Press.

Epstein, Cynthia Fuchs. 1993. *Women in Law* (3rd ed.). Urbana, IL: University of Illinois Press.

Erikson, Kai T. 1962. "Notes on the Sociology of Deviance." *Social Problems,* 9:307–314.

Erikson, Kai T. 1991. "A New Species of Trouble." In Stephen Robert Crouch and J. Stephen Kroll-Smith (Eds.), *Communities at Risk: Collective Responses to Technological Hazards.* New York: Peter Land, pp. 11–29.

Essed, Philomena. 1990. *Everyday Racism: Reports from Women of Two Cultures.* Claremont, CA: Hunter House.

Essed, Philomena. 1991. *Understanding Everyday Racism.* Newbury Park, CA: Sage.

Esty, Daniel C., Marc Levy, Tanja Srebotnjak, Alexander de Sherbinin. (2005). *2005 Environmental Sustainability Index: Benchmarking National Environmental Stewardship.* New Haven: Yale Center.

Evans, Robert G., Kimberlyn M. McGrail, Steven G. Morgan, Morris L. Barer, and Clyde Hertzeman. 2001. "Apocalpyse Now: Population and the Future of Health Care Systems." *Canadian Journal on Aging,* 20(suppl. 1):160–191.

Eyles, John, S. Martin Taylor, Jamie Baxter, Doug Sider, and Dennis Willms. 1993. "The Social Construction of Risk in a Rural Community: Responses of Local Residents to the 1990 Hagersville (Ontario) Tire Fire." *Risk Analysis,* 13(3):281–290.

Fagot, Beverly I. 1984. "Teacher and Peer Reactions to Boys' and Girls' Play Styles." *Sex Roles,* 11:691–702.

FAO. 1995. *FAO Yearbook 1995.* Rome, Italy: Food and Agricultural Organization of the United Nations.

Feagin, Joe R. 1975. *Subordinating the Poor: Welfare and American Beliefs.* Englewood Cliffs, NJ: Prentice-Hall.

Feagin, Joe R., and Clairece Booher Feagin. 1999. *Social Problems: A Critical-Conflict Perspective* (5th ed.). Upper Saddle River, NJ: Prentice Hall.

Feagin, Joe R., and Robert Parker. 1990. *Building American Cities: The Urban Real Estate Game* (2nd ed.). Englewood Cliffs, NJ: Prentice-Hall.

Feagin, Joe R., and Melvin P. Sikes. 1994. *Living with Racism: The Black Middle-Class Experience.* Boston: Beacon Press.

Feagin, Joe R., and Hernán Vera. 1995. *White Racism: The Basics.* New York: Routledge.

Feodorowycz, Orest. 2001. "Homicide in Canada." *Juristat,* 21(9).

"Fifty People Arrested in Europe and Canada in Anti Money-Laundering Operation." 2002. Canadian Press. (June 10). Retrieved June 15, 2002 (http://www.canada.com/search/site/story.asp?id=DAA8BD19-BECF-4B9E-8083-D3E784E89179).

Findlay, Deborah A., and Leslie J. Miller. 2002. "Through Medical Eyes: The Medicalization of Women's Bodies." In B. Singh Bolaria and Harley D. Dickinson. (Eds.), *Health, Illness, and Health Care in Canada* (3rd ed.) Scarborough, ON: Nelson.

Fine, Gary Alan. 1987. *With the Boys: Little League Baseball and Preadolescent Culture.* Chicago: University of Chicago Press.

Fine, Michelle. 1991. *Framing Dropouts: Notes on the Politics of an Urban Public High School.* Albany, NY: State University Press of New York.

Finkelhor, David. 1984. *Child Abuse: New Theory and Research.* New York: Free Press.

Firestone, Shulamith. 1970. *The Dialectic of Sex.* New York: Morrow.

Fishbein, Diana H., and Susan E. Pease. 1996. *The Dynamics of Drug Abuse.* Boston: Allyn and Bacon.

Fisher, Lawrence M. 1996. "Health on Line: Doctor Is In, and His Disk Is Full." *New York Times* (June 14):C1, C8.

Fitzgerald, Robin. 1999. *Family Violence in Canada: A Statistical Profile, 1999.* Statistics Canada.

Flanagan, William G. 1995. *Urban Sociology: Images and Structure* (2nd ed.). Boston: Allyn and Bacon.

Fleras, Augie. 2001. *Social Problems in Canada: Conditions, Constructions, and Challenges* (3rd ed.). Toronto: Prentice Hall.

Fleras, Augie. 2005. *Social Problems in Canada: Conditions, Constructions and Challenges* (4th ed.). Toronto: Pearson Prentice Hall.

Fleras, Augie, and Jean Leonard Elliott. 1992. *The Challenge of Diversity: Multiculturalism in Canada.* Scarborough, ON: Nelson.

Fleras, Augie, and Jean Leonard Elliott. 1996. *Unequal Relations: An Introduction to Race, Ethnic and Aboriginal Dynamics in Canada.* Scarborough, ON: Prentice Hall.

Fleras, Augie, and Jean Leonard Elliott. 1999. *Unequal Relations: An Introduction to Race, Ethnic, and Aboriginal Dynamics in Canada* (3rd ed.). Scarborough, ON: Prentice Hall/Allyn and Bacon.

Fleras, Augie, and Jean Leonard Elliott. 2003. *Unequal Relations: An Introduction to Race and Ethnic Dynamics in Canada* (4th ed.). Toronto: Prentice Hall.

Florida, Richard. 2002. "Toronto 2020." *Globe and Mail* (June 24):T8.

Flynn, Karen. 1998. "Feeding Kids on Tuna and Bologna: The Impact of the Cuts on Single Black Women in Toronto." In Luciana Ricciutelli, June Larkin, and Eimear O'Neill (Eds), *Confronting the Cuts: A Sourcebook for Women in Ontario.* Toronto: Inanna, pp. 143–148.

Forcese, D. 1997. *The Canadian Class Structure* (4th ed.). Toronto: McGraw-Hill Ryerson.

Fox, Mary Frank. 1995. "Women and Higher Education: Gender Differences in the Status of Students and Scholars." In Jo Freeman (Ed.), *Women: A Feminist Perspective* (5th ed.). Mountain View, CA: Mayfield, pp. 220–237.

Frank, Jeffrey. 2000. "Fifteen Years of AIDS in Canada." In *Canadian Social Trends 3.* Ottawa: Minister of Supply and Services Canada, and Toronto: Thompson.

Frankenberg, Ruth. 1993. *White Women, Race Matters: The Social Construction of Whiteness.* Minneapolis: University of Minnesota Press.

Frederick, Judith A., and Monica Boyd. 1998. "The Impact of Family Structure on High School Completion." *Canadian Social Trends,* (Spring):12–18.

Freeze, Colin. 2001. "Support for Death Penalty Plunges." *Globe and Mail* (February 16):A1.

Freidan, Betty. 1963. *The Feminine Mystique.* New York: Norton.

Freiler, Christa, and Judy Cerny. 1998. *Benefiting Canada's Children: Perspectives on Gender and Social Responsibility.* (March). Ottawa: Research Directorate, Status of Women Canada.

French, Dolores, with Linda Lee. 1988. *Working: My Life as a Prostitute.* New York: E.P. Dutton.

Freudenberg, Nicholas, and Carl Steinsapir. 1992. "Not in Our Backyards: The Grassroots Environmental Movement." In Riley E. Dunlap and Angela G. Mertig (Eds.), *American Environmentalism: The U.S. Environmental Movement, 1970–1990.* New York: Taylor & Francis, pp. 27–37.

Freund, Matthew, Nancy Lee, and Terri Leonard. 1991. "Sexual Behavior of Clients with Street Prostitutes in Camden, New Jersey." *Journal of Sex Research,* 28(4) (November): 579–591.

Frideres, James S. 1999, "Altered States: Federal Policy and Aboriginal Peoples," In Peter S. Li (Ed.), *Race and Ethnic Relations in Canada.* Toronto: Oxford University Press, pp. 115–146.

Frideres, Jim S. 2002. "Overcoming Hurdles: Health Care and Aboriginal People." In B. Singh Bolaria and Harley D. Dickinson. (Eds.), *Health, Illness, and Health Care in Canada* (3rd ed.). Scarborough, ON: Nelson.

Friedan, Betty. 1993. *The Fountain of Age.* New York: Simon & Schuster.

Friedmann, John. 1995. "The World City Hypothesis." In Paul L. Knox and Peter J. Taylor (Eds.), *World Cities in a World-System.* Cambridge, England: Cambridge University Press, pp. 317–331.

Friend, Tim. 1996. "Teens and Drugs: Today's Youth Just Don't See the Dangers." *USA Today* (August 21):1A, 2A.

Fullilove, Mindy Thompson, E. Anne Lown, and Robert E. Fullilove. 1992. "Crack 'Hos and Skeezers: Traumatic Experiences of Women Crack Users." *Journal of Sex Research,* 29(2):275–288.

Gabor, Thomas. 1995. *Responding to School Violence: An Assessment of Zero Tolerance and Related Policies.* Ottawa: Solicitor General of Canada.

Gabriel, Trip. 1995a. "A New Generation Seems Ready to Give Bisexuality a Place in the Spectrum." *New York Times* (June 12):C10.

Gabriel, Trip. 1995b. "Some On-Line Discoveries Give Gay Youths a Path to Themselves." *New York Times* (July 2):1, 9.

Gabriel, Trip. 1996. "High-Tech Pregnancies Test Hope's Limit." *New York Times* (January 7):1, 10–11.

Gailey, Christine Ward. 1987. "Evolutionary Perspectives on Gender Hierarchy." In Beth B. Hess and Myra Marx Ferree (Eds.), *Analyzing Gender: A Handbook of Social Science Research.* Newbury Park, CA: Sage, pp. 32–67.

Galt, Virginia. 2002. "Health Workers Stressed Out, Study Says." *Globe and Mail* (January 23):A5.

Gamson, Joshua. 1994. *Claims to Fame: Celebrity in Contemporary America.* Berkeley, CA: University of California Press.

Gamson, William. 1990. *The Strategy of Social Protest* (2nd ed.). Belmont, CA: Wadsworth.

Gans, Herbert. 1982. *The Urban Villagers: Group and Class in the Life of Italian Americans* (updated and expanded ed.). New York: Free Press.

Gardner, Carol Brooks. 1995. *Passing By: Gender and Public Harassment.* Berkeley, CA: University of California Press.

Gardner, Tracey A. 1994. "Racism in Pornography and the Women's Movement." In Alison M. Jaggar (Ed.), *Living with Contradictions: Controversies in Feminist Social Ethics.* Boulder, CO: Westview, pp. 171–176.

Garreau, Joel. 1991. *Edge City: Life on the New Frontier.* New York: Doubleday.

Gawin, F. H., and E. H. Ellinwood, Jr. 1988. "Cocaine and Other Stimulants: Actions, Abuse, and Treatment." *New England Journal of Medicine,* 318:1173–1182.

Gee, Ellen, and M. Kimball. 1987. *Women and Aging.* Toronto: Butterworths.

Gee, Ellen M. and Susan A. McDaniel. 1991. "Pension Politics and Challenges: Retirement Policy Implications." *Canadian Public Policy-Analyse de politiques,* 17(4):456–472.

Gerson, Kathleen. 1993. *No Man's Land: Men's Changing Commitments to Family and Work.* New York: Basic Books.

Gerstel, Naomi, and Harriet Engel Gross. 1995. "Gender and Families in the United States: The Reality of Economic Dependence." In Jo Freeman (Ed.), *Women: A Feminist Perspective* (5th ed.). Mountain View, CA: Mayfield, pp. 92–127.

Gertler, Meric S. 2001. "Urban Economy and Society in Canada: Flows of People, Capital and Ideas." *Isuma,* 2(3):119–130.

Gessen, Masha. 1993. "Lesbians and Breast Cancer." *The Advocate* (February 9):22–23.

Gfellner, Barbara M., and John D. Hundleby. 1995. "Patterns of Drug Use among Native and White Adolescents: 1990–1993." *Canadian Journal of Public Health,* 86:95–97.

Gibbs, Lois Marie, as told to Murray Levine. 1982. *Love Canal: My Story.* Albany, NY: State University of New York Press.

Gil, Vincent E., Marco S. Wang, Allen F. Anderson, Guo Matthew Lin, and Zongjian Oliver Wu. 1996. "Prostitutes, Prostitution and STD/HIV Transmission in Mainland China." *Social Science and Medicine,* 42(1):141–153.

Gilbert, Richard J. 1986. *Caffeine: The Most Popular Stimulant.* New York: Chelsea House.

Gilder, George. 1981. *Wealth and Poverty.* New York: Basic Books.

Gillespie, Kerry. 2006. "Thousands Waiting for Housing Relief." *Toronto Star* (October 26):A1, A6.

Gilovich, Paula. 2002. "Invisible Sex." *Seattle International Film Festival News* (February 1). Retrieved October 23, 2006 (http://www.seattlefilm.org/news/detail.aspx?NID=14&year=2002).

Giobbe, Evelina. 1993. "Surviving Commercial Sexual Exploitation." In Diana E. H. Russell (Ed.), *Making Violence Sexy: Feminist Views on Pornography*. New York: Teachers College Press, pp. 37–41.

Giobbe, Evelina. 1994. "Confronting the Liberal Lies about Prostitution." In Alison M. Jaggar (Ed.), *Living with Contradictions: Controversies in Feminist Social Ethics*. Boulder, CO: Westview, pp. 120–136.

Gladwell, Malcolm. 1997. "Damaged: Why Do Some People Turn into Violent Criminals?" *The New Yorker* (February 24–March 3):132–147.

Glaser, Barney, and Anselm Strauss. 1968. *Time for Dying*. Chicago: Aldine.

Glazier, Richard H., Elizabeth M. Badley, Julie E. Gilbert, and Lorne Rothman. 2000. "The Nature of Increased Hospital Use in Poor Neighbourhoods: Findings from a Canadian Inner City." *Canadian Journal of Public Health,* 91(4): 268–273.

Gleick, Elizabeth. 1996. "The Children's Crusade." *Time* (June 3):30–35.

Glick, Paul C., and Sung-Ling Lin. 1986. "More Young Adults Are Living with Their Parents: Who Are They?" *Journal of Marriage and the Family*, 48:107–112.

Globe and Mail. 2005. "Those Racial Statistics." Editorial (May 28):A24

Goffman, Erving. 1961. *Asylums: Essays on the Social Situation of Mental Patients and Other Inmates*. Chicago: Aldine.

Gold, Rachel Benson, and Cory L. Richards. 1994. "Securing American Women's Reproductive Health." In Cynthia Costello and Anne J. Stone (Eds.), *The American Woman, 1994–1995*. New York: Norton, pp. 197–222.

Goldberg, Carey. 1997. "Quiet Roads Bringing Thundering Protests." *New York Times* (May 23):A8.

Goldberg, Joshua. 1998. Personal correspondence to a friend. Author's Files. Victoria, BC.

Goldberg, Robert A. 1991. Grassroots Resistance: Social Movements in Twentieth Century America. Belmont, CA: Wadsworth.

Golden, Anne, William H. Currie, Elizabeth Greaves, and E. John Latimer. 1999. *Taking Responsibility for Homelessness: An Action Plan for Toronto*. Toronto: City of Toronto.

Goldie, Terry (Ed). 2001. *In a Queer Country: Gay and Lesbian Studies in the Canadian Context*. Vancouver: Arsenal Pulp Press.

Goldstein, Amy. 2002. "Health Coverage Falls: Uninsured Numbers Up after 2 Years of Decline." *Washington Post.* (September 30): A1.

Goode, Erich. 1989. *Drugs in American Society* (3rd ed.). New York: McGraw-Hill.

Goode, William J. 1976. "Family Disorganization." In Robert K. Merton and Robert Nisbet (Eds.), *Contemporary Social Problems* (4th ed). New York: Harcourt Brace Jovanovich, pp. 511–554.

Goode, William J. 1982. "Why Men Resist." In Barrie Thorne with Marilyn Yalom (Eds.), *Rethinking the Family: Some Feminist Questions*. New York: Longman, pp. 131–150.

Gordon, David M. 1996. *Fat and Mean: The Corporate Squeeze of Working Americans and the Myth of Managerial "Downsizing."* New York: Martin Kessler Books/ The Free Press.

Gordon, Frances Linzee. 2000. *Lonely Planet Guide to Ethiopia, Eritrea, and Djibouti* (1st ed.). Victoria, Australia: Lonely Planet.

Gordon, Milton M. 1964. *Assimilation in American Life: The Role of Race, Religion, and National Origins.* New York: Oxford University Press.

Gordon, Robert M. 2000. "Criminal Business Organizations, Street Gangs and 'Wanna-be' Groups: A Vancouver Perspective." *Canadian Journal of Criminology,* 42(1):39–60.

Gottdiener, Mark. 1985. *The Social Production of Urban Space.* Austin, TX: University of Texas Press.

Gover, Tzivia. 1996b. "Occupational Hazards." *The Advocate* (November 26):36–38.

Graham, Ian D., and Paul M. Baker. 1989. "Status, Age, and Gender: Perceptions of Old and Young People." *Canadian Journal on Aging*, 8(3):255–267.

Graham, John R., Karen J. Swift, and Roger Delaney. 2000. *Canadian Social Policy: An Introduction.* Scarborough, ON: Prentice Hall/Allyn and Bacon.

Graveline, Fyre Jean. 2000. "Lived Experiences of an Aboriginal Feminist Transforming the Curriculum." In Carl E. James (Ed.), *Experiencing Difference.* Halifax: Fernwood, pp. 283–293.

Gray, Paul. 1996. "Gagging the Doctors." *Time* (January 8):50.

Green, K. 1985. "Identification of the Facets of Self-Health Management." *Evaluation and the Health Professions,* 8:323–338.

Greenberg, Edward S., and Benjamin I. Page. 1993. *The Struggle for Democracy.* New York: HarperCollins.

Greene, Mark. 2003. Press Release for The Lysistrata Project. Retrieved March 2, 2003 (http://www.pecosdesign.com/lys/press1).

Greene, Vernon L., and J. I. Ondrich. 1990. "Risk Factors for Nursing Home Admissions and Exits." *Journal of Gerontology*, 45:S250–S258.

Grillo, Trina, and Stephanie M. Wildman. 1996. "Obscuring the Importance of Race: the Implication of Making Comparisons Between Racism and Sexism (or Other isms)." In Stephanie M. Wildman (Ed.), *Privilege Revealed: How Invisible Preference Undermines America.* New York: New York University Press, pp. 85–102.

Grobe, Jeanine (Ed.). 1995. *Beyond Bedlam: Contemporary Women Psychiatric Survivors Speak Out.* Chicago: Third Side Press.

Gross, Leonard. 1983. *How Much Is Too Much: The Effects of Social Drinking.* New York: Random House.

Guslits, Mark. 2002. "*Let's Build* Leads Toronto's Affordable Housing Plans." *Canadian Housing,* 19(1):23–24.

Ha, Tu Thanh. 2004. "Former Boxer's Daughter Breaks Silence on Incest." *Globe and Mail* (October 14):A9.

Hacker, Andrew. 1995. *Two Nations: Black and White, Separate, Hostile, Unequal* (rev. ed.). New York: Ballantine Books.

Haddock, Vicki. 1999. "Study: Kids Are Hooked on Media." *Austin American-Statesman* (November 21):A32.

Hagan, John, John H. Simpson, and A.R. Gillis. 1987. "Class in the Household: A Power-Control Theory of Gender and Delinquency." *American Journal of Sociology,* 92:788–816.

Hall, Roberta M., with Bernice R. Sandler. 1982. *The Classroom Climate: A Chilly One for Women?* Washington, DC: Association of American Colleges, Project on the Status and Education of Women.

Hall, Roberta M. 1984. *Out of the Classroom: A Chilly Campus Climate for Women.* Washington, DC: Association of American Colleges, Project on the Status and Education of Women.

Hannigan, John A. 1995. *Environmental Sociology: A Social Constructionist Perspective.* New York: Routledge.

Hansell, Saul. 1996. "Identity Crisis: When a Criminal's Got Your Number." *New York Times* (June 16):E1, E5.

Hantover, Jeffrey P. 1998. "The Boy Scouts and the Validation of Masculinity." In Michael S. Kimmel and Michael A. Messner (Eds.), *Men's Lives* (4th ed.). Boston: Allyn and Bacon, pp. 101–108.

Hardina, Donna. 1997. "Workfare in the U.S.: Empirically Tested Programs or Ideological Quagmire?" In Eric Shragge (Ed.), *Workfare: Ideology for a New Under-Class.* Toronto: Garamond Press, pp. 131–148.

Harper, Charles L. 2001. *Environment and Society: Human Perspectives on Environmental Issues* (2nd ed.). Upper Saddle River, NJ: Prentice Hall.

"Harper Questions 'Legitimacy' of Same-Sex Bill as Vote Nears." 2005. *CBC News* (June 28). Retrieved October 23, 2006 (http://www.cbc.ca/canada/story/2005/06/27/samesex050627.html).

"Harper's Index." 2002. *Harper's* (March 13).

Harris, Judith R. 1998. *The Nurture Assumption: Why Children Turn Out the Way They Do.* New York: Free Press.

Harrison, Susan. 1997. "Working with Women." In Susan Harrison and Virginia Carver (Eds.), *Alcohol and Drug Problems: A Practical Guide for Counsellors.* Toronto: Addiction Research Foundation, pp. 219–244.

Hartley, Nina. 1994. "Confessions of a Feminist Porno Star." In Alison M. Jaggar (Ed.), *Living with Contradictions: Controversies in Feminist Social Ethics.* Boulder, CO: Westview, pp. 176–178.

Hartmann, Heidi. 1976. "Capitalism, Patriarchy, and Job Segregation by Sex." *Signs: Journal of Women in Culture and Society,* 1(Spring):137–169.

Hartmann, Heidi. 1981. "The Family as the Locus of Gender, Class, and Political Struggle: The Example of Housework." *Signs,* 6:366–394.

Hartnagel, Timothy F. 2004. "The Rhetoric of Youth Justice in Canada." *Criminal Justice* 4(4):355–374.

Hauchler, Ingomar, and Paul M. Kennedy (Eds.). 1994. *Global Trends: The World Almanac of Development and Peace.* New York: Continuum.

Havighurst, Robert J., Bernice L. Neugarten, and Sheldon S. Tobin. 1968. "Disengagement and Patterns of Aging." In Bernice L. Neugarten (Ed.), *Middle Age and Aging.* Chicago: University of Chicago Press, pp. 161–172.

Hawaleshka, Danylo. 2002. "Measuring Health Care." *Maclean's* (June 17):23–31.

Hawley, Amos. 1950. *Human Ecology.* New York: Ronald Press.

Hawley, Amos. 1981. *Urban Society* (2nd ed.). New York: Wiley.

Hays, Constance L. 1995. "If the Hair Is Gray, Con Artists See Green: The Elderly Are Prime Targets." *New York Times* (May 21):F1, F5.

Health Canada. 1993. *Family Violence and Substance Abuse.* Ottawa: National Clearinghouse on Family Violence.

Health Canada. 1998. *Canada's Drug Strategy.* Ottawa: Minister of Public Works and Government Services Canada.

Health Canada. 2002. "45 000 Deaths a Year." Retrieved March 15, 2002 (http://www.gosmokefree.ca).

Health Canada. 2006. *Factsheets.* Retrieved October 19, 2006 (http://www.hc-sc.gc.ca/hl-vs/tobac-tabac/fact-fait/fs-if/index_e.html).

"Health Care Needs of Gay Men and Lesbians in the United States." 1996. *JAMA: The Journal of the American Medical Association,* (May 1):1354–1360.

Hendrick, Dianne. 1999. "Youth Court Statistics 1997–98: Highlights." Canadian Centre for Justice Statistics (Eds.), *The Juristat Reader: A Statistical Overview of the Canadian Justice System.* Toronto: Thompson, pp. 85–100.

Hendriks, Aart, Rob Tielman, and Evert van der Veen. 1993. *The Third Pink Book: A Global View of Lesbian and Gay Liberation and Oppression.* Buffalo, NY: Prometheus.

Henry, Frances, and Carol Tator. 1999. "State Policy and Practices as Racialized Discourse: Multiculturalism, the *Charter,* and Employment Equity." In Peter S. Li (Ed.), *Race and Ethnic Relations in Canada* (2nd ed.). Don Mills, ON: Oxford University Press, pp. 88–115.

Henry, Frances, and Carol Tator. 2000. "The Theory and Practice of Democratic Racism in Canada." In Madeline A. Kalbach and Warren E. Kalbach (Eds.), *Perspectives on Ethnicity in Canada: A Reader.* Toronto: Harcourt Brace, pp. 285–302.

Henry, Francis, Carol Tator, Winston Mattis, and Tim Rees. 2000. *The Colour of Democracy: Racism in Canadian Society.* (2nd ed.). Toronto: Harcourt Brace.

Herek, Gregory M. 1995. "Psychological Heterosexism and Anti-Gay Violence: The Social Psychology of Bigotry and Bashing." In Michael S. Kimmel and Michael A. Messner

(Eds.), *Men's Lives* (3rd ed.). Boston: Allyn and Bacon, pp. 341–353.

Hessing, Melody. 1993. "Mothers' Management of Their Combined Workloads: Clerical Work and Household Needs." *Canadian Review of Sociology and Anthropology*, 301:37–63.

Hessing, Melody. 1995. "The Sociology of Sustainability: Feminist Eco/nomic Approaches to Survival." In Michael D. Mehta and Eric Ouellet (Eds.), *Environmental Sociology Theory and Practice*. North York, ON: Captus Press, pp. 231–254.

Hewa, Soma. 2002. "Physicians, the Medical Profession, and Medical Practice." In B. Singh Bolaria and Harley D. Dickinson. (Eds.), *Health, Illness, and Health Care in Canada* (3rd ed.). Scarborough, ON: Nelson.

Higley, Stephen Richard. 1995. *Privilege, Power and Place: The Geography of the American Upper Class*. Lanham, MD: Rowman & Littlefield.

Hills, Stuart L. 1971. *Crime, Power, and Morality*. Scranton, PA: Chandler.

Hirschi, Travis. 1969. *Causes of Delinquency*. Berkeley, CA: University of California Press.

Hirschi, Travis, and Michael J. Hindelang. 1977. "Intelligence and Delinquency: A Revisionist Review." *American Sociological Review*, 42:571–586.

Hochschild, Arlie Russell, with Ann Machung. 1989. *The Second Shift: Working Parents and the Revolution at Home*. New York: Viking/Penguin.

Hoffman, Andrew J. 1994. "Love Canal Lives." *E Magazine* (November–December):19–22.

Holloway, Kelly. 2002. "Black Students Slam U of T for Law Tuition Hike." *Varsity* (February 25).

Holmes, Ronald M. 1983. *The Sex Offender and the Criminal Justice System*. Springfield, IL: Charles C. Thomas.

Holmes, Robert M. 1988. *Serial Murder*. Beverly Hills, CA: Sage.

Holt, John C. 1964. *How Children Fail*. New York: Dell.

Hooks, Bell. 1984. *Feminist Theory: From Margin to Centre*. Boston: South End Press.

Hooyman, Nancy R., and H. Asuman Kiyak. 1996. *Social Gerontology: A Multidisciplinary Perspective*. Boston: Allyn and Bacon.

Hou, Feng and Garnett Picot. 2004. "Visible Minority Neighbourhoods in Toronto, Montréal, and Vancouver." *Canadian Social Trends*, (Spring 2004):8–13.

Houseknecht, Sharon, Suzanne Vaughn, and Anne Macke. 1984. "Marital Disruption among Professional Women: The Timing of Career and Family Events." *Social Problems*, 31(1):273–284.

Hulchanski, J. David. 1990. "Planning New Urban Neighbourhoods: Lessons from Toronto's St. Lawrence Neighbourhood." In *UBC Planning Papers*. Vancouver: School of Community and Regional Planning, University of British Columbia.

Human Resources Development Canada (HRDC). 2002. *Advancing the Inclusion of Persons With Disabilities*. Ottawa: Government of Canada report (December). (http://www.hrdc-drhc.gc.ca/hrib/sdd-dds/odi/documents/AIPD/ fdr000.shtml).

Husk, Norma. 1998. "Men's Resistance to Men's Education: The Personal is Political." *Canadian Women's Studies*, 17–4:107–112.

Huston, Aletha C. 1985. "The Development of Sex Typing: Themes from Recent Research." *Developmental Review*, 5:2–17.

Illich, Ivan. 1975. *Medical Nemesis*. London: Calder and Brown.

Immem, Wallace. 2002. "Village Scores High Marks for Quality of Urban Life." *Globe and Mail* (August 5):A10.

Inciardi, James, Dorothy Lockwood, and Anne E. Pottieger. 1993. *Women and Crack-Cocaine*. New York: Macmillan.

Infertility Awareness Association of Canada. 2003. Retrieved April 20, 2003 (http://www.iaac.ca/english/articles/insurance.asp).

Ingram, Gordon Brent. 2001. "Redesigning Wreck: Beach Meets Forest as Location of Male Homoerotic Culture and Placemaking in Pacific Canada." In Terry Goldie (Ed.), *In a Queer Country: Gay and Lesbian Studies in the Canadian Context*. Vancouver: Arsenal Pulp Press, pp. 188–208.

International Lesbian and Gay Association. 2006. "Working to Achieve Equal Rights on a Global Scale Since 1978," Retrieved October 5, 2006 (http://www.ilga.org/aboutilga.asp).

Ipsos-Reid. 2002. "Canadians Say Computer Hardware (86%) and Teacher Training (82%) are the Two Main Barriers to Greater Use of Computers and Internet in Schools." Retrieved July 10, 2002 (http://www.ipsos-rcid.com).

"It's Alarming How Many Aboriginals Are in Prison." 2006. Editorial. *Globe and Mail* (October 19.) Retrieved October 20, 2006 (http://www.theglobeandmail.com/servlet/story/RTGAM.20061019.wenative19/BNStory/special Comment/).

Jackson, Robert, and Doreen Jackson. 1996. *Canadian Government in Transition: Disruption and Continuity*. Scarborough, ON: Prentice Hall.

Jaffee, David. 1990. *Levels of Socio-economic Development Theory*. Westport, CT: Praeger.

Jankowski, Martín Sánchez. 1991. *Islands in the Street: Gangs and American Urban Society*. Berkeley, CA: University of California Press.

Jiwani, Yasmin. 1997. "Reena Virk: The Erasure of Race." The FREDA Centre for Research on Violence against Women and Children, Simon Fraser University, BC. (December). Retrieved (http://www.harbour.sfu.ca/freda/articles/virk.htm).

Johnson, Bruce D., Paul J. Goldstein, Edward Preble, James Schmeidler, Douglas S. Lipton, Barry Spunt, and Thomas Miller. 1985. *Taking Care of Business: The Economics of Crime by Heroin Abusers*. Lexington, MA: Lexington Books.

Johnson, Holly. 1996. *Dangerous Domains: Violence against Women in Canada.* Toronto: Nelson.

Jolin, Annette. 1994. "On the Backs of Working Prostitutes: Feminist Theory and Prostitution Policy." *Crime and Delinquency,* 40(1):69–83.

Jones, Charles, Lorna Marsden, and Lorne Tepperman. 1990. *Lives of Their Own: The Individualization of Women's Lives.* Don Mills, ON: Oxford University Press.

"A Journey of 10,000 Miles Begins with the Shoes." 1996. *Time* (June 17):78.

JUMP. 2002. (http://www.jumptutoring.org).

Jung, John. 1994. *Under the Influence: Alcohol and Human Behavior.* Pacific Grove, CA: Brooks/Cole.

Kadie, Carl. 1993. *Computers and Academic Freedom* [online]. (http://www.eff.org.CAF/news/nov_28_1993).

Kalish, Richard A. 1985. *Death, Grief, and Caring Relationships* (2nd ed.). Monterey, CA: Brooks/Cole.

Kaminer, Wendy. 1990. *A Fearful Freedom: Women's Flight from Equality.* Reading, MA: Addison-Wesley.

Kane, Hal. 1995. "Leaving Home." *Transaction: Social Science and Modern Society* (May–June):16–25.

Kantrowitz, Barbara. 1993. "Live Wires." *Newsweek* (September 6): 42–48.

Kaplan, Robert D. 1996. "Cities of Despair." *New York Times* (June 6):A19.

Katz, Janet, and William J. Chambliss. 1995. In Joseph F. Sheley (Ed.), *Criminology: A Contemporary Handbook* (2nd ed.). Belmont, CA: Wadsworth, pp. 275–303.

Katz, Stephen. 2000. "Busy Bodies: Activity, Aging, and the Management of Everyday Life." *Journal of Aging Studies,* 14(2):135–152.

Kazemipur, Abdolmohammad, and Shiva S. Halli. 2000. *The New Poverty in Canada: Ethnic Groups and Ghetto Neighbourhoods.* Toronto: Thompson.

Kazemipur, Abdolmohammed, and Shiva S. Halli. 2001. "The changing colour of poverty in Canada." *Canadian Review of Sociology and Anthropology.* 38(2): 217–238.

Kemp, Alice Abel. 1994. *Women's Work: Degraded and Devalued.* Englewood Cliffs, NJ: Prentice Hall.

Kempadoo, Kamala. 1998. "Introduction: Globalizing Sex Workers' Rights." In Kamala Kempadoo and Jo Doezema (Eds.), *Global Sex Workers: Rights, Resistance and Redefinition.* New York: Routledge, pp. 1–28.

Kempadoo, Kamala. 2005. "Victims and Agents of Crime: The New Crusade against Trafficking." In Julia Sudbury (Ed.), *Global Lockdown: Race, Gender, and the Prison-Industrial Complex.* New York, NY: Routledge, pp. 35–55.

Kempe, C. Henry, F. Silverman, B. Steele, W. Droegemueller, and H. Silver. 1962. "The Battered-Child Syndrome." *Journal of the American Medical Association,* 181:17–24.

Kempe, Ruth S., and C. Henry Kempe. 1978. *Child Abuse.* Cambridge, MA: Harvard University Press.

Kendall, Diana. 2000. *Sociology in Our Times: The Essentials* (2nd ed.). Belmont, CA: Wadsworth.

Kendall, Diana. 2001. *Social Problems in a Diverse Society* (2nd ed.). Needham Heights, MA: Allyn & Bacon, p. 28.

Kendall, Diana. 2004. *Social Problems in a Diverse Society* (3rd ed.). Needham Heights, MA: Allyn & Bacon.

Kennedy, Paul. 1993. *Preparing for the Twenty-First Century.* New York: Random House.

Kessler-Harris, Alice. 1990. *A Woman's Wage: Historical Meanings and Social Consequences.* Lexington, KY: University Press of Kentucky.

Khayatt, Didi. 2001. "Addendum to What Makes Lesbianism Thinkable? Theorizing Lesbianism From Adrienne Rich to Queer Theory." In Nancy Mandell (Ed.), *Feminist Issues: Race, Class and Sexuality.* Toronto: Prentice Hall, pp. 49–74.

Kidron, Michael, and Ronald Segal. 1995. *The State of the World Atlas.* New York: Penguin.

Kiel, Douglas P., David T. Felson, Marian T. Hanna, Jennifer J. Anderson, and Peter W. F. Wilson. 1990. "Caffeine and the Risk of Hip Fracture: The Framington Study." *American Journal of Epidemiology,* 132:675–684.

Kimmel, Michael S. 1987. "The Contemporary 'Crisis' in Masculinity in Historical Perspective." In Harry Brod (Ed.), *The Making of Masculinities.* Boston: Allen and Unwin, pp. 121–153.

Kimmel, Michael S. (Ed.). 1990. *Men Confront Pornography.* New York: Crown Books.

King, Leslie, and Madonna Harrington Meyer. 1997. "The Politics of Reproductive Benefits: U.S. Insurance Coverage of Contraceptive and Infertility Treatments." *Gender and Society,* 11(1):8–30.

Kingsley, Cherry, and Melanie Mark. 2000. *Sacred Lives: Canadian Aboriginal Children and Youth Speak Out about Sexual Exploitation.* Vancouver: Save the Children Canada.

Kingstone, Barbara. 2002. "Invisible Women." *Forever Young,* (June):42.

Kinsman, Gary. 1996. *The Regulation of Desire: Homo and Hetero Sexualities* (2nd ed., rev.). Montreal: Black Rose Books.

Kipnis, Laura. 1996. *Bound and Gagged: Pornography and the Politics of Fantasy in America.* New York: Grove Press.

Kirsch, Max H. 2000. *Queer Theory and Social Change.* London: Routledge.

Kitzinger, Celia. 1987. *The Social Construction of Lesbianism.* London: Sage.

Kivel, Paul. 1996. *Uprooting Racism: How White People Can Work for Racial Justice.* Philadelphia: New Society Publishers.

Klockars, Carl B. 1979. "The Contemporary Crises of Marxist Criminology." *Criminology,* 16:477–515.

Knapp, Caroline. 1996. *Drinking: A Love Story.* New York: Dial.

Knox, Paul L., and Peter J. Taylor (Eds.). 1995. *World Cities in a World-System.* Cambridge, England: Cambridge University Press.

Kolata, Gina. 1996a. "Experts Are at Odds on How Best to Tackle Rise in Teen-Agers' Drug Use." *New York Times* (September 18):A17.

Kolata, Gina. 1996b. "On Fringes of Health Care, Untested Therapies Thrive." *New York Times* (June 17):A1, C11.

Kosmin, Barry A., and Seymour P. Lachman. 1993. *One Nation under God: Religion in Contemporary American Society.* New York: Crown Trade Paperbacks.

Kremarik, Frances. 2000. "One Hundred Years of Urban Development." *Canadian Social Trends,* (Winter): 18–22.

Krohn, Marvin. 1995. "Control and Deterrence Theories of Criminality." In Joseph F. Sheley (Ed.), *Criminology: A Contemporary Handbook* (2nd ed.). Belmont, CA: Wadsworth, pp. 329–347.

Kübler-Ross, Elisabeth. 1969. *On Death and Dying.* New York: Macmillan.

Kunisawa, Byron. 1996. "Designs of Omission." Workshop handout. Cultural Solutions. Author's Files, Victoria, BC. (http://www.byronkunisawa.com).

Kurz, Demie. 1989. "Social Science Perspectives on Wife Abuse: Current Debates and Future Directions." *Gender and Society,* 3(4):489–505.

Kurz, Demie. 1995. *For Richer, for Poorer: Mothers Confront Divorce.* New York: Routledge.

Kyratzis, Amy. 2001. "Emotion Talk in Pre-School Same-Sex Friendship Groups: Fluidity over Time and Context." *Early Education and Development,* 12(3):359–392.

Lalonde, Marc. 1974. *A New Perspective on the Health of Canadians.* Ottawa: Minister of Supply and Services.

Lamanna, Marianne, and Agnes Riedmann. 1994. *Marriages and Families: Making Choices and Facing Change* (5th ed.). Belmont, CA: Wadsworth.

Langelan, Martha J. 1993. *Back Off! How to Confront and Stop Sexual Harassment and Harassers.* New York: Fireside/Simon & Schuster.

Langlois, Stéphanie, and Peter Morrison. 2002. "Suicide Deaths and Attempts." *Social Trends,* (Autumn):20–25.

Lappé, Frances Moore, and Paul Martin Du Bois. 1994. *The Quickening of America: Rebuilding Our Nation, Remaking Our Lives.* San Francisco: Jossey-Bass.

Laqueur, Thomas. 1992. *Making Sex: Body and Gender from the Greeks to Freud.* Cambridge, England: Harvard University Press.

Larkin, June. 1994. *Sexual Harassment: High School Girls Speak Out.* Toronto: Second Story Press.

Larkin, June, and Pat Staton. 1998. "If We Can't Get Equal, We'll Get Even: A Transformative Model of Gender Equity." *Canadian Women's Studies,* 17–4:16–22.

Lauderback, David, and Dan Waldorf. 1993. "Whatever Happened to ICE: The Latest Drug Scare." *Journal of Drug Issues,* 23:597–613.

Lauer, Robert H. 1995. *Social Problems and the Quality of Life* (6th ed.). Madison, WI: Brown.

Lauer, Robert H., and Jeannette C. Lauer. 1991. "The Long-Term Relational Consequences of Problematic Family Backgrounds." *Family Relations,* 40:286–290.

Lauer, Robert H., Jeanette C. Lauer, Zelda Abramson, and Jeanette A. Auger. 2006. *Social Problems and the Quality of Life, Canadian Edition.* Toronto, ON: McGraw-Hill Ryerson.

Laurence, Leslie, and Beth Weinhouse. 1994. *Outrageous Practices: The Alarming Truth About How Medicine Mistreats Women.* New York: Fawcett Columbine.

Layton, Jack. 2000. *Homelessness: The Making and Unmaking of a Crisis.* Toronto: Penguin/McGill Institute.

Leaper, Campbell. 1994. *Childhood Gender Segregation: Causes and Consequences.* San Francisco: Jossey-Bass.

Leaper, C., K. Anderson, and P. Sanders. 1998. "Moderators of Gender Effects of Parents' Talk to Their Children: A Meta-Analysis." *Developmental Psychology,* 34:3–27.

Lee, Felicia R. 1996. "Infertile Couples Forge Ties within Society of Their Own." *New York Times* (January 9):A1, A7.

Lee, Kevin K. 2000. *Urban Poverty in Canada: A Statistical Profile.* Ottawa: Canadian Council on Social Development.

Lefrançois, Guy R. 1999. *The Lifespan* (6th ed.). Belmont, CA: Wadsworth.

Lehmann, Jennifer M. 1994. *Durkheim and Women.* Lincoln, NE: University of Nebraska Press.

Lehne, Gregory K. 1995. "Homophobia among Men: Supporting and Defining the Male Role." In Michael S. Kimmel and Michael A. Messner (Eds.), *Men's Lives* (3rd ed.). Boston: Allyn and Bacon, pp. 325–336.

Leinen, Stephen. 1993. *Gay Cops.* New Brunswick, NJ: Rutgers University Press.

Leland, John. 1995. "Bisexuality." *Newsweek* (July 17):44–50.

Lemert, Edwin. 1951. *Social Pathology.* New York: McGraw-Hill.

Lengermann, Patricia Madoo, and Jill Niebrugge-Brantley. 1992. "Contemporary Feminist Theory." In George Ritzer (Ed.), *Contemporary Sociological Theory* (3rd ed.). New York: McGraw-Hill, pp. 308–357.

Leong, Wai-Teng. 1991. "The Pornography 'Problem': Disciplining Women and Young Girls." *Media, Culture, and Society,* 13:91–117.

Levin, Jack, and Jack McDevitt. 1993. *Hate Crimes: The Rising Tide of Bigotry and Bloodshed.* New York: Plenum.

Levin, William C. 1988. "Age Stereotyping: College Student Evaluations." *Research on Aging,* 10(1):134–148.

Levine, Peter. 1992. *Ellis Island to Ebbets Field: Sport and the American Jewish Experience.* New York: Oxford University Press.

Levinthal, Charles F. 1996. *Drugs, Behavior, and Modern Society.* Boston: Allyn and Bacon.

Lewin, Tamar. 1995. "The Decay of Families Is Global, Study Says." *New York Times* (May 30):A5.

Lewis, Oscar. 1966. *La Vida: A Puerto Rican Family in the Culture of Poverty—San Juan and New York.* New York: Random House.

Lexchin, Joel. 2002. "Profits First: The Pharmaceutical Industry in Canada." In B. Singh Bolaria and Harley D. Dickinson.

(Eds.), *Health, Illness, and Health Care in Canada* (3rd ed.). Scarborough, ON: Nelson.

Ley, D.F., and L.S. Bourne. 1993. "Introduction: The Social Context and Diversity of Urban Canada." In L.S. Bourne and D.F. Ley (Eds.), *The Changing Social Geography of Canadian Cities*. Montreal: McGill-Queen's University Press, pp. 3–30.

Lian, Jason Z., and David Ralph Matthews. 1998. "Does the Vertical Mosaic Still Exist? Ethnicity and Income in Canada, 1991." *Canadian Review of Sociology and Anthropology*, 35(4):461–481.

Liebow, Elliot. 1993. *Tell Them Who I Am: The Lives of Homeless Women*. New York: Free Press.

Lin Lap-Chew 1999. "Global Trafficking in Women: Some Issues and Strategies." *Women's Studies Quarterly*, 1(2):11–18.

Lindsey, Linda L. 2005. *Gender Roles: A Sociological Perspective* (4th ed.). Upper Saddle River, NJ: Pearson Prentice Hall.

Lips, Hilary M. 1993. *Sex and Gender: An Introduction* (2nd ed.). Mountain View, CA: Mayfield.

Logan, Ron. 2001. "Crime Statistics in Canada, 2000." *Juristat*, 21(8).

Lombardi, Emilia L., Riki Anne Wilchins, Dana Priesling, and Diana Malouf. 2001. "Gender Violence: Transgender Experiences with Violence and Discrimination." *Journal of Homosexuality*, 42(1):89–101.

Lomborg, Bjorn. 2001. *The Skeptical Environmentalist: Measuring the Real State of the World*. Cambridge, UK: Cambridge University Press.

Lommo, Charlene. 2001. "Adult Correctional Services in Canada." *Juristat*, 21(5).

London, Kathryn A. 1991. "Advance Data Number 194: Cohabitation, Marriage, Marital Dissolution, and Remarriage: United States 1988." U.S. Department of Health and Human Services. Vital and Health Statistics of the National Center, January 4.

London, Kathryn A., and Barbara Foley Wilson. 1988. "Divorce." *American Demographics*, 10(10):23–26.

Lorber, Judith. 1986. "Dismantling Noah's Ark." *Sex Roles*, 14(11–12):567–579.

Lorber, Judith. 1994. *Paradoxes of Gender*. New Haven, CT: Yale University Press.

Lottes, Ilsa. 1993. "Reactions to Pornography on a College Campus: For or Against?" *Sex Roles: A Journal of Research*, 29(1–2):69–90.

Loury, Glenn C. 1997. "Integration Has Had Its Day." *New York Times* (April 23):A21.

Lowman, John. 1997. *Submission to the Subcommittee on Solicitation Laws of the Standing Committee on Justice, Human Rights, Public Safety and Emergency Preparedness*. Retrieved October 20, 2006 (http://users.uniserve.com/~lowman/).

Lowman, John. 2000. "Violence and the Outlaw Status of (Street) Prostitution in Canada." *Violence Against Women*, 6(9):987–1011.

Lowman, John, Chris Atchison, and Laura Fraser. 1997. *Sexuality in the 1990s: Survey Results—Men Who Buy Sex, Phase Two*.

Retrieved October 20, 2006 (http://users.uniserve.com/~lowman/ICSS/ icss.htm).

Lowman, John and Laura Fraser. 1995. *Technical Report: Violence against Persons Who Prostitute: The Experience in British Columbia*. Department of Justice Canada TR1996-14e, Research, Statistics and Evaluation Directorate Policy Sector. Retrieved October 20, 2006 (http://users.uniserve.com/~lowman/).

Luckenbill, David F. 1977. "Criminal Homicide as a Situated Transaction." *Social Problems*, 25:176–186.

Luffman, Jacqueline. 1998. "When Parents Replace Teachers: The Home Schooling Option." *Canadian Social Trends*, (Autumn).

Luker, Kristin. 1996. *Dubious Conceptions: The Politics of Teenage Pregnancy*. Cambridge, MA: Harvard University Press.

Lundy, Katherine Coleman. 1995. *Sidewalk Talk: A Naturalistic Study of Street Kids*. New York: Garland.

Lunman, Kim. 2002. "Privacy Watchdog Sues RCMP Over Cameras." *Globe and Mail* (June 22):A1.

Lytton, H., and D.M. Romney. 1991. "Parents' Differential Socialization of Boys and Girls: A Meta-Analysis." *Psychological Bulletin*, 109:267–296.

Maccoby, Eleanor E., and Carol Nagy Jacklin. 1987. "Gender Segregation in Childhood." *Advances in Child Development and Behavior*, 20:239–287.

MacCorquodale, Patricia, and Gary Jensen. 1993. "Women in the Law: Partners or Tokens?" *Gender and Society*, 7(4):582–593.

MacDonald, Eleanor. 2000. "Critical Identities: Rethinking Feminism Through Transgender Politics" (1998). In Barbara Crow and Lise Gotell (Eds.), *Open Boundaries: A Canadian Women's Studies Reader*. Toronto: Prentice Hall, pp. 282–290.

MacDonald, Kevin, and Ross D. Parke. 1986. "Parental-Child Physical Play: The Effects of Sex and Age of Children and Parents." *Sex Roles*, 15:367–378.

Macdonald, Gayle. 2004. "Bring Back Geezer TV." *Globe and Mail* (January 19):R3.

Macdonald, Scott. 1995. "The Role of Drugs in Workplace Injuries: Is Drug Testing Appropriate?" *Journal of Drug Issues*, 25(4):703–723.

Macfarlane, Ronald, Monica Campbell, and Sheela V. Basrur. 2000. *Toronto's Air: Let's Make It Healthy*. Toronto: Toronto Public Health.

Macionis, John J. and Linda M. Gerber. 2002. *Sociology* (4th Can. ed.). Toronto: Pearson.

MacIssac, Rob. 2002. "Regional Thinking." *Globe and Mail* (June 24):T3.

Mackenzie, Hugh. 2002. "Cutting Classes: Elementary and Secondary Funding in Ontario." The Canadian Centre for Policy Alternatives. Retrieved July 20, 2002 (http://www.policyalternatives.ca).

Mackie, Marlene. 1987. *Constructing Women and Men: Gender Socialization*. Toronto: Holt, Rinehart.

Mackie, Marlene. 1991. *Gender Relations in Canada: Further Explorations*. Toronto: Harcourt Brace.

MacKinnon, Catharine. 1987. *Feminism Unmodified: Discourses on Life and Law.* Cambridge, MA: Harvard University Press.

Maclean's. 1999. "Annual Poll." (December 20).

Maclean's. 2002. "Annual Poll." (December 30).

MacLeod, Jay. 1995. *Ain't No Makin' It: Aspirations and Attainment in a Low-Income Neighborhood.* Boulder, CO: Westview Press.

MacMillan, Craig S., and Myron G. Claridge. 1998. "Criminal Proceedings as a Response to Hate." Paper presented at the "Hatred in Canada" conference, University of Victoria, Victoria, BC. (September).

Macy, Marianne. 1996. *Working Sex: An Odyssey into Our Cultural Underworld.* New York: Carroll & Graf.

Mahoney, Jill. 2002. "Proposals Back Private Care." *Globe and Mail* (January 9):A3.

Makin, Kirk. 2002. "Ontario Court Upholds Parents' Right to Spank." *Globe and Mail* (January 16):A1, A8.

Malarek, Victor. 2002. "Ontario Teens Suing School Board Over Bullying." *Globe and Mail* (June 3):A4.

Males, Mike. 1994. "Bashing Youth: Media Myths about Teenagers." *Extra!* (March/April). Retrieved November 11, 1999 (http://www.fair.org/extra/9403/bashing-youth.html).

Malette, Louise, and Marie Chalouh (Eds.). 1991. *The Montreal Massacre.* Marlene Wildman (Trans.). Charlottetown, PEI: gynergy books.

Malinowski, Bronislaw. 1964. "The Principle of Legitimacy: Parenthood, the Basis of Social Structure." In Rose Laub Coser (Ed.), *The Family: Its Structure and Functions.* New York: St Martin's Press.

Malthus, Thomas R. 1965. *An Essay on Population.* New York: Augustus Kelley, Bookseller (orig. published in 1798).

"Man Guilty of Child Porn Cartoons." 2005. *XBiz News,* October 20. Retrieved October 23, 2006 (http://www.xbiz.com/news_piece.php?id=10887).

Mann, P. 1993. *Hostile Hallways: The AAUW Survey on Sexual Harassment in America's Schools.* Washington, DC: AAUW Educational Foundation Council.

Mann, Patricia S. 1994. *Micro-Politics: Agency in a Post-Feminist Era.* Minneapolis: University of Minnesota Press.

Marable, Manning. 1995. *Beyond Black and White: Transforming African-American Politics.* New York: Verso.

Marger, Martin. 1999. *Social Inequality: Patterns and Processes.* Toronto: Mayfield.

Marger, Martin N. 1994. *Race and Ethnic Relations: American and Global Perspectives.* Belmont, CA: Wadsworth.

Marlowe, Julian. 1997. "It's Different for Boys," In Jill Nagle (Ed.), *Whores and Other Feminists.* New York, NY: Routledge.

Marshall, Barbara L. 2000. *Configuring Gender: Explorations in Theory and Politics.* Peterborough, ON: Broadview Press.

Marshall, Katherine. 2006. "Converging Gender Roles." *Perspectives*: 5–17. Statistics Canada Catalogue no. 75-001-XIE.

Marshall, Robert. 2001. "Where Can We Get the Best Care?" *Maclean's* (June 11):31–43.

Marshall, Victor W. 1980. *Last Chapters: A Sociology of Aging and Dying.* Monterey, CA: Brooks/Cole.

Marshall, Victor W., and Judith Levy. 1990. "Aging and Dying." In Robert H. Binstock and Linda George (Eds.), *Handbook of Aging and the Social Sciences* (3rd ed). New York: Academic Press.

Matas, Robert. 2002. "B.C. Police Lashed over Probe." *Globe and Mail* (February 9).

Martin, Carol L. 1989. "Children's Use of Gender-Related Information in Making Social Judgments." *Developmental Psychology,* 25:80–88.

Martin, Dianne. 2002. "Demonizing Youth, Marketing Fear: The New Politics of Crime." In Joe Hermer and Janet Mosher (Eds.), *Disorderly People: Law and the Politics of Exclusion in Ontario.* Halifax, NS: Fernwood Publishing, pp. 91–104.

Martin, Patricia Yancy. 1992. "Gender, Interaction and Inequality in Organizations." In Cecilia Ridgeway (Ed.), *Gender, Interaction and Inequality.* New York: Springer-Verlag, pp. 208–231.

Martin, Teresa Castro, and Larry L. Bumpass. 1989. "Recent Trends in Marital Disruption." *Demography,* 26:37–51.

Marx, Karl, and Friedrich Engels. 1971. "The Communist Manifesto." In Dirk Struik (Ed.), *The Birth of the Communist Manifesto.* New York: International. (orig. published in 1847).

Marx, Karl, and Friedrich Engels. 1976. *The Communist Manifesto.* New York: Pantheon (orig. published in 1848).

Mascoll, Philip. 2005. "Canada Lags on Affordable Universities." *Toronto Star* (April 19):A16.

Mascoll, Philip, and Jim Rankin. 2005. "Racial Profiling Exists." *Toronto Star* (March 31):A1.

Massey, Douglas S., and Nancy A. Denton. 1992. *American Apartheid: Segregation and the Making of the Underclass.* Cambridge, MA: Harvard University Press.

Massey, James L., and Marvin D. Krohn. 1986. "A Longitudinal Examination of an Integrated Social Process Model of Deviant Behavior." *Social Forces,* 65:106–134.

Mastrofski, Stephen D. 1995. "The Police." In Joseph F. Sheley (Ed.), *Criminology: A Contemporary Handbook* (2nd ed.). Belmont, CA: Wadsworth, pp. 373–405.

Mathis, Nancy. 1996. "Clinton Urges Student Uniforms." *Houston Chronicle* (February 25):6A.

Maticka-Tyndale, Eleanor, Jacqueline Lewis and Megan Street. 2005. "Making a Place for Escort Work: A Case Study." *Journal of Sex Research,* 42(1):46–53.

Maugh, T. 1990. "Sex: American Style Trend to the Traditional." *Los Angeles Times* (February 18):A1, A22.

Maxwell, Milton A. 1981. "Alcoholics Anonymous." In Martin S. Weinberg, Earl Rubington, and Sue Kiefer Hammersmith (Eds.), *The Solution of Social Problems: Five Perspectives* (2nd ed.). New York: Oxford University Press, pp. 152–156.

Mayall, Alice, and Diana E. H. Russell. 1993. "Racism in Pornography." In Diana E. H. Russell (Ed.), *Making Violence Sexy: Feminist Views on Pornography*. New York: Teachers College Press, pp. 167–177.

Maynard, Joyce. 1994. "To Tell the Truth." In Jay David (Ed.), *The Family Secret: An Anthology*. New York: William Morrow, pp. 79–85.

McAdie, Patricia. 1998. "The Abandonment of the Pursuit of Equity and the Implications for Education." *Canadian Women's Studies*, 17(4):6–15.

McCall, Nathan. 1994. Makes Me Wanna Holler: A Young Black Man in America. New York: Random House.

McDonald, L. 2000. "Alarmist Economics and Women's Pensions." In Ellen M. Gee and Gloria M. Gutman (Eds.), *The Overselling of Population Aging: Apocalyptic Demography, Intergenerational Challenges, and Social Policy*. Don Mills, ON: Oxford University Press: 114–128.

McDonald, Lynn, Brooke Moore, and Natalya Timoshkina. 2000. *Migrant Sex Workers from Eastern Europe and the Former Soviet Union: The Canadian Case*. Ottawa: Research Directorate, Status of Women Canada.

McIntosh, Peggy. 1995. "White Privilege and Male Privilege: A Personal Account of Coming to See Correspondences through Work in Women's Studies." In Margaret A. Andersen and Patricia Hill Collins (Eds.), *Race, Class, and Gender: An Anthology*. Belmont, CA: Wadsworth, pp. 76–87.

McKeown, David. 2005. *Summary Report: Influence of Weather and Air Pollution on Mortality in Toronto*. Toronto: Toronto Public Health.

McKinlay, John B. 1994. "A Case for Refocusing Upstream: The Political Economy of Illness." In Peter Conrad and Rochelle Kern (Eds.), *The Sociology of Health and Illness*. New York: St. Martin's Press, pp. 509–530.

McLanahan, Sara, and Gary D. Sandefur. 1994. *Growing Up with a Single Parent: What Hurts, What Helps*. Cambridge, MA: Harvard University Press.

McLaughlin, Hannah. 1995. "Homophobia in the Schools." In Katherine Arnup (Ed.), *Lesbian Parenting Living with Pride and Prejudice*. Charlettetown, PEI: gynergy books, pp. 238–250.

McMullan, John L. 1992. *Beyond the Limits of the Law: Corporate Crime and Law and Order*. Halifax: Fernwood Publishing.

McMullin, J.A., and Victor W. Marshall. 1996. "Family, Friends, Stress, and Well-Being: Does Childlessness Make a Difference?" *Canadian Journal on Aging*, 15(3): 355–373.

McMullin, J.A., and Victor W. Marshall. 1999. "Structure and Agency in the Retirement Process: A Case Study of Montreal Garment Workers." In C.D. Ryff and Victor W. Marshall (Eds.), *The Self and Society in Aging Processes*. New York: Springer-Verlag, pp. 305–338.

McNamara, Robert P. 1994. *The Times Square Hustler: Male Prostitution in New York City*. Westport, CT: Praeger.

McNeill, J.R. 2000. *Something New Under The Sun: An Environmental History of the Twentieth-Century World*. New York: Norton.

McPherson, Barry D. 1990. *Aging as a Social Process: An Introduction to Individual and Population Aging* (2nd ed.). Toronto: Butterworths.

McWilliams, Peter. 1996. *Ain't Nobody's Business If You Do: The Absurdity of Consensual Crimes in Our Free Country*. Los Angeles: Prelude Press.

Mead, Margaret. 1966. "Marriage in Two Steps." *Redbook*, 127:48–49, 85–86.

Mead, Rebecca. 1994. "Playing It Straight: In and Out of the Closet." *New York* (June 20):40–46.

"Medical Marijuana Still Not Widely Available: Report." 2006. *CBC News*. Retrieved October 19, 2006 (http://www.cbc.ca/health/story/2006/06/14/medical-marijuana.html).

"The Megacity Summit." 1996. *New York Times* (April 8):A14.

Mehta, Bina, and Kevin Spooner. 2000. "Glimpses of a Canadian Interracial Relationship." In Carl E. James (Ed.), *Experiencing Difference*. Halifax: Fernwood, pp. 150–162.

Mellor, Mary. 1997. *Feminism and Ecology*. New York: New York University Press.

Merton, Robert. 1938. "Social Structure and Anomie." *American Sociological Review*, 3(6):672–682.

Merton, Robert King. 1968. *Social Theory and Social Structure* (enlarged ed.). New York: Free Press.

Michael, Robert T., John H. Gagnon, Edward O. Laumann, and Gina Kolata. 1994. *Sex in America: A Definitive Survey*. New York: Warner Books.

Michelson, William H. 1976. *Man and His Urban Environment: A Sociological Approach*. Don Mills, ON: Addison-Wesley.

Middlestaedt, Martin. 2001. "Poll Finds Global Climate Change Hot Issue." *Globe and Mail*. (July 10):A4.

Mies, Maria, and Vandana Shiva. 1993. *Ecofeminism*. Atlantic Highlands, NJ: Zed Books.

Mighton, John. 2002. "Breaking the Cycle of Ignorance." *JUMP Teaching Manual*. Toronto: Junior Undiscovered Math Prodigies.

Milan, Anne. 2000. "One Hundred Years of Families." *Canadian Social Trends*, (Spring):2–12.

Milkman, Harvey, and Stanley Sunderwirth. 1987. *Craving for Ecstasy: The Consciousness and Chemistry of Escape*. Lexington, MA: Heath.

Millar, Alison E. 2002. "Leaving the Trade: Exiting Experiences of Former Sex Trade Workers in the CRD." Unpublished master's thesis, University of Victoria, Department of Sociology, Victoria, BC.

Millar, Wayne J. 2001. "Patterns of Use—Alternate Health Care Practitioners." *Health Reports*, 13(1):19–20.

Miller, Casey, and Kate Swift. 1991. *Words and Women: New Language in New Times* (updated). New York: HarperCollins.

Miller, Eleanor M. 1986. *Street Woman*. Philadelphia: Temple University Press.

Miller, J.R. 2002. "Residential Schools." *The Canadian Encyclopedia*. Retrieved October 20, 2002 (http://www.thecanadianencyclopedia.com/index.cfm?PgNm= TCE& TCE_Version=A&ArticleId=A0011547&MenuClosed =0).

Miller, James. 1996. "Out Family Values." In Marion Lynn (Ed.), *Voices: Essays on Canadian Families*. Toronto: Nelson.

Miller, Michael W. 1994. "Quality Stuff: Firm Is Peddling Cocaine, and Deals Are Legit." *Wall Street Journal* (October 17):A1, A14.

Mills, C. Wright. 1959a. *The Power Elite*. Fair Lawn, NJ: Oxford University Press.

Mills, C. Wright. 1959b. *The Sociological Imagination*. London: Oxford University Press.

Minnich, Elizabeth Kamarck. 1995. "Transforming Knowledge." In Sheila Ruth (Ed.), *Issues in Feminism* (3rd ed.). Mountain View, CA: Mayfield, pp. 413–429.

Mitchell, Alanna. 2000. "Waste Not: How Tricks from Tiny Holland Can Tame Canada's Garbage Beast." *Globe and Mail* (November 18):F4–5.

Moloney, Paul. 2002. "Canadian Cities to Urge Ottawa for Tax Powers." *Toronto Star* (May 23):A9.

Monahan, John. 1992. "Mental Disorder and Violent Behavior: Perceptions and Evidence." *American Psychologist*, 47:511–521.

Montemurro, B. 2003. "Not a Laughing Matter: Sexual Harassment as 'Material' on Workplace-Based Situation Comedies." *Sex Roles*, 48:433–445.

Mooney, Linda A., David Knox, Caroline Schacht, and Adie Nelson. 2001. *Understanding Social Problems* (1st Can. ed.). Scarborough, ON: Nelson Thomson Learning.

Mooney, Linda A., David Knox, Caroline Schacht, and Adie Nelson. 2003. *Understanding Social Problems* (2nd Can. ed.). Scarborough, ON: Nelson Thomson Learning.

Morel, Sylvie. 2002. *The Insertion Model or the Workfare Model? The Transformation of Social Assistance within Quebec and Canada*. Ottawa: Research Directorate, Status of Women Canada.

Morgan, Robin. 1993. *The Word of a Woman: Selected Prose 1968–1992*. London: Virago Press.

Morgan, S. Philip, Diane N. Lye, and Gretchen A. Condran. 1988. "Sons, Daughters, and the Risk of Marital Disruption." *American Journal of Sociology*, 94(1): 110–129.

Mosher, Steven W. 1994. *A Mother's Ordeal: One Woman's Fight against China's One-Child Policy*. New York: HarperPerennial.

Mothers Against Drunk Driving (MADD) Canada. 2006. "MADD: 'Ensure Safe Roads by Passing Drug-Impaired Driving Law Now.'" (Press release). Retrieved July 18, 2005 (http://www.madd.ca/english/news/pr/p05jun16.htm).

Muggeridge, Peter. 2001. "Report on Ageism." *CARPNews* (December 5).

Muszynski, Alicja. 2000. "The Social Construction/Deconstruction of Sex, Gender, Race and Class." In B. Singh Bolaria (Ed.), *Social Issues and Contradictions in Canadian Society* (3rd ed.). Toronto: Harcourt Brace, pp. 95–131.

Muto, Sheila. 1995. "Student Uniforms Pay Off, One School District Says." *New York Times* (September 20):B6.

Myles, John. 2000. "The Maturation of Canada's Retirement Income System: Income Levels, Income Inequality and Low Income among Older Persons." *Canadian Journal on Aging*. 19(3):287–316.

Nangeroni, Nancy R. 2001. *Transgenderism: Transgressing Gender Norms. GenderTalk*. (http://www.gendertalk.com/tgism/tgism.shtml).

Nath, Pamela S., John G. Borkowski, Thomas L. Whitman, and Cynthia J. Schellenbach. 1991. "Understanding Adolescent Parenting: The Dimensions and Functions of Social Support." *Family Relations*, 40:411–420.

National Council of Welfare. 2001a. *Child Poverty Profile—1998*. Ottawa: Minister of Public Works and Government Services Canada.

National Council of Welfare. 2001b. *The Cost of Poverty*, 115 (Winter 2001–2). Ottawa, ON: Minister of Public Works and Government Services Canada.

National Council of Welfare. 2004. *Poverty Profile, 2001*. Ottawa, ON: National Council of Welfare.

National Council of Welfare. 2006. *Poverty Profile, 2002 and 2003*. Ottawa, ON: Minister of Public Works and Government Services Canada. July.

National Public Radio (USA). 1992. Untitled report on parental responses to children. (July 23).

National Victims Resource Center. 1991. *Juvenile Prostitution: Fact Sheet*. Rockville, MD: Victims Resource Center.

Nava, Michael, and Robert Dawidoff. 1994. *Created Equal: Why Gay Rights Matter to America*. New York: St. Martin's Press.

Navarro, Mireya. 1996. "Marijuana Farms Are Flourishing Indoors, Producing a More Potent Drug." *New York Times* (November 24):13.

Naylor, C. David. 1999. "Health Care in Canada: Incrementalism under Fiscal Duress." *Health Affairs*, 18(3):9–26.

Nechas, Eileen, and Denise Foley. 1994. *Unequal Treatment: What You Don't Know about How Women Are Mistreated by the Medical Community*. New York: Simon & Schuster.

Nelson, Adie. 2006. *Gender in Canada* (3rd ed.). Toronto: Pearson Prentice Hall.

Nelson, Adie and Barrie W. Robinson. 2002. *Gender in Canada* (2nd ed.). Toronto: Pearson.

Nelson, Fiona. 1996. *Lesbian Motherhood: An Exploration of Canadian Lesbian Families*. Toronto: University of Toronto Press.

Newman, Zoe. 2001. "The Bisexuality Wars: The Perils of Identity as Marginality." In Terry Goldie (Ed.), *In a Queer*

Country: Gay and Lesbian Studies in the Canadian Context. Vancouver: Arsenal Pulp Press, pp. 122–137.

Niebuhr, Gustav. 1996. "Bishop Who Ordained Gay Deacon Is Accused of Heresy." *New York Times* (February 28):A8.

North American Commission for Environmental Cooperation (CEC). 2001. Retrieved August 12, 2002 (http://www.cec.org/pubs_docs/documents/index.cfm?varlan= english &ID=141).

North American Commission for Environmental Cooperation (CEC). 2002. Highlights from *The North American Mosaic: A State of the Environment Report.* Retrieved July 16, 2002 (http://www.cec.org/files.PDFPUBLICATIONS/soehigh_en.PDF).

Novak, Mark and Lori Campbell. 2006. *Aging and Society: A Canadian* Perspective (5th ed.). Toronto: Nelson.

Oakes, Jeannie. 1985. *Keeping Track: How Schools Structure Inequality.* New Haven, CT: Yale University Press.

O'Connell, Helen. 1994. *Women and the Family.* Prepared for the UN-NGO Group on Women and Development. Atlantic Highlands, NJ: Zed Books.

Oliver, Melvin L., and Thomas M. Shapiro. 1995. *Black Wealth/White Wealth: A New Perspective on Racial Inequality.* New York: Routledge.

Olsen, Gregg M. 2002. *The Politics of the Welfare State: Canada, Sweden, and the United States.* Don Mills, ON: Oxford University Press.

Olzak, Susan, Suzanne Shanahan, and Elizabeth H. McEneaney. 1996. "Poverty, Segregation, and Race Riots: 1960 to 1993." *American Sociological Review,* 61(August):590–613.

Omi, Michael, and Howard Winant. 1994. *Racial Formation in the United States: From the 1960s to the 1990s* (2nd ed.). New York: Routledge.

Orenstein, Peggy. 1996. "For Too Many Schoolgirls, Sexual Harassment Is Real." *Austin American-Statesman* (October 4):A15.

Otis, Leah. 1985. *Prostitution in Medieval Society.* Chicago: University of Chicago Press.

Ouimet, Marc. 1999. "Crime in Canada and in the United States: A Comparative Analysis." *Canadian Review of Sociology and Anthropology,* 36(3):389–408.

Overall, Christine. 2000. "Heterosexuality and Feminist Theory." In Barbara A. Crow and Lise Gotell (Eds.), *Open Boundaries: A Canadian Women's Studies Reader.* Toronto: Prentice Hall/Allyn and Bacon, pp. 262–269.

Owens, Anne Marie. 2002. "Feminist Shifts Focus to Boys." *National Post.* Retrieved June 27, 2002 (http://www.nationalpost.com).

Oxfam Canada. 2002. "Coffee Facts." Retrieved September 19, 2002 (http://www.oxfam.ca/news/MakeTradeFair/Launch02.htm).

Parker, Robert Nash. 1995. "Violent Crime." In Joseph F. Sheley (Ed.), *Criminology: A Contemporary Handbook* (2nd ed.). Belmont, CA: Wadsworth, pp. 169–185.

Parsons, Talcott. 1951. *The Social System.* New York: Free Press.

Parsons, Talcott. 1955. "The American Family: Its Relations to Personality and to the Social Structure." In Talcott Parsons and Robert F. Bales (Eds.), *Family, Socialization, and Interaction Process.* Glencoe, IL: Free Press, pp. 3–33.

Parsons, Talcott. 1966. *Societies: Evolutionary and Comparative Perspectives.* Englewood Cliffs, NJ: Prentice Hall.

Pateman, Carole. 1994. "What's Wrong with Prostitution?" In Alison M. Jaggar (Ed.), *Living with Contradictions: Controversies in Feminist Social Ethics.* Boulder, CO: Westview, pp. 127–132.

Paul, Pamela. 2002. *The Starter Marriage and the Future of Matrimony.* New York: Random House.

Pear, Robert. 1996. "Health Costs Pose Problems for Millions, a Study Finds." *New York Times* (October 23):A14.

Pear, Robert. 1997. "Academy's Report Says Immigration Benefits the U.S." *New York Times* (May 18):1, 15.

Pearce, Diana M. 1978. *The Feminization of Poverty: Women, Work, and Welfare.* Chicago: University of Illinois Press.

Pedicelli, Gabriella. 1998. *When Police Kill: Police Use of Force in Montreal and Toronto.* Montreal: Vehicule Press.

Pepler, Debra, Wendy Craig, and J. Connolly. 1997. *Bullying and Victimization: The Problems and Solutions for School Aged Children.* Ottawa: National Crime Prevention Council of Canada.

Peritz, Ingrid. 2005. "Report Often, Judge Orders Homolka." *Globe and Mail* (June 4):A6.

Perry, David C., and Alfred J. Watkins (Eds.). 1977. *The Rise of the Sunbelt Cities.* Beverly Hills, CA: Sage.

Perry-Jenkins, Maureen, and Ann C. Crouter. 1990. "Men's Provider Role Attitudes: Implications for Household Work and Marital Satisfaction." *Journal of Family Issues,* 11:136–156.

Peterborough Social Planning Council. 1998. "A Report on Hunger in Peterborough." In Luciana Ricciutelli, June Larkin, and Eimear O'Neill (Eds.), *Confronting the Cuts: A Sourcebook for Women in Ontario.* Toronto: Inanna, pp. 124–132.

Petersen, John L. 1994. *The Road to 2015: Profiles of the Future.* Corte Madera, CA: Waite Group Press.

Peterson, R. Dean, Delores F. Wunder, and Harlan L. Mueller. 1999. *Social Problems: Globalization in the Twenty-First Century.* Upper Saddle River, NJ: Prentice Hall.

Peterson, V. Spike, and Anne Sisson Runyan. 1993. *Global Gender Issues.* Boulder, CO: Westview Press.

Petras, James F. 1983. *Capitalist and Socialist Crises in the Late Twentieth Century.* Totowa, NJ: Rowman and Allenheld.

Pheasant, Valerie Bedassigae. 2001. "My Mother Used to Dance." In Carl E. James and Adrienne Shadd (Eds.), *Talking About Identity: Encounters in Race, Ethnicity and Language.* Toronto: Between the Lines, pp. 38–43.

Philip, Margaret. 2003. "Gayby Boom." *Globe and Mail* (May 3):F4–F5.

Picard, A. 2004. "Dieting Commonplace among Preteen Girls." *Globe and Mail* (May 11):A21.

Picard, Andre. 2005. "Cannabis Painkiller Approved." *Globe and Mail* (April 20):A15.

Pierce, Jennifer L. 1995. *Gender Trials: Emotional Lives in Contemporary Law Firms.* Berkeley, CA: University of California Press.

Plant, Geoff. 2005. Letter (May 13). Stop Homophobia. Retrieved October 23, 2006 (http://www.geocities.com/mattsmem/editorial14.html).

Pocklington, Tom, and Allan Tupper. 2002. *No Place to Learn: Why Universities Aren't Working.* Vancouver: UBC Press.

Pollack, Andrew. 1996. "Square Pegs Stay Home from Japan's Schools." *New York Times* (September 15):A4.

Ponse, Barbara. 1978. *Identities in the Lesbian World: The Social Construction of Self.* Westport, CT: Greenwood Press.

Pope, C. Arden III, Richard T. Burnett, Michael J. Thun, Eugenia E. Calle, Daniel Krewski, Kazuhiko Ito, and George D. Thurston. 2002. "Lung Cancer, Cardiopulmonary Mortality, and Long-Term Exposure to Fine Particulate Air Pollution." *Journal of the American Medical Association,* 287(9):1132–1141.

Popenoe, David. 1988. *Disturbing the Nest: Family Change and Decline in Modern Societies.* New York: Aldine de Gruyter.

Popenoe, David. 1995. "The American Family Crisis." *National Forum: The Phi Kappa Phi Journal,* 73(Summer 1995):15–19.

Popenoe, David. 1996. *Life without Father: Compelling New Evidence That Fatherhood and Marriage Are Indispensable for the Good of Children and Society.* New York: Martin Kessler/Free Press.

Population Action International [formerly Population Crisis Committee.] 1992. *Human Suffering Index.* Washington, DC: Population Crisis Committee.

Porteous, S. 1998. *Organized Crime: Impact Study (Highlights).* Ottawa: Solicitor General of Canada.

Potterat, John J., Donald E. Woodhouse, John B. Muth, and Stephen Q. Muth. 1990. "Estimating the Prevalence and Career Longevity of Prostitute Women." *Journal of Sex Research,* 27(May):233–243.

Public Health Agency of Canada. 2005. *A Guide to HIV/AIDS Epidemiological and Surveillance Terms.* Retrieved October 23, 2006 (http://www.phac-aspc.gc.ca/publicat/haest-tesvs/faq_e.html).

Purvis, Andrew. 1996. "The Global Epidemic: AIDS Is Tightening Its Grip on the Developing World." *Time* (December 30):76–78.

Quadagno, Jill, and Catherine Fobes. 1995. "The Welfare State and the Cultural Reproduction of Gender." *Social Problems,* 42(2):171–190.

Queen, Carol. 1997. *Real Live Nude Girl: Chronicles of Sex-Positive Culture.* Pittsburgh, PA: Cleis Press.

Rabinovich, Jannit and Megan Lewis. 2001. *The Story of PEERS: Prostitutes Empowerment, Education and Resource Society.* Vancouver: Save the Children.

Rank, Mark Robert. 1994. *Living on the Edge: The Realities of Welfare in America.* New York: Columbia University Press.

Rankin, Robert P., and Jerry S. Maneker. 1985. "The Duration of Marriage in a Divorcing Population: The Impact of Children." *Journal of Marriage and the Family,* 47(February):43–52.

Raphael, Ray. 1988. *The Men from the Boys: Rites of Passage in Male America.* Lincoln, NE: University of Nebraska Press.

Ratner, Robert S. 1997. "Many Davids, One Goliath." In William K. Carroll (Ed.), *Organizing Dissent: Contemporary Social Movements in Theory and Practice.* Toronto: Garamond Press, pp. 271–286.

Rawls, John. 1971. *A Theory of Justice.* Cambridge, MA: Harvard University Press.

RCMP. 2006a. *National Child Exploitation Coordination Centre (NCECC).* Retrieved October 23, 2006 (http://www.rcmp.ca/factsheets/fact_ncecc_e.htm).

RCMP. 2006b. Virtual Global Taskforce. Retrieved October 23, 2006 (http://ncecc.ca/vgt_e.htm).

Reckless, Walter C. 1967. *The Crime Problem.* New York: Meredith.

Reiss, I. L. 1986. *Journey into Sexuality: An Exploratory Voyage.* Englewood Cliffs, NJ: Prentice-Hall.

Relman, Arnold S. 1992. "Self-Referral—What's at Stake?" *New England Journal of Medicine,* 327 (November 19): 1522–1524.

Renzetti, Claire M., and Daniel J. Curran. 1995. *Women, Men, and Society* (3rd ed.). Boston: Allyn and Bacon.

Reskin, Barbara F., and Heidi Hartmann. 1986. *Women's Work, Men's Work: Sex Segregation on the Job.* Washington, DC: National Academy Press.

Reskin, Barbara F., and Irene Padavic. 1994. *Women and Men at Work.* Thousand Oaks, CA: Pine Forge.

Reynolds, Cecilia. 2001. "The Educational System." In Nancy Mandell (Ed.), *Feminist Issues: Race, Class, and Sexuality* (3rd ed.). Toronto: Pearson, pp. 242–259.

Reynolds, Helen. 1986. *The Economics of Prostitution.* Springfield, IL: Charles C. Thomas.

Ricciutelli, Luciana, June Larkin, and Eimear O'Neill. 1998. "Preface." In Luciana Ricciutelli, June Larkin, and Eimear O'Neill (Eds.), *Confronting the Cuts: A Sourcebook for Women in Ontario.* Toronto: Inanna, pp. Iiii.

Rich, Adrienne. 1984. "Compulsory Heterosexuality and Lesbian Existence." In Ann Snitnow, Christine Stansell, and Sharon Thompson (Eds), *Desire: The Politics of Sexuality.* London: Virago Press, pp. 212–241.

Richardson, Laurel. 1993. "Inequalities of Power, Property, and Prestige." In Virginia Cyrus (Ed.), *Experiencing Race, Class, and Gender in the United States.* Mountain View, CA: Mayfield, pp. 229–236.

Richmond, Todd. 2002. 365gay.com. Retrieved December 18, 2002 (www.365gay.com/lifestylechannel/intime/months/02-february/bath.htm).

Risman, Barbara J. 1987. "Intimate Relationships from a Microstructural Perspective: Men Who Mother." *Gender and Society,* 1:6–32.

Roberts, Nickie. 1992. *Whores in History: Prostitution in Western Society.* London: HarperCollins.

Robertson, Angela. 1999. "Continuing on the Ground: Feminists of Colour Discuss Organizing." In Enakshi Dua and Angela Robertson (Eds.), *Scratching the Surface: Canadian Anti-Racist Feminist Thought.* Toronto: Women's Press, pp. 309–329.

Robinson, David, Frank J. Porporino, William A. Millson, Shelley Trevethan, and Barry McKillop. 1999. "The One-Day Snapshot of Inmates in Canada's Adult Correctional Facilities." In Canadian Centre for Justice Statistics (Eds.), *The Juristat Reader: A Statistical Overview of the Canadian Justice System.* Toronto: Thompson, pp. 54–66.

Rochlin, M. 1982. "The Heterosexual Questionnaire." *Changing Men*, (Spring).

Roos, Noralou P., and L.L. Roos. 1994. "Small Area Variations, Practice Style, and Quality of Care." In R.G. Evans, M.L. Barer, and T.R. Marmor (Eds.), *Why Are Some People Healthy and Others Not? The Determinants of Health of Populations.* Hawthorne, NY: Aldine de Gruyter.

Roos, Patricia A., and Barbara F. Reskin. 1992. "Occupational Desegregation in the 1970s: Integration and Economic Equity?" *Sociological Perspectives*, 35:69.

Ropers, Richard H. 1991. *Persistent Poverty: The American Dream Turned Nightmare.* New York: Plenum.

Rose, Arnold. 1951. *The Roots of Prejudice.* Paris: UNESCO.

Rosenberg, Janet, Harry Perlstadt, and William Phillips. 1993. "Now That We Are Here: Discrimination, Disparagement and Harassment at Work and the Experience of Women Lawyers." *Gender and Society*, 7(3):415–433.

Rosenberg, Matt. 2006 "Maquiladoros in Mexico." Retrieved Nov. 25, 2006 (http://geography.about.com/od/urbaneconomicgeography/a/maquiladoras.htm).

Rosenthal, Carolyn J. 1987. "Aging and Intergenerational Relations in Canada." In Victor W. Marshall (Ed.), *Aging in Canada Social Perspectives* (2nd ed.). Markham, ON: Fitzhenry and Whiteside, pp. 311–342.

Rosenthal, Elisabeth. 1997. "The H.M.O. Catch: When Healthier Isn't Cheaper." *New York Times* (March 16):E1, E4.

Ross, David P., Katherine J. Scott, and Peter J. Smith. 2000. *The Canadian Fact Book on Poverty.* Ottawa: Canadian Council on Social Development.

Rossi, Peter H. 1989. *Down and Out in America: The Origins of Homelessness.* Chicago: University of Chicago Press.

Rothchild, John. 1995. "Wealth: Static Wages, Except for the Rich." *Time* (January 30):60–61.

Rothman, Robert A. 1993. *Inequality and Stratification: Class, Color, and Gender* (2nd ed.). Englewood Cliffs, NJ: Prentice-Hall.

Rowan, Ruby. 2001. "Sleeping with the Enemy and Liking It: Confessions of a Bi-Sexual Feminist." In Allyson Mitchell, Lisa Bryn Rundle, and Lara Karaian (Eds.), *Turbo Chicks: Talking Young Feminisms.* Toronto: Sumach Press, pp. 238–244.

Rowland, Robyn, and Renate Klein. 1996. "Radical Feminism: History, Politics, Action." In Diane Bell and Renate Klein (Eds.), *Radically Speaking: Feminism Reclaimed.* London: Zed Books, pp. 9–36.

Rubin, J.Z., F.J. Provenzano, and Z. Luria. 1974. "The Eye of the Beholder: Parents' Views on Sex of Newborns." *American Journal of Orthopsychiatry*, 44:512–519.

Rubin, Lillian B. 1976. *Worlds of Pain: Life in the Working-Class Family.* New York: Basic Books.

Rubin, Lillian B. 1994. *Families on the Fault Line.* New York: HarperCollins.

Rusk, James and Johanna Boffa. 2005. "Regent Park." *Globe and Mail* (April 2):M7.

Russell, Diana E. H. 1993. "Introduction." In Diana E. H. Russell (Ed.), *Making Violence Sexy: Feminist Views on Pornography.* New York: Teachers College Press, pp. 1–20.

Ryan, William. 1976. *Blaming the Victim* (rev. ed.). New York: Vintage.

Sacco, Vincent F., and Leslie W. Kennedy. 1998. *The Criminal Event* (2nd ed.). Scarborough, ON: Nelson.

Sachs, Aaron. 1994. "The Last Commodity: Child Prostitution in the Developing World." *World Watch*, 7(4) (July–August):24–31.

Sadker, David and Myra Sadker. 2002. "The Mis-education of Boys" in *The Jossey-Bass Reader on Gender and Education.* Susan M. Bailey (Ed.). San Francisco, CA: Jossey-Bass. Pgs. 182–203.

Sadker, Myra, and David Sadker. 1994. *Failing at Fairness: How America's Schools Cheat Girls.* New York: Scribner.

Safilios-Rothschild, Constantina. 1969. "Family Sociology or Wives' Family Sociology? A Cross-Cultural Examination of Decision-Making." *Journal of Marriage and the Family*, 31(2):290–301.

Sallot, Jeff. 1999. "Latimer Sentence Too Harsh, Poll Told." *Globe and Mail* (January 11):A5.

Sambugaro, Elaine. 2000. "Money Laundering Is on the Rise." *Metro* (October 25):10–11.

Sampson, Robert J. 1986. "Effects of Socioeconomic Context on Official Reactions to Juvenile Delinquency." *American Sociological Review*, 51(December):876–885.

Sanday, Peggy Reeves. 1996. *A Woman Scorned: Acquaintance Rape on Trial.* New York: Doubleday.

Sandler, Bernice R. 2004. "The Chilly Climate: Subtle Ways in which Women are often Treated Differently at Work and in Classrooms" in Joan Z. Spade and Catherine G. Valentine (Eds.), *The Kaleidoscope of Gender: Prisms, Patterns and Possibilities.* Belmost, CA: Wadsworth, pp. 187–190.

Sanger, David E. 2000. "In Leading Nations, a Population Bust?" *New York Times* (January 1):YNE8.

Sangera, Jyoti. 1997. "In the Belly of the Beast: Sex Trade, Prostitution and Globalization". Paper presented to the South Asia Regional Consultation on Prostitution, Bangkok,

Thailand. (http://www.hsph.harvard.edu/organizations/healthnet/SAsia/repro2/jyoti_sangera.htm).

Sapon-Shevin, Mara. 1993. "Gifted Education and the Protection of Privilege: Breaking the Silence, Opening the Discourse." In Lois Weis and Michelle Fine (Eds.), *Beyond Silenced Voices: Class, Race, and Gender in United States Schools.* Albany, NY: State University of New York Press, pp. 25–44.

Sassen, Saskia. 1995. "On Concentration and Centrality in the Global City." In Paul L. Knox and Peter J. Taylor (Eds.), *World Cities in a World-System.* Cambridge, England: Cambridge University Press, pp. 63–75.

Satzewich, Victor. 1989. "Racism and Canadian Immigration Policy: The Government's View of Caribbean Migration, 1962–66." *Canadian Ethnic Studies,* 30(1):77–97.

Saunders, John. 2001. "Furor Erupts as Police Seize Spanked Children." *Globe and Mail* (July 6):A1, A7.

Saunders, Ron. 2005. *Lifting the Boats: Policies to Make Work Pay.* Ottawa: Canadian Policy Research Networks Inc. June.

Sauvé, Julie. 2005. "Crime Statistics in Canada, 2004." *Juristat.* 25(5).

Sawyer, Janet. 1989. "Internalized Dominance." *Quarterly Change,* 1(4):16–23.

Schlaadt, R.G. 1992. *Alcohol Use and Abuse.* Guilford, CT: Duskin.

Schneider, Keith. 1993. "The Regulatory Thickets of Environmental Racism." *New York Times* (December 19): E5.

Schur, Edwin M. 1965. *Crimes without Victims: Deviant Behavior and Public Policy.* Englewood Cliffs, NJ: Prentice-Hall.

Scott, Denise Benoit. 1996. "Shattering the Instrumental-Expressive Myth: The Power of Women's Networks in Corporate-Government Affairs." *Gender and Society,* 10(3):232–247.

Seabrook, Jeremy. 2002. *The No-Nonsense Guide to Class, Caste, and Hierarchies.* Carlisle, England: Carel Press.

Seager, Joni. 1997. *The State of Women in the World Atlas* (2nd ed.). London: Penguin.

Searight, H. Russel, and Priscilla R. Searight. 1988. "The Homeless Mentally Ill: Overview, Policy Implications, and Adult Foster Care as a Neglected Resource." *Adult Foster Care Journal,* 2:235–259.

Seavor, Jim. 1996. "Closing the Books on Homophobia." *Austin American-Statesman* (November 24):E11.

Segal, Lynn. 1990. "Pornography and Violence: What the 'Experts' Really Say." *Feminist Review,* 36:29–41.

Segall, Alexander, and Neena L. Chappell. 2000. *Health and Health Care in Canada.* Toronto: Prentice Hall.

Séguin, Rhéal. 2005. "Quebec's Health Minister Eschews Tax Hike." *Globe and Mail* (July 29):A6.

Seidman, Steven. 1992. "An Investigation of Sex-Role Stereotyping in Music Videos." *Journal of Broadcasting & Electronic Media* (Spring):212.

Sen, Amartya. 1999. *Development as Freedom.* New York: Knopf.

Serbeh-Dunn, Gifty, and Wayne Dunn. 2001. "We Are All the Same—Just Because You Are Black Doesn't Matter." In Carl E. James and Adrienne Shadd (Eds.), *Talking About Identity: Encounters in Race, Ethnicity and Language.* Toronto: Between the Lines, pp. 267–276.

Sexually Exploited Youth Committee of the Capital Regional District. 1997. *Report of the Sexually Exploited Youth Committee of the Capital Regional District, Victoria, British Columbia.* Victoria, BC: City of Victoria.

Shedler, J., and J. Block. 1990. "Adolescent Drug Users and Psychological Health." *American Psychologist,* 45:612–630.

Sheehan, Molly O. 2002. "CFC Use Declining." *Vital Signs 2002: The Trends That are Shaping Our Future.* New York: Norton.

Sheff, David. 1995. "If It's Tuesday, It Must Be Dad's House." *New York Times Magazine* (March 26):64–65.

Sheldon, William H. 1949. *Varieties of Delinquent Youth: An Introduction to Constitutional Psychiatry.* New York: Harper.

Sheley, Joseph F. (Ed.). 1995. *Criminology* (2nd ed.) Belmont, CA: Wadsworth.

Shelton, Beth Ann. 1992. *Women, Men and Time: Gender Differences in Paid Work, Housework and Leisure.* Westport, CT: Greenwood.

Shenon, Philip. 1996. "AIDS Epidemic, Late to Arrive, Now Explodes in Populous Asia." *New York Times* (January 21): A1.

Shepard, Dennis. 1999. "Dennis Shepard's Statement to the Court" (November 4). Retrieved November 15, 1999 (http://www.matthewsplace.com/dennis2.htm).

Sher, Kenneth J. 1991. *Children of Alcoholics: A Critical Appraisal of Theory and Research.* Chicago: University of Chicago Press.

Sherman, Lawrence, Patrick R. Gratin, and M.E. Buerger. 1989. "Routine Activities and the Criminology of Place." *Criminology,* 27(1):27–55.

Shilts, Randy. 1988. *And the Band Played On: Politics, People, and the AIDS Epidemic.* New York: Penguin.

Short, G. 1991. "Combating Anti-Semitism: A Dilemma for Antiracist Education." *British Journal of Educational Studies,* 39(1).

Shragge, Eric. 1997. "Workfare: An Overview." In Eric Shragge (Ed.), *Workfare: Ideology for a New Under-Class.* Toronto: Garamond Press, pp. 17–34.

Sidel, Ruth. 1996. Keeping Women and Children Last: America's War on the Poor. New York: Penguin.

Silver, Warren, Karen Mihorean, and Andrea Taylor-Butts. 2004. "Hate Crime in Canada." *Juristat,* (24)4. Catalogue no. 85-002-XIE.

Silverman, R.A., J.J. Teevan, and V.F. Sacco (Eds.). 1996. *Crime in Canadian Society* (5th ed.). Toronto: Harcourt Brace.

Simmel, Georg. 1950. *The Sociology of Georg Simmel.* Kurt Wolff. (Trans.). Glencoe, IL: Free Press (orig. written in 1902–1917).

Simon, Brenda M. 1999. "United States v. Hilton." Berkeley Technology Law Journal 14:385–403.

Simon, David R. 1996. *Elite Deviance* (5th ed.) Boston: Allyn and Bacon.

Singer, Bennett L., and David Deschamps. 1994. *Gay and Lesbian Stats.* New York: New Press.

Single, Eric, Minh Van Truong, Edward Adlaf, and Anca Ialomiteanu (Eds.). 1999. *Canadian Profile Alcohol, Tobacco and Other Drugs/Profil Canadien L'alcool, le tabac et les autres drogues.* Toronto: Centre for Addiction and Mental Health, and Ottawa: Canadian Centre on Substance Abuse.

Single, Eric, Linda Robson, Jurgen Rehm, and Xiadi Xie. 1999. "Morbidity and Mortality Attributable to Alcohol, Tobacco and Illicit Drug Use in Canada." *American Journal of Public Health,* 89:385–390.

Single, Eric, Linda Robson, Xiadi Xie, and Jurgen Rehm. 1996. *The Cost of Substance Abuse in Canada.* Ottawa: Canadian Centre on Substance Abuse.

Skolnick, Arlene. 1991. *Embattled Paradise: The American Family in an Age of Uncertainty.* New York: HarperCollins.

Skolnick, Jerome H. 1975. *Justice without Trial* (2nd ed.). New York: Wiley.

Sleeter, Christine E. 1996. "White Silence, White Solidarity." In Noel Ignatiev and John Garvey (Eds.), *Race Traitor.* New York: Routledge, pp. 257–265.

Small, Shirley. 1978. "Canadian Narcotics Legislation, 1908–1923: A Conflict Model Interpretation." In William K. Greenaway and Stephen L. Brickey (Eds.), *Law and Social Control in Canada.* Scarborough, ON: Prentice Hall.

Smith, Charlie. 2006. "Exposing the Boss's Pay." *Georgia Straight* Retrieved February 23, 2006. (http://www.matthewsplace.com/dennis2.htm www.straight.com/content.cfm?id=16227).

Smith, Graeme. 2002. "Doctors Reluctant to Form Networks." *Globe and Mail,* (March 1):A8.

Smith, Michael D. 1993. "Women's Fear of Male Violence." *Canada Watch,* 1:68–70.

Snell, Cudore L. 1995. *Young Men in the Street: Help-Seeking Behavior of Young Male Prostitutes.* Westport, CT: Praeger.

Snitow, Ann Barr. 1994. "Mass Market Romance: Pornography for Women Is Different." In Alison M. Jaggar (Ed.), *Living with Contradictions: Controversies in Feminist Social Ethics.* Boulder, CO: Westview, pp. 181–188.

Snyder, Benson R. 1971. *The Hidden Curriculum.* New York: Knopf.

Soble, Alan. 1986. "Pornography in Capitalism: Powerlessness." In Alan Soble, *Pornography: Marxism, Feminism and the Future of Sexuality.* New Haven, CT: Yale University Press, pp. 78–84.

Solyom, Catherine. 2001. "Pigment Matters in Montreal: Survey." *Gazette* (October 26).

Spafford, Marlee M., Neepun Sharma, Vicki L. Nygaard, and Christina Kahlou. 2002. "Diversity within the Profession, Part 1: Trends and Challenges." *Optometric Education,* 27(4/Summer):114–121.

Spanier, Graham, and Paul Glick. 1981. "Marital Instability in the U.S.: Some Correlates and Recent Changes." *Family Relations,* 30(July):329–338.

Special Committee on Pornography and Prostitution. 1985. *Pornography and Prostitution in Canada: Report of the Special Committee on Pornography and Prostitution.* Ottawa: Department of Justice Canada.

Squires, Gregory D. 1994. *Capital and Communities in Black and White: The Intersections of Race, Class, and Uneven Development.* Albany, NY: State University of New York Press.

Stanley, Alessandra. 1995. "Russian Mothers, from All Walks, Walk Alone." *New York Times* (October 21):A1.

Stanley, Julia P. 1972. "Paradigmatic Woman: The Prostitute." Paper presented at South Atlantic Modern Language Association, Jacksonville, FL, cited in Jessie Bernard, *The Female World.* New York: Free Press, 1981.

Stasiulis, Daiva K. 1999. "Feminist Intersectional Theorizing." In Peter S. Li (Ed.), *Race and Ethnic Relations in Canada* (2nd ed.). Don Mills, ON: Oxford University Press, pp. 347–397.

Statistics Canada. 1998a. "Deaths 1996." *The Daily* (April 16).

Statistics Canada. 1998b. "National Longitudinal Survey of Children and Youth, 1996–97." *The Daily* (October 28).

Statistics Canada. 1999a. "Assets and Debts Held by Family Units, Canada and Provinces, 1999." Retrieved April 23, 2003 (http://www.statcan.ca/english/pgdb/famil99d.htm).

Statistics Canada. 1999b. *A Portrait of Seniors in Canada* (3rd ed.). Ottawa: Ministry of Industry.

Statistics Canada. 2000. "Family Income, 1998." *The Daily* (June 12).

Statistics Canada. 2001a. "Crime Comparisons Between Canada and the United States." *The Daily* (December 18).

Statistics Canada. 2001b. "How Healthy Are Canadians?" *Health Reports,* 12(3).

Statistics Canada. 2001c. "Measuring Student Knowledge and Skills: The Performance of Canada's Youth in Reading, Mathematics and Science. *The Daily* (December 4).

Statistics Canada. 2001d. "School Performance of Children from Immigrant Families." *The Daily* (November 14).

Statistics Canada. 2001e. "Social Indicators." *Canadian Social Trends,* (Winter):25.

Statistics Canada. 2001f. "Trends in the Use of Private Education." *The Daily* (July 4).

Statistics Canada. 2001g. *Women in Canada: Work Chapter Updates.* Ottawa: Ministry of Industry.

Statistics Canada 2002. "Census family time series." Retrieved July 14, 2005 (http://www12.statcan.ca/English/census01/products/analytic/companion/fam/timeline/cfm).

Statistics Canada. 2002a. "Average Earnings by Sex and Work Pattern." CANSIM II, Table 202-0102. (http://www.statcan.ca/english/Pgdb/labor01a.htm).

Statistics Canada. 2002b. "Changes in Unmet Health Care Needs." *The Daily* (March 13).

Statistics Canada. 2002c. "Control and Sale of Alcoholic Beverages." *The Daily* (July 12).

Statistics Canada. 2002d. "Distance to School and University Participation." *The Daily* (June 24).

Statistics Canada. 2002e. "Divorces." *The Daily* (December 2).

Statistics Canada. 2002f. "Family Income, 2000." *The Daily* (October 30).

Statistics Canada. 2002g. "Housing: An Income Issue." *The Daily* (June 21).

Statistics Canada. 2002h. "Human Activity and the Environment: Annual Statistics." *The Daily* (November 6).

Statistics Canada. 2002i. *Low Income Cutoffs from 1992 to 2001 and Low Income Measures from 1991 to 2000.* Ottawa: Minister of Industry.

Statistics Canada. 2002j. "National Longitudinal Survey of Children and Youth: Childhood Obesity 1994 to 1999." *The Daily* (October 18).

Statistics Canada. 2002k. "Police Expenditures and Personnel in Canada 2001." *The Daily* (February 12).

Statistics Canada. 2002l. "Profile of Canadian Families and Households: Diversification Continues. Retrieved October 22, 2002 (http://www12.statcan.ca/english/census01/release/index.cfm).

Statistics Canada. 2002m. "Profile of the Canadian Population by Age and Sex: Canada Ages." Retrieved February 6, 2003 (http://www12.statcan.ca/english/census01/products/analytic/companion/age/contents.cfm).

Statistics Canada. 2002n. "A Profile of the Canadian Population. Where We Live." 2001 Census Analysis Series. Retrieved March 30, 2002 (http://www.statcan.ca/english/dai-quo/note.htm).

Statistics Canada. 2002o. "Social Indicators." *Canadian Social Trends,* (Spring):27.

Statistics Canada. 2002p. "2001 Census: Collective Dwellings." Retrieved November 6, 2002 (http://www12.statcan.ca/english/census01/products/analytic/companion/coll/contents.cfm).

Statistics Canada. 2002q. "2001 Census: Marital Status, Common-Law Status, Families, Dwellings, and Households." *The Daily* (October 22).

Statistics Canada. 2002r. "Wealth Inequality, 1984–1999." *The Daily* (February 22).

Statistics Canada. 2002s. "Youth in Transition Survey." *The Daily* (January 23).

Statistics Canada 2003a. "Canadian Community Health Survey: Mental Health and Well-being." *The Daily* (September 3).

Statistics Canada. 2003b. "Census of Population: Immigration, Birthplace and Birthplace of Parents, Citizenship, Ethnic Origin, Visible Minorities and Aboriginal Peoples." *The Daily* (January 21).

Statistics Canada 2003c. "Earnings of Canadians: Making a living in the new economy." *2001 Census* (Accessed June 29, 2005).

Statistics Canada 2004a. "Canadian Community Health Survey." *The Daily* (June 15).

Statristics Canada 2004b. "Divorces." *The Daily* (May 4).

Statistics Canada 2004c. "Joint Canada/United States Survey of Health." *The Daily.* (June 2).

Statistics Canada 2004d. "Measuring Up: Canadian Results of the OECD PISA Study." Retrieved September 16, 2005 (http://www.statcan.ca:8096/bsolc/english/bsolc?catno=81-590-X).

Statistics Canada 2004e. "National Graduates Survey: Student debt." *The Daily* (April 26).

Statistics Canada 2004f. "Parenting style and children's aggressive behaviour." *The Daily* (October 25).

Statistics Canada 2004g. "Profile of Disability in 2001." *Canadian Social Trends.* (Spring): 14-18.

Statistics Canada 2004h. "Social Indicators." *Canadian Social Trends.* (Winter): 35.

Statistics Canada 2004i. "Study: The Sandwich Generation." *The Daily* (September 28).

Statistics Canada 2004j. "University Tuition Fees." *The Daily* (September 2).

Statistics Canada 2005a. "Adult Literacy and Life Skills Survey." *The Daily* (May 11).

Statistics Canada 2005b. "Canadian Community Health Survey: Obesity among Children and Adults." *The Daily* (July 6).

Statistics Canada. 2005c. "Canadian Environmental Sustainability Indicators." *The Daily.* December 14.

Statistics Canada 2005d. "Crime Statistics." *The Daily* (July 21).

Statistics Canada. 2005e. "Family Income: 2003." *The Daily* (May 20).

Statistics Canada 2005f. "General Social Survey: Criminal Victimization." *The Daily* (November 24).

Statistics Canada 2005g. "International Adult Literacy and Skills Survey: Building our competencies." *The Daily* (November 30).

Statistics Canada. 2005h. "Social Indicators." *Canadian Social Trends* (Winter): 27

Statistics Canada 2005i. "Study: Exploring Crime Patterns in Canada." *The Daily* (June 29).

Statistics Canada 2005j. "Study: Trends in Income Inequality in Canada from an International Perspective." *The Daily* (February 10).

Statistics Canada. 2006a. *Family Violence in Canada: A Statistical Profile.* Catalogue no. 85-224.

Statistics Canada. 2006b. "General Social Survey: Paid and Unpaid Work, 2005." *The Daily* (July 19).

Statistics Canada. 2006c. "Income of Canadians: 2004." *The Daily* (March 30).

Statistics Canada 2006d. "Induced Abortions." *The Daily* (March 15).

Statistics Canada 2006e. "Women in Canada." *The Daily* (March 7).

Status of Women Canada. 2005. *National Day of Remembrance and Action on Violence Against Women. Fact Sheet: Statistics on Violence Against Women in Canada.* Ottawa, ON: Status of Women Canada. Updated and reviewed November 9, 2005. Retrieved July 31, 2006.

(http://www.swc-cfc.gc.ca/cgi-bin/printview.pl?file=/dates/dec6/facts_e.html**l).**

Steering Committee of the Physicians' Health Study Group. 1989. "Final Report on the Aspirin Component of the Ongoing Physician's Health Study." *New England Journal of Medicine*, 321:129–135.

Stefanac, Suzanne. 1993. "Sex and the New Media." *New Media* (April):38–45.

Stein, Peter J. 1976. *Single*. Englewood Cliffs, NJ: Prentice-Hall.

Stein, Peter J. (Ed.). 1981. *Single Life: Unmarried Adults in Social Context*. New York: St. Martin's Press.

Steingart, R. M., M. Packer, P. Hamm, et al. 1991. "Sex Differences in the Management of Coronary Artery Disease." *New England Journal of Medicine*, 325:226–230.

Stern, M., and K.H. Karraker. 1989. "Sex Stereotyping of Infants: A Review of Gender Labelling Studies." *Sex Roles*, 20:501–522.

Stevens, Patricia E. 1992. "Lesbian Health Care Research: A Review of the Literature from 1970 to 1990." *Health Care for Women International*, p. 13.

Stevens, William K. 1997. "How Much Is Nature Worth? For You, $33 Trillion." *New York Times* (May 20):B7, B9.

Stewart, Charles T., Jr. 1995. *Healthy, Wealthy, or Wise? Issues in American Health Care Policy*. Armonk, NY: M.E. Sharpe.

Stoll, Clifford. 1996. "Invest in Humanware." *New York Times* (May 19):E15.

Stoller, Robert J. 1991. *Porn: Myths for the Twentieth Century*. New Haven, CT: Yale University Press.

Strom, Stephanie. 2000. "Tradition of Equality Fading in New Japan." *New York Times* (January 4):A1, A6.

Sullivan, A. 1997. "The Conservative Case." In A. Sullivan (Ed.), *Same Sex Marriage: Pro and Con*. New York: Vintage, pp. 146–154.

Sutherland, Edwin H. 1939. *Principles of Criminology*. Philadelphia: Lippincott.

Sutherland, Edwin H. 1949. *White Collar Crime*. New York: Dryden.

Swanson, Jean. 1997. "Resisting Workfare." In Eric Shragge (Ed.), *Workfare: Ideology for a New Under-Class*. Toronto: Garamond Press, pp. 149–170.

Swanson, Jean. 2001. *Poor-Bashing: The Politics of Exclusion*. Toronto: Between the Lines.

Swift, Jamie, Jacqueline M. Davies, Robert G. Clarke, and Michael Czerny S.J. 2003. *Getting Started on Social Analysis in Canada* (4th ed.). Toronto: Between the Lines.

Swingewood, Alan. 2000. *A Short History of Sociological Thought* (3rd ed.). London: Macmillan Press.

Swol, Karen. 1999. "Private Security and Public Policing in Canada." In Canadian Centre for Justice Statistics (Eds.), *The Juristat Reader: A Statistical Overview of the Canadian Justice System*. Toronto: Thompson, pp. 15–25.

Sydie, Rosalind A. 1983. "Sociology and Gender." In M. Michael Rosenberg et al. (Eds.), *An Introduction to Sociology*. Toronto: Methuen, pp. 185–223.

Tadic, Vela, and Karen Hughes. 1998. "Sexual Harassment in the Service Economy: Exploring Women's Retail Work in Canada." *Canadian Women's Studies*, 18(1):86–91.

Tait, Heather. 1999. "Educational Achievement of Young Aboriginal Adults." *Canadian Social Trends*, (Spring).

Tallarico, Claire M. and Susan Black. 2005. "Latest Count of Top Women in Canadian Business Shows Little Progress Since Last Catalyst Census." *Catalyst News Release* (April 27). (http://www.catalystwomen.org).

Tannen, Deborah. 1990. *You Just Don't Understand: Women and Men in Conversation*. New York: William Morrow.

Tavris, Carol. 2002. "Are Girls Really as Mean as Books Say They Are?" *Chronicle of Higher Education*, 48(43):B7–B9.

Taylor, Leanne E. 2000. "Black, White, Beige, Other? Memories of Growing Up Different." In Carl E. James (Ed.), *Experiencing Difference*. Halifax: Fernwood, pp. 59–70.

Taylor, Verta, and Nicole C. Raeburn. 1995. "Identity Politics as High-Risk Activism: Career Consequences for Lesbian, Gay, and Bisexual Sociologists." *Social Problems*, 42(2):252–273.

Teeple, Gary. 2000. "The Decline of the Canadian Welfare State: Policies and Implications of Retrenchment." In B. Singh Bolaria (Ed.), *Social Issues and Contradictions in Canadian Society* (3rd ed.). Toronto: Harcourt Brace, pp. 434–468.

Tepperman, Lorne, and Jenny Blain. 2006. *Think Twice! Sociology Looks at Current Social Issues* (2nd ed .). Upper Saddle River, NJ: Prentice Hall.

Terkel, Studs. 1996. *Coming of Age: The Story of Our Century by Those Who've Lived It*. New York: St. Martin's Griffin.

Thomas, Cal. 1996. "Overrule Same-Sex Marriage." *Austin American-Statesman* (December 6):A15.

Thomas, Gale E. 1995. "Conclusion: Healthy Communities as a Basis for Healthy Race and Ethnic Relations." In Gail E. Thomas (Ed.), *Race and Ethnicity in America: Meeting the Challenge in the 21st Century*. Bristol, PA: Taylor & Francis, pp. 335–342.

Thomas, Mikhail. 2002. "Adult Criminal Court Cases." *Juristat*, 22(2).

Thompson, Jon, Patricia Baird, and Jocelyn Downie. 2001. *The Olivieri Report: The Complete Text of the Report of the Independent Inquiry Commissioned by the Canadian Association of University Teachers*. Toronto: Lorimer.

Thompson, Kenneth. 1998. *Moral Panics*. London: Routledge.

Thomson, Elizabeth, and Ugo Colella. 1992. "Cohabitation and Marital Stability: Quality or Commitment?" *Journal of Marriage and the Family*, 54:259–267.

Thorne, Barrie. 1998. "Girls and Boys Together... But Mostly Apart: Gender Arrangements in Elementary School." In Michael S. Kimmel and Michael A. Messner (Eds.), *Men's Lives* (4th ed.). Boston: Allyn and Bacon, pp. 81–100.

Thornton, Michael C., Linda M. Chatters, Robert Joseph Taylor, and Walter R. Allen. 1990. "Sociodemographic and Environmental Correlates of Racial Socialization by Black Parents." *Child Development*, 61:401–409.

Tibbetts, Janice. 2006. "Racist Web Postings Land White Supremacist in Jail." Canada.com. Retrieved October 19, 2006 (http://www.canada.com/globaltv/bc/news/story.html?id=24b848a3-9a77-4483-9b64-0695c2d02b5d&k=92331).

Tierney, John. 1994. "Porn, the Low-Slung Engine of Progress." *New York Times* (January 9):H1, H18.

Toner, Robin. 1995. "No Free Rides: Generational Push Has Not Come to Shove." *New York Times* (December 31):E1, E4.

Toner, Robin, and Robert Pear. 1995. "Medicare, Turning 30, Won't Be What It Was." *New York Times* (July 23):1, 12.

Toronto Dominion Bank. 2002. "A Choice Between Investing in Canada's Cities or Disinvesting in Canada's Future: Executive Summary." Retrieved November 1, 2002 (http://www.td.com/economics/index.html).

Torrey, E. Fuller. 1998. *Nowhere to Go: The Tragic Odyssey of the Homeless Mentally Ill.* New York: Harper and Row.

Tower, Cynthia Crosson. 1996. *Child Abuse and Neglect* (3rd ed.). Boston: Allyn and Bacon.

Towle, Evan B., and Lynn M. Morgan. 2002. "Romancing the Transgender Native: Rethinking the Use of the 'Third Gender' Concept." *GLQ: A Journal of Lesbian and Gay Studies*, 8(4):469–497.

Trainor, Cathy. 1999. "Canada's Shelters for Abused Women." *Juristat*, 19(6).

Trice, Harrison M., and Paul Michael Roman. 1970. "Delabeling, Relabeling, and Alcoholics Anonymous." *Social Problems*, 17(4):538–546.

Trocmé, Nico, Bruce MacLaurin, Barbara Fallon, Joanne Daciuk, Dianne Billingsley, Marc Tourigny, Micheline Mayer, John Wright, Ken Barter, Gale Burford, Joe Hornick, Richard Sullivan, and Brad McKenzie. 2001. *The Canadian Incidence Study of Reported Child Abuse and Neglect: Final Report.* Ottawa: Minister of Public Works and Government Services.

Trocmé, Nico, Lil Tonmyr, Barbara Fallon, Cindy Blackstock, Bruce MacLaurin, Ken Barter, Joanne Daciuk, Daniel Turcotte, Carline Felstiner, Richard Cloutier, and Tara Black. 2005. *The Canadian Incidence Study of Reported Child Abuse and Neglect: Major Findings 2003.* Ottawa: Public Health agency of Canada. Retrieved on October 20, 2005 (http://www.phac-aspc.gc.ca/cm-vee/csca-ecve/index.html).

Turk, Austin T. 1966. "Conflict and Criminality." *American Sociological Review*, 31:338–352.

Turk, Austin T. 1971. *Criminality and Legal Order.* Chicago: Rand McNally.

Turner, Francis J. 1995. "Social Welfare in Canada." In Joanne C. Turner and Francis J. Turner (Eds.), *Canadian Social Welfare* (3rd ed.). Scarborough, ON: Allyn and Bacon, pp. 2–11.

Tyler, Tracy. 2002. "More Women than Men Called to the Bar." *Toronto Star* (February 2):A18.

UNAIDS. 2005. *Epi Update 2004.* Retrieved June 15, 2005 (http://www.unaids.org/wad2004/EPIupdate2004_html_en/Epi04_13_enhtm#P251).

"Unionize Prostitutes, Nfld. Labour Leader Urges." 2004. *CBC News* (September 8). Retrieved October 16, 2006 (http://www.cbc.ca/canada/story/2004/09/06/prostitute040906.html).

United Nations. 1995. *The World's Women 1995: Trends and Statistics.* New York: United Nations.

United Nations Development Programme (UNDP). 1999. *Human Development Report: 1999.* New York: Oxford University Press.

United Nations Development Programme (UNDP). 2001. *Human Development Report 2001.* New York: Oxford University Press.

United Nations Environment Programme (UNEP). 1992. *Status of Desertification and Implementation of the United Nations Plan of Action to Combat Desertification.* Nairobi, Kenya: United Nations.

United Nations Environment Programme (UNEP). 2003. *The UN World Water Development Report.* Retrieved March 5, 2003 (http://www.unesco.org/water/wwap/wwdr/index.shtml).

U.S. Bureau of the Census. 1998. *Statistical Abstract of the United States, 1998* (118th ed.). Washington, DC: U.S. Government Printing Office.

U.S. Bureau of the Census. 2001. *Statistical Abstract of the United States, 2001.* Washington, DC: U.S. Government Printing Office.

Urschel, Joe. 1996. "How Girls Get Scared Away from Computers." *USA Today* (June 26):1D–2D.

Valpy, Michael. 2002. "Carey Speaks Out on Homosexuality." *Globe and Mail* (October 22):A8.

Valverde, Mariana. 1985. *Sex, Power and Pleasure.* Toronto: Women's Press.

Valverde, Mariana. 1998. "Sexuality." In Robert J. Brym (Ed.), *New Society: Sociology for the 21st Century* (2nd ed.). Toronto: Harcourt Brace, pp. 74–102.

Valverde, Mariana. 2000. "Lesbianism: A Country That Has No Language" (1987). In Barbara A. Crow and Lise Gotell (Eds.), *Open Boundaries: A Canadian Women's Studies Reader.* Toronto: Prentice Hall/Allyn and Bacon, pp. 255–261.

van Dijk, Jan J.M., Pat Matthews, and M. Killans. 1990. *Experiences of Crime around the World: Key Findings from the 1989 International Crime Survey.* Deventer, Netherlands: Klower.

Vanguard News Network. 2004. "Interview with George Burdi." Retrieved May 6, 2004 (http://www.vanguardnewsnetwork.com/2004b/42704burdiinterview.htm).

Vanneman, Reeve, and Lynn Weber Cannon. 1987. *The American Perception of Class.* Philadelphia: Temple University Press.

Vartiainen, Erkki, Meri Paavola, Alfred McAlister, and Pekka Puska. 1998. "Fifteen-Year Follow-up of Smoking

Prevention Effects in the North Karelia Youth Project." *American Journal of Public Health,* 88:81–85.

Vissing, Yvonne M. 1996. *Out of Sight, Out of Mind; Homeless Children and Families in Small-Town America.* Lexington, KY: University of Kentucky Press.

Vito, Gennaro F., and Ronald M. Holmes. 1994. *Criminology: Theory, Research and Policy.* Belmont, CA: Wadsworth.

Viviano, Frank. 1995. "The New Mafia Order." *Mother Jones* (May–June):45–55.

Vozoris, Nicholas, Barbara Davis, and Valerie Tarasuk. 2002. "The Affordability of a Nutritional Diet for Households on Welfare in Toronto." *Canadian Journal of Public Health,* 93:36–40.

Wagner, David. 1993. *Checkerboard Square: Culture and Resistance in a Homeless Community.* Boulder, CO: Westview.

Waldron, I. 1997. "Changing Gender Roles in Health Behavior." In D. Gochman (Ed.), *Handbook of Health Behavior Research I: Personal and Social Determinants.* New York: Plenum, pp. 303–328.

Walker, S.G. 1994. *Weapons Use in Canadian Schools.* Ottawa: Solicitor General of Canada.

Walker, S.L. 1994. "Critics Fume at Mayor of World Smog Capital. *San Diego Union-Tribune* (April 22). (Cited in Michael P. Soroka and George J. Bryjak, *Social Problems: A World at Risk.* 1995. Boston: Allyn and Bacon, p. 115.)

Wallerstein, Immanuel. 1984. *The Politics of the World Economy.* Cambridge, England: Cambridge University Press.

Wallerstein, Judith, and Sandra Blakeslee. 1989. *Second Chances: Men, Women and Children a Decade after Divorce.* New York: Ticknor & Field.

Wallis, Claudia. 1994. "A Class of Their Own." *Time* (October 31):53–61.

Wanner, Richard A. 1999. "Trends in Educational Opportunity in Canada, 1920–1994." *Canadian Review of Sociology and Anthropology,* 36(3):409–42.

Ward, Martha C. 1999. *A World Full of Women* (2nd ed.). Boston: Allyn and Bacon.

Warr, Mark. 1995. "Public Perceptions of Crime and Punishment." In Joseph F. Sheley (Ed.), *Criminology: A Contemporary Handbook* (2nd ed.). Belmont, CA: Wadsworth, pp. 15–31.

Warshaw, Robin. 1994. *I Never Called It Rape.* New York: HarperPerennial.

Watson, Roy E. L., and Peter W. DeMeo. 1987. "Premarital Cohabitation Versus Traditional Courtship and Subsequent Marital Adjustment: A Replication and a Follow-Up." *Family Relations,* 36:193–197.

Weedon, Chris. 1999. *Feminism, Theory and the Politics of Difference.* Oxford, England: Blackwell.

Weeks, John R. 1998. *Population: An Introduction to Concepts and Issues* (7th ed.). Belmont, CA: Wadsworth.

Weinberg, Martin S., and Colin Williams. 1975. *Male Homosexuals.* New York: Penguin.

Weinberg, Martin S., Earl Rubington, and Sue Kiefer Hammersmith. 1981. *The Solution of Social Problems: Five Perspectives* (2nd ed.). New York: Oxford University Press.

Weinberg, Martin S., Colin J. Williams, and Douglas W. Pryor. 1994. *Dual Attraction: Understanding Bisexuality.* New York: Oxford University Press.

Weiner, Jonathan. 1990. *The Next One Hundred Years: Shaping the Fate of Our Living Earth.* New York: Bantam.

Weisner, Thomas S., Helen Garnier, and James Loucky. 1994. "Domestic Tasks, Gender Egalitarian Values, and Children's Gender Typing in Conventional and Nonconventional Families." *Sex Roles,* 30:23–54.

Weiten, Wayne, and Margaret A. Lloyd. 1994. *Psychology Applied to Modern Life: Adjustment in the 90s.* Pacific Grove, CA: Brooks/Cole.

Weitz, Rose. 1996. *The Sociology of Health, Illness, and Health Care: A Critical Approach.* Belmont, CA: Wadsworth.

Weitzman, Lenore J. 1985. *The Divorce Revolution.* New York: Free Press.

Wellman, David T. 1993. *Portraits of White Racism* (2nd ed.). New York: Cambridge University Press.

Westoff, Charles F. 1995. "International Population Policy." *Society* (May–June):11–15.

Wildman, Stephanie M., and Adrienne D. Davis. 2002. "Making Systems of Privilege Visible." In Paula S. Rothenberg (Ed.), *White Privilege: Essential Readings on the Other Side of Racism.* New York: Worth, pp. 89–96.

Wilkie, Jane Riblett. 1993. "Changes in U.S. Men's Attitudes toward the Family Provider Role, 1972–1989." *Gender and Society,* 7(2):261–279.

Wilkinson, Sue, and Celia Kitzinger. 1996. "The Queer Backlash." In Diane Bell and Renate Klein (Eds.), *Radically Speaking: Feminism Reclaimed.* London: Zed Books, pp. 375–382.

Williams, Cara. 2001. "Family Disruptions and Childhood Happiness." *Canadian Social Trends,* (Autumn):2–4.

Williams, Christine L. 1995. *Still a Man's World: Men Who Do Women's Work.* Berkeley, CA: University of California Press.

Williams, Robin M., Jr. 1970. *American Society: A Sociological Interpretation* (3rd ed.). New York: Knopf.

Williamson, Robert C., Alice Duffy Rinehart, and Thomas O. Blank. 1992. *Early Retirement: Promises and Pitfalls.* New York: Plenum.

Willis, Ellen. 1981. *Beginning to See the Light.* New York: Knopf.

Willis, Ellen. 1983. "Feminism, Moralism, and Pornography." In Ann Snitow, Christine Stansell, and Sharon Thompson (Eds.), *Powers of Desire: The Politics of Sexuality.* New York: Monthly Review Press, pp. 460–466.

Wilson, David (Ed.). 1997. "Globalization and the Changing U.S. City." *The Annals of the American Academy of Political and Social Science,* 551(May). Special Issue. Thousand Oaks, CA: Sage.

Wilson, Susannah J. 2001. "Paid Work, Jobs and the Illusion of Economic Security." In Nancy Mandell (Ed.), *Feminist*

Issues: Race, Class, and Sexuality (3rd ed.). Toronto: Pearson, pp. 219–241.

Wilson, William Julius. 1996. *When Work Disappears: The World of the New Urban Poor.* New York: Knopf.

Wilton, Tamsin. 2000. *Sexualities in Health and Social Care: A Textbook.* Buckingham, England: Open University Press.

Wirth, Louis. 1938. "Urbanism as a Way of Life." *American Journal of Sociology,* 40:1–24.

Wirth, Louis. 1945. "The Problem of Minority Groups." In Ralph Linton (Ed.), *The Science of Man in the World Crisis.* New York: Columbia University Press, p. 38.

Wolf, Robin. 1996. *Marriages and Families in a Diverse Society.* New York: HarperCollins.

Wolff, Lee, and Dorota Geissel. 2000. "Street Prostitution in Canada." In *Canadian Social Trends 3.* Ottawa: Minister of Supply and Services Canada, and Toronto: Thompson, pp. 253–257.

Wolfgang, Marvin E., and Franco Ferracuti. 1967. *The Subculture of Violence: Towards an Integrated Theory in Criminology.* Beverly Hills, CA: Sage.

"Women CEOs" for Fortune 500 Companies. 2006. *Fortune,* (April 17). Retrieved July 30, 2006 (http://money.cnn.com/magazines/fortune/fortune500/womenceos/).

Women's International Network. 1995. "Sex Trade Flourishing in Japan." *WIN News* 21(Winter):42.

Wood, Julia T. 2001. *Gendered Lives: Communication, Gender and Culture* (4th ed.). Belmont, CA: Wadsworth/Thomson Learning.

Woods, James D., with Jay H. Lucas. 1993. *The Corporate Closet: The Professional Lives of Gay Men in America.* New York: Free Press.

Woog, Dan. 1995. *School's Out: The Impact of Gay and Lesbian Issues on America's Schools.* Boston: Alyson Publications.

World Health Organization (WHO). 1946. *Constitution of the World Health Organization.* New York: World Health Organization Interim Commission.

World Health Organization (WHO). 2000. *Female Genital Mutilation.* Fact Sheet No. 241. Retrieved July 31, 2006 (http://www.who.int/mediacentre/factsheets/fs241/en/print.html).

World Health Organization (WHO). 2002. *World Report on Violence and Health.* Retrieved February 15, 2003 (http://www5.who.int/violence_injury_prevention/main.cfm?p=0000000117).

World Health Organization (WHO). 2003. Retrieved February 16, 2003 (http://www.who.int/nut/obs.htm).

World Resources Institute. 1992. *World Resources 1992–93.* New York: Oxford University Press.

Wortley, Scot. 1999. "A Northern Taboo: Research on Race, Crime, and Criminal Justice in Canada." *Canadian Journal of Criminology,* 41(2):261–274.

Wren, Christopher. 1996. "Teen-Agers Find Drugs Easy to Obtain and Warnings Easy to Ignore." *New York Times* (October 10):A12.

Wright, Erik Olin. 1979. *Class Structure and Income Determination.* New York: Academic Press.

Wright, Erik Olin. 1985. *Class.* London: Verso.

Wright, Erik Olin. 1997. *Class Counts: Comparative Studies in Class Analysis.* Cambridge, England: Cambridge University Press.

Wright, Erik Olin, Karen Shire, Shu-Ling Hwang, Maureen Dolan, and Janeen Baxter. 1992. "The Non-Effects of Class on the Gender Division of Labor in the Home: A Comparative Study of Sweden and the U.S." *Gender and Society,* 6(2):252–282.

Wright, Richard T., and Scott Decker. 1994. *Burglars on the Job: Streetlife and Residential Break-ins.* Boston: Northeastern University Press.

WuDunn, Sheryl. 1996. "In Japan, Even Toddlers Feel the Pressure to Excel." *New York Times* (January 23):A3.

Yea, Sallie. 2005. "When Push Comes to Shove: Sites of Vulnerability, Personal Transformation, and Trafficked Women's Migration Decisions." *Sojourn,* 20(1):67–95.

Yinger, J. Milton. 1994. *Ethnicity: Source of Strength, Source of Conflict?* Albany, NY: SUNY Press.

York, Geoffrey. 2002. "Japan's Students Can't Spell Relax." *Globe and Mail* (June 10):A1, A12.

Young, J. H. 1961. *The Toadstool Millionaires: A Social History of Patent Medicine in America before Federal Regulation.* Princeton, NJ: Princeton University Press.

Young, Malcolm C. and Jenni Gainsborough. 2000. "Prosecuting Juveniles in Adult Court: An Assessment of Trends and Consequences" from *The Sentencing Project* (http://www.sentencingproject.org).

Young, Michael Dunlap. 1994. *The Rise of the Meritocracy.* New Brunswick, NJ: Transaction.

Zelizer, Viviana. 1985. *Pricing the Priceless Child: The Changing Social Value of Children.* New Haven, CT: Yale University Press.

NAME INDEX

A

Aalbers, M.B.,   171
Abbate, G.,   237
Abella, I.,   65
Abu-Laban,   94-95
Adams, K.L.,   112
Adams, T.,   17-18
Aday, D.P.,Jr.,   160
Adlaf, E.M.,   212, 214, 215. 323-324
Adler, P.A.,   97
Akers, R.L.,   211, 216-217, 221
Albrecht, G.L.,   263
Alexander, K.L.,   315
Alexander, P.,   171
Allen, P.G.,   186
Allman, D.,   172, 184-185
Allport, G.,   64
Almaguer, T.,   159
Altman, L.K.,   262
Alvi, S.,   13, 50
Alwin, D.,   292
Ambert, A.-M.,   301
Amott, T.,   78
Anders, G.,   272
Andersen, M.L.,   115
Anderssen, E.,   144
Anyon, J.,   316
Appelbe, A.,   38, 88, 91
Applebome, P.,   324, 328
Armstrong, H.,   277
Armstrong, P.,   277
Arnup, K.,   300
Ash, R.,   20
Atchison, C.,   186-187
Atchley, R.C.,   130
Aulette, J.R.,   290
Axinn, W.G.,   293

B

Bagby, M.,   313
Bailey, I.,   253
Baker, G.R.,   277
Baker, J.M.,   153-154, 158
Baker, P.M.,   123
Balakrishnan, T.R.,   301
Ballantine, J.H.,   313, 315-316
Bandura, A.,   12
Bane,   40
Bannerji, H.,   78
Barlow, H.D.,   232, 239-240, 244
Barofsky, I.,   279
Barrett, S.R.,   69-70
Barry, K.,   172, 189, 191
Basow, S.A.,   95-96, 100, 107
Basrur, S.V.,   367
Bauerlein, M.,   176
Bawer, B.,   145-147, 153
Beare, M.E.,   242
Becker, H.S.,   12, 189, 221, 249
Bedard, G.,   63
Beeghley, L.,   34
Beitel, A.H.,   95
Bélanger, A.,   295
Belle, M.,   299
Belsky, J.,   128
Bem, S.L.,   88
Bennett, N.G.,   293
Benoit, C.M.,   100
Benokraitis, N.V.,   88, 106, 108, 285, 299
Berger, P.,   5, 12, 291
Berger, R.J.,   198
Bergmann, B.R.,   110
Bernard, J.,   291
Bess, I.,   135
Besserer, S.,   232, 237, 239
Bibby, R.W.,   97, 181
Bishop, A.,   79
Black, S.,   109
Blackwood, E.,   144
Blain, J.,   305
Blakeslee, S.,   302
Blank, T.O.,   136
Blasius, M.,   152-154
Blauner, R.,   77
Block, J.,   221
Bluestone, B.,   32

Boffa, J.,   359
Bonacich, E.,   77
Bonger, W.,   248
Bonnin, J.,   218
Bosetti, L.,   328
Bouchard, L.,   144
Bourdieu, P.,   52, 315, 329, 331
Bourgeois, P.,   217, 227
Bourne, L.S.,   338, 358
Bowles, S.,   45, 315-316
Boyd, M.,   126, 292, 321-322
Bradsher, K.,   364
Brannigan, A.,   186
Brecher, J.,   19-20, 23, 384
Brennan, R.,   349
Brody, J.E.,   133
Brooke, M.,   173
Brown, P.,   269
Browne, J.,   172, 184
Buechler, S.M.,   21
Bullard, R.D.,   373
Bullough, B.,   172
Bullough, V.,   172
Bumpass, L.L.,   301-302
Burgess, E.R.,   7
Burke, M.A.,   129
Burke, R.J.,   109
Burns, J.F.,   262
Busch, R.C.,   285
Butler, R.N.,   122
Byrne, C.,   232

C

Cable, C.,   361-362, 370, 372
Cable, S.,   361-362, 370, 372
Cameron, D.,   369
Campbell, L.,   123, 127, 129-130,
   133-134, 138
Campbell, M.,   363
Cancian, F.M.,   291
Cannon, L.W.,   32
Capponi, P.,   30
Cargan, L.,   292

Carmichael, S., 65
Carol, N.J., 96
Carrier, J.G., 316
Carroll, W.K., 19
Carson, M., 144
Cass, V.C., 159
Castells, M., 357
Catalano, R.A., 269
Cavender, G., 249
Cerny, J., 40
Chalouh, M., 85
Chambliss, W.J., 242, 244
Chamie, J., 339, 354
Chapkis, W., 181
Chappell, N.L., 135-136, 264, 270, 276, 279
Chase-Lansdale, P.L., 299
Cherlin, A.J., 287-288, 301-302
Chermak, S.M., 232
Chesney-Lind, M., 249
Chidley, J., 196
Chudacoff, H.P., 122, 124
Chui, T., 126
Claridge, M.G., 157
Clark, J., 107
Clark, W., 301, 319-320, 326
Clarke, R.G., 385
Cleeland, N., 364
Clinard, M.B., 185
Coale, A., 343
Cochrane, J., 269
Cohen, L.E., 7, 247
Cohen, R., 107
Cohen, S., 10
Colella, U., 293
Coleman, E., 159
Coles, G., 316
Collenette, D., 349
Collins, P.H., 115, 186, 198
Collins, R., 316
Coltrane, S., 294
Compte, A., 6
Comstock, G.D., 157
Connell, C., 299
Connelly, J., 323
Corbeil, J.-P., 319
Cormack, E., 249
Corr, C.A., 124, 131
Corr, D.M., 124
Costello, T., 19-20, 384
Cottle, C.E., 199
Cottrell, B., 305
Coverman, S., 293
Cowan, G.C., 196
Cowley, G., 215
Cox, O.C., 77
Craig, W., 323
Crombie, D., 348
Crosette, B., 339
Crossette, B., 31, 354, 356
Crouter, A.C., 293
Cullen, D., 158
Curatolo, P.W., 213
Currah, P., 91, 152, 163

Curran, D.J., 112
Curry, B., 367
Czerny, M., 385

D

Dagg, A.I., 100
Daly, K., 249
Daniels, R.J., 326
Danziger, S., 31
Dauvergne, M., 85, 236, 240, 243
Davidson, J.O., 172, 176
Davies, J.M., 385
Davies, S., 328
Davis, A.D., 64
Davis, K., 52, 188, 287
Dawidoff, R., 146, 156, 160, 165
de Broucher, P., 322
Decker, S., 239
DeKeseredy, W., 13, 50, 106
Delk, J.L., 95
Demczuk, I., 144, 147-148
DeMeo, P.W., 293
DeMont, J., 373
Denton, M., 265
Denton, N.A., 353
DePasquale, K.M., 185
Deschamps, D., 155
Devereaux, A., 183
Devor, A., 91
Dews, P.B., 213
Diamond, J., 23
Diamond, S., 192, 197
Dickinson, H.D., 53, 267-268
Dieter, 101
Dietz, P., 236
DiFranza, J.R., 211
Dimmock, G., 195
Dobrzynski, J.H., 108-109
Doezema, J., 171
Dollard, J., 245
Donavon, T., 88-89
Donnelly, J., 261
Donziger, S.R., 243, 250
Doob, A.N., 10-11
Doyle, J.A., 144
Du Bois, P.M., 17
Dua, E., 78
Dubois, J., 42
Duffy, A., 38, 46, 107
Dull, D., 127
Duncan, D.F., 196
Dunlap, D.W., 147
Dunlap, R.E., 369
Durkheim, E., 7, 245-246, 289, 357
Dworkin, A., 199
Dynes, W.R., 146

E

Eckersley, R., 374
Eder, D., 318
Ehrenreich, B., 111
Ehrlich, A.H., 340-341, 344, 361-362, 371
Ehrlich, P.R., 340-341, 341, 344, 361-362, 371

Eichler, M., 360
Ellinwood, E.H.,Jr., 217
Elliot, J.L., 42, 62-63, 65, 67-71, 77, 79, 186
Ellis, D., 50
Ellis, Desmond, 13
Engels, F., 9, 53, 290, 371
Englehardt, H.T, Jr., 272
English, D., 111
Epstein, C.F., 102
Erickson, K.T., 249
Erikson, K.T., 370
Essed, P., 71-72, 78
Esty, D.C., 371
Evans, R.G., 134, 137
Eyles, J.S., 373, 374

F

Farr, 173, 175
Feagin, C.B., 32, 61-63, 65, 383
Feagin, J.R., 4, 32, 50, 61-65, 79, 88, 106, 108, 357-358, 383
Fedorowycz, O., 238
Felson, M., 247
Ferracuti, F., 247
Findlay, D.A., 279
Fine, G.A., 97, 99
Fine, M., 99
Finkelhor, D., 303
Firestone, S., 290
Fishbein, D.H., 206, 211-212, 215, 218, 220, 223, 225-226
Fisher, L.M., 278
Fitzgerald, R., 86
Flanagan, W.G., 346, 351, 357-358
Fleras, A., 42, 62-63, 65, 67-71, 77, 79, 86, 111, 114, 186
Florida, R., 345, 349, 359, 378
Flynn, K., 30
Fobes, C., 54
Fogot, B.I., 96
Foley, D., 279
Forcese, D., 57
Foucault, M., 162
Fox, M.F., 99
Frakenberg, R., 64
Frank, J., 155
Fraser, L., 177, 186-188
Frederick, J.A., 321-322
Freeze, C., 255
Freidan, B., 360
Freiler, C., 40
French, D., 189
Freudenberg, N., 369
Freund, M., 188
Frideres, J.S., 9, 261, 264, 268, 338
Friedan, B., 136
Friedmann, J., 355
Fullilove, M.T., 183

G

Gabor, T., 324
Gabriel, T., 159, 165, 296-297, 297

Gailey, C.W., 87
Gainsborough, 11
Galabuzi, 42
Galt, V., 274
Gamson, J., 152, 163
Gamson, W., 20
Gans, H., 359, 378
Gardner, C.B., 15
Gardner, T.A., 198
Garreau, J., 347
Gawin, F.H., 217
Gee, E.M., 133, 224
Geissel, D., 172, 177, 184–185
Gerber, L.M., 31, 36, 38, 46
Gerson, K., 285, 294
Gerstel, N., 293
Gertler, M.S., 349, 358–359
Gessen, M., 154
Gfellner, B.M., 220
Gibbs, L.M., 369
Gil, V.E., 176
Gilbert, R.J., 213
Gilder, G., 54
Gillespie, K., 350
Gilovich, P., 197
Gintis, H., 45, 315–316
Giobbe, E., 172
Gladwell, M., 245
Glaser, B., 131
Glazier, R.H., 350
Gleick, E., 43
Glick, P., 301
Glick, P.C., 302
Goffman, E., 268
Gold, R.B., 295–296
Goldberg, C., 368
Goldberg, J., 65
Golden, A., 352
Goldie, T., 152
Goldstein, A., 272
Goode, E., 217
Goode, W.J., 290, 301
Gordon, D.M., 53
Gordon, F.L., 93–94
Gordon, M.M., 76
Gordon, R.M., 237–238
Gottdiener, M., 358
Gottschalk, P., 31
Gover, T., 156
Graham, I.D., 123
Graham, J.R., 49
Gray, P., 272
Green, K., 279
Greenberg, E.S., 20
Greene, M., 19
Greene, V.L., 136
Grillo, T., 66, 74
Grobe, J., 268
Gross, H.E., 293
Gross, L., 209
Grossbard–Shechtman, A., 287
Guslits, M., 353

H

Ha, T.T., 304
Haddock, V., 125
Hagan, J., 250
Hall, R.M., 99
Halli, S.S., 53, 345, 354
Hamilton, C.V., 65
Hammersmith, S.K., 382
Hannigan, J.A., 373
Hansell, S., 240
Hantover, J.P., 97
Hardina, D., 48–49
Harper, C.L., 367
Harris, J.R., 301
Harrison, B., 32
Harrison, S., 223
Hartley, N., 191
Hartmann, H., 101, 114, 293
Hartnagel, T.F., 11
Hauchler, I., 337, 341–342, 363, 365, 367, 368
Havighurst, R.J., 136
Hawaleshka, D., 271, 349
Hawley, A., 357
Hays, C.L., 134
Healy, D., 280
Hendrik, D., 243
Hendriks, A., 161
Henry, F., 68, 71–75, 79
Herek, G.M., 145
Hessing, M., 111, 374
Hewa, S., 264
Higley, S.R., 357
Hills, S.L., 251
Hinch, R., 106
Hindelang, M.J., 245
Hirschi, T., 245, 247
Hochschild, A.R., 110, 293
Hoffman, A.J., 369
Holloway, K., 327
Holmes, R.M., 236, 240, 249
Holt, J.C., 315
hooks, b., 66
Hooyman, N.R., 123, 138
Hou, F., 354
Houseknecht, S., 301
Hughes, K., 107
Hulchanski, J.D., 351
Hundleby, J.D., 220
Husk, N., 100
Huston, A.C., 97

I

Illich, I., 277, 281
Immem, W., 349
Inciardi, J., 183

J

Jacklin, C.N., 96–97
Jackson, R., 290
Jaffee, D., 358
Jankowski, M.S., 238
Jensen, G., 107

Jiwani, Y., 14
Johnson, B.D., 219
Johnson, H., 85, 105
Jolin, A., 172, 190
Jones, C., 291
Jung, J., 209

K

Kadie, C., 196
Kalish, R.A., 130–131
Kaminer, W., 199
Kane, H., 338
Kantrowitz, B., 278
Kaplan, R.D., 355
Karracker, K.H., 95
Katz, J., 244
Katz, S., 137
Kazemipur, A., 53, 345, 354
Kellner, H., 291
Kemp, A.A., 105–107, 113–114
Kempadoo, K., 171, 175, 191
Kempe, C.H., 302–303
Kempe, R.S., 303
Kendall, D., 15, 17, 21, 328
Kennedy, L.W., 251
Kennedy, P., 342
Kennedy, P.M., 337, 341–342, 363, 365–367, 368
Kessler–Harris, A., 105
Kidron, M., 32
Kiel, D.P., 213
Kimball, M., 224
Kimmel, M.S., 197
King, L., 295
Kingsley, C., 171, 177, 183–186, 191
Kingstone, B., 127
Kinsman, G., 154–155, 198
Kipnis, L., 192, 197
Kirsch, M.H., 163
Kitzinger, C., 162
Kivel, P., 79
Kiyak, H.A., 123, 138
Klockars, C.B., 248
Knapp, C., 226
Knox, D., 52
Knox, P.L., 356, 358
Kolata, G., 224, 278
Kosmin, B.A., 146
Kremarik, F., 346, 364
Krohn, M.D., 247–248
Kübler–Ross, E., 131, 140
Kunisawa, B., 66
Kurz, D., 40, 42, 285, 290, 306

L

Lachman, S.P., 146
Lalonde, M., 277
Lamanna, M., 285, 291
Langelan, M.J., 105, 107
Langlois, S., 129–130
Lappé, F.M., 17
Laqueur, T., 87

Larkin, J., 98
Lauderback, D., 217
Lauer, J.C., 294
Lauer, R.H., 172, 183, 185, 187, 294, 306
Laurence, L., 279
Lavallée, L., 322
Layton, J., 350
Lee, F.R., 297
Lee, K.K., 354
Lefrançois, G.R., 129
Lehmann, J.M., 289
Lehne, G.K., 145
Leinen, S., 156
Leland, J., 165
Lemert, E., 249
Lengermann, P.M., 13
Leong, W.-T., 192
Leuchtag, 172, 175–176
Levin, J., 238
Levin, W.C., 123
Levine, P., 65
Levinthal, C.F., 205–206, 208–209, 211, 213, 219, 224
Levy, J., 130
Lew, R.A., 211
Lewin, T., 287
Lewis, J., 172, 175, 184
Lewis, M., 178
Lewis, O., 52
Lexchin, J., 277
Ley, D.F., 358
Lian, J.Z., 322–323
Liebow, E., 45
Lin, S.-L., 302
Lin Lap-Chew, 175
Lindsey, L.L., 95–101, 112–113
Lips, H.M., 101, 143
Lloyd, M.A., 245
Logan, R., 233, 239
Lombardi, E.L., 88–89, 91
Lomborg, B., 365, 368, 373
Lommo, C., 253
London, 351
London, K.A., 292, 302
Lorber, J., 92, 101, 105, 113
Lottes, I., 197
Loury, G.C., 329
Lowman, J., 177, 183, 185–188, 191
Luckenbill, D.F., 12
Luckmann, T., 12
Luffman, J., 328
Luker, K., 298
Lundy, K.C., 45
Lunman, K., 232
Lytton, H., 95

M

Maccoby, E.E., 96–97
MacCorquodale, P., 107
MacDonald, E., 88–91
MacDonald, G., 125
MacDonald, K., 95

MacDonald, S., 209
Macfarlane, R., 363
Macionis, J.J., 31, 36, 38, 46
MacIssac, R., 348–349
Mackenzie, H., 325
Mackie, M., 98, 114
MacKinnon, C., 199
MacLeod, J., 54
MacMillan, C.S., 157
Macy, M., 181, 184, 197
Mahoney, J., 260
Makin, K., 305
Malarek, V., 323
Males, M., 125
Malette, L., 85
Malinowski, B., 289
Malthus, T.R., 340–341
Mandell, N., 38, 46
Maneker, J.S., 301
Mann, P., 98
Mann, P.S., 290
Marable, M., 76
Marcus, F., 7
Marger, M., 4
Marger, M.N., 76
Mark, M., 171, 177, 183–186, 191
Marlowe, J., 184
Marsden, L., 291
Marshall, B.L., 92
Marshall, K., 110
Marshall, R., 271
Marshall, V.W., 130 132, 135
Martin, C.L., 96–97
Martin, D., 11
Martin, T.C., 301
Marx, K., 8, 9, 26, 32–33, 53, 160, 248, 371
Mascoll, P., 251, 325
Mason, 254
Massey, D.S., 353
Massey, J.L., 247
Mastrefski, S.D., 250
Matas, R., 86
Mathis, N., 324
Matika-Tyndale, E., 172, 175–177, 181–183
Matthaei, J., 78
Matthews, D.R., 322–323, 323
Maugh, T., 144
Maxwell, M.A., 16
Mayall, A., 198
Maynard, J., 209–210
McAdie, P., 99
McCall, N., 248
McConnell, W., 269
McDaniel, S.A., 109, 133
McDevitt, J., 238
McDonald, L., 173–175
McIntosh, P., 63–64
McKeown, D., 364
McKinlay, J.B., 261
McLanahan, S., 294
McLaughlin, H., 300
McMullan, J.L., 242

McMullin, J.A., 132, 135
McNamara, R.P., 172
McNeill, J.R., 368
McPherson, B.D., 122, 131
McQuillan, K., 299
McWilliams, P., 171, 186, 190
Mead, M., 292
Mead, R., 155
Meier, R.F., 185
Melko, M., 292
Mellor, M., 374
Merton, R.K., 6, 12, 246
Meyer, M.H., 295
Michael, R.T., 144
Michelson, W.H., 357
Middlestaedt, M., 366
Mies, M., 374
Mighton, J., 330–331
Mihorcan, K., 239
Milan, A., 288, 292, 299, 302
Milkman, H., 219
Millar, A.E., 177
Millar, W.J., 274–275
Miller, C., 112
Miller, E.M., 186
Miller, J., 300
Miller, J.R., 325
Miller, L.J., 279
Miller, M.W., 217
Mills, C.W., 5, 15
Minichiello, V., 172, 184
Minnich, E.K., 74
Mitchell, A., 369
Moloney, P., 348
Monahan, J., 269
Montemurro, B., 107
Mooney, L.A., 52, 114, 149, 154
Moore, B., 173–174
Moore, W., 52
Morel, S., 47–49
Morgan, L.M., 88–90
Morgan, R., 161
Morgan, S.P., 301
Morrison, P., 129–130
Mosher, S.W., 337
Mueller, H.L., 385
Muggeridge, P., 125
Muszynski, A., 53
Muto, S., 324
Myles, J., 138

N

Nabe, C.M., 124
Nangeroni, N.R., 88–89
Nath, P.S., 299
Nava, M., 146, 156, 160, 165
Navarro, M., 215
Naylor, C.D., 276
Nechas, E., 279
Nelson, A., 52, 85–86, 94–95, 104–110, 198
Nelson, F., 300
Neugarten, B.L., 136

Newman, Z., 162–163
Niebrugge-Brantley, J., 13
Niebuhr, G., 147
Norris, D., 292
Norris, Doug, 126
Novak, M., 123, 127, 129–130, 133–134, 138

O

Oakes, J., 315–316
O'Brien, M., 196
O'Connell, H., 287, 293, 344
Oliver, M.L., 33
Olivieri, N., 277, 280, 327
Olsen, G.M., 47
Olzak, S., 76
Omi, M., 62, 77
Ondrich, J.I., 136
Orenstein, P., 98
Otis, L., 172
Ouimet, M., 240–241
Overall, C., 161
Owens, A.M., 318

P

Padavic, I., 102, 104, 110, 116
Page, B.I., 20
Paglia, A., 212, 214
Palen, 351
Park, R.E., 7
Parke, R.D., 95
Parker, R., 357–358
Parker, R.N., 7, 13, 234, 247
Parker, S., 318
Parsons, T., 6, 113, 276, 289, 357
Passeron, J.-C., 52, 315, 329
Patel, D., 70
Pateman, C., 190
Paul, P., 292
Pear, R., 272–273, 344
Pearce, D.M., 40
Pease, S.E., 206, 211–212, 215, 218, 220,
   223, 225–226
Pedicelli, G., 2, 11
Pepler, D., 323
Peritz, I., 252
Perry, D.C., 358
Perry-Jenkins, M., 293
Petersen, J.L., 363, 368–370, 374
Peterson, 374
Peterson, R.D., 385
Peterson, V.S., 93, 112
Petras, J.F., 32
Philip, M., 300
Picard, A., 94, 216
Picot, G., 354
Pierce, J.L., 102, 107
Pocklington, T., 327
Pollack, A., 315
Ponse, B., 159
Pope, C.A., III., 363
Popenoe, D., 286, 289–290
Porteous, S., 224
Posterski, D.C., 97

Potterat, J.J., 185
Purvis, A., 176

Q

Quadango, J., 54
Queen, C., 191

R

Rabinovich, J., 178, 184
Raeburn, N.C., 165
Rank, M.R., 36, 54
Rankin, J., 251
Rankin, R.P., 301
Raphael, R., 189
Ratner, R.S., 18
Rawls, J., 272
Reckless, W.C., 247
Reiss, I.L., 197
Relman, A.S., 277
Renzetti, C.M., 112
Reskin, B.F., 101–102, 104, 110, 116
Reynolds, C., 99
Reynolds, H., 185
Ricciutelli, L., 30
Rich, A., 117, 161
Richards, C.L., 295–296
Richardson, L., 114
Richmond, T., 164–165
Riedmann, A., 285, 291
Rinehart, A.D., 136
Risman, B.J., 294
Roberts, N., 172
Robertson, A., 79
Robertson, D., 213
Robinson, B.W., 94–95, 97–98, 101–102,
   104–105, 108–110, 198
Robinson, D., 237, 245, 247
Robson, L., 205
Roman, P.M., 227
Romney, D.M., 95
Roos, L.L., 275
Roos, N.P., 275
Roos, P.A., 105
Ropers, R.H., 38, 43
Roscoe, T., 92
Rose, A., 79
Rose, D., 338
Rose, R., 144
Rosenberg, J., 107
Rosenberg, M., 356
Rosenthal, C.J., 135
Rosenthal, E., 272
Ross, D.P., 123–124
Rossi, P.H., 45
Rothchild, J., 38
Rothman, R.A., 31
Rubin, J.Z., 95
Rubin, L.B., 291, 306
Rubington, E., 382
Runyan, A.S., 93, 112
Rusk, J., 359
Russell, D.E.H., 193, 198–199
Ryan, W., 50

S

Sacco, V.F., 251
Sachs, A., 176
Sadker, D., 97–99
Sadker, M., 97–99
Safilios-Rothschild, C., 291
Sallot, J., 132
Sambugaro, E., 243
Sampson, R.J., 249
Sanday, P.R., 237
Sandefur, G,D., 294
Sandler, B.R., 99
Sanger, D.E., 337
Sangera, J., 175
Sapon-Shevin, M., 318
Sassen, S., 355
Satzewich, V., 77
Saunders, J., 305
Saunders, R., 30, 42
Sauvé, J., 124, 210, 233, 240, 243
Sawyer, J., 64, 153
Schacht, C., 52
Schissel, 11
Schlaadt, R.G., 222
Schneider, K., 373
Schur, E.M., 159
Scott, D.B., 113
Scott, K.J., 123
Seabrook, J., 50
Seager, J., 175–176
Searight, H.R., 269
Searight, P.R., 269
Seavor, J., 158
Segal, L., 198–199
Segal, R., 32
Segall, A., 136, 264, 270, 276, 279
Séguin, R., 274
Seidman, S., 101
Sen, A., 374
Shapiro, T.M., 33
Shedler, J., 221
Sheehan, M.O., 367
Sheff, D., 294
Sheldon, W.H., 244
Sheley, J.F., 250
Shelton, B.A., 110
Shenon, P., 262
Shephard, D., 157
Sher, K.J., 211
Sherman, L., 232
Shilts, R., 165
Shiva, V., 374
Short, G., 66
Shragge, E., 47–49
Sidel, R., 52
Sikes, M.P., 4
Silver, W., 239
Silverman, R.A., 251
Simmel, G., 12, 358, 378
Simon, B.M., 194
Simon, D.R., 242
Singer, B.L., 155
Single, E., 205, 209, 212, 214, 217, 219

Skolnick, A., 287
Skolnick, J.H., 250
Sleeter, C.E., 76
Small, S., 214
Smith, C., 53
Smith, G., 274
Smith, M.D., 106
Smith, P.J., 123
Snell, C.L., 172, 186
Snitow, A.B., 193
Snyder, B.R., 315
Soble, A., 198
Solyom, C., 354
Spafford, M.M., 154
Spanier, G., 301
Sprott, J.B., 10
Squires, G.D., 65
Stanley, J.P., 112
Stasiulis, D.K., 78
Staton, P., 98
Stefanac, S., 198
Stein, P.J., 292
Steingart, R.M., 279
Steinsapir, C., 369
Stern, M., 95
Stevens, P.E., 154
Stevens, W.K., 363
Stewart, C.T. Jr., 277
Stoll, C., 329
Stoller, R.J., 194
Strauss, A., 131
Street, M., 172, 175
Strom, S., 382
Sullivan, A., 160
Sunderwirth, S., 219
Sutherland, E.H., 241, 248
Swanson, J., 48–49
Swift, J., 385
Swift, K., 112
Swingewood, A., 14
Swol, K., 251
Sydie, R.A., 114

T

Tadic, V., 107
Tait, H., 323
Tallarico, C.M., 109
Tannen, D., 112
Tator, C., 72–74
Tavris, C., 318
Taylor, G., 65
Taylor, P.J., 356, 358
Taylor, V., 165
Taylor-Butts, A., 239
Teeple, G., 47, 50
Tepperman, L., 291, 305
Terkel, S., 122
Thomas, C., 163

Thomas, G.E., 79
Thomas, M., 251
Thomas, W.I., 12
Thompson, J., 277
Thompson, K., 10–11
Thompson, P.J., 100
Thomson, E., 293
Thorne, B., 96
Thornton, A., 293
Thorton, M.C., 75
Tibbetts, J., 70
Tierney, J., 194
Timoshkina, N., 173–174
Tobin, S.S., 136
Toner, R., 123, 138, 273
Torrey, E.F., 269
Tovée, 280
Tower, C.C., 123, 303
Towle, E.B., 88–90
Trainor, C., 86, 232, 237, 239
Trice, H.M., 227
Trocmé, N., 302, 303
Troper, H., 65
Tupper, A., 327
Turk, A.T., 248
Turner, F.J., 49
Tyler, T., 103

U

Urschel, J., 99

V

Valpy, M., 147
Valverde, M., 161, 165, 192, 197–198
van Dijk, J.J.M., 241
Van Truong, M., 209, 212, 214, 217, 219
Vanneman, R., 32
Vartiainen, E., 225
Vera, H., 64, 79
Vissing, Y.M., 186
Vito, G.F., 236, 240, 249
von Linne, C., 63
von Roosmalen, E., 109
Vozoris, N., 264

W

Wagner, D., 352
Waldorf, D., 217
Waldron, I., 224
Walker, S.G., 324, 364
Wallerstein, I., 355–356
Wallerstein, J., 302
Wallis, C., 328
Walters, V., 265
Wanner, R.A., 323
Ward, M.C., 94, 176
Ware, N.C., 112
Warr, M., 234

Warshaw, R., 237
Watkins, A.J., 358
Watson, R.E.L., 293
Weber, M., 5, 32–33
Weedon, C., 161–162
Weeks, J.R., 337, 340–344, 346
Weinberg, M.S., 144, 159, 164, 382, 384
Weiner, J., 365
Weinhouse, B., 279
Weisner, T.S., 96
Weiten, W., 245
Weitz, R., 134, 261, 263, 272
Weitzman, L.J., 40
Wellman, D.T., 64
West, C., 127
Wildman, S.M., 64, 66, 74
Wilkie, J.R., 290
Wilkinson, S., 162
Williams, C., 164, 301
Williams, C.L., 109
Williams, R.M., Jr., 7
Williamson, R.C., 136
Willis, E., 193, 199
Wilson, B.F., 302
Wilson, D., 356, 358
Wilson, S.J., 102–105, 110–111
Wilson, W.J., 52, 61
Wilton, T., 145–146
Winant, H., 62, 77
Wirth, L., 63, 358, 378
Wolf, R., 285, 292
Wolff, L., 172, 177, 184–185
Wolfgang, M.E., 247
Wood, J.T., 93–94, 95–96, 100–101
Woods, J.D., 155
Woog, D., 158
Wortley, S., 254
Wren, C., 215
Wright, B.H., 373
Wright, E.O., 9, 33, 36, 293
Wright, R.T., 239
WuDunn, S., 314
Wunder, D.F., 385

Y

Yea, S., 173
Yinger, J.M., 62
York, G., 315
Young, J., 10
Young, J.H., 213
Young, M.D., 316

Z

Zelizer, V., 297

SUBJECT INDEX

A

Aboriginal healing circle, 254
Aboriginal people. *See* Indigenous people
abortion, 295-296
absolute poverty, 31–32, 38
abuse of power, 107
accessibility, 270–271
accused
    homicide, 236
    sexual assault, 237
acid rain, 363
acquaintance rape, 237
active racism, 71
activity theory, 136–137
acute diseases, 261
acute phase, 131
adolescence, 124–125, 125, 234
adolescent prostitution, 185
adoption, 297–298
advanced industrialization and urbanization,
    341
affective-education programs, 225
affordable housing, 44
age
    chronological age, 122
    dependency ratio, 136, 138
    functional age, 122
    and heavy alcohol consumption, 207
    and the media, 125
    and pornography, 197
    and poverty, 40
    and prostitution, 185–186
    and social inequality, 123
age-based inequality
    see also ageism; aging
    age stratification, 131–132
    conflict perspective, 137
    elder abuse, 134
    family problems, 134–135
    feminist perspectives, 137
    functionalist perspective, 136
    homelessness, 135

interactionist perspective, 136–137
perspectives on, 136–137
reducing age-based inequality, 137–139
retirement, and changing roles, 133
social isolation, 134–135
victimization, 134
what you can do, 139
workplace discrimination, 132–133
age-based stereotypes, 123
age stratification, 131–132
ageism
    see also age-based inequality
    age-based stereotypes, 123
    defined, 122
    life course, 123–131
    mandatory retirement, 122, 133
    media ageism, 125
    social inequality, 123
    as social problem, 122–131
aggression, 244, 245
aging
    see also age-based inequality
    conflict perspective, 137
    death and dying, 130–131
    delayed initiation theory, 136
    disengagement theory, 136
    and family problems, 134–135
    feminist perspectives, 137
    feminization of aging, 134
    functionalist perspective, 136
    and health, 129, 133–134
    and health care, 133–134
    housing patterns, 135–136
    illness, 133–134
    interactionist activity theory, 136–137
    interactionist perspective, 136–137
    long-term-care facilities, 135–136
    perspectives on, 136–137
    primary aging, 126–127
    problems associated with, 131–136
    productive aging, 138
    secondary aging, 127

senescence, 126–127
social gerontology, 123
and suicide, 129–130
AIDS, 155, 176, 262
air pollution, 362–367
alcohol-related social problems
    alcoholic cirrhosis, 208–209
    cardiovascular problems, 208
    codependency, 210 211
    drinking and driving, 209, 210
    family problems, 209–211
    fetal alcohol effects (FAE), 208
    fetal alcohol syndrome (FAS), 208
    harms, described, 207
    health problems, 208
    nutritional deficiencies, 208
    workplace, 209
alcohol use and abuse
    and age, 207
    alcohol-related social problems. *See*
        alcohol-related social problems
    Antabuse, 226
    chronic alcohol abuse, 208
    and class, 207
    depressant, 206
    described, 206
    forms of alcohol, 206
    future of, 224–227
    and gender, 207
    and marital status, 207
    outpatient programs, 226
    prevention programs, 224–225
    short-and long-term services, 226–227
    therapeutic community approach,
        225–227
    treatment programs, 225–227
    what you can do, 227 228
alcoholic cirrhosis, 208
Alcoholics Anonymous (AA), 16, 226–227
alienation, 9
alternative health care, 274–275
alternative movements, 22

amalgamation, 76
amphetamine psychosis, 218
amphetamines, 217
anal sex, 148
androcentric, 13
androcentricity, 87
Anglo-conformity model, 76
anomie, 7
Antabuse, 226
anti-intellectualism, 318
anti-oppression work, 66
anti-racism initiatives, 75
anti-racist feminism, 78
anti-racist perspective, 78
anti-Semitism, 65–66
anticensorship feminists, 199
antipornography feminists, 199
ascribed status, 289, 320–323
assimilation, 76, 313
assisted reproductive technology, 297
assisted suicide, 132
atrophied human capital, 113
attention-deficit hyperactivity disorder (ADHD), 212
auto theft, 239
aversion therapy, 225

B

Bad Date Sheets, 177
bar girls and bar boys, 183
bawdy house, 183
beauty standards, 94–95
behavioural conditioning, 225
beliefs about elites, 20
billionaires, 33
binary polarization, discourse of, 73
binuclear family, 302
biological bases for gender roles, 88–92
biological definition of race, 62
biological division of labour, 113
biological explanations
    aggression, 244
    cortex, 245
    of crime, 244–245
    of drug abuse, 221
    positivist school, 244
    somatotype theory, 244
biosphere, 362
biotechnological revolution, 342
biphobia, 145
bisexual
    see also sexual orientation
    biphobia, 145
    classification as, 143–144
Black feminists, 115
blaming the victim, 50
blended family, 302
booster, 240
bourgeoisie, 9
breaking and entering, 239
brothels, 183
"Bubba" stereotype, 68–71

bullying, 323–324
business leaders, 151

C

C-Suite Survey, 150–152
caffeine, 213
call girls and call boys, 181
Canada
    affordable housing in, 44
    billionaires, 33
    child pornography and the Internet, 194–196
    cities, changes in, 346–348
    class inequality in, 32–38
    class structure, divisions in, 36–38
    crime in, *vs.* United States, 240–241
    democratic racism, 72–75
    education, problems in, 318–325
    family policies, 51
    global sex trade in, 173–175
    health care system, 269–275
    immigration and, 344–345
    immorality, beliefs about, 148
    meritocracy, 31
    minimum hourly wages, 37
    organized racism in, 68–70
    population, 128
    population change, 347
    poverty in, 38–46
    prostitution, 176–185
    racism in, 61
    sex tourism in, 175–176
    social classes in, 32
    social stratification, 32
    social welfare, 47–50
    urban problems, 348–354
    as welfare state, 47
    workfare, 47–49
Canada Assistance Plan (CAP), 47
Canada Health Act, 270
Canada Health and Social Transfer Act (CHST), 47–48
Canada's Drug Strategy, 223
Canadian business leaders, 151
Canadian Charter of Rights and Freedoms. See Charter of Rights and Freedoms
Canadian Employment Equity Act, 72
Canadian Safe Schools Network, 324
cannabis. *See* marijuana
capital punishment, 255
capitalism
    and aging, 137
    defined, 9
    "ebb and flow" cycle, 50
    exploitation of women, 114
    globalization of, 50
    and racialized exploitation, 77
    slavery, 77
    socialist feminist perspective, 114
capitalist class, 9
capitation, 274
cardiovascular problems, 208

carrying capacity, 362
censorship, 196, 199
Census families time series, 286
Census Metropolitan Areas (CMAs), 353
change, 313
Charter of Rights and Freedoms
    age discrimination, 132
    equality section (s. 15), 149
    health care, and private insurance, 273
    individual rights, guarantee of, 4
    and mandatory retirement, 122
    pornography and censorship, 199
    racism, erosion of, 71
    sex discrimination, 115
    sexual orientation, as protected ground, 150
charter schools, 328
child abuse, 302–305
child neglect, 302
child pornography, 194–196
child-related family issues, 295–300
child sexual abuse, 303–304
childhood, 123–124
childless couples, 359
children
    adolescence, 124–125
    aggression, and punitive parenting, 299
    in alcoholic families, 210–211
    born to crack-addicted mothers, 217
    and child abuse, 302–305
    child neglect, 302
    child-related family issues, 295–300
    children's rights, 10
    and domestic violence, 302–306
    and homelessness, 45
    maltreatment of, 302–303
    and one-parent households, 294
    and pornography, 198
    and poverty, 40
    problems of childhood, 123–124
children's rights, 10
chilly climate concept, 108–109
Chinese Immigration Act, 329
Christian ideology, 69
chronic diseases, 261
chronic malnourishment, 341
chronic phase, 131
chronically poor people, 37–38
chronological age, 122
churning, 274
cities. *See* urbanization
civil disobedience, 21
civilization, 68
class. *See* social class
class divisions, 36–38
class inequality
    in Canada, 32–38
    conflict perspective, 53
    divisions in Canadian class structure, 36–38
    feminist perspectives, 53–54, 78
    functionalist perspective, 52–53

income inequality, 34–36
interactionist perspective, 50–52
perspectives on, 50–54
reducing class inequality, 54
wealth, unequal distribution of, 33–34
what you can do, 54–55
class perspectives, 77
class system, 31
climate change, 364
clinical iatrogenesis, 277
clitoridectomy, 93
cocaine, 217
codependency, 210–211
cohabitation, 292–293
collective behaviour, 21
colonialism, 67–68, 77
colour blindness, discourse of, 73
coming out in homophobic culture, 153–154
commercialization of post-secondary education, 327
common-law, 292–293
communication styles, 112
community empowerment, 74–75
community policing, 251
comparable worth, 105
compulsory heterosexism, 145
conflict perspective
    on aging and age-based inequality, 137
    on class inequality, 53
    class perspectives, 77
    on crime, 248
    critical-conflict perspective, 8–9
    defined, 8
    described, 8
    on drug abuse, 222
    on education, 315–316
    on the environment, 371
    environmental justice framework, 372
    on ethnic inequality, 76–78
    on family-related problems, 290
    on gender inequality, 113–114
    on health care, 277–278
    hidden curriculum, 315–316
    iatrogenesis, 277
    on illness, 277–278
    internal colonialism, 77
    medical-industrial complex, 277
    political economy model, 357–358
    on population, 372
    on poverty, 53
    on prostitution, 189–190
    on racism, 76–78
    radical critical-conflict approach, 248
    on sexual orientation, 160–161
    on solving social problems, 383–384
    split-labour market theory, 77
    theory of racial formation, 77
    uneven development, 358
    on urban problems, 357–358
    value conflict perspective, 8
    on violence, 9–10
conformity, 246

congruence, 357
Constitution, 149
contingent work, 103–104
contraception, 295–296
control
    of fertility, 343–344
    of other people's labour, 9
    of property, 9
    social control, 188, 313
control theory, 247
Controlled Drugs and Substances Act, 214
core nations, 355
corporal punishment, 304, 305
corporate crime, 241–242
corporate death rate, 242
corporate downsizing, 53
cortex, 245
cosmopolites, 359
Council of Canadians, 22–23
courts, 251
crack babies, 217
cram school, 314
credit card fraud, 240
crime
    accused. *See* accused
    biological explanations, 244–245
    breaking and entering, 239
    Canada *vs.* United States, 240–241
    conflict perspective, 248
    control theory, 247
    corporate crime, 241–242
    credit card fraud, 240
    crime rates, selected offences, 235
    date rape, 237
    defined, 233
    delinquency, 234
    differential association theory, 248
    feminist perspectives, 249–250
    functionalist perspective, 245–248
    gang violence, 237–238
    hate crime, 4, 156–157, 238–239
    homicide, 234–236
    interactionist perspective, 248–249
    labelling theory, 248–249
    lifestyle-routine activity approach, 247
    manslaughter, 235
    mass murder, 235–236
    medicalization of crime, 249
    mens rea, 233
    occupational (white-collar) crime, 241
    official statistics, problems with, 232–233
    organized crime, 242, 243
    power-control theory, 250
    property crime, 239–240
    psychological explanations, 245
    radical critical-conflict approach, 248
    routine activities crime, 232
    self-reported victimization incidents, 234
    serial murder, 236
    sexual assault, 236–237
    shoplifting, 240
    social bond theory, 247

    as social problem, 232–234
    sociological explanations, 245–250
    strain theory, 246
    subculture of violence hypothesis, 247
    theft, 239
    types of, 234–243
    unintentional killing, 235
    victims. *See* victims
    violent crime, 234–239
    what you can do, 255
    youth crime, 234, 242–243
crime statistics, 232–233
crimes against the person, 86
Criminal Code
    bawdy house, 183
    child pornography, 194–195
    "communicating" (prostitution), 188
    decriminalization of sexual practices, 147–148
    hate crimes, 4, 157
    prostitution, 176–177, 183
    recommendations re sex industry, 174–175
    spanking, 305
    youth crime, 243
criminal intent, 233
criminal justice system
    the courts, 251
    death penalty, 255
    defined, 250
    incarceration rate, 253
    plea bargaining, 251, 252
    the police, 250–251
    prisons, 253
    punishment, 252–253
    restorative justice, 253–255
    what you can do, 255
criminal law
    indictable offences, 234
    summary conviction offences, 234
critical-conflict perspective, 8–9
crude birth rate, 337
crude death rate, 337
crude net migration rate, 338
cultural capital, 52, 315
cultural goals, 246–247
cultural iatrogenesis, 277
cultural racism, 72
cultural values, 72
culture
    and female genital mutilation, 93–95
    ideal culture, 8
    meaning of, 8
    rape culture, 101
    real culture, 8
    subculture, 360
    transmission of culture, 313

D

date rape, 237
death and dying, 130–131
death penalty, 255

decriminalization
    of marijuana, 216
    of sexual practices, 147
deforestation, 368
deindustrialization, 348
deinstitutionalization, 268–269
delayed initiation theory, 136
delinquency, 234
democratic racism, 72–75
demographic transition theory, 341
demography, 337
denial, discourse of, 73
dependency ratio, 136, 138
depressants, 206, 218
the deprived, 359
desertification, 368
deterrence, 253
deviance, 144–145, 188, 249
dieting, 94
differential association theory, 248
disability
    definitions of, 261–263
    employment rate, 43
    increase in number of disabled people,
      263–264
    and Indigenous people, 43
    mobility-related disabilities, 263
    pain-related disabilities, 263
    and poverty, 43
    rights organizations, 278
    as social problem, 263
disability-free life expectancy, 261–263
discretion, 250
discrimination
    anti-Semitism, 65
    defined, 4, 61
    described, 4
    individual discrimination, 65
    institutional discrimination, 65–66
    in medical care, based on sexual
      orientation, 154–155
    occupational, based on sexual
      orientation, 155–156
    sex discrimination, 115
    sexual orientation, 147, 153–157
    workplace discrimination, and age,
      132–133
disease. *See* illness
disengagement theory, 136
disposable societies, 369
distinct history and struggles, 66
division of labour
    biological division of labour, 113
    gendered division of labour, 92–93
    new international division of labour
      perspective, 32
divorce, 300–302
divorce rate, 286, 287, 288–289
domestic partnerships, 292–293
domestic violence
    child abuse, 302–305
    child sexual abuse, 303–304

ideology of non-intervention, 306
    incest, 303, 304
    parental abuse, 305
    social responses to, 306
    spouse abuse, 306
    women and children, 302
dominant group, 4, 63
double shift, 109–111
driving and drinking, 209, 210
dropout rate, 322
drug abuse
    biological explanations, 221
    caffeine, 213
    conflict perspective, 223
    defining, 205
    depressants, 218
    drug addiction, 205–206
    explanations of, 221–223
    feminist perspectives, 223
    functionalist perspective, 222–223
    future of, 223–227
    hallucinogens, 219
    illegal drugs, 213–221
    inhalants, 219
    interactionist perspective, 222
    labelling theory, 222
    lifetime use by Canadians, 214
    marijuana, 214–215, 216
    narcotics, 218
    objective component, 205
    opium, 213–214
    outpatient programs, 226
    over-the-counter drugs, 212–213
    overall harm from, 220
    past year drug use, 215
    percentage reporting harms from, 220
    potentiation, 218
    prescription drugs, 212
    prevention programs, 224–225
    psychological explanations, 221–222
    short-and long-term services, 226–227
    social learning theory, 221–222
    stimulants, 215
    subjective component, 205
    therapeutic community approach,
      225–227
    tolerance, 205
    treatment programs, 225–227
    what you can do, 227–228
    withdrawal, 206
drug addiction, 183–184, 205–206
drug subculture, 222
drugs
    caffeine, 213
    defined, 205
    illicit drugs, 205
    licit drugs, 205
    over-the-counter drugs, 212–213
    prescription drugs, 212–213
    recreational use, 205
    therapeutic use, 205
dual-earner marriages, 293–294

dying trajectory, 131
dysfunctions, 6–7, 313–314

E

early industrial stage, 341
earnings gap, 86, 104–105, 106
ebb and flow cycle, 50
ecofeminism, 374
economic growth, 362
ecosystem, 361–362
ecosystem services, 363
Ecstasy, 219, 220
ectomorphs, 244
edge city, 347
education
    ascribed statuses, and educational
      opportunities, 320–323
    bullying, 323–324
    change and innovation, 313
    charter schools, 328
    commercialization of post-secondary
      education, 327
    conflict perspective, 315–316
    cultural capital, 315
    defined, 312
    dropout rate, 322
    dysfunctions, 313–314
    educational attainment in population, 321
    elementary education, 325
    feminist perspective, 318
    financing problems, 325–327
    functionalist perspective, 313–314
    gender bias, 97–98, 99, 318
    and gender socialization, 97–100
    ghetto image, 317
    good teachers, importance of, 329
    hidden curriculum, 315–316
    home schooling, 328
    illiteracy, 319–320
    and immigrants, 320
    importance of, as social institution, 329
    interactionist perspective, 316–318
    in Japan, changes in, 314–315
    labelling, 316–318
    latent functions, 313
    level, and poverty, 42–43
    manifest functions, 313
    multiple jeopardy, 104
    perspectives on, 312–318
    post-secondary education, 323, 325–327
    and poverty, 45–46
    private schools, 328
    problems in Canadian education,
      318–325
    problems in the 21st century,
      327–330
    residential schools, 324–325
    school violence, 323–324
    schools, and homophobia, 158
    secondary education, 321–323, 325
    sexual harassment, 98–99
    social control, 313

social placement, 313
socialization, 313
tracking, 312
transmission of culture, 313
undergraduate tuition fees, 326
university degrees, and gender, 99–100
what you can do, 330–331
egalitarian family, 293–294
elder abuse, 134
elementary education, 325
elites, 20
emancipatory politics, 21
emigration, 338
employment
chilly climate concept, 108–109
comparable worth, 105
contingent work, 103–104
double shift, 109–111
employment rate, and disability, 43
gender-segregated work, 102
gendered division of paid work, 102–104
glass ceiling, 108–109
glass escalator, 109
and literacy, 319
occupational discrimination, based on sexual orientation, 155–156
occupational segregation by gender, 102–103
pay equity, 105
pink-collar ghetto, 103
sexual harassment, 105 107, 155–156
wage gap, 86, 104–105, 106
Employment Insurance program, 46
empowerment of communities, 74–75
endomorphs, 244
the Enlightenment, 67
environmental degradation, 361–363
environmental justice framework, 372
environmental problems
acid rain, 363
air pollution, 363–367
carrying capacity, 362
climate change, 364
conflict perspective, 371
deforestation, 368
desertification, 368
ecofeminism, 374
economic growth, 362
environmental degradation, 361–362
environmental justice framework, 372
environmental racism, 373
feminist perspective, 374–375
functionalist perspective, 370–372
in the future, 374
greenhouse effect, 364–365
interactionist perspective, 373–374
mining, 362
nuclear waste, 370
ozone layer, depletion of, 367
perspectives on, 370–375
smog, 363

soil depletion, 368
solid waste, 369
technological disasters, 370
toxic air pollutants, 367
toxic waste, 369
water shortages and pollution, 367–368
what you can do, 375
environmental racism, 373
environmental sociology, 370
environmental tobacco smoke, 211–212
equal opportunity, discourse of, 73
erotica, 193
escorts, 181, 183
ethnic group, 62
ethnic inequality
anti-racist perspective, 78
conflict perspective, 76–78
functionalist perspective, 76
reducing ethnic inequality, 79
as social problem, 61–64
symbolic interactionist perspective, 75–76
theory of racial formation, 77
what you can do, 79–80
ethnic pluralism, 76
ethnic villagers, 359
ethnicity
meaning of, 61–62
and pornography, 198
and poverty, 42
and prostitution, 186
ethnocentrism, 64–65
Eurocentric, 13
euthanasia, 132, 278
everyday racism, 71–72
excision, 93
expressive movements, 22
expressive tasks, 113
extended family, 285
extreme right-wing ideology, 69

F
families
see also family-related problems
abortion, 295–296
adoption, 297–298
binuclear family, 302
blended family, 302
Census families time series, 286
changing family structure and patterns, 285–286
changing views on, 288–289
child-related family issues, 295–300
cohabitation, 292–293
common-law, 292–293
contraception, 295–296
decline, issue of, 286–288
defined, 285
diversity in, 291–295
divorce, 300–302
divorce rate, 286, 287, 288–289
domestic partnerships, 292–293

dual-earner marriages, 293–294
egalitarian family, 293–294
extended family, 285
family of orientation, 299
family of procreation, 299
global perspective, 287
infertility, 296
kinship, 285
marriage, changing views of, 288–289
nature of families, 285–289
new reproductive technologies, 296–297
nuclear family, 286
one-parent households, 294–295
parenting style, 298–299
postponement of marriage, 292
principle of legitimacy, 289
remarriage, 302
reproductive freedom, 295–296
same-sex parenting, 300
single-parenthood, 287, 294–295
singlehood, 291–292
two-parent households, 294–295
and violence, 290, 302–306
Family Expenditures Survey (FAMEX), 39
family of orientation, 299
family of procreation, 299
family planning, 344
family policies, 51
family-related problems
see also families
and alcohol consumption, 209–211
child abuse, 302–305
codependency, 210–211
conflict perspective, 290
domestic violence, 302–306
feminist perspective, 290
functionalist perspective, 289–290
interactionist perspective, 290–291
parental abuse, 305
perspectives on, 289–291
spanking, 304, 305
spouse abuse, 306
in the 21st century, 306
teen pregnancies, 299
unmarried motherhood, 299
what you can do, 307
female circumcision, 93–95
female genital mutilation, 93–95
feminine, 87
feminist perspective
ecofeminism, 374
on education, 318
on environmental problems, 374
on family-related problems, 290
on health care, 279
on illness, 279
liberal feminists, 249
on population, 374
power-control theory, 250
radical feminists, 249
socialist-feminist perspective, 249

feminist perspective (*Continued*)
    on solving social problems, 384
    on urban problems, 360
    women's agency, 374
feminist perspectives
    on aging and age–based inequality, 137
    anticensorship feminists, 199
    antipornography feminists, 199
    Black feminists, 115
    on class inequality, 53–54, 78
    on crime, 249–250
    described, 13–14
    on drug abuse, 223
    feminist theories, variations in, 13–14
    feminists "of colour," 115
    feminization of poverty, 53
    on gender inequality, 114–115
    Indigenous feminists, 115
    liberal feminists, 114–115
    on poverty, 53–54
    on prostitution, 190–191
    on racism, 78
    radical feminists, 114
    on sexual orientation, 161–162
    socialist-feminist perspective, 53
    socialist feminists, 114
    on violence, 14–15
feminists "of colour," 115
feminization of aging, 134
feminization of poverty, 40, 42, 53
fences, 240
fertility, 337
fertility control, 343–344
fetal alcohol effects (FAE), 209
fetal alcohol syndrome (FAS), 209
financing education, 325–327
First Nations. *See* Indigenous people
fluoxetine (Prozac), 212
food banks, 44
freedom of expression, 73
frustration-aggression hypothesis, 245
functional age, 122
functionalist perspective
    on aging and age-based inequality, 136
    amalgamation, 76
    Anglo-conformity model, 76
    assimilation, 76
    on class inequality, 52–53
    control theory, 247
    on crime, 245–248
    defined, 6
    delayed initiation theory, 136
    described, 6
    disengagement theory, 136
    on drug abuse, 222–223
    dysfunctions, 6–7
    on education, 313–314
    on the environment, 370–372
    on ethnic inequality, 76
    ethnic pluralism, 76
    on family-related problems, 289–290
    on gender inequality, 113

on health care, 276
on illness, 276
latent functions, 6, 313
lifestyle-routine activity approach, 7, 247
manifest functions, 6, 313
mechanical solidarity, 357
organic solidarity, 357
on population, 370–372
on poverty, 52–53
on prostitution, 188–189
on racism, 76
segregation, 76
on sexual orientation, 159–160
social bond theory, 247
social disorganization, 7
on solving social problems, 382
strain theory, 246
subculture of violence hypothesis, 247
on urban problems, 357
on violence, 7–8
functionally illiterate, 319

G

gang violence, 237–238
gay
    see also sexual orientation
    classification as, 143–144
    stereotypical beliefs, 146
    as term, 143
gay advocacy, 164–165
gay-bashing, 154
Gay Liberation movement, 164–165
gender
    see also gender inequality
    and communication styles, 112
    defined, 87
    and health and illness, 264–265
    and heavy alcohol consumption, 207
    and pornography, 197–198
    and poverty, 40
    "third gender," 89
    transgender issues, 88–92
gender bias, 97–98, 99
gender differences, 87, 223
gender ideology, 92
gender inequality
    chilly climate concept, 108–109
    conflict perspective, 113–114
    contemporary gender inequality, 101–111
    double shift, 109–111
    feminist perspectives, 114–115
    functionalist perspective, 113
    gender role approach, 93
    gendered division of paid work, 102–104
    glass ceiling, 108–109
    glass escalator, 109
    interactionist perspective, 111–113
    language, 112
    persistence of, 85
    perspectives on, 111–115

reducing gender inequality, 115–116
sexual harassment, 105–107
as social problem, 83–93
and socialization, 93–101
structural approach, 93
wage gap, 104–105, 106
what you can do, 116–117
gender role approach, 93
gender-role socialization, 114–115
gender roles
    biological bases, 88–92
    defined, 88
    in the media, 100–101
    social bases, 92–93
gender-segregated work, 102
gender socialization
    and education, 97–100
    and the media, 100–101
    by parents, 95–96
    and peers, 96–97
gender subordination, 9
gendered division of labour, 92–93
gendered division of paid work, 102–104
gendered racism, 78
genderlects, 112
genocide, 77
gentrification, 351
gerontology, 123
GHB, 218
G.H.E.T.T.O. Movement, 330
glass ceiling, 108–109
glass escalator, 109
global activism, 23
global cities, 354–356
global perspective
    absolute poverty, 31–32
    cities, problems in, 354–356
    core nations, 355
    education in Japan, changes in, 314–315
    families, 287
    family planning, 344
    female genital mutilation, 93–95
    high-income nations, 31
    HIV/AIDS, 262
    life chances, 31
    low-income nations, 31
    Lysistrata Project, 19–20
    middle-income nations, 31
    migration, worldwide, 339
    new international division of labour perspective, 32
    organized crime, 243
    organized racism, 68–70
    peripheral nations, 355–356
    poverty, 31–32
    semiperipheral nations, 356
    sex trade, 173–175
    urban problems, 354–356
    violence, 3
    wealth, 31–32
global population
    see also population

fertility,   337
fertility control,   343–344
in the future,   374–375
impact of population growth,   340–341
migration,   338, 339
mortality,   337–338
population growth,   337–338
rapid growth, effect of, 354–355
world hunger,   341–342
zero population growth,   344
global sex industry,   172–176
globalization from below,   23
grassroots groups,   17–19
green revolution,   341–342
greenhouse effect,   364–365
greying of the population,   126
Grievous Bodily Harm,   218
gross domestic product (GDP),   31
groups
    dominant group,   4, 63
    ethnic group,   62
    grassroots groups,   17–19
    majority group,   63
    minority group,   63
    primary groups,   15
    racialized group,   62
    special-interest groups,   20
    subordinate group,   4
    subordinate groups,   63
    support groups,   16–17

H

Habitat for Humanity,   349
hallucinogens,   219
harassment,   98–99, 105–107
hard-core pornography,   193
Harper's Index,   370
hate crime,   4, 156–157, 238–239
health
    see also health care; illness
    and aging,   129, 133–134
    alcohol-related problems,   207–209
    alcoholic cirrhosis,   208
    cardiovascular problems,   208
    and class,   264
    disability-free life expectancy,   261–263
    and gender,   264
    gender differences in health behaviour,   223
    hospices,   131
    and Indigenous status,   264
    life expectancy,   260–261
    nutritional deficiencies,   208
    and obesity,   265–266
    and poverty,   44
    self-health management,   279
    and sex,   264–265
    as social problem,   260–266
    and structural variables,   265
    and telecommunications,   278
    what you can do,   280
    WHO definition,   260

health care
    accessibility,   270–271
    and aging,   133–134
    alternative health care,   274–275
    conflict perspective,   277–278
    costs and payment methods,   271–274
    coverage of care,   270
    "crisis" in Canadian health care,   269–275
    current issues,   270–275
    development of national health care system,   270
    discrimination, based on sexual orientation,   154–155
    feminist perspective,   279
    functionalist perspective,   276
    health care professionals,   274
    iatrogenesis,   277
    infant mortality,   261
    interactionist perspective,   278–279
    medical-industrial complex,   277
    perspectives on,   276–279
    quality of care,   275
    technology, use of,   275
    in United States,   272–273
    urban health care crisis,   349–350
    what you can do,   280
health care professionals,   274
health maintenance organization,   272
heel,   240
heroin,   219
heterosexism,   145
heterosexual questionnaire,   145
hidden curriculum,   315–316
high-income nations,   31
higher education,   42–43
historical roots of race,   63
historical roots of racism,   67–68
HIV,   155, 176, 262
home schooling,   328
homelessness,   45, 135, 269, 351–353
homicide,   234–236
homophobia,   145, 158
homosexual
    see also sexual orientation
    classification as,   143–144
    homophobia,   145
    as term,   143
hospices,   131
Hospital Insurance and Diagnostic Service Act,   270
house girls,   183
household composition, and poverty,   40
housing
    and aging,   135–136
    discrimination, based on sexual orientation,   153–154
    and poverty,   44–45
    problems,   350–353
housing shortage,   350–351
human rights legislation,   71
Human Suffering Index (HSI),   340

Hunger Count 2002,   38, 45
hustlers,   183

I

iatrogenesis,   277
ideal culture,   8
ideology of non-intervention,   306
illegal drugs
    depressants,   218
    hallucinogens,   219
    inhalants,   219
    marijuana,   214–215, 216
    narcotics,   218
    stimulants,   215
illicit drugs,   205
    see also illegal drugs
illiteracy,   319-320
illness
    see also health
    acute diseases,   261
    and aging,   133–134
    chronic diseases,   261
    and class,   264
    conflict perspective,   277–278
    feminist perspective,   279
    functionalist perspective,   276
    and gender,   264
    HIV/AIDS,   155, 176, 262
    and Indigenous status,   264
    interactionist perspective,   278–279
    manufacturers of illness,   261
    medicalization,   279
    perspectives on,   276–279
    and sex,   264–265
    sexually transmitted diseases,   296
    sick role,   276
    as social problem,   260–266
    and structural variables,   265
    what you can do,   280
immigrants, and education,   320
immigration,   338, 344–345
immigration legislation,   77, 174–175
immorality, beliefs about,   148
impaired driving,   209
incarceration rate,   253
incest,   237, 303, 304
inclusion,   38
income
    defined,   34
    gap,   104
    inequality,   34–36
    median total family income,   35
    share of total income,   35
Indigenous feminists,   115
Indigenous people
    disability rates,   43
    genocide,   77
    healing circle,   254
    and health and illness,   264–265
    overrepresentation of, in prison,   253
    population in Canada,   79
    residential schools,   324–325

Indigenous people (*Continued*)
    sentencing circle, 253–255
    sexual promiscuity stereotype, 186
individual discrimination, 65
individual sexism, 102
individual solutions, 15–16
individualism, 73
industrial production, 362
industrialization, 7
infant mortality rate, 261, 338
infertility, 296
infibulation, 93
inhalants, 219
innovation, 246, 313
insider trading, 241
institutional designs of omission, 67
institutional discrimination, 65–66
institutional racism, 71
institutionalized sexism, 102
instrumental tasks, 113
interactionist activity theory, 136–137
interactionist perspective
    on aging and age-based inequality,
        136–137
    on class inequality, 50–52
    on crime, 248–249
    defined, 11
    described, 11–12
    differential association theory, 248
    on drug abuse, 222
    on education, 316–318
    on the environment, 373
    on ethnic inequality, 75–76
    on family-related problems, 290–291
    on gender inequality, 111–113
    on health care, 278–279
    on illness, 278–279
    interactionist activity theory, 136–137
    labelling theory, 12, 222, 248–249
    on population, 373
    on poverty, 50–52
    on prostitution, 189
    racialized socialization, 75
    on racism, 75–76
    on sexual orientation, 159
    situational approach, 12–13
    social construction of reality, 12
    on solving social problems, 384
    on urban problems, 358–360
    on violence, 12–13
internal colonialism, 77
internalized dominance, 64, 153
Internet
    censorship, 196
    child pornography, 194–196
    prostitution, advertising for, 172–175
    and solving social problems, 384
interpersonal racism, 68–71
intersectionality, 42, 43
intersexed, 87
intimate relationships
    cohabitation, 292–293

common-law, 292–293
diversity in, 291–295
domestic partnerships, 292–293
dual-earner marriages, 293–294
one-parent households, 294–295
postponement of marriage, 292
singlehood, 291–292
two-parent households, 294–295
involuntary commitment, 268, 269
IQ, 245
irreconcilable differences, 301
issue focus, 20

J

jails, 253
johns, 186–188
joint, 215
JUMP, 330

K

Keynesian welfare state, 47–50
kinship, 285
kleptomaniac, 240
Kyoto Protocol, 365–367, 372

L

labelling theory, 12, 222, 248–249, 316–318
labels, 12
language, and gender, 112
latent functions, 6, 313
later maturity, 128
law, and sexual orientation, 147–152
law and order approach, 10
legalization of marijuana, 216
lesbian
    see also sexual orientation
    classification as, 143–144
    stereotypical beliefs, 146
    as term, 143
liberal feminists, 114–115, 249
liberal values, discourse of, 73
licit drugs, 205
life chances, 31
life course
    adolescence, 124–125
    age and social inequality, 123–131
    childhood, 123–124
    death and dying, 130–131
    described, 123
    later maturity, 128
    middle age, 126–128
    old age, 128–129
    suicide, 129–130
    young adulthood, 124–126
life expectancy, 126, 260–261, 338
life politics, 21
lifestyle-routine activity approach, 7, 247
linguistic sexism, 112
Liquid X, 218
living will, 131
lobbies, 20
lone-parent women, 40

long-term-care facilities, 135–136
long-term strategies, 15
low income cut-off (LICO) line, 39
low income measure (LIM), 39–40
low-income nations, 31
low-level literate, 319
lower class, 36
lower upper class, 36
LSD, 219
Lysistrata Project, 19–20

M

macrolevel analysis, 5
macrolevel attempts at solutions, 19–24
mainlining, 219
majority group, 63
male circumcision, 94
malice aforethought, 234–235
Malthusian perspective, 340
managed care, 272
mandatory retirement, 122, 133
manifest functions, 6, 313
manslaughter, 235
manufacturers of illness, 261
maquiladora plants, 356
marijuana, 214–215, 216
marital rape, 237
marital status, and heavy alcohol
    consumption, 207
marriage
    changing views on, 288–289
    dual-earner marriages, 293–294
    postponement of, 292
    remarriage, 302
    second shift, 293
masculine, 87
mass murder, 235–236
master status, 159
MDMA (Ecstasy), 219, 220
mechanical solidarity, 357
the media
    ageism, 125
    drunken driving, 210
    education and the ghetto, 317
    and gender socialization, 100–101
    incest, 304
    poor-bashing, 41
    preferring age groups, 125
    Regent Park, perceptions of, 359
    social policy newspeak words, 41
    and youth violence, 10–11
Medical Care Act, 270
medical-industrial complex, 277
medical marijuana program, 216
medical treatment model, 225
medicalization, 279
medicalization of crime, 249
megalopolis, 348
men
    fathers, after divorce, 294
    as johns, 186–188
    male prostitutes, 184–185

in middle age,   127–128
younger than 40, earnings of,   127
mens rea,   233
mental disorder,   266, 267, 268
mental illness
deinstitutionalization,   268–269
homelessness,   269
involuntary commitment,   268, 269
rates of,   266–268
as social problem,   266–269
total institution,   268–269
treatment of,   268–269
vs. mental disorder,   266
meritocracy,   31
mescaline,   219
mesomorphs,   244
methylphenidate (Ritalin),   212
microlevel analysis,   5
microlevel attempts at solutions,   15–16
mid-range attempts at solutions,   16–19
middle age,   126–128
middle class,   36
middle-income nations,   31
middle-term strategies,   15
migration,   338, 339
minimum hourly wages,   37
mining,   362
minority group,   4, 63
mobility-related disabilities,   263
monogamy,   288
moral entrepreneurs,   12, 249
moral panic, discourse of,   73
mortality,   337 338
Mothers Against Drunk Driving (MADD),
18, 210
multiculturalism, discourse of,   73
Multilateral Agreement on
Investments (MAI),   22
multilevel facilities,   135
multiple issues,   20
multiple jeopardy,   104
murder,   234–236
myths,   4

N

narcotics,   218
Narcotics Anonymous (NA),   16
national activism,   22
national identity, discourse of,   73–74
national social movements,   20–24
negative-education programs,   224
negative ethnocentrism,   64–65
neo-Malthusians,   340–341
new international division of labour
perspective,   32
new reproductive technologies,   296–297, 297
nicotine,   211–212
no-fault divorce laws,   301
non-violent protest,   21
norms
defined,   7
male gender norms,   99

and prostitution,   188–189
sexuality,   144
nuclear family,   286
nuclear waste,   370
nutrition, and poverty,   44
nutritional deficiencies,   208

O

obesity,   265–266
obscenity,   192
occupational discrimination,   155–156
occupational segregation by gender,   102–103
occupational (white-collar) crime,   241
official crime statistics,   232–233
old age,   128–129
older people. *See* ageism
one-parent households,   294–295
one-sex-model of humanity,   87
opiates,   219
opium,   213–214
oppressions,   115
organic solidarity,   357
organized crime,   242, 243
organized racism,   68–70
outpatient programs,   226
over-the-counter drugs,   212–213
overdoses,   213
ozone layer depletion,   367

P

pain-related disabilities,   263
parasitical transcendence,   374
parental abuse,   305
parenting style,   298–299
parents, and gender socialization,   95–96
Participation and Activity Limitation Survey
(PALS),   43
passive racism,   71–72
patent medicines,   213
patriarchy,   85, 102, 114
pay equity,   105
PCP,   219
peer groups
described,   96
and gender socialization,   96–97
peripheral nations,   355–356
personal problems,   260
perspective,   6
see also sociological perspectives
peyote,   219
phobias,   145
physical tasks,   131
pink-collar ghetto,   103
playground interactions,   96
plea bargaining,   251, 252
pluralism,   76
police,   250–251
polite racism,   71
political action committees (PAC),   20
political change,   20
political correctness,   73
political economy model,   357–358

political roots of race,   63
pollution
air pollution,   363–367
water pollution,   367–368
Pollution Probe,   17–18
poor-bashing,   41
population
see also population growth
of Canada,   128
carrying capacity,   362
change, in Canada,   347
conflict perspective,   371–372
defined,   337
demography,   337
educational attainment,   321
feminist perspective,   374
functionalist perspective,   370–372
in the future,   374–375
global population. *See* global population
greying of the population,   126
incarceration rate,   253
interactionist perspective,   373
perspectives on,   370–375
what you can do,   375
of world's ten largest cities,   355
zero population growth,   344
population composition,   340
population growth
see also global population
demographic transition theory,   341
fertility,   337
impact of,   340–341
Malthusian perspective,   340
migration,   338
mortality,   337–338
neo-Malthusians,   340–341
and population composition,   340
pornography
and age,   197
anticensorship feminists,   199
antipornography feminists,   199
censorship,   199
child pornography and the Internet,
194–196
and class,   197–198
defined,   191–192
and digital media,   194–195
distribution of,   193
and ethnicity,   198
extent of,   193–194
future of,   198–200
and gender,   197–198
hard-core pornography,   193
liberal view,   198–199
nature of,   193–194
obscenity,   192
and racialization,   198
religious conservative view,   199
research on,   196–197
social construction as social problem,
192–193
social context,   192

pornography (*Continued*)
soft-core pornography, 193
supply and demand, 194
vs. erotica, 193
what you can do, 200
positive ethnocentrism, 64
positive reinforcement, 222
positivist school, 244
post-secondary education, 323, 325–327
postindustrial stage, 341
postponement of marriage, 292
potentiation, 218
poverty
and ability, 43
absolute poverty, 31–32, 38
and age, 40
blaming the victim, 50
in Canada, 38–46
child poverty, 40
and children, 40
chronically poor people, 37–38
conflict perspective, 53
consequences of, 43–46
cultural capital, lack of, 52
and education, 45–46
and education level, 42–43
and ethnicity, 42
feminist perspectives, 53–54
feminization of poverty, 40, 42, 53
functionalist perspective, 52–53
and gender, 40
global perspective, 31–32
and health, 44
and household composition, 40
and housing, 44–45
how Canada deals with, 46
inclusion, 38
as individual problem, 46
interactionist perspective, 50–52
intersectionality, 42, 43
lone-parent women, 40
low income cut-off (LICO) line, 39
low income measure (LIM), 39–40
and nutrition, 44
perspectives on, 50–54
poverty line, 38, 39–40
poverty rate, 38–39
racialization of poverty, 42
reducing poverty, 54
relative poverty, 38
remaining poor in Canada, 36–37
risk of poverty, 40–43
spatial separation of the poor, 353–354
structural poverty, 46
underclass, 37–38
in United States, 38
what you can do, 54–55
"poverty industry," 53
poverty rate, 38–39
power
abuse of power, 107
defined, 32

differentials among groups, 63
imbalance, 99
johns and prostitutes, 186
power-control theory, 250
preferred provider organization (PPO), 272
preindustrial stage, 341
prejudice
anti-Semitism, 65
defined, 64
socially determined prejudices, 145
prescription drugs, 212–213
pressure groups, 20
prestige, 32–33
prevention programs, 224–225
preventive self-care, 279
primary aging, 126–127
primary deviance, 249
primary groups, 15
primary prevention, 224
primary sex characteristics, 88
principle of legitimacy, 289
prisons, 253
private schools, 328
productive aging, 138
proletariat, 9
property crime, 239–240
prostitution
adolescent prostitution, 185
and age, 185–186
agency personnel, 183
bar girls and bar boys, 183
broad definition, 171–172
brothels, 183
call girls and call boys, 181
in Canada, 176–185
city bylaws, 182–183
conflict perspective, 189–190
decriminalization, 189–190
defined, 171–172
drug addiction, 183–184
entry into sex trade, 184–185
escorts, 181, 183
and ethnicity, 186
extent of, in Canada, 185
feminist perspectives, 190–191
functionalist perspective, 188–189
globalization of, 172
HIV/AIDS, 176
house girls, 183
hustlers, 183
industrialization of, 172
interactionist perspective, 189
jargon of the profession, 181–182
"johns" or customers, 186–188
male prostitutes, 184–185
narrow definition, 171
normalization of, 172
perspectives on, 188–191
and racialization, 186
second-tier prostitutes, 183
sex tourism, 175–176
and sexual orientation, 184

social class, 186
streetwalkers, 183
strippers, 183
table dancers, 183
third-tier prostitutes, 183
top-tier prostitutes, 181
and victimless crime, 190
as "world's oldest profession," 172
protest crowds, 21
Prozac, 212
psychedelic trip, 219
psychological explanations
aggression, 245
of crime, 245
of drug abuse, 221–222
IQ, 245
psychological tasks, 131
public housing projects, 351
punishment, 222, 252–253

Q

quality of care, 275
Queer theory, 162–163
quid pro quo harassment, 106

R

race
see also racism; visible minority
biological definition, 62
feminization of poverty, 42
historical roots of, 63
internalized dominance, 64
intersectionality, 42
meaning of, 61–62
political roots of, 63
and poverty, 42
as social construct, 62
sociological definition, 62
White privilege, 63–64
"racial" purity, myth of, 63
"racial" supremacy doctrine, 67
racialization
meaning of, 61–62
and pornography, 198
of poverty, 42
and prostitution, 186
sexual promiscuity stereotype, 186
racialized beauty standards, 95
racialized group, 62
racialized inequality. *See* racism
racialized socialization, 75
racialized subordination, 9
racism
active racism, 71
anti-racism initiatives, 75
anti-racist perspective, 78
binary polarization, discourse of, 73
in Canada, 61
colour blindness, discourse of, 73
conflict perspective, 76–78
cultural racism, 72
defined, 64

democratic racism,   72–75
denial, discourse of,   73
empowerment of communities,   74–75
environmental racism,   373
equal opportunity, discourse of,   73
everyday racism,   71–72
feminist perspectives,   78
forms of, in Canadian society,   68–72
functionalist perspective,   76
gendered racism,   78
historical roots of,   67–68
institutional racism,   71
interpersonal racism,   68–71
liberal values, discourse of,   73
major institutions, role of,   75
moral panic, discourse of,   73
multiculturalism, discourse of,   73
national identity, discourse of,   73–74
organized racism,   68–70
passive racism,   71–72
polite racism,   71
political correctness, discourse of,   73
redneck racism,   71
reducing racism,   79
reflective skills and practices,   74
responses to allegations of,   74
reverse racism, discourse of,   73
as social problem,   61–64
societal racism,   71–72
symbolic interactionist perspective,
      75–76
systemic racism,   71
theory of racial formation,   77
what you can do,   79–80
white victimization, discourse of,   73
radical critical-conflict approach,   248
radical demands,   20
radical feminists,   114, 161, 249
rape culture,   101
reactive self-care,   279
real culture,   8
rebellion,   247
recreational drug use,   205
redneck racism,   71
reefer,   215
reflective skills and practices,   74
reform movements,   21
refugees,   338
Regent Park,   359
regulatory self-care,   279
rehabilitation,   252–253
relative poverty,   38
religion, and sexual orientation,   146–147
religious movements,   22
remarriage,   302
reproductive freedom,   295–296
residential schools,   324–325
resistance movements,   22
restorative justice,   253–255
restorative self-care,   279
retirement principle,   133
retreatism,   247

retribution,   252
reverse racism, discourse of,   73
revolutionary movements,   21–22
Ritalin,   212
ritualism,   246–247
Rohypnol,   218
romantic love,   291
roster,   274
routine activities crime,   232
rural areas,   357

S

same-sex marriages,   146–147, 149–152
same-sex parenting,   300
sandwich generation,   138
scam artists,   134
scapegoat,   245
scare tactics,   224–225
schizophrenia,   269
school violence,   323–324
schools, and homophobia,   158
second shift,   293
second-tier prostitutes,   183
secondary aging,   127
secondary deviance,   249
secondary education,   321–323, 325
secondary prevention,   224
secondary sex characteristics,   88
segregation,   76
self-care,   279
self-esteem enhancement,   225
self-fulfilling prophecy,   12
self-health management,   279
self-help organizations,   16–17
self-identification,   144
self-reported victimization incidents,
      234–235
semiperipheral nations,   356
senescence,   126–127
sentencing circle,   253–255
serial monogamy,   289
serial murder,   236
sex
      defined,   87
      and health and illness,   264–265
      intersexed,   87
      one-sex-model of humanity,   87
      primary sex characteristics,   88
      secondary sex characteristics,   88
      two-sex model,   87
sex differences,   87
sex industry
      future of,   198–200
      global sex industry,   172–176
      pornography,   191–192
      prostitution. *See* prostitution
sex tourism,   175–176
sex trade. *See* prostitution
sexism
      defined,   85
      gendered racism,   78
      individual sexism,   102

institutionalized sexism,   102
      linguistic sexism,   112
sexual abuse of children,   303–304
sexual assaults,   85
sexual attraction,   143–144
sexual harassment,   98–99, 105–107, 155–156
sexual involvement,   144
sexual orientation
      biphobia,   145
      changing sexual orientation,   163–164
      classification of,   143–144
      coming out in homophobic culture,
            153–154
      compulsory heterosexism,   145
      conflict perspective,   160–161
      defined,   143
      discrimination based on,   153–157
      equal rights,   163, 165
      feminist perspectives,   161–162
      functionalist perspective,   159–160
      gay advocacy,   164–165
      hate crime,   156–157
      heterosexism,   145
      homophobia,   145
      housing discrimination,   153–154
      ideological bases of inequality,   145–152
      interactionist perspective,   159
      lack of knowledge about,   154
      law,   147–152
      medical care, discrimination in,   154–155
      nature and extent of inequality,   144–145
      occupational discrimination,   155–156
      perspectives on,   157–163
      as prohibited ground for discrimination,
            147
      prostitution,   184
      Queer theory,   162–163
      radical feminists,   161
      reducing inequalities,   163–165
      religion,   146–147
      same-sex marriages,   146–147, 149–152
      same-sex parenting,   300
      schools, and homophobia,   158
      sexual harassment,   155–156
      stereotypical beliefs,   146
      victimization,   156–157
      violence against gays and lesbians,   157
      what you can do about inequality,
            165–166
sexual promiscuity stereotype,   186
sexuality,   144
sexually transmitted diseases,   296
shantytowns,   356
shooting,   219
shoplifting,   240
short-term strategies,   15
sick role,   276
single issues,   20
single-parenthood,   287, 294–295
single-room occupancy (SRO) hotels,   135
singlehood,   291–292
situational approach,   12–13

slavery, 77
smog, 363
smoking, 211–212
snitch, 240
social bases for gender roles, 92–93
social bond theory, 247
social change
    defined, 15
    long-term strategies, 15
    middle-term strategies, 15
    and reducing social problems, 15–24
    short-term strategies, 15
social class
    see also class inequality
    class divisions, 36–38
    class perspectives, 77
    class system, 31
    determination of, in Canada, 32
    and health and illness, 264–265
    and heavy alcohol consumption, 207
    and hidden curriculum, 315–316
    lower class, 36
    lower upper class, 36
    middle class, 36
    of parents, and education, 322
    and pornography, 197–198
    prostitution, 186
    working class, 36
social construct, 62
social construction approach, 373
social construction of reality, 12
social control, 188, 313
social deviance, 7
social disorganization, 7
social gerontology, 123
social iatrogenesis, 277
social isolation, 134–135
social learning theory, 221–222
social mobility, 31
social movements, 17–18, 20–24
social placement, 313
social policy
    American model of health care,
      272–273
    Canadian *vs.* Western European family
      policies, 51
    coming out in homophobic culture,
      153–154
    democratic racism, state responses to,
      72–75
    euthanasia, 132
    Kyoto Protocol, 365–367
    marijuana, 216
    newspeak words, 41
    plea bargains, 252
    saving our cities, 348–349
    schools and homophobia, 158
    spanking, 305
    transgender issues, 88–92
    workfare, 47–49
social problems
    see also specific social problems

ageism, 122–131
    crime, 232–234
    defined, 2
    described, 2–4
    disability, 263
    ethnic inequality, 61–64
    in global perspective. *See* global
      perspective
    grassroots groups, 17–19
    health, 260–266
    illness, 260–266
    individual solutions, 15–16
    long-term strategies, 15
    macrolevel attempts at solutions,
      19–24
    mental illness, 266–269
    microlevel attempts at solutions,
      15–16
    mid-range attempts at solutions, 16–19
    middle-term strategies, 15
    myths about, 4
    national social movements, 20–24
    perceived problems and possible
      solutions, 383
    political change, 20
    racism, 61–64
    reducing social problems, 15–24,
      382–385
    self-help groups, 16–17
    short-term strategies, 15
    social change, 15–24
    social movements, 17–18
    sociological examination of, 4, 5
    sociological imagination, 5
    sociological perspectives. *See* sociological
      perspectives
    special-interest groups, 20
    study of, 4–5
social protection, 252
social stratification, 32
social structure, 7
social tasks, 131
social welfare in Canada, 47–50
socialist-feminist perspective, 53, 249
socialist feminists, 114
socialization
    education, 313
    gender-role socialization, 114–115
    gender socialization, 93–101
    racialized socialization, 75
    White racialized socialization, 76
socially determined prejudices, 145
societal racism, 71–72
society, 3
sociological imagination, 5
sociological perspectives
    on aging and age-based inequality,
      136–137
    on class inequality, 50–54
    conflict perspective, 8–10
    on crime, 245–250
    on education, 312–318

    on the environment, 370–375
    on family-related problems, 289–291
    feminist perspectives, 13–15
    functionalist perspective, 6–8
    on gender inequality, 111–115
    on health care, 276–279
    on illness, 276–279
    interactionist perspective, 11–13
    on population, 370–375
    on poverty, 50–54
    on prostitution, 188–191
    on sexual orientation, 157–163
    solving social problems, 382–385
    on urban problems, 356–360
sociology
    defined, 3
    macrolevel analysis, 5
    microlevel analysis, 5
    theoretical perspectives, 4
"sodomy," 148
soft-core pornography, 193
soil depletion, 368
solid waste, 369
solving social problems, 382–385
somatotype theory, 244
spanking, 304, 305
special-interest groups, 20
specialism, 352
spiritual tasks, 131
split-labour market theory, 77
spouse abuse, 306
stable employment, 43
stage-based approach, 131
standpoint analysis, 78
stereotypes
    age-based stereotypes, 123
    "Bubba" stereotype, 68–71
    defined, 65
    older employees, 132
    sexual orientation, 146
    sexual promiscuity stereotype, 186
stimulants, 211, 215
straight, 143
    see also sexual orientation
strain theory, 246
streetwalkers, 183
strippers, 183
structural approach, 93
structural functionalist perspective. *See*
    functionalist perspective
structural poverty, 46
struggle for survival, 67
student loans, 42
subculture, 360
subculture of violence hypothesis, 247
subordinate groups, 4, 63
substance abuse. *See* drug abuse
substance dependence, 268
suicide, 3, 129–130
summary conviction offences, 234
sunna, 93
support groups, 16–17

survival of the fittest, 67
sustainable development, 336, 371
symbolic interactionist. *See* interactionist perspective
systemic racism, 71

T

table dancers, 183
task-based approach, 131
tasks
    expressive tasks, 113
    instrumental tasks, 113
    physical tasks, 131
    psychological tasks, 131
    social tasks, 131
    spiritual tasks, 131
technological change, 53
technological disasters, 370
technology, and health care, 275
teen pregnancies, 299
teenagers, 124–125, 125, 185–186
terminal phase, 131
tertiary prevention, 224, 225
Thailand, 176
theft, 239
theory, 5–6
theory of racial formation, 77
therapeutic community approach, 225–227
therapeutic drug use, 205
"third gender," 89
third-tier prostitutes, 183
Tobacco Act, 211, 223
tobacco (nicotine)
    environmental tobacco smoke, 211–212
    and life expectancy, 211
    as social problem, 211–212
    stimulant, 211
tolerance, 205
top-tier prostitutes, 181
total institution, 268–269
toxic air pollutants, 367
toxic waste, 369
tracking, 312
tradition, 73
transgender issues, 88–92
transitional industrial stage, 341
transmission of culture, 313
the trapped, 359
treatment
    drug and alcohol abuse treatment programs, 225–227
    of mental illness, 268–269
truth, 73
two-parent households, 294–295
two-sex model, 87

U

UN World Water Development Report, 368
underclass, 37–38
undergraduate tuition fees, 326
uneven development, 358
Uniform Crime Report, 232

unintentional killing, 235
United States
    crime in, *vs.* Canada, 240–241
    health care model, 272–273
    poverty in, 38
    public schools in, 328
Universal Declaration of Human Rights, 148–149
universalism, 73
university-corporation partnerships, 327
unmarried motherhood, 299
unmarried people, 359
urban problems
    see also urbanization
    in Canada, 348–354
    conflict perspective, 357–358
    deindustrialization, 348
    feminist perspective, 360
    fiscal crisis in cities, 348–349
    functionalist perspective, 357
    in the future, 361
    global problems, 354–356
    health care crisis, 349–350
    homelessness, 351–353
    housing problems, 350–353
    housing shortage, 350–351
    interactionist perspective, 358–360
    perspectives on, 356–360
    political economy model, 357–358
    saving our cities, 348–349
    spatial separation, 353–354
    uneven development, 358
urbanism, 358
urbanization
    see also urban problems
    Canadian cities, changes in, 346–348
    contemporary urban growth, 346–348
    defined, 7
    early urban growth and social problems, 346
    edge city, 347
    gentrification, 351
    megalopolis, 348
    organic solidarity, 357

V

value conflict perspective, 8
values, 7
victimization
    and aging, 134
    and sexual orientation, 156–157
victimization surveys, 238, 239
victimless crime, 190
victims
    of homicide, 236
    of sexual assault, 237
violence
    ambivalence about, 2
    conflict perspective, 9–10
    defined, 2
    domestic violence, 302–306
    elder abuse, 134
    in the family, 290, 302–306

feminist perspectives, 14–15
functionalist perspective, 7–8
gang violence, 237–238
against gays and lesbians, 157
global perspective, 3
hate crime, 4
interactionist perspective, 12–13
lifestyle-routine activity approach, 7
murder of women, 85–86
school violence, 323–324
sexual assaults, 85, 236–237
sexual harassment, 98–99, 105–107
situational approach, 12–13
subculture of violence hypothesis, 247
victimization, 7
against women, 85–86
youth violence, 10–11
violent crime, 234–239
visible minority
    see also race
    spatial separation of, 353–354
    status, 79

W

wage gap, 86, 104–105, 106
wage squeeze, 53
water shortages and pollution, 367–368
wealth
    defined, 32
    global perspective, 31–32
    high-income nations, 31
    unequal distribution of, 33–34
welfare state, 47–50
Western European family policies, 51
white-collar crime, 241
White privilege, 63–64
White racialized socialization, 76
White supremacist groups, 68–70
white victimization, discourse of, 73
withdrawal, 206
women
    see also feminist perspective; gender inequality
    chilly climate concept, 108–109
    and contingent work, 103–104
    and division of labour, 92–93
    and domestic violence, 302–306
    double shift, 109–111
    female genital mutilation, 93–95
    feminization of aging, 134
    gendered racism, 78
    glass ceiling, 108–109
    glass escalator, 109
    labour force participation, 102, 109–110
    lone-parent women, 40
    in male-dominated businesses, 109
    in management, 109
    in middle age, 127–128
    multiple jeopardy, 104
    murder of, 85–86
    parental abuse, 305
    pink-collar ghetto, 103

women (*Continued*)
   and retirement, 133
   second shift, 293
   sexism. *See* sexism
   sexual assaults, 85
   sexual harassment, 98–99, 105–107
   spouse abuse, 306
   trafficking of, 173–175
   under 30, earnings of, 126
   violence against, 85–86

   wage gap, 86, 104–105, 106
   and work, 108
women's agency, 374
workfare, 47–49
working class, 9, 36
working poor, 36
workplace, alcohol in, 209
workplace discrimination, 132–133
World Health Organization (WHO), 3, 260
world hunger, 341–342

Y

young adulthood, 124–126
Young Offenders Act, 10
youth crime, 234, 242–243
Youth Criminal Justice Act (YCJA), 10–11, 242
youth violence, 10–11

Z

zero population growth, 344

PHOTO CREDITS